THE SOUTHERN COMMON PEOPLE

Recent Titles in
Contributions in American History
Series Editor: Jon L. Wakelyn

The Politics of Wartime Aid: American Economic Assistance to France and French Northwest Africa, 1940–1946
James J. Dougherty

The Oil Cartel Case: A Documentary Study of Antitrust Activity in the Cold War Era
Burton I. Kaufman

The Social Bases of City Politics: Atlanta, 1865–1903
Eugene J. Watts

Two Nations Over Time: Spain and the United States, 1776–1777
James W. Cortada

Transatlantic Revivalism: Popular Evangelicalism in Britain and America, 1790–1865
Richard Carwardine

The Mess in Washington: Manpower Mobilization in World War II
George Q. Flynn

City and Hinterland: A Case Study of Urban Growth and Regional Development
Roberta Balstad Miller

Biography of a Progressive: Franklin K. Lane, 1864–1921
Keith W. Olson

Farmers Without Farms: Agricultural Tenancy in Nineteenth-Century Iowa
Donald L. Winters

The Half-Opened Door: Discrimination and Admission at Harvard, Yale, and Princeton, 1900–1970
Marcia Graham Synnott

The Tarnished Dream: The Basis of American Anti-Semitism
Michael N. Dobkowski

Sobering Up: From Temperance to Prohibition in Antebellum America, 1800–1860
Ian R. Tyrrell

Alcohol, Reform and Society: The Liquor Issue in Social Context
Jack S. Blocker, Jr.

THE SOUTHERN COMMON PEOPLE
Studies in Nineteenth-Century Social History

Edited by EDWARD MAGDOL and
JON L. WAKELYN

Contributions in American History, Number 86

GREENWOOD PRESS
WESTPORT, CONNECTICUT • LONDON, ENGLAND

Library of Congress Cataloging in Publication Data
Main entry under title:

The Southern common people.

(Contributions in American history; no. 86
ISSN 0084–9219)
Bibliography: p.
Includes index.
1. Middle classes—Southern States—History—19th century. 2. Southern States—Social conditions. 3. Southern States—Economic conditions. I. Magdol, Edward. II. Wakelyn, Jon L.
HT690.U6S68 301.44'1 79–7724
ISBN 0–313–21403–4

Library of Congress Catalog Card Number: 79–7724
ISBN: 0–313–21403–4
ISSN: 0084–9219

First published in 1980

Greenwood Press
A division of Congressional Information Service, Inc.
51 Riverside Avenue, Westport, Connecticut 06880

Printed in the United States of America

10 9 8 7 6 5 4 3 2 1

To my brother Murray
and my sister Rosanne
—E.M.

To David and Meredith
—J.L.W.

Contents

Part II: The Common People of the Postwar South

Preface
Who Were the Common People?

Over the past two decades, the nineteenth-century South has inspired much historical writing, including studies of the South's prewar planters and postwar commercial elites, politics and leadership, and slavery and freedom. Books and articles on slavery and the freedman have given special attention to family life, work habits, religious beliefs, and how blacks related to the white upper classes. The postwar decline of plantation society, economic upheavals, and the populist movements have received excellent treatment. These works, many of which employ the techniques of the new economic and social history, have made the nineteenth-century South more intelligible to the scholar and the student.

However, the social life and labor experiences of the great mass of the white folk have received neither the quantity nor the quality of study that has been given to slaves and elite planters, politicians, and intellectuals. Yet those non-elites included, among others, small farmers, herdsmen, common and skilled laborers, artisans, shopkeepers, and "poor whites," who had important roles in the economic growth, the political changes, and the social life of the nineteenth-century South. Along with the emerging professionals—lawyers, doctors, and bankers—they made up the so-called middle classes. In this volume, space permits concentration only on the landowning farmers, herdsmen, and urban merchants and laborers. Slaves and free blacks, lawyers and bankers, and relations of "poor whites" to the middle classes are often mentioned. For the sake of historical accuracy, we prefer to use the accepted term of the period, the "common people," rather than "middle class" to refer to the southerners described in this volume.

It becomes evident by our simple grouping of the common people that the major task of those who would study the part they played in the momentous upheavals of the nineteenth century—settlement of the West, agricultural rise and decline, civil war, the end of slavery, urbanization, and agrarian unrest—is to clarify just who belonged to that class or interest. Americans have been somehow reluctant to discuss social and economic groups in class terms, and they have generally lumped the non-elites into an amorphous group known as the middle class. Only those poorest people who somehow were outside the freely competitive, property-owning citizenry have been considered to be in the lower class. To add to the confusion, romantic nostalgia for a lost agrarian paradise led southerners themselves to call the large white majority simply the "yeomanry." But the yeoman farmer group did not include the urban worker, the shopkeeper, or the small planter, let alone the professional class that appeared during the middle of the nineteenth century. The class terms used in the past simply will not be of much help in trying to understand the complexity of social, kinship, status, and economic relations that divided and united the people of the South.

Knotty problems abound for any group classification. Did the common people consist largely of non-slaveholders? Did the size of farms or urban commercial property separate the common people? How did occupation or professional outlook determine economic allegiance? To what extent did the geographical subregions with different soil fertility, types of terrain, and degrees of urban growth influence class distinctions? Did geographical mobility and the belief in equal opportunity mitigate class feeling? Certainly any attempt to trace the rise in status of southerners over a period of years is made more difficult by the number of times the average head of family moved. Is there any evidence that the common people at any time thought or acted in class terms? During the colonial and revolutionary periods, there is an indication that class hostilities influenced political and economic events. Did those conflicts continue into the nineteenth century? Or did the political changes of the Jacksonian period disrupt class feelings and influence attitudes toward social status?

Only a few social commentators and historians have attempted to overcome those obstacles and analyze class and status distinctions among the southern people. In *Social Relations in Our Southern States*, published in 1860, Daniel R. Hundley classified people according to family name and occupation. An upper-class Alabama lawyer who had lived outside the South for many years, Hundley wrote his book to correct northern misconceptions of the southern class structure and to explain to himself just how individuals among the crude, uneducated masses had risen to positions of social and financial prominence. His version of a social structure included merchants, lawyers, bankers, and other businessmen in the urban middle class. The amount of land owned and the number of slaves held separated the small planter from the yeoman farmer, although both belonged to the middle class. A large planter without proper family connections could never enter the elite circles of society. Hundley admired the self-made merchants, professionals, and most of the planters, especially when they had no political or social ambitions. But class was fixed and status was predetermined in the world that Hundley constructed.

The only modern scholar to devote a book entirely to the common people is Frank L. Owsley. In *Plain Folk of the Old South*, Owsley described the common people as non-slaveholding, property-owning farmers. They were financially successful people, ambitious for their childrens' future, and at ease with the planter elites. Owsley believed that they made up fully 80 percent of the white heads of families in the late antebellum South.

We found these studies to provide interesting insight into social and economic conditions and class attitudes. However, they are unsuitable for understanding just who were the common people. Hundley's use of status alone to structure class is rigid and static, and Owsley's data are often simply wrong. For example, his statistics often include slaveholding families whom he believed did not belong to his plain folk. Otto Olsen's assertion in "Historians and the Extent of Slaveownership in the Southern United States" that 31 percent of the white heads of families owned slaves certainly called Owsley's classification into question. Owsley completely omitted the crossroads merchant, the urban work force, and other non-agrarian members of southern society. The concept of a system based on income and agricultural production has proved too narrow for use in deciding who were the common people.

Recent studies of the common people ask further questions about pre-emancipation classification. Ira Berlin believes that any determination of social and economic class should consider what, how much, and for whom a particular occupational group produced. Frank J. Huffman's valuable statistical analysis, included in this volume, shows the importance of noting class changes through the study of income and property ownership from one generation to the next. Other works point out that job training and work habits often reveal how occupational groups classified themselves. Studies of the culture, including family life, educational levels and values, religious beliefs, and common folk treatment and status under the law, help us to understand class identities. Thus in defining the common people we have largely been guided by occupational and personal social relations. These relations include the quantity and type of commodities produced for specific markets, occupational status, social distance and proximity to other non-elites as well as elite groups, political behavior, and aspects of distinctive middle- and laboring-class cultures and values.

We would suggest, therefore, the following as a preliminary profile of southern social classes that include the common people: In the agricultural regions, the common people were those farmers and small planters who owned their own land, produced staple crops, and food for themselves, the large planters, and urban consumers. Planters who owned more than twenty slaves and who grew staple crops are considered part of the elite. In the postwar emancipation years many of those planters and their sons would move into the ranks of the common people. The herdsmen, often considered members of the lower class because they owned no land, provided meat for the towns and plantations. Ownership of land was important to the people, but they certainly considered herdsmen a vital part of the economy and included them among the common folk. The war devastated the herds of swine and contributed to the herdsmen's decline in status and wealth. Country store owners, in small towns or rural villages, considered themselves members of the common folk. Urban mechanics who held steady jobs or owned their own businesses, whether they were property owners or not, belonged to the common folk. Unskilled seasonal day laborers who had no steady employment were one component of the lower class. Most antebellum factory laborers seldom held permanent jobs, often shifted from urban to rural occupations, and belonged to the laboring lower classes. Their numbers would swell in the postwar years as many families lost their land. Lawyers, physicians, bank clerks, small merchants, and factory managers made up the professional middle classes, although a few believed themselves to be members of the elite.

Most of these occupational groups are studied in the essays included in this volume. The authors of the selections have also pointed to useful analytical categories. First, they deal with values, mores, habits, and thoughts of the social groups. Lawrence Goodwyn tells us that the relationship between what the rank-and-file Populists believed and how they acted is important for understanding the movement itself. Second, the essays deal collectively with the problems of class confrontation, domination and challenge, in a society having ill-defined classes. The connections between attitudes and conflict have been applied to the antebellum period as well as the postwar years of economic and political turmoil in order to view both continuity and change in the nineteenth-century South. Hopefully, the authors in this collection have assisted in the task of writing a complete history of nineteenth-century southern society.

We have incurred debts in producing this volume, first of all to the authors of the various selections. The assistance and cordiality of journal editors and publishers were invaluable. The editors of Greenwood Press deserve special praise for their unwavering support for this scholarly study of all of the common people. Ira Berlin places this volume into historiographical perspective in his afterword. Herbert G. Gutman helped us to select those topics that would best give the reader an understanding of the lives of the common people. George Rawick lent an ear to many of our ideas. His standard of prodigious research in the slave narratives serves as a model for all who would seek to understand the lives of the supposedly inarticulate. As is evident from the selection of articles, we acknowledge the debt all students of social history owe to Peter Stearns and his invaluable *Journal of Social History*. Vernon Burton shared his knowledge of the local history of the South. Since none of the above friends and colleagues agreed on just who comprised the common people, we absolve all of them from responsibility for the final selections.

E.M.
J.L.W.

Part I

THE COMMON PEOPLE OF THE ANTEBELLUM SOUTH

Introduction

According to Frank L. Owsley, the antebellum southern common folk were socially deferential to but economically independent of the planter elites. In his *Plain Folk of the Old South*, the only book devoted entirely to the lives of the common people, Owsley revised the prevailing view of a servile and dependent white lower class and a small, insignificant yeoman farmer population. Owsley believed that the great majority of the common folk had a financial stake in the future of cotton cultivation and thus supported the expansion of southern cotton lands into the Southwest, which furthered sectional tensions. They also had family and cultural ties to the upper classes that resulted in a lifestyle that emulated that of their betters. Emotional and material attachments to the homeland, and deference to the wishes of the planter elites, Owsley claimed, even united the southern people on secession.

Owsley's studies, however, received scant praise from the scholarly community. Although many historians admitted that Owsley had described a much larger and more affluent common folk than had previously been thought to exist, his research was found faulty. He was criticized for not making a chronological analysis of the labor activities and land development of the common folk. A few scholars claimed that Owsley made the common people mere exponents of elite cultural and social values, whereas others believed he missed seeing just how dependent their lives actually were. Later historians have revised Owsley's approach and have suggested additional approaches to the study of the common folk—just what they produced and for whom, how they lived, and their relations with other classes. We still do not know how the common people descended from the lower-class colonial tradition, what role they had in populating the great Southwest, to what extent they actually deferred to the upper classes, and why they seemed to support both secession and the Confederate war effort.

If the common people supported southern secession, their ancestors were not united over the American Revolution in the southern colonies. In fact, many scholars have shown that the Revolution in the South was more like a civil war in which the people were divided over class and political issues. An earlier generation of historians believed the civil war was fought by conflicting geographical interests, with the southwestern colonials usually in support of the British cause in hopes of gaining political power after the Revolution ended. In *American Slavery, American Freedom*, Edmund P. Morgan contradicted the views of political divisions in the colonial period. Instead, he discovered that the need for labor in those agricultural societies as well as the desire for political order led the elites to offer a form of equality to the common folk based on race prejudice. But Jackson T. Main has suggested that the southern colonies were indeed divided over class interests. He believes that further research on the development of skilled trades, regional markets, and religious competition could shed more light on colonial society and its divisions on the eve of the Revolution.

In this volume's initial selection, Walter J. Fraser, Jr., discusses the tensions between the elite officer corps and the rank-and-file recruits of the revolutionary army in South Carolina. Fraser finds that few members of the lower class became officers and that officers claimed class privileges in dictating orders to common soldiers. Still, the common folk enlisted in the army in large numbers because of recruitment promises of western lands and larger participation in the political future of the new states formed during the war. Others, especially urban and rural poor with no land, were drafted into the army, as is evident from the Vagrancy Act of 1778. The common soldier often deserted to the British side because of cruel punishment for the slightest offense against the elite officers. Fraser rejects the view that the war led to class leveling; instead, he claims that the conflict between soldier and officer actually reflected the intense class antagonisms that existed in the late colonial period. Without the opportunities for westward migration brought about by the war, he implies, that conflict would have intensified in the new nation.

Thus having a clear picture of the lives of the common folk during the colonial period is important to our understanding of those people during their transition from a colonial to a westward-migrating population in the new American nation. Land speculators, the politically ambitious, the bounteous financial opportunities, and the brutality of the frontier have been studied in depth. But one still wonders why historians discovered so little class conflict in the Southwest. Did the mutual need for protection from the Indians and cooperation for material survival mitigate frontier conflict? Or did the development of a planter hierarchy based on financial wealth and slave property condemn the common folk to the support of a racial caste system?

Frank L. Owsley has written the most thorough study of the occupation and permanent settlement of the Southwest by the common folk. In the chapter from the *Plain Folk of the Old South* included in this volume, he claims that the first settlers were nomadic herdsmen who bypassed the rich farmlands for grazing lands. They were eventually driven off the land into the hill country to become the so-called poor whites of the antebellum South. As farmers replaced the herdsmen, they competed for the best soil, with proper land selection and hard work as the primary divider between yeoman farmer and planter elite. Recent research challenges Owsley's conclusions on where the farm groups settled and just who profited most from the land. By the 1830s many small farmers became dissatisfied with their economic opportunities and moved even farther west, into the Arkansas and Texas frontier. Who were they and what other reasons made them leave? Above all, what kind of economic and social life had they left behind?

Scholars have also suggested that social relations along with economic success created a bond between the common folk and the elites. Owsley believed that family connections, based on frequent intermarriage among the classes, and unity of social and cultural values, mitigated feelings of class resentment. His description of the plain folk as crude and happy people, wildly enthusiastic in their religion, content to have their children accept a common-school education, and generally subscribing to the social values of the elites, is overly simplistic. Owsley allowed his understanding of the life-styles of the elites to determine how he viewed the social lives and cultural values of the common people. Perhaps detailed observation of southern society may reveal more about class relations.

Popular hopes and fears were reflected in the appeals of competing religious sects. Scholars such as Walter Posey and Donald Matthews have studied the attitudes of the rural and urban populations toward religion. They discovered a remarkable similarity of beliefs among the classes of the South. The most recent analysis of common-folk religion, Dickson K. Bruce's *And They All Sang Hallelujah*, looks only at the camp meeting. Bruce found a downtrodden, depressed people, wholly subservient to the planters. He ignored the relationship between the minister and his flock, the implications of class politics in the sermons, and the many changes among the religious sects, such as the drive toward an educated clergy during the late antebellum period. After all, popular change in attitudes toward preaching and education among the fundamentalist churches suggests a relatively sophisiticated common folk.

Randall Miller's essay written for this volume looks at the Catholic church in its attempts to thrive among the slaves, the urban white masses, and the small farmers. His depiction of the decline of the Catholic church among slaves and common folk of the lower South revealed a resistance to institutionalized and ritualized religion. Humorless and strict, the mostly foreign-born clergy frightened blacks and whites alike. Miller also discovered that the clash of economic interests among the urban free blacks and white unskilled laborers fed class-based religious conflicts that were destructive to the growth of the Catholic church in the South. In view of one church's failure to gain converts, we might then ask how other churches functioned in the economic and social milieu of the antebellum period.

Just as much of our understanding of religion comes from the point of view of the elites, and education appears so much a part of religion, so are most of the studies of education based on the schools and schooling of the elites. Numerous accounts of the social life of college students as well as biographies of the self-made individuals tell us little about the role of education in the lives of the common people. Owsley's claim that any farmer's son who wanted a college education could have one does not conform to the facts of college attendance. Actually, the common people were opposed to taxes for education, and many refused to send their children to public schools. One wonders what stigma may have been attached to public education. More important, if education is reflective of societal values, then the curriculum, the social and economic composition of the classroom, and parent and student expectations from education are of utmost importance in understanding the economic as well as the social life of the southern common people. As Ruth Miller Elson has shown in *Guardians of Tradition,* the antebellum southern classroom became a place to propagandize for a united South as well as to deny class feelings.

Guion G. Johnson suggests a connection between primary and secondary education, family expectations, and employment patterns in antebellum North Carolina. She claims that many middle-class families believed that education meant social advancement for their children, or at least their male children. Others saw the school as a place of discipline for unruly offspring. One wonders just how much status was attached to the private academy over the public school. What role did the fundamentalist religious sects have in that relationship between family life and education? Would the amount of literacy of the society tell us about job opportunities and professionalism? There is, Johnson believes, a connection between common folk class feeling and social values and the classroom. Her comments serve as a beginning in discovering the nature of the relationship between education and society.

As with religion and education, scholars believe that an understanding of the laws of the South also may tell us about class relations. In a celebrated study of crime and punishment in eighteenth-century England, *Albion's Fatal Tree*, E. P. Thompson claims that the elites used the law and the threat of imprisonment to control the social and economic behavior of the masses. Perhaps the planter and merchant elites used the same tactics with regard to the southern common people. Jack Kenny Williams in *Vogues in Villainy*, however, suggests that lawlessness in antebellum southern society created an intense popular demand to write laws to protect property and life from criminal elements. No doubt conditions in the South—such as the absence of a police force on the frontier, conflicts over land titles, and the uncontrolled growth of urban population—also contributed to violent criminal behavior and influenced the laws passed to control that behavior. If the elites used the law and criminal prosecution to control the common folk, the common folk in turn desired those laws for self-protection.

An essay in this volume concerning violent crime and control of criminal activities in Savannah during the 1850s captures the relationship between violence and the dynamic economic growth and social change in much of the urban South. Richard H. Haunton shows that fraternization between blacks and whites, especially among white immigrant merchants and tradesmen and slave thieves, was common in the urban retail trades. Judges locked up vagrants, paupers, the insane, as well as rowdy seamen, with black and white criminals, thus merging many types of deviant behavior in the popular mind. Free blacks, slaves, and the white lower classes received stiff jail sentences. Juries rarely convicted prominent merchants, lawyers, or planters, or at least they seldom served prison terms. Does this mean that the urban elites and their supporters used the legal system to control the common folk as well as the criminals? Did similar uses of elite power obtain in the rural South?

Haunton in part describes social and economic relations between urban free blacks and certain white laborers. It is evident that the free blacks influenced common-folk work patterns. In the next selection in this volume Ira Berlin discusses the work habits as well as the social relations among the free blacks in the Old South. They competed for jobs with urban day laborers and often replaced white laborers on the plantations and farms. One wonders to what extent the urban middle classes cooperated with the elites in using free black labor as a means of dominating the work patterns of the white common folk. Did the same strategy obtain in the rural sections of the South? Berlin's study suggests that further study of free black labor would reveal much about white occupations, job competition, and caste and class social relations.

In delineating distinctions between occupation and status among the free blacks in different southern regions, Berlin also suggests that geographical divisions caused occupational and status differences among the white common people. The availability of cheap, good land in the lower South meant that the common people profited more from their agricultural investments and owned more slaves than their counterparts in the upper South. The production of food for the midwestern and eastern urban markets showed that farmers in the upper South had strong economic ties to the North. As slavery declined in the upper South, the farm economy shifted radically from that of the lower South. The more rapid growth of urban life in the upper South created a larger urban middle class than in the lower South. More detailed study of those differences in employment status, wealth, and production interests among the common people would help us understand the economic tensions that divided the citizens of the many southern regions.

Studies such as Berlin's show just how much we need to understand working habits and changing job patterns in the various southern regions. The excellent works of economic historians such as Stanley Engerman, Robert Gallman, William Parker, Morton Rothstein, and Gavin Wright have brought to light regional differences as well as planter and slave work habits, the division of labor on the plantation, and the economic ties among the elites. Historians can no longer realistically claim that the South had only a simple agrarian economy. Yet, of this recent research, only Sam B. Hilliard, in *Hogmeat and Hoecakes*, studied the agricultural and commercial lives of the common people. His commentary on food production, eating habits, and internal commercial trading routes opens many questions about the variety of occupations and the work ethic in the economic system. Hilliard, however, neglected to analyze class ties or the business relationships between those who produced food for home consumption and the large number of farmers and planters who grew staple crops for export.

Forrest McDonald and Grady McWhiney provide a detailed description of one group of the southern work force, the herdsmen. The authors claim that the herdsmen, long thought to be part of the class of poor whites, were actually successful, if not affluent, members of common-folk society. By showing that the herdsmen chose a nomadic life-style and had no need to own land, the authors have disabused us of Owsley's classification of the agrarian middle class by landownership. One may ask whether other southern labor groups chose to unburden themselves of landownership, thus affecting their social and class status in the views of their contemporaries. The herdsmen also traded with the country store owners and the small farmers, as well as the urban merchants and the planters. The interconnectedness of the labor force also revealed many economic ties among the common folk. Further study of the common-folk labor force may reveal even more detailed financial connections.

Failure to understand the occupational structure as well as the social values and class attitudes of the common people also obscures their roles in the secession crisis. In *Toward a Patriarchal Republic*, Michael Johnson suggests that after the election of Lincoln the elites forced secession on the lower South out of fear of common-folk and lower-class Unionist sentiment. Johnson believes that because the common people had no interest in the slave economy, the planter leaders suspected they would not support the southern cause. In the view of Eugene D. Genovese, in "Yeoman Farmers in a Slaveholders' Democracy," the common folks' support of secession was inimical to their material and class interests. They owned few slaves and did not really have an economic stake in the society. Genovese claims that family connections, other social ties, and a body of common beliefs provided by the planter elites led the common folk to support secession. In short, although Genovese and Johnson do not agree on the actual role the common people had in secession, they concur that the elites controlled society and led the lesser folk to secession and civil war.

In large part the central question on the role of the common people in the secession crisis is their stake in society, or their interest in the future of slavery. Many scholars have concluded that race fear, based on the potential loss of white status and jobs, led the common folk to support secession. In a most provocative essay, reprinted in this volume, Robert R. Russel claims that the non-slaveholder shared the slave owners' financial interests and therefore supported any means to perpetuate slavery. Russel discounts the racist argument and shows that urban merchants, rural storekeepers, and small farmers traded with the planters and were united with them economically. Russel, however, misunderstood common-folk slave ownership and therefore discounted it as a reason to support secession. Before the Genovese theory of hegemonic powers of the elites may be given credence, we must clarify the relationship between common-folk slave ownership and the mutual financial interests of all the southern people.

Lack of clarity about which segments of the common folk supported secession and why also has confused our understanding of their behavior during the Civil War. Studies of common-folk good humor in the face of material deprivation and of their tenacious pursuit of the war effort rarely discuss the meaning of loyalty. Those who write about disloyalty claim that scarcity and the Confederate government's inability to inspire the troops and the people back home actually led to desertion to the Union cause. A few authors have suggested that the slave owners' unwillingness to serve in the army or fully support the Confederate government's confiscation practices fomented class conflict. In short, there is no consensus among scholars about the relationship between class interest and loyalty to the Confederacy.

One reason for the lack of understanding regarding common-folk loyalty is that the people left few records of how the war affected them materially and socially. Alden B. Pearson, Jr., discovered the diaries of a minister and his wife, which reflected the impressions of the common folk about the Civil War. Through the diaries, Pearson describes the depths of popular disillusionment with the war, the tragedies of internal conflicts, and the lasting animosity of many southerners because of northern soldiers' behavior in occupied territory. The diaries also relate how those hardships destroyed families, ruined incomes, and forced people to leave their homes permanently. Hostility toward the failed Confederate leadership and divisions among the people notwithstanding, Pearson believes that losing the war united most southerners against the victors.

During the early postwar years, as Michael Perman discusses in *Reunion Without Reaction*, persistent class and regional animosities in the South kindled northern hopes that many southerners would support the early Union plans for reconstruction. But the former Confederate state governments, probably with popular support, passed the "black codes," which limited the freedom of the ex-slaves. Northerners retaliated by imposing reconstruction on the southern people. Perhaps racial control was indeed more important to the southern common people than their own class or regional hostilities. This is another question that remains unanswered because of our ignorance of the lives of the common people. One thing is certain, northern-directed Reconstruction forced most southerners to unite against outsiders, even though they may have remained divided internally.

Recent scholarship on those postwar years has concentrated on the war's effect on the people of the South. Although decline in status, income, and landownership actually began before the war, the war ended slavery; many of the common people as well as some of the elites lost their land, or were forced onto smaller holdings, and their livestock was destroyed. Determining which classes lost the most in the war or during Reconstruction remains the subject of further investigation. The postwar depression in the world demand for cotton drastically changed the social composition of the New South. Part II of this volume shows the results of common folks' loss of land, jobs, and social status. Many of the selections in that part demonstrate that to understand what the war and Reconstruction contributed to the bitter conflict in the Populist era requires knowledge of class and financial relations in the Old South.

Walter J. Fraser, Jr.

Reflections of "Democracy" in Revolutionary South Carolina? The Composition of Military Organizations and the Attitudes and Relationships of the Officers and Men, 1775–1780

Since "armies are but projections of the societies from which they spring," historians of the Consensus School and the New Left are essentially agreed that studies of military organizations in Revolutionary America could offer "some broad insights into American life"; and at the same time such studies would reveal more about the Revolutionary Era "from the bottom up."[1]

Prominent members of the Consensus School have already reached conclusions supporting their school of thought. Professor Don Higginbotham has written: "What provocative questions about American society arise when we learn that numerous American officers avoided the customary lash as a form of punishment, and that many officers fraternized with their enlisted men and discussed the issues of the war with them."[2] Within militia organizations, Higginbotham found a "lack of social cleavage between most officers and their men." This "made for a familiarity that more than occasionally bred ill-discipline and disobedience."[3] Professor Daniel Boorstin, also a Consensus School historian, finds a "leveling spirit" within Revolutionary Era military organizations. He too discovers "an unmilitary familiarity between officers and men" which sometimes led to disobedience in the ranks and desertions.[4] Higginbotham and Boorstin would agree that an independence of spirit, poor pay, inadequate food, clothing, and lodging rather than a desire to join the enemy prompted these desertions among the rank and file. Both historians also would agree that the officers came from "the vast free holding middle class" while the rank and file were represented by the "sturdy yeomen" or "embattled farmers" who united in a "people's war for political independence."[5]

Source: South Carolina Historical Magazine 78 (July 1977): 202–12. Reprinted with permission.

The assumptions of the Consensus School of historians, then, reflect a society wherein social distinctions are blurred, where there is considerable "democracy," and a society in which there is much agreement, unanimity, and little class conflict. This paper will test these general conclusions against fragmentary data assembled on the composition of certain military organizations in Revolutionary South Carolina and the attitudes and relationships of the officers and men.

On June 1, 1775, the Provincial Congress assembled in Charles Town, South Carolina. Aware of the events at Lexington and Concord and amidst rumors that the British were planning to incite Indian attacks and slave rebellions across South Carolina, the Congress ordered the raising of two regiments of foot and one of rangers. By February, 1776, the Second Provincial Congress had added an artillery regiment and two rifle regiments. In late 1776 these six regiments became part of the Continental Establishment.[6]

From the first raising of the regiments both the field grade and company grade officers were selected by the South Carolina Legislature. They chose men like themselves, "gentlemen of fortune and family," who had "a stake in society." Generally they were men who had become rich, gradually or overnight, in trade, land, and slaves. These Carolina men were described by a northern-born contemporary as "haughty and insolent"; the ownership of slaves had accustomed them "from infancy to tyrannize. They carry with them a disposition to treat all mankind in the same manner."[7]

Of the twelve officers appointed by the Legislature who rose to the rank of colonel or general in the six regiments, ten were members of the Provincial Congress and the remaining two were younger men from prominent families.[8] Of the one-hundred and eight men who were elected to company grade positions (captains), twenty were members of the Legislature when first elected; another thirty-six were subsequently elected to the Legislature or held elective posts as magistrates in their districts; at least twelve others were identified as younger relatives of influential Carolinians.[9] Therefore a substantial majority of those men positively identified as being elected to a captaincy in South Carolina's six regiments were men, like their superiors, who held a substantial "stake in society."

Upon election, South Carolina's "aristocratic" officer corps sought to raise an army. It was one of their most vexing problems.

Initially "belles, barbecues, and bounties" were used as inducements for recruiting. Employing these tactics in scouring the backcountry in July, 1775, to fill up the ranks of the Second Regiment, Captain Bernard Elliott found the type of men the elite officer corps wanted in its army—"young men (who) would be very proper for the Service as they have little, and some no property, but live on the cattle of the Neighbouring stocks, and the Deer they kill by fire hunting at Night," Captain Elliott wrote. However, he met with very limited success in enlisting recruits.[10]

The officer class continued to lament the lack of recruits to fill up the ranks. In early 1777, Captain Thomas Pinckney wrote to his sister from Charles Town: "I am much chagrined at the bad success we have met with in recruiting."[11] By 1778 the regiments remained at half-strength and a Charles Town resident moaned: "It is difficult to fill them when the inhabitants don't incline to enlist for Soldiers. But, we are in hopes to fill them by a Vagrant Act."[12]

The Vagrant Act passed the South Carolina Legislature in March, 1778, Desperate for troops, the Legislature ordered the immediate enlistment of all "idle men, beggars, strolling or straggling persons" as privates in South Carolina's six regiments. Persons voluntarily enlisting were offered 100 acres of land in South Carolina in addition to the 100 acres offered by the Continental Congress. Also sizeable bounties were paid to all physically fit recruits not over forty-five years of age.[13]

Despite such arbitrary measures and attractive inducements, troop strength remained down. A French official at Charles Town in late 1778 observed that the garrison numbered only 600 men and these were "recruited with some difficulty."[14]

Those that did enlist came under a disciplinary system initially tempered with paternalism. During the early months of 1776, officers like Colonel Charles Cotesworth Pinckney, Colonel Francis Marion and Captain Bernard Elliott paternalistically admonished their troops to behave like soldiers. The officer's lectures on Christian habits often carried both a strong puritanical strain and an ultra-patriotic theme.

Holding duty, honor, and service sacred, Colonel Pinckney told his men that "the most glorious of all characters" was the "good soldier." Pinckney urged his men to eschew the "Dissipation and Seduction of" Charles Town; then "we shall have the heart felt Satisfaction of having done our duty, and Shall not be unworthy of the praises of our Country." For "Country, Love of Military Glory, which should swell the soldier's breast and Lead him to Renown," Pinckney told his recruits, "exert every Endeavour to preserve and Increase the Discipline of the Regiment that when our County Shall call us forth to real action we may add to and not diminish it." By this discipline, he concluded, "the Grecians Routed the numerous house of Persia, the Romans gained their amazing victories."[15]

Captain Bernard Elliott also sought in a paternalistic fashion to awaken his men to their duty. He composed and read to them a prayer:

> O Lord God of Hosts . . . instruct and enoble us to behave ourselves. . . . O make us faithful soldiers of Jesus Christ. Preserve us our God from the profaneness and blasphemy, the Lewdness and debauchery. . . . Help us our Supreme Commander . . . so to live that we may find it the greatest gain to die; and let us go on (as Christ's faithful) soldiers so conquering and to conquer the enemies of thy Glory . . . that having overcome we may sit down in thy Kingdom. . . .[16]

But such paternalistic lectures, pious and patriotic appeals appear to have fallen on deaf ears. The exhortations may have even rankled the enlisted men.

When the recruits showed little disposition to behave as their superiors admonished them to do, a sterner tact was taken. Regimental officers posted orders promising swift and severe disciplinary action for gaming and drunkenness. The men were ordered to be "decently dressed" and "to shave at least three times a week"; they were ordered "not to sleep" in their clothes; they were commanded to follow the examples of "the officers in having their hair cut short" and not kept at "an effeminate length"; the enlisted men were instructed "to touch" their caps "and give the wall to every Continental officer whom they shall meet."[17] Despite this barrage of orders, the enlisted men showed no inclination to conform to regulations. And they demonstrated particularly a disposition to "hassel" their officers.

Perhaps rankling the enlisted men were the visible signs of the great social cleavage beween themselves and the "aristocratic" officer corps. An English traveler in South Carolina on the eve of the Revolution described the officer class as "all people of property (who) cutt a pretty good regular appearance having handsome uniforms." However, he found that the enlisted men, "if possible, make a worse figure than the Train Bands of London."[18] French officials visiting in South Carolina during 1777 and 1778 also noted the motley appearance of the enlisted men. One French official commented that the clothing of the rank and file "is not . . . uniform, since they lack cloth and other articles"; another wrote that the "troops are in a rather bad state both as regards dress and discipline."[19]

Besides dress, the enlisted men no doubt noted the great inequities in lodging, food, and leisure-time activities between themselves and their officers. They observed the black body servants attending officers from generals to lieutenants. They observed such officers as Captain Thomas Pinckney receiving a steady flood of luxury items denied to them. Over a period of several months Pinckney requested and received from his family dozens of bottles of the best brandy and wines, turkeys, hats lined with "Pink Silk," Cassimere waist coats, butter, silver shoe buckles, a bath tub, mosquito net and table linens. While stationed near Charles Town Pinckney's men noted that he frequently attended parties, teas, and balls "with the ladies" although they were not permitted to attend such activities.[20]

It became quite apparent to the enlisted men that while they were neither well quartered nor well cared for, denied even the basic necessities; while they suffered during the winter months from lack of blankets and fuel, their officers lived high and well.[21] This awareness of the great inequities in life-styles intensified their hostility toward the elite officer class. Perhaps this is partly the reason that many simply refused to obey the orders constantly handed down on dress and behavior. Maybe these feelings account for the continuing assaults on the property of the officers.

Regimental records abound with accounts of enlisted men stealing their officer's silk stockings and linen shirts; of stealing the parson's fences and insulting the regimental chaplains. As well, the records are replete with incidents of rioting of the enlisted men, of their firing off salvos from their barracks in the dead of the night and of drunkenness. And there is ample evidence of more serious offenses like refusing to obey a direct order, threatening an officer, desertions, and treason.[22]

When their paternalistic appeals failed to bring order and discipline to their reluctant recruits, the South Carolina officer class adopted the disciplinary system authorized by the Continental Congress with the advice of General Washington. Now courts martial convened with astounding frequency in South Carolina's six regiments.

During an eleven month period about two-hundred-and-fifty men out of three-hundred-and-sixteen men of the second regiment were court-martialed for various offenses—over eighty percent of the unit! Though the records of the fourth regiment are less complete, thirty-nine separate courts martial were convened over a two-year period.[23] And frequently the cases of five to eight men were taken up at a time by these boards. Within a period of four months, December 5, 1777, to April 14, 1778, forty-three courts martial were "ordered to sit" on cases involving men of the first regiment. An order book of the same unit covering a different time period shows that only seventeen men were court-martialed during a seven month period. However, the officer keeping this order book recorded only the most serious breeches of discipline.[24] Ten courts martial were convened in the third regiment during a four month period.[25]

These fragmentary records of the first, second, third and fourth South Carolina regiments show specifically that 297 enlisted men were court-martialed. If, however, added to this figure is the number of men facing charges before the ninety-two boards during which no specific charges or names were recorded, a conservative estimate of the men court-martialed would be 481. The combined strength of these units during these periods probably never exceeded 900 enlisted men. Therefore, approximately fifty percent of the rank and file faced court martial boards during this brief time span in four of the six South Carolina regiments.[26]

The men in these units were court-martialed for a wide variety of offenses. Desertions accounted for nearly thirty-five percent of the disciplinary action; neglect of duty, allowing prisoners to escape, disrespect to officers, and treason account for nearly seventeen percent of the offenses; being drunk on duty and displaying riotous behavior account for approximately thirteen percent; about eleven percent of the men who faced court martial boards were charged with being absent from guard and sleeping on sentinel duty; stealing, forgery, gambling and quarrelling constituted about six percent of the offenses. The men were also court-martialed for losing their weapons, selling their equipment, beating their wives or someone else's wife, and one private was court-martialed for threatening "to take away the life of a fifer when in the execution of his office."[27] In about six percent of the cases, the charges against the men were undetermined.

For all offenses, the punishment most frequently handed down by the boards was flogging. The Continental Congress initially authorized thirty-nine lashes, but on September 20, 1776, the Congress raised the maximum number of stripes to 100.[28] However, not only did the number of lashes frequently seem to exceed the offense in the South Carolina units, some sentences were illegal. In January, 1776, an enlisted man stationed on Sullivan's Island near Charles Town was tried for mutiny, convicted, and sentenced to 250 lashes.[29]

Cruel and unusual punishments unauthorized by the Continental Articles were also imposed by South Carolina's court martial boards. In December, 1776, Levi Coleman was convicted of sleeping on his post and sentenced to "sit down and have one gun under his hams, and another over his neck, and brought as close together as possible, and tied fast, there to remain for the space of ten minutes, and at the expiration of the time the upper gun to be fired off.[30] On January 3, 1777, another enlisted man convicted of sleeping on his post was sentenced "to ride the wooden horse," a particularly cruel punishment.[31]

The most severe punishments were reserved for the enlisted men who were judged disrespectful toward their officers or who exhibited treasonable behavior. Within a period of a few months in 1777 four men of the second regiment were punished severely for disrespect to their officers. John Griffin was sentenced to 100 lashes for "misbehavior to Lt. Welch"; Thomas Walker for "misbehavior and insolence" to Lt. Evenigh received 100 lashes; because "his misbehavior to his officer Lt. Dunbar was insolent and criminal in a very high degree contrary to all good order & discipline," Sgt. O'Neal was reduced to private and sentenced to "receive 100 lashes on his bare back." It was charged that private James Orange, who while confined for desertion, did, in the "most outrageous and grossest manner insult and abuse Lt. Preveaux . . . threatening him with a knife in his hand & in the course of the abuse he repeatedly damned the Continental Congress saying he was good English Blood & would support the cause of Great Britain to his last." Tried and found guilty, Orange was sentenced to receive 200 lashes because of the "atrociousness of his crime."[32] When Michael Wall of the first South Carolina regiment and Conrad Besinger were tried and adjudged guilty for desertion and being "found in arms against the United States" they were sentenced "to be hanged by the neck til dead." Phillip McQuire and William Hogh of the first South Carolina regiment were tried for desertion and being in arms against the United States. Both men were sentenced to be shot.[33] It appears too that the following men were executed for the following reasons: Thomas Metcalf, "Enemy to the States," George Rardall, "Treason," and James Sims "for endeavouring to make the soldiers discontented with the Constitution & attempting to induce them to desert."[34]

Although the usual sentences for simple desertion were 100 lashes, occasionally the court martial boards handed down sentences imposing capital punishment. In March, 1778, James Oliver, John McNamara and James Harlock of the first regiment were charged with desertion and sentenced to "suffer death by being shot."[35] The Reverend Oliver Hart has left a rather gruesome account of an execution for desertion. Attending in the capacity of chaplain to the condemned, Hart watched as a Sergeant Malcom was blindfolded and made to drop to his knees. He was then shot; "which was thrice repeated before he was quite dead."[36]

If "armies are but projections of the societies from which they spring," the fragmentary records bearing on the composition of South Carolina's six regiments of the Continental Line, and the attitudes and relationships of the officers and men reflect a sharply different society than that pictured by the Consensus historians. South Carolina's units were led by a haughty, arrogant, and "aristocratic" officer corps, wealthy in land and slaves. They commanded grossly understrength units composed of reluctant, unpropertied, and vagrant recruits, not "sturdy yeomen." Sharp distinctions in dress, lodging, and food highlighted the social cleavage between the officers and men and there is little indication of a "leveling spirit" within these units. Nor is there any evidence that the officers fraternized with their enlisted men or discussed the issues of the war with them. Rather, when the officer class discovered that a paternalistic approach failed to quell the rebelliousness of the men, they came to use the lash unsparingly.

Accepting the fact that a well disciplined military organization is necessary in war time, the punishments meted out, however, seem at great variance with the alleged humanitarian cause for which the Revolution was fought—"life, liberty and the pursuit of happiness." Were the severe punishments, then, an indication that the elite recognized that there were deep-seated antagonisms toward them among the rank and file? Does not the endemic rebelliousness and hostility of the enlisted men toward the "glorious cause" and their officers indicate this? It is significant to note that the Consensus historians have accounted for the behavior of the enlisted men in the same way that one of South Carolina's elite, David Ramsey, accounted for their behavior. The rank and file, Ramsey wrote, were "accustomed to activity on their farms (and) they could not bear the languors of an encampment. Having grown up in habits of freedom and independence on their freeholds, they reluctantly submitted to martial discipline."[37]

In sum, the desertions, neglect of duty, insolence toward their officers and general misbehavior of the poor white rank and file is analogous to the behavior of black slaves in the antebellum South toward their masters. Also the response of the master class, first with paternalism and then the lash, bears striking similarities. As the black slave resisted class oppression,[38] perhaps so too were members of South Carolina's enlisted ranks resisting class oppression. And as slave resistance and rebelliousness was a manifestation of class war,[39] so too was the behavior of South Carolina's rank and file who discovered little in the way of common goals with the "aristocratic" revolutionaries.

In view of these conclusions, then, more studies are needed "from the bottom up." Perhaps they too might question the confronting Consensus School's conclusions that the Revolution was not fought to gain, but to preserve democracy. Such studies may thereby promote a new appreciation of Carl Becker's thesis: the Revolution was not only a struggle for home rule, but also one to determine who would rule at home.

Notes

1. Don Higginbotham, "American Historians and the Military History of the American Revolution," *American Historical Review*, 70 (October, 1964): 33-34; Don Higginbotham, *The War of American Independence: Military Attitudes, Policies and Practice*, 1763-1789 (New York, 1971): xv, 7; John Shy, "A New Look at Colonial Militia," *William and Mary Quarterly*, 20 (April, 1963): 176; John Shy, *Toward Lexington: The Role of the British Army in the Coming of the American Revolution* (Princeton, N.J., 1965): viii, 393; Jesse Lemisch, "The American Revolution Seen from the Bottom Up," in Barton J. Berstein (ed.), *Towards a New Past: Dissenting Essays in American History* (New York, 1969): 27.

2. Higginbotham, "American Historians," 34.

3. Higginbotham, *The War of Independence*, 12.

4. Daniel J. Boorstin, *The Americans: The Colonial Experience* (New York, 1958): 365-367.

5. Ibid.

6. A. S. Salley, Jr. (ed), "Records of the Regiments of the South Carolina Line, Continental Establishment," *South Carolina Historical and Genealogical Magazine*, 5 (January, 1904): 15; Edward McCrady, *The History of South Carolina in the Revolution, 1775-1780* (New York, 1969): 10-14; David Duncan Wallace, *South Carolina: A Short History, 1520-1948* (Chapel Hill, N.C., 1951): 260, 283.

7. McCrady, *History of South Carolina*, 13; H. Roy Merrens, "A View of Coastal South Carolina in 1778: The Journal of Ebenezer Hazard," *South Carolina Historical Magazine* 73 (October, 1972): 190.

8. Wilmot G. DeSaussure, *The Names as far as can be Ascertained of the Officers who Served in the South Carolina Regiments on the Continental Establishment* (Columbia, S.C., 1886); William E. Hemphill and Wylma Anne Wates (eds.), *Extracts from the Journals of the Provincial Congress of South Carolina, 1775-1776* (Columbia, S.C., 1960): 43-48, 269-299; William E. Hemphill and Wylma Anne Wates (eds.), *Extracts from the Journals of the Provincial Congress of South Carolina, 1776-1780* (Columbia, S.C., 1970): 331-371; A. S. Salley, Jr. (ed.), "Records of the Regiments of the South Carolina Line, Continental Establishment," *South Carolina Historical and Genealogical Magazine*, 5 (October, 1904): 216-217. The names of the officers who rose to be colonels or generals were: Christopher Gadsden, Isaac Huger, Owen Roberts, William Moultrie, Isaac Motte, William Thompson, James Mayson, William Henderson, Edmund Hyrne, John Laurens, Francis Marion, Thomas Sumter.

9. DeSaussure, *The Names . . . of the Officers who Served*; Hemphill and Wates, *Extracts . . . 1775-1776*, 269-299; Hemphill and Wates, *Extracts . . . 1776-1788*, 331-371; Richard Walsh, *The Writings of Christopher Gadsden, 1746-1805* (Columbia, 1966), 184n.

10. Joseph W. Barnwell (ed.), "Bernard Elliott's Recruiting Journal, 1775," *South Carolina Historical and Genealogical Magazine* 17 (July, 1916): 95-98.

11. Jack L. Cross (ed.), "Letters of Thomas Pinckney, 1775-1780," *South Carolina Historical Magazine* 58 (July, 1957): 77.

12. Raymond Starr, "Letters from John Gervais to Henry Laurens, 1777-1778," *South Carolina Historical Magazine* 66 (January, 1965): 29.

13. McCrady, *History of South Carolina*, 309.

14. Lee Kennett (ed.), "Charleston in 1778: A French Intelligence Report," *South Carolina Historical Magazine* 66 (April, 1965): 110.

15. A. S. Salley (ed.), "Order Book of the 1st Regiment, South Carolina Line," *South Carolina Historical and Genealogical Magazine* 7 (July, 1906): 133-134; Marvin R. Zahniser, *Charles Cotesworth Pinckney: Founding Father* (Chapel Hill, N.C., 1967): 38.

16. Order Book of Captain Bernard Elliott, MS., South Carolina Historical Society, Charleston.

17. Ibid.; A. S. Salley (ed.), "Order Book of the 1st Regiment, South Carolina Line," *South Carolina Historical and Genealogical Magazine* 7 (January, October, 1906): 79-80, 196; John Bennett, "A List of Non Commissioned Officers and Private Men of the Second South Carolina Continental Regiment of Foot," *South Carolina Historical and Genealogical Magazine* 16 (January, 1915): 28-29.

18. John Bennett, "Charleston in 1774 as Described by an English Traveler," *South Carolina Historical and Genealogical Magazine* 47 (July, 1946): 179-180.

19. Paul G. Sifton, "Some Sources of South Carolina Revolutionary History, with Two Unpublished Letters of Baron de Kalb," *South Carolina Historical Magazine* 66 (April, 1965), 107; Lee Kennett, "Charleston in 1778: A French Intelligence Report," 110.

20. Jack L. Cross (ed.), "Letters of Thomas Pinckney, 1775-1780," *South Carolina Historical Magazine* 58 (January, April, July, October, 1957): 25-26, 28-29, 31, 72, 74, 76, 80, 81, 147, 237.

21. Bennett, "A List of Non Commissioned Officers and Private Men," 32-33.

22. Ibid.; [Captain Isaac] DuBose Order Book, January 15-November 22, 1777, MS. South Carolina Historical Society; Order Book of Captain Barnard Elliott; "Order Book of John Faucheraud Grimke, August 1778 to May 1780," *South Carolina Historical and Genealogical Magazine* (April, 1912, July 1916, October 1917, April, 1918); A. S. Salley, Jr. (ed.), "An Order Book of the 1st Regiment, South Carolina Line, Continental Establishment," *South Carolina Historical and Genealogical Magazine* 7 (January, 1906).

23. Dubose Order Book; Bennett, "A List of Non Commissioned Officers and Private Men," 32.

24. A. S. Salley, Jr. (ed.), "An Order Book of the 1st Regiment, South Carolina Line, Continental Establishment," *South Carolina Historical and Genealogical Magazine* 7, 8 (January, July, October, 1906, April, 1907): 19-25, 75-80, 130-40, 194, 196, 197, 200-201; 69-73, 75, 79, 83; Moultrie-Lincoln Order Book, MS., South Carolina Historical Society.

25. Salley (ed.), *Order Book of the Third Regiment*, 1, 11, 16, 17, 26, 27, 29, 31, 32, 33.

26. List of the Division of the Army of the State of the United States of America Under the Command of the Honorable Maj. Gen. Robert Howe in the State of South Carolina, 1778," *South Carolina Historical and Genealogical Magazine* 13 (April, 1912): 94; Bennett, "A List of Non Commissioned Officers and Private Men," 32.

27. Moultrie-Lincoln Order Book.

28. Maurer Maurer, "Military Justice Under General Washington," *Military Affairs* 28 (Spring, 1964): 12.

29. A. S. Salley, Jr., *The History of Orangeburg County, South Carolina* (Baltimore, 1969): 342.

30. Robert W. Gibbes, *Documentary History of the American Revolution* (3 vols. New York, 1855-1857), II, 50-51.

31. Ibid., II, 51; Maurer, "Military Justice," 11.

32. Dubose Order Book.

33. Moultrie-Lincoln Order Book.

34. A. S. Salley (ed.), "Records of the Regiments of the South Carolina Line, Continental Establishment," *South Carolina Historical and Genealogical Magazine* 5 (April, 1904): 85.

35. Salley (ed.), "An Order Book of the 1st Regiment," 73.

36. Diary of the Reverend Oliver Hart," *Year Book, 1896, City of Charleston, South Carolina* (Charleston, 1896): 395.

37. David Ramsay, *History of South Carolina From Its First Settlement in 1670 to the Year 1808* (2 vols. Newberry, South Carolina, 1858), I, 169.

38. Eugene D. Genovese, *Roll, Jordon, Roll: The World the Slaves Made* (New York, 1974): 597-598.

39. Ibid., 588.

Frank L. Owsley

The Farmers Possess the Land

The second wave of settlers to come into the public domain were, as previously observed, the farmers and planters, who desired the ownership of the land rather than its free use. They cleared and fenced off large areas, turned out their own little herds of cattle and swine to graze on the unimproved public and private lands of the community and thus forced the graziers to withdraw and seek ranges undisturbed by the plow and ax. It was agriculture, then, and not slavery—as has been said repeatedly in the discussion of the pastoral economy of the frontier—that drove the herdsmen from frontier to frontier and finally into the pine barrens, hills, and mountains. After the Civil War this phenomenon was repeated when the farmers or nesters swarmed into the Great Plains and crowded the cattle ranchers farther into the more arid regions.

If slavery did not drive out the herdsmen from the good lands, what of the farmers, both the nonslaveholders and the small slaveholders? Were they crowded from the good lands by the planter and compelled to settle upon the inhospitable soil of the pine barrens and mountains? The answer to this is no. The plain farmers, who comprised the bulk of the Southern people, lived, as a rule, neither in the piney woods nor in the mountains, except in the valleys. They lived dispersed over all the arable regions of the South and were settled in considerable numbers on every type of soil adapted to agricultural uses except the swamp and river lands. The immigrant farmer usually avoided such regions because of the deadly malaria, and because of the great expense of clearing off the heavy timber and dense canebrakes and of constructing canals and dykes. Because of this unhealthfulness and the cost of bringing such lands under culti-

Source: Reprinted by permission of Louisiana State University Press from *Plain Folk of the Old South* by Frank L. Owsley, copyright ©1949.

vation, even the richest planters usually shunned these swamps as long as other moderately rich land was available. The truth of the matter is that the plain farmers settled where they chose and stayed as long as it suited them. There were, however, several factors that determined the farmers' choice of location when they migrated to the new lands in the West.

The agricultural immigrant, far more than the herdsman, tended to seek out a country as nearly as possible like the one in which he formerly lived, in the matter of soil, rainfall, temperature, and appearance. The similarity of appearance was of great importance for both psychological and practical reasons. The fact that the emigrant shook from his feet the dust of his old community did not mean that he divested himself of the mental picture and love of the old countryside, of those rich limestone valleys, rolling hills, and sandy levels where the odor of the resinous pine scents the air and the tall trees moan in the wind, or of the rugged mountains with purple shadows and smoke hanging above the cove in the late afternoon, announcing the cheery news of supper cooking or the still making a run. A settler simply could never be entirely happy and feel at home unless he was surrounded by a landscape much like the one where he had spent his earlier years. Those accustomed to rugged country seldom debouched upon the plains, but migrated to a country where there were other hills, mountains, and valleys. The Ozarks, for example, were largely settled by pioneers from the Appalachians. Likewise, those who had inhabited level country usually avoided the hills unless they could settle in a wide valley with the hills in the distance. Others, who had lived in an open country, preferred to settle on an open prairie. Farmers accustomed to sandy loams and even poor sandy soils would not usually pre-empt or purchase a homestead in a region of stiff clay or "gumbo" soils.

Aside from sentiment that grows into acute nostalgia in strange surroundings, the agricultural migrants have scientific and practical reasons for selecting a country similar to the one from which they emigrate. The farmer who seeks a country similar in appearance, climate, and soil to the old community in which he has lived makes the basic and sound assumption that he can continue in the new country to grow the field crops, fruits, and vegetables, the tillage, habits, and marketing of which are part of his mental furniture. William H. Sparks, who himself had migrated west, remarked that the immigrants were sure to select their new home, whenever they could, "in the same parallel, and with surroundings as nearly like those they had left as possible. With the North Carolinian, good springwater, and pineknots for his fire, were the *sine qua non*."[1] Paul Vidal de La Blache, the geographer, applies this principle to the migratory movements of the Chinese into the unsettled areas within their own country. "How," he asks, "could such individuals contrive to get along there, if unable to live in customary ways, and with customary means?" They must "find an environment similar to the one which they have been obliged to leave."[2] Isaiah Bowman observes that the primary function of the individuals who went out upon the American frontier to locate a fit place for settlement for themselves and their neighbors usually "consisted merely in finding soils and slopes that resembled those back at home that were known to be good."[3] The letters and diaries of pioneers abound with reports to those in the East that the soil and climate of the new country were like those back at home. As a result of such reassuring knowledge, "one great bugbear of pulling up stakes and removing to a distant home was greatly neutralized by this comfortable feeling that, however great the distance and the consequent toil, men knew toward what kind of haven they were faring and that they would meet there conditions which they had mastered before."[4]

It was soon known by the average person in the Eastern states, that, outside the highlands, the temperature, rainfall, and soil of the country lying to the west, until the Great Plains were approached, were sufficiently like those in the East to permit the continuation of the same types of agriculture. This information was derived in part from land prospectors and the emigrant guides prepared by such writers as William Darby, who made a careful study of these and related matters, but it came chiefly from the reports of the herdsmen, who had raised their little patches of corn, truck, tobacco, and cotton while hunting and grazing their livestock on the frontier. By 1860 the trend of migration had been scientifically examined by the Census Office on the basis of the nativity reports in the census tables of 1850 and 1860, and the superintendent of the census was able to state the fact that "the almost universal law of internal migration is, that it moves west on the same parallel of latitude. . . . Men seldom change their climate, because to do so they must change their habits."[5]

Although the necessity of continuing to grow the usual crops compelled the immigrant farmer to stay within certain parallels of latitude or isothermal zones, it was not the sole practical motive that prompted him to settle upon land similar to that which he had cultivated in the East. Of great importance was the need to continue to employ the methods and tools with which he was familiar. Those accustomed to the use of certain farm implements adapted to one kind of soil had great difficulty in changing to another type of soil, even though such a change did not entail any change in their farm economy. This was particularly true of those who, having cultivated sandy or loamy soils, moved into gummy clays and lime soils. Indeed there has been since ancient times a preference among agricultural folk for a soil with a sand or silt content because of the greater ease with which it can be cultivated. Vidal de La Blache observes, for example, that the early agricultural communities of Europe were located on "the most easily cultivated" and "not always the most fertile" soils. "Mellow friable lands forming a sort of band from southern Russia to northern France" were the early abode of agricultural settlers. "Men began to seek out certain localities because they were easy to cultivate."[6] Another consideration of great importance in selecting a place of settlement was the character of drinking water to be found in the new country. Such consideration is easily overlooked by an urban people who take for granted a good water supply. The character of the water is largely determined by the character of the soil, except in the case of water from artesian wells and wells bored to a deep stratum. The best water was always to be found in a country with a rolling surface and light, sandy, poor soil. People who were accustomed to the cool limpid, freestone, soft water of the sandy hills could seldom be induced to remain long in a limestone region where the water was never clear and was hard and bitter. The women folk had their say at this point: washing and cooking in such water was too much for those accustomed to soft, freestone water.

The implication of this prejudice in favor of a country similar in climate, surface appearance, streams and springs, soil, and the natural growth of grass, timber, and wild flowers, is this: the farmers making new homes in the West were, in the majority of cases, not in search of the richest lands of the public domain, but merely the richest of the particular type of land to which they were accustomed back in the East. Perhaps in most cases they were content with land almost identical with that left behind, however poor such land had been. The only advantages that the new land would have were that it was fresh and cheaper, and the range would be better for livestock and game.

Naturally, therefore, the rural folk of the upper South dwelling in the limestone valleys and highlands, whose pattern of farm husbandry had been the growing of grain and livestock, did not in migrating erupt into the lower South where climate and soil would force a radical change in farm economy and methods of cultivation. On the contrary, when they migrated, it was usually into the highlands, limestone basins, and valleys of Tennessee, Kentucky, Missouri, and northern Arkansas, and into the wooded lands across the Ohio River, where climate, soil, timber and the grasses indicated that the new country would be hospitable to the familiar old crops.

The authors of the emigrant guides, gazetteers, and geographies were thoroughly cognizant of the westward trend and of the principles of human geography governing it; and they counseled the prospective immigrant in accordance with these principles. Baird, in traveling over the West was struck with the manner in which that country had been colonized.

"The emigration to the Valley of the Mississippi," says Baird, "seems to have gone in columns, moving from the East almost due west, from the respective states from which they originated. From New England the emigrating column advanced through New York, peopling the middle and western parts of that state in its progress; but still continuing, it reached the northern part of Ohio, then Indiana, and finally Illinois. A part of the same column . . . is diverging into Michigan. . . . The Pennsylvania and the New Jersey column advanced within the parallels of latitude of those states in west Pennsylvania, and still continuing, advanced into the middle and southern parts of Ohio, and extended even into the middle parts of Indiana and Illinois. The Virginia column advanced first into the western part of the state and Kentucky—which was long a constituent part of it—, thence into the southern parts of Indiana and Illinois, until it had spread over almost the whole of Missouri. The North Carolina column advanced into East Tennessee, thence into West Tennessee, and also into Missouri. And the South Carolina and Georgia column has moved upon the extensive and fertile lands of Alabama [and Mississippi]. . . . In Arkansas, the emigrating columns of Kentucky and Tennessee predominate. . . .

"The above mentioned fact furnishes a better key than any other that I know of, to furnish a correct knowledge of the diversities of customs and manners which prevail in the Valley of the Mississippi. For if one knows what are the peculiarities of the several states east of the Allegheny mountains, he may expect them, with some shades of difference, occasioned by local circumstances, in the corresponding parallels in the West. Slavery keeps nearly within the same parallels. And so does every other peculiarity."[7]

William Darby, John M. Peck, S. H. Collins, Samuel Brown, and Timothy Flint, to name only a few of the better known authors of emigrant guides, give similar descriptions of the characteristics of the westward migration. They all give what has proved to be reasonably accurate advice as to the several temperature zones and the crops and fruits best suited to them.[8]

The Federal censuses of 1850 and 1860 fully sustained these observations on migration. In 1850 there were 142,102 free natives of Virginia living in the upper Southern states of Missouri, Kentucky, and Tennessee, and 155,978 living in the Old Northwest; but in the lower Southern states of Georgia, Florida, Alabama, Mississippi, Louisiana, Arkansas, and Texas there were only 38,311 such Virginians. The Virginians had settled chiefly in the tobacco, grain, and livestock regions. Maryland exemplifies better than Virginia the zonal trend of the migration of agricultural folk. In 1850 over 30,000 free natives of that state were living in Virginia and Pennsylvania—obviously the western portions—54,310 in the Old Northwest, 12,277 in Tennessee, Kentucky, and Missouri, and only 4,722 in the seven states of the lower South mentioned above. Thus Maryland contributed little either to the upper or lower Southern states west of the mountains. North Carolina which, outside of the highlands, is essentially a state of the lower South, had 103,315 free natives living in Tennessee, Kentucky, and Missouri, 52,467 in the Old Northwest, and 107,912 in the newer states of the lower South.

The cotton farmers and planters of the lower states of the seaboard South did not settle to any great extent in the grain and livestock-growing states of the upper South. The Carolinas settled Georgia, and also, with considerable aid from Virginia, colonized Tennessee. The remainder of the states of the lower South were the children and grandchildren of the Carolinas, Georgia, and Tennessee. In 1850 there were 140,261 free native South Carolinians, 140,041 Georgians, 99,140 North Carolinians, and 79,640 Tennesseans living in the newer states of the lower South compared with about 43,000 from Virginia and Maryland. Though Tennessee and North Carolina had contributed heavily to the upper slave states and to the Old Northwest, South Carolina and Georgia had only 12,000 free natives in that region in 1850.[9]

The census of 1860 continues to show the westward trend of population in the South, the newer states such as Alabama, Missippi, Tennessee, and Kentucky contributing heavily to the states in the same zones to the west.[10]

The first agricultural settlers in the new farm lands in the Southwest as a rule came from the Piedmont or "up country" of the Carolinas and Georgia, where they had already been engaged in the cultivation of cotton and where the soil was similar in its clay and sand contents to much of the soil of the new country. Local pioneer writers agree that the early settlers of the Southwest—especially Alabama and Mississippi—were up-country Carolinians or Tennesseans, many of whom had originally come from up-country South Carolina. For example, most of the South Carolinians who moved into Blount, Jefferson, and Pickens counties in Alabama, were from the York, Abbeville, and Fairfield districts,[11] very similar both in soil and in topography to the country in which they settled. More recent studies show that in all parts of Alabama, as late as 1828, most of those immigrants whose origin could be ascertained came not from the Tidewater regions of the South Atlantic states, but from the Piedmont, where they had been cultivating the short-staple cotton. They were usually farmers and small planters with few slaves. Few of the Tidewater planters migrated into the Southwest during this period, probably because their heavy investments in land, the stability of their principal money crops—rice, tobacco, and long-staple cotton—and their established social position tended to hold them where they were.[12] But it may well be that the climate of the Southwest, which was not hospitable to the culture of rice, tobacco, and long-staple cotton, was a decisive factor in retarding the migration from the low country.

These up-country cotton farmers and planters who settled in the newer lands selected, as has been suggested, the lighter sandy loam and sand and clay soils in preference to the stiff clays and rich black prairie lands. A. J. Brown, in his *History of Newton County, Mississippi*, observed that the early settlers in that region preferred the poorer sandy lands to the richer prairies and clay soils. "The prairies of the county," he wrote, "were very open; thousands of acres of this kind of land were entirely unobstructed by timber or undergrowth, and were very easily brought into a state of cultivation. The level, sandy and uplands were much more in demand, as the people much preferred the level uplands to the ridges or prairies."[13] Nettie Powell noted the same thing in Marion County, Georgia. "The section south of where Buena Vista now is and leading towards Draneville was known as 'turkey ridge,' and was not attractive to early settlers on account of the hard red clay soil [indicating rich soil] which was not easy to cultivate with the wooden plows that were then in use. The most of this region was left vacant until the middle thirties."[14]

The method of migration and settlement in the South, for rich and poor, was fairly uniform during the pioneer period. Friends and relatives living in the same or neighboring communities formed one or more parties and moved out together, and when they had reached the promised land they constituted a new community, which was called a "settle-ment"—and still is so called. Settlements were frequently miles apart, and the inhabitants of a single settlement would be more scattered than they had been in the old community in the East. After the first trek other settlers would come in smaller groups or in single families and fill in the interstices. These later comers would often be relatives or friends of these who had come first, or friends of their friends. Frequently church congregations would move in a body into the Southwest, or an entire hamlet or community would simply evacuate and march together into the "land of milk and honey." In describing the settlement of Wilkinson County, Georgia, Victor Davidson observes that "frequently large tracts were purchased and whole communities (from the older parts of the state and the Upper South) would move and settle on them. There were instances where congregations would follow their pastors here." One entire community from Virginia "came in a body from that State and purchased lands near each other."[15]

The migration of a family group from Abbeville, South Carolina, to Cherokee County in the Coosa River Valley of Alabama in 1835, has been described by one of the members of the group. "In November 1835," he says, "we bade adieu to friends and left the old homestead never to look upon it again. . . . Late in the afternoon of our first day's travel we were joined, as we rolled on, by my maternal grandparents and several other members of the family, the party thus numbering forty or fifty souls."[16] One of the most interesting group migrations into the wilderness was that of the Presbyterian congregation of Bethel Church, which came in a body from Williamsburg district of Columbia, South Carolina, and settled in Maury County, Tennessee, in 1808, where they established their church, "Zion," and the Zion community, which has remained virtually intact until this day.[17] The settlements at Watauga and in neighboring valleys, the Cumberland settlements, and those of the Kentucky bluegrass basin, such as Harrodsburg and Boonesboro, are all too well known as group undertakings to need more than mention. Such examples might be endlessly repeated. Thus the early communities of the newer states and territories were often transplanted organisms rather than synthetic bodies.

These groups did not move into the public domain in ignorance of their exact location; but rather, like the children of Israel, they sent their Calebs and Joshuas ahead to spy out the land and prepare the way. An early description of Blount County, Alabama, relates how the pioneer farmers chose their location and how they made ready for the families to settle in a new community. As they prepared to move into the wilderness, the prospective immigrants usually sent ". . . a few strong men, generally their sons, without families, deep into the then wilderness in the fall, to make corn and prepare for them. The father generally went with them and chose the place, and then went back to prepare for moving when the corn was made. A bushel of meal will suffice a man one month, and if he has no other than wild meat, he will require even less bread. In the fall season, place three or four men, one hundred miles in a wilderness, with proper tools and two horses, they will pack their bread stuff for the hundred miles—procure their meat—clear land—and produce corn sufficient to bread one hundred persons one year."[18] Blount County, which comprised much of northern and western Alabama at the time of the first settlement in 1816 and 1817, was settled in this fashion.

The same preparations are easily traced in the case of the family and neighbors of Senator Charles Tait. The Taits lived in Elbert County, Georgia, from which many of the early settlers of Alabama migrated. Charles Tait commissioned his son, Captain James A. Tait, to go into the public domain of Alabama territory to select a future home for the family. On February 2, 1817, the son, in company with his wife's brother and father, set out for Alabama territory on a journey of exploration.[19] The father and son had agreed on the type of place to select. There were certain characteristics that the place should possess, which the elder Tait later described in a letter to his son. It must unite salubrity, fertility, and navigation, and possess other advantages "... such as a stream near at hand for a mill and machinery—a never failing spring at the foot of a hillock, on the summit of which a mansion house can be built in due time; that it have an extensive back range where our cattle and hogs can graze and fatten without the aid of corn houses, that on the right and left there is an extensive body of good land where will settle a number of good neighbors and from whom the pleasure and benefits of society will soon be realized."[20]

In December, 1817, following his journey of exploration, Captain Tait wrote his father that he would soon go to the Alabama territory, taking two or three Negroes with him, and would buy a few Negroes in Alabama, where they would make a corn crop. Later when it was safe, the family was to be brought to the new home.[21] With several Negroes—and, presumably, several of his neighbors—he proceeded to the present Wilcox County and became a squatter on the public domain, where he raised a crop of corn just as had the small farmers who came to Blount County in northern Alabama in the same year. After a year on the public domain he purchased some land at two dollars an acre; but the government held most of the land off the market, and he complained to his father that "we shall have to make another crop on the public land. The failure of the sale of all the townships advertised is a grievous and most mortifying disappointment to those generally settled on the land and to us in particular."[22]

In the meantime, the neighbors were moving into Alabama territory, many of them to become neighbors of the Taits at their new home near Fort Claiborne, where a place on the bluffs of a river were selected with the requirements that met the elder Tait's specifications. The son's letters show that the trek from Elbert County had begun even before he himself had selected a plantation. "Mr. Goode and family started yesterday for the Alabama territory," he reported in November, 1817. "Gov. Bibb will start on Thursday I believe, Esquire Barnet was to have broke ground on Thursday last, his son-in-law Taliafero, follows in about three weeks, and I suppose his son Thomas in the course of the winter. Thus you see the present inhabitants are moving off."[23] Two weeks later James wrote his father, who was in Washington: "My cousin Davidson Hudson is here at our house now. He is just returned from Fort Claiborne and is determined to settle at that place or at some other town in that country; he will move out in the spring.

"The Miss Olivers are willing to go out with their sister [Mrs. Hudson] and if you are willing as their gardian and can make some suitable arrangement with regard to the disposition of their property. . . . I am determined to start before Christmas."[24] By the beginning of 1819 the migration from Elbert County, Georgia, to the neighborhood of Fort Claiborne seemed to be nearly completed. On January 20, 1819, Charles Tait wrote his son that "by this time, I hope, the last party under the direction and protection of Captain Goode have reached the Peach Tree-Bluff, in safety."[25]

The long move from the older states into the new territory was seldom the final move. Like a great drove of blackbirds lighting in a grain field, with each bird milling about, making short flights within the field in search of a more satisfactory location, the agricultural immigrant after reaching the region of his choice often moved about several times within the same general community before making a permanent settlement. The Tait papers imply that the Georgia immigrants followed this pattern more or less after reaching the Fort Claiborne community. They do not, however, supply the particulars that one would like to have. Nevertheless, occasionally the immigrant left accounts of the final phase of settlement after the frontier was reached. Such was true of the Ramsey family that migrated to southeast Mississippi, and the Robbins family that settled in Coosa County, Alabama. The records of these people are especially significant, since both families were of plain, farmer stock, which as a rule, left few personal letters and diaries.

In the winter of 1807–1808 the Ramsey family—consisting of the father, mother, two young boys, and a Negro woman—migrated from Georgia to the lands freshly ceded by the Choctaw Indians in southeast Mississippi. After a hazardous journey through the Indian country, made on horseback and on foot, the family reached Wayne County, Mississippi, in the late winter or early spring of 1808. The father immediately erected a log cabin on government land, and as soon as he had provided shelter for his family he commenced preparations for farming. He cut down the dense canebrake and fired the cane as soon as it would burn, thus killing the timber and clearing the ground. Without further preparation Ramsey planted his crop. "The planting [J. C. Ramsey, a son, later wrote] was done by making holes at proper distances, depositing the seed, covering with . . . earth taken out in making the hole. No fences nor plowing necessary, all that it needed was to keep down the mutton cane, [and] butter weed with the hoe. . . . But this preparation required time and labor, so that on the 4th day of July Father finished planting his corn and pumpkins. Such was the richness and character of this loam soil at that time that it required a short time for corn to mature; early killing frosts were also uncommon; so that although Father was late getting his in the ground, yet in gathering it in the fall, he not only made a plenty for home consumption but a surplus for market, and as to his pumpkin crop I recollect distinctly to have heard him say repeatedly that he 'could nearly walk all over his field stepping on pumpkins.' "[26]

Having little or no money, the family not only grew its own food but made its own clothing, shoes, and hats. The father bartered for a spinning wheel made by one of the neighbors, procured a pair of cotton cards, and made a loom "Georgia style." Ramsey then bargained for cotton with some of the neighbors who had been there long enough to grow a patch of cotton. He and his wife agreed to spin thread and weave cloth, with the aid of Dinah, the Negro girl, in payment for the cotton, which had to be picked from the seed by hand. Later, a hand gin, operated by some younger member of the family, was acquired.

"With these facilities, [says J. C. Ramsey] rough and unhandy as they were, Mother not only clothed the family but made surplus for market, which Father in the fall of that year [1808] carried to Mobile and sold for $2.50 per yard. Mobile was then under Spanish control and country produce or manufactured [was] very high."[27]

During the first year on the Mississippi frontier, the Ramsey family and the other settlers of the neighborhood "were often much annoyed with the Indians; although no violence was ever attempted by them." The Ramseys lived on the trail leading from the main Choctaw villages to Mobile, where the Indians sold their furs, deerskins and bearskins and purchased powder, shot, and whiskey. On their way home, the Indians, who traveled in large groups, usually made it a point, continues Ramsey "to camp near the houses of the white settlers . . . bringing great loads of whiskey . . . conveyed in kegs." They would stay in the camp near the white settlers until they had consumed most or all of their supply of whiskey; and they would stage a big drunk. "Fighting, scratching and yelling was generally kept up as long as the whiskey held out." "They had system however in their drunken sprees. One would remain sober to protect and keep the drunken ones out of the fires, and prevent them from killing each other in their fights, and do police duty in general" and "to keep them from interrupting the white people especially the ladies."[28]

At the end of the year (1808) the elder Ramsey sold his squatter's rights—a cabin and some cleared land and other improvements—and moved two or three miles further down the Chickasawha River, a tributary of the Pascagoula River. "He appeared to take up the idea," observes his son, "that improving new places and selling them out to other new comers (and there were many) was better for him; more money in it; than to remain at one place and make larger improvements." By this method he hoped to "accumulate money sufficient to buy, or enter him a permanent home, when the government lands were put into the market; which he anticipated would be at no distant day, which was even so." On this new place, says the son, the father "made improvements like unto his former one, made one or two crops, and sold out again."[29] The next move was again down the Chickasawha River, across the Wayne County line into Greene County and in the neighborhood of Bethel Church (Methodist), of which he had been a member since coming to Mississippi. "Here he was associated with a community of excellent citizens such as John McRae; William Martin; Norman McDuffie; Roderick McDuffie; Alex McIntosh; Daniel McIntosh; McInnis McLeod; Smith and others . . . most of whom were Scotch from North Carolina." These Scotch had built a church and, though doubtless Presbyterians, had "united with the Methodist church," probably because of their inability to obtain a Presbyterian minister. "Father McRae was a leading and zealous spirit in the church," observes the diarist, "occupying the position of class leader and with whom my father was soon associated in the same office." The Ramseys did not become squatters at this particular place, but rented river land. It was a sickly location, however, and after one year the family moved back some distance from the river.[30] The next year Ramsey sold his improvements and moved a short distance down the river where he again built a cabin, cleared land, and made a good crop. In 1815 he moved once more down the river, but was still only five miles from Bethel Church.[31]

At last the elder Ramsey had found the place that he wished to make his permanent home, and by his hard and unceasing toil had accumulated enough cash to make the purchase. When the government land in this community was put up for sale in 1816–18, Ramsey journeyed over to the land office at St. Stephens, on the Tombigbee River in Alabama, to make the purchase, only to find that "a brother in the church" was going to bid against him for the land on which he had built a cabin and cleared fields. Finally he and the "brother" agreed to divide the land, and Ramsey at last acquired a farm. He was, however, grievously disappointed both in his farm and in his neighbor and "brother in the church," and he quickly sold his farm and purchased land on Pearl River in Lawrence County, a distance of about one hundred miles from his home in Greene County. A move to this new community would end his connections with the Bethel Church neighborhood in or near which he had lived for ten years.[32]

But this last move was never made. Ramsey's unremitting toil, year in and year out, in clearing and improving government lands and selling to squatters had broken his health. He "consequently decided to move to the range and give up trying to make a living by cultivating river lands," his son informs us. He accordingly disposed of his land on Pearl River and with the proceeds purchased cattle, sheep, and swine. These together with the livestock which he already owned gave him, as his son puts it, "a pretty good start of stock." In the fall of 1819 he "gathered up his cattle, hogs, and sheep and drove them to the range on the South side of Red Creek . . . a distance of about twenty miles" from Bethel Church. Here on government lands and in the midst of a grazier's paradise, where the nearest two neighbors were four and eight miles away, Ramsey "selected him a place in the woods; a beautiful bluff on . . . Red Creek."[33] Here he built a substantial log home and acquired title to his land as soon as it was put on the market.

Even though it was winter when the livestock were turned upon the range, the younger Ramsey remarks that "our stock of cattle that roamed around us looked fine and fat." "The grass [was] thick, long and tender, the ravines or branches, creek bottoms, covered with a thick cane or reed brake; no frost had fallen to kill off the luxuriant grass which then covered and carpeted the large plateaus of pine forest." Not only were cattle and sheep kept fat on the grass and cane but "the hog range here was equal to the necessities of the people, requiring no corn to prepare them for pork." Indeed "large fine fat porkers could be killed from the woods."[34]

The younger Ramsey was exultant over the new home and the pastoral life. Never had the family had such an abundance and variety of food: milk, butter, cheese, fat beef, pork from the range; and turkey, venison, bear meat, fish, and other wild game from woods and stream.

The Ramseys now followed the pattern of the herdsmen described previously. They cleared and cultivated fields large enough to supply themselves with vegetables, fruits, corn, wheat, and cotton for their clothing; but for money they depended on the sale of cattle and hogs and other products of the range and the forest. Each year they marketed, in Mobile, cattle, hogs, butter, eggs, chickens, peltries, venison hams, and wild turkeys "by which means many luxuries and necessities of life were supplied."[35] Eventually, however, when the population of the pine woods had become too dense for grazing as a major occupation, the Ramseys turned more and more to agriculture.

Soloman Robbins, who migrated to Alabama a few years after Ramsey settled in Mississippi, had been in Alabama during the Creek War as a private soldier, and had been entranced with the rich lands ceded by the Indians to the United States government. He returned to his home in North Carolina when the war ended, and prepared to move to the Alabama frontier. In 1816 he arrived on the Tallapoosa River, a few miles north of the future city of Montgomery. Here he opened up a farm; but the swampy river lands soon proved unhealthful and he moved to Autauga County on the Alabama River, a few miles to the southwest. He lived in this place about fifteen years and apparently accumulated considerable property, including a few slaves.

But Robbins was not content with his land, level and rich though it was. Indeed, it seems that he desired nothing so much as to get away from rich, level land and make his permanent home in the hilly country, for no sooner had the Creeks ceded the rugged lands north of Montgomery to the United States than Robbins moved in. His daughter, Mrs. Kate Grayson, described the migration and settlement of the family. After the Creek treaty of 1832, Robbins "moved with his family to Coosa County among the Creek Indians, and was the first settler to find a home in that county. As he moved from Autauga County [the adjoining county before Elmore was formed] he opened up his road as he went, with the help of the hands who assisted in driving his wagons and stock, horses, cattle, sheep, hogs, etc., of which he owned vast numbers, they cleared the road heading from Wetumpka to Nixburg—via Central Institute, which road is in use to this day. He bought a large tract of land from the Indians, paying them in silver (they would accept no other kind of money), and having the entire county to select from, of course he made a judicious selection and bought land unexcelled in fertility of soil, fine timber, most excellent range for stock, and watered by at least a dozen large, bold springs of never failing clear, cold, sparkling free stone water. Wild game was abundant, so plentiful indeed that father could go out any morning before breakfast and kill a deer or bring as many wild turkeys as he could carry. I have heard my mother say she often had as much as a large wash tub full of turkey breasts alone salted down at a time. I have often heard my father remark—even when eighty years of age—that if he knew of a country as fine as that when he went there, he would go to it even at his advanced age."[36] But Robbins made this their home and many of the descendants have remained within twenty-five miles of the original settlement through the fourth and fifth generations. The county was hilly, and the soil was of only moderate fertility as compared with that on the Tallapoosa and Alabama River bottoms where Robbins had first settled. But it was a healthful region, and its surface, soil, trees, and streams were like those of the Piedmont region of North Carolina, which doubtless explains why Robbins left the rich black belt and chose a rugged but beautiful country.

In the main outline, then, the migration and settlement of the agricultural population on the Southern frontier followed a pattern. The agricultural folk in migrating into the public domain sought a country as similar as possible to the country in which they had lived. The reasons for this were the natural love of familiar environment and the necessity of continuing the accustomed farm husbandry, which only a country similar to the old one in climate, soil, and natural growth could meet. The migrants thus found themselves moving in a westerly direction along those isothermal lines or temperature zones in which they had lived in the East. Grain and cattle farmers of the upper South remained such, and settled in the upper South to the west of the mountains and in the lower portion of the Old Northwest. Tobacco and cotton farmers did likewise and moved into the middle and lower Southern territories and states. Before migrating, one or more representatives of a group spied out the land, whereupon the group—which was frequently a congregation or neighborhood—moved out together and became neighbors in the new country. Here, in searching for a suitable place, they often moved about several times in the same community before making a permanent settlement.

This pattern of migration and settlement had a significant bearing upon the social and economic structure of the Old South and the New. The herdsmen, who withdrew to the rugged and sterile land in order that they might continue the occupation that they preferred, placed drastic limitations upon their own future economic well-being. As long as the pine belt and highlands were not overcrowded by man and beast, the range remained good and these semi-pastoral folk lived well and possessed a strong sense of security. They were certainly not poor whites as a class; but neither were many of them wealthy. Eventually, when these regions began to be crowded—and this was happening in a few places prior to the Civil War—the people would be compelled to graze fewer cattle and cultivate more and more land until they would find themselves farmers cultivating poor soil without much knowledge of agriculture.

Those agricultural immigrants who had deliberately shunned the fertile but tough clay and lime soils and had settled upon inferior sandy-loam lands placed limitations, though not as severe, upon their future economic prosperity in a way similar to the piney-wood and mountain folk. While many became well-to-do, few became rich; for the economic level of an agricultural people can rise but little above the level of the fertility of the soil. On such lands there were many large farmers and small planters with ten or fifteen slaves, but there were few if any large planters.

Those who moved into the rich lands were most fortunate; for while the majority of them were possessed of only moderate means at the time of settlement, nearly all rose in the economic scale and many who were poor in the beginning became immensely wealthy before 1860.

There were thus several regions differing greatly in fertility of soil, and consequently in wealth. Between these regions there was segregation; but within each region there was very little except in the swampy, river lands, where only the Negro, who had considerable immunity to malaria, could dwell in safety. Here large plantations were developed, through the means of slave labor, by planters usually living in a village or town in a more healthful locality. In the black belt outside of these sickly lowlands the property of the nonslaveholders, the small slaveholders, and the great planters lay more or less intermingled, and the census and tax lists show that the values of their lands and their agricultural productions per acre were about the same.

The former dependence upon large capital and slave labor to develop and maintain these large, swampy, river plantations may be better realized by viewing those areas at the present time. Many, perhaps most, such plantations have been abandoned since 1865. The ditches have long since filled with muck and trees and a dense growth of gum and cypress has brought back the primeval wilderness. Even white men of means have usually avoided such places, and there are few if any Negroes who have cared to become pioneers in clearing and ditching swamplands.

Notes

1. Sparks, *Memories of Fifty Years*, 20.

2. Vidal de La Blache, *Principles of Human Geography*, 68, Cf. Flint, *The History and Geography of the Mississippi Valley*, 217.

3. Isaiah Bowman, *The Pioneer Fringe* (New York, 1931): 6.

4. Archer B. Hulbert, *Soil: Its Influence on the History of the United States* (New Haven, Conn., 1930): 78. See also ibid., 21-23; Albert B. Faust, "German Americans," in Francis J. Brown and Joseph S. Roucek (eds.), *Our Racial and National Minorities; Their History, Contributions, and Present Problems* (New York, 1937): 171; and Laurence M. Larson, *The Changing West and Other Essays* (Northfield, Minn., 1937): 11-12, 69-70, 71, for settlement of the Northwest by Europeans from similar regions.

5. *Eighth Census, Population*, xxxv.

6. Vidal de La Blache, *Principles of Human Geography*, 62, 65.

7. Baird, *View of the Valley of the Mississippi*, 100-101.

8. Darby, *Emigrant's Guide to the Western and Southern States*, 121, 231; Peck, *A New Guide for Emigrants*, 62, 63, 108; S. H. Collins, *The Emigrant's Guide to and Description of the United States of America* (4th ed.; Hull, n.d.): 97, 98, *passim*; Flint, *The History and Geography of the Mississippi Valley, passim.*

9. *Seventh Census*, Table XV, xxxvi-xxxviii.

10. *Eighth Census, Population*, xxxiv, and 616-23. See also William O. Lynch, "The Westward Flow of Southern Colonists Before 1861," in *Journal of Southern History*, 9 (1943): 303-27.

11. George Powell, "A Description of Blount County," in *Transactions of the Alabama Historical Society, July 9th and 10th, 1855* (Tuscaloosa, 1855): 37-41; Nelson F. Smith, *History of Pickens County, Alabama* (Carrollton, Ala., 1856): 37-49. See also A. B. McEachin, "History of Tuscaloosa" (MS. copy in Alabama Department of Archives and History; also published in Tuscaloosa *Times*, 1880); and Ezekiel Abner Powell, "Fifty Years in West Alabama" (MS. copy in Alabama Department of Archives and History; also published in Tuscaloosa *Gazette*, August 12, 1886-September 5, 1889).

12. See especially Thomas P. Abernethy, *The Formative Period in Alabama, 1815-1828* (Montgomery, 1922): 25-26.

13. Brown, *History of Newton County*, 54.

14. Nettie Powell, *History of Marion County, Georgia* (Columbus, 1931), 21.

15. Davidson, *History of Wilkinson County*, 147, 162.

16. J. D. Anthony, *Life and Times of Rev. J. D. Anthony: An Autobiography with a Few Original Sermons* (Atlanta, 1896): 14.

17. Records of Zion Church, Maury County, Tennessee (microfilm copies in Joint University Libraries, Nashville, Tennessee).

18. Powell, "Description of Blount County," 42. See also, Brewer, "History of Coosa County," 48, for the example of Joel Speigner "spying out the lands for a group back in South Carolina."

19. Elizabeth Caroline Tait to Charles Tait, February 5, 1817, Tait Papers, Family Letters I (B) (Alabama Department of Archives and History). At the time this letter was written Charles Tait was United States Senator from Georgia.

20. Charles Tait to James A. Tait, January 20, 1819, Tait Papers, Family Letters I (A).

21. James A. Tait to Charles Tait, December 15, 1817, Tait Papers, Family Letters I (B).

22. *Id.* to *id.*, January 21, 1818, and January 17, 1819, Tait Papers, Family Letters I (B).

23. *Id.* to *id.* November 16, 1817, ibid.

24. *Id.* to *id.* December 2, 1817, ibid.

25. Ibid., (A).

26. A. C. Ramsey, Diary, 3-4 (MS. in Alabama Department of Archives and History). This manuscript is called a diary, but is really a memoir.

27. Ibid., 4-5.

28. Ibid., 6-7.

29. Ibid., 7-8.

30. Ibid., 10-13.

31. Ibid., 16-20.
32. Ibid., 20 ff.
33. Ibid., 36.
34. Ibid., 36-38.
35. Ibid., 53a.
36. Mrs. Kate Grayson to her nephew, W. O. Robbins of Elmore County. The original letter is enclosed in Brewer, "History of Coosa County." It was written about 1903.

Randall M. Miller

The Failed Mission: The Catholic Church and Black Catholics in the Old South

The story of black Catholics in the Old South is largely unwritten. It is easy to see why. The population was small and elusive. Except for the Gulf region and pockets in Maryland, South Carolina, Florida, and Kentucky, Catholicism rarely touched black slaves, or whites too for that matter. Catholicism among black slaves in America left no legacy of resistance; it built no solid foundation for future black social and political activity; and it declined steadily among blacks throughout the nineteenth century. The black church in America grew out of the slaves' secret gatherings in groves and hollows—out of the Afro-American community's striving for cultural and spiritual autonomy. Catholicism was no part of this process. The few Catholic slaves in the Old South lived as a people apart. As such, they slipped into historical obscurity.[1]

This is understandable, if unfortunate. The records on Catholicism among enslaved Afro-Americans are fragmentary and misleading. Few Catholic slaves left autobiographies or personal accounts of what their religion meant to them in their daily lives. Few remnants of their beliefs are preserved in Afro-American folklore. Catholic masters and the church either cared so little about the slaves' religious lives or were so ignorant of the slaves' private world that they did not observe or record religious activity in the quarters. Much of the story of Catholicism among slaves of the Old South must be stitched together in a patchwork design from scattered, randomly created, and sometimes doubtful and conflicting evidence. There are many tantalizing clues, but the researcher should proceed with extreme caution.

Still, the records suggest patterns of slave values and behavior that provide revealing, if brief, glimpses into the interior world of the slaves. They also adumbrate the nature of master-slave relations on the sensitive subject of religion. The history of Catholicism among slaves in the Old South reiterates the central theme of much of Afro-American life—the quest for a distinct identity. The Catholic slaves, like their Protestant counterparts, adapted the master's religion to fit their own community needs. They were not passive recipients of the slaveholder's culture. They defined and preserved their own religious values capable of surviving the rigors of bondage. In so doing, they put distance between themselves and their masters. But they also put distance between themselves.

The Afro-American experience has been one of division as well as common struggle. Real differences in occupational status, proximity to the master, social status, and sometimes age divided the slaves.[2] Real differences in religious values and style also separated the black slaves in the Old South. These divisions grew in the variegated social and cultural climates in which the slaves lived. Slaves in the upper South, for example, responded to different religious cues than those in the Gulf region. Urban slaves had a wider range of denominational choices than did rural slaves. African-born slaves had less to do with Christianity than did American-born bondsmen. Catholic slaves lived in greater social isolation than did Protestant slaves.

The best estimates put the number of black Catholics in the South at 100,000 persons in 1860. But these people did not compose a distinct ethnic group. They were divided by culture, geography, and circumstance. Even though Catholics lived throughout the South, they tended to congregate in particular neighborhoods. There were five regional divisions among Catholics and within these several caste divisions. An older white and black Catholic population existed in Maryland and spilled over into Virginia. A small colony of French and German Catholic settlers in western Kentucky kept some slaves who professed Catholicism. Low country South Carolina, especially Charleston, harbored a Catholic population, many of whom were émigrés from the West Indies. Florida also had a tiny Catholic enclave. The largest concentration of Catholics was in the Gulf region, particularly in and around New Orleans. The American acquisition of Florida and Louisiana significantly altered the character of the American Catholic population, as did the migration of several thousand black and white Catholic refugees from the Caribbean between 1790 and 1810. Increasingly, the Catholic population derived from non-British origins, and in the case of the refugees, it became an urban population. But most Catholics continued to reside on farms, and with the westward movement in the early nineteenth century, Catholics in the Gulf region became a minority population.

Within the regional concentrations of black Catholics caste barriers sometimes separated slaves, free blacks, and creole free persons of color. The latter group was peculiar to Louisiana and established a unique ethnic identity that has survived into this century. They constituted a recognized and self-perpetuating third caste in antebellum Louisiana. They occupied a precarious middle ground between white and black, and they jealously guarded their autonomy. They celebrated their French and Spanish heritage, sloughed off their African cultural ties, and staked off clear racial and cultural boundaries between themselves and their own black slaves, indeed all blacks.[3] Likewise, free blacks did not always identify with the aspirations and interests of their enslaved Afro-American brethren. Much depended on their economic status and place of residence of course—free black urban entrepreneurs being the most isolated in culture and attitude from the slaves and poorer free blacks—but real tensions sometimes marked relations between free and enslaved black people.[4] Although many black Catholic slaves lived or worked in New Orleans, they largely remained a rural people in residence and mind-set. In time, many in the city succumbed to "Americanizing" pressures and gave up their faith. On the farms, however, many Catholic slaves retained a Catholic identity of sorts, although the insidious American influence steadily corroded their Catholic attachment. The haughty manner of colored creole and white Catholic masters took its toll; so too did the prejudices and hostility of poor farmers and Irish immigrants toward the slaves. The process of religious survival and accommodation among the slaves on the farms forms the substance of this essay.

Except perhaps in lower Louisiana, the Catholic church in the Old South was not equipped to be the guardian of the slaves' moral and physical health. It was not the arbiter of the planters' or poor whites' social and moral lives. The church recognized slave marriages, but it lacked the power to enforce planter compliance in allowing, or honoring, the sacrament of marriage among slaves. Unlike the church in Spanish America, the church in the Old South largely abdicated its evangelical role among the slaves. Local parish records indicate a high rate of baptisms among slaves throughout the antebellum period, particularly in lower Louisiana. But there is little evidence of high rates of slave identification with Catholicism in terms of attendance at mass, marriage in the church, or other signs of Catholic activity and devotion.[5]

During the nineteenth century, the church was besieged with financial and staffing problems that interrupted or prevented it from reaching out to the rural folk of the South. Perhaps the most fundamental cause of the church's meager achievements in evangelizing was the church's dependence on immigrant clergymen. As Jay Dolan has shown, the church recognized the need to evangelize among its scattered and declining population. In the voluntaristic world of America the church had to compete for converts. Parish missions staged revivals and rekindled Catholic commitment in the nineteenth century, but the church's revivalistic efforts in the antebellum period were sporadic and largely confined to the cities. New Orleans was well served by revival preachers. Central and northern Louisiana hardly saw them. Too many of the priests who did come to the South were foreign-born. Many came from provincial farming backgrounds in Europe, and so at least had an affinity to the rural folk. But even the best of them missed the nuances of southern religious and social culture.

The worst alienated Protestant and Catholic alike and set back Catholic efforts to win converts and social acceptance—the necessary preconditions to establish permanent missions in the countryside.[6]

Foreign-born priests frequently had trouble with the language. As late as the Civil War, the church continued to rely on priests with a poor command of English. In 1862, for example, a white Catholic girl in Louisiana observed that her family avoided mass because they did not want to suffer Father Larneudie's preaching. As always in such things, the priest's reputation preceded him. The previous Sunday he had "preached one hour and a half," but nobody understood anything he had said. The word was passed. Avoid the good father thereafter. John Nevitt, an Adams County, Mississippi, planter who was a member of the board of trustees of the local Catholic church, briefly drifted away from attendance at mass because he found local Protestant preachers more comprehensible than the local priest. His church was later without a priest and turned to itinerant Protestant preachers for Sunday services. Unlike the immigrant priests before them, these preachers evoked a positive response from the otherwise taciturn Nevitt. The evidence of the general inadequacy of preaching among foreign-born priests was ubiquitous in the Old South, and it hurt.[7]

The faithful chafed under the burden of poor preaching and alien ministers. The less devout stayed away. As the Catholic population shifted and hordes of non-Catholics invaded the Gulf region, Catholic attendance declined and Catholic power evaporated. And the church was slow to respond in the South. It was not until 1850 that Archbishop Antonie Blanc provided organized religious and educational life for Catholics in Louisiana, the stronghold of Catholicism in the South. And the establishment of dioceses and parish missions rarely extended real Catholic influence into the backcountry. The rich Catholics could travel to towns to participate in organized religious life, and they could send their children to Catholic schools. The poor, black and white, waited on the priests' annual visits to remind them of their Catholic sacramental life. Churches fell into disuse for want of clergy and lay interest. Indignities occurred. The church at St. Stephens, Alabama, for example, was sold and converted to a brothel. In St. Mary's Parish, Louisiana, which had four Catholic churches in 1860 capable of seating fourteen hundred persons, church attendance was so low that one observer wryly remarked that the situation would not improve unless the grogshops were closed on Sunday. Catholic planters put plantation duties before religious ones. Church was not sufficiently appealing or necessary to them to warrant a trip to town. One Catholic woman confessed that she chose not to attend mass during the summer and fall simply because it was "two hot." The church at Houma, Louisiana, tried to make it easier for parishioners to attend services by paving a walk from the main street of the town to the church, but its efforts were not rewarded. Poor roads were not the problem. It was indifference on the part of the Catholic parishioners, whatever their income or social status. This religious indifference would not go unnoticed by the slaves of Catholic masters. A faith that was not worth observing when it was hot or inconvenient was no faith at all.[8]

Catholicism had an image problem in the nineteenth century. It was a religion of "foreigners" who professed loyalty to a foreign power. It was a religion that exercised few social restraints on its followers—witness the drunkenness and poverty of the immigrant Irish, who were despised equally in the North and the South by Protestant whites and blacks. It was a religion that lacked the directness and simplicity of messasge of "American" religion. Catholics engaged in too much chanting, too much "idolatry," too much elaborate ritual, and too much hierarchical organizing for American egalitarian tastes. And American Protestants would have none of it. During the Civil War, even when the church labored mightily for the Confederate war effort, one Louisiana woman reacted strongly to the nature of the Catholic service. Given her location, she should have been less sensitive about such things. But when a Catholic companion commented on her refusal to participate in a Catholic mass that she had attended, the woman replied sharply that she did not care what the priest thought of her actions and would not worship when she did not know what was going on. It is significant that even in lower Louisiana, the seat of Catholicism, non-Catholics remained suspicious and ignorant of Catholic services and intentions.[9]

Worse, many non-Catholics believed that Catholics were ungodly. Southerners regarded Catholics as inveterate gamblers and drunkards, and they deemed the foreign-born priests to be the worst of the lot. Such attitudes led to ugly doings. In Louisiana in 1857, for example, an Italian-born priest was murdered at a grocery across from his church. Twenty persons had witnessed the crime, but nobody helped the priest. Indeed, his body lay in the street all night. A local Protestant blamed the priest's alleged lust for women and craving for money as the cause of the murder. This response neatly fit prevailing interpretations of the "low life" of Catholic immigrants. Nativism ran strong in the 1850s. Anti-Catholic feelings discouraged conversions to Catholicism. During the Civil War, when religious intensity swelled in the South, one brave lady came out for Catholicism. She had wanted to convert "for a long time but had not the courage, to resist so much opposition as she knew she would be sure to encounter." But not everyone was brave. The Catholic church in the South did not grow significantly during the great wave of religiosity in the 1850s and 1860s. It remained on the defensive and too weak to be a bastion for the slaves and the poor, or an attraction to them.[10]

The Catholic church in America traditionally has followed a course of political caution. In the nineteenth century, particularly in the South, the church lacked the numbers, wealth, and internal strength to stride with confidence into political and social controversy. Whenever possible, the church avoided conflicts with local powers. In the Old South to be different was often to be damned. Catholic leaders were sensitive to the church's minority status in the Protestant South and so tried not to be different on the basics. It was having enough trouble establishing control over church finances and policy. The laity held the purse strings in most parishes, and wealthy laymen exercised a decisive influence in church affairs. They ensured that their churches would serve their needs alone. This often meant ignoring the social needs of poor parishioners, black and white, and it even led to the exclusion of black parishioners from services.[11] If a priest challenged lay power, he often suffered humiliation and defeat. The wardens of one church settled a dispute with their parish priest by locking him out of the church during Holy Week. At another church the white parishioners resisted the priest's efforts to allow blacks to worship there, and although the priest had enough prestige to prevent the whites from harming the blacks, his own ministry never fully recovered after the incident. In this instance, the planters knew what they were doing, for however much slaves and lower-class whites distrusted one another, they could make common cause against planters. For that reason planters encouraged rivalries between slaves and poor whites—letting the whites bully the blacks and allowing the slaves to denigrate the poor whites as "trash." Hostilities between Irish Catholic immigrants and slaves only intensified this rift separating lower-class black and white Catholics.[12]

Church leaders got the message. Only the most devout Catholics heeded church teachings that ran against their material interest in slavery. The southern bishops comforted them that compliance was not always necessary. Indeed, by their public support for southern "rights" and planter hegemony, the bishops pointed the way to Catholic acceptance in the South. With declining numbers of white Catholics, rising Protestant opposition to Catholic missions, and the return of agricultural "flush times" in the 1850s, the church was in no mood to offend anyone on the issue of slavery. As Madeleine Rice has shown, Catholic leaders opposed antislavery reform as a New England Protestant movement closely aligned with nativism and anti-Catholic activity. In addition, many Catholic clergymen who came from Europe linked abolitionism in America with the rationalism and anticlericalism that threatened Catholic teaching in Europe. Like the dominant Protestant churches of the Old South, the Catholic church mirrored the racial values of its followers and reinforced planter hegemony by supplying biblical justifications for slavery and a conservative social order. In neither teaching nor example did the church create a moral climate conducive to manumissions or humane treatment of slaves. Individual clergymen interceded on the slaves' behalf and called for Christian charity, but their numbers were few and their power illusory. Catholic masters remained the sole arbiters of discipline and treatment on their plantations and in their communities. The slaves had to fend for themselves and to reach accommodations with their masters; the poor white farmers had to defer to the stronger economic and social power of the planters. The church did not figure in the lower-class whites' and enslaved blacks' strategies for survival.[13]

Bishop William Henry Elder of Natchez summed up the problem in a letter to the Society for the Propagation of the Faith, written in 1858. He noted that few slaves of Catholic masters and few poor white farmers received regular spiritual instruction. Several planters hired preachers to attend to their plantations and to deliver sermons on Sundays, but the preachers were generally Protestants. Many masters refused to let their Catholic slaves attend services off their plantations because the masters feared that the slaves might run away. Planters sometimes encouraged black slaves to preach, but this naturally excluded the Catholic priest from control or direction of the slaves' religious concerns. As teachers of catechism, the masters performed poorly, if at all. The masters failed to do their part in bringing up their slaves as Catholics. With widely scattered churches, few priests, and no money, Elder and the other bishops could not meet the needs of the slaves or the white Catholics. The priests who were available devoted their attention to winning and holding white Catholics, and some priests evoked fear or, worse, ridicule among the slaves who did not understand them or perceived them to be arms of the masters' authority.[14]

No sermon notes survive to tell us what the priests said on those occasions when they ministered to the slaves. The few contemporary accounts suggest that priests did not avoid special pleading, which surely alienated the slaves. How could the slaves in Colonel Carroll's Maryland plantation respect the priest who insisted that they obey their master and who defended slavery as good for their upbringing and maintenance? The problems of style and language aside, the priests lacked credibility among the slaves. To be sure, some priests displayed kindness and concern for the slaves. They tried to provide health care and educational and spiritual guidance for Catholic slaves. Other priests, however, betrayed confidences, which had a devastating effect on the slaves' loyalty. The church, after all, was the servant of the slaveholders, and the priests knew their masters. So did the slaves. One Catholic slave woman said it all when she quit Catholicism because her confessor was a proslavery apologist who informed on slaves expressing sentiments for freedom.[15] Slaves might suffer dull priests, but they were not about to countenance hypocritical ones.

In the end, the priests did not count for much in the Catholic slaves' religious world. The priests were transient figures who passed hurriedly and often unnoticed through the slaves' lives. Their visits to the plantations were too infrequent to establish rapport with the slaves, and their ministry, although often well intentioned, was too unrelated to the slaves' daily sufferings to have much meaning for them. Catholic slaves and slaves of Catholic masters rarely commented on the priests in their past. And that silence speaks volumes. Catholicism then would be a product of plantation circumstances. As in so many things, the master would put his imprint on the religion, and the slaves would accept and adapt those parts of it that met their peculiar needs.

In the absence of priests, Catholic masters held prayer meetings, taught catechism, and otherwise tried to conduct religious services for the slaves. If mixed with good treatment and if culturally isolated, the slaves responded favorably to such training. Each Sunday, for example, the Catholic mistress of one Kentucky plantation drilled the slave children in catechism and the Lord's Prayer. Although many of the children later became Baptists or Methodists, they gratefully acknowledged her teachings and thanked her for leading them to Christ.[16]

But countervailing forces often undermined the Catholic masters' efforts to bring up their slaves as good Catholics. Many slaves recoiled from the embarrassment of sitting in segregated pews or galleries in the rural Catholic churches.[17] The presence of black slave preachers, who were not Catholics, competed effectively for the slaves' attention, and the advance of Protestant culture among slaves overwhelmed the small number of Catholic slaves. More directly important was the relationship between the master's treatment of the slaves and their acceptance of his religion. The slave La Son Mire refused to attend mass, partly because he found the segregated seating obnoxious and degrading, but largely because his Catholic master exhibited no evidence of Christian character in his regular dealings with the slaves. Catholic masters who broke the Sabbath, whipped their slaves excessively, denied food and adequate shelter to their slaves, and in other ways abused the slaves obviously earned the enmity of the slaves, but they also discredited Catholicism. The slaves noted that Catholic mass failed to temper the wickedness of one Maryland slaveholder who repeatedly began "fighting amongst the colored people" after mass. She was "never satisfied" and once beat a slave woman viciously with a walking stick. A Virginia slave showed no respect for his master or his master's faith because the master, "a good Catholic, though very disagreeable," drove the slaves hard and abused them with coarse language. Odel Jackson of Mississippi put it more succintly in describing the character of her Catholic owner, whom she would never follow: "De ole Missus was mean."[18] Catholic masters were no better or no worse than Protestant masters in their treatment of the slaves. Neither in Louisiana nor outside of it did Catholicism restrain the excesses of barbaric masters or otherwise serve to ameliorate the conditions of bondage for the slaves. For that reason, Catholicism deserved no special attention from the slaves.

Masters generally allowed their slaves to follow the religion of their choice. Masters won respect for setting up chapels for slaves and not interfering in the slaves' religious practices. In the Gulf states wise Catholic masters who purchased slaves from the Protestant upper South acquiesced in the inevitable by allowing the non-Catholic slaves to go to their own churches or to listen to black preachers.[19]

There was not much masters could do to impose their own religious values on the slaves because the slaves resisted the slaveholders' often clumsy attempts to rule their private lives. In this regard, the case of John Thompson is instructive. Thompson, a Methodist slave, was once hired to a Catholic tobacco farmer in Maryland. All the slaves on the tobacco farm were Catholics, save for Thompson, who lived in isolation due to the circumstances of his religion and his status as a hired slave. The master prayed three to four times daily, and on Sunday he called the slaves to prayer. Thompson refused to participate, and he further enraged the Catholic slaveholder by singing Methodist hymns while working. Eventually, Thompson could no longer stand the pressures to conform or the abusive master, and he fled the plantation. For Thompson, as for many slaves, religion was too important to be left to a white man's direction and misuse.[20]

Slaves used religion to insulate themselves from their masters and to preserve their own heritage. In so doing, they showed that they did not love their masters so much that they sought to accept the masters' religion. And the slaves suffered much to nurture their own religious culture free from the slaveholders' interference.[21] Elizabeth Ross Hite, a former slave of a French Catholic master in antebellum Louisiana, described the slaves' struggle to define their own religious identity. She recalled that at Pierre Landro's "Trinity Plantation" the slaves were christened as Catholics and were "supposed to be Catholics." But "lots didn't like that 'ligion." Some slaves were from Virginia, where they had been practicing Protestants, and their children sought to follow the religion of their parents. The slaves also had a deeper commitment to religion than the master. For them, religion was no casual affair; rather, it was the central feature of their Afro-American community's identity. Landro tried to raise the slaves in the Catholic faith. He brought a black man from France to teach the slaves "how to pray, read and write." The slaves, particularly the women who were more religiously vocal than the men, disliked French-trained preachers because they would not let the slaves "shout an pray lak ya wanted to." But "Prayin and be free to shout" was the essence of the slaves' religion. "Gawd says dat ya must shout if ya want to be saved. Dats in de Bible." The slaves preferred to risk Landro's wrath rather than God's, so they turned to their own black exhorters, who let them shout and pray all night. Another reason for their preference for black exhorters was that the slave exhorters worked on the plantations "lak ev'rybody else." The exhorter at the Landro place was a trusted member of the slave community who knew the slaves' sufferings by his personal experience. The Catholic priests, however, espoused a stiff, foreign religion, and they were outsiders. In the closed world of the plantation all outsiders were suspect—the master's hirelings more so. This was a major obstacle confronting Catholic preachers, and they never broke down the barriers of suspicion.

The slaves at Landro's plantation attended their own church, which was hidden "in de brick yard way out in de field." Every night they gathered there to sing, pray, and hear Bible lessons from "Old man Mingo." Although he prided himself as a religious man, Landro opposed the slaves' nightly services. He feared that an excess of slave religiosity would "give him all religion an' no work." By staying up late each night, the slaves were too tired to work or started late on the next day's tasks. Still, the slaves persisted in their nocturnal devotions despite frequent whippings from Landro. In that way they demonstrated their independence and their real devotion to religion. Needless to say, Landro won no converts by his actions.[22]

It worked both ways. Catholic slaves sold to Protestant masters might demand the right to attend mass, even if this meant traveling to town, and some masters gave in rather than risk unnecessary and dangerous confrontations. When a Protestant master prevented his Catholic slaves from praying during the week, they sneaked off to do so. For them, religion was a means of expressing their autonomy. It was not so much what Catholicism or Protestantism taught theologically that counted among the slaves as it was who controlled the churches and how the religious affiliation affected the masters' collective behavior. Living away from any Catholic church, one slave refused to accept Protestantism and kept alive his Catholic identity by observing dietary and personal religious customs. In that way he retained a link to his personal past, and he set himself apart from his new master's total control.[23]

Catholicism had a material attraction for some slaves. The priest's visit meant a holiday on the plantation, and many slaves of Catholic masters took part in the mass for that reason. Charity Parker, a former slave from Louisiana, remembered how "when dere was Communion on de place dere was a big celebration. De marse an' mistres would send down cake and ice cream and nobody worked dat day." Another slave was happy to see the master bring a priest to the farm to baptize the slave children because the master treated the slaves to "real beef meat" after each baptism. Matthew Hume of Kentucky confessed that despite assiduous efforts of the devout Catholic mistress to teach the slaves their catechism, he attended classes solely to get the sugar and candy that were dispensed afterward. Vanity also served God. Slave girls looked forward to christenings because they received pretty dresses for the occasions. At the Dermot Martine plantation in Louisiana the Catholic slave girls enjoyed primping in front of the mirror to see who was "pretty enough to go to church." Attending mass promised a trip to town or a nearby plantation. Such events broke the monotony and loneliness of rural life, but the slaves' participation did not always lead to a greater Catholic devotion on their part.[24]

Catholicism was of course more than presents and holidays. The mysticism and high moral code of nineteenth-century Catholicism appealed to some slaves. Charity Parker of Louisiana is a case in point. As a girl, she was disappointed that the outbreak of the Civil War prevented her from making her first communion. She was "lookin forward to havin' dat white dress, veil an' candle dat dey gave everyone of dem slaves" at their first communion. But, for her, Catholicism also meant spiritual cleansing. In old age, after converting to Protestantism, she sometimes wished that she had remained a Catholic. As she put it: "If you pure to de Lord, yer pure to everythin'. When you go to confession you gotta have in yo' mind dat you ain't gonna do anythin' ya tell da priest ya ain't gonna do, an' yo' gonna say 'Lord, when I go befo' de priest, don' let me do no more behind his back den I confess to his face.' "[25] Catholicism was a personal religion that demanded daily devotion and an honest self-assessment of one's moral life. It was also a sedate religion that had few of the public displays of unbridled emotion that sometimes characterized southern evangelical religion. Some slaves found in this a greater measure of truth in religion. They recoiled from the crude religious practices of their more vocal Protestant counterparts. Thus Donaville Broussard of Louisiana distinguished Catholic slaves as civilized because they "didn't have to half-drown when they got religion." And Carlyle Stewart of Louisiana identified himself as a Christian who "never got that 'ligion that makes you shout and carry on." Rather, he prayed in his home at night—a sure sign of genuine commitment.[26]

The syncretic process of Afro-Catholicism that developed in the Caribbean never flowered in the Old South, but enough elements of the slaves' African heritage must have transferred to Catholicism to give it some appeal among them. Direct evidence of this transfer, however, is not available. Catholic feast days, the use of candles, burial rites, and liturgy all provided disguises for African religious traditions. The syncretism that occurred, however, largely took place in and around New Orleans, which had a large concentration of black Catholics and fresh infusions of African culture. There are examples of slaves who elevated Catholic priests to the status of healers, thus comparing them with the healer/exhorter of West African religions. Even proximity to the Catholic clergy suggested divine powers. The slave Simon, who lived with the Daughters of the Cross mission in Louisiana, was "esteemed by his people who consult him like they would an oracle." Indeed, one day "a negro came to ask him to bless his marriage." But the syncretic process in the Old South is too elusive to document with confidence.[27]

Catholics in the rural South lacked the properties necessary for the emergence of a vigorous, syncretic Afro-Catholicism. Catholic feast days and religious ceremonies were observed too infrequently, and after the American acquisition of Louisiana, the Gulf South was overrun by Afro-American slaves carrying an Afro-Protestantism that effectively challenged Catholic teaching among the slaves. An illiterate people must be shown religion. This can be accomplished through miracles and through the good example of religious leaders. Catholic masters and priests were not providing miracles. Indeed, their religion was hardly visible in large areas of the Gulf South, the most "Catholic" of regions. And white priests and masters could not win the slaves' confidence. Inexorably, the Afro-Protestantism of the newcomers took hold and captured the Catholic slaves' attention and affection.

The meeting of Catholic and Protestant slaves in the Old South revealed the different cultural reference points among the slaves. Black Protestants and black Catholics approached one another warily. Initially at least, each group practiced endogamy, but in time the rising number of Protestant slaves and the declining number of Catholic slaves throughout the South made this impossible for Catholics. Some Catholic masters tried to preserve Catholicism among their slaves by selling Catholic slave families intact and only to Catholic masters. Others tried to retain a French cultural and language orientation on the plantations to combat the Americanizing influences.[28] But economic pressures and, more generally, planter ignorance of or indifference to the slaves' religious preferences led to increased mingling of Protestant and Catholic slaves. Still, as late as 1863, Thomas Wentworth Higginson could wonder how his black regiment of ex-slaves from South Carolina would react to a contingent of new recruits: "we have recruits on their way from St. Augustine, where the negroes are chiefly Roman Catholics; and it will be interesting to see how their type of character combines with that elder creed."[29]

Higginson need not have worried. Catholic and Protestant slaves were combining everywhere in the South by 1860. The war only accelerated the process. The decline of Catholic influence among slaves in the rural South occurred at different times in different places of course, but by 1860 the pattern of Afro-Protestant absorption of Catholic slaves was well established. Many Catholic slaves were familiar with the broad outlines of southern Protestantism through the preaching of itinerant ministers employed by their masters or through the appearance of revival meetings in their neighborhoods. Others discovered Afro-Protestantism by listening to black preachers in the shadows of the quarters. Others still had relatives or close fellow bondsmen who were Protestants. Catholic slaves who left the church did not wander aimlessly in a spiritual wasteland; rather, as "churched" slaves they sought a spiritual home in some kind of organized religion. The Afro-Protestantism of the slaves offered the most inviting opportunities for spiritual and psychological fulfillment.

The migration westward and southward of slavery introduced blends of Afro-Protestantism to the Gulf region. By sheer numbers the Protestant-oriented slaves simply overwhelmed the Catholics. For some Catholic slaves the "new" religion heralded a total transformation of values. They traded the dignity and solemnity of formal Catholicism for the emotional richness of Afro-Protestantism. Rather than worship alone, they joined the Afro-Protestant community to sing and dance together in the new religion. One slave woman nicely detailed her conversion to what she significantly termed the "American" religion. She had been raised a Catholic but "never knowed how good the 'Merican religion was till I married John. He was a member of the 'Merican church, and he got me to go with him on Sundays to his church; and the more I went the more I liked it." She had been a practicing Catholic for many years and had denigrated Protestantism until she met her husband. She reported that since she joined his church, "I been changed, I feel like I been new born." The

American religion "makes any body feel happy all over; it runs through you, down from your head to the very soles of your feet!" As for Catholicism, it was "all doings and no feeling in the heart." Likewise, Henry Reed of Louisiana observed that he did not know "how to talk" until he met a "real American" who drew him away from Catholicism and French culture.[30] Like so many others, they were guided by family interests. Reed's mother was a Baptist, and Reed credited her example as the principal cause of his conversion. Charity Parker left a congenial Catholicism to follow the religion of her Baptist mother. Religion meant community and family solidarity.[31]

The only rural Catholic group of any size to survive the American acculturation onslaught was the colony of creoles of color centered at Isle Brevelle in Louisiana. In their self-imposed isolation they established Catholicism as the only religion. They ruthlessly stamped out Africanisms among the slaves and insisted that all men, slave and free, practice their brand of Catholicism. Despite segregated worship and a denial of their African heritage, the slaves apparently followed Catholic teaching. Religion is both a public and a private event. To be successful, it must be visible, and in the chapels and religious festivals at Isle Brevelle it was very much so. The Catholic calendar of feast days and special devotions and regular attendance at mass fixed the timetable of life in the colony and reinforced Catholic identity for creole and slave alike—something that also occurred in diluted form among Catholics in New Orleans. Cultural isolation, of course, was crucial to this process, but until the barriers fell during the Civil War, the colony existed as a historical anomaly out of time and place in the American and Protestant Old South.[32]

Emancipation allowed most southern blacks to express their religious preferences openly. Most visibly, the freedmen retreated from white churches to form their own. Just as they sought economic and political independence, they refused to take religion from their former masters. For Catholics this was not so easy. The church lacked the resources to establish separate black and white churches, and congregational autonomy was not a recognized church practice. To remain of the faith meant having to suffer the humiliation of sitting in segregated galleries or pews in the old churches. In some cases it meant having to travel thirty miles or more to find a Catholic church. Not everyone wanted to or was able to make the journey.[33] Black Catholics pressed for changes in seating policy and for their own churches. Black Catholics in St. Martinville, Louisiana, for example, petitioned the state legislature to repeal an 1858 statute that allowed only whites to incorporate churches there.[34]

But many former slaves of Catholic masters were not interested in removing such legislative obstacles or facing white racism each Sunday. They left the church. This move made the break with their former masters and slavery complete. It reflected the freedmen's desire to locate in a religious environment more compatible with their own peculiar spiritual, psychological, and social needs. The freedmen's movement out of the Catholic church was also an attempt to reclaim their family roots. Recall Henry Reed: During slavery he had regularly attended mass with his Catholic master. Catholicism, however, had kept him in cultural isolation in rural "French" Louisiana, and he found Catholicism to be an empty faith. He later blamed his "ignorance" of American ways on his sheltered religious life, and after emancipation he became a Baptist preacher. The reasons were complex, but one stood out: "I had a good maw," he said, and "she was the cause of me being converted." He became part of the larger Afro-American community, growing in the seedbed of the black Protestant churches of the postwar South.[35]

French-speaking Catholic freedmen, however, did not generally join the exodus out of the Catholic church. They were already a people apart from the larger Afro-American community, and many chose to remain so. They married in the Catholic Church, baptized their children there, and worshipped there. Each act of participation reconfirmed their faith. Even in the face of evangelizing by northern Protestant missionary-teachers, who were often aghast at the Sabbath breaking of the French-speaking ex-slaves, they stood their ground.[36] Perhaps they liked a religion that allowed them to work on Sundays—no mean consideration for farmers scratching out a living. More likely, they were simply prisoners of their cultural and physical isolation from American blacks, or they fondly remembered the good priests and paternalistic Catholic masters who had comforted them when they were sick and otherwise had treated them decently.[37]

On the whole, however, the Catholic record during Reconstruction was not good. Many Catholic ex-slaves left the church, and others grew angry and frustrated with the church's halting and fumbling ministry. The church was slow to meet the needs of the freedmen. The Second Plenary Council of Baltimore (1866) promised a fresh approach to establishing missions among southern blacks. The bishops addressed the problems of providing educational and material assistance to the freedmen, but little came of their deliberations. The bishops quarreled over the amount and the direction of such assistance. Only Bishop Augustine Verot of Savannah recognized the desperation of the freedmen in the dislocated postwar South. But special efforts to educate and to support the ex-slaves were not forthcoming. Waves of new immigrants from Europe after the war exhausted the church's attention and resources nationally, and the general confusion of southern and national political, social, and economic life after the war dissipated reform efforts. The church's brief interest in southern blacks lapsed. It would not revive until the Third Plenary Council of Baltimore in 1884.[38]

In the meantime, the Catholic ex-slaves were left to themselves. What aid the church did provide was often disorganized. Individual priests attempted to establish schools for the ex-slaves, but outside of the cities few prospered. In one case, however, a Catholic school brought together ex-slave children and the children of creoles of color who had refused to mix with blacks before the war. The church school thus showed a potential for socializing black and creole Catholics and forging a larger Catholic community among the colored lower classes of the South. Generally, the few freedmen who received instruction in the parish schools described it as poor. One Catholic ex-slave in Texas, for example, attended classes run by some nuns and a German priest, but he thought that the education they offered did not amount to anything.[39] Despite propitious conditions to win friends among blacks by imitating the Protestant missionary associations, the church continued to lose influence among the blacks.

Catholicism was a captive religion that was unable to reach a captive people. The history of Catholicism in the South suggests that institutional religion adjusted to fit local norms and conditions. Representing a minority religion and population, the church catered to those in power, and in so doing ignored the powerless. Catholicism in the Old South operated within the peculiar world that the slaveholders made, and its limited role as teacher and arbiter for the slaves, and for lower-class whites too, cannot be understood apart from that context. For the slaves, Catholicism too often lacked immediate purpose. It did not provide a place for slave preachers and exhorters; it did not hold out the promise of temporal release from slavery's torments; it did not function independently from the formal, and for the slaves alien, institutional structure of the planter-dominated church. The wonder is not that Catholicism declined among the slaves of the rural South but that it survived at all.

Notes

Research for this essay was completed under a faculty research grant from Saint Joseph's College, Philadelphia, and a grant from the American Philosophical Society.

1. For a general survey of the literature on the subject see Randall M. Miller, "Black Catholics in the Slave South: Some Needs and Opportunities for Study," *Records of the American Catholic Historical Society* 86 (1975): 93-106.

2. On ranking within the slave community see John W. Blassingame, "Status and Social Structure in the Slave Community: Evidence from New Sources," in Harry P. Owens, ed., *Perspectives and Irony in American Slavery* (Jackson, Miss., 1976), pp. 137-51.

3. On this point see Gary B. Mills, *The Forgotten People: Cane River's Creoles of Color* (Baton Rouge, La., 1977), *passim*; and Sister Frances Jerome Woods, C.D.P., *Marginality and Identity: A Colored Creole Family Through Ten Generations* (Baton Rouge, La., 1972), chap. 3.

4. Ira Berlin, *Slaves Without Masters: The Free Negro in the Antebellum South* (New York, 1974), pp. 271-83.

5. My observation is based on samples of church records in Louisiana, Mississippi, Alabama, and Maryland.

6. On Catholic revivalism see Jay P. Dolan, *Catholic Revivalism: The American Experience, 1830-1900* (Notre Dame, Ind., 1978), pp. 3-12, 15-24, 33-49, 65-66, and *passim*.

7. [Tennessee Robertson] to Mary Jane Robertson, April 1862, Mary Jane Robertson Papers (Louisiana State University); John C. Nevitt Journal, May 31, 1829, March 11, 1832 (Southern Historical Collection—University of North Carolina at Chapel Hill).

8. A. B. Moore, *History of Alabama and Her People* (Chicago, 1927), p. 182; Franklin (La.)

Planter's Banner, August 2, 1849; Tennessee Robertson to Mary Jane Robertson, June 29, 1861, Robertson Papers; Raleigh A. Suarez, "Religion in Rural Louisiana," *Louisiana Historical Quarterly* 38 (January 1955): 62. It is worth noting that in rural, lower Louisiana the number of churches grew steadily from 1850 to 1860, but attendance did not keep pace with the growth. On religious indifference among Catholics see Mother Mary Hyacinth Le Conniat to her parents, December 6, 1856, August 19, 1857, in Sister Dorothea Olga McCants, ed., *They Came to Louisiana: Letters of a Catholic Mission, 1854-1882* (Baton Rouge, La., 1970), pp. 56, 66-67. As Dickson D. Bruce, Jr., argues in *And They All Sang Hallelujah: Plain-Folk Camp Meeting Religion, 1800-1845* (Knoxville, Tenn., 1974), p. 45, southerners "generally displayed a good deal of apathy and even hostility toward organized religion" in general, and even revivals did not change that. Indifference to and ignorance of formal religion was not peculiar to Catholics, and even after a wave of Protestant revivals only about 20 percent of the whites in the Old South were churched by 1860.

9. Priscilla "Mittie" Munnikhuysen Bond Diary, January 24, 1864 (Louisiana State University).

10. Effingham Lawrence comments in Magnolia Plantation Journal, October 4, 1857, Henry Clay Warmoth Papers (Southern Historical Collection—University of North Carolina at Chapel Hill); Kate Sully to Mary Jane Robertson, June 28, 1864, Robertson Papers.

11. On the church's position see John T. Gillard, *Colored Catholics in the United States* (Baltimore, 1941), pp. 42-43; Madeleine H. Rice, *American Catholic Opinion in the Slavery Controversy* (New York, 1944), *passim*; and James J. Pillar, *The Catholic Church in Mississippi, 1837-1865* (New Orleans, 1964), *passim*. On lay control of the churches see James J. Pillar, "Catholicism in the Lower South," in Lucius F. Ellsworth, ed., *The Americanization of the Gulf Coast, 1803-1850* (Pensacola, Fla., 1972), pp. 38ff.

12. Minutes of the Meetings of the Fabrique (Archives of St. Paul's Church, Mansura, La.); *American Catholic Quarterly Review* 14 (1889): 483. On the relations between the Irish immigrants and slaves see, for example, Earl F. Niehaus, *The Irish in New Orleans, 1800-1860* (Baton Rouge, La., 1965), pp. 49-54; Frances Anne Kemble, *Journal of Residence on a Georgia Plantation* (New York, 1863), pp. 79-80.

13. Rice, *American Catholic Opinion*, pp. 90-103; Maria G. Caravaglios, *The American Catholic Church and the Negro Problem in the XVIII-XIX Centuries* (Rome, 1974), pp. 182-84; Michael V. Gannon, *Rebel Bishop: The Life and Era of Augustine Verot* (Milwaukee, Wisc., 1964), pp. 33-39; Niehaus, *Irish in New Orleans*, pp. 47-55, 160-62.

14. Elder letter printed in John Tracy Ellis, ed., *Documents of American Catholic History* (Milwaukee, Wisc., 1956), pp. 335-36. For a Catholic priest's account of planter resistance to his mission in Louisiana see John M. Odin's letter of August 2, 1823, printed in "Letters Concerning Some Missions of the Mississippi Valley, 1818-1827," *Records of the American Catholic Historical Society* 14 (1903): 189. A vigorous priest could win converts and acceptance; for some examples see Pillar, *Catholic Church in Mississippi*, pp. 37-42; and Joe Gray Taylor, *Negro Slavery in Louisiana* (Baton Rouge, La., 1963), p. 140. On scattered Catholic churches in the South see Edwin S. Gaustad, *Historical Atlas of Religion in America*, rev. ed. (New York, 1976), p. 105.

15. William Howard Russell, *My Diary North and South* (New York, 1863), p. 184; Octavia V. Rogers Albert, *The House of Bondage, or Charlotte Brooks and Other Slaves* (New York, 1860), p. 69.

16. George Rawick, comp., *The American Slave: A Composite Autobiography*, 19 vols. (Westport, Conn., 1972), volume on *Indiana*, VI, p. 108. See also Rawick, comp., *Texas*, IV(2), pp. 60, 62; *Mississippi*, VII, pp. 120-21.

17. Segregated seating was the norm outside of New Orleans.

18. Rawick, comp., *Texas*, V(3), pp. 107-9; William Still, *The Underground Railroad: A Record of Facts, Authentic Narratives, Letters, &c.* (Philadelphia, 1872), pp. 71, 461, 524; Odel Jackson narrative, Louisiana W.P.A. Slave Narratives (Louisiana Department, Louisiana State Library, Baton Rouge).

19. Rawick, comp., *Texas*, IV(2), p. 62; *North Carolina*, XV(2), pp. 336-37.

20. John Thompson, *The Life of John Thompson, Fugitive Slave* (Worcester, Mass., 1856), pp. 52ff.

21. On the place of religion in the emerging Afro-American community of the quarters see John W. Blassingame, *The Slave Community: Plantation Life in the Antebellum South* (New York, 1972), especially pp. 60-75; Vincent Harding, "Religion and Resistance Among Antebellum Negroes, 1800-1860," in August Meier and Elliott Rudwick, eds., *The Making of Black America*, 2 vols. (New York, 1969), 1: 179-97; Donald Mathews, *Religion in the Old South* (Chicago, 1977), pp. 185-236; and Eugene Genovese, *Roll, Jordan, Roll: The World the Slaves Made* (New York, 1974), especially pp. 159-284.

22. Elizabeth Ross Hite narrative, Louisiana W.P.A. Slave Narratives (Louisiana Department, Louisiana State Library, Baton Rouge).

23. James B. Sellers, *Slavery in Alabama* (University, Ala., 1950), pp. 322, 323; Rawick, comp., *Texas*, V(4), p. 132; Pillar, *Catholic Church in Mississippi*, pp. 120-21.

24. Charity Parker narrative, Louisiana W.P.A. Slave Narratives, Dillon MSS, Melrose Collection (University of Northwestern Louisiana), copy courtesy of Margaret Dalrymple; Rawick, comp., *Texas*, IV(1), p. 308; *Indiana*, VI, p. 108; *Texas*, IV(2), p. 226.

25. Charity Parker narrative.

26. Rawick, comp., *Texas*, IV(1), p. 151; Carlyle Stewart narrative, Louisiana W.P.A. Slave Narratives (Louisiana Department, Louisiana State Library, Baton Rouge).

27. On the syncretic process see Roger Bastide, *African Civilisations in the New World*, trans. by Peter Green (New York, 1971), Chap. 7. On the priest as comforter and healer see for example Rawick, comp., *Texas*, IV(2), p. 226, for a planter-initiated call; and Adam Hall narrative, Louisiana W.P.A. Slave Narratives (Louisiana State University), for a black's turning to a priest for healing. On Simon see Mother Mary Hyacinth Le Conniat to her parents, December 6, 1856, in McCants, ed., *They Came to Louisiana*, p. 56. The veneration of Catholic saints and observance of Catholic rites could blend with voodoo: See, for example, "External Love Christian Faith No. 1," in "Life Histories for *Gumbo-Ya-Ya*," folder 5, Box 11, Lyle Saxon Collection (Tulane University).

28. On Catholic masters' selling slaves to other Catholics see, for example, Louisville (Ky.) *Catholic Advocate*, January 26, 1836, September 14, 1839. On the French culture among slaves see, for example, Frances and Theresa Pulszky, *White, Red, Black: Sketches of Society in the United States*, 3 vols. (n.p., 1853), 2: 271-72; and especially Henry Reed narrative, Louisiana W.P.A. Slave Narratives (Louisiana Department, Louisiana State Library, Baton Rouge).

29. Higginson quoted in Miles Mark Fisher, *Negro Slave Songs in the United States* (Ithaca, N.Y., 1953), p. 149.

30. Albert, *House of Bondage*, pp. 68-69; Henry Reed narrative.

31. Henry Reed narrative; Charity Parker narrative.

32. Mills, *Forgotten People*, Chap. 6; Louis Joseph Piernas narrative, Mississippi W.P.A. Slave Narratives (Mississippi Department of Archives and History).

33. On the tendency of Freedmen to leave white churches see, for example, Peter Kolchin, *First Freedom: The Response of Alabama's Blacks to Emancipation and Reconstruction* (Westport, Conn., 1972), Chap. 5; and Edward Magdol, *A Right to the Land: Essays on the Freedmen's Community* (Westport, Conn., 1977), Chap. 3. On traveling long distances to church see, for example, Henri Necaise narrative, Mississippi W.P.A. Slave Narratives (Mississippi Department of Archives and History).

34. Charles Vincent, *Black Legislators in Louisiana During Reconstruction* (Baton Rouge, La., 1976), p. 161.

35. Henry Reed narrative. See also Charity Parker narrative; and Rawick, comp., *Texas*, IV(2), p. 60.

36. Rawick, comp., *Texas*, IV(1), pp. 92, 252-53, IV(2), p. 227, V(3), pp. 274-75. For a northern missionary's description of a creole settlement see Edmonia G. Highgate to the American Missionary Association, December 17, 1866, American Missionary Association Archives (Amistad Research Center, Dillard University).

37. See, for example, Rawick, comp., *Texas*, IV(2), pp. 226-27.

38. On the Plenary Council see Edward J. Misch, "The American Bishops and the Negro from the Civil War to the Third Plenary Council of Baltimore (1865-1884)" (Ph.D. dissertation, Gregorian University, Rome, 1968), Chap. 3. The priests were not idle. An energetic priest supported by an interested bishop could win converts to Catholicism and deliver much aid to people in need. For one case see William Henry Elder to John B. Mouton, September 14, 1866, Elder Papers (Natchez-Jackson Diocesan Archives).

39. Louis J. Piernas narrative; Rawick, comp., *Texas*, V(3), p. 93.

Guion Griffis Johnson

Public Schools

North Carolina approached the subject of public education slowly and reluctantly, but, once having adopted it, developed by the close of the ante-bellum period a creditable state system supported by public taxation. Although in colonial North Carolina[1] education was largely associated in the minds of the people with the functions of the church, the idea of education as a public duty was expressed before the middle of the eighteenth century. A bill for the establishment of free schools was introduced in the colonial Assembly as early as 1749 and again in 1752, only to be defeated. In 1754 the Assembly actually appropriated £6,000 for building and endowing a school, but later used the money for military purposes.

When the time came to frame the State Constitution in 1776, sentiment for free schools was sufficiently strong to write into it a section on education providing "That a school or schools be established by the Legislature, for the convenient instruction of youth, with such Salaries to the Masters, paid by the Public as may enable them to instruct at low prices; and all useful Learning shall be duly encouraged and promoted in one or more Universities."

But in the crucial periods of the Revolution and of the Confederation, men were more concerned with establishing order out of confusion than they were in the education of youths at the public expense. In 1800 a correspondent of the *Raleigh Register* wrote regretfully that nine-tenths of the people in North Carolina were buried in "brutish ignorance."[2] Eleven years later Dr. Jeremiah Battle estimated that in Edgecombe County "about two thirds of the people generally 'can read'; & one half of the males 'write' their names: but not more than one third of the women can write." The progress of learning, he thought, had been slow "for '25 years back.' "[3]

Agitation

The battle smoke of the Revolution had scarcely cleared when a few public men, zealous for education, began to agitate for free schools. A judge in his charge, such as that of Judge Taylor to the Superior Court at Edenton in 1801,[4] might present the establishment of schools as a duty of first importance for the consideration of the grand jury; a newspaper correspondent, such as "Cervantes" in the *Raleigh Register*, might plead in behalf of "public seminaries of learning";[5] a governor in his message to the Legislature, such as Benjamin Williams' in 1802, might recommend "the provision of means for the general diffusion of learning"; but the public in general showed little interest in the subject. Nevertheless, these few advocates kept the question alive. In their eagerness for public education, they exaggerated its benefits and thus gave rise to the legend that education is a guaranty of happiness and goodness.

Although the agitation for public education was intimately associated with politics, it was never a political issue.[6] Federalists might differ on the subject as much among themselves as they did with Anti-Federalists; and Whigs with other Whigs as much as with Democrats. The subject, however, was closely related to political theory. Out of the crisis of the Revolution new philosophies arose. Some argued that the functions of the government were purely political. It was unwise, therefore, for a State to assume the education of its youth, for the State thus would be encroaching upon the personal liberties of the individual, one of the inalienable rights of man. Moreover, public education was unrepublican, for it taxed all for the benefit of some.

This was the reason which the Senate Committee on Education in 1829 gave for reporting unfavorably on a "bill for the education of poor children."[7] "It would from the vast expenditure required in its practical operation require a proportional imposition of taxes upon the people which at this period they would but little sustain and to which they would never submit without a murmur," wrote Tryam McFarland, chairman of the Committee, "and more than all would from equal contribution of all for the benefit of some be equally irreconcilable with strict justice and the sentiments of the Community at large."[8]

As McFarland stated, many in the State opposed public education, not only because they considered taxation for its support incompatible with their theory of a free government, but also because they had, since colonial times, been opposed to increased taxation on any ground. "Should schools be established by law, in all parts of the State, as in the North," wrote "X" in the *Raleigh Register* in 1829, "our taxes must be considerably increased, possibly to the amount of one per cent, and six pence on a poll; and I will ask any prudent, sane, saving man if he desires his taxes to be higher? . . . You will doubtless be told that our State is far behind her sister in things of this sort,—and what does this prove? . . . We shall always have reason enough to crow over them, while we have power to say, as I hope we may have, that our taxes are lighter than theirs."[9]

Many who were bitterly opposed to an increase in taxes, would have been glad to see public schools if any other means for their establishment could have been devised. They frequently argued, however, that the whole scheme was impracticable and unfair. For instance, McFarland's committee in 1829 objected to establishing public schools in each county, because such a plan "would fail to assist the children of the poorest classes." "These could not be educated on this system," the committee argued, "because their labor a great portion of their time is indispensible to the support of their parents and themselves."[10]

There were others who would go a step further and say that poor children need have no education at all. "Would it not redound as much to the advantage of young persons, and to the honour of the State, if they should pass their days in the cotton patch, or at the plow, or in the cornfield, instead of being mewed up in a school house, where they are earning nothing?" asked a correspondent of the *Register*. "Gentlemen," he continued, "I hope you do not conceive it at all necessary, that *everybody* should be able to read, write and cipher. If one is to keep a store or a school, or to be a lawyer or physician, such branches may, *perhaps*, be taught him; though I do not look upon them as by any means indispensable: but if he is to be a plain farmer, or a mechanic, they are of no manner of use, rather a determent."[11] Those in the "lower sphere of life" were better suited to their work when left uneducated, for education made the laborer discontented.[12]

The poorer classes themselves frequently opposed public schools on the ground that education led to aristocracy, and many, rich and poor alike, objected because they did not wish their children to be educated at the public expense.[13] Those who could afford to have their children educated would do so; those who could not would not humble themselves by making their children objects of charity.

The friends of education had an answer for all these objections. Those who held that public education was an encroachment upon man's personal liberties were confronted with the theory that it is the duty of a republican form of government to educate its voters. Accepting Thomas Jefferson's theory that popular intelligence is the basis of successful popular government, the friends of education argued that the diffusion of knowledge among the masses was one of the foremost duties of the state. "The more ignorant the people are, the more they are subject to be led astray by erroneous opinions, to be deluded by misrepresentations, and imposed upon by artifice," wrote "P. S." from Lincolnton in 1824. The failure of North Carolina to establish public schools had reacted against the State. North Carolina was everywhere held in ill repute.

"The character and honor of our state imperiously demand increased intelligence in the mass of our population," he declared. "It is humiliating in the highest degree, to behold the gigantic strides by which our sister states have surpassed us in the march of improvement. . . . Our agriculture is nearly what it was in the days of our fathers; enterprise, of every kind, seems to have taken wings, and fled to some congenial abode; our political existence has been but barely acknowledged; and, with very few exceptions, our representation at Washington has been such as to corroborate the degrading opinions entertained of our state. It is now high time to retrieve our lost honor, and establish our character for intelligence, patriotism and enterprize." If the state will improve the intelligence of the "lower classes" by the establishment of public schools, agriculture will prosper; "commerce will wave its flag; talents and ability will mark our representatives; . . . and our state assume that rank to which its resources and its political duration so eminently entitle it."[14]

Not only is education necessary for the success of popular government, but it is necessary for a well ordered social structure. The public school is a training school for life.[15] Ignorance debases man's faculties and hurries him into "gambling and drunkenness and lewd debauchery";[16] education brings with it an "attendant train of morality, honesty, temperance and happiness."[17] Governor Owen used this argument as one of the main points in his message on education to the Legislature of 1830. "If then it be true," he asked the Legislature, "that the vice, irreligion, and consequent poverty and misery of a large portion of our fellow citizens are to be attributed to their intellectual condition, are these not indispensable considerations to the virtuous legislator?"[18]

Following the argument of Gray's "Elegy," the friends of education warned their adversaries that they might be sending "some mute inglorious Milton" to his grave. "Who of us can tell but that in the bosom of some obscure little cottager there lives a spark which once kindled into a flame, might enlighten and warm the universe?" asked President Caldwell of the State University in his "Letters on Popular Education Addressed to the People of North Carolina."[19] Joseph B. Hinton and thirty-seven others from Beaufort County lamented in a petition for free schools the great waste of genius in North Carolina and spoke of "the immensity of talent and usefulness, now dormant, which would anon, blaze in the State" if public schools were only established.[20]

Those who were crusading for public schools sought to meet the opposition of the poor classes by telling them that an education would elevate their social status. "To the poor talented youth . . . who might otherwise be bred up in ignorance and vice," public education would be "a stepping stone to honor and preferment."[21] Education refines the sensibilities and elevates conversation, and "instead of the rawness, the awkwardness and the uncouth manners which give offence, and repress sociability," the poor would be able to "participate in the advantages which result from a refined and reciprocal interchange of the courtesies of life."[22]

As the years passed by and still North Carolina did not adopt a system of public schools, the claims for education became more extravagant. Education was the "breath of life." Only facilitate the spread of "useful learning" and you will animate "The People . . . our husbandmen, our mechanics, and our militia," wrote an advocate from Edgecombe County in 1824. "You will infuse into this great body a SOUL."[23] Only adopt public education and it "will work a vast revolution in the intellectual, moral and physical conditions of North Carolina." It will "resuscitate the sinking energies of the State, and ultimately elevate her to that proud and eminent station among the members of this Confederacy to which she is justly entitled."[24] It will bring a millennium in which there is no poverty, no evil, and no strife. "Our wildernesses and solitary places will then blossom like the rose."[25] In time, education was to become in this State, as in all others of the Union, the greatest dogma of salvation next to Christianity.

Early Free Schools

Since colonial times, a few children in North Carolina had received a little schooling free. The apprenticeship system of binding our poor orphans was a practice which the settlers brought with them from England. As early as February, 1695, the General Court for Albemarle County bound "W^m^ ye son of Timothy Pead . . . Dec^d^ being left destitute" to "Thomas Harvey esq^r^ and Sarah his wife until he be at ye age of twenty one years and the said Thomas Harvey to teach him to read."[26] In 1715 the Colony passed its first law regulating the system of apprenticeship, and this law, with a few subsequent alterations, was the basis of the ante-bellum practice.[27]

Other poor children on rare occasions also received a little free schooling. The teacher might offer to give his services without cost to a "select number" of poor children, or some prosperous planter or merchant might contribute funds for this purpose. In 1744 James Winwright of Carteret County left a small legacy for the establishment of a free school in Beaufort, and in 1769, James Innes left £100 sterling and other property "For the Use of a Free School for the benefite of the Youth of North Carolina." Out of this legacy the trustees established Innes Academy in Wilmington. In 1766 the General Assembly incorporated the "Society for promoting and establishing a Public School in Newbern," which it had previously aided in 1764 by a grant of certain town lots. The act of incorporation allowed the trustees funds arising from a tax of one penny a gallon on all spirituous liquors brought into the Neuse River for seven years. These funds were to be applied in part to the free education of at least ten poor children annually. In 1813 an act to establish free schools in Wayne County, the funds for which were to be raised by lottery, actually passed the Legislature, but the school was never established. The following year Alexander Dixon of Duplin County left $12,000 for a charity school in the county, from which the county is still receiving interest.

Early in the ante-bellum period, groups of women in various towns in the

State began to organize societies for the education of "poor female children."[28] The first of these societies was the Newbern Female Charitable Society incorporated in 1812. Later there followed the Female Orphan Asylum Society of Fayetteville, the Raleigh Female Benevolent Society, the Wilmington Female Benevolent Society, the Ladies of the Congregation of St. John's Church, Fayetteville, and others. The societies usually rented a house which they turned over to a woman teacher. Since most of the girls were illegitimate children born of mothers who haunted the village brothels, the societies frequently converted the school building into an orphanage. Here the teacher was also housemother and counselor. The children were taught an elementary education, "neatness, correct deportment," and "those useful branches of home industry." At one time the Raleigh school had as many as thirty or forty pupils.[29]

The men's clubs also occasionally contributed to the education of the poor. The theatrical societies occasionally gave the proceeds from one of their performances for this purpose. On July 24, 1800, Mr. and Mrs. Hardinge, assisted by some gentlemen of the town, gave a performance at the theater in Fayettefille "for the benevolent and humane purpose of extending to poor children, and such as are deserted by their parents, the benefits of Education."[30] Almost every incorporated academy gave instruction free to a few poor children. Sometimes their charters made this requirement of them in consideration of the privileges granted.

About 1814 the Joseph Lancaster system of teaching was hailed in the State as a means of educating the poor. It was thought that by this system one teacher could instruct great numbers in half the time ordinarily required. In 1814 Governor David Stone established a Lancaster school where those who were unable to pay tuition were taught "without reward."[31] A few other Lancaster schools opened in the State, but they did not achieve the marvelous results their friends expected.

The Public School Movement

North Carolina still retained its reputation for ignorance and unprogressiveness as the nineteenth century wore on. In 1824 an Edgecombe correspondent of the *Raleigh Register* wrote regretfully, "It is a melancholy fact, that many of our farmers of wealth and character, nay, even many of our instructors and clergy, are notoriously deficient in Orthography, and Reading and Writing, and the commonest rules of vulgar Arithmetick."[32] In 1829 President Joseph Caldwell of the University of North Carolina declared that the State was three centuries behind in public improvements and education.[33] Several years later, the Reverend A. J. Leavenworth, a Presbyterian minister of Charlotte, estimated that "we have probably 120 thousand children between the ages of 5 and 15 years, who are destitute of a common school education."

In some parts of the State, many large families might be found, "not one of whom, parents or children, can read their alphabet; and in others, whole neighborhoods of forty and fifty families exist, among whom but few individuals can read their Bible."[34] So many in the State were without education that politicians often found it profitable to declare on the stump that they had never spent a penny on an education and to call those who had been to school the "ruffled-shirted gentry."[35]

So far, the opponents of education had won. The same forces which had retarded the progress of the State in its program for internal improvements and in the agitation for constitutional reform were now preventing the adoption of a public school system: the low per capita wealth, a narrow theory of the functions of state government, the dread of taxation, and sectional jealousies.[36]

But the friends of education were not content to let the subject rest. The *Journal* of the House of Commons for 1802 records that "Mr. Calvin Jones moved for leave and presented a bill to establish schools; which was read the first time and rejected."[37] From 1802 until the establishment of public schools in 1839 scarcely a year passed without some mention of the subject in the Legislature. Every governor except two from 1802 until 1838 recommended the establishment of public schools. In 1805 the Joint Committee replied to Governor Turner's message on education that the "Committee have duly considered" the subject "and are of opinion that although the situation of the State requires legislative aid; yet for the want of sufficient funds, your committee are of opinion, that an interference at this time would be inexpedient."[38] Invariably legislators expressed sympathy for the cause of education, but invariably pleaded insufficient funds as the reason for ignoring it.

By 1815, however, the cause had gained sufficient friends to enable both the House and Senate to appoint special committees on education, the first in the history of the State. The following year Governor Miller's recommendations on education to the Legislature were referred to a committee of which Archibald D. Murphey, senator from Orange County, was chairman, and he prepared a report, expressing vigorously the Jeffersonian theory of public education and recommending that the speakers of the two houses appoint a committee to digest "a judicious system of public education" based upon the principles which his report outlined.[39] Although others had expressed these views earlier than he, it was left to Murphey to popularize them and to win for himself the title of "father of the common schools" in North Carolina.

Born near Milton about 1777, Archibald DeBow Murphey,[40] son of Colonel Archibald Murphey, of local fame in the Revolution, was easily the most distinguished socially-minded statesman in anti-bellum North Carolina even when compared with such distinguished men as William Gaston, Joseph Caldwell, Charles Fisher, John M. Morehead, Edward B. Dudley, and William A. Graham. He was graduated from the University of North Carolina in 1799, and, after having taught there two years, was admitted to the bar and shortly afterward began practice in Hillsboro. From 1812 to 1818 he represented Orange County in the Senate. In these few years he constantly astonished conservative senators with his revolutionary views. He outlined a program of internal improvements which would tie the various sections of the State together by a system of navigable rivers and macadamized roads obtained through taxation. He drew up a system of public schools whereby every county in the State would have adequate schools maintained by public taxation. He favored amending the State Constitution to make it conform to "the first Principles of a Republican System of Government."[41] He did not live to see any of these measures adopted, but he set in motion forces which were later to jar the State out of its lethargy.

In 1817 John M. Walker of Warren County presented a report[42] on teacher-training as a member of the Joint Committee appointed by Murphey's resolution of the previous year, and Murphey himself presented his famous report on education as a member of the Senate Committee on Education. This report crystallized the thinking on public education and was the basis of the act of 1839 which established the public school system in the State. It called for the creation of a school fund, the appointment of a state school board, the organization of schools, and the establishment of "an asylum for the deaf and dumb." Murphey based the school system upon primary schools, academies, and the University of North Carolina. He outlined "the course of studies to be prescribed" for each of these three divisions in the system. He went a step further and gave his views on teaching methods and discipline. His plan called for the free education of poor children in the primary schools and the maintenance, as well as education, of a select number in the academies and the University.[43]

The Legislature ordered Murphey's report printed, but promptly killed his bill to carry the report into effect. The following year William Martin of Pasquotank presented a bill "to establish and regulate schools in the several counties of this State," and in 1819 the Education Committee started a movement which was later to culminate in the creation of the Literary Fund. The Senate Education Committee, of which Emanuel Shober of Stokes County was chairman, recommended the creation of a "School Fund" which might be raised "either by drawing it from the lands lately acquired from the Cherokee Indians or by appropriating a part of the stock holden by the state in the bank."[44] But it was not until 1825 that the school fund was actually created. In this year the friends of education were able for the first time to push a bill through the Legislature. The bill, drawn by Bartlett Yancey, speaker of the Senate, and introduced by Charles A. Hill, created a fund, known as the Literary Fund, from special sources[45] which was to be used to establish common schools when it had grown sufficiently large. For the management of the fund, the bill created a board composed of the governor, the chief justice, the speakers of the two Houses of the Legislature, and the State treasurer.

The Literary Fund grew slowly. In 1827 it amounted to little more than

$36,000. By 1836 it had grown to $243,162, all of which the Board had invested in bank stock except $3,845 in cash. During these years the fund had suffered losses through dishonesty, bad investments, and misappropriations. Unwilling to use the money for schools because of the insufficiency of the fund, the Legislature did not hesitate to apply it to other purposes, including the payment of their own salaries. The Legislature was always conscientious about repaying the amount borrowed as soon as the taxes "afforded the means," but never conscientious to the extent of paying interest on the loans.[46]

Nevertheless, the cause in behalf of public education was growing in popular favor. Newspapers offered their space to all who would write on the subject. No Fourth of July speech was complete without reference to "a system of general instruction" as one of "the cardinal objects of North Carolina."[47] In 1830 a writer in the *Raleigh Register* proposed a state teacher's association and in 1831 a convention of teachers met in Chapel Hill to organize the North Carolina Institute of Education.[48] In 1832 Joseph Caldwell of the University of North Carolina addressed his *Letters on Education* to the people of the State.[49]

In the Legislature the friends of education would not let the subject rest. Not a session passed without their introducing a bill, making a report, or inquiring into the state of the Literary Fund. Beginning in 1829, Tryam McFarland introduced a bill for three successive years calling for the education of poor children. In 1829 Charles R. Kinney submitted a plan for primary schools to Governor Owen which the governor in turn submitted to the Legislature. In 1834 Hugh McQueen, senator from Chatham County, introduced a bill calling for the collection of educational statistics and the increase of the Literary Fund through certain taxes. In 1836-1837, the first session of the Legislature after the change in representation[50] by the Constitutional Convention of 1835, the friends of education won their first real victory since 1825. In this year the Legislature passed a bill vesting certain swamp lands in the literary board and appropriating $200,000 for their drainage and improvement; it instructed the literary board "to digest a plan for Common Schools, suited to the conditions and resources of this State, and report the same to the next General Assembly"; and it greatly increased the Literary Fund by the addition of a large portion of the surplus revenue received from the Federal Government.

It is doubtful whether the Legislature would have adopted a system of public schools for another decade had not Congress in 1836 voted to distribute the surplus revenue in the United States Treasury among the States on the basis of their representation in Congress. North Carolina received $1,433,757.39 of this fund. The distribution which the Legislature of 1836-1837 made of the money received was a victory for education and a tribute to North Carolina statesmanship. All but $100,000, which was used for contingent expenses, went eventually to the Literary Fund;[51] so that in 1840 the fund for popular education amounted to more than two million dollars.

The plan for a system of public schools which the Literary Board submitted to the Legislature of 1838-1839 followed closely Murphey's plan of 1817. Governor Dudley approved the bill in his message to the Legislature and William W. Cherry, senator from Bertie, and Frederick J. Hill, representative from Brunswick, introduced bills in their respective houses to carry the plan into effect. The bill which finally passed the Legislature January 7, 1839, provided for the division of the State into school districts, the establishment of a primary school in each district through county taxes supplemented by appropriations from the Literary Fund, and the creation of county and district school boards to put the schools into operation.[52] But schools were to be established only in those counties which approved the bill by a vote to be cast in August, 1839. Those who had supported the cause of education from the beginning conducted a feverish campaign during the summer, but the people as a whole were only mildly interested. The vote for schools carried in all but seven of the sixty-eight counties, and the public school system went into operation the following year. These counties, Edgecombe, Wayne, Columbus, Rowan, Lincoln, Yancey, and Davidson, later voted in favor of public schools.

Public Schools at Last

The act of 1839 outlined a public school system in broad details. It did not fix responsibility for the operation of the system; it did not even make the erection of school houses or the support of the schools by county taxation mandatory. It did not require the local school committees to make reports on the number and progress of the schools within their districts. The school system thus established was a bitter disappointment to those who had expected so much of it.

When the act passed, its friends hoped that every district in the State, out of public spirit, would at once erect a schoolhouse "sufficient to accommodate at least fifty scholars," as the bill suggested.[53] But schoolhouses which had to be built by private subscription of money and labor were built slowly. In 1840 there were only 632 primary schools of any kind in the State.[54] Lacking public schoolhouses, the district committees might use their allotment from the State fund in various ways. They might honestly spend it on schools, distributing it, perhaps, as the Lincolnton Committee did, among the academies and private schools in the community. W. H. Abernethy of Lincolnton wrote to Calvin H. Wiley in 1856:

> At our last Superior Court I was appointed one of the District School Committee [.] Before this I never had paid any attention to free Schools . . . I found it a disjointed business [.] in the first place it has been customary here to get up a School in the Academies (we have two, male and female) for five months, on subscription (these schools were controlled by Trustees), and there was generally one or two petty schools in town (besides, taught by female teachers on subscription) [.] the District School Com. would

distribute the Free School fund among all these Schools and the teachers would divide it as they pleased. . . .[55]

Being less honest than the Lincolnton Committee, the officers might decide to use the fund for private purposes. In 1850 Governor Manly thought that it might "be safely stated that thousands of dollars remain from year to year in the hands of the [county] Superintendents; and if a rigid settlement were enforced, the public would be astonished at the aggregate sum thus withheld from its legitimate destination."[56] The act of 1852 which created the office of state superintendent also gave the superintendent authority "to see that moneys distributed for the purposes of education are not misapplied."[57] In 1854 Wiley obtained a more definite law on this subject whereby misapplication of educational funds was made a misdemeanor; county superintendents, district committeemen, and clerks of county courts might be fined $50 for neglect of duty; and chairmen of county boards of superintendents might be fined $500, to be recovered by the state superintendent in Wake County Superior Court, for failure to make a report on the disbursement of educational funds.[58]

While the counties were eager to accept the $40 for each school district due them from the Literary Fund by the act of 1839, they were not always willing to raise by taxation the $20 per district required by law. In 1840 the Legislature modified the school tax law so that county courts were merely "authorized and empowered" to levy a tax which should "not exceed one half of the estimated amount to be received" from the Literary Fund. Four years later the Legislature permitted county courts "in their discretion" to levy a school tax.[59] As early as 1848 Governor Graham had suggested that the counties be required to raise a sum equal to one half the amount received from the Literary Fund, and William B. Shepard introduced a bill in the Senate authorizing the Literary Board to withhold the State fund from counties which did not submit yearly a statement showing that they had raised a sum equal at least to a third of the amount due them from the Literary Fund,[60] but the bill failed to pass, and no other Legislature sought to remedy this defect during the ante-bellum period.[61]

There was no way to penalize a county for resolving, as the Cumberland County Court did in 1855, that "the school tax is for the present dispensed with."[62] The Edgecombe County Court, although the county had voted for schools under the act of 1841, did not consider levying a school tax until 1853. In that year the Court decided to take a vote at the next election of congressmen "whether [a] county tax should be levied to aid the present fund received semi-annually from the State," but, it was not until 1855 that the county collected its first school tax.[63] In those counties which actually levied a tax, the tax itself frequently varied from year to year. For instance, the tax in Pasquotank County in 1851 was 34¼ cents on the $100 valuation of property and 31¼ cents on the poll, but in 1852 the tax fropped to 5 cents on property and 10 cents on the poll. In Orange County the school tax varied over a period of five years from 6 cents to 7½ cents on property and from 8 cents to 22¾ cents on the poll.[64]

The chief reason for the fluctuation of the county school taxes and for the failure of some counties to levy a tax was that the county superintendents frequently found that the funds which they had on hand were sufficient to meet their school requirements. It did not occur to some county officials that they might use the surplus to improve the schoolhouses and equipment or to lengthen the school term. Even had some counties desired to lengthen the school term to six months instead of three they probably could not have found children to attend or teachers to conduct the schools, for, at least in the first decade of the operation of free schools, there were not enough teachers in the State for each of the 1,250 school districts created.

The public school system was further handicapped by the inefficiency of the county boards of superintendents and the district committeemen. Since the State exercised no administrative control over the county boards, they were left to their own devices. Few county boards took the trouble to make reports to the Literary Board on the number and condition of the schools as required by the act of 1846. It was often difficult to find capable men who were willing to serve on the school boards. Sometimes a county court appointed "one of the most illiterate of our citizens" chairman of the board of superintendents, as R. W. Millard of Sampson County complained in 1856.[65] It was even more difficult to obtain efficient committeemen. "Men who are the most capable will not serve as committeemen and the consequence is the people Elect men who are totally unfitted for this office [.] some men have been Elected for this office who could neither Read nor write,"[66] wrote A. W. Brandon of Rowan County in 1854. Sometimes "a popular, noisy fellow" would engineer the election of the district committee so that his favorite would be employed to teach.[67]

In 1841 the Legislature unfortunately passed an act which retarded the development of public schools. The act made federal population instead of white population the basis of distributing the Literary Fund. It clearly discriminated against the West with its small amount of Negro population.[68] Sectional strife which had so long prevented the adoption of a public school now appeared to handicap the operation of the system.

Moreover, the school districts were too large to make the location of the schoolhouses convenient to all in the districts. The act of 1839 had advised the county boards of superintendents to lay off districts "containing not more than six miles square, but having regard to the number of white children in each."[69] "Our districts are generally quite large or extend over a considerable extent of county," wrote a committeeman from Hyde County in 1854, "& it seems that now we are obliged to have them large to get anything like a decent sized school [.] when a school commences in a good sized district the scholars will number perhaps 55 or 50 or even more for 4 or 5 weeks & then a falling off takes place until the end of the quarter when the number is hardly 10."[70] He overlooked the fact that some families in the district lived so far from the school that their children could not possibly make the trip every day.

The defects in the public school system itself probably would not have been so apparent had there been a general sentiment in the State in favor of public schools. "I do not think the Public Schools will ever prosper and work well until a new generation arises," wrote A. W. Brandon, chairman of the Rowan Board of superintendents, in 1854. "The people take but little Interest in the schools in this County."[71] James Avery of Burke County thought that "the greatest difficulty in the way of success in our Common Schools . . . is the apathy and indifference manifested by the Upper Classes who do not send their children much to Common Schools."[72] On this same subject S. D. Wallace wrote, "I am sorry to say that in Wilmington our common schools are not patronized except by those who have not the means to send to other schools & hence the numbers that attend are limited & their character not very flattering."[73] Others objected to the public schools because they were coeducational. In Washington there were more than 450 children of school age in 1857 but not more than 60 ever went to the "Free Schools in their mixed character," for many parents would not "send Females where males go."[74] Accordingly, the committeemen in 1857 were "about to have a male & Female School seperate [*sic*]."

In addition to this lack of public support, the common schools were further handicapped by the opposition which they encountered from the old-field schools and academies and by the scarcity of good teachers.[75] Committeemen quarreled and neglected their duties; county chairmen misapplied school funds; prosperous families patronized private schools for fear of contamination from the poor; poor families kept their children out of school to work on the farm; schoolhouses went without repairs and finally fell in ruins.

Calvin H. Wiley and the Common Schools

At last the Legislature, after refusing in 1839 to provide for a state superintendent of public schools, saw the necessity of one. Calvin H. Wiley of Greensboro had introduced a bill in the Legislature of 1850-1851 providing for a state superintendent but the measure failed. At the next meeting of the Legislature he was more successful. The act of 1852 created the office of superintendent and defined the duties. The superintendent was to codify the educational laws of the State, to enforce these laws, to see that the school funds were properly applied, to obtain annual reports from county boards, to collect full information concerning the condition and operation of schools in each county, to find the causes which promoted and those which retarded the schools, to consult and advise with teachers, to instruct the examining committees concerning the proper qualifications of teachers, to attend meetings of the State Literary Board, to deliver educational addresses, to make an annual report to the governor on the progress of the public school system, and otherwise to promote the cause of public education.[76] This new officer was to receive only $1,500 for such an undertaking, but Calvin H. Wiley, state superintendent of public instruction from 1853 to 1865, was equal to the task.

If Murphey was the father of public education Wiley was the savior. Born in Guilford County in 1819 of Scotch-Irish descent, a student at Caldwell Institute in Greensboro and a graduate of the University of North Carolina, Wiley was already popular in the State as a lawyer, author, editor, and politician before his appointment as state superintendent of public instruction.[77] He took to his office an enthusiasm for his work and a genuine devotion to North Carolina. His theory of education was the old Jeffersonian doctrine which had been expressed in the State since the time of the Revolution: popular education is the basis of a republican form of government. It was Wiley, however, who sought to popularize the theory in North Carolina. From Cherokee to Currituck, in his speeches, letters, and reports, he constantly preached the doctrine that a "system of common schools for a great and growing state is a vast and sublime moral obligation."

When Wiley began his work as state superintendent in 1853 he found the public school system "obscured in darkness." After spending the most of his first year in office traveling over the State, visiting schools, inquiring into conditions, sounding out public opinion, he said in his first report to the governor, "I feel bound to say that money is not our greatest want— . . . We want more efficient management—a constant embodiment and expression of public opinion—a watchful supervision—a liberal course of legislation, good officers, and patience and energy in all having an official position in the system."[78] During the twelve years that he was state superintendent, he made the accomplishment of these objectives the chief duties of his office. He seldom had difficulty in obtaining legislation for improving the machinery of the school system. He gradually won the cooperation of the county and district committees, and in the end made the public schools a credit to the State. It was no idle boast when he declared in 1860, "North-Carolina has the start of all her Southern sisters in educational matters."[79]

In his second report to the governor, Wiley pointed out three serious defects in the school system: the failure of the county boards of education to make annual reports as required by law, the difficulty of obtaining good teachers, and the lack of organization in the schools.[80] By constantly reminding the county boards of their duties and bringing suit in cases of extreme misconduct or neglect, Wiley was able to report in 1858 that "the spirit of chairmen of county boards has now undergone a complete revolution."[81] The character of the teachers had also greatly improved, and with the improvement in teachers there came also an improvement in the organization of the schools.

In 1860 Wiley had been in office only seven years; yet in that short period he had revolutionized the public school system of North Carolina.[82] The number of school districts had increased from about 3,000 in 1853 to 3,471 in 1860; the number of schools from 2,500 to 3,082; the number of children in school from 95,000 to 118,852; the number of licensed teachers from 800 to 2,752; the expenditures from $150,000 in 1854 to $278,000 in 1860.[83] He had been unable, however, to lengthen the school term; it remained at about four months until the close of the anti-bellum period.

The establishment of common schools in North Carolina was an achievement of North Carolina statesmanship. The anti-bellum period opened and closed with the majority of the people in the State indifferent to education; some, yeomen and gentry alike, were actually opposed to the principle of public education. A few farseeing men had always been in favor of a general instruction of the masses; others were converted to the theory by the Revolution. These few, the articulate members of the State community, advocated the subject constantly in the pulpit, the press, and the legislative hall. They slowly won converts; finally achieved their goal. After 1840 the State boasted of its system of common schools as proudly as it previously had boasted of its State University and its statue of Washington. A few men in their devotion to a cause had forced a State, ridiculed by its neighbors as backward and ignorant, into a step as progressive as any taken by its scorners.

Notes

1. See Knight, *op. cit.*, pp. 1-41; Connor, *North Carolina*, I, 177-81; C. L. Raper, *Church and Private Schools in North Carolina*, pp. 3-71; C. L. Smith, *History of Education in North Carolina*, pp. 9-50; M. C. S. Noble, *A History of the Public Schools of North Carolina*, pp. 3-24.
2. March 25.
3. MS in Thomas Henderson Letter Book; Newsome, "Twelve North Carolina Counties," *NCHR*, VI, 91.
4. *Raleigh Register*, November 3, 1801.
5. Ibid., March 25, 1800.
6. In 1854 the Democratic platform pledged the party to continue the development of common schools "until the blessings of education shall have been afforded to all children of the State," and the party repeated the pledge in subsequent platforms.
7. This was not the McFarland Bill which was approved by the Committee, of which Tryam McFarland of Richmond, the author, was chairman.
8. MS in Legislative Papers. In Senate December 24, 1829. Mr. Coon stated that he was unable to find this report in the Legislative MSS (see his *Beginnings of Public Education in North Carolina*, I, 447 n).
9. November 9; Coon, *Beginnings of Public Education in North Carolina*, I, 432-33.
10. MS in Legislative Papers, in Senate, December 24, 1829.
11. November 9, 1829; Coon, *Beginnings of Public Education in North Carolina*, I, 432.
12. See North Carolina Grand Lodge of Freemasons, *Circular on the Subject of Education*, December 28, 1847, p. 2, for an argument against this theory.
13. See Coon, *Beginnings of Public Education in North Carolina*, I, xi.
14. Ibid., I, 254-55. For further support of this theory see Caldwell's "Letters on Popular Education," in ibid., II, 599; Address of Joseph A. Hill before the North Carolina Institute of Education, printed in *Raleigh Register*, February 25, 1843; and *Fayetteville Observer*, October 25, 1827.

15. *Raleigh Register*, March 25, 1800.
16. *Hillsborough Recorder*, February 13, 1822.
17. *Catawba Journal*, December 7, 1824.
18. *House Journal*, 1830-1831, p. 157; Coon, *Beginnings of Public Education in North Carolina*, I, 456.
19. Ibid., II, 605.
20. MS in Legislative Papers, in Senate, December 12, 1825.
21. *Raleigh Register*, April 6, 1839; Coon, *Beginnings of Public Education in North Carolina*, II, 899.
22. *Raleigh Register*, December 3, 1824; Coon, *Beginnings of Public Education in North Carolina*, I, 248.
23. Coon, *Beginnings of Public Education in North Carolina*, I, 247.
24. B. L. Beall and C. Brummell in *Raleigh Register*, July 13, 1839; Coon, *Beginnings of Public Education in North Carolina*, II, 903.
25. Ibid., I, 247. See especially the articles written during the educational campaign of 1839, ibid., II, 893-912.
26. *CRNC*, I, 448.
27. *Infra*, p. 703.
28. *Supra*, pp. 162-64; *infra*, pp. 425, 702.
29. *Raleigh Register*, August 2, 1822, April 18, 1849; *Fayetteville Observer*, April 22, 1830.
30. *Raleigh Register*, August 19, 1800.
31. Coon, *North Carolina Schools and Academies*, p. 516.
32. December 3; Coon, *Beginnings of Public Education in North Carolina*, I, 246.
33. *Raleigh Register*, February 4, 1830; Coon, *Beginnings of Public Education in North Carolina*, I, 434.
34. Ibid., II, 813.
35. *Raleigh Register*, September 3, 1838.
36. *Supra*, pp. 36-38.
37. *House Journal*, 1802, p. 46.
38. *Senate Journal*, 1805, p. 24.
39. For the report see Coon, *Beginnings of Public Education in North Carolina*, I, 105-13.
40. See R. D. W. Connor, *Ante-Bellum Builders of North Carolina*, Chaps. I-II; S. A. Ashe, *Biographical History of North Carolina*, IV, 340-49; and *The Papers of Archibald D. Murphey*.
41. *The Papers of Archibald D. Murphey*, II, 58.
42. Coon, *Beginnings of Public Education in North Carolina*, I, 147-64.
43. Ibid., I, 123-46; also in *The Papers of Archibald D. Murphey*, II, 63-83.
44. Coon, *Beginnings of Public Education in North Carolina*, I, 186.
45. *Sessional Laws*, 1825-1826, Chap. I; Coon, *Beginnings of Public Education in North Carolina*, I, 280-82. The fund was to consist of "the dividends arising from the stock now held, and which may hereafter be acquired by the State in the Banks of Newbern and Cape Fear, and which have not heretofore been pledged and set apart for internal improvements; the dividends arising from stock which is owned by the State in the Cape Fear Navigation Company, the Roanoke Navigation Company, and the Clubfoot and Harlow Creek Canal Company; the tax imposed by law on licenses to the retailers of spirituous liquors and auctioneers; the unexpended balance of the Agriculture Fund, which by the Act of the Legislature, is directed to be paid into the public Treasury; all monies paid to the State for the entries of vacant lands, (except the Cherokee Lands;) the sum of twenty-one thousand and ninety dollars, which was paid by this State to certain Cherokee Indians, for reservations to lands secured by them by treaty, when the said sums shall be received from the United States by this State; and all the vacant and unappropriated swamp lands in this State, together with such sums of money as the Legislature may hereafter find it convenient to appropriate from time to time."

46. See W. K. Boyd, "Finances of the North Carolina Literary Fund," *South Atlantic Quarterly*, XIII, 270-79.

47. From Fourth of July Toast of William Gaston in 1825, in Coon, *Beginnings of Public Education in North Carolina*, I, 256.

48. Ibid., pp. 452-543; 510-21.

49. Ibid., II, 545-613.

50. *Supra*, pp. 34-35.

51. See Boyd, *History of North Carolina*, pp. 227-28. The distribution of the fund was as follows: $300,000 for the State's subscription to stock in the Bank of North Carolina; $300,000 for the debt of the Literary Fund on stock taken in the Bank of Cape Fear; $200,000 to drain swamp lands appropriated to the Literary Fund; $100,000 for contingent expenses; and $533,757.39 to the Board of Internal Improvements for investment in stock of the Wilmington and Raleigh Railroad Company. The State's holdings in the two banks and in the railroad company were assigned to the Literary Board.

52. *Sessional Laws*, 1838-1839, Chap. VIII; Coon, *Beginnings of Public Education in North Carolina*, II, 886-90.

53. *Star*, May 8, 1839.

54. "Extracts from the Third Annual Report of the Superintendent of Common Schools," *NCJE*, I, 63.

55. MS in Wiley Papers: W. H. Abernethy to Calvin H. Wiley, Lincolnton, May 30, 1856.

56. *House Journal*, 1850-1851, p. 478.

57. *Sessional Laws*, 1852-1853, Chap. XVIII, secs. 7, 16.

58. Ibid., 1854-1855, Chap. XXVI, secs. 46-49, 57.

59. Ibid., 1840-1841, Chap. VII, sec. 6; ibid., 1844-1845, Chap. XXXVI, sec. 6.

60. MS in Legislative Papers, in Senate, December 23, 1848.

61. The Legislature of 1854-1855 passed a meaningless section of the common school bill (*Sessional Laws*, Chap. XXVII, sec. 28), stating that county courts "shall levy a tax . . . which shall not be less than one-half of the estimated amount to be received . . . from the literary fund."

62. MS in Cumberland County Court Minutes, 1849-1852, March term, 1855.

63. MS in Edgecombe County Court Minutes, 1853-1857, May term, 1854, February term, 1855.

64. MSS in Orange County Court Minutes, 1851-1855, February terms of court in 1851, 1852, 1853, 1854, 1855.

65. MS in Wiley Papers: R. W. Millard to C. H. Wiley, April 11, 1856.

66. Ibid.: A. W. Brandon to C. H. Wiley, 1854.

67. Ibid.: R. H. Ballard to C. H. Wiley, 1854.

68. See Zebulon B. Vance on this subject in *Raleigh Register*, December 20, 1854. Governor Manly said in his message to the Legislature in 1850 (*House Journal*, 1850-1851, p. 476): ". . . those counties in the State containing a sparse white population, and but few white children to educate, yet containing many slaves and free negroes, receive the larger proportion of this public bounty; while those counties having a large white population and many children to educate, yet having few slaves and free negroes, receive the smaller share. This arrangement I hold to be wrong."

69. *Revised Code*, 1855, Chap. LXVI, sec. 34, inserted a provision that boards of superintendents lay off "school districts (and number the same,) of such form and size for one school, as they think most convenient for the inhabitants of the county." See Wiley on this point in his digest of school laws, *NCJE*, IV, 147-49.

70. MS in Wiley Papers, December 3, 1854.

71. Ibid.: A. W. Brandon to C. H. Wiley, 1854.

72. Ibid.: James Avery to C. H. Wiley, 1854.

73. Ibid.: S. D. Wallace to C. H. Wiley, January 22, 1856.

74. Ibid.: Joseph Potts to C. H. Wiley, April 20, 1857; see also *Raleigh Register*, April 18, 1849.

75. *Infra*, pp. 318-23.
76. *Sessional Laws*, 1852-1853, Chaps. XVIII.
77. For brief sketches of Wiley's life see Connor, *Ante-Bellum Builders of North Carolina*, pp. 93-115; Ashe, *Biographical History of North Carolina* II, 427-41; S. B. Weeks, *Beginnings of the Common School System in the South*, Chap. XXIX; H. C. Renegar, "Problems, Policies and Achievements of Calvin Henderson Wiley" (unpublished typescript).
78. *Legislative Documents*, No. 12, Session 1854-1855, p. 36.
79. Ibid., No. 10, Session 1860-1861: "Report of the Superintendent of Common Schools," pt. II, p. 9.
80. Ibid., Session 1854-1855: "Second Annual Report of the General Superintendent of Common Schools," pp. 8-23.
81. Ibid., No. 9, Session 1858-1859, pp. 13-17.
82. The following questionnaire which Wiley sent to the counties shows his method of work and at the same time presents valuable information concerning the status of the common schools (MS in Calvin H. Wiley Papers, Returns from Counties):

Question I. What is the number of Common School Districts in your county?
Answer—Thirty nine

2. How are the Districts laid off? are they generally intended for one school, or for several.
Ans. Surveyed regularly about 3¼ miles squ—intended for only one school
3. What is the size of the Districts generally?
Ans. About 3¼ miles square
4. Could your county, in your judgment, be so laid off in Districts, that no one District would be too large for one school, and few Districts so very small that a distribution of the Fund, according to Districts, would not be unjust?
   not too large, but too populous. the size near equal
5. Were the Districts laid off by actual survey?
   Yes,—varied in size to suit water courses
6. Can your county be so Districted as to bring each child, or a very large portion of the children within reach of a school?
   Yes, in the way it is now laid off
7. When did the Common School System go into practical operation in your county?
   On May 1850
8. When did you begin to have Examining Committees?
   from the beginning or shortly after
9. What is your observation of the effect of Examining Committees, good or bad?
   has a good effect
10. Has there been complaint of the want of capacity and fidelity in teachers?
   at first there was but some improvement
11. Do the people generally elect Committee-men? do many vote in each election?
   the people Elect. do not many attend & vote
12. What is the general opinion as to the best method of choosing Committee-men?
   By County Superintendant
13. Is it difficult to get good men to act as Committee-men?
   very difficult
14. Do you lay a school tax? if so when did you begin, and what is the amount levied on each poll, and on each hundred dollars' worth of land?
   Yes. commencement, 8 cts on Poll 6 on land present amt about 700 $ from the county
15. Have you school houses in all your Districts?
   Yes. One with 3—5 with 2 schools
16. How many Common Schools are there in your county?
   forty-six

17. Is there a supply of teachers moderately qualified?
    not in the county
18. What is the probable cause of the want of more teachers?
    the want of proper information
19. Are your schools gradually improving?
    They are
20. Do you know how many Academies, Classical and Select schools there are in your county?
    One Male— (no) Female
21. What is the average character of the school houses in your county, comfortable or otherwise?
    largest number comfortable
22. How do you divide your portion of the common School Fund?
    By the number of children in each District of proper age
23. Does this method give general satisfaction?
    It does, was adopted by bord of county superintendants
24. Have you ever divided on any other plan?
    none
25. Do the people generally build the school houses, furnish wood &c., at their own expense?
    About 4/5 do balance do not
26. At what seasons are the schools generally taught?
    Too much in winter
27. Do your teachers ever have public examinations?
    But a few cases yet but increasing
28. How will the wages of school teachers compare with the general prices for labor, clerking, &c., &c., favorably or otherwise?
    reasonably favorable ranging from $12 to $20 per month—prices and qualification increasing
29. Are your teachers native, or from other places?
    Two thirds natives one third from abroad
30. Has the Chairman of your county been often changed?
    No change
31. Is there complaint of want of uniformity in books? or of the use of bad books, or of frequent changes?
    Verry great need of uniformity of Books, at least one third lost for want of such

. . . Make such suggestions as may occur to you, in regard to the deficiencies of the Law, the difficulties in the way of greater success of the Common Schools, and the want of proper attention or management on the part of all concerned.

It would be of Great benefit for som one qualified to visit all the schools and impart som more interest and attention to duties of the committeemen som of whom are very inatten to there duties also to see how the Teachers fullfiled their duties I would also recommend that female schools be taught in the warm season of the year.

Legislative Documents, No. 12, Session 1854-1855, pp. 32-34; No. 10, Session 1860-1861, pp. 3-6. These figures are Wiley's estimates based upon actual returns from most of the counties.

Richard H. Haunton

Law and Order in Savannah, 1850–1860

Savannah was a rapidly growing port city on the eve of the Civil War. This had not always been the case. Incorporated in 1789, the city grew slowly during the first half-century of its corporate existence. Population, which stood at 5,166 in 1800 and 5,215 ten years later, increased to 7,523 in 1820 but then dropped to 7,303 in 1830.[1] The third decade of the century was, in fact, the most disappointing one for Savannah. Hard hit by both fire and yellow fever in 1820, the city was slow to recover in the years following. Not only did population dip, but the annual value of foreign exports declined steadily as well, and the city showed little disposition to remedy the situation by undertaking large-scale works of internal improvement.[2] Savannah, wrote William Gilmore Simms in 1831, "remains stationary and has an air of utter stagnation and languishment."[3]

The rise of Savannah port in the ensuing years was a direct result of the construction of the Central Railroad of Georgia. Running 190 miles from Savannah to Macon, the line was built between 1836 and 1843 for the express purpose of competing with Charleston for the upcountry cotton trade. During the late 1840's and 1850's, the Central was expanded into a railroad system; with extensive financial backing from Savannah, other lines were constructed, merging or connecting with the Central and linking Savannah to Tennessee, Alabama, and states beyond.[4] The effects of railroad building were clearly shown in increased receipts of goods at the Georgia port between 1849 and 1860. By the latter year, Savannah had edged past Charleston in total cotton exports, foreign and domestic, and moved into third position among America's

Source: Georgia Historical Quarterly 56 (Spring 1972): 1–24. Reprinted by permission of the Georgia Historical Society.

cotton ports.[5] Territorial and population growth accompanied the rise in Savannah's economic fortunes. From the figure of 7,303 in 1830, population climbed to 11,214 in 1840 and then to 15,312 at mid-century. By 1860, Savannah would have 22,292 inhabitants.[6]

Even the most efficient of city administrations, with police and court systems immune to the influences of party politics, would have been hard pressed to keep the peace in Savannah during the 1850's. The Savannah *Daily Morning News* noted in 1851 that as the city's population increased, so did the evils and disorders; hitherto known as a city of good order and "thrifty enterprise," commented the Savannah *Daily Georgian* in 1854, Savannah "bids fair soon to become quite as notorious in character for crime."[7] Several thousand new citizens, a majority of them migrants from foreign countries or Northern states, came within the purview of the law during the decade,[8] and as the city prospered, there was a larger floating population with which to contend. Negro slaves,[9] many of whom were already accustomed to living out and hiring their own time, became more difficult to control within the extended limits of the city. Locally-owned bondsmen, runaway slaves from surrounding counties, free Negroes, seamen, and Irish laborers congregated in Savannah's outlying districts, where they engaged in various illicit activities and committed crimes against one another. Narrow streets, lanes, and alleys, as well as the absence of gas lighting in the fringe areas, complicated law enforcement.

Reporting to the City Council in 1855 on the city's "bad spots," the police chief pointed up other inducements to lawlessness. In the northwest part of town—west of Whitaker Street and north of South Broad Street—were seventy-three liquor shops, three boarding houses for sailors, and four well-known brothels; this section included the iniquitous Oglethorpe Ward. Currytown and Robertsville, on the southwest side, accounted for another forty liquor shops. The worst area comprised the wards east of Habersham Street, which included "over one hundred liquor vending shops, twenty-six sailor boarding houses, five large houses of ill fame, besides numerous small ones," and supplied "an average of two in four of those persons arrested for disorderly conduct." All of these districts contained populations described as "very mixed."[10]

In an urban environment the control of slaves perforce became a public responsibility. "From Jan'y to Decr.," complained the Savannah planter John Stoddard, "many owners cannot tell where their servants are, or what they are doing."[11] Private letters bear out the accuracy of the statement. "I have not seen Maria," wrote one resident, "for she is in a part of town to which I cannot walk."[12] Rose has been absent nearly a week," wrote another. "I will use every endeavor to hear of her, . . . as I fear she is getting into bad company."[13] Even if the slave did not work out or live out, he was apt to be constantly running errands into the urban world about him.

By the 1850's Savannah possessed a full complement of laws governing the economic and social life of the Negro when away from the master's premises. If hired out, the slave had to wear a badge, for which the owner paid the city $2.50 to $10, depending on the hireling's skill and sex. Negroes working in stores were forbidden to do any selling, except in the presence of the employer or an adult white employee. Movement of Negroes was regulated by the pass system. A "general ticket" signed by the slaveowner or by the guardian of a free Negro passed the bearer until bell-ring at ten o'clock in the evening, after which time the Negro had to have a "special ticket" stating the exact hour of expiration. No black could be out after midnight unless his ticket "distinctly specified" the time when it was given, the purpose of the errand, and the destination.

Fraternizing of Negroes outside the owner's premises was frowned upon by the law. Except for funerals and Sunday worship, no more than seven of them could assemble in any house, building, lot, street, or lane, and there could be no meeting for dancing "or other merriment" without written permission from the mayor or two aldermen. Nor could the Negro play or bet at any game of cards, dice, dominoes, or billiards. He was denied the simplest pleasures. Instruction in reading and writing—indeed, the mere possession of printed matter or articles of stationery—was forbidden. No person could sell "or furnish" him any intoxicating beverage. He could not smoke in public, view a military or civic parade, ride a horse on the Sabbath (unless sent on a mission by his master), or own a dog. Should he ever commit the human error of "quarreling or fighting" with his compeers, the law required his arrest and punishment.[14]

Available evidence indicates that the slave code was frequently ignored. In grand jury presentments, newspaper articles, and private letters, the white community lashed out at failures in law enforcement. Early in the decade, one Savannahian appealed to Congressman Howell Cobb for assistance in obtaining a company of "flying artillery" for the city. "Such a company here," wrote Dr. W. C. Daniell, "will have a very desirable influence on our slave population . . . which is becoming very licentious & give occasional indications of insubordination which tell badly of the future."[15]

Yet the same white community, knowingly or unknowingly, very often aided and abetted the Negro in his transgressions of the law. It was not uncommon for the white employer to hire a slave who was without a badge or a written permit from his owner.[16] "From the numbers in the streets, though not great," wrote Nehemiah Adams, "you would not suspect that the blacks are restricted at night." Passes were "freely given; so that, after all, the bondage is theoretical, but still it is bondage."[17] Slaveowners' children were cajoled by servants into granting passes, while out in town there were many individuals, according to the *News*, "who never hesitate to give tickets to Negroes, over whom they have no authority." The whole system, said the *News*, was a "perpetual annoyance."[18]

Nothing undermined the slave code so much, however, as the Negro's persistent urge, whatever the consequences, to partake of the momentary freedoms and delights which urban life afforded him. In 1856, Charles C. Jones, Jr., advised selling the slave Jane, who had run away from his father's plantation in Liberty County, because "her tales of Savannah, & of high life in the City" would have a harmful effect if she were returned to the plantation. "Savannah," he noted, "is the last place in the world for servants inclined to evil." Four years later, Jones sent one of his own slaves to the plantation for a week while he made a short trip out of the city. "[I] am afraid," he wrote, "to let George run at large in the city, while we are away, as he most assuredly will do,—it being almost an impossibility to prevent the contraction of idle, vagrant habits by especially young servants in this place."[19] Jones was not alone in his fears, apparently, since Savannah's jail records for the period show that there were always a sizable number of slave occupants who had been committed by their owners merely for "safe keeping."[20]

Undeterred by penalties inflicted on them, Negroes continually violated every one of the ordinances regulating their behavior. They smoked in public, kept dogs as pets, rode horses on Sunday without permits, and visited their friends and mates after bell-ring without tickets.[21] More worrisome to the authorities was what often happened when blacks congregated in large numbers. Entries on the Fine and Information Docket of the Police Court for "unlawful assemblage" were common, the assemblage frequently including both slaves and free Negroes.[22] The *News*, in May, 1854, complained that groups of Negroes, "blacks of 'elegant leisure'—the snobs of our 'colored population,' " met regularly to test their marksmanship with pistols. During the same month, some two dozen Negroes were arrested when a ball they were holding at Giles and Bradley's sawmill ended in a riot. The owners had approved the dance, they contended, not knowing that the mill was within the city's jurisdiction.[23]

Some relatively trivial Negro offenses were construed by whites as acts of boldness and arrogance—"evils," said one Savannahian, "which unless checkd. at once, will cause great damage to us & our children."[24] A typical grievance was expressed in untypical fashion by a writer to the *News* in 1855:

> Frequent and constant use of the Park, (especially on Sunday afternoon), by negroes [is a nuisance]. . . . It is bad enough, while riding on the roads in the vicinity of Savannah, to have the dust whirled into your face by some fast mulatto buck driving out his yellow wench, at the fastest rate at which a hired horse can travel. If the roads are to be given up to these gentry, let us, at least, have the use of the city side-walks, crossings, and promenades. . . . Gaudily dressed mulatto girls, and mustachio'd fellows who ought to be engaged hauling cotton and sweeping stores, are never allowed in [other] cities, and should not be allowed in this city, to pollute the atmosphere with their peculiar aroma, and the additional odor of their strong segars.[25]

Others complained of the boisterousness and coarse language of Negroes, and of their failure to move to the outside when passing whites on the street.[26]

Though such practices were not always in direct violation of the city code, they often led to arrest and punishment, as evidenced by the Savannah *Daily Journal and Courier's* listings of cases before the Police Court in 1855: "Jeffrey and Sam, slaves, ... obstructing the side walk. To be flogged"; "Adam, a slave ..., using vulgar language in a public place, sentenced to receive thirty-nine lashes in jail."[27]

Nehemiah Adams must have caught Savannah at a rare moment when he wrote that he saw no Negroes frequenting saloons or indulging in "unsuitable behavior"; "the slaves are generally free as to street brawls and open drunkenness."[28] Quite to the contrary, hardly a day passed when Negroes were not brought before the mayor for "Fighting & Disorderly Conduct" or drunkenness or both.

Few subjects occasioned more concern during the 1850's than the evil effects of spirituous liquors on the community in general and on Negroes in particular. The liquor traffic, according to the Chatham County grand jury in May, 1851, was "demoralizing to the black population, ruinous to their health, and destructive of their usefulness as labourers";[29] In January, 1852, the grand jury estimated that three-fourths of its indictments were for crimes "committed or originating in dram shops."[30] Not only did Savannah's grocery and grog shops sell liquor to Negroes on the premises—particularly on Sundays, a further violation of the law—, but they were the source of a host of other illicit activities as well. In some instances, Negroes were installed as tenants in houses adjoining the grog shops, there to be used as agents for the dispensing of ardent spirits to other blacks. The *Journal and Courier* reported in 1855 that Negroes were retailing liquor on the river front "at fashionable restaurant prices—12½ cents per glass."[31]

Liquor shops also served as gambling centers for Negroes and as markets for stolen property. Despite laws prohibiting most trade with slaves, except by written consent of the owner, shopkeepers received goods purloined by country Negroes from their masters' storehouses and by city slaves from ships, wharves, stores and warehouses, and private residences. Receipts from the urban slave might include jewelry, silverware, food, clothing, tobacco, or even a load of iron, but the usual offering was cotton. According to the *News*, some forty to sixty bales of stolen cotton, re-packed into round bales, were shipped out of Savannah every week during the winter season. The equivalent given by the shopkeeper in exchange for stolen items was generally liquor.[32]

Attempts to cope with these problems met with little success. The Chamber of Commerce, in 1851, posted rewards for the apprehension of whites or Negroes selling or receiving stolen cotton, and in 1853 the Savannah Total Abstinence Society sought to have the state legislature prohibit traffic in spirituous liquors. A Grocers' Association was immediately organized to oppose the move.[33] In 1854 and 1855, and again between 1859 and 1861, reform-minded city administrations made serious efforts to suppress the practices of the shopkeepers. Liquor license fees were increased, as were the fines for violation of liquor ordinances. A law of 1859 authorized the police to enter grog shops after bell-ring and arrest any Negro who was not the property of the shopowner and who did not possess a ticket from his master or employer designating his reason for being there; shopkeepers entertaining such Negroes were also to be arrested.[34] The following year, however, the grand jury delivered the usual presentment, calling attention to "the *grievous injuries resulting from the selling of spiritous* [*sic*] *intoxicating liquors to our slaves & free persons of colour—and the keeping of disorderly & gambling houses for the same*," and recommending "*nothing less than confinement in the penetentiary* [*sic*]" for those committing the offenses.[35]

Of the more serious crimes perpetrated by Negroes, none was so common as theft. Constantly exposed to an affluent white society, they took by stealth what they could seldom hope to gain by honest labor. The deeds were committed night and day, by blacks acting alone or in groups. The city's Negro youth were particularly active. Describing the arrest, in 1854, of four slaves who had burglarized a jewelry shop, the *News* noted that the oldest was eighteen years of age and that each belonged to a different master; in 1855 it was reported that bands of young Negroes had become "so emboldened as to enter houses in broad day light, and help themselves to whatever comes most convenient to their reach." The stolen items might be a means to an end—the shopkeeper's liquor—or treasures in their own right. Found on the person of the slave Stephen, following a clothing store robbery in 1858, were "socks, silk neck ties, pants and shoes, with which, it being Sunday, he had dressed himself."[36]

The steady association of slaves, free Negroes, and whites inevitably bred crimes against person as well as property. Among slaves there were frequent cases of assault and battery and a surprising number of murders;[37] and in spite of—or, to some contemporary observers, because of—the permissive nature of urban slavery, the bondsman often vented his hostility towards the system in acts of violence against whites. When apprehended for night visiting without a ticket, the slave Jane, according to her owner, "swore no white man should carry her to the Guard house & from appearances (for I saw her) had made a *good fight*."[38]

Policemen were not the only targets of slave animosity. The information docket for June 9, 1860, contained the entry "Monday [slave] . . . Knocking mistress down on the street. . . . Turned over to owner for punishment," while newspapers during the course of the decade listed such assault or murder victims as a German shopkeeper, a sawmill superintendent, and "a young lady walking along the canal."[39] Available evidence suggests that much Negro violence was the result of direct provocation by whites. The City Council, in 1854, heard the interesting case of a Negro who had become boisterous "when a number of white men . . . annoyed him in various ways for their sport,"[40] and court records for the period are abundant with cases of whites striking or beating slaves.[41]

Savannah was a haven for runaways during the ante-bellum era. Many of the fugitives were city slaves who had wandered off from their master's residence or business establishment, but the great majority were from plantations in Georgia and South Carolina. Plantation Negroes always numbered large among the occupants of the city jail.[42] Newspapers were filled with advertisements, both from the jailer in search of owners and from planters in pursuit of their property. For city authorities the apprehension of runaways was a constant chore, as well as a profitable one. "These constables are themselves notorious rascals," Charles C. Jones, Jr., advised his father. "It would not be amiss . . . to give $30, as rewards are running quite high." The jailer received a fee of $5 for his services.[43]

Once arrived at Savannah, the runaway usually merged with other Negroes in the more populous areas of town, resident slaves, and even whites, often helping to conceal him when necessary.[44] While he might attempt to pass as a free Negro, he customarily represented himself as a slave who had been allowed to come to the city to hire his own time.[45] Runaways also gathered in camps outside the city, generally supporting themselves by thievery.[46] Savannah not only afforded the fugitive an exciting, if precarious, taste of freedom, but it might be the avenue to escape from bondage as well. In late 1849 the slave Henry "passed himself off as a French cook" in order to gain passage on a ship to Boston, and in 1851 lawyers secured the return of Thomas Sims, a bricklayer's apprentice, after he had turned up among abolitionists in the same city. Later in the decade four slave stowaways were found on the *Nicholas Biddle*, about to sail for Liverpool; according to the Savannah *Daily Republican*, they had been enticed aboard by Negro crew members.[47]

The occasional departure of vessels from Liberia, under the sponsorship of the American Colonization Society, was a further source of difficulty. Following reports that some three hundred runaways had flocked to Chatham County in anticipation of one such voyage in 1856, and that local slaves had been approached by agents of the Colonization Society, the Council, in effect, terminated the Society's work in Savannah by imposing a tax of $200 on any slave or free Negro entering the city for the purpose of being transported to Liberia.[48]

Besides the detection of runaways and stowaways, the city had to cope with a considerable traffic in stolen Negroes during the 1850's. Local bondsmen were abducted and taken elsewhere to be sold, and numerous attempts were made to dispose of stolen plantation Negroes to slave dealers in Savannah. In 1850 alone, according to the *Georgian*, four such efforts were foiled by the broker William Wright.[49]

While the steady erosion of Savannah's slave system kept the Negro in the public eye, there is no reason to believe that he was more responsible than the white man for undermining the general peace and order of the community. In due proportion to population totals, there were usually at least twice as many whites as blacks in the city jail. During any term of the Chatham County Superior Court, such as that for January, 1856, the presentments revealed the extent and range of white crime: malicious mischief, larcency from the house, larcency from the person, buying and receiving stolen goods, forgery, fraud and embezzlement, illegal voting, assault and battery, assault with intent to murder, and murder.[50]

Adopted citizens were the worst offenders. The Irish were entered regularly on the Police Court docket for disorderly conduct and drunkenness, entries for the latter often being accompanied by the words "and lying down in street." "Charles McCarty was found lying on the ground, holding on to the grass, in order to keep from falling off," reported the *Journal and Courier* in 1855. "Such a situation being thought *Prima facie* evidence of too great indulgence in liquid comforts, he was arrested."[51] In one way or another, the foreign-born were usually linked with election irregularities. Observing the municipal election of 1851, the New Yorker Henry Cathell noted that the Irish were "the grand movers in all disturbances. The green horns or 'Country crakers [*sic*],' suffered when they got among the Hibernians. This all appeared to me very natural with exception, that here, Bowie Knives, Revolvers, and Clubs were used, and with us fists only."[52] Prior to the city election of 1854, the *Republican* claimed that immigrants were being admitted to citizenship who already possessed registry tickets entitling them to vote, a reversal of the usual procedure; and according to the same journal, the American party would have carried the county in the 1855 state elections if men of foreign birth had been required to present naturalization papers at the polls.[53]

As grog shop owners, the foreign-born were the usual corrupters of city slaves, and as landlords of sailor boarding houses, they victimized visiting seamen. River piracy had been tolerated for so many years, commented the mayor in 1855, that those engaged in it had come to regard it as "almost an established right."[54] Such notorious landlords and "shipping agents" as James Kelly, William Dunn, and Christopher Hussey employed runners to abduct or entice seamen from incoming ships. At the boarding house, the sailors were presented exorbitant bills—as high as $40.75 and $39.75 per day, according to samples in possession of the *News* in 1855—for lodging, food, and especially drink. Rendered destitute, they were then shipped out on other vessels, the landlords usually appropriating any advance pay.[55]

Even the upper class white too often failed to set a good example by his public behavior. Urging the Chatham County grand jury, in 1854, to drive gambling establishments from the city, Judge George T. Howard addressed himself especially to the evil of gambling "in high life, among gentlemen." Far from being an exception to the law, said Howard, gentlemen should be dealt with more severely "because their position in society . . . gives tone and character to their actions."[56] Statements in letters and travel accounts of the period indicate that drinking was rife among the wealthy. Though he saw no intoxication, James S. Buckingham noted that "wine is universally drank [*sic*] here, and champaigne [*sic*] in abundance, of which the ladies partake as freely as the gentlemen."[57]

Quick to deplore lawlessness among the lower orders, the aristocrat exhibited his own penchant for violence in the *code duello*. To many Savannahians dueling was "a barbarous custom,"[58] but it was a custom, nevertheless. While the need for it was unfortunate, wrote the young lawyer George A. Mercer, "it at least tends to preserve gentlemanly deportment, & a healthy social tone" and "is not . . . half so debauching in its tendency as those brutal prize fights that constantly occur at the north."[59] In 1827 an "Anti-Duelling Association" had been formed for the purpose of "restraining, and if possible . . . suppressing" the practice of dueling, but its published essays and successful mediations had little effect on the public mind. The organization was defunct by the mid-1840's. For the remainder of the ante-bellum era, Savannahians, as well as South Carolinians and other Georgians, repaired regularly to Screven's Ferry or another spot on the Carolina side of the Savannah River to settle their differences with pistols or rifles. However, dueling fatalities were few in number.[60]

The likelihood that a member of the gentry would have to answer for his actions before a court of law was small, as evidenced by merchant William W. Gordon's description of a quarrel between "two young bloods" in February, 1855. According to Gordon, one of the participants was seriously wounded, but "as they were both . . . of respectable family, the papers make no mention of it nor does the law take cognizance of it, Laws in this community resembling what the Grecian robber said of all Laws—'cobwebs made to catch poor flies but thro' which respectable wasps break with impunity.' "[61] Writing to a correspondent in New Orleans the same month, Savannah merchant Charles A. L. Lamar pointed up the advantages of Chatham County as the starting point for a filibustering expedition to Cuba. Conviction for violation of the neutrality laws, said Lamar, would be difficult. "Gen'l Pierce and his whole Cabinet, were they *here*, could not convict me or my friends. That is the advantage of a small place. A man of influence can do as he pleases."[62] Two years later, Lamar wrote similarly of a project to land African slaves near Savannah: "One thing is certain. Nothing can be done in the way of conviction."[63]

It is noteworthy that the remarks made by Gordon and Lamar in 1855 came at the moment Savannah was undergoing the unique experience of over-enforcement of the law. Under the Democratic administration of John E. Ward in 1854, a serious effort was made to regulate the shopkeepers and, for the first time, to enforce the longstanding Sunday blue laws. These laws forbade whites to work on the Sabbath and prohibited most forms of recreation; except for medicine, ice, and milk, no goods, liquid or solid, were to be sold. To help implement his policies, Ward introduced mounted patrolmen into the city's police system.[64] The changes became the key issue in the municipal election later in the year. In that contest, a Democratic slate nominated by the shopkeepers was defeated by a "People's Ticket" pledged to preserve the new police system. Ward, along with most of the other incumbents, repudiated the shopkeepers' ticket and, in his words, "voted for correct principles."[65]

The new regime, headed by Mayor Edward C. Anderson, did more than continue the reforms of its predecessor. The Anderson administration was praised for suppressing river piracy, enforcing health ordinances, and curtailing minor disorders, but there was also talk of oppression and "Jacobinism."[66] In January, 1855, the *News* accused the Council of enforcing "the letter of the law in its most arbitrary, illiberal construction, against citizens admitted to be guilty of no intentional offense." According to the *Georgian*, people were being penalized for entering their stores on Sunday, even to feed their cats, and a lady had been fined for permitting wine to be served in her parlor on the Sabbath; "ere long it will be considered in the Council Chamber a finable misdemeanor for a man to kiss his wife on that holy day."[67] City officers were not immune, it being reported in June that several, including the marshal, had been fined for "various slight omissions and derelictions."[68] Opposition to the system took the form of court appeals, letters to the press, and the formation of a Citizens' Protective Association, but most Savannahians probably followed the advice of "Citizen," in the *Journal and Courier* of January 15, 1855, and resolved to "bear with it"; some found new ways of doing old things, such as buying on Saturday night the liquor they intended to drink on Sunday—thus becoming "their own retail consumers"—or purchasing it from apothecaries on Sunday for "medicinal" purposes.[69] In the city election of December, 1855, a Democratic majority was returned to power. Within five months the *Republican* was accusing the new Council of undermining the reforms of the preceding administrations.[70]

To cope with the misdoings of an enlarged population, Savannah was compelled to reorganize its police system during the 1850's. In the early years of the decade, law enforcement at night was in the hands of the so-called "watch," numbering some one hundred men by 1854; during the day, the city was guarded by five constables, the marshal, and several watchmen detailed for the purpose.[71] Appointments to these positions were usually on an annual basis. To most observers, the system was pitiable. The daytime force was clearly inadequate in size, and the members of the watch, though efficient at bloc voting on election days,[72] seemed seldom to be at the right place at the right time on their evening rounds. With exasperation, the *Republican* reported a series of burglaries in 1851, heading its notices with the caption "Watch! Watch!"[73] The watchmen, said the same journal in 1853, were not very watchful, a statement which the Savannah *Evening Journal* thought overly generous:

We are really at a loss to know what to make of our up-town neighbor lately—does he mean to say that there is such a thing as a police force in this city! Brother, beware how you draw such long bows! You'll impair your credit for veracity if you seriously put such rumers [*sic*] afloat. A 'watch' in Savannah! Capital joke. We just begin to see the cue, our neighbor refers to time-pieces in the jewellery stores.[74]

At a salary of $25 per month, the watchmen had small incentive to perform efficiently. Most worked at other jobs during the day in order to supplement their own income; fatigued at night, they were frequently found asleep on duty. Their knowledge of the city and its ordinances was limited. Nor was the night guard sufficiently large or mobile to cover the entire city; in the unlighted districts—the fringe areas and wharves—there were not enough watchmen, and in some wards there were none at all. The first important move away from this system occurred during the administration of Mayor Ward in 1854. The position of constable was eliminated and the number of watchmen cut nearly in half. The vacancies were filled by twenty mounted men, who, along with the police captain, two lieutenants, and four sergeants, were to serve three-year terms and be "at all times at the command and in the service of the city." Five years later, the night watch was done away with entirely, all policemen being made subject to duty both day and night. The salary of privates, mounted and foot, was increased to $500 per annum, and they were forbidden to engage in other pursuits.[75]

The reforms did not solve all problems. According to the grand jury in 1860, drinking and gambling among slaves were daily permitted "by the culpable indifference, inactivity or collusion" of police officers; police brutality had continued and little had been done to separate law enforcement from party politics.[76] Yet the increased activity in the Police Court and the plaudits from governing officials in other cities attest to the fact that Savannah's police department functioned more efficiently at the end of the decade than at the beginning.[77]

Once apprehended by the police, the transgressor of the law was likely to be confined in the guard room of the Oglethorpe barracks, a place, said the police captain in 1856, "not fit to put any man . . . who had any claims to decent treatment." Built originally in the 1830'sto house federal troops, the barracks served as headquarters for the local police from 1854 to 1861.[78] Negroes taken up after bell-ring could be released from the guard house upon the payment, usually by the owner but sometimes by the offender himself, of a one dollar fine,[79] but most violations of city ordinances, by Negroes or whites, entailed appearance before the mayor in the Police Court. Violations of state law would ordinarily be heard in one of Savannah's four magistrates' courts, the presiding justice either passing immediate sentence or ordering the accused to stand trial at the next session of the Chatham County Superior Court. Lines of jurisdiction were indistinct, however, with both city and county courts handling indictments for such offenses as assault and battery, riot, theft, receipt of stolen goods, gambling, and the sale of liquor to slaves.[80]

In the punishments meted out by these courts, the distinction between Negro and white was clear. Whites convicted of misdemeanors were usually ordered to pay a fine. Slaves and, especially, free Negroes might occasionally escape with a fine, but whipping was the common mode of punishment for both. The most frequent sentence was thirty-nine lashes, the maximum allowable by law for a single day, but the punishment might be extended over several days for more serious violations—thirty-nine lashes on one day and twenty on the next, or three times thirty-nine lashes administered on successive days or at intervals of two or three days. Frequently there was little consistency in the punishments imposed for a particular offense. The mere act of smoking in public by a Negro might bring a penalty of two dollars, three dollars, eight lashes, or thirty lashes.

The inequity of the law was apparent in the sentences handed down for major crimes. Negro stealing or horse stealing sent the white man to the penitentiary for several years, but for the murder of a Negro he paid a fine of several hundred dollars and spent thirty days in jail. The murder of a white by a Negro was rare, but when it occurred it brought the maximum punishment and aroused the full passion of the community. In March, 1861, an Irishman was killed by a Negro; when found, secreted in a brick oven at the residence of two other bondsmen, the supposed murderer was shot and wounded by an onlooker. "It was with considerable difficulty," reported the *News*, "that his captors prevented his being lynched." and the next day the mayor had to summon a special military force to prevent the removal of the prisoners from jail for that purpose.[81] The prospect was not much brighter for the slave who murdered another slave. Though hanging was common in such cases, the felon might get by with three hundred or five hundred stripes administered in doses of fifty on the bare back.[82]

If there was discrimination in the courtroom, the situation was quite the reverse at the city jail. There resided one of the most heterogeneous groups in the city, including those serving sentences or awaiting trial for felonies or misdemeanors, vagrants and paupers, the insane, free Negro seamen waiting for their vessels to depart, runaway slaves, and slaves committed by their owners for safekeeping. All mingled together, irrespective of sex, color and condition.[83] The jail was also the scene of daily whippings inflicted on the Negro in accordance with court orders or written requests from slaveowners. While recalcitrant bondsmen sometimes were punished at home, the usual procedure was to send them to the jail to receive a designated number of lashes; the master was then billed by the jailer for services rendered.[84] Jail records indicate that few owners failed to take advantage of the system, although one Savannahian wrote that the thought of sending "Georgianna" to jail "almost thru' me in convulsions, the idea of so faithful a creature to be so publicly whipped, she has her faults but she is kind to me and watchful if I am the least sick."[85]

Criticism of the jail facilities increased during the 1850's. Ventilation and sanitation were inadequate, according to the grand jury's report in 1850; conditions were "inhuman" and "demoralizing." Jail revenue had dropped, the mayor reported three years later, because "many masters are unwilling to expose their servants to the dangers of such a residence." Others who complained about the ease of escape and the absence of any program of employment whereby inmates might assist in their support received small satisfaction when the jailer had to be summoned before Council in 1857 for allowing Negro prisoners to go at large and for detailing them to his private residence to perform chores.[86] In 1857 the state legislature authorized Savannah to erect a workhouse, and for the remainder of the decade the city aldermen and justices of the Chatham County Inferior Court debated each other's responsibilities in the matter. No workhouse or new jail had been built when the Civil War broke out.[87]

While lawlessness was by no means peculiar to Savannah during the 1850's, the fact remains that it was an important part of her constitution. This was as true in 1860 as in 1850. With the rapid growth in the city's population, particularly in the early years of the decade, the problem of controlling the diverse elements which comprised that population was intensified. The municipal government responded by seeking and obtaining from the legislature increased jurisdiction over crimes committed within and outside the city limits.[88] In 1854 began the re-organization of the police, and between 1850 and 1861 annual expenditures for the police system, always the largest item in the city's budget, jumped from $24,318.09 to $45,676.26.[89] But the funds and reforms seemed to have but slight impress on the network of crime which pervaded the port city environment. Periods of vigorous law enforcement, in 1854–1855 and during the emotion-charged atmosphere of the secession crisis, were followed by periods of casual enforcement. Still present at the end of the decade were the dens of iniquity—the liquor shops, gambling houses, brothels (the City Court grand jury, in 1860, merely urged that they be removed from the "central and respectable portion" of the city), and sailor boarding houses.[90] For runaways from the interior, Savannah remained the logical destination. There was no discernible weakening of the slave's desire to pursue the "high life" of the city or of the aristocrat's cavalier attitude toward the law.

Notes

1. *Return of the Whole Number of Persons within the Several Districts of the United States, according to "An act providing for the second Census of Enumeration of the Inhabitants of the United States." Passed February the twenty eighth, one thousand eight hundred* (New York, n.d.), 2-0; *Census for 1820* (Washington, 1821): 28; U. S. Census, 1830, Georgia, microfilm at Georgia Historical Society, Savannah, of original at National Archives; *The Seventh Census of the United States: 1850 . . .* (Washington, 1853): lii.

2. *An Official Register of the Deaths Which Occurred Among the White Population in the*

City of Savannah, During the Extraordinary Season of Sickness and Mortality which prevailed in the Summer and Fall Months of the Year 1820 . . . (Savannah, 1820): 23; William R. Waring, *Report to the City Council of Savannah, On the Epidemic Disease of 1820* (Savannah, 1821), 3-4; E. Merton Coulter, "The Great Savannah Fire of 1820," *Georgia Historical Quarterly*, 23 (1939): 1-2 (hereafter cited as *GHQ*); Robert G. Albion, *The Rise of New York Port, 1815-1860* (New York, 1939): 390.

3. Mary C. Simms Oliphant, Alfred T. Odell, and T. C. Duncan Eaves, eds., *The Letters of William Gilmore Simms* (5 vols., Columbia, S. C., 152-56), 3 (1954): 19.

4. The corporation of Savannah alone invested nearly two and three-quarter million dollars in railroads between 1835 and 1860, over half of the total municipal investment in Georgia for that purpose. Milton S. Heath, *Constructive Liberalism: The Role of the State in Economic Development in Georgia to 1860* (Cambridge, Mass., 1954), 287. The expansion of the Central Railroad can be followed to best advantage in *Reports of the Presidents, Engineers-in-Chief and Superintendents, of the Central Rail-Road and Banking Company of Georgia, From No. 1 to 19 Inclusive* . . . (Savannah, 1854) and *Reports of the Presidents and Superintendents of the Central Railroad and Banking Co. of Georgia, From No. 20 to 32 Inclusive* . . . (Savannah, 1868). See also Ulrich B. Phillips, *A History of Transportation in the Eastern Cotton Belt to 1860* (New York, 1908).

5. E. J. Donnell, *Chronological and Statistical History of Cotton* (New York, 1872), 372-504, *passim*.

6. U. S. Census, 1840, Georgia, microfilm at Georgia Historical Society of original at National Archives; *Seventh Census of the United States:* 1850, p. 366; Joseph C. G. Kennedy, comp., *Population of the United States in 1850; Compiled from the Original Returns of the Eighth Census* . . . (Washington, 1864): 74.

7. Savannah *Daily Morning News*, July 14, 1851 (hereafter cited as *News*); Savannah *Daily Georgian*, May 16, 1854 (hereafter cited as *Georgian*).

8. Between 1850 and 1860, the number of foreign-born in Savannah increased from 2,434 to 4,652 and the number of Northern-born from 744 to 1,471. The influx of foreigners and Northerners accounted for at least 53 per cent of the 5,499 increase in the free population of Savannah during the 1850's. Compiled from J. D. B. De Bow, *Statistical View of the United States . . . Being a Compendium of the Seventh Census* (Washington, 1854): 399; Kennedy, comp., *Population of the United States in 1860*, xxxii; U. S. Census, 1860, Georgia, Schedule I (Free Inhabitants), microfilm at Georgia Historical Society of original at National Archives.

9. Savannah's slaves numbered 6,231 in 1850 and 7,712 in 1860. *Seventh Census of the United States: 1850*, p. 366; Kennedy, comp., *Population of the United States in 1860*, p. 74.

10. Report of the Chief of Police [March 20, 1855]," in Savannah *Daily Republican*, March 24, 1855 (hereafter cited as *Republican*).

11. John Stoddard to Hon. Thomas M. Turner, Mayor of Savannah, January 8, 1859, in Copy and Daybook of John F. Hamilton, Marmaduke Hamilton Papers, Duke University Library, Durham, North Carolina.

12. Sarah A. Lawton to Mrs. A. L. Alexander, December 1, 1851, in Alexander-Hillhouse Papers, Southern Historical Collection, University of North Carolina Library, Chapel Hill.

13. H. T. Campbell to George Jones, December 27, 1855, in George Noble Jones Papers, Georgia Historical Society.

14. On provisions of the slave code, see Edward G. Wilson, comp., *A Digest of All the Ordinances of the City of Savannah, and Various Laws of the State of Georgia, Relative to Said City, Which Were of Force on the 1st January, 1858* . . . (Savannah, 1858): 7-8, 129, 181-84, 186, 393, 416-19, 425, 515 (hereafter cited as Wilson, *Digest of Ordinances, 1858*); *News*, January 10, 1851, January 25, 1853; Richard C. Wade, *Slavery in the Cities: The South, 1820-1860* (New York, 1964): 40-41.

15. Dr. W. C. Daniell to Hon. Howell Cobb, January 4, 1850, in Howell Cobb Papers, University of Georgia Library, Athens.

16. Charles C. Jones, Jr., to his father, October 1, 1856, in Charles Colcock Jones, Jr., Collection, University of Georgia Library; Savannah City Council, Council, Minutes, February 10, 1853, City Hall, Savannah.

17. Nehemiah Adams, *A South-Side View of Slavery; or, Three Months at the South, in 1854* (Boston, 1854): 25.

18. Julia E. Harn, "Old Canoochee-Ogeechee Chronicles. III. Life among the Negroes," *GHQ*, XVI (1932), 149; *News*, April 10, 1850, November 4, 1852, October 28, 1859; *Republican*, November 27, 1851.

19. Charles C. Jones, Jr., to his father, October 1, 1856, in Jones, Jr., Collection; Jones to his father and mother, February 24, 1860, *ibid.*

20. See City of Savannah, Jail Records, 1855-1863, microfilm at Georgia Department of Archives and History, Atlanta, of originals at Georgia Historical Society.

21. According to a visitor, nearly every slave possessed one or two dogs, which were "exceedingly numerous" in Savannah; efforts were made by the city to reduce their number, but the owners could usually conceal them. Emily P. Burke, *Reminiscences of Georgia* [Oberlin, Ohio], 1850): 92. On violations of the slave code, see especially the Fine and Information Dockets of the Savannah Mayor's Court, 1850-1860, microfilm at Georgia Department of Archives and History of originals at Georgia Historical Society, and the daily listings of cases before the Police Court in Savannah *Daily Journal and Courier*, April-December, 1855.

22. See, for example, the entry for June 15, 1860, involving fourteen slaves and two free Negroes, and that for November 12, 1860, involving eight slaves and one free Negro.

23. *News*, May 16, 19, 1854; *Georgian*, May 16, 1854.

24. John Stoddard to Hon. Thomas M. Turner, January 8, 1859, in Copy and Daybook of John F. Hamilton, Hamilton Papers.

25. *News*, May 5, 1855.

26. *Ibid.*, June 18, 1851, April 26, 1854; Savannah *Journal*, May 6, June 25, 1852; Savannah *Evening Journal*, August 29, 1853; Presentment of the Grand Jury, Chatham County Superior Court, May, 1859, in *News*, June 8, 1859; John Stoddard to Hon. Thomas M. Turner, January 8, 1859, in Copy and Daybook of John F. Hamilton, Hamilton Papers.

27. Savannah *Daily Journal and Courier*, July 11, 12, 1855.

28. Adams, *A South-Side View of Slavery*, 25.

29. Presentment of the Grand Jury, May, 1851, in Chatham County Superior Court, Minutes, XX, 185, original at Chatham County Courthouse, Savannah; *News*, May 28, 1851. The statement was not without foundation. In 1851, Francis L. Sweet, a minor, gained permission from the Chatham County Superior Court to sell a slave, earlier bequeathed to him, because "said Negro woman Nelly, is in the habit of using to excess intoxicating liquors, so that she is become a cause of constant inconvenience & expense . . . by reason of her drunken [n]ess, instead of a source of profit to him." Chatham County Superior Court, Proceedings, January 30, 1851, original at Chatham County Courthouse. See also Hugh W. Mercer to his wife, June 23, 1849, in Mercer Papers, Georgia Historical Society.

30. Presentment of the Grand Jury, January, 1852, in Chatham County Superior Court, Minutes, XX, 256-57; *News*, January 30, 1852.

31. Savannah *Daily Journal and Courier*, February 6, 1855.

32. *News*, July 2, 1851, July 9, August 17, November 5, 1855, October 20, 1858, May 11, October 27, 28, 1859; *Republican*, April 12, June 5, 1851, May 3, June 20, 1854, May 20, 1856, April 5, 1858; *Georgian*, April 12, June 25, 1854; City Council, Minutes, April 24, 1851; Richard D. Arnold to John W. Forney, December 18, 1850, in Richard H. Shryock, ed., *Letters of Richard D. Arnold, M.D., 1808-1876, Mayor of Savannah, Georgia, First Secretary of the American Medical Association*, Trinity College Historical Society Papers, Double Series XVIII-XIX (Durham, 1929), 44-45 (hereinafter cited as Shryock, ed., *Arnold Letters*.

33. *News*, April 18, 1851, September 17, 1852, February 18, March 1, May 6, 1853; *Georgian*, February 18, 1853.

34. Wilson, *Digest of Ordinances, 1858*, pp. 411-12; City Council, Minutes, December 8, 1859; *News*, November 28, 1859. See also *Acts of the General Assembly of the State of Georgia . . . 1855-'56* (Milledgeville, Ga., 1856): 388.

35. Presentment of the Grand Jury, January, 1860, in Chatham County Superior Court, Minutes, XXIV, 43. See also Presentment of the Grand Jury, City Court of Savannah, November, 1860, in *Republican*, November 24, 1860.

36. *News*, October 25, 1854, July 26, 1858; Savannah *Daily Journal and Courier*, July 9, 1855.

37. On the crime of murder, committed by slaves against other slaves, see Gov. Herschel V. Johnson to George W. Anderson, August 18, 1856, in Executive Department of the State of Georgia, Minutes, November 7, 1855-December 26, 1859, p. 131, original at Georgia Department of Archives and History (hereafter cited as Georgia Executive Department, Minutes, 1855-1859); Gov. Johnson to Sheriff of Chatham County, March 12, 1857, ibid., 174-75; George A. Mercer, "Diary, June 15, 1860-December 17, 1865," entry of August 26-28, 1860, typewritten copy at Georgia Historical Society of original in Southern Historical Collection, University of North Carolina Library; Savannah *Daily Journal and Courier*, September 18, 1855; *News*, March 30, 1854, June 28, August 23, 1856, March 16, 1857, July 10, 1858.

38. George S. Owens to "Sal," July 22, 1857, in Wallace-Owens-Thomas Papers, Collections, Georgia Society, Colonial Dames of America, Georgia Historical Society.

39. *News*, February 26, 1852, July 24, 26, 1858; *Georgian*, May 1, 1852.

40. City Council, Minutes, June 15, 1854; *News*, June 16, 1854.

41. See the Fine and Information Dockets of the Savannah Mayor's Court, 1850-1860; presentments in Chatham County Superior Court, Minutes, XX-XXV; *News*, December 5, 1854.

42. City of Savannah, Jail Records, 1855-1863.

43. Charles C. Jones, Jr., to his father, October 1, 1856, in Jones, Jr., Collection; bill from Savannah jail to "John Houston," September 13, 1853, in Mary Williamson Houstoun Papers, Georgia Historical Society.

44. See *News*, September 13, 1851, February 4, 1852, February 28, 1853, August 30, 1856, December 23, 1857, March 25, 1861; Savannah *Daily Journal and Courier*, November 3, 1855; City of Savannah, Jail Records, 1855-1863.

45. Charles C. Jones, Jr., to his father, October 1, 1856, in Jones, Jr., Collection; *Republican*, August 2, 1851; *News*, February 28, May 2, November 11, 1853, August 26, 1858.

46. Ibid., June 29, 1850; Savannah *Daily Journal and Courier*, February 15, 1855.

47. *Georgian*, March 25, 1850; *News*, April 7, 9, 11, 21, 1851; *Republican*, October 29, 1860; Harold Schwartz, "Fugitive Slave Days in Boston," *New England Quarterly*, 27 (1954), 197-201. The law forbade any fellowship between free Negro seamen and slaves, but they were occasionally found together. See, for example, Savannah Mayor's Court, Fine and Information Docket, July 9, 1860.

48. City Council, Minutes, June 26, July 24, August 7, 1856; *News*, June 27, July 25, August 8, 1856.

49. *Georgian*, December 20, 1850; *News*, January 22, April 30, 1855, August 19, 1858, March 7, 1860; Charles Lyell, *A Second Visit to the United States of North America* (2 vols., New York, 1868), I, 232; City of Savannah, Jail Records, 1855-1863.

50. Chatham County Superior Court, Minutes, XXII, 96-97, 105-106, 111-12, 116-20, 173-74.

51. Savannah *Daily Journal and Courier*, October 30, 1855.

52. Henry L. Cathell, Diary, December 1, 1851, in Southern Historical Collection, University of North Carolina Library. See also the comments of Richard Arnold in Shryock, ed., *Arnold Letters*, 39, 46-47.

53. *Republican*, December 1, 1854, October 2, 1855.

54. *News*, May 19, 1855.

55. Ibid., March 22, April 6, May 18, August 2, 9, 27, September 7, 1855, March 7, 1857, March 11, 1859; *Republican*, February 2, 1852; Savannah *Daily Journal and Courier*, May 19, 1855; City Council, Minutes, June 17, 1852; Richard D. Arnold to John W. Forney, December 18, 1850, in Shryock, ed., *Arnold Letters*, 47.

56. "Charge of His Honor George T. Howard, to the Grand Jury," Chatham County Superior Court, May, 1854, in *News*, May 9, 1854.

57. James S. Buckingham, *The Slave States of America* (2 vols., London, 1842), I, 125. See also Richard D. Arnold to his wife, May 16, 1845, in Shryock, ed., *Arnold Letters*, 26; Arnold to Howell Cobb, November 15, 1858, in ibid., 92; Sir Frederick Pollock, ed., *Macready's Reminiscences, and Selections from His Diaries and Letters* (New York, 1875), 543.

58. See H. J. Wayne to Mary G. Harden, November 2, 1843, in Edward Harden Papers, Duke University Library.

59. George A. Mercer, "Diary, 1855-1860," entry of October 18, 1859, typewritten copy at Georgia Historical Society of original in Southern Historical Collection, University of North Carolina Library. Further comment on dueling and the preservation of "a healthy social tone" is contained in George A. Mercer, Meditations, 1859-1861, p. 31, original in possession of Louise Mercer Duncan, Savannah. "It has ever been to me a dear fancy," Mercer reflected, "that a lofty self-respect born of the ancient chivalry & native pride, was necessary to regulate the dealings of men with their fellows, to mitigate the asperities of society and soften the ha[r]sh yoke which the Law places upon our necks. This like the subtle ether, which is necessary in the operations of the physical world, comes in to the aid of the Law & makes duty pleasant & justice mild. Upon this ground I advocate a military taste, & excuse duelling, because they foster this sense of self-respect."

60. On the subject of dueling in Savannah, see George A. Mercer, "Diary, 1855-1860," entry of June 6, 1860; George S. Owens to his mother, June 14, 1852, in Wallace-Owens-Thomas Papers; Wallace Cumming to Harriet V. Alexander, September 8, 1852, in Alexander-Hillhouse Papers; Pollock, ed., *Macready's Reminiscences*, 543; *Georgian*, June 11, 1851; *News*, February 17, 1857, November 15, 16, 1859; City Council, Minutes, November 14, 1859; Jack K. Williams, "Georgia As Seen By Ante-Bellum English Travelers," *GHQ*, 32 (1948): 168; Thomas Gamble, Jr., *A History of the City Government of Savannah, Ga., from 1790 to 1901* ([Savannah, 1901]): 242 (hereafter cited as Gamble, *History of the City Government*); and especially Thomas Gamble, Jr., *Savannah Duels and Duellists, 1733-1877* (Savannah, 1923): 183-259. The Georgia Historical Society has in its possession the Constitution and Minutes (1827-1838) of the "Savannah Anti-Duelling Association."

61. William W. Gordon to Eleanor L. Kinzie, February 17, 1855, in Mrs. William W. Gordon Series, Gordon Family Papers, Southern Historical Collection, University of North Carolina Library.

62. Charles A. L. Lamar to J. S. Thrasher, February 25, 1855, in Anon., ed., "A Slave-Trader's Letter Book," *North American Review*, 143 (1886): 448.

63. Charles A. L. Lamar to L. Viana, December 26, 1857, in ibid., 452.

64. City Council, Minutes, May 18, June 22, July 27, 1854; John E. Ward, *Report of John E. Ward, Mayor of the City of Savannah. For the Year Ending 31st October 1854 . . .* (Savannah, 1854): 5-6 (hereafter cited as Ward, *Mayor's Report, 1854*, and similarly for other mayors' reports; all reports for the period were published at Savannah during the same year in which the individual report was made); Wilson, *Digest of Ordinances, 1858*, pp. 187-88, 391-94, 411; *News*, May 16, 19, July 14, 28, 1854; *Republican*, June 7, July 26, 1854. With barrooms and groceries closed on Sunday, reported the *Republican*, attendance at Negro churches was larger than it had been for years. Ibid., August 2, 1854.

65. John E. Ward to Hon. Howell Cobb, December 20, 1854, in Cobb Papers; *Republican*, November 20, December 2, 4, 1854; *News*, December 5, 1854.

66. Presentment of the Grand Jury, Chatham County Superior Court, May, 1855, in *News*, May 28, 1855; Edward C. Anderson, *Mayor's Report, 1855*, p. 6; Wilson, *Digest of Ordinances, 1858*, pp. 404-406; *News*, January 18, March 27, April 6, June 1, 15, 1855; Savannah *Daily Journal and Courier*, January 15, 1855; *Republican*, March 15, 22, 1855.

67. *News*, January 24, 1855; *Georgian*, January 14, 1855.

68. *News*, June 1, 15, 1855.

69. Savannah *Daily Journal and Courier*, May 21, 1855; *News*, January 18, February 7, March

7, 1855, February 22, 1856.

70. *Republican*, April 22, 1856. Income from fines imposed in the Police Court dropped from $2,660.63 for the year ending October 31, 1855, to $1,321.36 for the year ending October 31, 1856. Richard D. Arnold, *Mayor's Report, 1860*, p. 26.

71. Charles Seton Henry Hardee. *Reminiscences and Recollections of Old Savannah* (Savannah, n.d.): 57-58; City Council, Minutes, December 29, 1853, May 18, 1854; *News*, December 31, 1853, May 19, 1854.

72. Richard D. Arnold to John W. Forney, December 18, 1850, in Shryock, ed., *Arnold Letters*, 46.

73. See *Republican*, January 24, 1851.

74. Savannah *Evening Journal*, January 18, 1853.

75. City Council, Minutes, January 15, 1852, May 18, June 22, 1854, January 24, 1856, December 22, 1859; Ward, *Mayor's Report, 1854*, pp. 5-6; Arnold, *Mayor's Report, 1860*, p. 8; *News*, May 19, 1854, January 25, 1856. Detection of crime was made easier by the introduction of gas lighting on the river front in 1855 and into the city's outlying districts in 1860. Anderson, *Mayor's Report, 1855*, p. 6; Thomas M. Turner, *Mayor's Report, 1859*, p. 6; Arnold, *Mayor's Report, 1860*, p. 3.

76. Presentment of the Grand Jury, January, 1860, in Chatham County Superior Court, Minutes, XXIV, 43; *News*, June 16, 1860.

77. Arnold, *Mayor's Report, 1860*, p. 26; Charles C. Jones, Jr., *Mayor's Report, 1861*, pp. 14, 18; *News*, January 17, 1856; *Georgian*, May 25, 1856; Wade, *Slavery in the Cities*, 101.

78. *News*, June 27, 1856; James P. Screven, *Mayor's Report, 1857*, p. 13; Jones, Jr., *Mayor's Report, 1861*, p. 6; Gamble, *History of the City Government*, 155, 240.

79. Wilson, *Digest of Ordinances, 1858*, p. 325; Hardee, *Reminiscences and Recollections of Old Savannah*, 57-58; Adams, *A South-Side View of Slavery*, 24; *News*, July 22, 1852.

80. The Court of Common Pleas and Oyer and Terminer, after 1853 the City Court, heard mainly civil cases, though it also had jurisdiction over misdemeanors committed within the corporate limits of the city. See Wilson, *Digest of Ordinances, 1858*, pp. 44-45, 527-29; Edward J. Harden, comp., *A Code of Laws Relating to Health and Quarantine, Inspection, Pilotage, Shipping and Seamen, . . . And of the Various Statutes of the State Having Direct Reference to Savannah* (Savannah, 1860): 52 (hereafter cited as Harden, *Code, 1860*); *News*, December 29, 1855; Gamble, *History of the City Government*, 451-53; and especially the Proceedings of the City Court for the years 1850-1852 and 1856-1857, microfilm at Georgia Department of Archives and History of originals at Georgia Historical Society. The United States District Court and the United States Circuit Court for the Southern District of Georgia also met at Savannah, much of their work consisting of maritime cases, civil and criminal—damage suits arising from ship collisions, libels against vessels for debts, smuggling or "passing false invoices through Custom House," piracy, mutiny, maltreatment of sailors, and importation of African Negroes. Dockets and Minutes of the two federal courts are at the Federal Records Center, General Services Administration, East Point, Georgia. On the functions of the local magistrates' courts, as well as on the corruption connected with them, consult Harden, *Code, 1860*, pp. 70-72; Wilson, *Digest of Ordinances, 1858*, p. 45; *News*, March 31, May 1, 1854, August 30, 1856, July 10, 1858; Savannah *Daily Journal and Courier*, June 30, 1855; *Republican*, August 30, 1856; Savannah *Evening Journal*, January 4, 1853; Gov. Joseph E. Brown to Justices of the County Inferior Court, Minutes, February 2, 1861, Vol. H, p. 48, microfilm at Georgia Department of Archives and History of original at Chatham County Courthouse; George A. Mercer, "Diary, 1855-1860," entry of June 12, 1860.

81. *News*, March 4, 7, 1861.

82. Conclusions as to the variation in the punishment of Negroes and whites are based mainly on newspaper reports of court cases, the Fine and Information Dockets of the Savannah Mayor's Court, 1850-1860, and the Minutes and Proceedings of the Chatham County Superior Court for the same period. On the punishment of slaves convicted of murdering other slaves, see also Gov. Herschel V. Johnson to George W. Anderson, August 18, 1856, in Georgia Executive Department,

Minutes, 1855-1859, p. 131; Gov. Johnson to Sheriff of Chatham County, March 12, 1857, ibid., 174-75.

83. Presentment of the Grand Jury, Chatham County Superior Court, May, 1850, in *News*, May 28, 1850; Presentment of the Grand Jury, Chatham County Superior Court, January, 1855, in ibid., January 27, 1855; City of Savannah, Jail Records, 1855-1863.

84. Wilson, *Digest of Ordinances, 1858*, p. 227; Burke, *Reminiscences of Georgia*, 43; Richard D. Arnold, Receipt Book, 1848-1859, in Richard D. Arnold Papers, Duke University Library.

85. Mrs. J. Scarborough to R. M. Goodwin, March 5, 1850, in Godfrey Barnsley Papers, Duke University Library.

86. Presentment of the Grand Jury, Chatham County Superior Court, May, 1850, in *News*, May 28, 1850; Presentment of the Grand Jury, Chatham County Superior Court, January, 1855, in ibid., January 27, 1855; "Mayor's Report [November 30, 1853]," in *ibid.*, December 3, 1853; City Council, Minutes, November 27, 1856, November 26, 1857; *News*, March 3, 1855, November 28, 1856, November 28, 1857.

87. *Acts of the General Assembly of the State of Georgia . . . 1857* (Columbus, Ga., 1858), 166-67; Screven, *Mayor's Report, 1857*, p. 12; Turner, *Mayor's Report, 1859*, pp. 8-9; Arnold, *Mayor's Report, 1860*, p. 33; City Council, Minutes, February 2, October 11, 1860; *News*, April 17, 1860; Gamble, *History of the City Government*, 414-15.

88. Wilson, *Digest of Ordinances, 1858*, pp. 44-45, 325, 503-504, 524, 529; Georgia Executive Department, Minutes, 1855-1859, p. 110.

89. Arnold, *Mayor's Report, 1860*, p. 26; Jones, Jr., *Mayor's Report, 1861*, p. 14.

90. Presentment of the Grand Jury, January, 1860, in Chatham County Superior Court, Minutes, XXIV, 43; Presentment of the Grand Jury, City Court of Savannah, November, 1860, in *Republican*, November 24, 1860; City Council, Minutes, December 5, 1860.

Ira Berlin

The Structure of the Free Negro Caste in the Antebellum United States

Of late, historians of slavery in the Americas have turned their attention from the slave to that peculiar product of the peculiar institution, the free Negro.[1] They have generally agreed that Negro freemen were important far beyond their numbers. Increasingly, they have given the free Negro a central role in determining the nature of slavery and race relations generally. But perhaps the most important reason for the renewed interest in free Negroes is an understanding that they set precedents, both for white-black relations and for relations among blacks when slavery ended. Far more than the status and treatment accorded the slave, the status and treatment accorded the freeman was a harbinger of the postemancipation world. Often the laws, attitudes, and institutions which victimized Negro freemen during the slave years—political proscription, segregation, and various forms of debt peonage—became the dominant modes of racial oppression ensnaring all blacks after slavery. In a like manner, the free Negro's years of liberty profoundly influenced the pattern of postemancipation black life. Free Negroes moved in disproportionate numbers into positions of leadership in the black world when slavery ended, and they carried their preemancipation ideals and institutions with them. In the United States, for example, nearly half of the twenty-two blacks who served in Congress between 1869 and 1900 were drawn from the ranks of those who had been free before the Civil War, although only one black in nine enjoyed liberty in 1860.[2] The freemen's unique experience continued to shape black life long after free Negroes lost their special status.

Although the free Negro's importance has been generally acknowledged, historians are only beginning to learn about the anomalous caste. Even the free

Source: Journal of Social History 9, no. 3 (1975): 297–318. Reprinted by permission.

Negro in the United States, the most intensively studied group in the Western hemisphere, can claim no general history. Instead, scholars have been forced to rely on state and regional studies of uneven quality, supplemented by histories of slavery which occasionally devote a chapter to the free Negro or monographs on related subjects like manumission or colonization.[3] The absence of a general overview has fragmented knowledge of the anomalous caste, misleading historians who have compared free Negroes in the United States with those in other slave societies or who have looked upon free Negroes as precursors of postemancipation patterns of race relations and black life.

Much of the confusion about the free Negro caste in the United States has been caused by viewing it as a monolithic group. Free Negroes have usually been depicted as more black than free in a society that admitted only black slaves and white freemen. While this assessment contains much truth, it tends to mute important differences within the free Negro caste and ultimately to inhibit analysis. Actually, three major groups of free Negroes existed in the United States: a Northern caste, an Upper South caste, and a Lower South caste.[4] Each had its own distinctive demographic, economic, social, and even somatic characteristics. These differences bred different relations with whites and slaves and, most importantly, distinctive systems of values and modes of social action.

Distinctive social and sometimes racial origins stood at the root of these pervasive intracaste differences. More than anything else, the nature of emancipation shaped the character of a free Negro population. Whether manumission was inspired by a master's economic, ideological, or personal concerns, whether it was selective or indiscriminate, and whether it led to the continuance or ultimate liquidation of slavery determined—by the various combinations within specific historical situations—whether freemen would be numerous or few, rich or poor, skilled or unskilled, black or brown, granted social recognition or condemned as pariahs. These same factors, of course, also created differences within the free Negro populations of the North, the Upper South, and the Lower South. But regional distinctions transcended these subregional differences and become the starting point for any analysis of Negro freemen in the United States.

The Free Negro in the North

The American Revolution transformed the North from a slave to a free society, greatly enlarging its free Negro population. Before the Revolution, few blacks enjoyed liberty in the northern colonies. Although rarely numerous enough to induce census takers to enumerate them as a distinct group, they nevertheless raised white fears of subversion. During the colonial era, northern lawmakers steadily eroded the freemen's liberty, taxing them with numerous proscriptions on their civil, political, and social rights.[5] On the eve of the

Revolution, northern whites, even those who opposed slavery, showed little inclination to increase the number of free Negroes. But the events of the Revolutionary era moved in unpredictable and uncontrollable ways. As the war dragged on, grim necessity forced the British and then, more grudgingly, colonial Americans to muster black slaves into their armies by offering them freedom in exchange for their services.[6] The libertarian ideology which Patriots used to justify their rebellion further added to the free Negro population, weakening and eventually destroying slavery. Many masters, inspired by the egalitarian nature of Revolutionary ideology, freed their slaves and emancipationists, carrying Revolutionary principles to their logical conclusion, demanded liberty for all. Slavery fell first in New England, where blacks were few in number and never an important part of the labor force or a threat to white dominance. In the Middle Atlantic States, where slaves were more numerous, slavery proved more resistant to Revolutionary change. But the influx of white immigrant workers assured employers of an adequate supply of labor and undermined the most persuasive argument against abolition. By 1804, every northern state had provided for eventual emancipation.[7]

Still, slavery died hard. In 1820, almost twenty thousand slaves remained in the North. Although that number fell dramatically in succeeding decades, slavery lingered on. There were over one thousand bondsmen in the "free" states in 1840. Moreover, in many of the new northern states, slaveholders and their allies tried to overthrow the antislavery provisions of the Northwest Ordinance and reinstate the peculiar institution. Failing that, they enacted various forms of long-term indentureships which allowed chattel bondage to flourish covertly until the Civil War.[8] Nevertheless, the fate of slavery had been sealed and the number of free Negroes, augmented by natural increase and fugitives from the South, continued to grow. In 1860, about a quarter of a million blacks, slightly less than half of the nation's free Negroes, lived in the North (see Tables 1–4).

As in every slave society, the nature of emancipation determined the char-

Table 1. Free Negro Population, 1790–1860[a]

	1790	1800	1810	1820	1830	1840	1850	1860
United States	59	108	186	234	320	386	434	488
North	27	47	78	99	138	171	196	226
South	32	61	108	134	182	216	238	262
Upper South	30	57	94	114	152	174	204	225
Lower South	2	4	14	20	30	41	34	37

Source: Population of the United States in 1860 (Washington, D.C., 1864), pp. 598–605.
[a]In thousands, figures do not always add up owing to rounding.

Table 2. Percentage of Increase of Free Negroes, 1790–1860

	1790-1799	1800-1809	1810-1819	1820-1829	1830-1839	1840-1849	1850-1859
United States	82.3%	72.0%	25.2%	36.9%	20.9%	12.5%	12.3%
North	73.9	65.8	27.0	38.5	24.1	15.0	15.2
South	89.3	76.8	24.0	35.6	18.4	10.5	10.0
Upper South	88.5	65.5	21.2	33.1	14.8	16.8	10.4
Lower South	99.5	223.3	42.1	49.8	36.5	–16.3	7.2

Source: Population of the United States in 1860 (Washington, D.C., 1864), pp. 598–605.

acter of the free Negro caste. Emancipation in the North was ideologically inspired, indiscriminate, and ultimately complete.[9] Masters, convinced of the evil of chattel bondage or forced to liberate their slaves by legislative or judicial edict, freed all their slaves, black as well as brown, unskilled laborers as well as skilled artisans, field hands as well as house servants. Thus, the free Negro population of the North was largely black. In 1850, when the United States census first distinguished between blacks and mulattoes—meaning anyone who appeared to have white ancestry—over 70 percent of northern free Negroes were determined to be of unmixed African origins[10] (see Table 5).

Indiscriminate, complete emancipation left northern blacks a largely urban group and their disproportionate urban residence increased during the antebellum years. Except for a few areas of Rhode Island, the Hudson Valley, and southern New Jersey, slaves had been largely an urban group in the colonial North. Most newly liberated blacks remained in the cities. They were soon joined there by free Negroes from the countryside who found the anonymity of urban life a welcome relief from the proprietary attitudes of the rural freeholders who had known them as slaves. Between 1790 and 1810, the number of free Negroes in New York City increased over 600 percent, while the number of slaves declined by less than 30 percent. Negro freemen in other Northern

Table 3. Proportion of Negroes Free, 1790–1860

	1790	1800	1810	1820	1840	1860
United States	7.9%	10.8%	13.5%	13.2%	13.4%	11.0%
North	40.2	56.7	74.0	83.9	99.3	100.0[a]
South	4.7	6.7	8.5	8.1	8.0	6.2
Upper South	5.5	8.1	10.4	10.6	12.5	12.8
Lower South	1.6	2.1	3.9	3.5	3.1	1.5

Source: Population of the United States in 1860 (Washington, D.C., 1864), pp. 598–605.

[a]virtually all

Table 4. Regional Distribution of Free Negroes, 1790–1860

	1790	1800	1810	1820	1840	1860
North	45.6%	43.5%	41.9%	42.5%	44.2%	46.3%
South	54.4	56.5	58.1	57.5	55.8	53.7
Upper South	50.7	52.5	50.5	48.9	45.1	46.1
Lower South	3.7	4.0	7.6	8.6	10.7	7.6

Source: Population of the United States in 1860 (Washington, D.C., 1864), pp. 598–605.

cities registered similar, if not as rapid, rates of growth.[11] Progress made by this first wave of black immigrants in establishing churches, schools, and benevolent societies in the urban North encouraged a steady influx of free Negroes from the northern countryside and fugitives and freemen from the slaveholding South. Although the growth rate of urban blacks slowed perceptively after the first flush of freedom, the number of free Negroes in the cities of the North continued to increase throughout the antebellum period. By 1860, fully 60 percent of all northern blacks lived in cities [12] (see Table 6).

Indiscriminate and complete emancipation also meant that the Northern free Negro caste was no more skilled than the slave population it replaced. Since as a group northern slaves were not particularly skilled, most blacks carried their low occupational status from slavery to freedom. The egalitarian ideology that inspired emancipation did little to strengthen the freemen's economic position, and indeed it might have weakened it. At best, the Revolutionary ideology promised freedom. It made no provision for former slaves to be trained in a craft and it offered them no guarantees of steady work or a living wage. Certainly, there was never a hint of compensation for the long years of bondage; slaveholders might be compensated, not slaves. Northern whites believed that those who enjoyed liberty, worked hard, were clever enough and lucky enough would prosper. Those who did not, should not—and with justice. So when the largely unskilled blacks, many without experience in the free marketplace, fell to the bottom of the social order, whites believed they knew the reasons why: blacks were lazy, stupid, and corrupt. Masters, once having freed

Table 5. Proportion of Free Negroes of Mixed Racial Ancestry, 1850

United States	36.7%
North	28.9
South	43.0
Upper South	38.5
Lower South	68.6

Source: Negro Population of the United States, 1790–1915 (Washington, D.C., 1918), p. 221.

their slaves, need feel no concern for their fate. But the newly freed blacks did not merely fall in occupational standing—whites anxious to confirm their cherished racial ideas frequently pushed them down. Many slave craftsmen had difficulty finding work at their old trades once they were free. White workers frequently refused to labor alongside blacks, and white employers often refused to hire blacks for any but the most menial tasks.[13]

Northern attitudes toward work compounded the freemen's difficulties. Work was central to the developing "free labor" ideology of the North. From it sprang the virtues which northern society celebrated: family stability, religious freedom, political independence, and social mobility. A man's social status and that of his posterity depended upon his ability to work to his fullest ability. What whites valued, they were not about to share with a people they despised. Although the demand for labor increased rapidly during the antebellum years, blacks found it impossible to improve their economic status. The influx of immigrants allowed white workers and employers to maintain their racial preferences. Indeed, during the 1830s, the growing number of newly arrived Irish and German immigrants began to muscle free Negroes out of many of the low-paying trades they controlled, steadily shrinking the range of menial labor at which blacks might earn a living. Ironically, the presence of white immigrant workers which had earlier assured emancipation now froze freemen on the lowest rung of the economic ladder. In 1855, nearly 90 percent of all New York City blacks worked at menial, unskilled jobs (see Table 7). The situation was not materially better anywhere in the North.[14]

While the indiscriminate and ideologically inspired nature of emancipation in the North reduced blacks to profitless drudgery, complete emancipation provided them with certain rights. The abolition of slavery in the North freed whites from their fear of servile revolt. With slaves gone, whites did not look upon every gathering of free blacks as the beginning of an insurrection. Although ingrained racism induced northern whites to limit severely the political rights of blacks, they still allowed freemen certain crucial civil liberties. Northern free Negroes maintained the right to travel freely, organize their own institutions, publish their own newspapers and journals, and petition and protest. Here the ideology of the Revolution, which elevated freedom of movement, the

Table 6. Proportion of Free Negroes, Urban,[a] 1860

United States	47.3%
North	61.4
South	35.2
Upper South	32.3
Lower South	53.2

Source: Population of the United States in 1860 (Washington, D.C., 1864).

[a]Places, incorporated and unincorporated, over 2,500 in population

Table 7. Proportion of Free Negroes Engaged in Skilled Trades in New York, Richmond, and Charleston, 1855–1860

	% Skilled
New York City[a]	12.5
Richmond[b]	32.0
Charleston[b]	76.0

Sources: Robert Ernst, "The Economic Status of New York City Negroes, 1850–1863," *Negro History Bulletin* 12 (1949): 131–2, 139–43; Richmond and Charleston manuscript census, 1860, National Archives, Washington, D.C.

[a]1855 [b]1860

press, assembly, and petition to a place of honor in the American pantheon, helped protect the free Negro's liberty. But, in the final analysis, only the absence of slavery made whites secure enough to allow blacks these basic freedoms.

The expansion of the white population also bolstered white confidence. Although the number of free Negroes grew rapidly during the antebellum years, the white population, swollen by foreign immigrants, increased much faster. The surety of dominance created by their overwhelming numerical superiority eased white fear of the free Negro. But the combination of white confidence and white racism mixed to form a powerful segregationist ethos. "In virtually every phase of existence," Leon F. Litwack has observed, northern "Negroes found themselves systematically separated from whites. They were either excluded from railway cars, omnibuses, stagecoaches, and steamboats or assigned to special 'Jim Crow' sections; they sat, when permitted, in secluded and remote corners of theaters and lecture halls; they could not enter most hotels, restaurants, and resorts, except as servants; they prayed in 'Negro pews' in the white churches, and when partaking of the sacrament of the Lord's Supper, they waited until the whites had been served the bread and the wine."[15] Throughout the North, whites and blacks lived in different worlds.

While segregation reduced blacks to second-class citizens, it allowed them to create their own autonomous communities. Many freemen welcomed the opportunity to escape the white world. From the first years of freedom, blacks built their own churches and schools and hired their own ministers and schoolmasters.[16] With a secure base of communal support, black leaders transformed the liberties whites allowed them into a powerful organizational and political tradition. From Richard Allen and Prince Hall to Frederick Douglass and Martin Delany, the primary mode of social action for northern blacks was organizing institutions to protect themselves from the rigors of the white world and using these same institutions to demand full equality.

The segregationist ethos which alienated blacks from whites and pushed freemen together also united free Negroes and slaves. Ties between free and bond Negroes, rooted in familial, racial, and personal loyalties and strengthened by common living and working conditions, remained strong as northern slavery waned in the early years of the nineteenth century. Since emancipation doomed slavery and all blacks would eventually be free, status distinctions—free and slave—never took on the importance they would in the southern states. Free blacks not only pushed for the final liquidation of slavery in the North, but also for abolition of bondage wherever it remained. Black leaders turned the organizational machinery of the northern free Negro community against southern slavery. They petitioned state legislatures and Congress to abolish slavery and encouraged antislavery whites to take a stronger stand against the peculiar institution. The growing number of southern fugitives in the North stoked the militance of northern freemen. Free Negro opposition to slavery grew during the 1840s and 1850s and many northern blacks came to see their own elevation as contingent on abolition in the South. By the eve of the Civil War, northern blacks were fully identified with the cause of the slave.[17]

Northern antislavery organizations also became the most important link between black leaders and the larger white community. Indeed, since segregation and economic proscription barred free Negroes from meaningful participation in white society, antislavery organizations often became the only common meeting ground for northern blacks and whites. Abolition societies offered blacks and whites an opportunity to share their diverse experiences and to cultivate the dream of a common future. Equally important, they gave black leaders a chance to rise to prominence outside the bounds of their own community. It was as abolitionist spokesmen—not as ministers and schoolmasters—that black leaders gained national recognition. Ambitious freemen seemed to compensate for their lack of economic opportunity by pouring their energies into antislavery politics. With the transformation of organized antislavery from a sectarian crusade to a political party, free Negroes found they could earn more than recognition within the antislavery movement. The political patronage that accompanied the success of the Republican party offered blacks "higher wages, more security, and greater status and prestige" than any other available work, as economic proscription grew and professional opportunities narrowed in the North. Political patronage increasingly became the lifeblood of the black elite. Entree to public office, observed the historian of Detroit's black community, "might comprise a son's most important inheritance or a daughter's dowry." For northern freemen and the elite in particular, politics was more than a means of racial advancement; it was a way of life.[18]

The Free Negro in the Upper South

As in the North, the free Negro in the Upper South was largely a product of the American Revolution. Before the Revolution, there were few free Negroes in the southern colonies. A 1775 Maryland census, the only known prewar enumeration of Upper South freemen, counted slightly more than 1,800 free Negroes or roughly 4 percent of the colony's black population.[19] The ideals and events of the Revolution combined to increase the number of free Negroes many fold. Legislators and judges, taking the words of the Declaration of Independence to heart, liberalized manumission codes and relaxed the strictures against freedom suits. In the border states, emancipationists organized abolition societies and demanded an end to slavery. Although they failed to topple the slave regime, liberalized manumission laws encouraged masters to free their slaves. Economic changes in the Upper South, especially in Maryland, Delaware, and northern Virginia, also encouraged manumission. The increased worldwide demand for foodstuffs induced farmers in this region to switch from tobacco to cereal agriculture and, concomitantly, stimulated the growth of towns and light industry. This economic transformation reduced the need for slaves, as wheat agriculture on small units, under existing technology, thrived on free labor. Many farmers found themselves with a surplus of bondsmen. Most sold their excess slaves at a profit, but some, touched by Revolutionary ideas of equality, freed them. Moreover, the growth of towns and manufacturing induced slaveowners to hire their slaves out, giving some bondsmen an opportunity to buy their way out of slavery.[20]

The sharp increase in manumission and self-purchase deeply affected blacks still in bondage. Many, seeing friends and relatives shed the shackles of slavery, hearing rumors of freedom in the North or imminent emancipation in the South, seized their liberty by running away. These fugitives, finding safety in greatly enlarged free Negro communities, frequently invited family and friends to join them and often eased their passage from bondage with a forged pass, a quick change of clothes, and a fast horse. The growing number of manumitted and fugitive blacks swelled the tiny colonial free Negro population. Between 1755 and 1790, when the first federal census was taken, Maryland's free Negro population increased 350 percent. During the succeeding two decades it doubled and nearly doubled again, so that by 1810 there were over thirty thousand Negro freemen in the state who constituted almost a quarter of Maryland's black population. Freemen increased at a rate only slightly behind Maryland's pace throughout the states of the Upper South. By 1810 these states contained nearly one-hundred thousand free Negroes who made up 8 percent of the black population of the region and almost 60 percent of the free Negroes in the United States.[21]

The rapid increase in the number of free Negroes during the early years of the Republic stunned and frightened slaveholders. They moved quickly to stem the flood of manumissions and runaways by reenacting strictures against freeing slaves and by tightening runaway codes.[22] This new legislation, combined with informal pressure on would-be manumitters, slowed the growth of the free Negro caste. Between 1810 and 1820, Upper South free Negroes increased at a third of the previous decade's rate. In the years that followed the freemen's rate of growth continued to tumble, as manumission declined and immigration to the North, Canada, and Africa increased. Although the number of free Negroes in the Upper South continued to grow, the proportion of the nation's freemen living in that region dwindled. By the eve of the Civil War, less than 50 percent of American free Negroes resided in the Upper South.[23]

Restrictions on manumission and stiffer runaway regulations enacted during the late eighteenth and early nineteenth centuries inaugurated a new pattern of free Negro growth. Some masters still freed their slaves or allowed them to purchase their liberty; a few slaves escaped from bondage and remained in the South; and the free Negroes continued to increase by natural means. But in most places, the number of slaves passing from slavery to freedom was a trickle compared to an earlier flood. Moreover, the libertarian idealism that had accompanied emancipation in the Revolutionary era rarely motivated masters in the later period. Instead, slaveowners generally acted from personal and often paternal considerations. Masters who emancipated slaves for personal reasons naturally tended to be highly selective; usually, they manumitted only those slaves they knew best. These were not field hands, but a small circle of house servants, artisans, and foremen. Thus, the new pattern of growth not only altered the size of the free Negro caste, but changed its character as well.[24]

The free Negro population of the Upper South was therefore the product of two different patterns of manumission. The first and most important was large-scale, relatively indiscriminate, and rooted in ideological and economic changes. The second was smaller, extremely selective, and originated in personal relationships between masters and slaves. Both were incomplete. These distinctive patterns of manumission, by sometimes complementing and sometimes countering one another, shaped the development of the free Negro caste in the Upper South.

The large-scale, indiscriminate manumission of the Revolutionary era, founded in changes in economy and society, produced a largely black—as opposed to a mulatto—free Negro population in the Upper South as it had in the North. But the smaller, selective emancipation which followed tended to lighten the color of the free Negro caste. When personal relations between master and slave became the surest route to freedom the master's Negro mistress and mulatto children had the best chance of winning their liberty. While only a few masters freed their children by black women, many more placed them in privileged positions within the plantation hierarchy. From these positions, they frequently prevailed upon their owners to free them or accumulated enough money to buy their way out of bondage. The majority of free Negroes in the Upper South were black, but the caste was significantly lighter than its Northern counterpart. In 1850, about 40 percent of Upper South freemen were of mixed racial origins.[25]

Changing patterns of manumission affected the free Negroes' place of residence as well as their color. The relatively indiscriminate manumission which followed the Revolution liberated blacks throughout the slave society. In the North, where most slaves had lived in cities, it produced a largely urban free Negro population. But southern slavery flourished in the countryside and most newly emancipated blacks remained rural folk. In 1860, two of three Upper South freemen lived in the countryside. Even Baltimore, whose twenty-five thousand free Negroes composed the largest urban black population in the nation, contained only a third of Maryland's free Negroes. Nevertheless, the advantages of an urban residence drew blacks to southern cities just as it had drawn them to northern ones. Despite legal restrictions and prohibitions, many freemen migrated to the cities of the Upper South. Selective, personal manumission of the later period added disproportionately to the urban free Negro population. The cramped conditions of city life pushed slaveholders and slaves together in ways which fostered manumission. Masters who knew their slaves were more likely to free them than those who did not. Urban conditions also allowed slaves far greater opportunities to work on their own, and slaves who had saved a few dollars had a better chance of winning their master's favor than those who had not. Thus, although the mass of free Negroes remained in the countryside, Upper South freemen were a disproportionately urban group. In 1860, more than a third of Upper South free Negroes lived in cities, and they were almost twice as urban as whites and more than five times as urban as slaves.[26]

As in the North, the relatively indiscriminate manumission of the post-Revolutionary era left many Upper South free Negroes without skills or trades. The more selective manumission that followed tended to counteract that trend. Masters who freed their slaves for personal or paternal reasons frequently trained them in a trade and helped them find work or open a shop of their own. After emancipation, they often patronized their former slaves and encouraged friends to do the same. But paternal emancipation accounted for just a small portion of the free Negro population of the region, and freemen remained largely an unskilled group. Moreover, even those who carried skills out of bondage had difficulty finding steady work. Many southern whites believed blacks could perform only the simplest tasks. "A negro can never be a competent mechanic, because he is intellectually and mentally incapable of such elevation," intoned a Tennessee newspaper. "He is unfit for everything save plantation and menial services."[27] Racial prejudice relegated most free Negroes to the meanest drudgery at the lowest pay. In the countryside, free Negro men generally worked as farm laborers, turpentine hands, and fishermen, and in the cities, they found employment as teamsters, factory workers, and day laborers. Free Negro women usually served as domestics, cooks, and laundresses, and frequently did field work as well. Thus freedom added little to the occupational status of most Upper South free Negroes. The proportion of freemen working in unskilled occupations was higher than any other free group in the region.

Still, as a group, Upper South freemen achieved considerably higher levels of skill than free Negroes in the northern states. In Richmond, for example, over 30 percent of the free Negro population worked at skilled trades in 1860. Free Negroes composed about one-sixth of Richmond's bricklayers and blacksmiths, half its plasterers, and more than half its barbers. Several factors helped Upper South free Negroes reach this comparatively high occupational standing: perhaps the most important were southern attitudes toward race and work. In a racially based slave society, whites eschewed labor, especially jobs identified with blacks. A Virginia farmer told Frederick Law Olmsted that "no white man would ever do certain kinds of work . . . , and if you should ask a white man . . . he would get mad and tell you he wasn't a nigger."[28] Although many of the jobs deemed "nigger work" were drudgery deserving of that epithet, others provided steady work and lucrative wages. Frequently, they were skilled trades which demanded craftsmanship of the highest order. Upper South freemen practiced and sometimes dominated trades which whites monopolized in the North. The enslavement of some blacks ironically elevated the economic status of others.

But while the presence of slavery improved the economic standing of Upper South free Negroes, it severely limited their political and organizational opportunities. Just as abolition had eased fear of free Negro subversion in the minds of northern whites, the continued presence of slavery intensified it in the minds of southern whites. With little supporting evidence, Upper South whites clung to the belief that free Negroes were the chief source of inspiration and leadership for slave unrest.

It could hardly be otherwise. Although slaveholders throughout the Americas feared that Negroes free of the bonds of servitude would become an insurrectionary nucleus around which slaves would rally, whites in the American South held free Negroes in special awe. Their egalitarian heritage told them that blacks, like whites, were rational, if culturally inferior, beings capable of improvement and desirous of liberty. Although harsh repression might constrain black people's desire for freedom, it could never obliterate it. "History furnishes no instance of one people residing in the midst of another as a lower caste and excluded from an equality of civil rights that have stopped short of violence and rebellion as soon as their strength has given them reasonable hope of success," observed Virginia petitioners in 1849.[29] Upper South whites did not merely fear that blacks would revolt; they fully expected them to. The free Negro's presence, contaminating slaves with the idea that blacks could be free, just might breed such a "reasonable hope of success." Free Negroes did not have to organize insurrectionary plots, aid runaways to freedom, or pass abolitionist literature to be deemed subversive in the white mind. "Their mere presence, the simple act of walking our streets, and traveling our highways by the farms of the countryside," cautioned one Tennessee lawmaker, "is sufficient to incite insurrection in the slaves, for the desire for freedom is innate in the human breast."[30]

White fear of free Negro subversion affected every aspect of free Negro life. In the North, the segregationist ethos had created nascent ghettos which for all their attendant social disorders, provided common ground for blacks to solve common problems. Although the conditions of free Negro residence in the South were as dismal as any in the North, the pattern was considerably different. Southern whites were reluctant to create a unified black community where freemen and bondsmen could mix freely and form revolutionary combinations. This allowed freemen to reside near their place of work or near other people, black or white, of similar class status. Unlike their northern counterparts, southern free Negroes lived scattered throughout the cities of the slave states.[31] Their disparate pattern of residence placed inherent limitations on their organizational abilities.

Upper South whites took other more direct steps to limit the free Negro's subversive potential. Whites feared that free Negroes, by their presence if not their actions, would awaken blacks to the possibilities of liberty. But, as one Virginia legislator early recognized, if 'blacks see all of their color slaves, it will seem to them a disposition of Providence, and they will be content."[32] Thus whites limited the freemen's liberty and, whenever possible, equated them with slaves. In doing so, they went far beyond the proscriptions placed on Negro political rights in the northern states. Not only were southern free Negroes prohibited from voting, sitting on juries, and testifying against whites in court, but they were also barred from traveling without white permission and meeting without white supervision. These legal limitations were only part of a more general pattern of racial oppression, for any free Negro who presumed himself equal to a white implicitly challenged the system of slavery and was subject to summary punishment.[33]

Taken together, the disparate pattern of residence and the legal and extralegal constraints on free Negro liberty severely circumscribed the organizational and political opportunities of southern freemen. No black newspapers were published and no black conventions met in the slaveholding states. Black churches, schools, and fraternal societies met openly in most of the larger southern cities, and clandestinely—or with the quiet connivance of sympathetic officials—in many towns and rural localities, but never on the scale of northern organizations. There were no southern free black organizations to equal the AME Church or any southern black spokesmen to rival Frederick Douglass.

Barred from politics in even the narrowest sense, ambitious blacks channeled their energy in other directions. Just as leading northern freemen, proscribed from the world of business, poured themselves into organizational activity, so southern free Negroes, proscribed from the world of politics, concentrated their energy in economy activity. As tradesmen and artisans, freemen scored considerable gains in the Upper South. Their wealth grew steadily during the antebellum years. In Richmond, for example, the number of black real propertyholders increased fourfold and the value of their property grew from $18,000 to $185,000 between 1830 and 1860, a rate of growth far greater than the freemen's numerical increase. Although further research is needed to delineate fully the nature and size of black property ownership and compare it with that of whites, Richmond suggests the general trend.[34] Most free Negroes remained poor and propertyless, but the success of a significant minority shaped the development of free Negro leadership and influenced the relationship between free Negroes and whites and other blacks.

The freemen's search for economic security in the marketplaces of the South created tensions between freemen and slaves and among the free Negroes themselves. Since free Negroes had limited purchasing power and slaves had almost none, whites provided the most important customers for free Negro goods and services. Indeed, given the extent of white racism, Negro freemen frequently needed the support of white leaders to open a shop or practice a trade. To guarantee that support, leading free Negroes pursued alliances with their white patrons by adopting their standard of values and dissociating themselves from the mass of slaves and poor freemen whose friendship might tarnish their reputation as a "good Negro." The possibility for economic success at once made the marketplace, not, as in the North, the political arena, the common meeting ground for successful free Negroes and whites and created barriers between free and slave blacks.

Common origins, color, and circumstance transcended those barriers, especially at the lower and middle levels of free Negro society. Poor free Negroes and slaves worked together in the same shops and factories, prayed together in the same churches, and rubbed elbows in the same back-alley retreats. Many intermarried, dissolving still further differences in status and sealing the bonds of racial unity.

Still, the insoluble distinction between free and slave remained, and it grew with the freemen's ability to improve their lot. Successful free Negroes also suffered the pains of white oppression, but they could look down to slavery as well as up to complete freedom. Standing a step above the slave, these freemen could see how their status might degenerate and they knew whites needed only the flimsiest excuse to grab their liberty. They had learned to squeeze a few precious benefits from their middle-caste status, and they were not willing to surrender them without a guarantee of something better. Slaves were in no position to offer such an assurance. Freedom within the context of slavery thus pushed freemen and bondsmen apart. If northern blacks found it easy to identify with the cause of the slave, many southern free Negroes found the commitment to universal black liberty a luxury they could not afford. And yet racial loyalties could not be ignored, if for no other reason that whites would not permit them to be forgotten. Even at the upper reaches of free Negro society, freemen felt the tug of common racial bonds. Many successful Upper South free Negroes dangled uncomfortably between free and slave, unable to resolve the conflicting ties of status and caste.

The Free People of Color of the Lower South

Unlike the free Negro populations of the North and the Upper South, Lower South free people of color were relatively untouched by the events of the American Revolution. During the war, Lower South whites rejected the pleas of the Continental Congress to arm slaves in the Patriot cause. With Independence, no antislavery societies appeared and few masters freed their slaves. Instead, fear of servile insurrection fed by the numerical superiority of blacks in the low country hardened the Lower South's commitment to slavery. While the transformation of the Upper South's economy has stimulated manumission, economic changes in the Lower South sealed the door to black freedom. The expansion of rice culture in the lowlands and later the spread of cotton culture to the upcountry undercut the egalitarian thrust of Revolutionary ideology and snuffed out any hint of antislavery action. Emancipation, as a Savannah newspaper observed, was simply "not a prudent subject of discussion in Georgia."[35] During the 1770s and 1780s, while the number of northern and Upper South freemen grew rapidly, the free Negro population of the Lower South stagnated. In 1790, most Lower South freemen were descendants of those few slaves who had wriggled out of bondage during the colonial era.

That changed dramatically during the 1790s as events in Saint Domingue drove hundreds of free Negroes toward American shores. Like the colonial American free Negro caste, the *gens de couleur* of Saint Domingue had their origins in the illicit relations between white men and black slave women. But unlike their American counterparts, the French adventurers who came to Saint Domingue did not settle with their families. Instead, they hoped to make their fortunes in the booming sugar economy and return to France as quickly as possible. The absence of white women and the lack of a commitment to permanent settlement not only promoted stable alliances between these men and black women, but, more importantly, permitted them to recognize their brown children without raising the ire of their legitimate families. French colonials generally freed their mulatto offspring as a matter of course, and many saw to it that they were trained in a trade or educated for a profession. Some provided their children with substantial fortunes. Moreover, the relatively small number of nonslaveholding whites on the Island allowed people of color to advance themselves comparatively free from the competition free Negroes faced on mainland English North America. Although the *gens de couleur* suffered increasingly harsh racial proscription, they had a place in the economy and society of Saint Domingue and they made the most of it. Allied with their fathers, they served the plantation economy as artisans, tradesmen, overseers, soldiers, and slave catchers. A few became wealthy planters in their own right.[36]

Nevertheless, they too yearned for full equality, and their success only sharpened the sting of racial discrimination. In 1789, when the Bastille fell and the French Revolutionary Assembly promulgated its Declaration of the Rights of man, they believed their chance had come. In Saint Domingue and in Paris, the *gens de couleur* pressed their demands for equal rights. But white planters, jealous of their racial prerogatives and mindful of the effects on slavery, resisted and violently repressed any move toward equality by the free people of color. Still, the new repression could not crush the hopes aroused by the Revolutionary promise of equality, and open fighting between free people of color and whites broke out in many parts of the Island. Slaves, seeing their masters in disarray, quickly grabbed their liberty. By late 1792, what had begun as a dispute within the free caste had become a war between slave and free, black and white. The slave rebellion thrust the free people of color squarely and uncomfortably between the two factions. Forced to take sides, many joined Toussaint's army and rose to leadership in the struggle against slavery and white domination. But others had enjoyed their elevated caste position too long; for them, any alliance with African slaves was repugnant. They hurriedly repaired their ties with whites and fought under the French flag. When the blacks emerged victorious, these free people of color fled the Island with Toussaint burning the wharves behind them.[37]

Refugees from Saint Domingue spread throughout the Caribbean basin. Most migrated to the French colony of Louisiana, but others took refuge in Cuba and Jamaica and some found their way to the nearby mainland ports, especially Charleston and Savannah. American slaveholders welcomed the white emigres from Saint Domingue with whom they deeply sympathized. Free people of color naturally did not find as warm a reception. Americans were hostile towards free Negroes under the best of circumstance, and they viewed blacks who had witnessed the events on Saint Domingue with special horror. But once again, free people of color found that their service in the cause of slavery paid dividends. In spite of popular opposition and legal proscriptions, their influx continued. Between 1790 and 1810, the number of free Negroes in South Carolina more than doubled and those in Georgia increased well over 200 percent. The Louisiana Purchase in 1803 incorporated still more free people of color of similar origins into the United States. By 1810, there were over fourteen thousand free Negroes residing in the Lower South.[38] This largely mulatto, often French-speaking caste composed less than 10 percent of the American free Negro population, but their wealth, education, connections with influential whites, and long experience as freemen gave them special standing not usually accorded free Negroes in other parts of the nation.[39]

As the temper of internal warfare cooled in the new Republic of Haiti, immigration of free people of color into the United States slowed and may well have been reversed. The free Negro caste in the Lower South grew at a correspondingly slower pace. Much of this new growth was the product of natural increase of an existing population, but, as in the Upper South, some masters freed their slaves or allowed them to purchase their freedom. Almost all of these bondsmen were former members of the slave elite. The expansion of plantation culture in the Lower South gave little encouragement to anyone to challenge slavery. Manumission was generally paternal in origin and extremely selective. Few slaves found their way out of bondage who did not have close connections with their owners. Similarly, the rising price of slaves limited self-purchase to the best-connected and most skilled craftsmen. Thus native additions to the Lower South's free Negro population, like immigrant *gens de couleur*, were generally the children of white planters and slave women or privileged bondsmen who might win their master's approbation and permission to purchase their own liberty. Lower South freemen were an overwhelmingly urban, mulatto caste. In 1860, over half of the free people of color resided in the cities of the Lower South and fully three-quarters were of mixed racial origins.[40]

Wealthy refugees from Saint Domingue, the sons and daughters of American slaveholders, and the skilled black artisans who somehow bought their way out of bondage quickly achieved an elevated place in the economy of the Lower South's port cities. Their level of skill not only far exceeded that of the free Negroes of the Upper South, but it compared well with that of most urban whites. In Charleston, for example, nearly 80 percent of the city's free people of color did skilled work in 1860. This nearly equalled that of Irish immigrant workers. In some trades, colored freemen controlled a good part of the work and even monopolized some of it. Fully one-quarter of the city's carpenters, nearly 40 percent of the tailors, and three-quarters of the millwrights were free Negroes, although free Negro men composed only 15 percent of the city's free male work force.[41]

The stigma of "nigger work," which guarded free Negro jobs in the Upper South, offered even greater protection in the Lower South, where slavery was more deeply entrenched and the defense of slavery more explicit. Edward Laurens, a leader of the South Carolina nullification movement, rejected the common cant that the pleasures of urban life dissipated Charleston's best young men and turned them into idlers. "The true state of the case is," Laurens insisted, "that we first degrade the occupation by employing colored persons, and are then surprised that our young men, (whose spirit and high mindedness we endeavor almost daily to excite), will not enter the arena with them."[42] Skills learned with the patronage of well-connected whites and protected by the powerful stigma of "nigger work" enabled free people of color to enjoy a growing prosperity.

Their wealth, high occupational status, West Indian origins, French language and culture, urban residence, brown skin, indeed, their very name elevated the Lower South's free people of color in the white man's eyes and encouraged whites to consider them a caste apart from the overwhelmingly rural black slaves. Unlike those in the Upper South, whites in the Lower South resisted the tendency of jumbling free and slave Negroes together. As late as 1856, the Louisiana Supreme Court affirmed that "in the eyes of Louisiana law there is . . . all the difference between a free man of color and a slave that there is between a white man and a slave." Many Lower South whites believed free Negroes were useful members of society who strengthened, not weakened, the slave regime. "The relation of the free colored people and the slave is not one which gives any apprehension as to the quiet and contentment of the latter," observed a leading New Orleans daily. "Those who are free and in good circumstances regard the slave with more disdain and antagonism than the white man."[43] Although whites were not willing to reward the most loyal free people of color with equality, their special place in Lower South society, elevated above the slave but locked below all whites, was protected by the belief that free people of color were reliable allies in time of danger and the fear that tampering with the freemen's rights would drive them into an insurrectionary alliance with the slaves. Whites did not soon forget the twin lessons of Saint Domingue.

Lower South whites did not try to equate free Negroes with slaves or pack them off to Africa. Instead, their racial policy centered upon the delicate task of building the freemen's middle position, allowing free people of color just enough latitude to assure their loyalty but not so much as to encourage them to challenge white dominance. The three-caste system inherited from French and Spanish rule in Louisiana and introduced into other parts of the Lower South by West Indian emigres flourished in the ports of the Lower South and to a lesser degree in the hinterland. Although it was only rarely powerful enough to receive explicit legal sanction, whites supported the development of a loyal middle caste by patronizing free Negro tradesmen, lending them money, selling them land and slaves, and protecting them in moments of danger. Occasionally, whites granted the most successful free people of color additional rights and quietly allowed them to vote, attend school, testify in court, and occasionally to pass into the white caste.[44] But, like any essentially informal social practice, the extent of the three-caste system did not become fully manifest until it was challenged. When some whites threatened the long established prerogatives of the free people of color, commonplace notions that there was "nothing to single them out as the universal enemy of the whites" were rushed to the fore, often with good effect. Fear that pushing free Negroes too hard would break down "the barrier which now separates the free colored man from the slave and assigns him an intermediary *caste* between the slave and the master" not only restrained white racism but allowed the free people of color to wring additional concessions from whites.[45]

The benefits of their third-caste position encouraged the free people of color of the Lower South to think of themselves as a caste apart from the slaves. While a profound ambivalence characterized the attitude of Upper South free Negroes toward the slaves, Lower South free people of color demonstrated little interest in those in bondage except perhaps as property. They generally eschewed the African Baptist and Methodist churches into which slaves and poor free blacks crowded, and, when they could, they joined Catholic or Episcopal congregations. They used the liberties that whites allowed them to form their own exclusive associations, like the Société des Artisans in New Orleans, the Creole fire companies of Mobile, and the Brown Fellowship Society of Charleston. Many of these organizations not only stipulated that their members be free but also that they be of mixed racial origins, thus adding still another barrier between the largely light-skinned free people of color and the overwhelmingly dark-skinned slaves. Around these institutions, the free people of color organized their own communities apart from whites, who rejected them, and from blacks, whom they rejected. These communities offered freemen a small and comfortable if limited world where they could be masters of their own fate. Behind the walls of these elite communities, free people of color soothed their bruised egos by flaunting their position on top of black society. Their exclusive balls and parties asserted their elevated status and distinguished them from the mass of blacks whose crude lives, emotional religion, and strange dialect so horrified them. The security of these communities allowed elite freemen to prosper and to transfer their high status to their children, thereby compensating in some measure for the white man's rebuff. But these refugees came to depend on skin color and ancestry as well as wealth. They married among themselves and often it seemed their purpose was to breed themselves closer to the white ideal, perhaps with the hope of someday winning the full acceptance they craved.[46]

Different patterns of emancipation and manumission and diverse social, economic, and racial circumstances thus created three distinct groups of free Negroes in the United States. The distance between the free blacks of the North and the free people of color of the Lower South was measured in more than miles. In almost every aspect of their social life—economic standing, political and social status, characteristic modes of social action, indeed, physical being—light years separated northern and southern freemen.[47]

Differences among free Negroes explain much about the history of black people in the United States and American history generally. It suggests why so few southern freemen sought to leave the slave states for "freedom" in the North or, for that matter, why so few northern blacks went South in search of better jobs. While southern free Negroes could explain their political and social liberties greatly by migrating to a free state, they could do so only at the expense of their economic opportunities. A Charleston carpenter might say and do things in Philadelphia which would be suicidal if said and done in South

Carolina, but he would have great difficulty finding work at his chosen profession. In many parts of the North, it would be impossible for him to get work at any skilled trade. Similarly, northern freemen might be tempted to migrate south in search of work, but they understood their social and political liberties would be severely constrained.[48]

The reluctance of free Negroes to trade one set of opportunities and liabilities for another points to the vast differences in priorities and goals between them. These differences also help to explain the absence of significant interregional cooperation among freemen not only in the war against slavery but also in the movement for racial uplift. Although problems in communication and different patterns of repression would have inhibited the development of such a national movement under the best of circumstances, more fundamental cultural differences among free Negroes prohibited them from trying to establish such organizations.

The full meaning of the tripartite division of the free Negro caste becomes apparent only after the general Emancipation of 1863 and 1865. For if free Negroes were precursors of postemancipation race relations and black life generally, differences among antebellum freemen should also be an important element in the postemancipation world. The lack of detailed knowledge of the structure of black society following emancipation makes it hazardous to generalize about continuities between the pre- and postwar periods at this time. Yet, it is clear that northern freemen remained disproportionately important in black political affairs despite their continued numerical minority. Of the 22 blacks who served in Congress from the South during the nineteenth century, almost a third were born, educated, or spent their formative years in the northern states although only 5 percent of the black population of the United States resided in the North in 1860.[49] Frederick Douglass remained the dominant black political figure until his death in 1895. The preeminence of northern blacks as spokesmen for all blacks in national politics and their disproportionate presence in the expanding network of churches and schools and even in some Southern legislatures suggests the continuing power of a political tradition nearly a century in the making. Only with the death of Douglass and the rise of Booker T. Washington did the locus of black leadership shift to the South and then only briefly as northern blacks led by Monroe Trotter and W. E. B. DuBois challenged Washington's hegemony. But if northern blacks remained politically dominant, the center of black economic enterprise remained in the South. And perhaps it is not surprising that two of the three founders of the largest and most successful black-owned business, the North Carolina Mutual Insurance Company, descended from southern free Negroes.[50]

Neither the structure of black society nor the intense ideological disputes within the black community at the end of the nineteenth century can be fully understood without reference to the diverse traditions of the free Negro caste.

The emergence among southern blacks of an ideology which emphasized self-help and economic improvement may not only speak to the changes in black life that followed the failure of Reconstruction, but to the mode of racial advancement established by antebellum southern freemen. Indeed, much of the struggle for leadership within the black community at this time may not be, as is often depicted, between an old elite rooted in freedom and a new elite up from slavery,[51] but between elements of an elite with very different traditions of social action.

How the structure of antebellum black society influenced the development of black society after the Civil War remains a matter of intensive investigation. One starting point is the diverse traditions of the antebellum free Negro caste.

Notes

1. During the past three years, six book-length studies of Negro freemen have been published: David W. Cohen and Jack P. Greene, eds., *Neither Slave Nor Free, The Freedman of African Descent in the Slave Societies of the New World* (Baltimore, 1972); Letitia Woods Brown, *Free Negroes in the District of Columbia, 1790-1846* (New York, 1972); Herbert E. Sterkx, *The Free Negro in Antebellum Louisiana* (Rutherford, N.J., 1972); Marina Wikramanayake, *A World in Shadow: The Free Black in Antebellum South Carolina* (Columbia, S.C., 1973); Jerome S. Handler, *The Unappropriated People: Freedmen in the Slave Society of Barbados* (Baltimore, 1974); Ira Berlin, *Slaves Without Masters: The Free Negro in the Antebellum South* (New York, 1974); also Frederick P. Bowser, *The African Slave in Colinial Peru, 1524-1650* (Stanford, Calif., 1974), chs. 10-11. Recent comparative studies of slavery and race relations have also emphasized the free Negro's importance. See, for example, Carl N. Degler, *Neither Black Nor White: Slavery and Race Relations in Brazil and the United States* (New York, 1971) and H. Hoetink, *Slavery and Race Relations in the Americas: Comparative Notes on Their Nature and Nexus* (New York, 1973).

2. Samuel D. Smith, *The Negro in Congress, 1870-1901* (Chapel Hill, N.C., 1940), p. 8; free Negroes enjoyed the same disproportionate influence in state legislatures. Luther P. Jackson, *Negro Officeholders in Virginia, 1865-1895* (Norfolk, Va., 1945), pp. 1-43, 50; Joel Williamson, *After Slavery: The Negro in South Carolina During Reconstruction, 1861-1877* (Chapel Hill, N.C., 1965), pp. 376-7; Peter Kolchin, *First Freedom: The Responses of Alabama's Blacks to Emancipation and Reconstruction* (Westport, Conn., 1972), pp. 163-7; David C. Rankin, "The Origins of Black Leadership in New Orleans During Reconstruction," *Journal of Southern History* 40 (1974): 417-40.

3. The most significant regional and state studies of the free Negro in the United States are Leon F. Litwack, *North of Slavery: The Negro in the Free States, 1790-1860* (Chicago, 1961); Berlin, *Slaves Without Masters*; Emma Lou Thornbrough, *The Negro in Indiana: A Study of a Minority* (Indianapolis, 1957), chs. 1-8; Luther P. Jackson, *Free Negro Labor and Property Holding in Virginia, 1830-1860* (New York, 1942); John Hope Franklin, *The Free Negro in North Carolina, 1790-1860* (Chapel Hill, N.C., 1943); E. Horace Fitchett, "The Traditions of the Free Negro in Charleston, South Carolina," *Journal of Negro History* 25 (1940): 139-51 and Fitchett, "The Origins and Growth of the Free Negro Population of Charleston, South Carolina," *ibid.*, 26 (1941): 421-37; Wikramanayake, *World in Shadow;* and Sterkx, *Free Negro in Antebellum Louisiana.* Outdated in conception and method, but still useful are John H. Russell, *The Free Negro in Virginia, 1619-1865* (Baltimore, 1913) and James M. Wright, *The Free Negro in Maryland, 1634-1860* (New York, 1921).

4. Throughout this essay, I have defined the North as the states which made provision for emancipation following the American Revolution or which later entered the Union as free states. Delaware, Kentucky, Maryland, Missouri, North Carolina, Tennessee, Virginia, and the District of Columbia constitute the Upper South; Alabama, Arkansas, Florida, Georgia, Louisiana, Mississippi, South Carolina, and Texas the Lower South.

5. Winthrop D. Jordon, *White Over Black, American Attitudes Toward the Negro, 1550-1812* (Chapel Hill, N.C., 1968), pp. 122-6; Lorenzo J. Greene, *The Negro in Colonial New England* (New York, 1942), pp. 298-304; Edgar J. McManus, *Black Bondage in the North* (Syracuse, N.Y., 1973), pp. 68-70, 111, 122, 130, 162.

6. Benjamin Quarles, *The Negro in the American Revolution* (Chapel Hill, N.C., 1961); Donald L. Robinson, *Slavery in the Structure of American Politics, 1765-1820* (New York, 1971), pp. 98-130.

7. Arthur Zilversmit, *The First Emancipation: The Abolition of Slavery in the North* (Chicago, 1967); Jordan, *White Over Black*, pp. 315-74; Litwack, *North of Slavery*, pp. 3-14; McManus, *Black Bondage*, pp. 160-79; Gary B. Nash, "Slaves and Slaveowners in Colonial Philadelphia," *William and Mary Quarterly* 30 (1973): 231-2, 236-56, especially 254, 256; Robert William Fogel and Stanley L. Engerman, "Philanthropy at Bargain Prices: Notes on The Economics of Gradual Emancipation," *Journal of Legal Studies* 3 (1974): 377-82, 385-93.

8. Jacob P. Dunn, Jr., *Indiana: A Redemption from Slavery* (Boston, 1888); Theodore C. Pease, *The Story of Illinois* (Chicago, 1949), pp. 72-8.

9. Historians have spent a good deal of energy trying to distinguish between the ideological and the economic causes of manumission. Needless to say, except for determinists of one brand or another, this is a thankless task. The essential point is that Revolutionary ideology gave northern emancipationists the leverage to attack slavery successfully. If the demand for slaves or long-term commitment to slavery had been greater in the North, their task would have been more difficult and perhaps impossible. Yet, even where slavery played a marginal economic role, abolitionists met firm resistance. Only the impetus of Revolutionary ideology allowed them to triumph.

10. *Negro Population of the United States, 1790-1915* (Washington, D.C., 1918), p. 221. Census enumerations of color—black and brown—are not without their problems, since perception of color and sensitivity to black-mulatto differences varied from person to person and, perhaps more significantly, from region to region. Lawrence Glasco, in the fullest exploration this question has thus far received, has concluded that "the census figures are probably adequate. Certainly, if one finds consistent, strong patterns, then the skeptic must be able to find equally consistent errors which could account for such patterns. And, when using the census to compare the characteristics of the ante-bellum mulatto and black, there *do* emerge consistent, sharp differences" ("The Mulatto: A Neglected Dimension of Afro-American Social Structure" [unpublished paper, courtesy of the author]).

11. *Return of the Number of Persons Within the Several Districts of the United States* [for 1790] (Washington, D.C., 1802); *Aggregate Amount of Persons Within the United States in the Year 1810* (Washington, D.C., 1811).

12. Computed from *Population of the United States in 1860* (Washington, D.C., 1864).

13. Lorenzo J. Greene, *Negro in Colonial New England*, pp. 100-123; Nash, "Slaves and Slaveowners in Philadelphia," pp. 248-52; McManus, *Black Bondage*, pp. 184-5, 196-7; Litwack, *North of Slavery*, pp. 5-6, 101-3, 153-86.

14. Robert Ernst, "The Economic Status of New York City Negroes, 1850-1863," *Negro History Bulletin* 12 (1949): 131-2, 139-43; Theodore Hershberg, "Free Blacks in Antebellum Philadelphia: A Study of Ex-Slaves, Freeborn, and Socio-economic Decline," *Journal of Social History* 5 (1972): 186, 198-9; J. D. B. DeBow, *Statistical View of the United States* (Washington, D.C., 1854), pp. 80-81. The "free labor" ideology is discussed in Eric Foner, *Free Soil, Free Labor, Free Men: The Ideology of the Republican Party Before the Civil War* (New York, 1970).

15. Litwack, *North of Slavery*, p. 97.

16. Biographical studies still offer the best insights into the early church movement in the

North; see Charles H. Wesley, *Richard Allen, Apostle of Freedom* (Washington, D.C., 1935) and Carol V.R. George, *Segregated Sabbaths, Richard Allen and the Rise of Independent Black Churches, 1760-1840* (New York, 1973). These two studies of Allen may be supplemented by Lorenzo J. Greene, "Prince Hall: Massachusetts Leader in Crisis," *Freedomways* 1 (1961): 238-52.

17. Litwack, *North of Slavery*, pp. 214-46; Benjamin Quarles, *Black Abolitionists* (New York, 1969).

18. David M. Katzman, *Before the Ghetto: Black Detroit in the Nineteenth Century* (Urbana, Ill., 1973), pp. 175-206.

19. *Gentlemen's Magazine and Historical Chronicle* 34 (1764): 261.

20. Berlin, *Slaves Without Masters*, pp. 15-50; for a full explication of economic changes in the Upper South, see Carville Earle and Ronald Hoffman, *The Urban South: The First Two Centuries* (forthcoming).

21. Berlin, *Slaves Without Masters*, pp. 36-45, and especially 46-7.

22. Ibid., pp. 101-3, 138-9.

23. *Population of the United States in 1860*, pp. 598-605.

24. Berlin, *Slaves Without Masters*, pp. 135-7.

25. *Negro Population of the United States*, p. 221.

26. Computed from the *Population of the United States in 1860.*

27. *Nashville Republican Banner*, 12 June 1858.

28. Frederick Law Olmsted, *A Journey in the Seaboard Slave States* (New York, 1856), pp. 91-2; Richmond Manuscript Census, 1860, National Archives, Washington, D.C. Occupational data on Richmond and Charleston freemen were graciously supplied by Professor Herbert Gutman of City College of New York.

29. *African Repository* 25 (1849): 73.

30. *Nashville Union and American*, 19 November 1860.

31. Richard Wade, *Slavery in the Cities: The South, 1820-1860* (New York, 1964), pp. 55-79, 275-7; Berlin, *Slaves Without Masters*, pp. 251-8.

32. Richmond *Virginia Argus*, 17 January 1806.

33. Berlin, *Slaves Without Masters*, pp. 90-99, 316-42.

34. Jackson, *Free Negro Labor and Propertyholding*, 138 and *passim*; Wright, *Free Negro in Maryland*, pp. 186-7; Dorothy Provine, "The Economic Position of Free Blacks in the District of Columbia, 1800-1860," *Journal of Negro History* 58 (1973): 67-72; Russell Garvin, "The Free Negro in Florida Before the Civil War," *Florida Historical Quarterly* 46 (1967): 12.

35. Savannah *Columbian Museum & Savannah Advertiser*, 11 March 1796.

36. Laura Foner, "The Free People of Color in Louisiana and St. Domingue, A Comparative Portrait of Two Three-Caste Slave Societies," *Journal of Social History* 3 (1970): 406-30; Cohen and Greene, eds., *Neither Slave Nor Free*, pp. 172-92.

37. James G. Leyburn, *The Haitian People* (New Haven, Conn., 1941), ch. 1; C.L.R. James, *The Black Jacobins: Toussaint L'Ouverture and the San Domingo Revolution*, 2nd rev. ed. (New York, 1963).

38. Petitions from Charleston, 11 December 1797, ? September 1798, South Carolina Legislative Papers, Grand Jury Presents, Beaufort, November 1793, Charleston, November 1792, South Carolina Archives, Columbia, S.C.; Charleston *City Gazette*, August-December 1793; Proceedings of the Savannah City Council, 5 July 1795, Savannah City Hall, Savannah, Georgia; *Population of the United States in 1860*, pp. 598-601.

39. Berlin, *Slaves Without Masters*, pp. 128-32.

40. *Negro Population of the United States*, p. 220; urban population computed from *Population of the United States in 1860.*

41. Charleston Manuscript Census, 1860, National Archives.

42. Edward Laurens, *A Letter to the Hon. Whitemarsh B. Seabrook* (Charleston, 1835), pp. 9-10.

43. Helen T. Catterall, ed., *Judicial Cases Concerning Slavery and the Negro*, 5 vols. (Washing-

ton, D.C., 1926-1937), 3: 649; *New Orleans Daily Delta*, 17 July 1852; *Charleston Courier*, 9 December 1835.

44. Berlin, *Slaves Without Masters*, pp. 192-9, 212-6.

45. [Edwin C. Holland], *A Refutation of the Calumnies Circulated Against the Southern and Western States, Respecting the Institution of Slavery* (Charleston, 1822), pp. 83-5; *Journal of the Louisiana House of Representatives*, 1846 (adjourned session), p. 71; quote in *Charleston Courier*, 9 December 1835.

46. An insider's view of this society can be gleaned in William R. Hogan and Edwin A. Davis, eds., *William Johnson's Natchez: The Ante-Bellum Diary of a Free Negro* (Baton Rouge, La., 1951); also R. L. Desdunes, *Nos Hommes et Notre Histoire* (Montreal, 1911); Fitchett, "Traditions of the Free Negro in Charleston," pp. 139-51; Wikramanayake, *World in Shadow*.

47. Again, it must be emphasized that the physical characteristics, social circumstances, or modes of social action of any one of these three groups of freemen did not exist exclusively in any one geographical region. Some northern freemen shaped the exclusivist tendencies of the free people of color of the Lower South and some Lower South free people of color fully identified with the cause of the slave. Each region had its share of subthemes. An excellent beginning to a fuller understanding of these has been made by Theodore Hershberg, "Mulattoes and Blacks: Intra-Group Color Differences and Social Stratification in Nineteenth Century Philadelphia," *Journal of American History* (forthcoming).

48. When they did migrate North, southern freemen carried their cultural traditions with them. This may account for the higher social status enjoyed by slave-born blacks in antebellum Philadelphia when compared to that of those blacks born in freedom. Theodore Hershberg, whose ongoing study of nineteenth-century Philadelphia unearthed this seeming anomaly, suggests that the destructiveness of the urban experience accounts for the failure of free-born blacks to do as well as those born in slavery. Yet, as Hershberg acknowledges, most Philadelphia blacks who had been born in slavery were migrants from the Upper South either as long-time or newly emancipated freemen, while most free-born blacks were probably natives of Philadelphia or the surrounding free states. The real comparison, then, may not be between slave and free-born blacks, but between southern freemen who traditionally looked to the marketplace as a source of advancement and northern freemen who looked elsewhere for their social status. In this light, it is interesting to observe that although free-born blacks had lower socioeconomic status, they generally belonged to more prestigious social organizations (Hershberg, "Free Blacks in Antebellum Philadelphia," pp. 183-209 and especially the tables on pp. 186 and 188 and note 26 on p. 208).

49. Smith, *Negro in Congress, passim.*

50. Walter B. Weare, *Black Business in the New South: A Social History of the North Carolina Mutual Life Insurance Company* (Urbana, Ill., 1973), pp. 50 and *passim.*

51. August Meier, "Negro Class Structure and Ideology in the Age of Booker T. Washington," *Phylon* 23 (1963): 258-66.

Forrest McDonald and
Grady McWhiney

The Antebellum Southern Herdsman: A Reinterpretation

In 1860 hogs and other southern livestock were worth half a billion dollars—more than twice the value of that year's cotton crop. Not all of the Old South's animals were sold each year, of course, but in 1850 the Patent Office (the statistics-gathering predecessor of the Department of Agriculture) reported that one relatively small area of the South—some two hundred miles square of piney woods in southern Mississippi, eastern Louisiana, and western Alabama—had "raised, . . . for 20 years past, one million head of cattle yearly" and sold them for "from $10 to $12 per head." Two-thirds of the nation's hogs were grown in the South. In 1860 ten southern states—Alabama, Texas, Georgia, Mississippi, Arkansas, Kentucky, North Carolina, Missouri, Tennessee, and Virginia—could boast of a hog population of more than a million; only four northern states—Illinois, Indiana, Ohio, and Pennsylvania—could claim so many. Nor were these southern animals merely valueless "razorbacks," so often described as bone and gristle. In 1860 the hogs and other livestock slaughtered in the South were worth some $106,555,000; this was $327,000 more than all the livestock slaughtered in the North.[1]

Despite their numbers and value, southern animals—as well as the people who raised them—have received far less attention than their importance in the economy warranted.[2] Hogs especially have been neglected. This neglect of livestock in works on the South seems to be the result of a strong historiographical tradition. Part of the problem is that historians, especially those who synthesize, usually write about what other historians have written about. This is necessary, of course, because no individual can become an expert on all

Source: Journal of Southern History 41 (May 1975): 147–66.

topics and in all areas. So historians borrow from and build upon previous scholarship; they also follow trends, just as do other people. Textbook writers and other generalists have ignored the importance of animals in the South's history because specialists have ignored livestock. In 1965 a distinguished agricultural historian stated: "There are no works dealing with southern farm livestock except for rather sketchy and inadequate treatment of livestock production in the Tennessee-Kentucky region."[3]

Another reason why livestock and those who raised it have received little attention[4] may be that historians have been intimidated by one or both of two overwhelming historiographical influences. No single individual has exerted more influence upon interpreting the history of the South, especially the antebellum South, than Ulrich Bonnell Phillips. In his two most important works—*American Negro Slavery* and *Life and Labor in the Old South*—Phillips insisted that plantations and slavery determined the nature of southern society. At the top were the agriculturists who owned much land and many Negroes and grew the great staple crops. Because his interests centered on the plantation, Phillips neglected those people who were not large slaveholders and landowners. He failed to mention hog raisers in *American Negro Slavery* though he noted that bacon was a staple in the slave diet and was, along with chicken, one of the plantation's "standard meats."[5] It is not that Phillips totally ignored southerners who raised and drove livestock to market. He was aware that such people existed, but he minimized their importance by giving them little space in his books. He spent less than a page on livestock drovers in *Life and Labor*.[6]

By allotting so little space to people like drovers, who were not a part of the plantation itself but without whom the plantation system could not have existed, Phillips distorted both the composition of antebellum southern society and the importance of certain occupations. He also perpetuated the misconception that almost every antebellum southerner was, or wanted to be, a grower of great staple crops. "Wanted: lands like those of the Bluegrass, in the climate of middle Georgia, on rivers flowing smoothly to the sea, under laws favorable to the holding of Negroes in bondage. Such a notice," Phillips contended, "might well have been signed by any of ten thousand men in the 'teens; and the 'twenties, 'thirties, 'forties and 'fifties brought no end to the demand."[7]

Phillips arranged his evidence to convince readers that the only worthwhile activity in the Old South was the growing of plants, *and that success, not occupation, determined a man's place in society*. What caused the differences in wealth between planters and farmers, he argued, was simply "the variance of talent, resolution, health and mere luck. The divergencies furthermore, were not sharply between rich and poor but of continuous gradation from millionaires to paupers; and the classes were by no means constant in personnel." Long before Frank Lawrence Owsley wrote a book about the "plain folk" Phillips had "discovered" them—only to obscure them by painting them in false colors. "These and their fellow millions," he wrote, "cannot be lumped as 'poor whites' and dismissed. . . ." They were yeoman farmers who grew plants;

all of them aspired to possess land and slaves, many owned land, and some owned a few slaves. "Their standards of comfort and propriety, their manners and morals, varied with the vicinage, with health and wealth, with education and opportunity, and with individual proclivities and predilections," Phillips claimed,[8] but he saw all as a part of a competitive agricultural society and system in which everyone tried to better himself by acquiring land and slaves.

What Phillips completely missed in his analysis of antebellum society was the importance of the herdsmen. In some ways this is a curious oversight, since Phillips used certain references to herdsmen which suggest that their role was far more significant than his brief mention of them would indicate. For example, he quoted a Virginia mountaineer, who wrote in 1828: "I am not making any money at present, and cannot until I sell my corn to Hog-drovers, from which I never have failed to make every fall something like four or five hundred dollars." This letter alone suggests that hog driving was a sizable—and distinct—economic operation. Such a conclusion is confirmed by another letter quoted by Phillips from a settler near Chattanooga who complained in 1850 that a drought had reduced local crops by half: "I do not know what the poor hog drovers will do for corn this season if they drive as many as they did last. They must have drove some 80 thousand . . . last season, and it would take no inconsiderable part of the corn raised in our valley . . . to feed that number during their passage this season. The mules have commenced going already. For the last two weeks there has hardly been a day that a drove or two has not passed."[9]

Apart from Phillips, the man most responsible for distorting the southern herdsmen's role was Frederick Jackson Turner. If Phillips's vertical model of antebellum southern society minimized the importance of the herdsmen by placing them near the bottom of a chain of ambition, Turner's horizontal model of successive frontiers relegated the herdsmen to a transitory and impermanent existence. They were to him merely a stage in frontier development—"fur-trader, miner, cattle-raiser, and farmer." As Turner described this process, "each type of industry was on the march toward the West, impelled by an irresistible attraction. Each passed in successive waves across the continent. Stand at Cumberland Gap and watch the procession of civilization, marching single file—the buffalo following the trail to the salt springs, the Indian, the fur-trader and hunter, the cattle-raiser, the pioneer farmer—and the frontier has passed by. Stand at South Pass in the Rockies a century later and see the same procession. . . ."[10]

This Turnerian emphasis upon the herdsman as a transitory figure always being pushed westward by farmers is evident in even the most careful studies of southern livestock raisers. Lewis Cecil Gray, who devoted considerable space to animal husbandry in his massive history of agriculture in the Old South, concluded: "Before the outbreak of the Civil War the advance of agriculture was driving the herding industry into the semiarid districts of western Texas."[11]

Turner's influence is also apparent in the best analysis of the antebellum southern livestock grazers ever written—the twenty-eight pages Frank L. Owsley allotted to herdsmen in his study of the Old South's plain folk.[12] Owsley made a valuable contribution to the understanding of the livestock industry by showing that "grazing was a major occupation in the South . . ." and that grazers were "a large and important element" in antebellum southern society.[13] But he also argued that herdsmen "were the typical pioneers." Some, essentially hunters and trappers who grazed animals only as a "secondary pursuit," constantly moved "from place to place in search of better pastures and more game"; others, "who were the main body of frontiersmen, occupied the zone of unsurveyed lands at a reasonably safe distance from the Indian border. They were the genuine herdsmen."[14] Owsley believed that, as a rule, herdsmen ultimately either became farmers or were driven out as grazing regions became more settled. "A cattleman usually began as a poor young man, and if he became wealthy he settled down in some well-selected spot, usually as a planter . . . ," he wrote. "Frequently, too, the smaller herdsmen settled as farmers on land which they had purchased. . . ." But "Many others . . . grazed their cattle and hunted from one frontier to another until at last there was no frontier left except the great pine barrens and the broken mountainous regions."[15]

Owsley's explanation of why the herdsmen moved so often was the same as Turner's though with a twist that explained how herdsmen could remain in the East while being pushed ever westward—namely, that they were driven to the "inner frontier." "It was agriculture . . . ," insisted Owsley, "that drove the herdsmen from frontier to frontier and finally into the pine barrens, hills, and mountains. After the Civil War this phenomenon was repeated when the farmers or nesters swarmed into the Great Plains and crowded the cattle ranchers farther into the more arid regions."[16]

Though Owsley believed that farmers drove out the herdsmen, he did not believe that slavery and the plantation system drove out the small farmers. Indeed, he argued that small and large plant growers managed to live together in harmony. But, astonishingly, he did not go on to observe that animal growers and plant growers could also coexist in large areas of the South. As a result, he ignored the probability that half or more of the people he listed as small farmers (Owsley estimated that 70 percent of the people of the lower South owned farms)[17] raised animals worth more than their crops and that many of the rest raised plants such as corn primarily to supply animals. (Table 1 illustrates the prevalence of livestock culture in precisely those counties that Owsley used to illustrate the opposite.)

Livestock growers have suffered some misunderstanding in the works of Phillips and even the most conscientious Turnerians, such as Owsley, because all these historians shared a Jeffersonian bias; their ideal types—Phillips's planter and the Turnerians' independent yeoman—were dirt farmers. These writers considered livestock growers as primitive, passing, and inferior to the

Table 1. Farms and Production in Selected Alabama Counties, 1860

Counties	Farms Under 50 Acres	Farms over 500 Acres	Total Number of Farms	Total Number of Hogs	Total Value of Livestock	Average Number of Hogs per Farm	Average Value of Livestock per Farm	Average Value of Cotton per Farm*
Black Belt:								
Dallas	116	193	711	55,145	$1,716,129	78	$2,414	$3,567
Greene	72	166	793	49,701	1,746,454	63	2,202	2,919
Lowndes	249	160	1,033	56,394	1,661,362	55	1,608	2,078
Marengo	187	166	778	58,457	1,699,142	75	2,184	3,210
Monroe	299	39	764	30,661	673,257	40	881	954
Montgomery	117	169	800	63,134	1,748,273	79	2,185	2,944
Perry	229	118	926	41,767	1,305,872	45	1,410	1,927
Black Belt Counties	1,269	1,011	5,805	355,259	$10,550,489	61	$1,818	$2,474
Pine Belt and Upland:								
Bibb	370	7	878	42,158	$608,458	48	$693	$878
Coffee	433	4	829	23,859	392,032	29	473	255
Coosa	841	24	1,631	35,810	909,070	22	557	343
Covington	312	5	517	20,527	324,362	40	627	156
Fayette	758	0	1,189	21,963	501,713	18	422	184
Lauderdale	456	71	996	24,101	845,171	24	849	444
Randolph	1,508	3	2,202	37,596	679,785	17	309	117
Washington	136	117	725	15,314	295,576	21	408	190
Pine Belt and Upland Counties	4,814	231	8,967	221,328	$4,556,167	25	$508	$250

Source: Agriculture in the United States in 1860, pp. 2–5, 193. The counties are those selected by Owsley, *Plain Folk*, 157–62, 181–93.

*An average price of 10 cents per pound was used for cotton.

superior and more permanent plant growers. The epitome of this whole attitude can be found in the words of the most distinguished living Turnerian.

> Far below the yeoman farmers in the South's social scale [wrote Ray Allen Billington] were the poor whites who, as "crackers," "hillbillies," or "sandhillers," were scattered in small communities through the poorest southern lands: the Georgia pine barrens, the sandy-woods section of southern Mississippi, the piney forests of Alabama, and the worn-out soils abandoned by cotton planters. Most of them made a pretense of planting a crop but lethargy overcame them once the seed was in the ground. They depended for food less on their weed-choked fields than on omnipresent hogs who cared for themselves and on game they brought down with their long rifles. Unkempt, illiterate, shiftless, and lazy, these miserable by-products of the plantation system were condemned to their squalid existence by more fortunate neighbors who pushed them into unproductive lands, then kept there by the ravages of the parasitical hookworm which left them lethargic and listless. Yet they too defended slavery, largely because they subconsciously realized that this artificial barrier alone kept them from the very bottom of the social scale.[18]

A special word needs to be added about Sam Bowers Hilliard's excellent recent work on the southern food supply, *Hog Meat and Hoecake*. Hilliard is often brilliant and sometimes profound, and as a result of his diligent labors we know a great deal more about the raising and consumption of livestock (especially hogs) in the antebellum South than we ever knew before. But he, too, is caught up in the Phillips-Turner trap. He recognizes that enormous quantities of hogs are raised but vacillates between believing that they were incidentally raised by plant growers who aspired to become planters, a la Phillips, and by frontiersmen who were being pushed ever westward or toward "internal frontiers," a la Turner and Owsley. Only now and again does Hilliard depart from a two-character model of southern society (that is, "subsistence farmers" and the people they aspired to become, slaveowning cotton planters) and note that there may have been a third "class" of antebellum southern whites, namely herders.[19]

In 1962 Eugene D. Genovese subjected what he regarded as the Owsley "thesis"—and what, more properly, can be regarded as some suggestions Owsley made—to a harsh critique. But Genovese missed Owsley's point and inadvertently supplied information supporting the point we propose to make about the importance of livestock drovers in the antebellum southern economy. Genovese addressed himself toward proving that the great slave plantations—whether planting tobacco, rice, sugar cane, or cotton—produced far from enough livestock even for plantation consumption and that what they did produce was of inferior quality. He pointed out that hogs slaughtered in Chicago in 1860 averaged 228 pounds—as against a southern average, *determined by study of the records of twenty-four southern plantations*, of a mere 140 pounds. Indeed, Genovese says, the 140-pound figure is inflated by "inclusion of the heavier hogs bought from drovers to be slaughtered on the plantations."[20]

That is just it: the raising of livestock was a function performed not only by yeoman farmers and the operators of plantations but also by people who raised cattle and hogs as their principal occupation and who did so out of both tradition and choice. In 1840 a traveler in southern Mississippi noted that "The people are for the most part pastoral, their herds furnishing their chief revenue." This trade in animals, he concluded, "has enriched many people. . . ." A resident of northeastern Texas stated in 1850 that many of his neighbors raised livestock for sale in Louisiana: "Two thousand head or upwards [of cattle] are annually shipped to New Orleans." During the antebellum period, a preacher recalled, "most of the people [of northern Florida and southern Georgia] . . . lived by raising stock." And in 1848 a visitor reported: "The principal revenue of the people [of East Tennessee] . . . is derived from the business of raising cattle."[21]

Though additional research is needed to determine exactly who these livestock growers were and where they came from, there is enough available information to make some fairly confident suggestions. Lewis C. Gray as well as Percy Wells Bidwell and John Ironside Falconer print maps and other data that show the geographical distribution of cattle and swine, as reflected in census figures; *Hog Meat and Hoecake*, along with several studies of agriculture in particular states, offers valuable (if often misunderstood) information; and studies of migration, both from Europe to America and inside the South, afford enough material to warrant a few general observations.[22]

At the outset it must be understood that the raisers of livestock in the Old South were not one group but three—each with countless gradations both in the extent of their specialization and the volume of their business. Abundant evidence indicates that many planters kept herds, though, as Genovese notes, they tended to be small and of less than first-rate quality and though, as E. Merton Coulter says, many planters disdained to raise swine on the ground that it was beneath their dignity.[23] Second, there were the yeoman farmers, growers of plants, who almost universally kept some hogs and often raised sizable herds. Third, and possibly most important, there were drovers, whose main or sole occupation was that of herding, and who, when they raised any crops at all, did so only incidentally or for fattening their stock.

Many of the American drovers of both the eighteenth and nineteenth centuries came from the Celtic areas of the British Isles, meaning the southwestern, western, and northern parts of England, the Scottish Lowlands and Highlands, and most especially the "Scotch-Irish" plantations of Lowland Scots in Ulster, northern Ireland. Not all Celts were drovers, and not all drovers were Celts, of course, but if one tracks down where the Scotch-Irish went in their great migration that began soon after 1715, involved perhaps half a million souls, and did not abate until after the panic of 1837, one has pinned down important antebellum livestock country. They went to Philadelphia, thence to the uplands around that city, and thence to the uplands of the Pennsylvania valleys. From there they moved in two general directions: westward along the Ohio Valley, on both the Ohio and Kentucky sides of the river, and southwestward down the several valleys of Maryland and Virginia, back up to Virginia's Southside, down through the Piedmont of the Carolinas, and then into Tennessee and northern parts of Georgia, Alabama, and Mississippi, and ultimately into Arkansas, northern Louisiana, and Texas. Throughout, from 1715 to 1837 and beyond, as the Scotch-Irish went they took their cattle-and-hog culture with them.[24]

Moreover, the migration of the Scotch-Irish was attended all the way by what, when they reached the Great Plains, was called the "open-range system." Thanks to Billington, Walter Prescott Webb, John Wayne, and a host of movies and television shows, every schoolboy knows about the open range: the cattle barons of the Great Plains reaped fortunes by grazing their herds on public lands until the hated sheep farmers and the grubby plowmen began to fence the ranges in the 1880s. Rather less known is that the open range had been part of the tradition of the antebellum South for some decades, and of the British uplands for some centuries before that, and had in fact been the indispensable condition of Celtic livestock tending for a long, long time.

A quick survey will illustrate the point. Land tenure in the Lowlands and in Ulster until 1715, and in the Highlands until late in the eighteenth century, implicitly or explicitly contained a provision that grazing and foraging rights pertained to every person who lived on the land, no matter how high or low his station; the lowliest cotter could graze his hogs on the uncultivated lands of the most lordly landholder. The enclosure movement, which had had profound effects upon English farming in the preceding two centuries, now hit the Scots, but its meaning was different, for the Scots were primarily drovers who disdained to be mere tillers of the soil.[25]

When the Lowlanders and the Scotch-Irish made their exodus to America they carried their habitual ways with them. Moreover, colonial and state laws protected them in those ways. Gray indicates that it was not until the mid-1830s that Virginia passed its first laws permitting fencing on an extremely limited basis and another decade before South Carolina followed suit; until then, and to a considerable extent afterward, anybody owning cattle and hogs could graze them in the pastures and woods of any planter, excepting only land that was both fenced and in crops—to the chagrin of Edmund Ruffin and many another "progressive" planter. Indeed, Ruffin labored for twenty years before being able to obtain in 1858 a special act of the Virginia legislature permitting planters in Prince George County to limit the open-range rights of drovers by erecting fences around entire estates or adjoining estates—which attests to the numbers and political strength of the herdsmen. This "reform & revolution in this heretofore fixed policy of Va," Ruffin hoped, might soon be extended to other counties—despite what he called the "pig-headed" opposition of men like J. B. Cocke—and if so, it would be "almost as great a benefit for the agricultural interests of Virginia, as I had before rendered in any other way."[26]

What actually evolved in Virginia was what amounted to a local-option system: landowners in particular counties could by special acts of the legislature acquire the right to fence their property. Meanwhile, North Carolina had long since made it criminal to interfere with livestock grazing on any land not under cultivation and fenced no matter who owned the land or the animals, and that law remained on the books long after the Civil War; the open range or commons was the norm in Louisiana and Mississippi throughout the antebellum period; Tennessee did not pass laws permitting the fencing of entire farms until late in the nineteenth century; the local-option system continued in Texas and Louisiana until after World War II; practice in Florida, whatever the law, retained common grazing and foraging rights as late as the 1950s; and local-option laws remained in force in Georgia until 1957, when a statewide law ended the open range after a prominent businessman, Walter Candler, was killed when his car hit a cow that was asleep in the road.[27]

And yet Owsley, for all his perceptiveness, was able to write: "By 1840 the better agricultural lands in the older states and in many parts of the newer ones had been sufficiently settled by farmers to interfere with grazing upon the open range, and the herdsmen had largely disappeared from such lands." And in 1972 Hilliard could echo: "The herder either was pushed out by the farmer and the planter or, more likely, joined their ranks. In discussing former occupations of early settlers, many writers of the postwar period referred to the 'old-timers' as being cattlemen. Apparently they were cattle herders during the early years and shifted to crops later."[28]

Obviously, the variety of livestock that could be raised by the traditional Celtic method—if simply allowing one's animals to run wild and root for themselves on just anybody's land can be called a method—was limited or determined by the available natural food supply. The Scotch-Irish had long raised hogs and cattle indiscriminately, for the two get along well enough together; for a surprising reason, to be related below, sheep and goats were not acceptable. In America the same pattern held, but the predominance of woodland over open pasture east of the Mississippi dictated that swine would fare better than cattle, and so it was. In southern and central Indiana and Illinois, in the Nashville Basin and the bluegrass region of Kentucky, and on the Gulf coastal plain cattle were as important as hogs, and once the Scotch-Irish penetrated the Prairie Plains and then the Great Plains cattle became far more important. But in most of the Old South the hog was king.

The Celtic herdsmen's way required little expenditure of either labor or money. In many areas of the South natural vegetation was so abundant that, as one contemporary noted, "The [sheep] require no feed, summer or winter. . . ." "We raise our hogs by allowing them to range in our woods, where they get fat . . . on acorns. . . ," insisted a South Carolinian. "The cost of raising cattle amounts to nothing more than the time consumed in marking and branding," claimed a man from northeastern Texas. "Cattle require no feeding. In spring and summer, the grass upon the prairies furnishes excellent grazing, and the wild rye, cane, and winter-grass in the bottoms, furnish food during the winter. . . . Hogs are never fattened upon corn, from the fact that they fatten themselves in the woods, upon acorns, which, of course, is the cheapest method of producing pork and bacon. Bacon and pork fattened upon acorns is considered by many as being sweeter and better flavored than that fattened upon corn."[29]

The herdsmen's life-style had another peculiar attribute as well: the wealth of the grazers was largely invisible to outside observers. From James Boswell's account of his travels through Scotland with Samuel Johnson in the eighteenth century until Frederick Law Olmsted's account of his travels through the South in the 1850s travelers uniformly reported scenes of poverty and squalor among the open-range herdsmen. All saw the cattle and hogs roaming the woods but noted them only incidentally or in passing; Olmsted, typically, saw only poverty by day and ate good pork every night. To this day there are "poor farmers" from west Florida to Colorado who appear, to the untrained eye, to be quite impoverished, but whose wealth in animals foraging the woods is such that the authors—and most of our readers—would readily exchange net worths with them.

Finally, there was, complementary to the commons or open-range system, a tradition of driving great herds over long distances to market—a tradition antedating the Chisholm trail by centuries. The origins of the cattle and hog drives were in thievery; for several centuries prior to the Act of Union in 1707 many Highland and several Lowland clans had made their livelihood by going south, stealing stock, and driving herds long distances to secluded and well-protected places. (It was mainly for that reason that the prejudice against sheep and goats developed; those animals were noisy and difficult to drive at night and thus harder to steal than the more tractable cows and pigs.) Over the years the rustlers' trails were worn into roads, and when England and Scotland were merged, the same roads were used to drive animals long distances to markets in the Midlands, London, and the south of England.[30] By the middle of the eighteenth century, when the Scotch-Irish and the Scots were arriving in America in large numbers, the long drive to market was an established norm. By 1800 drives originating in the Carolina uplands terminated in Savannah, Charleston, Norfolk, and Philadelphia; animals were being driven from the Shenandoah Valley to Richmond and Baltimore; and herds were driven from Tennessee and Kentucky to Pittsburgh, Baltimore, and Philadelphia. After the War of 1812 drives were extended to the rapidly expanding lower South.[31]

By the 1830s the "industry" had become regularized into a pattern that was to prevail for a half century or more and had begun to be specialized as well. As farmers joined the herdsmen in populating a particular area the two became complementary: that is, far from displacing the herdsmen, or ranking above them as the Turner and Phillips schools maintained, many farmers were dependent upon the drovers as their principal market and geared their production to the drovers' needs by producing corn for fattening the livestock just before marketing. The principal farm crop raised by the sturdy yeoman of North Carolina, Mississippi, and Tennessee thus came to be not cotton but corn; indeed, more than half the cultivated acreage in the South in the 1850s was devoted to raising corn, first and foremost for feeding to animals, mainly hogs, just before and during the drives. "For the want of a market," noted a Kentucky farmer, "we are compelled to feed our grain to horses, mules, cattle, and hogs, and thus we realize about 20 cents per bushel for corn, which is a profit of about 100 per cent on the cost. Our grasses and clover yield about the same profit in livestock."[32]

Fortunately, we have one excellent account of what the great antebellum southern pig drives were like—and from a most unexpected source. Edmund Cody Burnett, the distinguished editor and historian of the Continental Congress, grew up in the Scotch-Irish area of the French Broad River of eastern Tennessee, and toward the end of his life he wrote up and published an account of hog driving in his home area. His own memories went back to the 1870s, he had interviewed oldtimers who could remember the 1850s, and meticulous research carried him another twenty years—and to the conclusion that methods had remained fundamentally the same throughout the nineteenth century.[33]

The French Broad River (now largely flooded by the Douglas Dam in the TVA system) meandered for twenty-five to thirty miles between Newport and Dandridge, and its bottom lands were of varying width. In that area 20,000 to 30,000 hogs were fattened for market every year, which means *a thousand hogs a mile.* Hog drives originating there and in the surrounding countryside went along the French Broad Road to Asheville, North Carolina, a distance of about fifty-five miles, and involved 150,000 to 160,000 hogs a year. Many hogs were butchered in Asheville, but many more were driven on elsewhere, for Asheville was a gathering place from which drives were continued to Savannah, Charleston, Norfolk, and the plantations in between.

Burnett also provides information about how the business had become specialized by mid-century and how the dirt farmers fitted into the larger scheme of things. East of the mountains, for example, the people who conducted the drives were called drovers, for herdsmen there took their own stock to market. In the west the drives were conducted by people who specialized in that function and were called drivers, as opposed to the drovers who "raised" the animals in the traditional way. Hog drives normally took place between August and November (cattle drives, at least in the Ohio country, began when the hog drives ended). Drives were in herds of 300 to 2,000 hogs, the average being about 400. Normally there was one "pigboy" for every hundred head of swine, plus a manager for every herd. Hogs could be driven eight to ten miles a day; they stopped at night at stock stands or hog "hotels." The best-known stand in the area—famous "from Cincinnati to Charleston"—was that at Alexander, some ten miles north of Asheville, built about 1828 by Captain James Mitchell Alexander, a Revolutionary War veteran, and operated fifty years later by his descendants. The Alexander stand contained stores and a variety of manufactories, and could accommodate 4,000 hogs and fifty men at a time.

There were fifteen hog hotels on the fifty-five-mile road from Big Creek to Asheville, and their practices were fairly uniform. It took eight bushels of corn per hundred hogs per day on the drives—meaning 25,000 bushels a year for the hogs driven on the French Broad Road—and most of the corn was supplied to the standkeepers by neighboring farmers. The standkeepers paid the farmers fifty cents a bushel and charged the drivers seventy-five cents a bushel. The drivers paid either in due bills or in lame hogs at the South Carolina market prices. Hog prices, in turn, hinged on cotton prices, roughly at a ratio of one to two. That is, if cotton was at fourteen cents a pound, hogs were seven cents on the hoof. (Presumably, the price of hogs was geared to the price of other staples elsewhere.) The driver obviously took some chances in buying hogs from the drovers, for staple prices did fluctuate during the driving season. Too, he had to reckon both on the cost of boarding his animals and on the weight losses on the drives: from Big Creek to Asheville, over the mountains, 200-pound hogs would lose on the average twelve pounds, but from Asheville to South Carolina markets they would hold their weight or even gain weight.

There is every reason to believe that Burnett's account of the French Broad region is applicable to so many areas in the South as to constitute a virtually universal pattern. Gray points out that in the late 1830s and throughout the 1840s as many as 55,000 hogs passed over Point Mountain, North Carolina, that upwards of 80,000 were driven through Cumberland Gap (the "Kaintuck Hog Road"), 60,000 apiece through Buford's Gap and on the Kanawha route, and 40,000 to Alabama and Georgia, from Kentucky alone. Patterns of the drives began to shift somewhat by the 1850s, with the development of packinghouses in Louisville, Cincinnati, Nashville, Gallatin, and a number of other places on navigable rivers. But the drives themselves continued and grew greater every year.[34]

Because livestock, and especially hogs, constituted such an important product of the antebellum South—though neither contemporary observers nor later historians have been fully aware of this fact—it behooves us, we believe, to consider some of the implications thereof. The first implication, for historians, is that we and our graduate students should be turned loose to forage the sources even as the hogs were turned loose to forage the oak ridges and the piney woods. Doubtiess, there are in the publications and manuscripts of small, local historical societies reminiscences as valuable as Burnett's, and there must be other sources that are equally valuable—as a perusal of Owsley's and Hilliard's footnotes suggests.

Another implication is that the history of southern land laws and land-tenure practices, and perhaps those of the entire United States, needs thorough restudy, despite the tons of ink that have been spilled on the subject. Walter Webb once said that an enterprising graduate student could make quite a reputation for himself by doing a history of the law of riparian rights in America. Such a student could do even better by doing a study of grazing rights, fencing laws, and related matters.

Still another set of implications has to do with the importance of droving in assessing the economic and social impact of the Civil War and Reconstruction. The capital losses in the form of animals destroyed by both Confederate and Union troops during the war were as important to the drovers, relatively, as were the capital losses to the planters that resulted from emancipation. In South Carolina, for example, the hog population was reduced from 965,000 in 1860 to possibly no more than 150,000 at war's end. In describing the "devastation" of South Carolina by the Federal army, one observer noted that "the larger portion of the Country . . . [has been] utterly stript of its Stock. . . ." Eight years after the war there were still only 332,000 hogs in the state.[35]

The recovery of grazers in most other parts of the South seems to have been equally slow despite their life-style, which required little in the way of cash capital, land, or labor. In 1860 the South had raised two-thirds of the nation's swine, but in 1880 it raised less than half. And these figures tell only part of the story. Eight of the former slave states produced some 2,600,000 fewer hogs in 1880 than they had in 1860. Only in southern states with relatively small black populations and where there had been little fighting during the Civil War were there significant gains in the number of hogs between 1860 and 1880.[36]

Though these statistics are suggestive, more research is needed to determine exactly what happened to the herdsman and his way of life in the decades after the Civil War. It has long been a cliché that the "poor white"—by which, it should now be clear, is often meant herdsmen—oppressed blacks as intensely as they did because blacks were the only people beneath them on the social scale, and the poor white intended to keep them there. Yet another reason also seems plausible, at least as far as herdsmen were concerned. The freedmen threatened the open-range system far more seriously than had the likes of Edmund Ruffin; they foraged widely and stole and butchered the hogs and cattle they found roaming the woods. "We cannot raise a turkey, chicken, or a hog," reported James H. Clanton of Alabama in 1871. He had quit raising livestock "in consequence of the stealing by the negroes" and was paying twenty-five cents a pound for bacon that had sold for five cents before the war because "We dare not turn stock out at all."[37] In 1868 a Freedmen's Bureau official noted that livestock owners in his South Carolina district "still complain that their hogs and hens disappear; and, during my official term of fifteen months, I procured the liberation of, perhaps, twenty negro thieves from jail, . . . while at least as many more were sentenced by the courts. . . ." Liberation was usually contingent upon the accused leaving the area. "Andy [a freedman who] had stolen a pig . . . was in jail, awaiting trial," observed this same official; "but the sheriff was willing to release him on condition that he would take a [labor] contract out of the State. . . ."[38]

Complaints against black thieves were widespread throughout the Reconstruction period.[39]

All in all, [admitted Vernon Lane Wharton, a liberal scholar] the source of the great majority of the Negro's trouble with the law from 1865 to 1890 was his penchant for petty thievery. . . . With the coming of freedom sheer poverty and hunger gave an added incentive for such forays. The Negro found himself surrounded by temptation. Effective fences were rare, and hogs, sheep, turkeys, and cattle wandered untended in the uncultivated stretches of almost every plantation. The theft of such livestock, frequent enough in ordinary times, increased to alarming proportions in years of poor crops.[40]

In 1867, for example, the Federal army commander in Mississippi reported: "The crop . . . having gathered, the freedmen are now idle, and without, in a great majority of instances, means of support. The result is great complaints from every section of the state of depredations being committed on live stock, hogs, sheep and cattle." Exasperated owners of animals sought ways to protect their property. A newspaper editor wrote: "Our advice to hog-raisers is, if a man is found under very suspicious circumstances in the woods, drop him, and let the buzzards hold an inquest over his remains." Wharton concluded that "The result of such agitation was the passage by the first Democratic legislature of a bill which declared the theft of any property valued at more than ten dollars, or of any kind of cattle or swine, regardless of value, to be grand larceny, subjecting the thief to a term up to five years in the state penitentiary. This was the famous 'pig law,' which was largely responsible for an increase in the populaiton of the state prison from 272 in 1874 to 1,072 at the end of 1877."[41]

To move to a somewhat grander plane, the persistence and the importance of the drover suggests that he may have had a great deal to do with shaping that elusive but quite real quality known as the southern character. Indeed, we believe that Phillips's famous aphorism—that it was "the inescapable presence of the Negro" that made the South what it was—may be in want of revision, for the ineradicable presence of the Scotch-Irish drover seems at least equally influential. The drover was an independent cuss, for his wealth was mobile, he had the use of the land of even the greatest planters, he was much less dependent upon the weather than farmers were, and there was always a demand for his product. His life-style encouraged leisure rather than the compulsive pursuit of wealth that dominated both the northern commercial man and (despite their protests to the contrary) most southern planters as well; to the outsider, caught up in the race for profits, the herdsman appeared to be both indolent and shiftless.[42] His unhurried pace was reflected in his manners, in his speech, and in the very way he walked. Courteous, modest, and even deferential, he could yet be deadly if provoked, and the readiest way to provoke him was to treat him or his kin disrespectfully; he never forgot or forgave an insult. Though far from class-conscious, at least in a Marxian sense, he was proud and possessed of strong ethnic and racial prejudices and was intensely clannish and suspicious of outsiders. His hostility to governmental restraint was as striking as his skill in the political arts.

Finally, a word is in order about "models" of southern society and of American society as a whole. By and large southern historians have been more wholesomely skeptical of artificial social models than other historians have been. But abstract models, those of U. B. Phillips and F. J. Turner, have also dominated the descriptions and understanding of southern society. Phillips's model of a society organized on vertical and ambitional lines is highly questionable; what is needed, instead, is an organic model that takes into account the fact that society was organized around symbiotic and functional relationships. Turner's horizontal model of "stages of development" in frontier after frontier is equally questionable. Much of what Turner and his disciples regarded as uniquely southern or uniquely American characteristics, bred on the ever-passing frontier, were actually Celtic characteristics that predated both the South and the American frontier by many centuries.

Notes

1. *Agriculture of the United States in 1860 . . . Compiled from . . . the Eighth Census . . .* (Washington, 1864), 184-87; *Report of the Commissioner of Patents, for the Year 1850:* Part II, *Agriculture* (Washington, 1851), 260; cited hereinafter as *Patent Office Report, 1850.* The average price for middling upland cotton between 1856 and 1860 was 11.5 cents on the New York market and 6.7 cents on the Liverpool market. The weighted average price in 1860 on the New Orleans market was 11.1 cents per pound. M. B. Hammond, *The Cotton Industry: An Essay in American Economic History* (New York, 1897), Appendix I; Lewis C. Gray, *History of Agriculture in the Southern United States to 1860* (2 vols., Washington, 1933), II, 1027. For this study an average price of 10 cents per pound was used. It should be noted that cotton prices fluctuated "as much as 5 cents per pound—and more—throughout the season in every market. . . ." Harold D. Woodman, *King Cotton & His Retainers—Financing & Marketing the Cotton Crop of the South, 1800-1925* Lexington, 1968), 19-20.

This essay presents a tentative and a preliminary statement of a thesis on this and related subjects on which we are currently doing research toward a book. We offer it now, complete with possible imperfections, on the ground that it will be several years before we publish the book and we would like to stimulate criticism and research in this immensly rich area right away. For critical comments and suggestions, we are grateful to Professors James C. Bonner, E. Merton Coulter, David Herbert Donald, Ari Hoogenboom, John Hebron Moore, Charles P. Roland, V. Jacque Voegeli, and Bennett H. Wall.

2. Julian A. C. Chandler *et al.*, eds., *The South in the Building of the Nation* (13 vols., Richmond, 1909-1913), V, 242-57, allot a mere fifteen pages to the animal industry of the South and only a short paragraph (125 words) to hogs; Wendell H. Stephenson and E. Merton Coulter, eds., *A History of the South* (9 vols. to date, [Baton Rouge], 1947-   ), devote only thirty of the more

than four thousand pages in these volumes to livestock. See also Francis B. Simkins and Charles P. Roland, *A History of the South* (4th ed., New York, 1972); William B. Hesseltine and David L. Smiley, *The South in American History* (2d ed., Englewood Cliffs, N.J., 1960); and Monroe L. Billington, *The American South: A Brief History* (New York, 1971). An exception to this pattern is Charles P. Roland's forthcoming volume on the recent South, which has much information on livestock and poultry production since World War II.

3. James C. Bonner, "Plantation and Farm: The Agricultural South," in Arthur S. Link and Rembert W. Patrick, eds., *Writing Southern History: Essays in Historiography in Honor of Fletcher M. Green* ([Baton Rouge], 1965), 169.

4. There are some exceptions. Gray, *History of Agriculture,* devotes many pages to livestock. So does Sam B. Hilliard, *Hog Meat and Hoecake: Food Supply in the Old South, 1840-1860* (Carbondale and Edwardsville, Ill., London, and Amsterdam, 1972). Other scholars who have not ignored the subject include John H. Moore, *Agriculture in Ante-Bellum Mississippi* (New York, 1958); James C. Bonner, *A History of Georgia Agriculture, 1732-1860* (Athens, 1964); Everett Dick, *The Dixie Frontier: A Social History of the Southern Frontier from the First Transmontane Beginnings to the Civil War* (New York, 1948); Clement Eaton, *A History of the Old South* (New York, 1949); Clement Eaton, *The Growth of Southern Civilization, 1790-1860* (New York, 1961); Paul W. Gates, *The Farmer's Age: Agriculture, 1815-1860* (New York, 1960); and, of course, Frank L. Owsley, *Plain Folk of the Old South* ([Baton Rouge], 1949). See also note 22.

5. Phillips, *American Negro Slavery: A Survey of the Supply, Employment and Control of Negro Labor as Determined by the Plantation Régime* (New York and London, 1918), 265, 276, 279, 297, 312 (quotation).

6. Phillips, *Life and Labor in the Old South* (Boston, 1929), 144-45.

7. Ibid., 99.

8. Ibid., 346, 340.

9. Ibid., 144-45.

10. Turner, "The Significance of the Frontier in American History," in Turner, *The Frontier in American History* (New York, 1920), 12.

11. Gray, *History of Agriculture,* 11, 834.

12. Owsley, *Plain Folk,* 23-50; see also Owsley, "The Pattern of Migration and Settlement on the Southern Frontier, *Journal of Southern History,* XI (May 1945), 147-76.

13. Owsley, *Plain Folk,* 27, 24.

14. Ibid., 24-25.

15. Ibid., 33-34, 25.

16. Ibid., 51.

17. Ibid., 9.

18. Billington, *Westward Expansion: A History of the American Frontier* (4th ed., New York, 1974), 315.

19. Hilliard, *Hog Meat and Hoecake,* 9, 40-45, 56-59, 92-140, *passim.*

20. Genovese, "Livestock in the Slave Economy of the Old South—A Revised View," *Agricultural History,* 36 (July 1962), 143-49.

21. John F. H. Claiborne, "A Trip Through the Piney Woods," Mississippi Historical Society, *Publications,* 9 (1906), 514-38 (quotations on pages 515 and 522); *Patent Office Report, 1850,* p. 189; Simon P. Richardson, *The Lights and Shadows of Itinerant Life: An Autobiography . . .* (Nashville and Dallas, 1901), 26-27; Charles Lanman, *Letters from the Alleghany Mountains* (New York, 1849), 153; see also William Faux, *Memorable Days in America: Being a Journal of a Tour to the United States . . .* (London, 1823), 135, 143-45; Frederick W. C. Gerstaeker, *Wild Sports in the Far West* (London and New York, 1854), 166, 214-17, 284, 293; [J. Goldsmith], *The Present State of the British Empire in Europe, America, Africa and Asia* (London, 1768), 323, 361, 373; Charles W. Janson, *The Stranger in America . . .* (London, 1807), 186; Francois A. Michaux, *Travels to the West of the Allegheny Mountains . . .* (Paris, 1804), 236-37, 239, 257; Frederick L.

Olmsted, *A Journey in the Seaboard Slave States with Remarks on Their Economy* (New York, 1856), 65-66, 100, 271, 709; John F. D. Smyth, *Tour in the United States of America* . . . (2 vols., London 1784), I, 161; David B. Warden, *A Statistical, Political, and Historical Account of the United States of North America*... (3 vols., Edinburgh, 1819), II, 215, 221, 339, 362, 390, 391; III, 18, 149-50, 257, 341.

22. Gray, *History of Agriculture*, II, 831-57; Bidwell and Falconer, *History of Agriculture in the Northern United States, 1620-1860* (Washington, 1925), 387, 388, 398, 438, 440; Hilliard, *Hog Meat and Hoecake*, 92-140; Moore, *Agriculture in Ante-Bellum Mississippi*; Herbert Weaver, *Mississippi Farmers, 1850-1860* (Nashville, 1945); Blanche H. Clark, *The Tennessee Yeoman, 1840-1860* (Nashville, 1942); Cornelius O. Cathey, *Agricultural Developments in North Carolina, 1783-1860* (Chapel Hill, 1956); James W. Thompson, *A History of Livestock Raising in the United States, 1607-1860* (Washington, 1942); James G. Leyburn, *The Scotch-Irish: A Social History* (Chapel Hill, 1962); Marcus L. Hansen, *The Atlantic Migration, 1607-1860: A History of Continuing Settlement of the United States* (Cambridge, Mass., 1940); Ian C. C. Graham, *Colonists from Scotland: Emigration to North America, 1707-1783* (Ithaca, 1956); Barnes F. Lathrop, *Migration into East Texas, 1835-1860: A Study from the United States Census* (Austin, 1949).

23. Coulter states that although planters "kept some hogs, in many parts of the Lower South many people had a prejudice against raising swine, probably because they thought it was not dignified." Coulter, *The Confederate States of America, 1861-1865* ([Baton Rouge], 1950), 246. It would be foolish to raise livestock, an Alabama planter thought, "for cotton at 10 to 12½ cents per pound is much more profitable." And a Mississippian claimed that planters "could, were we not so absorbed in cotton raising, raise hogs enough for our own meat. A few sensible old farmers do this, but the most of us abandon every thing for the sake of cotton, and so we depend almost entirely upon the more northern States to furnish us with this most essential commodity," *Patent Office Report, 1850*, pp. 301-302, 187-88.

24. Leyburn, *The Scotch-Irish*, and Lathrop, *Migration into East Texas*, provide much information on this pattern of movement. In 1790 Scots and Scotch-Irishmen (including those from outside Ulster) already constituted just under a fourth of the total white population of the South, and they may well have formed a majority in those parts of the South emphasized in the text; extrapolated from "Report of Committee on Linguistic and National Stocks in the Population of the United States," American Historical Association, *Annual Report, 1931*, I (Washington, 1932), 107-408, but especially 206-70. The geographical distribution of the Scots and Scotch-Irish in 1776 can be inferred from the religious maps in Charles O. Paullin, *Atlas of the Historical Geography of the United States*, edited by John K. Wright (Washington, 1932), plates 82-88; virtually all of the Presbyterians and many of the southern Baptists were of Scots background. The maps for 1860 are suggestive but less conclusive. Customarily, at least until the Tennessee frontier was reached, westward and southwestward migration was not a generalized movement of the whole Scotch-Irish population with existing frontiersmen leading the way. Rather, the latest arrivals moved farthest out on the frontier. Highland Scots followed a different pattern: they headed straight for the interior of North Carolina and were much less mobile.

25. R. A. Gailey, "Agrarian Improvement and the Development of Enclosure in the Southwest Highlands of Scotland," *Scottish Historical Review*, 42 (October 1963), 105-25; James E. Handley, *Scottish Farming in the Eighteenth Century* (London, 1953); Leyburn, *The Scotch-Irish*; T. C. Smout, *A History of the Scottish People, 1560-1830* (New York, 1969).

26. Gray, *History of Agriculture*, II, 843; William K. Scarborough, ed., *The Diary of Edmund Ruffin* (1 vol. to date, Baton Rouge, 1972-), I, 150, 358.

27. Michaux, *Travels to the West of the Allegheny Mountains*, 236-39; Gray, *History of Agriculture*, II, 843; Cathey, *Agricultural Developments in North Carolina*, 51*n*; Moore, *Agriculture in Ante-Bellum Mississippi*, 62-63; Olmsted, *Journey in the Seaboard Slave States*, 709; Edmund C. Burnett, "Hog Raising and Hog Driving in the Region of the French Broad River," *Agricultural History*, 20 (April 1946), 95; interview with Valton G. Midgett, Rodanthe, Outer Banks,

North Carolina, August 28, 1974; Charles P. Roland to the authors, June 26, 1974; interview with John Henry Cassidy, Walton County, Florida, March 1974; James C. Bonner to the authors, July 19, 1974. E. Merton Coulter, *The South During Reconstruction, 1865-1877* ([Baton Rouge], 1947), 228, traces the gradual development of local-option laws after the Civil War.

28. Owsley, *Plain Folk*, 34; Hilliard, *Hog Meat and Hoecake*, 117.

29. *Patent Office Report, 1850*, pp. 260, 233, 189.

30. Archibald R. B. Haldane, *The Drove Roads of Scotland* (London and New York, 1952), 2-46, 199-201. An additional reason for the prejudice against sheep and goats, as many historians have observed, was the southerner's habit of keeping hunting dogs. A Virginian also reported that wolves ate the sheep in his area, but a Georgian stated that the people in his region were unwilling to raise sheep on a large scale, "owing to the depredations of dogs," and a North Carolinian, who had lost sheep to dogs, wished for "extermination of the whole canine race." *Patent Office Report, 1850*, pp. 367, 395, 369.

31. Data regarding drives are from travel accounts, such as Johann David Schopf, *Travels in the Confederation, [1783-1784]*, translated and edited by Alfred J. Morrison (2 vols., Philadelphia, 1811), II, 108-10, and those cited in note 21. A map showing the main droving routes is in Hilliard, *Hog Meat and Hoecake*, 194.

32. Gray, *History of Agriculture*, II, 837; Clark, *Tennessee Yeoman*, 126; *Patent Office Report, 1850*, pp. 266-67.

33. This and the three following paragraphs are derived from Burnett, "Hog Raising and Hog Driving," 86-103; see also the same author's delightful, "The Hog Drivers' Play-Song and Some of Its Relatives," *Agricultural History*, 23 (July 1949), 161-68.

34. Gray, *History of Agriculture*, II, 840-41; *Report of the Commissioner of Patents, for the Year 1847* (Washington, 1848), 531-34. About one-fourth of all the hogs slaughtered by packing-houses were processed in or around Cincinnati.

35. James Chesnut, Jr., to Jefferson Davis, March 15, 1865, Jefferson Davis Papers (Duke University Library, Durham, N. C.); Francis B. Simkins and Robert H. Woody, *South Carolina During Reconstruction* (Chapel Hill, 1932), 258. On the theft and destruction of livestock by Union and Confederate forces in states other than South Carolina see Nimrod Porter Diary, January 16, 19, 23, February 15, March 5, 16, 22, 26, 27, 1865 (Southern Historical Collection, University of North Carolina Library, Chapel Hill, N.C.); John Houston Bills Diary, July 10, 12, September 26, October 19, 26, November 29, December 3, 10, 1863; January 20, March 7, May 1, July 4, 20, August 8, October 18, 1864, John Houston Bills Papers (Southern Historical Collection); Bayside Plantation Record, May 3, 1863 (Southern Historical Collection); S. L. Norwood to Walter W. Lenoir, April 24, 1865 (typed copy), Lenoir Family Papers (Southern Historical Collection); Bell I. Wiley, *The Plain People of the Confederacy* (Baton Rouge, 1944), 21-23.

36. *Report on the Productions of Agriculture as Returned at the Tenth Census (June 1, 1880)* (Washington, 1883), 4-5; *Agriculture of the United States in 1860*, pp. 184-87. In 1880 every former slave state except Arkansas, Delaware, Florida, Missouri, and Texas had fewer hogs than in 1860. The big gainers were Missouri (over 2,000,000), Texas (nearly 580,000), and Arkansas (nearly 400,000). The big losers were Virginia (nearly 133,000, without counting the 511,000 hogs credited to West Virginia in 1880); Georgia (565,000), North Carolina (430,000), Alabama (496,000), Mississippi (381,000), South Carolina (338,000), Tennessee (187,000), and Kentucky (105,000).

37. Quoted in Walter L. Fleming, ed., *Documentary History of Reconstruction* (2 vols., Cleveland, 1907), II, 279.

38. J. W. DeForest, "The Man and Brother," *Atlantic Monthly*, 22 (September and October 1868), 344, 415.

39. See for example Porter Diary, January 22, March 23, August 20, 26, September 15, 26, October 15, December 7, 1865; January 12, September 24, 1866; Bills Diary, August 21, 1863; October 25, 1866; Everard Green Baker Diary, April 20, 1867 (Southern Historical Collection).

40. Wharton, *The Negro in Mississippi, 1865-1890* (New York, Evanston, and London, 1965), 236-37.

41. Ibid., 237.

42. A full (and typical) description of the "poor white" is in Simkins and Roland, *History of the South*, 138-39. If allowance is made for a bit of exaggeration and minor errors this account accurately captures many qualities of the southern herdsmen. They were not as a rule, however, either Anglo-Saxon or impoverished, as Simkins and Roland describe the poor white as being.

Robert R. Russel

The Effects of Slavery upon Nonslaveholders

Perhaps no interpretation of the economic history of American Negro slavery is more generally accepted today than that the institution was detrimental to the nonslaveholding whites of the South. There have been frequent expressions of the view that the master class knew its own interest. Occasional admissions of doubt that emancipation conferred economic benefits upon the typical Negro are encountered, but it would be difficult to find any divergence from the opinion that the peculiar institution was a curse to the nonslaveholding whites. The fact that the latter did not become abolitionists is usually attributed to ignorance of their own interests, domination by the slaveholders, racial prejudice, or fond expectations of rising into the master class.[1] It is the purpose of this article to attempt to show that the commonly accepted interpretation requires great qualification to bring it into accord with the truth.

In 1860 approximately one-fourth of the white families of the South were slaveholding and three-fourths nonslaveholding; and of the slaveholding families a great many had only one or two slaves each. In earlier years of the period, the proportion of slaveholders was slightly larger.

The slaves and slaveholders were very largely concentrated in belts—the so-called black belts—which coincided with the areas devoted to the growing of staples, chiefly cotton, tobacco, sugar and rice.[2] There were also many slaves in the cities and towns in or near the staple-growing areas. These had been marked out by climate, the character of the soil, and, not least, by accessibility

Source: Critical Studies in Antebellum Sectionalism by Robert R. Russel, used with the permission of the publisher, Greenwood Press, Inc. The selection appeared originally in *Agricultural History*, 15 (April 1941): 54–71. Reprinted by permission of the Agricultural History Society and the author.

to market. Cotton, for example, for climatic reasons could not be grown to advantage north of an irregular line crossing North Carolina, Tennessee, and Arkansas. South of this line cotton was grown on the better lands which lay within reasonable distances of navigable rivers or of railroads. Some of the best of the present-day cotton lands were not utilized for that crop as late as 1860, because they were too far from navigable rivers while railroads had not yet penetrated into their vicinity.[3]

The great majority of the nonslaveholding whites lived outside the principal staple-growing districts in what is commonly called back, up, or hill country, or in mountainous regions. In these areas there were comparatively few slaves. The people were mostly small farmers and, because of lack of markets or inaccessibility to them, were engaged in a more or less self-sufficing agriculture with much household manufacturing.

It is difficult to see how people living in the back country could be injured by slavery in the black belts. Except possibly to a slight extent and in a most indirect way, it was not slavery which prevented them from producing staple crops for market; it was inaccessibility. Such markets as they had for their surplus bacon, lard, mules, whiskey, etc. were chiefly among the planters or in the towns which served the staple-producing districts. In so far as it was slavery which caused planters to concentrate on the growing of the great market crops while purchasing various supplies elsewhere, the institution created markets for back-country farmers and thus benefited them.

It is said that slavery had driven nonslaveholding whites out of the black belts and out of staple production and had thus worked them a great injury; that, had it not been for slavery, more of them would have lived in the staple-producing regions and raised the great market crops and would have had a higher standard of living on that account.

This time-honored indictment of the peculiar institution has such great plausibility that its validity has seldom been questioned. The black belts were a fact. Even nonslaveholding whites who lived in the staple-growing areas did not produce the staples in quantities proportionate to their numbers. Virtually all the sugar and rice and the bulk of the cotton and tobacco were produced by slave labor. In 1850, according to J. D. B. DeBow, there were about 800,000 slaves engaged in cotton growing and only about 100,000 whites, and there is no reason to doubt the essential accuracy of his estimate.[4] Much the greater part of the cash farm income of the South was received by a comparatively small number of planters, all of whom employed slave labor, of course. In the cotton States in 1850, according to William E. Dodd, "A thousand families received over $50,000,000 a year, while all the remaining 666,000 families received only about $60,000,000."[5] This may also be accepted as approximately accurate. Yet, in spite of such prima facie evidence, the contention that slavery drove nonslaveholding whites out of staple production and thus did them a great injury contains considerably less than a half truth. Both the extent to which slavery excluded nonslaveholding whites from commercialized agriculture and the extent of the injury caused by such exclusion have been greatly exaggerated.

It is recognized at the outset that the problem involves not only the question of the comparative effectiveness of Negro slave labor and free white labor, but also that of the efficiency of the plantation as compared with the small farm as a unit of agricultural organization. The plantations of the ante bellum South were operated with slave labor almost exclusively. Almost all white agricultural workers were employed on small farms; very few served as wage earners on plantations. Moreover, the plantation system could not have existed extensively in the ante bellum South without slave labor, for the simple reason that, where land was cheap and plentiful and it was easy to become an independent farmer, free whites would not work for low enough wages, in large enough numbers, and with a sufficient degree of regularity to permit large-scale farming.[6] White indentured servitude, with which the earliest plantations had been started, was an impossibility in the ante bellum period. Therefore, any competitive advantages which the plantation may have possessed over the small farm as a unit of farm organization must be accredited to the institution of slavery.

In sugar and rice culture the plantation undoubtedly had great competitive advantages over the small farm.[7] Sugar growers who owned sugar-making machinery had a great advantage over those who did not, and the machinery was so expensive that only large producers could afford it. The cost of building levees also was conducive to large-scale operations. The plantation had similar advantages over the small farm in rice growing. Since plantations would have been impossible without slavery, it is proper to conclude that slavery kept small farmers from growing sugar cane and rice or, at least and more probably, from growing other crops on lands which were actually devoted to sugar and rice.

In the growing of cotton and tobacco, however—and these staples employed about eight slaves to every one in sugar and rice—it is very doubtful that the plantation was superior to the small farm as a unit of agricultural production.[8] The planter might buy supplies, sell his produce, and obtain credit—a very doubtful advantage—on somewhat better terms than the small farmer. Joseph C. Robert has described the marketing of tobacco in ante bellum Virginia in great detail. The buyers were very numerous, widely distributed, and quite competitive. The planter seems to have had little advantage over the small farmer in selling his product.[9] In a newer community where marketing facilities were not so well developed, the advantage of the large-scale farmer in buying and selling may have been considerable. In a district where the large planters bought and sold through nonresident merchants or agents and the small farmers were too few and too poor to support competitive buyers and retail merchants adequately, the small farmers would receive considerably less than the planters for what they might sell and pay considerably more for what they might buy.[10]

The planter was able to effect a division of labor among his hands that was not possible on a small farm, but the operations and the machinery required in farming in those days were too simple to permit any considerable advantage to be gained from that. In fact the division of labor on a large plantation tended to become fixed and, by its inflexibility, may have impaired rather than promoted efficiency. For example, there would have been a moral difficulty about sending a dignified coachman to the field to plow or "chop." A farm worker of a reasonable degree of competence probably increases his efficiency by making the frequent changes from one sort of common task to another which are necessary on the farm.

The slaveholder had no compunctions about putting female slaves in the field gangs. White women and girls of small-farm families also worked in the fields to a considerable extent. Frederick Law Olmsted reported: "I have, in fact, seen more white native American women at work in the hottest sunshine in a single month, and that near mid-summer, in Mississippi and Alabama than in all my life in the Free States, not on account of an emergency, as in harvesting, either, but in the regular cultivation of cotton and of corn, chiefly of cotton."[11] However, white farm women and girls certainly did not go into the fields as regularly as slave women and girls. The planter had an advantage here as far as production of field crops was concerned.

The cotton planter usually had his own gin and press while his small-farm neighbor had to pay toll. Whether the planter had a competitive advantage in his ownership depended upon the tolls paid by the farmer. The advantage may have been the other way. Other implements and tools used in cotton production and the implements and tools used in tobacco farming were too simple and cheap to give any advantage to the large-scale farmer in their use; it would be a poor farmer indeed who could not afford a plow and a mule.

These competitive advantages of the plantation over the farm, to the extent that they existed, were at least partially offset by certain disadvantages. The overhead expenses of the large planter were proportionally greater than those of the small farmer. The large planter had to hire an overseer or overseers and often had various other functionaries such as manager, foreman, drivers, and yard boy. The production and curing of tobacco required especially close supervision because care in handling greatly affected the quality, which was an important factor in determining price. The number of slaves which could be supervised efficiently by one overseer was, therefore, small.[12] The planter himself, the mistress, and the sons and daughters did not ordinarily engage in physical labor, as did members of the small-farm family. The plantation house was often literally overrun with domestic servants.

If large-scale farming had possessed any considerable competitive advantages over small-scale farming in producing cotton and tobacco, there would not have been so many small farms and small plantations devoted to their production. Perhaps one-half the cotton was grown on farms where there were either no slaves at all or fewer than ten or a dozen.[13] Such farms were too small to possess in any material degree the alleged advantages of large-scale production. Probably an even larger percentage of Southern tobacco was produced on small farms or small plantations. Robert has shown that even in Charlotte County, Virginia, where, in 1850, the average size of the tobacco farms was greater than in any other county of the State, about 53 percent of the crop was produced on plantations employing not more than ten or twelve hands. Robert presents a frequency table showing for seven Virginia counties the number of farms which produced tobacco in 1859 in quantities falling within each of several sets of limits. This table seems to show that, except that farms with two hands were more numerous than those with one—probably because large families were more numerous than small—the numbers of tobacco farms employing the several respective numbers of hands varied in regular fashion inversely with the numbers of hands employed.[14] If the plantation had possessed any appreciable advantages over the smaller farm this inverse variation would not have been so regular.

The laborers employed on the typical small farm, that is the members of the white farm family, were almost certainly as efficient as the slaves on the plantations, if and when the whites chose to exert themselves to a reasonable extent. The qualification is essential, for many whites did not choose to exert themelves very much. In the days of the great slavery debate, Southern controversialists often enthusiastically asserted that their slaves constituted the best trained and most efficient labor force in the world. An occasional model writer has placed a high estimate on the effectiveness of the slaves.[15] The typical slave was certainly a more effective worker than the free Negro after emancipation,[16] but the great weight of the evidence is that slaves were not as efficient as white workers of good quality. Ulrich B. Phillips seems to have aptly characterized slave efficiency: "The generality of planters, it would seem, considered it hopeless to make their field hands into thorough workmen or full-fledged men, and contented themselves with very moderate achievement. Tiring of endless correction and unfruitful exhortation, they relied somewhat supinely upon authority with a tone of kindly patronage and a baffled acquiescence in slack service."[17] The fathers of the Constitution expressed the prevailing estimate of their time regarding the relative productiveness of whites and slaves in the famous three-fifths clause.[18] Olmsted, in the 1850s, thought slaves were not nearly so effective as white farm workers in New York State.[19]

It has been quite common for writers, in trying to determine the relative efficiency of Negro slave labor and free white labor, to compare the slaves with the white wage labor of the plantation regions, but this method is unsound. The plantation slaves were of average quality. The wage earners were usually the poorest quality of whites, who worked neither very hard nor very regularly.[20]

Whites of any competence either got land and farmed on their own account or found other employment which was more remunerative than farm labor for hire.

Slave labor was efficient enough, if employed at tasks for which it was adapted, to produce for the masters, taking one year with another, an appropriable surplus over the cost of maintenance. However, the appropriable surplus of the individual slave was normally so small that a master could not enjoy a large income unless he had a large number of slaves.[21] A farmer with a few slaves worked along with them and made a somewhat better living than his neighbor who had no slaves. A farmer with a larger number of slaves might escape physical toil and enjoy a still higher standard of living. Only the great planters could live in a liberal style. The evidence seems conclusive that planters with fewer than about fifteen slaves did not live well.[22]

Except, then, in special cases like sugar and rice where much capital other than slaves was required for effective production, the much touted advantage of the plantation with slave labor over the small farm with white labor reduces to about this: The plantation could not produce more in proportion to land and equipment or to the number of hands employed; if large enough it could produce more goods and leisure for the white family. That, in all common sense, was why people acquired slaves and ran plantations. The small farm with reasonably good management and reasonable industry on the part of members of the farm family afforded at least as high a standard of living as the plantation afforded the planter family and the slaves averaged together.

Why, then, if Negro slave labor was not inherently superior to free white labor, and if the plantation possessed little, if any, competitive advantage over the small farm as a unit of agricultural organization, did nonslaveholding whites fail to produce a larger share of the cotton and tobacco? There were several reasons.

First and foremost come the major matters of enterprise and managerial ability. Nowadays, the more competent and industrious farmers in any community generally get the better land and larger acreages. In slavery days in the South, the better farmers got the more desirable lands, larger holdings, and also the slaves to work them and grew more cotton and tobacco. If a small farmer in the cotton or tobacco belt prospered by growing the staple of his region or otherwise, the natural and attractive thing to do was to buy land and slaves as he could. If he continued to thrive, he would eventually become a planter. Thus a small farmer would have been "driven out" by a planter. Of course the man who inherited land and slaves had a better chance of remaining in the planter class than one who had inherited nothing had of entering it. However, many a young man who inherited wealth in slavery days mismanaged his patrimony, lost it in whole or in part, and ended his days in "reduced" circumstances, while many a young man who started with neither land or slaves became a prosperous planter. Thomas J. Wertenbaker has shown that the planter class originated in this latter fashion in colonial times.[23] Olmsted admitted that small farmers were not debarred from becoming planters in the ante bellum period.[24] One suspects that most farmers who prospered did so not because they had come by land and slaves but because they attended to business and managed well, while most of those who failed did so because they took life too easy and managed badly. Credit has too often been given to slavery or the farm organization which rightfully belongs to the master.

Secondly, even in the staple-growing districts, the small farmers did not have as strong incentives to grow the staples for market as the planters had. They found it to their advantage to do a more general type of farming with more household manufacturing. In contrast, planters almost of necessity produced for the market. There would have been few planters if it had not been possible to grow market crops profitably on plantations. As a rule, a master will not employ a large force in a self-sufficing economy, because, after a certain volume of production has been reached, an additional application of labor can contribute but little to satisfy the wants of the farmer and his family but only to raise the standard of living of the laborers, something in which an employer is only mildly interested.[25] In a self-sufficing economy in America a family with a considerable number of slaves would have enjoyed a rude plenty and have been freed from grinding toil but would have had the various cares and worries involved in slaveholding. A family without slaves would have enjoyed the same rude plenty, and although it must have engaged in hard labor, would not have had the cares and worries of the slaveholding family. A planter in the ante bellum South produced the various necessary and desirable articles for home consumption which could be produced cheaper on the plantation than they could be bought in the market. However, the wants of the slaves were simple, perforce, and easily satisfied, and the demand of the planter's family for such articles was limited. These wants having been satisfied, the planter sought to produce as large a salable surplus as possible in order that he might command for his slaves certain things from outside the community which might be necessary for their continued efficiency and for himself and family the various articles of necessity, comfort, and luxury which could not, or at least not advantageously, be produced on the plantation. The small nonslaveholding farmer, on the contrary, found it desirable to devote a large share of his labor to the production of the numerous articles for consumption which could be produced advantageously at home, because, in proportion to numbers, the farmer family consumed larger quantities of such things than did the planter family and the slaves together.

The small farmer of the nineteenth century had a further reason for carrying on more self-sufficing activities than the planter. This was the feeling, already mentioned, that white women and girls, although allowed to work at various household industries which were just as useful and productive as plowing and hoeing, nevertheless, should not be expected to labor in the fields. The planter was under no moral pressure not to send his female slaves into the fields.

The planter had a further reason to concentrate his efforts on the growing of cotton or other staples in the fact that Negro slave labor was relatively more efficient therein than in the production of the various other things commonly produced on Southern farms in slavery days, for examples, fruit, poultry, dairy products, bacon, lard, soap, candles, whiskey, coarse textiles, clothing, and axe and hoe handles. The planter, on this account, sometimes found it to his advantage to grow more cotton or tobacco and buy other things. The small farmer and his family, on the other hand, could produce the varied articles of the general farm more effectively than could the slaves and, therefore, more often found it advantageous to produce them at home instead of buying them at the store.[26] The fact that in a given community planters specialized more in producing the great Southern staples while small farmers went in more for general farming does not of itself prove that white labor was less efficient than slave labor in cotton and tobacco, as has so often been assumed; it can just as well prove that white labor was more efficient than slave labor in general farming.

In comparisons of slave-labor plantations with small white-labor farms this simple fact has been too frequently overlooked: Even if the former had competitive advantages over the latter in the production of a crop, say cotton, the small farmers nevertheless would have grown that crop for a living if thereby they could have made a better or easier living than by producing something else. Nowadays small farmers in large areas of the South find it advisable to devote their major efforts to producing cotton, tobacco, or some other crop or crops for market while buying at the store a great variety of articles formerly produced at home; but the fact that they do so now does not prove that they would have done so in the 1830s and 1850s if it had not been for slavery. The abolition of slavery almost certainly made the Negroes of the South less effective as producers of farm products. It is certainly wrong to assume that it was the abolition of slavery only, or even principally, which gave the small farmers their "opportunity." The same general factors have operated to further commercialize agriculture in the South that have operated elsewhere, namely, cheap transportation, which has enabled people to get more for what they sell and to pay less for what they buy; the industrial revolution, which has made it possible to manufacture more and better goods in the mills and factories in towns and cities at incomparably lower costs than they can be made on farms; and the agricultural revolution, particularly the introduction of improved farm machinery, which has encouraged specialization and commercialization by making it too expensive to own machinery applicable to more than one or two crops and too great a handicap in competition not to adopt some of it.[27]

Since planters had such strong incentives to produce staple crops for market, they must remain where there was access to markets. Small farmers, who did relatively more subsistence farming regardless of location, were not under such pressure to remain in the commercialized farming districts. Therefore, if planter neighbors made attractive offers for the land, the farmers might find it to their advantage to sell and move to a more remote region where land was cheaper but about as well adapted to their type of farming.

The American people during the slavery period were already a race of land speculators. Large numbers moved to the frontier and submitted for the time to frontier living conditions with the hope that the "progress of the country" and especially the development of means of transportation would soon catch up with them and give their lands a value far in excess of the original cost. Masters with numerous slaves would not or could not be frontiersmen unless the frontier had natural facilities for transportation to market and could almost at once be reduced to cultivation. If they had debts, as most masters did, they were under strong economic compulsion to get cash incomes every year. It follows, therefore, that the proportion of small farmers in the commercialized-farming districts would tend to be reduced by this movement toward the frontier. If a few years later the planter followed the small farmer to the erstwhile frontier and bought up his farm, the farmer was not injured; at least he had done what he had hoped to do and could move on to a new frontier to repeat the process.[28]

Once a given district became rather thickly settled with masters and slaves, small farmers moved out to get away from the "niggers" and live in a neighborhood where there were more of their own kind. Repelling them from good neighborhoods was probably the principal way in which slavery worked to the economic detriment of nonslaveholding whites. Some of the best lands in the South today are being cultivated by Negroes, who are in general less efficient farmers than whites, because once the Negroes were there in great numbers, the whites would not move in.[29]

It is true, of course, that if slavery had never been established in the United States and, therefore, the plantation system had not developed extensively, the lands held by planters would have been held by small farmers who, in many instances no doubt, would have been the same persons who were planters. In that hypothetical case, being located near transportation facilities and finding prices, at least of cotton, somewhat higher than they actually were by reason of the smaller production which would have occurred, small farmers would have grown greater quantities of cotton and tobacco, but considerably less than actually were grown in the South by planters and farmers combined. In this sense, then, slavery may be said to have "driven" nonslaveholding farmers out of staple production and deprived them of an economic opportunity. This is far different from the usual implication, namely, that plantations produced a great quantity of cotton and tobacco very cheaply and thereby depressed prices so greatly that, while planters continued to make money, small white farmers could not make a living by growing the staples. Furthermore, even this concession requires qualification. It may well be that, if slavery had never been established in the South or, although established, had been abolished later, the direct benefits conferred upon small farmers by the absence or removal of competition from plantations and slaves would have been more than offset by the possible injury to the prosperity of the section as a whole.[30]

The farmer folk of the South who received the most meager rewards were the "poor whites." Slavery has so often been blamed for the condition and even the existence of the poor whites that their relation to the institution seems to require special mention.

The poor whites were the ne'er-do-wells of the Southern countryside. They were poor, ignorant, shiftless, and almost utterly lacking in pride and the desire to improve their lot. They lived on the poorer lands interspersed among the plantations and better farms or in the pine barrens, sand hills, or other undesirable locations. In some cases they owned the land they occupied, in others they were merely squatters. They lived from hand to mouth. They farmed in a feeble sort of way, raising a little corn and garden truck and keeping a few hogs. Sometimes they raised a little cotton or tobacco. They hunted and fished a little. Some of them made corn whiskey and sold it to the planters and the slaves. They did odd jobs now and then for neighboring planters or farmers but shunned steady employment. They were often suspected of doing a lot of petty stealing from their more provident neighbors. Occasionally the terms "low whites" and "mean whites" were used to denote them.[31]

The abolitionists were fond of denominating all the nonslaveholding whites of the Southern countryside as poor whites. This was a libel on the great majority of the small farmers of the section, who were reasonably industrious and self respecting and, in general, made a fairly comfortable living. There were, however, thousands of poor whites. William Gregg, a public-spirited cotton manufacturer of South Carolina, once estimated that one-third of the white population of his State belonged to the class.[32] However accurate his estimate may have been, they were found in all the Southern States and the proportion was too high in all.

There seem to have been several causes for the development of the poor-white class. The poor quality of a large proportion of the indentured servants, so numerous in the South in colonial days, may explain it in part. The comparative ease of getting a living of a sort in a country where land, at least poor land, was so cheap, where corn, vegetables, and fruits grew without much care, where game, fish, and edible wild plants abounded, and where winters were short and mild, contributed to easy-going ways. Because of various historical factors, which will readily occur to anyone familiar with American colonial history, there had not been the feeling of community responsibility in the South that there had been in Puritan New England to insist that individuals conform to community standards of industry, thrift, and morality. Perhaps the principal cause was hookworm and repeated attacks of malaria, which sapped people's vitality and robbed them of hope and ambition, although it is not entirely clear whether people became poor whites because they had contracted hookworm or got hookworm because they were poor whites. The class of poor whites in all probability would have developed if slavery had never been introduced. There are poor whites now two generations after emancipation, and in spite of a greater density of population, better health services, more varied industry, public schools, and the many inducements to exertion offered by modern civilization. Similar classes, under different names, although perhaps not so great in numbers, are to be found in other parts of the country; and, for that matter, the same general type may be found in varying proportions in every country on the globe.

However, in at least two ways slavery seems to have contributed to the formation of the poor-white class of the South. Contrary to the usual rule, many of the poorer whites might have been better off as farm laborers under supervision than as independent farmers, but slavery retarded the development of a wage-earning class in the plantation districts. Originally planters had resorted to the use of bound servants because competent free laborers were scarce in a country where it was so easy for people of any competence at all to become independent farmers on land of their own. Once slavery was firmly established in a district, it in turn discouraged the development of a free-labor class.[33] Planters preferred slaves to the poorer sort of whites. They also hesitated to attempt to use wage laborers instead of slaves, because, until a large wage-earning class should have developed, they could feel no assurance of being able to fill the vacancies that were certain to occur. Whites would not work in field gangs along with slaves under overseers. If it had not been for slavery, people with managerial ability might have made greater efforts to get the poor whites to work for wages or to rent the better lands and might have succeeded, as they did, in a measure, other things contributing, after the War for Southern Independence. By creating the black belts in ways described in preceding paragraphs, slavery created a social condition conducive to the development of such a class of poor whites. The more enterprising and intelligent of the small farmers either got out of the staple belts or graduated into the planter class leaving the less enterprising and less intelligent behind on poor lands which the planters could not use. Planters, having their own social life, took little interest in and felt little responsibility for their poor-white neighbors, except, perhaps, at election time. If the small-farmer population had remained larger, there might have been churches, more schools, and a more wholesome community life in general, which would have given some stimulus, encouragement, and aid to the weaker and less fortunate members of society.[34]

Slavery was certainly no more detrimental to nonslaveholding whites engaged in nonagricultural occupations than it was to small farmers. There seems to have been no dearth of employment in the Southern countryside for such white artisans as there were. It is true that planters often had slaves trained in various skilled crafts, and they often became excellent workmen. They were, indeed, frequently hired out by their masters to neighbors who needed their services.[35] In general, however, the Negro artisans were not as competent as the white, and the latter were preferred. It was the scarcity of the white artisans which caused planters to resort to training slaves in the trades. This scarcity, in turn, was due to the strong inducement there was all through this period for people of good quality to get land and live on it.

In the cities and towns of the slaveholding States, white wage earners had to compete with free Negroes and with Negro slaves, who were either employed in their masters' businesses, hired out by their masters to other employers, or allowed to hire their own time. Such free Negroes and slaves worked at practically every sort of task.[36] They had a monopoly of domestic service. Either because of its character, or because Negroes had so long predominated in it, or both, the whites had come to look upon such service as menial and degrading, and employers preferred the Negroes because they were more obsequious. In other occupations the whites and Negroes, sometimes of both sexes, worked side by side, usually, but not always, with some distinction in tasks in favor of the whites. For example, in the Tredegar Iron Works at Richmond, Virginia, each white master workman was given a Negro "assistant."[37]

The white workers frequently resented the presence of the blacks, either because of race prejudice, or dislike of their competition, or both, and sought to have them excluded from the pursuits concerned. There was, for example, a strike of the white workers in the Tredegar works having this object, but it was unsuccessful, as well all other efforts to exclude Negroes. Employers could not afford to allow such a principle to be established, as white workers were not sufficiently numerous and permanent in most localities to permit reliance on them alone. The use of slaves, if they belonged to the owners of the business, gave the employers assurance that operations would not be interrupted or wages forced to too high levels by strikes and withdrawals; and, even if the slaves were hired from others, the assurance was nearly as great, for still there could be no strikes, and labor contracts were usually made for a year at a time.[38]

In the skilled trades the white workingmen were more efficient and were, therefore, preferred. Negro competition was not keen.[39] In unskilled and semiskilled labor the superiority of white workers to slaves was not so great, if, indeed any existed, but in general white workers had no difficulty in getting jobs, excepting, of course, that they sought none in domestic service. As the middle period wore on and the demand for labor in the cotton and sugar belts grew, there was a tendency for slave labor to be drawn from the towns to the farms where white labor was not available, leaving places in towns open to the whites. This tendency was reinforced by the increasing difficulty of handling slaves amid urban surroundings and by the better adaptability, generally speaking, of slaves to agriculture than to urban occupations.

Nonslaveowning employers of labor in the cities had no particular disadvantage in competition with slaveowning employers as they would have had in the country, for they were able to hire either whites, slaves, free Negroes, or all three. In fact, railroad companies, manufacturing concerns, etc. usually found it necessary or desirable to start with hired labor, free or slave, because with hired labor it was not necessary to raise so much capital at the outset. Employers sometimes preferred to hire their hands also, because this permitted a selection more in accord with existing needs and enabled the employers to expand or contract their labor forces and more readily adjust production to the state of business.[40]

In slavery days the cities and towns of the South, being neither numerous nor large, derived their support principally from plantation districts, where there were many slaves, rather than from small-farming regions, where there were few. It was chiefly the planters who bought, sold, borrowed, travelled, and sent their children to academies and colleges. It seems quite certain, therefore, that if it had not been for plantations and slavery, the cities and towns of the South would have been even fewer and smaller, resulting in even less opportunity for nonslaveholding whites.

In the days of the great slavery debate, the abolitionists, when pressed closely to show how slavery injured the nonslaveholding whites, always replied that it did so by inspiring a contempt for manual labor among all whites who came in contact with it. This answer still finds favor in the textbooks. The writer has examined the contention at some length in another place and found that there was a grain of truth in it but little more than a grain.[41]

In conclusion, Negro slavery was in some respects to the economic advantage of many of the nonslaveholding whites of the slaveholding regions; in others it was to their disadvantage. To many nonslaveholding whites it was a matter of economic indifference. It is impossible to strike a balance in which confidence can be placed. It is certain that the net injury, if there was any, has commonly been grossly exaggerated. The fact that nonslaveholding whites did not seek to destroy the institution as injurius to their economic interests may only show that their common sense operating upon a familiar matter was sounder than the economics of abolitionists theorizing at a distance or of some modern historians theorizing after a long lapse of time.

Notes

1. See, for example, William E. Dodd, *The Cotton Kingdom*, 32 (New Haven, Conn., 1921).
2. Ulrich B. Phillips, "The Origin and Growth of the Southern Black Belts," *American Historical Review*, 11 (July 1906): 798-816.
3. Very illuminating on this point is Charles W. Ramsdell, "The Natural Limits of Slavery Expansion," *Mississippi Valley Historical Review*, 16 (September 1929): 151-171.
4. J. D. B. De Bow, *The Industrial Resources, etc., of the Southern and Western States*, 1 (New Orleans, 1852-1853): 175. See also A. N. J. Den Hollander, "Tradition of 'Poor Whites'" in William T. Couch, ed., *Culture in the South* (Chapel Hill, 1934), 411.

5. *Cotton Kingdom*, 24.

6. This point has been developed at greater length in Robert R. Russel, "The Economic History of Negro Slavery in the United States," *Agricultural History*, 11:308-321 (October 1937). Only whites of the poorest quality worked as farm laborers in the Old South—that is, when they worked at all. Often young men of a better sort worked for neighbors for hire (sometimes as overseers) until they could accumulate the little capital required to start farming on their own account. People who worked regularly at trades or other occupations occasionally worked for farmers at harvest or other special seasons when wages were temporarily high. Plantations obviously could not be run with such labor.

7. There is a well-reasoned statement of this fact in Edward C. Kirkland, *A History of American Economic Life*, 181-182 (New York, 1932). See also Lewis Cecil Gray, *History of Agriculture in the Southern United States to 1860* (Washington, 1933), 479-480.

8. U.S. Census Office, Seventh Census, 1850, *Statistical View of the United States . . . Being a Compendium of the Seventh Census . . .*, by J. D. B. DeBow, 178, Cf. Ulrich Bonnell Phillips, *American Negro Slavery*, 309-330 (New York, 1918); M. B. Hammond, *The Cotton Industry: An Essay in American Economic History* (New York, 1897), 98-110; Gray, *History of Agriculture in the Southern United States*, 478-480; Kirkland, *History of American Economic Life*, 182-183; Rosser H. Taylor, *Slaveholding in North Carolina: An Economic View* (Chapel Hill, 1926), 81, 86-91; Frederick L. Olmsted, *A Journey in the Back Country in the Winter of 1853-4* (Putnam's Sons edition, New York, 1907), 1: 73, 131, 141, 167; 2: 65-70, 119.

9. *The Tobacco Kingdom: Plantation, Market, and Factory in Virginia and North Carolina, 1800-1860* (Durham, 1938), 94-117. The facts are given by Robert. The conclusion has been drawn therefrom by the writer.

10. Olmsted, *Journey in the Back Country*, 2:65-67.

11. Ibid., 56. Cf. Gray, *History of Agriculture in the Southern United States*, 362-363, 471.

12. Robert, *Tobacco Kingdom*, 18; Taylor, *Slaveholding in North Carolina*, 89; Gray, *History of Agriculture in the Southern States*, 545.

13. Phillips, *American Negro Slavery*, 226.

14. These references are based on Robert, *Tobacco Kingdom*, 245-247, 249-250.

15. For example, Gray, *History of Agriculture in the Southern United States*, 361-364, 464-471.

16. Hammond, *Cotton Industry*, 186; Alfred Holt Stone, *Studies in the American Race Problem*, 125-208 (New York, 1908); U. B. Phillips, "The Economics of Slave Labor in the South," in *The South in the Building of the Nation*, 5: 121 (Richmond, 1909); Edward Bryon Reuter, *The American Race Problem: A Study of the Negro*, 227-256 (ed. 2, New York, 1938).

17. *Life and Labor in the Old South*, 200 (Boston, 1929).

18. Max Farrand, ed., *The Records of the Federal Convention of 1787*, 1: 580-588; 3:253, 255, 342, 400, 428-430 (ed. 2, New Haven, 1937). C. C. Pinckney, when reporting to the South Carolina House of Representatives put it thus: "As we have found it necessary to give very extensive powers to the federal government both over the persons and estates of the citizens, we thought it right to draw one branch of the legislature immediately from the people, and that both wealth and numbers should be considered in the representation. We were at a loss, for some time, for a rule to ascertain the proportionate wealth of the states. At last we thought that the productive labor of the inhabitants was the best rule for ascertaining their wealth. In conformity to this rule, joined to a spirit of concession, we determined that representatives should be apportioned among the several states, by adding to the whole number of free persons three fifths of the slaves."—p. 253.

19. *Journey in the Back Country*, 1:64, 83, 90; 2:51, 106, 115, and *A Journey in the Seaboard Slave States* (New York, 1856), 185, 203, 717. See also Charles H. Wesley, *Negro Labor in the United States, 1850-1925: A Study in American Economic History* (New York, 1927), 3-6.

20. Taylor, *Slaveholding in North Carolina*, 80, Gray, *History of Agriculture in the Southern United States*, 468; Frederick Law Olmsted, *Journeys and Explorations in the Cotton Kingdom* 1 (London, 1861): 82, and *Journey in the Back Country*, 1: 255; 2: 12-13, 29.

21. Gray, *History of Agriculture in the Southern United States*, 474.

22. Olmsted made this point over and over again with much illustrative detail. For examples, see his *Journey in the Seaboard Slave States*, 329, 384-386, 393, 559-563, and *Journey in the Back Country*, 1: 174-196, 230-231, 261-266; 2: 22, 88, 167-174.

23. *The First Americans, 1607-1690* (New York, 1929), 22-48.

24. *Journey in the Back Country*, 1: 141, 177; 2:66, 121-124.

25. Gray, *History of Agriculture in the Southern United States*, 475.

26. Cf. Walter L. Fleming, "The Slave-Labor System in the Ante-Bellum South," in *The South in the Building of the Nation*, 5:16. A planter told the English geographer, Robert Russell, that the reason more planters did not raise hogs and make their own bacon was that the Negroes would steal the little pigs and roast them. *North America, Its Agriculture and Climate*, (Edinburgh, 1857), 265.

27. Cf. Den Hollander, "The Tradition of 'Poor Whites,'" 422-25.

28. Olmsted, *Journey in the Seaboard Slave States*, 576-577; Frederick Jackson Turner, *Rise of the New West* (New York and London, 1906), 90-92; Fleming, "The Slave-Labor System in the Ante-Bellum South," 107, 113-114.

29. Phillips, *American Negro Slavery*, 396.

30. Robert R. Russel, "The General Effects of Slavery upon Southern Economic Progress," *Journal of Southern History*, 4 (February 1938): 34-54.

31. Good descriptions are Paul H. Buck, "The Poor Whites of the Ante-Bellum South," *American Historical Review*, 31 (October 1925): 41-54; and Den Hollander, "The Tradition of 'Poor Whites'," 403-431. Frank L. and Harriet C. Owsley almost reason the poor whites away.—"The Economic Basis of Society in the Late Ante-Bellum South," *Journal of Southern History*, 6 (February 1940): 24-45.

32. *DeBow's Review*, August 1851, p. 133. Cf. Gray, *History of Agriculture in the Southern United States*, 487.

33. This point is developed more fully in Robert R. Russel, "The Economic History of Negro Slavery in the United States," 317-319.

34. Fleming, "The Slave-Labor System in the Ante-Bellum South," 113; Phillips, *American Negro Slavery*, 396; Olmsted, *Journey in the Back Country*, 2:61-70.

35. Wesley, *Negro Labor in the United States*, 6-7; Stone, *Studies in the American Race Problem*, 149-208; Reuter, *American Race Problem*, 227-256; Gray, *History of Agriculture in the Southern United States*, 500, 566; Ulrich B. Phillips, ed., *Plantation and Frontier* (*A Documentary History of American Industrial Society*, v. 1-2), 1 (Cleveland, 1910): 172, 253, 334.

36. Phillips, *American Negro Slavery*, 402-424; Wesley, *Negro Labor in the United States*, 1-28; Gray, *History of Agriculture in the Southern United States*, 467, 566; Kathleen Bruce, *Virginia Iron Manufacture in the Slave Era*, ch. 6 (New York and London, 1931); A. H. Stone, "Free Contract Labor in the Ante-Bellum South," in *The South in the Building of the Nation*, 5: 142.

37. For reasons not entirely clear, the hands in Virginia tobacco factories were nearly all Negroes,—Bruce, *Virginia Iron Manufacture*, 238-240; Robert, *The Tobacco Kingdom*, 197-208.

38. Wesley, *Negro Labor in the United States*, 69-86; Phillips, *American Negro Slavery*, 413; Robert Royal Russel, *Economic Aspects of Southern Sectionalism, 1840-1861* (Urbana, 1924), 53, 218-220; Olmsted, *Journey in the Back Country*, 1: 199-200; 2: 57; Bruce, *Virginia Iron Manufacture*, 234-237, 243-244.

39. Phillips, *American Negro Slavery*, 403, table.

40. Robert, *Tobacco Kingdom*, 199; Gray, *History of Agriculture in the Southern United States*, 566; Russel, *Economic Aspects of Southern Sectionalism*, 210-211, 219.

41. Robert R. Russel, "The General Effects of Slavery upon Southern Economic Progress," 37-40; See also Phillips, *American Negro Slavery*, 397-398.

Alden B. Pearson, Jr.

A Middle-Class, Border-State Family During the Civil War

An unusual insight into the impact of the Civil War on the South emerges from the diaries of George Eagleton and his wife Ethie. Neither wealthy planters nor poor whites, the Eagletons were examples of the solid, middle-class citizens of the South. George, a preacher's son and a preacher himself, numbered among his brothers three merchants and a doctor. Both he and Ethie came out of family backgrounds rooted in the early settlers and farmers of East Tennessee. They were part of that substantial, comfortably situated group which provided community leadership in the towns and rural areas of the South.

Yet, they were not exactly a typical couple; for they were better educated than most of the people among whom they lived and worked and, unlike most of their contemporaries, they kept diaries. Despite the turmoil of the war years they somehow found the time and energy to record the terrible experiences, the anguish and loneliness of separation, the fear and the hatred, as well as the love and fleeting joys of this time when their country, their institutions, their communities and their families were being torn apart. This essay presents a grass-roots view of the war as George and Ethie saw it and as it affected them; it is an attempt to convey a feeling for the war, a sense of what the struggle meant to the people whose lives it transformed.[1]

George Ewing Eagleton was a Presbyterian preacher and teacher in Middle Tennessee when the war began. Born in 1831 in Murfreesboro, where his father spent thirty-seven years as pastor of the First Presbyterian Church, educated at Union University there, at Maryville Theological Seminary in East Tennessee and at Union Theological Seminary in New York City, George had

Source: Civil War History 22, no. 4 (December 1976): 318–36, Kent State University Press.

imbibed strong anti-slavery and pro-Union sentiments from his family and his educational contacts. Although he was unable to accept the abolitionist program and resented the arrogant self-righteousness of abolitionist speakers (many of whom he heard in person in New York in 1853–54), he vigorously opposed secession. But he sadly went with his state when it refused to yield to the threat of Federal coercion in 1861. Ethelinda Foute Eagleton, born in 1835 in Maryville, was the daughter of Daniel Davis Foute, one of the early settlers and at one time a large landowner in the Montvale Springs and Cades Cove regions of East Tennessee. She had attended schools in Greeneville and Maryville, where she met George while he was studying at the seminary there.[2]

George's and Ethie's records of his enlistment and first few weeks in the 44th Tennessee Infantry reveal the confusion and lack of organization in the Army of Tennessee while disclosing his own reactions to the crisis. In 1861 George was pastor of three country churches and principal of a rural school in Lincoln County (directly south of Nashville on the Alabama state line). In November, in response to Governor Isham G. Harris' call for more militia to defend the state, George "volunteered as a private soldier to aid in driving the invader from Southern soil." Immediately problems arose, for there was still confusion about the relationship of the state militia to the Confederate States Army. Harris then instructed the militia to stay at home and the army volunteers to leave for their training camps. When the volunteers met to elect officers before proceeding to camp, many naturally decided that they would prefer to be considered militia. George was one of several men whose speeches prevented the dissolution of the company, at least for the moment.[3]

Under the impact of difficult conditions in Camp Trousdalc (on the Kentucky line north of Nashville) the original doubts and fears of many were multiplied. George described the problems and his own actions in some detail. On arriving at the camp, the volunteers were

> put into a frame building large enough to afford sleeping room for about 100 men—no ceiling and no floor, with 3 rows of bunks on each side, no fireplace and no stove. And there we learn that we must provide ourselves with cooking utensils, which thing we proceeded to do. . . .
>
> Our company refuses to be sworn in. The reason? So many have deserted us that the company is not full. We have been deserted especially by men who were secessionists 12 months ago—noisy, ready for war, and cursing men who were then of union preferences!!! Our men fear that, once sworn in, the company will be disorganized and scattered about in small squads. Great confusion! . . .
>
> I was called at midnight, after I had cast about me the drapery of my couch and retired to pleasant (?) dreams, to use my influence in quelling a rebellious spirit that was fast gaining ground in our company. Certain disaffected ones are trying to break up the company in order to get back home themselves! I got good attention and talked for half an hour. Took vote of the company. They vote to be sworn in. Gov. I. G. Harris has thrown the military arrangements of Tenn. into the wildest confusion. He has acted like

a man in a drunken spree. This confusion and the disgraceful cowardice of many who were last winter for secession and war (if need be) but are now refusing self and means for the prosecution of the war into which they have plunged the country—these things are disorganizing companies all over the country.

Only fifty-two of the more than eighty who originally volunteered for this company were actually sworn into the army.[4]

In the nearly six years of Ethie's marriage to George she had often expressed in her diary her loneliness during George's frequent absences of as much as a week at a time while he preached at extended "sacramental meetings" and attended various denominational gatherings. But this parting was infinitely more painful than the others. In her diary she poured out the anguish which women throughout the ages have felt as they watched their men march off to war:

Mr. Eagleton's school dismissed—and what for? O my God, and must I write it? He has enlisted in the service of his country—to war—the most unrighteous war that ever was brought on any nation that ever lived. Pres. Abe Lincoln has done what no other Pres. ever dared to do—he has divided these once peaceful and happy United States. And Oh! the dreadful dark cloud that is now hanging over our country—'tis enough to sicken the heart of any one.

'Tis a dark, gloomy day to me. I feel more like I was preparing for Mr. E's funeral than any thing else. . . .

Mr. E. is gone. Oh, my poor wretched self! What will become of me, left here without a home and relatives, a babe just nine months old and no George. Oh, this desolate heart! . . . What a long day! True, too true what Dr. Eagleton [George's father] says—that our marriage life has been short, but, oh, how oft have we sipped from the cup of affliction. But all the sickness and death that ever I had in our family is nothing to compare to giving up Mr. E.

Such a long day this has been. How oft have I looked round to see if Mr. E. was not coming in. Davis [infant son] is quite sick—uneasy about him. I always had Mr. E. with me to help nurse him, but now I am alone.

Ethie soon found some support and companionship when she moved to Murfreesboro to live with George's sister Elvira (Mrs. Samuel Campbell) on a plantation just outside the city; she was also much closer to George.[5]

Although Christmas day found them still separated, Ethie was at least warm and comfortable with George's family. Just before Christmas, however, George's company, with only three weeks training and still without arms, was moved some thirty miles north to Bowling Green, Kentucky. General Albert Sidney Johnston was strengthening the center of his long defensive line which stretched from Cumberland Gap on the east to Columbus, Kentucky, on the west. Johnston expected the main Federal thrust into Tennessee to come from General Don Carlos Buell's army through Bowling Green and Nashville. The cold, uncomfortable trip by rail in "fireless and seatless" stock cars failed to overcome George's sense of humor even though the men had to spend the night in the cars far outside the town. "Major 'Somebody' comes round," George wrote,

> and tells us to "do the best we can till morning." No drinking water, no fire, not even a rail fence to burn, for the soldiers have been here before! No room for sleeping. "Do the best you can"—yes, and since I have sworn to obey orders, I'll just roll me up in my blanket and set myself up against the side of this dirty stock car and thus watch for the break of day. It is bitter cold; some curse and swear, others laugh, and some others threaten to burn the old cars to keep us warm. But thus and so passes the night and the light of the morrow dawneth.[6]

At Bowling Green George's regiment began to feel and act more like soldiers; on December 28, as rumors of the gradual approach of a horde of Federal forces and of an imminent battle circulated among the men, they at last received their muskets and rifles. The battle did not come, but the troops suffered from long hours of drilling and guard duty in exceptionally cold, wet weather. Some came down with measles; others, like George, were hit by fever and vomiting. On January 6, 1862, only one-third of George's regiment reported for duty. Despite his illness he preached to the men and held prayer meetings whenever possible, conducted funerals and was elected chaplain of his company. In mid-January he obtained a twelve-day leave for the purpose of arranging his financial affairs back in southern Tennessee, "so that," he said, "if I should never return from this war, my wife will have as little trouble in settling up as possible."[7]

On his trip George and Ethie were able to enjoy a couple of extra days together because rail traffic from Murfreesboro to Nashville was so jammed and confused that he could not get on a train. Ethie was delightfully surprised when George walked in, especially since she had just received a letter from him communicating his fear that he was about to go into battle. George walked the three miles from the station through a hail and snow storm to see her. No wonder she was surprised:

> Oh! how my heart leaped for joy to see him once more safe at home and know that he would have a good comfortable house and a warm bed to sleep in this bitter cold night. Bless his dear soul, how I wish I could keep him all the time. . . . Noble-hearted fellow! may God spare your life and health in the hour of battles! . . . May God spare him from the hands of the enemy. May he be spared to return to his little family.

In only two weeks George did return but under far less favorable circumstances.[8]

In mid-January, Confederate forces under General George B. Crittenden were demolished in the battle of Mill Springs in eastern Kentucky leaving Johnston's right flank exposed at Bowling Green and eastern Tennessee virtually undefended. Even more serious was the threat which developed to the west, where on February 6, General U.S. Grant's Federal forces easily captured Fort Henry, the only Confederate defensive position on the Tennessee River, thereby opening that river as far as Muscle Shoals in northern Alabama. Grant's forces then turned eastward toward Fort Donelson, which protected the Cumberland River route to Nashville and Johnston's rear. Johnston and General P. G. T. Beauregard, who had recently joined him on his way to take over the forces in western Tennessee and Kentucky under Johnston, decided to pull General William J. Hardee's command back from Bowling Green to Nashville.[9]

Caught up in this retreat, George shared the general confusion and suspicions of the men as they marched south in extreme cold and snow. Approaching Nashville, they learned of the fall of Fort Donelson (Feb. 16), then moved on toward Murfreesboro on the Nashville and Chattanooga Railroad. George expressed what many of his comrades felt:

On the march again . . . we get sad intelligence that after 3 or 4 days hard fighting Fort Donelson has surrendered and all our men save the dead are prisoners in the hands of the Federals! As we march, silently, sadly, we shed many a tear for our unfortunate fellow soldiers, for our Country, our families, and our homes! But above us floats a beautiful flag and on that flag is emblazoned, "Liberty or Death!" We mean it! We pass through Nashville and camp. . . . Our men are greatly annoyed at the reported surrender of Nashville! No foe there! But our generals have a sad view of things thus,—no—there's a trick in this surrender! Our men don't understand the move; and indeed, if this surrender be just as it appears to be, then I for one had rather burn Nashville (if it must be given up), the Capital of my native state, to ashes and there in its ashes fight to the death for every inch of soil! We have backed far enough. If we yield this grain growing state to the foe, where will we get bread for the army? If we yield this state with its important railroads and tributaries to the Ohio River, we only have built and surrendered the best avenues to the heart of the Southern Confederacy! But enough of this until we can see the design of our military chiefs. . . . Generals Hardee, [Gideon] Pillow, [John B.] Floyd, etc., visit our regiments and address the troops, trying to reconcile them to the giving up of the Capital, etc. Some lift hat and voice in rousing approval, but others are downcast and retire to their tents to weep at such thoughts as the leaving of their families and homes behind them to the mercy of a merciless foe.[10]

The slow march to Murfreesboro through cold and rain took three more days and left George and so many others sick that they filled all six hospitals and many private homes in the town. George, however, had a better time than most of his fellows, having received permission to stay with his family while the army was there. As the army moved south toward Decatur, Alabama, and an eventual union with Beauregard's forces at Corinth, Mississippi, George was too sick to march:

Sick in bed, but about sun-up, I heard our brigade moving. Yes, they are off for . . . for lower down in Dixie, and I'm left here sick of a fever. Another "advance moving back-

> ward." It is said that the federals will enter this place so soon as our men are out. What shall I do? The devilish Yankees will take me prisoner if I remain. So in company with brother John [who was also in Hardee's brigade, in the 45th Tennessee Infantry] I get in my buggy and travel. . . .

For almost a month George and his brother followed Hardee's slow movement to Corinth, sometimes stopping for several days with friends as George gradually recovered from his fever and finally catching up with their regiments on March 23.[11]

In Ethie's distress at her husband's difficulties she vented her feelings against leaders on both sides of the conflict. Her animosity toward Lincoln brought forth the most violent sentiments expressed in the diary of this usually mild and pious young woman:

> . . . Poor George! I never hated to part with you so much; not able to sit up and yet have to go. Would that I could go with you and nurse you through your sickness. If I just had it in my power, how willingly could I kill old Lincoln. . . .
> Oh, what a dark day to me. If I could just hear from dear George—where or how he is tonight. . . . But scamp Lincoln has deprived me of that pleasure. Oh, he will surely get his portion in that lake that burneth with fire and brimstone for causing our once happy land to become so distracted and wretched. . . .
> I am afraid that the generals in Middle Tennessee are not doing their duty. Johnston and Crittenden are drunkards.[12]

In mid-March, before George caught up with his regiment at Corinth, Murfreesboro came under Federal occupation as Buell moved south then west to join Grant at Pittsburg Landing, leaving detachments at strategic points to guard bridges and railroads. At first the Federal occupation did not weigh heavily on Ethie and her family although the Campbells' farm was visited frequently by the troops, searched for arms, and looted for provisions (including not only eggs but also setting hens). For a while pickets were posted on the farm and restricted the visiting of neighbors, which had always been one of Ethie's few simple diversions. The requirement for passes for even the simplest travel to visit friends or even to go to church especially irked Ethie: "A person cannot go to a neighbor's house—nay!—even over his own farm without a pass, and that from an invader; and this is freedom, is it? This is a free country?" Lacking any close companions outside George's family and shut off from church attendance for long periods, Ethie felt her loneliness more acutely. Her diary demonstrates her increasing longing to see George or even to hear from him; she heard of at least one letter which he sent but which was burned when Federal troops searched the house of the person who had it at the time. In her loneliness Ethie found some solace in her son, Dave, now about a year old: "Ah! I am so lonely today. No one to keep me company. Yes, here is my noble boy. . . . Oh, my proud and happy boy—may God help me to bring you up in the 'fear and admonition of the Lord.' May you be a good boy and a happy and useful man."[13]

As regimental chaplain George was exempt from combat duty; and, while Beauregard and Johnston were reorganizing their forces in preparation for fighting Grant before Buell could join him, George searched out a suitable building for a regimental hospital, visited the sick, preached and conducted Bible study classes. He also had some free time for visiting friends in the area, shaving for the first time since he enlisted and even getting a haircut. George complained of frustration and depression at this time. Whether the time hanging heavy upon him (even driving him to busy himself with washing dishes and cooking) gave him too much opportunity to meditate upon his situation or whether the concentration of his associates on the task of getting ready to kill and destroy the enemy in the battle which seemed inevitable troubled his Christian conscience is not clear from his diary. "For the first time, during the past two or three days," he recorded on March 28, "I have felt homesick, or tired of my position, or wanted a discharge, or something. In the discharge of my official duties I meet with no encouragement from men or officers; consequently I feel rather melancholy." Little time remained for such thoughts, however, for on April 2 Johnston decided to attack the Federals at Pittsburgh Landing, some twenty-three miles north of Corinth.[14]

George's account of the battle of Shiloh reveals nothing new to the historian but demonstrates several well-known features of that struggle and conveys the feeling of horror which its participants experienced. As part of General S. A. M. Wood's Third Brigade of Hardee's Third Corps, George's regiment was one of the first to leave Corinth, escaping some of the confusion that prevented the other Confederate forces from reaching their assigned positions on time. They marched twelve miles before pitching camp at midnight on April 3. Hardee's corps was in battle line ready to lead the attack virtually according to Beauregard's schedule on the fourth but had to wait until the morning of the sixth for the other troops to move into position. George's record of the firing and skirmishing on the fourth and fifth increases the mystery about the Federal failure to realize the presence of Johnston's army until the surprise attack hit Grant's forces on Sunday morning, April 6. From his position in the hospital George saw little of the actual fighting but much of the effects of it; his account of the struggle, the Confederate advance on Sunday and retreat on Monday, the rain and the suffering is worth quoting in full.

April 4, Friday—Early in line of march again till 9 miles brings us near the foe. A body of our cavalry brought on an attack and were routed, but a fire from one of our regiments and from a battery stopped and turned the foe. Several Yankee officers and privates brought in as prisoners. Much fire during night in line; wore our arms all night. The casualties are yet unknown.

April 5, Saturday—A gloomy morning but after a little while the clouds break away.

Gen. Johnston had intended a general attack on the enemy this morning, but Gen. Leonidas K. Polk's division is not up yet. I am very busy—no breakfast. No general fighting, but skirmishing and fighting all day. Our men are in battle line for several miles. Within a few miles of Tenn. River and in plain hearing of the enemies' drums our pickets go up to the enemies' line. I rode about 9 miles and worked hard all day fitting up our hospital.

April 6, Sabbath—Cool night and a beautiful clear morning, a lovely day—but how little like the Sabbath, for about the dawn of day the pickets of both armies begin the work of death. Then is heard the sound of firing by platoons, by wings, by regiments. The dread time has come; the battle of battles during this war has opened. There are here two of the largest and best drilled armies that have ever met on American soil. The first and heaviest firing comes from the direction of our brigade. Soon the wounded begin to be brought into the hospital. Blood! Blood! Agony! Death! Gaping flesh wounds, broken bones, amputations, bullet and bomb fragment extractions. As we try and toil to relieve the suffering, to bind up a wound or speak a word of comfort to the expiring soldier, our souls are cheered by the palpable fact that the enemy is being routed and driven back along the whole line. A total defeat. The noise of musketry and cannons becomes constantly fainter, more, more distant, then ceases altogether. Today's fight has closed, but many on both sides have fallen—some 4, 5, or 6,000 prisoners reported—a number of batteries, nearly all their camps, commisary, etc. taken. After night it rains hard—a bad night for the exposed soldier, especially the sick and wounded. Our regiment is very much scattered and many are wounded. In marching through the thick wood, over fences, across branches, and in the undergrowth, and the charging of some 4 batteries, they became much separated by falling in with other regiments; but they fought on and on! Sad to relate, Gen. Johnston is wounded and dies; thus have we lost our commander-in-chief. Rains.

April 7, Monday—Still sprinkling a little. I go over the battlefield in search of wounded soldiers with several wagons. Death and destruction! It seems that all the Hell hounds have been crying havoc, and been turned loose as the dogs of war. I passed amid scenes that beggar all description. But, hark, what means that noise? The battle opens again; and once more the whistling of Minié balls, the bursting of bombs, and the crushing of tree tops by cannon balls is heard. We are ordered back; and returning to the hospital, we bury one of our regiment—no coffin and in a shallow grave dug with wooden paddles. Prayer at the grave—a solemn time.

April 8,—After a hotly contested yesterday the fighting ceases—a drawn fight. Both armies remain in part upon the field; the enemy have recovered some of the ground lost on yesterday, but they were reinforced by the army of Gen. Buell from Middle Tennessee—so that our troops, worn down by forced marches, loss of sleep and yesterday's fight, were forced to contend against fresh troops. A portion of our army started back for Corinth last evening. I remained with the wounded of our regiment at hospital. Our colonel with tears in his eyes bade us farewell as he left us. This morning I gave up my horse to the last one of the wounded at our hospital and set out afoot carrying the gun of another. It was feared the enemy would advance and capture us, but we got to our camps near Corinth after dark. My feet were blistered, the blisters broke and were bleeding—very sore feet. Weary, I at once fell down in open air asleep but was soon called up to supper. There had been so much rain that the roads were almost impassable, and consequently an awful destruction of property by the way. Much of the spoil of war had to be given up.

Although Beauregard, who assumed command when Johnston died, claimed a victory of Shiloh, George's account supports the conclusion which he and many others soon reached—that the most the Confederacy could claim was a draw in the battle itself and that in the long run the Union came out ahead.[15]

While Beauregard's troops nursed their wounded and reorganized at Corinth, General Henry W. Halleck, the new Federal commander, slowly brought his forces toward Corinth, pausing to dig entrenchments each night in order to prevent a recurrence of the devastating surprise of April 6, George's diary for the rest of April and most of May records mostly routine events and situations—numerous funerals and a few regular preaching services, food shortages, inactivity and boredom, paydays, skirmishing and picket clashes with increasing frequency as Halleck drew nearer in May, rumors and dissatisfaction among the troops especially about the reorganization and their new officers, and complaints about the personal hazards of camp life—body lice, ticks, gnats, mosquitoes, spiders and the "camp itch."[16]

At the end of May, as Halleck edged closer to the Confederate lines just north of Corinth, Beauregard decided to avoid being flanked and entrapped by the much larger Federal force by retreating down the Mobile and Ohio Railroad to a stronger defensive position, which he found at Tupelo, some fifty miles to the south. George recorded the experience of the first several days of this withdrawal, but before it was completed he received the honorable discharge for reasons of health which he had requested late in April. On the retreat there was the usual wondering and questioning among the troops about their destination and whether their generals really knew what they were doing. Excessive dust and inadequate water sources in this drought-ridden area, harassment from Union cavalry, worry about the safety of the baggage wagons, shortage of food for men, mules and horses contributed to George's sense of relief when his discharge came through on June 2. But George's troubles were far from over; he still had to make his way through more than three hundred miles of Union-held territory to his family at Murfreesboro.[17]

Meanwhile, garbled accounts and rumors of the fighting at Shiloh had heightened Ethie's fears for George's safety. At first she had heard of a Union victory, then, on the following day, of a great Confederate triumph. The Sunday after Shiloh found her praying for George while still not knowing whether he had survived the battle: "Dear George! Today is he among the living or numbered with the dead? O God, spare his life for thy name's sake. Amen. O, that I could just hear from him." Not until April 22 did Ethie at last learn through a letter from George's brother John to his wife, who was also staying with the Campbells, that her husband was safe. By the spring of 1862 inflation and shortages were affecting the state, and Ethie for the first time in her life spun her own wool from her own sheep. Troubled for several weeks with a debilitating illness which amplified her sense of loneliness and sadness, Ethie found only a brief return of joy when George unexpectedly arrived on June 14.[18]

Beauregard's withdrawal to Tupelo had left the Union forces in control of almost the whole length of the Memphis and Charleston Railroad across northern Mississippi and Alabama, most of which they had held since mid-April. When George and his brother John (who had also been discharged) left Tupelo on June 3, they had no illusions about their probable fate if they should meet Union troops. Winding through the back woods, avoiding major towns, nursing a sick horse, sometimes traveling by night, receiving bed, food and information from sympathetic residents, they slipped quietly into the Campbell home after twelve days riding. Summing up the trip, George attributed their success to divine guidance.

> One night [he said] we passed through a drove of beef cattle of the enemy between their camp fires in sight on either hand . . . Providence has guided us; several times we missed the enemy not knowing it until afterwards. These infernal Yankees garrison every important town in this region; but our cavalry occasionally pounces on them, and guerilla parties are doing sad work with some of them.[19]

Difficult as this trip had been, George and John soon decided that roaming the countryside was safer for two Confederate veterans than remaining within easy reach of the Murfreesboro garrison. Three days later they were off again—this time to Marshall County (the next one to the southwest), where, most importantly, there were no Union garrisons but only frequent patrols, and also where they had many relatives and friends (George had lived there, had been pastor of one church there and had preached in several others). Returning almost three weeks later on the day which Ethie called the "glorious no longer" fourth of July, the two brothers soon found that their fears had not been without foundation—and that their absence had not been long enough.[20]

Soon after their departure the Union authorities in Murfreesboro began putting pressure on local residents to accept amnesty by taking the oath of allegiance to the Union, as the new military governor, Andrew Johnson, specified in his inaugural proclamation. George's father spent one or two nights in jail for refusing to take what Ethie called "the vile oath." Indignantly but fearfully and silently in her diary she cried "Shame! Shame!" against those who prevented doctors, lawyers and businessmen from working unless they took the oath; but her deepest concern was for the church:

> I can't think that God in his 'tender mercy' will allow such a state of things much longer. Surely he will not allow his church doors to be closed by a set of vile invaders. Are there not enough of good people in his church to send up petitions to the throne of grace for the opening of their church and the renewal of their minister's labors? "The prayers of the righteous availeth much.'

She soon had cause for even more worry when the requirement of the oath hit even closer to her.[21]

George and John with their families had enjoyed a quiet, pleasant Sunday (July 6) when in the late afternoon "four low-down, vile, . . . *nasty* Yankees" (Ethie's description and emphasis) galloped up with orders to arrest the brothers and take them into Murfreesboro. George's description of the proceedings in the office of the Provost Marshal reveals the mental anguish of a man torn between the clear dictates of his conscience and the necessity to accommodate to an evil world for the sake of his loved ones.

> We are before a self-important, tyrannical upstart, dubbed and befooled by the title "Provost Marshall." "Pride goeth before a fall." After some conference I asked to be banished beyond the Federal lines. "No—*the oath.*" I positively refuse to take it to friend after friend that advise and urge it. I owe no allegiance to the Lincoln Dynasty or to the Northern Despotism. A plain friend suggests that better men than I have already pined, languished, and some died in their military bastilles and their abolition inquisitions. I hesitate; I meditate—I dream: Behold, a highway robber! The traveler *gives him* his money to save his life? Behold, the midnight assassin! The *father deceives* him to save his wife and children? I am in the clutches of Robber, Assassin (and if there be baser titles, give them to him also). What ought I do? I'll go to jail, to the guillotine, before binding myself to support the Federal Government as it is. But here are two great evils! May I choose the less? Then here is compulsion! "*force!*" the bayonet! The oath *thus* administered, and that *without authority*-the oath thus taken (as Socrates swallows the hemlock;) is *without moral obligation*? I waiver. One by my side takes it; it is laid before me. I subscribe—and go forth to hate ten fold more this Yankee despotism and to teach my children forever to hate it! This oath I expect to *keep*, of course, but only *just as I have taken it*?!!. When *under bayonet constraint* I may observe it.[22]

Such intense hatred and determination to resist appear rarely in George's diary. What aroused these violent feelings was the element of coercion, which had brought forth similar diatribes against the abolitionists in the prewar period and against Lincoln's attempt to force the southern states to remain in the Union. Combining a heritage of fierce independence, which derived from his family roots in the mountains of East Tennessee, with the individualism and devotion to freedom of conscience of his Calvinistic religion, George regarded attempts to dictate matters of conscience and personal freedom as one of the worst of man's sins against his fellow man. This experience of the oath left an indelible mark on George although he soon escaped from at least the legal restrictions which it imposed upon him.

George's inning against the Yankees at Murfreesboro came the following Sunday, when Nathan Bedford Forrest's cavalry totally surprised them, captured the town, and proceeded to rip up the tracks and burn the bridges of the Nashville and Chattanooga Railroad. This raid helped to force Buell to abandon his move toward Chattanooga and settle for a defensive position between that city and Murfreesboro. Both of the Eagletons discussed the raid at some length in their diaries. Ethie concentrated on the human interest side—Captain O. C. Rounds being dragged from under a bed where he had hidden, women and children hiding in their cellars then fleeing to the country without pausing to eat anything. Her first experience of war left a vivid impression: "O, what times. I never want to hear of the like again. I have often read of war, but I have never felt it before. George was in town until late in the evening."[23]

And what kept George in town so late in the evening? George was enjoying himself immensely—and also clearing the record of reference to the hated oath which he had taken a week earlier. George admitted to playing a small but active role in the raid, but his cryptic reference to his part raises more questions than it answers. Let him tell it himself.

> Another eventful day. As the shades of night disappear, the Federal garrison here... are aroused by the terrible clatter of Gen. Forrest's cavalry horses. Excepting 2 companies of Ky. cavalry, Gen. Forrest captured or killed the whole garrison. Thank God for this sudden and (for the instant) complete deliverance from this plague of "body lice," etc. Literally and figuratively, physically and morally, I got my oath back again—"Bond" and all! And had the pleasure of seeing this whole pandemonium of garrisoning devils taken out as prisoners of war; after having contributed to this desired consummation my mite of "aid and comfort," it becomes me to change my local habitation instanter, ere a new garrison is sent in.[24]

Having recovered and destroyed the document which he had recently signed, and having enjoyed assisting the raiding party, George became more active in support of the Confederate cause. At the same time he temporarily removed himself from the Murfreesboro area and the possibility of immediate retaliation by Union authorities there. He spent more than a week roaming through the region southwest of Murfreesboro, providing information for the Confederate cavalry operating there and at the same time collecting debts owed to him by parents of his former pupils at Boonshill Institute. He must have been contemplating moving his family out of such a disturbed area, for he returned as the owner of a one-horse rockaway—a low, light open-sided carriage with a fixed top. On his return to Murfreesboro he was surprised to learn that Buell had already sent a full division to garrison the town. That was enough for George. Two days later he set out in his new rockaway with Ethie and Dave and a few possessions for East Tennessee, where Confederate forces were still in control.[25]

Using his intimate knowledge of the area, George picked his way eastward, avoiding Union scouts, pickets and garrisons. Four days' travel brought him through the Union lines to the Cumberland Mountains and Confederate territory; then a more leisurely trip over the Holston River to Maryville and on to Ethie's parents' home in Cades Cove almost on the North Carolina line put them among friends and relatives on both sides of the family. Here Ethie and

George enjoyed over a year of nearly normal life. Ethie, glad to be back among her own people, neglected her diary for long periods, noting only a few short trips and visits and, of course, the birth of their fourth child, significantly named Campbell Exile, in April of 1863.[26]

George took up preaching duties in several of the vacant Presbyterian churches in the Knoxville-Maryville area. As long as Confederate troops were in control of the region, he had little difficulty with the Unionists, or Tories, who, as the more numerous faction in East Tennessee, had steadfastly opposed secession even after Lincoln called for troops in April, 1861. Many of George's and Ethie's relatives here were Unionists, but no difficulty appears to have arisen among them on that score. George noted occasional problems in the churches caused by political differences although he was careful to refrain from discussing "the state of the country" from the pulpit. During this period he blasted the Yankees in his diary only once—when he saw his parents at the home of his father's half-brother near Maryville after they had fled Murfreesboro in December 1862.

> At the house of Uncle John Eagleton (a kind-hearted tory) I met with my venerable parents—refugees—homeless in their old age. This war! and these infernal Yankees! Last summer severe and protracted illness (in the mercy of God) kept my aged sire from an abolition prison at a place where he has quietly labored as pastor since 1829. And now!

A month later more refugees from Middle Tennessee joined the exiles as George's brother John brought his family to the relative security of Cades Cove.[27]

In the late summer of 1863 the war came to northeastern Tennessee as Union forces under General Ambrose Burnside began moving down from Kentucky forcing General Simon Buckner to withdraw down the Tennessee valley toward Chattanooga. By early September Knoxville had fallen, and Burnside was moving on down the valley in pursuit of Buckner. In the meantime George had accepted a call to the Presbyterian church in New Market, twenty-five miles northeast of Knoxville. There he moved not only his own family but also his mother, father and sister, the wife and three children of his brother John, and three slaves. Here in the rented house which he called "Refugee Retreat" his father baptized his new son with the symbolic name "Exile." For nearly a year George had relatively few difficulties in New Market; the church and its Sunday school were growing despite the defection of some Unionists who refused to worship with the "rebels" after the Union troops moved in.[28]

In November, 1863 General James Longstreet's foray up the valley from Georgia and unsuccessful attempt to dislodge Burnside from Knoxville presented George an opportunity to observe and comment on the differences in behavior of the two occupying forces. After his failure at Knoxville Longstreet moved into winter quarters to the northeast (at Morristown and Russellville) and for several weeks during the winter held the New Market area. George was impressed by the differences in the treatment of the churches by the Yankees and the Confederates. The Yankees, he charged, used his church for a guard-house, stole the furnishings, including the Morocco leather binding of the pulpit Bible, and rarely listened to a sermon. The Confederates during their brief stay repaired the damages to the churches and attended daily services with some even joining the church. Such experiences only confirmed the Eagletons' contempt for the "invaders [who were] turning this valley into a desert. Such robbing, plundering, destroying, burning and general vandalism!![29]

Almost from the beginning of George's ministry in New Market a few Unionists, including some church members, had been trying to force him to leave by means of "anonymous letters, irresponsible messages of advice, warnings, threatenings, etc., a regular system of espionage at the church," even threats to his friends about his own safety. In August, 1864 this opposition took more forceful action. False reports about him to the authorities at Knoxville brought soldiers to search his house (and in the process to steal his possessions). Almost immediately he was ordered never to preach again in New Market. Defying this order, George received more specific and direct threats, to which also he refused to bow. Then came one of the most traumatic experiences of his life.

I had just retired to bed when a knock is heard at the door. I am ordered to report to the officer commanding, "Tomorrow won't do." So I dress, go out and am decoyed out of town and then I felt sure that I was bound for Knoxville jail. But no, I am halted below town in a rail road cut—ordered to draw my shirt, but refuse. Another order with terrible and cocked Repeaters at my head and breast. Boldly, I assure them that they can't muster Blue Coats "enough to make me heap *that indignity upon myself*." They leave my *pants on me*, and upon my naked breast and back they inflict bloody stripes "forty save one", perhaps thrice fold! Twice was I felled to the earth by the stroke of a club, inflicting an ugly wound first over one eye, then over the other—the scars of which, and of these many stripes I must carry to my grave. The men who inflicted this merciless scourging were mere tools, in the hands of the disaffected minority in New Market Presbyterian Church! A part of this party have failed in a nine-months effort to run me from my post of duty, where (before God I believe that) my usefulness and acceptability is increasing. I have not breathed a syllable in the pulpit (during the Federal sway in E. Tenn. nor before except on the set "Days") in regard to state of the country. Luther once said he would attend the Diet "though the devils there were as thick as the tiles on the houses". My motto is "Do your duty and leave results to God."
Esqr. Wm. Dick, Dr. A. B. Blackburn etc. are guilty in this whole affair. The least that may be said against them is that when they heard and knew of the cry "Crucify him, Crucify him"! they did not even ask "Why, *What evil hath* he done." The *heathen* Pilate did, but these *Presbyterian Elders* did not.[30]

Even after this beating George was determined to do his duty, affirming that he would "rather die in New Market pulpit than anywhere else on earth."

Threats of similar treatment for his friends or for anyone showing sympathy for him did not deter some of his friends and church members from visiting him and assisting Ethie in caring for his wounds, but the added threat against all active male members of the church if services were not suspended convinced George to step down. Ethie also was "trembling for him" and urging him to flee as soon as he was physically able. George reluctantly acquiesced and added greatly to his store of resentment against the Unionists for forcing him once more to compromise his conscience.[31]

For the next five months George led a rambling, insecure existence wandering over northeastern Tennessee, southwestern Virginia and western North Carolina, sometimes joining Confederate cavalry units, always avoiding Union troops. His odyssey almost ended just as it began. Attempting to cross the Holston River at a ford north of Strawberry Plains in order to catch up with General Joseph Wheeler's cavalry, which was on a sweeping raid up from Georgia, above Knoxville and on into Middle Tennessee, he and the other two Presbyterian ministers who were traveling with him were met in the middle of the river by a "shower of Yankee Minié balls." Turning back, they fled eastward then north to Bristol and on as far as Lexington, Virginia. In a friendly country once more George did some preaching, attended church meetings and watched for an opportunity to return to his family.[32]

His chance came in November when General John C. Vaughn's cavalry came out of Virginia and drove the Union forces back into Knoxville for a short while. After a cold, wet four-day, hundred-mile trip from Bristol on a lame, sick horse, George spent a few days with his family before Vaughn began to retreat back to Virginia. George scrambled after Vaughn on another worn-out horse. Mid-December found him and about fifty other refugees from the Unionists virtually surrounded by hostile forces and finally heading across the mountains into North Carolina. Among Ethie's relatives near Statesville in Iredell County in the western part of the state, George settled down to await the end of the war and the return of safe enough traveling conditions to enable him to bring his family to join him. He accepted a call to the Concord Presbyterian Church in Iredell County, where there were few raiding Yankee troops and few violent tories (he did, however, have his horse confiscated by Union raiders just as the war was officially ending).[33]

While George was dodging Unionists and Yankees and finally settling down in the safety of North Carolina, Ethie was struggling to care for three small children in the midst of hostility, inflation and shortages—and worst of all for her, loneliness. She reacted to George's flight in August, 1864 with determination to care for her children. From this point until she rejoined George in North Carolina in August, 1865, Ethie's diary received more attention than in the preceding years. Although she received less hostility from the tories than had George, she was forced to move from New Market out into the country soon after he left; here her contacts were narrower and her few friendships more precious to her. Her accounts of visits by foraging Yankee soldiers "stealing the bread out of the oven and under the bed looking for apples," taking chickens and hogs, and demanding to know whether her husband was in the Confederate army rang true to life. Occasionally a note of bitterness against the tories in New Market crept into her diary, as in her rhetorical question on learning that a prayer meeting had been organized at the local college—"Why did they not go to the church? Were they afraid George's ghost would haunt them?" She also noted, however, that the tories were very kind to her children and that she frequently received gifts of food and offers of assistance from some of them. Much of her diary for this period records ordinary events and activities—preparing food (drying vegetables and fruit for winter use, making preserves, taking wheat to the mill to be ground, reboiling molasses), making clothes, trading rawhide for finished leather and having shoes made from it, sending wool to a weaver and getting it back as cloth, sewing and knitting, trading bacon or flour for a day's work chopping wood, even chopping wood herself when necessary, recording titles of books she read, nursing sick children. Her time was thus well-filled with providing the basic necessities of life.[34]

Yet the war was constantly in the background of her life and often intruded into her diary. She noted with interest reports and rumors of military activities of both sides, especially when they might affect George. Saddened by news of the death of her father because he had been dragged out of his sick-bed in Cades Cove and imprisoned in Knoxville, she worried about the fate of her homeless and penniless mother and sister. Inadequate communications added to the burden of worry. One of the longest and most expressive passages in Ethie's diary was evoked by the news that her father was in prison in Knoxville; it seems to speak not just for Ethie but for all women who have ever sat at home while their men were fighting.

> I heard that my poor old papa was in Knoxville. Where, O Where is my mother and sister? Their only protector taken from them. Tell me. Kind heaven, is this cruel way of living our doom? See old gray-headed men torn from the bosom of their families, from their pleasant firesides. 'Tis not on man that these partings fall heaviest. He goes forth into the fierce strife of the world and enters into its business and turmoils until he has no time for sorrow, little for remembrance. He gives a thought once and a while to the hearth he has left behind. He thinks sadly for a while of the tear-wet face of one to whom he bade goodbye with a kiss long ago. Perhaps a tear dims his eye at the remembrance, but the whirl of his active life soon brushes it from his memory. Woman thinks always; he is never absent from her thoughts. The last dream at night is of him and with the first thought of the morning his thought is blended. His footsteps seem sounding upon every wind. She lives over a thousand times the days they have passed together, she remembers every soft word he has spoken. Every thing for which he expressed a preference she cherishes. The past is her treasure. She lives not in the present but in hope and in memory.[35]

The end of the war did not bring immediate peace to Tennessee or any noteworthy improvement in Ethie's situation. In fact, in May a close friend of

George and Ethie was taken out in the middle of the night and whipped just as George had been, although not quite so severely. In June, Ethie left New Market and moved back to Cades Cove although she was unable to inform George of her move.[36]

George's account of his trip back to Tennessee paints a vivid picture of conditions in that area immediately after the war ended. Sometimes coming dangerously close to bands of renegades in the mountains, he and his two companions found even greater threats in the area of New Market, where George discovered that his family had gone to Cades Cove.

> Now what shall we do? We hold a 'council of war.' We have entered this 'Paradise of Devils' (E. Tennessee) with our lives in our hands. We dare not pause here; the tories are worse than before the late surrender, robbing, cowhiding, hanging, shooting, etc. To reach my family's present whereabouts we must pass through 70 miles of bad country where I may meet many who will recognize me. There be some to meet with whom is to kill or be killed. I don't wish to see them but am prepared for the worst.[37]

They reached the Cove safely but took the back route to North Carolina through the Great Smoky Mountains. George's party encountered nothing more dangerous than washed-out roads and bridges, blockades, torrential rains, clumsy oxen which lost one wagon into the Little Tennessee River, and swarms of hornets and yellow jackets. All these, George noted, "give variety to the monotony of travel."[38]

The Eagletons spent about a year and a half in Iredell County before George accepted a call from a church in southern Arkansas. Ever since the end of the war he had expressed his determination to leave the scene of so much trouble and bitterness for the trans-Mississippi region. Here he could make a new start far from the "Yankee and tory vandals," who had "driven from home and scattered, robbed and persecuted" his and Ethie's families. Moreover, out West he would not have to endure so much the tragic effects which he expected from the Union's act of "turning loose 4,000,000 lazy blacks among the people of the Confederate states."[39]

Because the Eagletons lived in a state where there were strong sentiments on both sides in the civil struggle, their experiences were probably more devastating than those of residents of less sharply divided states. Surely George would not have had as much trouble as a Confederate veteran in Mississippi or Georgia as he did in Tennessee. Overall, however, the war affected them in ways which were characteristic for large numbers of southerners. The war shattered the world that they had known and scattered and destroyed their families. It alienated them from the state of their birth and of their ingrained loyalty; ironically, George refused to return to the state whose rights and soil he had gone to war to protect. The war created enduring hatred and loathing for the "Yankees and tories" and all that they stood for. The psychological impact of forced decisions against one's conscience, of long and painful separation from loved ones, of unrelieved worry over their safety cannot be measured. For many men like George the war brought violence and brutal death directly into their lives, lives which theretofore had been relatively untouched by such horrible facts. Yet, like countless others, George and Ethie not only survived but went on to build new lives out of the ruins of the old. Their courage, their determination to do what was right, their love and devotion for each other and for their family to a large degree overcame the tragic experience of the war. George became a fruitful and respected leader in church, school and community affairs in Arkansas, then in Texas, where he died in 1899.

Notes

1. George's *Day Book* and Ethie's *Stray Thoughts* are in the possession of their granddaughter, Elvie Eagleton (Mrs. Ottis C.) Skiplper, Huntsville, Alabama.

2. For Eagleton's prewar attitudes and his pro-Confederate decision, see the author's "The Tragic Dilemma of a Border-State Moderate: The Rev. George E. Eagleton's Views on Slavery and Secession," *Tennessee Historical Quarterly*, 32 (Winter 1973), 360-73. Parts of Ethie's diary appear in Elvie Eagleton Skipper (ed.), "'Stray Thoughts': The Civil War Diary of Ethie M. Foute Eagleton," Foreword by Ottis C. Skipper, *East Tennessee Historical Society's Publications*, 40 (1968): 128-37, and 41 (1969): 116-28.

3. *Day Book*, Nov. 26, 28, 1861.

4. Ibid., Nov. 28, Dec. 1, 7-9, 1861.

5. *Stray Thoughts*, Nov. 26-30, Dec. 20-21, 1861.

6. Thomas Lawrence Connelly, *Army of the Heartland: The Army of Tennessee, 1861-1862* (Baton Rouge, La., 1967), 65-77, 91-92; Stanley F. Horn, *The Army of Tennessee: A Military History* (Indianapolis and New York, 1941), 57-58; *Day Book*, Dec. 23, 1861.

7. *Day Book*, Dec. 25, 1861-Jan. 21, 1862.

8. *Stray Thoughts*, Jan. 13, 25, 1862.

9. Connelly, *Heartland*, pp. 78-99, 103-25, 131; *Army*, pp. 80-99.

10. Connelly, *Heartland*, pp. 78-85, 109-25, 133-37; Horn, *Army*, pp. 83-99; *Day Book*, Feb. 16, 17, 1862.

11. Connelly, *Heartland*, pp. 131-35, 138-39, 145; Horn, *Army*, pp. 99, 109; *Day Book*, Feb. 28-Mar. 23, 1862.

12. *Stray Thoughts*, Feb. 27, Mar. 1, 6, 1862. On March 31, 1862, at Iuka, Miss., Crittenden was arrested and deprived of his command for drunkenness. Connelly, *Heartland*, p. 146; Wiley Sword, *Shiloh: Bloody April* (New York, 1974), 85-86.

13. Connelly, *Heartland*, pp. 149-50; *Stray Thoughts*, Mar. 17-May 30, 1862.

14. Connelly, *Heartland*, pp. 145-53; Horn, *Army*, pp. 109-21; Sword, *Shiloh*, pp. 73-99; *Day Book*, Mar. 25-April 1, 1862.

15. Connelly, *Heartland*, pp. 152-75, 179-80; Horn, *Army*, pp. 122-43; Sword, *Shiloh*, pp. 100-442. George's regiment, the 44th Tennessee, suffered 350 casualties out of its 470 participants. [Goodspeed Publishing Co.] *History of Tennessee* (Nashville, 1886), 587.

16. *Day Book*, April 11-May 25, 1862.

17. Connelly, *Heartland*, pp. 176-80; Horn, *Army*, pp. 150-54; *Day Book*, May 29-June 3, 1862.

18. *Stray Thoughts*, April 11-June 14, 1862.

19. Connelly, *Heartland*, p. 178; *Day Book*, June 3-14, 1862.

20. *Day Book*, June 17-July 4, 1862; *Stray Thoughts*, July 4, 1862.

21. James W. Patton, *Unionism and Reconstruction in Tennessee, 1860-1869* (Chapel Hill, N.C., 1934), 34; Stanley J. Folmsbee, Robert E. Corlew, and Enoch L. Mitchell, *Tennessee: A Short History* (Knoxville, Tenn., 1969), 342-44, *Stray Thoughts*, June 19, 21, 22, 1862.

22. *Day Book*, July 6, 1862.

23. Connelly, *Heartland*, pp. 201-02; Horn, *Army*, pp. 161, 452 n. 23; Folmsbee, *et al.*, *Tennessee*, p. 334; *Stray Thoughts*, July 13, 1862.

24. *Day Book*, July 13, 1862.

25. Connelly, *Heartland*, p. 202; *Day Book*, July 22, 24, 1862.

26. *Day Book*, July 24, 1862-Sept. 6, 1863; *Stray Thoughts*, July 24, 1862-April 22, 1863.

27. *Day Book*, Oct. 26, Dec. 8, 1862, Jan. 15, 1863. The Cove was a pocket of Confederate sentiment surrounded by the prevailing Unionist influence. Inez E. Burns, *History of Blount County, Tennessee: From War Trail to Landing Strip* (Maryville, Tenn., 1957), p. 122.

28. Thomas Lawrence Connelly, *Autumn of Glory: The Army of Tennessee, 1862-1865* (Baton Rouge, La., 1971), pp. 94, 99, 121, 138, 149-50, 172, 192; Horn, *Army*, pp. 242, 244-45; Goodspeed, *History*, pp. 490-91, 558; *Day Book*, Sept. 10, 1863-July 24, 1864.

29. Connelly, *Autumn*, pp. 261-67, 295-96; Horn, *Army*, pp. 294-95; Goodspeed, *History*, pp. 491-93, 558; *Day Book*, Feb. 13, 1864; *Stray Thoughts*, Feb. 13, 1864.

30. *Day Book*, Aug. 3-18, 1864; *Stray Thoughts*, Aug. 3-25, 1864.

31. *Day Book*, Aug. 20-21, 1864; *Stray Thoughts*, Aug. 18-25, 1864. For evidence that such action was common to both sides see Patton, *Unionism*, pp. 51-74.

32. Connelly, *Autumn*, pp. 434-35; Horn, *Army*, p. 363; *Day Book*, Aug. 25-Nov. 17, 1864.

33. Goodspeed, *History*, pp. 495-96, 559; *Day Book*, Nov. 17, 1864-April 14, 1865.

34. *Stray Thoughts*, Aug. 26, 1864-July 16, 1865.

35. Ibid., especially Dec. 7, 1864, Jan. 20, 22, 24, 1865; Burns, *Blount County*, p. 65.

36. *Stray Thoughts*, May 5, June 15-21, July 16, 1865.

37. *Day Book*, July 4-20, 1865.

38. Ibid., July 20-31, 1865.

39. *Day Book*, April 29, Dec. 3, 1865; May 27, Oct. 25, Dec. 18, 1866, Sept. 18, 1867.

Part I:

Suggested Readings

Owsley's *Plain Folk of the Old South* (1949), is still the only attempt to survey the lives of the common people. Also see the work of Owsley's students, Blanche H. Clark, *The Tennessee Yeoman, 1840–1860* (Nashville, Tenn. 1942), Herbert Weaver, *Mississippi Farmers, 1850–1860* (Nashville, Tenn., 1945), and Harry L. Coles, Jr., "Some Notes on Slaveownership and Landownership in Louisiana, 1850–1860," *Journal of Southern History* 9 (August 1943). The best critique of Owsley is Fabian Linden, "Economic Democracy in the Slave South: An Appraisal of Some Recent Views," *Journal of Negro History* 31 (April 1949). Also see Barrington Moore, Jr., *Social Origins of Dictatorship and Democracy* (Boston, 1966). Classical studies of the South with comments on the common folk are William E. Dodd, *Statesmen of the Old South* (1911); Ulrich B. Phillips, *Life and Labor in the Old South* (New Haven, Conn., 1929); and, Roger W. Shugg, *Origins of Class Struggle in Louisiana* (Baton Rouge, La., 1939).

Attempts to classify the common folk have been infrequent. Serious investigation should begin with Daniel Hundley, *Social Relations in Our Southern States* (New York, 1860). More systematic work may be found in Wilbert E. Moore and Robin M. Williams, "Stratification in the Ante-bellum South," *American Sociological Review* (1942); Ira Berlin, "White Majority," *Social History* (May 1977). Tommy W. Rogers, "D. R. Hundley; A Multi-class Thesis of Social Stratification in the Ante-bellum South," *Mississippi Quarterly* (1970), Robert P. Sutton, "Sectionalism and Social Structure," *Virginia Magazine of History and Biography* (1972); D. L. A. Hackett, "The Social Structure of Jacksonian Louisiana," *Louisiana Studies* (Spring 1973); Eugene D. Genovese, " 'Rather Be a Nigger Than a Poor White Man' ": Slave Perceptions of Southern Yeomen and Poor Whites," in Hans L. Trefousse (ed.), *Toward a New View of America: Essays in Honor of Arthur Charles Cole* (New York, 1977); Eugene D. Genovese, "Yeoman Farmers in a Slaveholders' Democracy," *Agricultural History* (1974); Otto H. Olsen, "Historians and the Extent of Slave Ownership in the Southern United States," *Civil War History* (June 1972).

Eyewitness accounts by northern and foreign travelers of the southern people rarely are accurate on the common people. If used with caution, antebellum southern writers of folk literature and humorous tales reveal much about the lives of the people. See William Tappan Thompson, *Major Jones's Courtship* (Philadelphia, 1848); Johnson Jones Hooper, *Adventures of Captain Simon Suggs* (Philadelphia, 1848); and George Washington Harris, *Sut Lovingood* (New York, 1867). Works about the folk writers include William Stanley Hoole, *Alias Simon Suggs* (University Alabama, 1952); Jennette Reid Tandy, *Crackerbox Philosophers in American Humor and Satire* (New York, 1925); and Kenneth S. Lynn, *Mark Twain and Southwestern Humor* (Boston, 1959).

There are many important studies that touch on the lives of the common folk in the colonial and revolutionary period. See Richard B. Morris, *Government and Labor in Early America* (New York, 1946); James P. Whittenburg, "Planters, Merchants, and Lawyers: Social Change and the Origins of the North Carolina Regulation," *William and Mary Quarterly* (April 1977); Ronald Hoffman, "The 'Disaffected' in the Revolutionary South," in Alfred F. Young (ed.), *The American Revolution: Explorations in the History of American Radicalism* (DeKalb, Ill., 1976); Jackson Turner Main, *The Social Structure of Revolutionary America* (Princeton, N.J., 1965); Julia Cherry Spruill, *Women's Life and Work in the Southern Colonies* (Chapel Hill, N.C., 1938); Henry Roy Merrens, *Colonial North Carolina in the Eighteenth Century* (Chapel Hill, N.C., 1964); Rhys Isaac, "Evangelical Revolt: The Nature of the Baptists' Challenge to the Traditional Order," *William and Mary Quarterly* (1974); James A. Henretta, "Families and Farms: *Mentalité* in Pre-industrial America," *William and Mary Quarterly* (January 1978); D. Alan Williams, "The Small Farmer in Eighteenth-Century Virginia Politics," *Agricultural History* (1969); Carville V. Earle, *The Evolution of a Tidewater Settlement System* (Chicago, 1975); Harold E. Davis, *The Fledgling Province: Social and Cultural Life in Colonial Georgia, 1733–1776* (Chapel Hill, N.C., 1976); Edmund S. Morgan, *American Slavery, American Freedom* (New York, 1975); Aubrey C. Land, "Economic Behavior in a Planting Society: The Eighteenth-Century Chesapeake," *Journal of Southern History* (1967); Timothy H. Breen, "A Changing Labor Force and Race Relations in Virginia, 1660–1710," *Journal of Social History* (Fall 1973).

For southerners' westward migration see Conrad and Irene B. Tauber, *The Changing Population of the United States* (New York, 1958); Thomas P.

Abernathy, *The South in the New Nation, 1789–1819* (Baton Rouge, La., 1961); John D. Barnhart, "Frontiersmen and Planters in the Formation of Kentucky," *Journal of Southern History* (February 1941); William O. Lynch, "The Westward Flow of Southern Colonists Before 1861," *Journal of Southern History* (August 1943); Tommy W. Rogers, "The Great Population Exodus from South Carolina, 1850–1860," *South Carolina Historical Magazine* (January 1967); Tommy W. Rogers, "Origins and Destination of Tennessee Migrants, 1850–1860," *Tennessee Historical Quarterly* (Summer 1968); Charles D. Lowery, "The Great Migration to the Mississippi Territory, 1798–1819," *Mississippi History* (August 1968).

On religion in the Old South among the common folk see Donald G. Mathews, *Religion in the Old South* (Chicago, 1977); Dickson D. Bruce, Jr., *And They all Sang Hallelujah: Plain-Folk Camp-Meeting, 1800–1845* (Knoxville, Tenn., 1975); Charles Albert Johnson, *The Frontier Camp Meeting* (Dallas, 1955); Walton B. Posey, *Frontier Mission: A History of Religion West of the Southern Appalachians to 1861* (Lexington, Ky., 1966); William Warren Sweet, *Religion on the American Frontier: The Baptists, 1785–1830* (New York, 1931); Clement Eaton, *The Mind of the Old South* (Baton Rouge, La., 1964); Bertram Wyatt-Brown, "Antimission Movement in the Jacksonian South," *Journal of Southern History* (1970); Darward T. Stokes, "North Carolina and the Great Revival of 1800," *North Carolina Historical Review* (October 1966); James Banner, "Religious Benevolence as Social Control," *Journal of American History* (1973).

The only book that deals specifically with the education of the common folk is Edgar W. Knight, *Public Education in the South* (New York, 1922). Also see David B. Potts, "Baptist Colleges in the Development of American Society, 1812–1861," (Harvard Ph.D. 1967); Marcus C. S. Noble, *A History of the Public Schools of North Carolina* (Chapel Hill, N.C., 1930); Albea Godbold, *The Church College of the Old South* (1944); William Arthur Maddox, *The Free School Idea in Virginia Before the Civil War* (New York, 1918); Alfred James Morrison, *The Beginnings of Public Education in Virginia, 1776–1860* (Richmond, 1917); John Furman Thompson, *The Foundations of the Public School in South Carolina* (Columbia, S.C., 1925); Dorothy Orr, *A History of Education in Georgia* (Chapel Hill, N.C., 1950); David F. Allmendinger, Jr., "The Dangers of Ante-bellum Student Life," *Journal of Social History* (Fall 1973); Ruth Miller Elson, *Guardians of Tradition* (Lincoln, Nebraska, 1963).

Fascinating studies of the relationship of class violence to crime and legal controls are Douglas Hay *et al.*, *Albion's Fatal Tree* (New York, 1975), Scott and Patricia O'Brien, "Crime and Punishment as a Historical Problem," *Journal of Social History* (Summer 1978). For an introduction to elite use of the law in the Old South see Eugene D. Genovese, *Roll, Jordan, Roll* (New York, 1974). Criminal behavior and punishment may be found in James M. Bonner,

"The Georgia Penitentiary at Milledgeville, 1817–1874," *Georgia Historical Review* (1974); Ralph Simpson, "Campus Violence and Moderation in the Ante-bellum South," *Research Studies* (1970); Howell M. Henry, *The Police Control of the Slave in South Carolina* (Columbia, 1914); James Flanigan, "The Criminal Law of Slavery and Freedom," Ph.D. Diss., Rice University, 1973; James C. Scott, "Protest and Profanation," *Theory and Society* (Spring 1977); Jack Kenny Williams, *Vogues in Villainy; Crime and Retribution in Ante-bellum South Carolina* (Columbia, S.C., 1959); Arthur F. Howington, "Violence in Alabama: A Study of Late Ante-bellum Montgomery," *The Alabama Review* (July 1974). Robert M. Saunders, "Crime and Punishment in Early National America: Richmond, Virginia, 1784–1860," *The Virginia Magazine of History and Biography* (January 1978).

For the free blacks see Ira Berlin, *Slaves Without Masters* (New York, 1974); Laura Foner, "The Free People of Color in Louisiana and St. Dominque," *Journal of Social History* (Summer 1970); John H. Russell, *The Free Negro in Virginia, 1619–1865* (Baltimore, 1913); H. E. Sterkx, *The Free Negro in Ante-bellum Louisiana* (Rutherford, N.J., 1972); James Martin Wright, *The Free Negro in Maryland, 1634–1860* (New York, 1971), Letitia Woods Brown, *Free Negroes in the District of Columbia, 1790–1846* (New York, 1972); Charles S. Sydnor, "The Free Negro in Mississippi Before the Civil War," *American Historical Review* (July 1927); John Hope Franklin, *The Free Negro in North Carolina, 1790–1860* (Chapel Hill, N.C., 1943); George R. Woolfolk, *The Free Negro in Texas, 1800–1860* (Ann Arbor, Mich., 1976).

The question of subregional distinctions among the common people may be previewed in the bibliography on southern westward settlement. Also see Frederick Jackson Turner, *The United States, 1830–1850* (New York, 1935); David M. Potter, *The South and the Sectional Conflict* (Baton Rouge, La., 1968); and William W. Freehling, "The Editorial Revolution, Virginia, and the Coming of the Civil War: A Review Essay," *Civil War History* (March 1970).

There are few studies of common people's work habits. Urban work patterns may be seen in David R. Goldfield, *Urban Growth in the Age of Sectionalism: Virginia, 1847–1861* (Baton Rouge, La., 1977), and Mary Fulton Green, "A Profile of Columbia in 1850," *South Carolina University Magazine* (1969). For common folk's occupations see Lewis E. Atherton, *The Southern Country Store, 1800–1860* (Baton Rouge, La., 1949); Daniel Harvey Calhoun, *Professional Lives in America: Structure and Aspiration 1750–1850* (Cambridge, Mass., 1965); William K. Scarborough, *The Overseer* (Baton Rouge, La., 1966); Harold D. Woodman, *King Cotton and His Retainers* (Lexington, Ky., 1968); Tom E. Terrill, "Eager Hands: Labor for Southern Textiles, 1850–1860," *Journal of Economic History* (1976); Ernest M. Lander, *The Textile Industry in Antebellum South Carolina*

(Baton Rouge, La., 1969); Randall M. Miller, "Daniel Pratt's Industrial Urbanism: The Cotton Mill Town in Antebellum Alabama," *Alabama Historical Quarterly* (Spring 1972); Richard B. Morris, "Labor Militancy in the Old South," *Labor and Nation* (May–June 1948); Sam B. Hilliard, *Hog Meat and Hoecakes* (Carbondale, Ill., 1973).

The role of the common folk in the secession crisis has been most recently discussed in Michael P. Johnson, *Toward a Patriarchal Republic: The Secession of Georgia* (Baton Rouge, La., 1977). Comments that supplement Russell's views of the nonslaveholder and secession may be seen in Heywood Fleisig, "Slavery, the Supply of Agricultural Labor, and the Industrialization of the South," *Journal of Economic History* (September 1976); Robert E. Gallman, "Southern Antebellum Income Reconsidered," *Explorations in Economic History* (1975); Eugene D. Genovese, "Yeoman Farmer in a Slaveholder's Democracy," *Agricultural History* (1978).

In addition to the works cited in the second section on the behavior of the common folk during the Civil War, see Gary B. Mills, "Alien Neutrality and the Red River Campaign: A Study of Cases Heard Before the International Claims Commissions," *Southern Studies* (Summer 1977); Harry M. Scheiber, "Pay of Confederate Troops, Problems of Demoralization: A Case of Administrative Failure," *Civil War History* (September 1969); Georgia Lee Tatum, *Disloyalty in the Confederacy* (Chapel Hill, N.C., 1934); Joseph Howard Parks, *Joseph E. Brown of Georgia* (Baton Rouge, La., 1977).

Part II

THE COMMON PEOPLE OF THE POSTWAR SOUTH

Introduction

New issues and new relationships arising from the Civil War's disruptions and postwar capitalist agriculture dominate Part II of this volume. Reconstruction era race and class relations, farmer and artisan political protest, and the conditions of life and labor during the South's belated industrial transformation are some of the major concerns of this section.

During the war, significant proportions of the white lower classes had defied and disobeyed the planters and their spokesmen in the Confederacy by large-scale desertions from the army, by organizing Unionist sentiment, and by forming outlaw bands and other associations that weakened the planters' war for southern independence. The war meant gross physical devastation, property losses, and the abolition of chattel slavery. Most profoundly, war exposed class differences and produced class friction but little visible change in antebellum social structure, except for the destruction of slavery.

Every southerner, black and white, suffered some kind of impoverishment during the following decades as a result of the war and Reconstruction policies. Planters suffered less than other groups despite black self-emancipation and white disloyalty and disobedience. Planters and farmers temporarily overcame the costly effects of farm destruction, losses of livestock, buildings, tools, and seeds. Black slaves seemed at first to have gained most—their freedom—but soon suffered more than others from post-emancipation class realignments, race policies of apartheid, and economic change. Black freedmen and white tenant farmers appear to have continued as the base of planter wealth. The plantation system proved a resilient institution, adaptable to "free" and tenant farm labor as well as to slave; and many antebellum plantation owners retained their properties and their dominance, through alliance with industrial interests and with the aid of coercion and violence, according to recent studies by Jonathan Wiener, Jay Mandle, and Michael Schwartz. (The works of these and other authors mentioned in this Introduction will be found in the Suggested Readings for this part of the book.)

Recently, economists and economic historians of the South have contributed helpful studies analyzing the post-Reconstruction decline of southern agriculture. Roger L. Ransom and Richard Sutch maintain that emancipation affected antebellum yeomen least among white classes; by 1880 white owner-operator farms of fifty acres or less comprised 28 percent of all the farms in the cotton South. Gavin Wright, in studying the political economy of that commodity, pointed out that by 1880 one-third of the white farm operators in the cotton states were tenants. Yet, as Harold Woodman notes, the rise of post-Reconstruction tenantry represents more than the classical responses of "risk takers and risk averters" in the agricultural marketplace. The various forms of tenant farming after the war also were part of the emergence of "new classes and relationships." In this Woodman offers a path for social historians to follow in searching for the history of the white middle and lower classes.

Students of the South should be stimulated by both Woodman's suggestions in a thoughtful essay, "Sequel to Slavery: The New History Views the Post-bellum South" (*Journal of Southern History* 43, November 1977), and the essays in the following pages. They illuminate what is now known about post-emancipation southern lower- and middle-class groups. They continue in newly sophisticated ways an approach of historians of a generation ago.

Southerners and other Americans rediscovered poverty and their history during the Great Depression of the 1930s. Writers of southern history in those crisis years initiated a reversal of the mythic "tragic era" of defeated slave owners and their lost world and the imperfect "Solid South" of post-Reconstruction Bourbon Redeemers. Behind them, scholars revealed, stood their retainers, the landowning banks and insurance companies, railroad, steel and iron, coal, timber, cotton, tobacco, and sugar corporations. But, historians demonstrated, the "plain people" did not constitute a parternalistically suffocated universe of dependency, although racism exacted a high price from southern society. Its members are still making payments.

A flood of afflictions in the 1930s uncovered a new southern self-consciousness expressed by Progressive middle-class reformers, by intellectuals nostalgically idealizing agrarianism, and by abundant southern literary art seeking a truth for life to imitate. A new southern class awareness was expressed by striking coal miners, and organizing drives by sharecroppers, tenant-farmers, and unemployed millworkers. Frank Owsley reflected a yearning for relief from the ill effects of a profoundly disturbed industrial capitalism by turning to history. There he rediscovered the antebellum yeoman farmers and their ways of life, the Jeffersonian ideal reawakened. (But you could not go home again to the storied South.)

When he wrote of the Reconstruction years, Owsley assigned a major role to the white "plain folk" as saviors of the South from "final ruin." The yeoman farmer's resourceful ingenuity surmounted Civil War and Reconstruction hardships in contrast to the supposed plantation owners' paralysis of production. But that sturdy class of farmers who emerged from the Tennessee and Appalachian up-country did not exclusively remake the South or save it from destruction. Although Owsley erred in this, he stimulated the search for the white middle and lower classes. Their history in the last third of the nineteenth and early twentieth centuries has been investigated in the past two decades by such historians as William Ivy Hair, Lawrence C. Goodwyn, Robert C. McMath, William Warren Rogers, J. Morgan Kousser, and William F. Holmes. Generally, they have approached their work with heightened appreciation of small-farmer and agricultural-laborer roles, values, and culture and their struggles for political and economic power.

Southern intellectuals politicized during the depression ironically pursued the ideologically conservative Owsley's lead. They explored the social forces that made the "New South." The beginnings of a new historiographical revisionism were ushered in by histories of class conflict in antebellum Louisiana, of black slave labor effecting self-emancipation, of postbellum agrarian protest, and of political and industrial unrest that confronted southern upper-class institutions and ideology with threatening alternatives. Southern workers and farmers proved to be no dropouts from a national upheaval in the 1880s and 1890s. Those works by Roger Shugg, W. E. B. Du Bois, Alrutheus Ambush Taylor, C. Vann Woodward, Vernon L. Wharton, Albert D. Kirwan, and others were the cutting edge of a new history of the South and of America. Their contribution was to reveal that in political and economic affairs a new set of social relationships was accompanied by powerful remnants of the old and that these comprised the central experience of southern social history after 1861. They showed that suppressed antebellum industrialism took on new life, even in a predominantly agricultural world. It entered the twentieth century as a major component of a national system with headquarters in major northern cities and some southern ones as well.

A product of the South's industrial development was the formation of an industrial working class that organized itself in the Knights of Labor, across race lines, claimed its equal rights, and later supported the Populist party. Labor joined farmers in calling for cooperative enterprise to curb monopolies, and they advanced other proposals for national ownership of basic sectors of the economy. Skilled white labor later responded to industrialism by turning to its own forms of control over the labor market that excluded blacks and women. But before the century was over, black and white workingmen and women had challenged the railroads in the Great Southwest strike, the sugar field owners in Louisiana strikes in 1886 and 1887, the shipping interests in New Orleans by the general strike of 1892, and miners took on the Tennessee Coal, Iron, and Railroad Company in 1891.

Racism persisted in the postbellum South and took on open and brutal forms as the opposition to industrialism and Democratic political domination mounted. Former slave-owning planters were transformed into wage and share-paying plantation owners, merchants, and investors in industrial enterprise. After slavery had been destroyed, their domination was exercised in great measure by race division, disfranchisement of black and white lower-class voters, and by legal and extralegal violence. The former slaves were denied land on which to develop their own ways of life and their own communities. A sort of enclosure movement pushed economically depressed whites from the tobacco and cotton fields and the countryside generally into the cotton mills, where they became a tightly controlled proletariat. They continued to be depressed. And racist ideology kept them from association with black labor, with whom they might have found common ground for common action as miners, iron workers, and farmers had found a basis for collaboration.

The complexity and variety of southern society became more evident in the final third of the nineteenth century. A Frank Owsley or a post-slavery David Hundley was not required to refute simplistic class structures created by opponents of the slave system. The implication of unity and continuity in southern history that W. J. Cash perceived charmingly in *The Mind of the South* could be disturbed by Ella Lonn's study of disloyalty and desertion during the Confederacy, Woodward's puncture of the "Solid South" myths, and Clement Eaton's antebellum "federalism of cultures." Woodward and Du Bois showed that the plain people stepped into the pages of history in their own right, claiming a share in the shaping of southern society. Shugg demonstrated the discontinuities and disunities in Louisiana society and culture. These historians of the depression era and their students have taught us much about the "mudsills and bottom rails," and about the propertied and powerful who dominated the South.

A new generation of scholars informed by liberal social science and historical materialism, and by the uprisings of lower classes and colonial peoples throughout the world since World War II, have opened anew the possibilities for social history. Their explorations of the turbulent and the quiet periods point the way to richer understandings of the people's life and labor, their subcultures, and their roles in making southern society. They are asking questions that were ignored by, or escaped, older historians addressing the race question in southern historiography or who were preoccupied with explications of the "lost cause" or with the Progressive political consensus and its ramifications.

We are obviously at the beginning of a great turn in the road leading us to the minds and deeds of white and black southern industrial workers and their cultures, farm laborers, tenants and owners, women, Indians, Hispanic, Irish, German, Italian, and other immigrant subcultures and communities in the South. The very richness and diversity of late nineteenth- and early twentieth-century southern society suggest complex social relationships. Paternalism and dependency, racial imbalances and injustices and their correction, the intersections of cultures during the major socioeconomic rearrangements, the active participation of disinherited, despised, and disenfranchised plebeians in politics invite exploration of their lives and labors. Folklorists and novelists have contributed much to our knowledge of that social history of the South, and some may have introduced or perpetuated harmful stereotypes. Although we must be grateful, for example, for Ellen Glasgow's turn-of-the-century novels that gracefully portrayed changing personal and communal relations in Virginia, we should at the same time regret the misuses of Erskine Caldwell's Georgia backcountry folk. However, the major responsibility for rehabilitation of the plain people's past remains with social historians.

Many of those groups of southerners receive serious and sophisticated attention in the essays in this collection. At the same time these writings suggest that further work is necessary. The articles in Part II of this book follow a rough chronological arrangement. They begin with Reconstruction and conclude with an aspect of industrialization. The essays are concerned with Southern popular consciousness and with distinctive expressions of some lower-class and middle-class world views. Farm and factory, city and country are represented in these articles. In Jeffrey's, farm women emerge toward equality with men from a cocoon placed around southern women in general. In Magdol's, an isolated Indian group asserts its identity and its interests against the former slave-owning gentry. In Burton's, black freedmen contest and comply with the dictates of the white-line Democratic party leadership. In Goodwyn's, farmers balk at that party's complicity in the monopolization and depletion of southern natural resources and the degradation of the nation's democratic values and aspirations.

The essays enter the worlds of the middle and lower classes in novel and illuminating ways. Frank Huffman's statistical comparison of a Georgia town and countryside social structure over three decades affords a starting point for any appreciation of changes in class and property status from prewar to postwar times. The cases of Athens and Oconee county residents appear to be prototypes of the small city and rural South from 1850 to 1880. Huffman begins to answer the need for demographic studies of southern social change through the war and Reconstruction years. His essay reveals no destruction of property or losses directly due to the war, which may make the cases of limited value. However, the indirect effects of war may be seen in declining trade in the city. This could have been the result of prewar soil exhaustion as well as of the drain of men and resources by the war. What remains appears to be a serious change in property ownership and status, which at least helps us to witness a postwar change in the social structure suggested by Owsley and others: The yeoman farmer was depressed into tenant farming or urban occupations.

Huffman's distillation and analysis of census data deal with population persistence and in-migration, occupational status and black-white occupational differences, the striking growth of farm tenantry over ownership, personal property ownership, and the advance of rural poverty. The essay reveals an economically stable urban but fragile rural society on the eve of protracted urban and rural social conflict. Athens and Oconee may prove to be a yardstick by which to measure the populations in other southern communities. Understandably this concise statistical study must leave for other scholars the task of retrieving the range of emotions and thoughts and responses of the town and country folk.

W. E. B. Du Bois sensitively described the texture of life among rural black laborers and peasants in that era in Dougherty County, Georgia. Amid the "forlorn and forsaken" land Du Bois found a black community striving to keep body and soul together. Like their white counterparts, Dougherty County blacks also labored under the impositions of the Cotton Seed Oil Trust, high rents, and low cotton prices. Their lot was poverty and especially peonage, marked by child and prison labor, debt, and the denial of schooling and opportunity for self-improvement. Du Bois took the numbers in the census and the local tax records and breathed life into them with his descriptions of real human beings. He left a grim picture of depression in Dougherty County. The stir made by Farmers' Alliances and other organizations in the southern countryside in the same period prompts an inquiry: Had the spirit of freedmen self-assertion in the 1860s been so thoroughly curbed as Du Bois's essay of the 1890s suggests? Like other microcosms, the Dougherty County example may obscure the larger picture of southern agrarian woes and responses to them. Yet it may be considered a standard for comparisons with other southern counties. Surely, we could stand to have a comparable exposition of white tenants and sharecroppers in the same period.

That there may have been a tradition in the black community that gave substance to its survival is suggested in the essays by Vernon Burton and Edward Magdol. The essay on Grimes County populism by Lawrence Goodwyn also suggests that the stability of black organization since Reconstruction not only served survival purposes but contributed a substantial base for white political protest a generation later in the 1890s and early 1900s. The selections yield strong clues to important historical continuity in the black lower-class world over two generations and to the lost possibilities of agrarian class harmony. In these essays, Edgefield, South Carolina, blacks; Robeson County, North Carolina, Lumbee Indians and black freedmen; and (in Leon Fink's recent study) Richmond, Virginia, Knights of Labor, suggest that the non-white South developed not only ethnic but distinctive class cultures, values, and mechanisms for survival and success. But defeat and failure were the palpable facts. They may be explained in considerable measure by examples such as the inability of Grimes County Populists to prevent White Man's Union murders and other intimidations of voters or the timidity of Richmond Knights of Labor in resisting attacks on the organization's short-lived racial equality. In this regard, Leon Fink's discussion of Richmond politics sheds much needed light upon the impulses and inhibitions of white craftmen and others. Much as his paper and Goodwyn's and Montgomery's essays on populism improve our perception of black and white cooperation, the field remains open to further exploration of white common people's attitudes and their motivations to action and inaction.

These works underscore the need for research in white farmer, industrial worker, and lower middle-class communities and cultures to match the sort of study the black people have received. Sterling Stuckey, Lawrence Levine, and Herbert G. Gutman provide a few examples of scholars whose work recently has revised Afro-American history and destroyed shibboleths and stereotypes. Moreover, William Ivy Hair's study of Louisiana post-Reconstruction politics and society sets an example of high quality in the scholarship of that state's popular forces. Similarly, J. Morgan Kousser's acute quantitative study of low-income whites' and blacks' disenfranchisement in the Gilded Age and the Populist upheaval is a methodological tour de force that reflects upper-class anxieties about lower-class political behavior. On the road to a social history of the southern plain people are William F. Holmes's studies of Arkansas sharecroppers and rural laborers in the colored and white southern Farmers' Alliances, and Holmes's and William W. Rogers's studies of whitecapping and agrarian protest in Alabama. They elevate our knowledge from the level of the political biographies of grass-roots politicos from Tom Watson to Huey Long which have become a genre in southern historiography. The scholarly emphasis has begun to shift from the charismatic and self-proclaimed middle-class leadership toward the rank and file of southern social movements.

Among works in progress in this new southern social history two that have recently been completed appear in this volume. One is Julie Roy Jeffrey's refreshing review of southern women's roles in general through her examination of women in a North Carolina Farmers' Alliance local organization. While liberating themselves, as Jeffrey demonstrates, they played vital roles in the sub-alliances. As Robert McMath has shown, these organizations expressed a white rural subculture and its values. The second is Dale Newman's novel contrast of workers in spinning and weaving mill villages. Through her recent in terviews with mill village residents Newman has retrieved a considerable record of textile industry life and labor conditions. Although just outside of the intended chronological framework of this collection, the experiences and ideas of the villagers reflect little change in conditions and relationships from the nineteenth- and early twentieth-century establishment of those factory towns. Where a plentiful mill village scholarship approached their worker-inhabitants as repressed objects of an all-embracing paternalism, Newman transports us to the inner world of the despised "lintheads" themselves. They appear tentatively, belatedly, and self-consciously resistant to the corrosiveness of millowner hegemony. In this sense, Newman provides a substantial component of social history missing from Liston Pope's landmark 1940 study of religion and church as instruments of class control.

Most of the contributors revise older versions of southern history. First of all, their close attention to lower-class perceptions and actions in itself constitutes a significant new contribution. Burton's article adds to our appreciation of the self-determinative roles of free blacks in the Reconstruction era. Burton examines changing class and race relations in Edgefield, South Carolina. His findings show black competitive and self-assertive behavior ranging from militant and forceful confrontation to defensive accommodation. Burton thus importantly joins recent historians of the free people in modifying Woodward's interpretation of southern race relations and in reversing Eugene D. Genovese's assertions of black political impotence engendered by planter paternalism during slavery.

The actions of Robeson county, North Carolina, blacks and Indians illustrate the rapidly adaptive capacities of repressed people who move from pre-political to more modern forms of action. Their distinctive behavior and thought revise concepts of lower-class dependency and black manipulability by the powerful.

Fink, Goodwyn, and Montgomery question and refute "status anxiety" theories for farmer and labor behavior. Richmond Knights in Fink's paper demonstrate distinctive artisanal approaches to political action setting them apart from reformist middle-class allies. Goodwyn's essay reverses a formerly accepted version of Populist regressiveness. Montgomery reinforces Goodwyn's interpretation in his larger work, *Democratic Promise*, but also cautions against a vision of populism limited to the money question. Montgomery's brief review essay corrects the tendency to isolate southern history from national history and calls attention to the radical prescription of socialism in the movement's program. Finally, he restores the awakened industrial working class to an influential role in analysis of the Populist movement.

Revisionism was implicit in Du Bois's observations in the Georgia Black Belt. He furnished a corrective to the traditional sources of his time, against which Goodwyn also would later caution. If one were to rely upon traditional Grimes County white middle-class sources, both written and oral, then serious distortion entered the record, or omissions occurred, according to Goodwyn. As his essay demonstrates, he found it necessary and enlightening to speak to non-traditional participant-observers, some of the victims of repression themselves. Goodwyn's, Du Bois's, and Newman's recourse to neglected primary sources, the "plain people," represents both conceptual and methodological gains.

These essays unitedly affirm the active class and ethnic diversity of southern postbellum society and thought. They do not approach exhaustion of the possibilities for southern social history. They may inspire controversy and skepticism, which would be contributions enough. But the editors anticipate that readers will be moved to press ahead with further reexamination of assertions made in these essays and to new explorations of questions and groups neglected here.

Edward Magdol

Against the Gentry: An Inquiry into a Southern Lower-Class Community and Culture, 1865–1870

Beginning with W. E. B. Du Bois in the Progressive period, revisionist writers of Reconstruction history have rendered tragic-era interpretations incredible. They have admirably redressed the balance of ethnicity but left us only at the threshold of the former slaves' world. The task remains to step over that threshold, to reconceptualize Reconstruction historiography from the point of view of the Southern lower classes. This essay suggests a need for such a new approach toward Reconstruction social history. The evidence of vital lower-class cultures as expressed in their values, views and activity indicates that until that need is met Reconstruction history is incomplete.[1]

Lower-class groups in the Americas have demonstrated a lively talent for creating viable subcultures. "Outlaw," creole and mestizo free peoples have sustained communities and subcultures in defiance of local gentries and distant political rulers. Runaway slave villages enjoyed varying degrees of success from the seventeenth to the nineteenth century. Notable were the quilombos and palenques—the runaway slave communities in Cuba, Brazil, Jamaica and Florida. "Fugitive" mestizo communities existed in western South Carolina mountains during the eighteenth century. From time to time maroon communities appeared and disappeared on the swamps, bayous and mountains of the southeastern United States. All have enriched the history of Atlantic and Caribbean cultures.[2]

One such subculture flourished in Robeson County, North Carolina, during post–Civil War years. A mixed community of seven thousand lower-class blacks and Anglo-Indians, it emerged from relative isolation to participate in

Source: This essay was originally published in the *Journal of Social History* 6, no. 3 (Spring 1973): 259–83. Reprinted by permission.

the Reconstruction process. The two ethnically diverse components shared considerable cultural homogeneity, partly a function of their lower-class status. Available evidence points to two responses to the gentry and its power. The first, cultural resistance against white upper-class rule, was the essential dynamic of the Anglo-Indians. The second response was a combination of political, economic and cultural activities asserted by the blacks. The Anglo-Indians were concentrated in a swampy enclave called The Settlement, labeled "Scuffletown" by the whites. The blacks, who were more numerous, were widely dispersed throughout the county. This community of mestizos and freedmen appears to have been fashioned to some extent by propinquity. It became cohesive and vigorous when it confronted the local cotton-planter and turpentine-manufacturing gentry.[3]

The most dramatic expression of this lower-class multi-ethnic world was its support of a daring social bandit, Henry Berry Lowry, from 1865 to 1872 in defiance of state and local authorities. This picaresque young Anglo-Indian carpenter and his gang, made up of 8 to 20 Indians, Blacks and one poor white youth, robbed and killed Confederate officials, planters and Klansmen. Like some other primitive rebels, they began their bandit and outlaw careers trying to avenge the murders of their kinsmen. Their criminal activity was intended to establish justice, with a slight redress for grievances from booty for Robeson's poor people. Despite their social deviance the gang won at least the tacit sanction of Indians and former slaves. Today Lowry is the folk hero of about 50,000 Lumbee Indians.[4]

Although he was a surrogate for Robeson's poor people, Lowry's social brigandage was not a substitute for the concurrent and lawful effort of the freedmen to assert themselves. Both kinds of activities were intimately related. The poor sought justice and respect for their identities. Their efforts toward these ends brought them together to confront the power of the gentry over them and the land. The bases for their protests derived not only from their origins, material conditions, economic and social status, but also from their conceptions of justice, marriage and family and modes of self-expression. These were the meaningful elements of a culture and a community that deserve a place in social history.

The way into the complex, obscure and baffling history of Robeson's peasant and rural proletarian world is beset with almost as much difficulty as the way through the swamps of the Lumber River area where some of its members lived. The historian must avoid the sentimentality of lower-class hero-worshippers and even more the judgments of self-centered middle-class white contemporaries who left the principal written records of their post–Civil War experiences. "Scuffletown" loomed large in their intellectual and emotional perceptions. "Scuffletown's" residents, as they viewed them, were a decadent social formation infecting the slaves of white planters in an otherwise moral community. In postwar years Scuffletonians did not improve, but rather worsened, their profligate image in the eyes of the defeated cotton gentry and turpentine manufacturers. Indeed, "Scuffletown" was their derogatory label for that community. On the other hand, an opposite set of values may be inferred from "The Settlement," the label applied to this Anglo-Indian and/or Anglo-Afro-Indian enclave. With these subjective differences in mind, this inquiry sought relatively more objective sources, such as manuscript census data and Freedmen's Bureau records.[5]

Another problem, for the historian, is the obscurity that surrounds the origins of The Settlement and the identity of its peoples. Firm evidence is scant and there appears little likelihood of finding new data. White middle-class writers of the 1870s, relying on oral traditions, were vague about how "Scuffletown" began. Later, ethnologists accepted a view that Robeson County Indians were descendants of Croatan Indians and members of Sir Walter Raleigh's "Lost Colony." The North Carolina legislature in 1885 authorized the Croatan name, based on research and assertions of Hamilton McMillan, a white local historian and Democrat. He asserted a link between English Roanoke Island refugees and their supposed Indian hosts with whom they probably intermarried, and the brown- and dark-skinned people in Robeson three centuries later. Before the legislature's act, Robeson mestizos had no Indian designation. They spoke English and appeared to have the same folkways as neighboring English-speaking poor white farmers. Some had apparently become assimilated and were prosperous yeoman farmers; some even had owned slaves. The adult males exercised the right of franchise up to 1835. Some of their children up to that time attended white schools; most of those in schools attended separate subscription schools that their elders organized and conducted. There is no evidence of tribal organization. The absence of an Indian language when they were "discovered" by eighteenth-century Scots immigrants further complicates identification. The continuity of family names over almost two centuries suggests strong kinship ties as one mechanism of community and of ethnic identification.[6]

The confusion is not relieved by other white designations during the nineteenth century. When the 1835 North Carolina constitution was adopted, mestizos lost their rights to vote, to bear arms and to send their children to white schools. Thereafter they were officially designated "free persons of color." This meant they were placed in a resented classification with free black people, who also were disfranchised and stripped of educational and other civil rights. Printed census compendia of 1860 and 1870 used "colored" to include all non-whites, and, as in manuscript census forms, they were differentiated as "black" or "mulatto." Alongside hundreds of "mulatto" entries, census takers recorded Lowry, Lowrie, Oxendine, Locklear, Chavis, Dial, Revels, Brayboy and other family names of people who in the 1880s claimed Indian identity. One wealthy Lumberton, N.C., lawyer testified in 1871 that these were among people commonly called "mulattoes." "That is the name they are known by," he explained, "as contradistinguished from negroes." Whether Indian or "mulatto" or "free person of color," their claim to some *independent* identity was supported by their refusal from 1868 to 1885 to send their children to black schools. While being barred from white schools, they won separate Indian schools essentially on the grounds that they were rejected as whites and refused to be classified as blacks.[7]

The supposed genesis of The Settlement was described by two white observers in the 1870s. One was Mrs. Mary Norment, widow of a Lowry gang victim. The other was former North Carolina Adjutant General John Gorman. According to them, eighteenth-century slaves and Tuscarora Indians who had been forced off their lands by white planters, settled in these "sandy patches of land situated among the slashes and swamps of the Pee Dee and Lumber Rivers." The Indians came into a section already inhabited by a number of "Free Negro" families "whose manner of life was similar to that of the half-breed Indians." Mrs. Norment named probable runaway slave families who formed a nucleus for the future community. Miscegenation produced the people Gorman was to confront when he was in command of forces pursuing the Lowry band. "Here the people lived," he wrote, "without schools or churches, in a sort of savage freedom, though subject to the laws of the State," until the outbreak of the Civil War.[8]

This area was commonly known, Mrs. Norment explained, as "a large free negro or mulatto settlement, without streets or public buildings, having no municipal laws or regulations." It was, however, a country "interspersed and traversed by swamps, covered at wide intervals with hills, with here and there a log cabin of rude and simple construction." These were called "mulatto cabins." A *Nation* reporter in 1865 had labeled them "Negro huts." They appeared poor when compared to homes built by skilled carpenters. Generally the log huts were surrounded by a patch of cleared dry land of three or four acres plowed and planted in corn, potatoes and rice. The crops "come up *puny*, grow *puny*, and mature *puny*," Mrs. Norment reported. A local militia officer recorded a visit to one such homestead, "ten by fourteen made of pine boards; and no floor, only dirt." The family occupying the house consisted of a couple and their "seven children, a gun and four dogs. One broken chair, two plates, one broken fork, no cups or anything of the kind."[9]

The poverty of Settlement people resulted from their low wages when they worked for others and from their possession of marginally productive lands sufficient for bare subsistence. The people lived by "riving shingles, tending turpentine 'orchards,' hunting and fishing, and by occasional jobs from nearby planters." A New York *Herald* reporter in 1872 wrote from Lumberton that Settlement people "labored as ditchers for neighboring farmers who pay them the magnanimous wages of $6 a month." This "pocoson land" (swamp in Indian language) was rich in whortleberries and blackberries, from which Scuffletonians earned some money. A farmhand earned about $10 a month with board. In Robeson County, by 1870, a farmhand hired by the year, earned $6 a month with board. A day laborer received 50¢ with board, 75¢ without. This represented deterioration from common-labor daily wages in North Carolina, which averaged 77¢ in 1860 and 82¢ in 1869. Moreover, North Carolina common labor wages for both years was the lowest in the United States and in the war-torn South. In South Carolina, for example, the daily rate was 82¢ in 1860 and $1.01 in 1869; in Virginia, 81¢ and $1.01. Average monthly earnings with board in North Carolina also declined over the Civil War decade: from $10.37 to $8.39. While Robeson County real wages or purchasing power data have not been computed, common laborer and farm-hand conditions may be inferred from downward trends in United States real wages from 1860 to 1870. A British investigator in 1870 observing high prices in Richmond, Virginia, shops, for example, explained a Southern plight for his readers at home: "The labourer cannot command the same comfort as the labourer of other countries, save at a much higher monetary rate of wages. . . . People speak, in giving an estimate of values, of 'ante-bellum' and 'post-bellum' prices." It can only be surmised that marginal "Scuffletown" fared worse than more developed areas.[10]

Mrs. Norment may have had these conditions in mind when she tried to trace the origin of the name. "It was generally a scuffle with the mulattoes to live—to keep body and soul together, owing to their improvident habits," was one of her theories. A second was that eighteenth-century "mulattoes" in the swamp country congregated at Lowry's Inn at Harper's Ferry (maintained by an ancestor of the future social bandit) to imbibe whiskey. When full of liquid spirits they engaged in the "broad shuffle."[11]

The black and Indian population grew despite the poor conditions. In 1860 it totaled 6,917 persons. Slaves numbered 5,329 blacks and 126 mulattoes. "Free colored persons" were 1,459 so-called "mulattoes" (in the manuscript census) and three black men. Total population in the county was 15,489. Ten years later colored people numbered 7,654, white 9,214. Illiteracy was high among the colored, with 4,528 over ten years of age not being able to write. It is unclear from the 1870 census what number could not read.[12]

Some social stratification was exhibited in a sampling of four Settlement townships in or near Scuffletown and the town of Lumberton, the county seat. In the main, the sample points to a laboring and settled population. At the top were 77 black and 116 "mulatto" farmers. Below them an ethnically heterogeneous rural proletariat was formed. Many listed as "farm-laborers" were children in farmers' nuclear families. On the other hand, many heads of households and other adults were also designated farm-laborers. The largest occupational category in the sampling is 960 farm-laborers, 547 black and 413 mulatto. Domestic service occupations total 124; turpentine and day-laborers, 122; and women "keeping house," that is, the wives of farmers, laborers and some artisans, total 372. Only 34 artisans appear in these dominantly colored townships. Among them, ten were black blacksmiths. There were also six carpenters and five coopers. Only eight mulatto artisans appeared. Among seven miscellaneous occupations was an 85-year-old male basketmaker in Lumberton, born in Africa.[13]

As in other preindustrial societies, artisans here furnished a leadership for Robeson County's lower-class world. Allan Lowry, father of the future outlaw, was recognized as a kind of leader of the colored community although he did not live in "Scuffletown." He was a skilled house carpenter and had trained his several sons in the trade. Their work was evident in their own home and in the frame buildings of their rich white neighbor John McNair. Their skill was also displayed in buildings they erected in the towns of Lumberton and Shoe Heel. The Lowrys and Oxendines and a few other families of mixed ancestry appear to have enjoyed better status than most of their free colored neighbors. In part, their prominence probably was an inheritance from generations of Lowrys who had been among eighteenth-century settlers. The large Lowry clan was "moderately prosperous" and contained "skilled craftsmen, yeoman farmers, and several clergymen." Reverend Patrick Lowry was an older brother of Henry Berry Lowry.[14]

Mrs. Norment inadvertently tells us that Scuffletown people did have a settled way to life. She reveals that they lived in families, on family farmsteads, to sustain the large broods of children that she found deplorable. Above all, they lived in the same community for generations. While they may not have suited Mrs. Norment's standards, blacks and Indians chose their own for marriage and family. Herbert Gutman has adduced considerable data to demonstrate such self-determined behavior, particularly among former slaves emerging into freedom. In Robeson County, he found hundreds of freed men and women with ten and more years of "cohabitation" who registered their marriages during 1866. My own sampling of the county marriage and cohabitation records reveals 76 registrations of such lengthy pre-emancipation marriages out of a total of 176 certified by one justice of the peace on August 11, 1866.[15]

Further support for the picture of settled family patterns emerges from the 1870 census. For the first time black people were described as more than mere aggregations of slaves. Thus the census revealed more particular data about family structure. In Burnt Swamp Township, where colored people outnumbered whites 1,038 to 473, a distinct pattern of nuclear households emerged among blacks as well as Indians. This configuration had already been evident for the latter group in 1860. My survey of the 161 colored families in this Scuffletown township revealed 78 percent of all black families to be nuclear male-headed, with father and mother and children residing in the same household. Among mulattoes the nuclear family portion was 77.5 percent. In a smaller sampling within the township, eight out of 13 black nuclear families were headed by male turpentine laborers. More study is required for greater statistical precision. But the high proportion of nuclear families shown here among lower classes casts great doubt upon Mrs. Norment's and General Gorman's notions of profligacy and the state of "savage freedom," in Burnt Swamp at least.[16]

When Settlement people were perceived through white, Presbyterian or Methodist, and class-conscious eyes, they provided a cultural shock to their observers. Scuffletown became "*a great incubus—a great drawback* on Robeson County, not only in religion, and morals, but in a money point of view." In the first place, before the Civil War "Scuffletown demoralized the entire slave population and not a few of the 'white trash.' " Scuffletown provided refuge for runaway slaves of Robeson County cotton planters. Moreover, Mrs. Norment complained, the "interminable diabolism" of the Scuffletonians even forced the county to foot the bill for extra terms of court to try the cases on the crowded dockets. Robeson taxes consequently were high in comparison to other North Carolina counties. "From time immemorial," Mrs. Norment asserted, "the denizens of Scuffletown" frequently stole pigs and chickens and killed sheep (presumably other people's) for mutton. Even so, she found the habits of these racially mixed peoples to be "peculiar and eccentric." Sometimes they would be of a "religious aspect as austere as the most rigid Pharisee could desire." At other times, Scuffletonians descended headlong into "immoral excesses degrading to human nature," such as the drinking of whiskey, quarrelsomeness under the influence of alcohol, fighting and cutting and stabbing each other. Moreover, the widow asserted, they were superstitious, believing in "fairies, elfs, spirits, ghosts and goblins and in conjuration." Yet, when they became adults, they joined either the Baptist or Methodist church. Both sects as well as Presbyterian ministers preached to the "mulattoes" in Scuffletown and sent ministers among them "to impart spiritual instruction to their benighted minds."[17]

Mrs. Norment's view of degradation and disorderly conduct in The Settlement varies considerably from the opinion of H. W. Guion who testified before a joint committee of Congress in 1871. Guion, a former director of the Wilmington, Charlotte and Rutherford Railroad, said that Robeson's "free persons of color" were "very innocent and inoffensive in those days before the war." He went on to state that "they had their own body of land together; they were very poor; and depended a great deal upon the county wardens of the poor." But he also considered Settlement people "very worthless, trifling people" when he knew them in 1863 or 1864. He had tried to hire them to dig a canal, as his company was building its road through the county, but the people refused to go to work "until bacon got up to 25 cents a pound." Then, he complained, "they would go out and work just long enough to get a little bacon and then they would carry it away." What he failed to appreciate was their insistence on working on their own terms. These were the terms of preindustrial peoples out of tune with the demands of time and money and capital accumulation. A wealthy white Lumberton lawyer, born among the "free colored people," called them "thriftless, lazy, thievish, and indolent." This remained the upper-class whites' social portrait of Scuffletown for the ante-bellum period as well as for the war and Reconstruction years.[18]

Such observers failed to explain the durability of Scuffletown. According to their descriptions, Scuffletonians possessed no moral or material strength, no sense of propriety or order, no sense of right and justice. If theirs was the correct view of the lower-class multi-ethnic world of Robeson County, then Scuffletown should have been severely damaged, if not destroyed, by two events. The first of these was the 1835 disfranchisement and erasure of Indian identity. Lacking a tribal structure and an Indian language, Scuffletonians in 1835 could not fall back on those cultural defenses against the attack. A lingering and growing resentment resulted, although these so-called mulattoes did bear the burden of their humiliation in apparent passivity for thirty years.[19]

The second blow, after a generation, came when the Confederacy resorted to labor impressment in 1862 and 1863. As its military and economic position deteriorated during the Civil War, the Confederacy adopted Draconian measures. The North Carolina legislature complied with Confederate demands by establishing quotas of slaves for labor battalions. Robeson County was expected to deliver one fourth of the male slave population for labor on state defenses. Hard-pressed slave-owners protested. Slaves, they asserted, should be used as a last resort. They pointed to the "free persons of color" not subject to militia duty as preferable labor conscripts. The legislature responded in 1863 and thereafter by recruiting officers who began to dragoon such "free persons of color," including Robeson County mestizos. They were sent to build the revetments of Fort Fisher at the mouth of the Cape Fear River. Working alongside black slaves, they often toiled standing in the water digging sod from the marsh, "in rafting timber and lumber, and water transportation." These laborers were poorly fed, inadequately clad and suffered from lack of fuel, proper quarters and hospitalization, plus being supervised by taskmasters who proved harsh and unrelenting. In February 1865, when it was already too late to correct abuse, General Braxton Bragg pledged that he would provide remedies.[20]

The irritation of the mestizo laborers' self-conception was already producing resistance. Working with slaves meant to them that they were reduced to bondsman status. Moreover, their claims to Indian or white identity had been trampled and ignored. The freedom they had enjoyed before 1835 was made even more remote. Had they been as decadent as Mrs. Norment and other white conservatives portrayed them, these mestizos should have been crushed and dispersed. Instead, in this situation, during 1864 and 1865, they enacted their own principle of right by running away from the Cape Fear River works and hiding in Robeson's swamps. In order to survive a fugitive life, they formed gangs and resorted to robbery. The Settlement people at least did not betray these fugitives, some of them being members of their own families. They became symbols of Robeson lower-class discontent. More significantly, they became instruments of that community's revitalization.

Robeson's cotton and turpentine gentry were vexed by these fugitive laborers. Their Home Guard in 1864 hunted down two such runaways, the sons of George Lowrie, who were arrested as deserters and killed. Their cousin, Henry Berry Lowry, sought to avenge their deaths and to punish their murderers. He and his brothers killed two minor Confederate officials who had recruited and gathered laborers. One was a liquor dealer who had settled in Scuffletown. He had offended whites and Indians by his overbearing and abusive manner as a recruiting officer and by his reputation for "familiarity with the wives and daughters of his customers." It would appear that young Lowry simultaneously was executing a sentence and asserting an established moral code that sanctioned his behavior.[21]

The breakdown of the gentry's social control under the impact of General W. T. Sherman's advances early in 1865 further hastened the severity of Home Guard actions against The Settlement. Allan Lowry and his son William were accused of thievery and were killed by a Home Guard force taking the law into its own hands in March 1865. In May the guard executed Hector Oxendine because he had allegedly stolen a horse and guided invading Yankees in "stealing" horses and stock.[22]

During an investigation of these lynchings, Sinclair and Calvin Lowry listed among the Home Guard "some of the most prominent men of the county of Robeson, N.C.—ministers of the Gospel, Justices of the Peace, Farmers and an Attorney at Law." Hugh Oxendine, as the plaintiff in the case of Hector, deposed that ". . . a clube of rebs met and tuck him off and put him to death just because he went of with the Yankey raid." Two ministers accused of killing Allan and William Lowry tried to defend their actions on grounds that the Confederate government was defenseless and unable to protect itself; able-bodied men had been conscripted and only defenseless families were left to face robberies; local civil authorities were equally powerless; and there was "no security for life or property."[23]

The latter presented a problem, and was a costly concern of Robeson's cotton planters and turpentine manufacturers. Moreover, their ultimate security, their hegemony, had been breached. Their desperation may be appreciated by considering one planter's efforts to hold a labor force and exercise old ways of command. Robert McKenzie, a wealthy former slaveowner, one of the accused lynchers of Allen Lowry, tried to force another member of the family, Sinclair Lowry, to labor for him. The young mestizo declared that McKenzie had told him that "he would get him clear of being shot if he would work six months for him and not leave the said McKenzies house either day or night." The planter, however, failed in this coercion. Moreover, his domination was seriously challenged by robbers who had taken clothing and jewelry from his house and 1500 pounds of meat from his storehouse. Throughout the Reconstruction years he and other planters were robbed of personal possessions and suffered depletion of their smokehouses and storehouses. The robbers often blamed were the men who made up the Lowry band.[24]

Lowry was outlawed by the Democratic-Conservative government in 1866 and was not relieved of that status by subsequent and allegedly friendly Republican administrations. During those years he hid out in the swamplands, when he was not to be found in his own cabin with his family. He gathered around him his kin. The nucleus of his band of seven or eight (sometimes swelling to possibly twenty or thirty including Confederate deserters and escaped Union prisoners) consisted of his brothers Steve and Tom; his wife's brothers Andrew and Boss Strong; Calvin and Henderson Oxendine; and John Dial, all the above being Indians; George Applewhite, a black former slave who had married an Oxendine girl; Eli Ewin known as "Shoemaker John," another black former slave; and, finally, for a short time the white Buckskin Scots boy Zachariah T. McLauchlin. The chief was and still is a legendary figure in the folklore of Robeson County. In addition to being a house carpenter, he was known to have worked as a beekeeper during his outlaw years. (North Carolina, it should be recalled, was the prime honey-producing state in the Union in 1860.) John Dial was an apprentice blacksmith. Eli Ewin's occupation was plainly described in his nickname. Applewhite was a skilled mason and plasterer. Steve Lowry was once a locomotive fireman on the Wilmington, Charlotte and Rutherford Railroad. Andrew Strong was a logger who worked with black crews in the lumber industry.[25]

These proud young artisans and skilled men were held responsible for murders and robberies beginning in April 1864 and ending in 1871. An inventory of their loot demonstrates that they provided not only for themselves as outlaws cut off from their normal livelihoods, but they also played the role of Robin Hood. Their wealthy neighbor John McNair suffered their depredations repeatedly through those years. In 1864 a feather bed was stolen, along with a quilt. McNair's smokehouse was often emptied of pork. In some twenty robberies, his home lost beds, bolsters, pillows, sheets, combs, brushes, clothing, crockery, cutlery, cash, guns and a watch. Clothing, and thousands of pounds of bacon, hams, and other "eatables" were taken from other planters. In the act of robbery, the Lowry band sometimes would demand that a breakfast or a dinner be served to them seated in the dining rooms of their victims, as if to savor a life style unjustly denied to them. Indeed, when they raided Mrs. William McKay's home they ordered her step-daughter to "play some on the Piano-Forte for them, which she did, in order to keep them in good humor."[26]

The bandits also felt moved to justify their crimes, as if they were novices or alien to such a life. They told Mrs. McKay "that they needed everything they had taken, that they had to *live as well as other people, etc.*" A few months later, Henry Berry Lowry confronted John McNair with a demand that he intervene to release the wives of the bandits from jail. "They have put my wife in jail for no crime but because she is my wife; that aint her fault and they can't make it so. You people," Lowry told McNair, "won't let me work to get my living, and I have got to take it from you; but God knows, she'd like to see me make my own bread." To some other anonymous person, Henry Berry Lowry was reported to have said, "We are not allowed to get our living peaceably and we must take it from others. We don't kill anybody but the Ku Klux." In 1872, Townsend reported from Lumberton, "In the interrupted enjoyment of family happiness Henry Berry Lowry expressed a desire to quit the swamps and return to his carpenter's trade and peaceful society."[27]

Even if society would not recognize his plea, Henry Berry Lowry had to live and so did his people. Thus, in 1871 he and his band went into nearby Richmond County, took two mules and a wagon from a farmer, loaded it with corn and drove to Scuffletown. "The corn was equally distributed," according to Townsend, and the wagon and team were returned to the owner the same day. We do not know for certain that the food, clothing, bedclothing and other booty was "equally distributed." We can safely surmise that the band took more than it needed for its own families, including the leader's wife and three children. And, these acts earned for Lowry's band wide support and protection among Scuffletown's poor people. The New York *Herald* reporter, who appeared somewhat sympathetic toward Lowry, wrote, "There isn't probably a Negro in Scuffletown who would betray him. . . . Frequent exhibitions of magnanimity distinguish his bloody course and he has learned to arrogate to himself a protectorate over the interests of the mulattoes, which they return by a sort of hero worship." A conservative observed, "It became a proverb in Robeson County that the mulattoes and negroes were as true to the Lowrie bandits as the needle is to the pole." But Aunt Phoebe, an aged black woman and ex-slave, probably expressed the meaning of the Lowry band when she said, "Oh, dis was a hard country, and Henry Berry Lowery's jiss a payin' 'em back. He's only a payin' 'em back! It's better days for de brack people now. Massta, he's jiss *de king o' dis country.*"[28]

We do not know if a specific king served as the model for Aunt Phoebe's characterization of Lowry. However, we do know that the concept of a just king was held by European lower classes who similarly sustained social brigandage. Their own "poor boy" represented to them the surrogate for their failures to break out of their circle of poverty. Eric Hobsbawm has brilliantly shown how peasant societies also lent a sort of super-human power, or at least the power of a just king, to *their* bandits. How different, then, is Aunt Phoebe's notion of Lowry from the thoughts of Carpathian peasants about their Oleksa Dovbush of whom it was said, "for seven years he fought in our country, and while he lived things went well with the people"?[29] In this connection Aunt Phoebe and Henry Berry Lowry do explain something of the weight of prepolitical standards of right and justice in the post–Civil War South.

Just as other social bandits failed to change the world in which their peasant supporters bore their oppressions, so Henry Berry Lowry and his band failed. They symbolized the renewal of a people's energies but could not effect change for the better. They had thrust toward justice and respect for their people's identity and way of life. But they were insufficient and archaic; inappropriate, alone, to get beyond the defense of custom and tradition. The destruction of slavery, the serious dislocation and dispersal of planter power and the birth of a freedman laboring class created the need for modern instruments in the contest for community control.

That new class of rural laborers produced by emancipation was both contrast and complement to the Lowry gang. While the latter pursued justice on a narrow field, freedmen assertiveness, as a more modern effort, confronted the gentry and the new order of capitalist agriculture. Significantly, in the new way of life men and women who only yesterday were slaves demonstrated that they had a vision of the world that they wished to make. Their newly released energies were directed toward the creation of schools, economic justice, political equality, religious autonomy and stabilized family life. We turn to them, the largest and probably most decisive component of Robeson's multi-ethnic lower-class community.

An Aunt Phoebe could poignantly state the nature of the problems of the poor and could symbolize their response in supporting the Lowry gang. But support for the 1868 State Constitution, for example, required organized communities and a leadership capable of mobilizing and speaking for such communities. The more numerous freedmen among Robeson's lower classes took their first step toward such organized political action and found men in their midst who could lead. To be sure, blacks were not alone among the poor in doing so. Indians became active Union Leaguers and Republicans. In addition, some native Southern whites in the wartime pro-Union, clandestine Heroes of America, or Red Strings, supported the 1868 Constitution and the Republican Party. Finally, the poor received support from some middle-class whites and "mulattoes."[30]

Robeson county slaves were declared free on May 15, 1865. To the great dismay of the Reverend Washington Sanford Chaffin, conservative circuit preacher, they rapidly asserted themselves. In the process they contradicted notions of their alleged decadence or indolence or insolence. By the end of June a church composed of black people and led by Presbyterian Reverend James Sinclair was meeting in Lumberton. Whites had many reasons to hate Sinclair and this activity aroused them even more, but blacks accepted his help at this time. On the other hand, they did not accept his class values. Sinclair complained in October than some of Robeson's blacks were developing "extravagant ideas in relation to confiscated lands." Ironically, on the same date he wrote those words, Reverend Chaffin complained to his diary that "Sinclair is still stirring the people." But the blacks apparently needed no white stirring to congregate in large numbers in Lumberton on Emancipation Day, January 1, 1866. They had developed their own ideas about land and freedom.[31]

They clearly appreciated their new status and celebrated it. Moreover, they were aware of the need to defend their freedom. When Sinclair was bound by a county court for his part in a fight with a conservative white, blacks held a meeting at the Lumberton court house on March 5 and signified their support for him. The freedman Wesley McQueen made a strong speech in the minister's defense, recognizing him as a symbol of freedmen aspirations.[32]

Freedmen suffered economic as well as political and social oppression under the state's Black Code. Even with a Freedmen's Bureau agent in Lumberton they were unable to work without abuse from their employers. During the summer of 1866, for example, when most of them engaged in cultivating cotton, they contracted for a share of the crops or for wages. But some employers tried to evict them without paying shares or wages. Freedmen took their complaints to the Bureau. But real redress seemed to wait on Radical Reconstruction when they made use of the rights of free men, especially of lawful assembly.[33]

In the face of these hardships, freedmen had already begun to send their children to a school conducted by Sinclair in Lumberton. Later, while the Radical Reconstruction Acts of 1867 were being implemented, freedmen made "several applications" to the Bureau agent to establish a school. "They are anxious to learn," he reported. Freedmen had already been conducting their own night school, attended by about sixty children and youths. "Two or three colored men" were their teachers, but they lacked enough books for their students. Three months later, in November 1867, the Bureau man reported that the freedmen "show an increased desire for Books and Schools and to educate themselves. A frame is already cut for a schoolhouse 36' × 25' at no expense to the Bureau."[34]

Robeson's freedmen asserted themselves even more demonstratively in Reconstruction politics. Chaffin's diary alone records 27 dates between July 5, 1865, and January 4, 1869, on which freedmen participated in parades, meetings, celebrations or elections. After the 1867 Reconstruction Acts enfranchised non-whites in the South, Robeson County's blacks and mestizos made effective use of the ballot. They comprised 45 percent of the population. Those eligible to vote were 48 percent of the electorate. These "Negro" voters (a loose term, for it probably included Anglo-Indians) furnished 71 percent of the ballots cast for the state constitutional convention. A similar pattern developed in three other Cape Fear counties. In the 1868 contests for elective offices, Republicans won majorities in four of the seven lower Cape Fear counties. Robeson was one of them. "Colored" voters were responsible for 56 percent of the Republican party votes there.[35]

The challenge presented to planter power by the freedmen in the Leagues and party was reflected in the Klan murders of Benjamin Bethea and Henry Revels. These two former slaves, one black and the other mulatto, were deemed by the Klan to be too active and "saucy" in Republican affairs. But Lowry understood the importance of Ben Bethea to Robeson's poor and to justice. When the gang discovered his body, they made sure to bring it to County Coroner Robert Chaffin, turpentine manufacturer and son of the Lumberton preacher, and to notify the U.S. Army commander. What the gang lacked in respect for planter law and order they made up in their ironical hope for justice in the case of Ben Bethea. They apparently also hoped to pay homage to Bethea's political leadership. He had combined "politics and the wrongs of the colored people into his prayers."[36]

Freedmen self-assertiveness is further reflected in Reverend Chaffin's several diary entries in 1868 complaining of colored people's boycotts of his prayer meetings. This defection he attributed to the corrosive effects of radical Republicanism. He failed to note that after Emancipation a black, brown, or red person *chose* not to listen to him simply because they were free to choose. But more disturbing to Chaffin was the plan of a colored people's congregation to receive the black radical preacher John Williams at Chaffin's church in Lumberton. Chaffin adamantly refused to participate in the service or to allow the use of the building. On the other hand, he seemed self-satisfied when colored people in 1869 invited him to speak at *their school.*[37]

Probably the most profound expression of Black and Indian desires for cultural self-determination centered on the Robeson County churches. Partial evidence for one denomination, the Baptist, indicates that through the Reconstruction years, colored people steadily withdrew from the white controlled churches. In the case of the Ashpole Baptist Church, situated in The Settlement, the colored people's choice is clear. Consistently, in 1863, 1865 and 1867, it had the largest "Black" membership of the county's nine churches reporting to the Cape Fear Baptist Association. But in 1869 the annual meeting of the assocation reported *no* "colored" people in the Ashpole church. Negro Baptists had organized their own general association in 1867 and state convention in 1869. The local removal may have followed the state leadership. In 1872 the First Baptist Church of Lumberton granted dismission to all of its 20 Negro members. They joined the Sandy's Grove Colored Church. Finally, in 1879, a group of Anglo-Indians led by Locklear, Jacobs, Chavis, Lowrie and Oxendine families, succeeded in breaking away from white dominated churches to establish the first of many of their own Missionary Baptist Churches. This was the Burnt Swamp Baptist Church, in the heart of The Settlement. Earlier, Mrs. Norment, in bristling at the idea of blacks and "mulattoes" controlling their own churches, gave us a standard for their norms. She wrote, "They have shut the doors of their churches against all ministers of the white race and installed in their places in the pulpit persons of their own color 'to explanify' the Scriptures and elucidate them into 'a mist of obscurity,' literally 'the blind leading the blind.'"[38]

A white visitor to black Baptist churches in another North Carolina county lifted the veil a little further. He noted that the churches increased by 10 or 15 members each Sunday but that their spiritual progress lagged. "An impression prevails among many of them," he reported, "that their own feelings and impulses afford better evidences of the teachings of the Holy Ghost, than the Bible. They profess to think that while the Scriptures may instruct white Christains, their instruction comes more directly from the great source of light." This was startling independence from white belief and custom. Yet some black churchmen exercised prerogatives of self-governance much like those exercised by the white churches. They excommunicated and otherwise disciplined backsliders. Whatever whites might think of their practice and thought, black freedmen declared at least this measure of cultural independence. These alterations and adaptations of religious form and content may possibly furnish a model for understanding Robeson County lower-class colored churches.[39]

Another cross-cultural adaptation occurred in Settlement folk music and dance. Steve and Henry Berry Lowry spent hours playing the banjo, that distinctively American instrument introduced by seventeenth-century African slaves. When Henry Berry could elude his pursuers he found relaxation in "one of the huts of Scuffletown and plays to the dancing of the mulatto girls and his companions by the hour, his belt of arms unslung and thrown at his feet." A New York *Herald* reporter on returning from a visit to the gang's swamp hideout was led away through waist-high water and then was entertained by them in one of the cabins. Andrew Strong " 'picked' the banjo, played on the violin and sang . . . and the peculiar airs which he was accompanied on the banjo were novel and exceedingly pleasant." Unfortunately the journalist did not report the words or musical style. Grimly, the banjo proved to be an instrument of Steve Lowry's death. He was betrayed by its chords while playing in a supposedly secure hideaway. Sheriff Rod McMillan told of another occasion when he and his men stood an all-night vigil outside Henry Berry's cabin: "That banjo was everlastingly thrumming and we could hear the laughter and Juba beating nearly the whole night long." The Juba dance was common among Robeson blacks and "mulattoes" as it was wherever black Africans had found themselves, "whether in the West Indies or South Carolina." It was an African step-dance resembling a jig, "with elaborate variations."[40]

As with other lower classes some traditional folk society beliefs persisted. Steve Lowry, for example, was described as being "a firm believer in conjuration, and always kept on hand a supply of roots, bones, etc." Mrs. Norment interpreted Settlement people's beliefs in "fairies, elfs, spirits, ghosts and goblins" as signs of degradation. For Settlement people this persistence probably represented rejection of Mrs. Norment's religious and class values. Finally, the manner in which Henry Berry Lowry's disappearance in 1872 was explained or not explained dramatically expressed folk culture. It is not clear whether the outlaw carpenter was shot or shot himself by accident or simply stole away. Legend has it that he escaped from Robeson County and found a peaceable life in the West or in Mexico or in. . . . Perhaps one day he would come back, as saviours must for oppressed peoples. For a generation he was periodically reported in various places. Above all, for the poor farmers and laborers in Robeson County, the symbol of their struggles never died.[41]

It appears paradoxical that folk beliefs and behavior should persist in a way of life clearly moving in a modern direction. Robeson's lower-class culture contained both tendencies, for it was involved in the end of one tradition and the beginning of another. Moreover, it is useful to focus on the matter of choices: archaic ones such as support of the Lowry gang and modern ones such as self-created community institutions and organizations; choices about how to work and whether to work. For example, when a sprout of industrialism appeared, canal workers in RobesonCounty refused to be deferential to the entrepreneurs and their values. They chose instead to be "archaic" and work to their own rhythms of need. Yet, cotton laborers later brought their protest to the Freedmen's Bureau over wages not paid and crops not shared according to contract. They undoubtedly aided in the reconstruction of the former slaveowners such as Robert McKenzie. A cotton planter before the war and a turpentine manufacturer as well after it, he ceased lording it over his subjects. In 1866 he offered wages and houses and gardens for turpentine laborers. Slaves and masters were transformed. If the former masters briefly practiced enlightened self-interest under the pressure of Radical Reconstruction policies, they were also forced to do so when they confronted transformed and self-conscious black and Indian laborers and poor farmers.[42]

In their experiences with the gentry, Robeson's lower-class community devised modes of action that would guard its ways of living. At thc heart of their culture, the two ethnic groups shared conceptions of right. If upper-class whites thought that Settlement people or the freedmen lacked their standards of good behavior and proper beliefs, it did not follow that they lacked any at all. We have seen indications of their sense of community, of honor and justice, of family responsibility. Each of these was further expression of what they perceived to be theirs by right. Outlawry and ties of kinship, on the one hand, and modern institutions—schools, churches, government (Freedmen's Bureau)—on the other hand, were the available instruments they chose to effect change in their lives so that they could "live as well as other people." That was right for them. Right was involved in the mutual reinforcement among Blacks and Indians, as in Lowry's concern that black Benjamin Bethea should not have been sacrificed to injustice, and in Aunt Phoebe's faith in Lowry as the minister of justice "for de brack people."

Robeson's multi-ethnic lower classes were revitalized by their experience during Reconstruction. They emerged with renewed energies and rediscovered consciousness as distinct peoples. The process was hastened by the charismatic Henry Berry Lowry during their springtime of self-consciousness. Finally, the disruption of planter power and the emergence of self-assertive black rural proletarians produced a way of life temporarily changed for the better. Scuffletown-Settlement is important as one of many isolates of mestizo culture in the United States. The remarkable growth of the Croatan or Lumbee Indians of Robeson County since the 1870s suggests a pivotal experience in Reconstruction. The Robeson freedmen are important as a typical emergent Southern lower-class black community. Strikingly, this upheaval was not produced by a messianic or religious movement, nor by an esoteric type of "crisis cult." Clearly, revitalization proceeded through the medium of social experience.[43]

As with other such cultural upheavals and renewals, success was not ordained. In this case, Reconstruction was aborted by Klan violence and by the new dominant men of finance, manufacture, railroads and plantations. Emergent lower-class subcultures were repressed by the weight of economic and political power arrayed against them. Yet even such external forces failed to eliminate all of the changes in black and Indian ways of living. Blacks and Indians had gained a measure of control over their lives, their values and their community.

The people of Robeson's lower-class community emerge as neither depressed and deplorable victims of social change nor as the social deviants that some portrayed them to be. Instead they appear as proud peoples mobilizing their meager material but strong moral resources to establish their own culture and community.

Notes

1. W. E. B. Du Bois, *The Souls of Black Folk* (1903), Ch. II, "Of the Dawn of Freedom," (N.Y., 1953, Jubilee edition); "Reconstruction and Its Benefits," *American Historical Review*, 15 (1910); A. A. Taylor, *The Negro in the Reconstruction of Virginia* (Washington, D.C., 1926); *The Negro in South Carolina During Reconstruction* (Washington, D.C., 1924); W. E. B. Du Bois, *Black Reconstruction in America* (New York, 1935); Vernon Lane Wharton, *The Negro in Mississippi, 1865-1890* (Chapel Hill, N.C., 1947); Horace M. Bond, "Social and Economic Forces in Alabama Reconstruction," *Journal of Negro History*, 23 (1938); Joel Williamson, *After Slavery, The Negro in South Carolina During Reconstruction 1861-1877* (Chapel Hill, N.C., 1965), among others.

2. Richard Maxwell Brown, *The South Carolina Regulators* (Cambridge, Mass., 1963); Kenneth W. Porter, "Negroes and the Seminole War, 1835-1842," *Journal of Southern History*, 30 (November, 1964), pp. 427-40; Orlando Patterson, *The Sociology of Slavery, An Analysis of the Origins, Development and Structure of Negro Slave Society in Jamaica* (London, 1967), pp. 263-64; Franklin W. Knight, *Slave Society in Cuba During the Nineteenth Century* (Madison, Wis., 1970), pp. 80-81; Carl N. Degler, *Neither Black Nor White* (New York, 1971), pp. 48-52. See also James McKaye, *The Mastership and Its Fruits: The Emancipated Slave Face to Face with His Old Master. A Supplemental Report to Hon. Edwin M. Stanton, Secretary of War* (New York, 1864), pp. 8, 10-11; Herbert Aptheker, "Maroons Within the Present Limits of the United States," *Journal of Negro History*, 24 (April 1939), pp. 167-84; Roger Bastide, *African Civilizations in the New World* (London, 1967), chs. 3 and 4, 46-88.

3. *Population of the United States in 1860; Compiled from the Original Returns of the Eighth Census Under the Direction of the Secretary of the Interior* (Washington, D.C., 1864), p. 359; Sid-

ney W. Mintz, "The Folk-Urban Continuum and the Rural Proletarian Community," *American Journal of Sociology*, Vol. 59 (1953-54), 136-43, furnishes a rough analytical model for study of Robeson lower-class life. This is his revision of Robert Redfield's "folk society" concept. Mintz derived his formulation from a study of modern Puerto Rican plantation laborers who were ethnically heterogeneous but exhibited "a very real kind of cultural homogeneity, partly class determined." Bastide, *African Civilizations*, p. 78, for the concept of mestizo communities formed through propinquity.

4. W. McKee Evans, *To Die Game, The Story of the Lowry Band, Indian Guerrillas of Reconstruction* (Baton Rouge, 1971); Mary C. Norment, *The Lowrie History, As Acted in Part by Henry Berry Lowry, The Great North Carolina Bandit, with Biographical Sketches of his Associates, Being A Complete History of the Modern Robber Band in the County of Robeson and the State of North Carolina* (Wilmington, N.C., 1875; Lumberton, N.C., 1909); Thomas M. Gorman Papers (1863-1917), North Carolina Department of Archives and History, Raleigh; George Alfred Townsend, *The Swamp Outlaws: or the North Carolina Bandits, Being a Complete History of Modern Rob Roys and Robin Hoods* (New York, 1872).

For European models and experiences of social brigandage, see Eric J. Hobsbawm, *Primitive Rebels, Studies in Archaic Forms of Social Movement in the 19th and 20th Centuries* (New York, 1959, 1965), Ch. II, "The Social Bandit."

A case of acceptable social deviant behavior by Nicolas Gomez, a Tarascan village "bad guy," in Durazno, Mexico, may be a useful comparison with Lowry's. It is described in Paul Friedrich, "An Agrarian Fighter," in Melford E. Spiro, ed., *Context and Meaning in Cultural Anthropology* (New York, 1965), pp. 117-43. Friedrich writes: "Nico's history demonstrates how a man can be deviant but still acceptable in a changing cultural system and how a particular mode of deviancy is tightly articulated with the norms of his group" (p. 141).

5. Norment, *Lowrie History; Report of the Joint Select Committee to Inquire into the Condition of Affairs in the Late Insurrectionary States* (Ku Klux Conspiracy) (13 vols.; Washington, D.C., Government Printing Office, 1872) North Carolina, pp. 253, 284 (Testimony of Giles Leitch and H. W. Guion).

6. Evans, *To Die Game*, pp. 28, 29; Norment, *Lowrie History*, pp. 4-9; Gorman Papers, pp. 1-3; J.R. Swanton "Probable Identity of the 'Croatan' Indians," Senate Report No. 204, 73rd Congress, 2nd Session (January 23, 1934), pp. 3-5; Lew[is Randolph] Barton, *The Most Ironical Story in American History: An Authoritative, Documented History of the Lumbee Indians of North Carolina* (Charlotte, N.C., 1967).

7. Evans, *To Die Game*, p. 32; *Ku Klux Conspiracy*, North Carolina, p. 284; *Population of the United States in 1860* (Washington, 1864), pp. 351. 353, 355, 359; *A Compendium of the Ninth Census: 1870* (Washington, 1872, pp. 225, 424; also manuscript censuses, Robeson County, 1860 and 1870, National Archives, Washington, D.C.; Clifton Oxendine, *A Social and Economic History of the Indians of Robeson County, North Carolina.* Unpublished master's thesis, George Peabody College, 1934, p. 16.

8. Norment, *Lowrie History*, pp. 4-9, 26-29; Gorman Papers, pp. 1-3; Bastide, *loc cit.* for a comparable settlement of Black Caribs and Indian Caribs: "Such communities, which exhibit no liaison with tribal *lignages*, are simply groups formed through propinquity; there is no tribal organization, since the Negroes are forcibly subjected to the laws and civil constitution of the country which they inhabit: On the other hand, their *social* life is highly developed, with numerous lively festivals."

9. Norment, *Lowrie History*, pp. 22, 24, 29; Gorman Papers, pp. 2, 8; John Richard Dennett, *The South As It Is* (Ed. Henry M. Christman: New York, 1967) (from Lumberton, N.C., October 23, 1865, dispatch to *The Nation*), p. 178; Evans, *To Die Game*, pp. 66-67.

10. Townsend, *The Swamp Outlaws*, p. 44; Gorman Papers, p. 2; Barton, *The Most Ironical Story*, p. 119; 1870 Census, Schedule 5, Social Statistics, Robeson County; Hugh T. Lefler and Albert R. Newsome, *North Carolina; The History of a Southern State* (Chapel Hill, 1963), p. 379; Stanley Lebergott, "Wage Trends, 1800-1900," in [National Bureau of Economic Research],

Trends in the American Economy in the Nineteenth Century; Studies in Income and Wealth, Vol. 24 (Princeton, 1960), 493; Stanley Lebergott, *Manpower in Economic Growth, The American Record Since 1860* (New York, 1964), pp. 539, 541; Robert Somers, *The Southern States Since the War, 1870-71* (New York, 1871), p. 18.

11. Norment, *Lowrie History*, p. 7.

12. *Ninth Census*, p. 424.

13. Manuscript Ninth Census, Robeson County, North Carolina, 1870. The townships sampled are Back Swamp, Burnt Swamp, Howellsville and Smith's. Total white and "colored" population respectively in each is 359/441; 473/1038; 782/241; 635/1049. The town of Lumberton reported 331 white and 284 "colored."

14. Norment, *Lowrie History*, p. 30; Evans, *To Die Game*, pp. 10, 69; Gorman Papers, p. 8.

15. Manuscript Ninth Census, Robeson County; Robeson County Marriages and Cohabitation Records, 1850-1866, pp. 227-32.

16. Manuscript Ninth Census, Burnt Swamp Township, Robeson County, 1870.

17. Norment, *Lowrie History*, pp. 25-26, 28-29.

18. *Ku Klux Conspiracy*, North Carolina, pp. 253, 284.

19. Gorman Papers, p. 5; Evans, *To Die Game*, pp. 28, 32.

20. B. H. Nelson, "Some Aspects of Negro Life in North Carolina During the Civil War," *North Carolina Historical Review*, 25, No. 2 (April 1948), 143-66; Braxton Bragg to Jefferson Davis, Wilmington, N.C., February 9, 1865, *The War of the Rebellion: A Compilation of the Official Records of the Union and Confederate Armies* (128 vols., Washington, D.C., 1880-1891) Series 1, Vol. 47, part 2, pp. 1137-38; Evans, *To Die Game*, pp. 3-7.

21. Evans, *To Die Game*, p. 39; Norment, *Lowrie History*, p. 42.

22. Evans, *To Die Game*, pp. 3-18; U.S. War Department, Records of the Army Commands, Second Military District (Lumberton, N.C., Post) (Record Group 393, National Archives). I am indebted to Professor W. McKee Evans, California State Polytechnic College, for this material which was a source for his book, *To Die Game*.

23. Record Group 393, (Letters received, 1867) National Archives; Ibid., J. H. Coble and L. McKinnon to Lieut. William Birnie, June 8, 1867, in Letters Received.

24. Ibid., Sinclair Lowry deposition, June 1, 1867, in "Investigation" by Lieutenant Birnie, Freedmen's Bureau Agent at Lumberton, N.C.; Norment, *Lowrie History*, pp. 62-63; RG393, National Archives, Deposition of Robert McKenzie, May 29, 1867.

25. Evans, *To Die Game*, pp. 74, 100, 134, 202; Goldsboro, N.C., *Carolina Messenger*, July 5, 1875; Norment, *Lowrie History*, pp. 8-22.

26. Norment, *Lowrie History*, pp. 43-45, 90; Townsend, *Swamp Outlaws*, pp. 16-17, 26; New York *Herald*, February 27, 1872.

27. Ibid.

28. Townsend, *Swamp Outlaws*, pp. 26, 27, 56; Norment, *Lowrie History*, pp. 9, 157.

29. Hobsbawm, *Primitive Rebels*, pp. 25-27.

30. Ibid., Sidney Andrews, *The South Since the War* (Boston, 1866) pp. 119-31, 162; W. E. B. Du Bois, *Black Reconstruction*, p. 530; Evans, p. 90; RG105, National Archives (Alfred Thomas, Freedmen's Bureau Agent to Thos. A. Norment, Esq., Chairman, County Court, February 25, 1868); Charlotte *Observer*, June 11, 1905, reprint of Wilmington *Daily Journal* article, 1875; Manuscript Journal of Washington Sanford Chaffin, (1865-1871), Duke University Library, Durham, N.C., May 25, 1867; (". . . negro political lecturers going among the negroes and I apprehend evil from it.") A. J. McDonald, et al., to W. W. Holden, May 10, 1868, Holden Private Papers, North Carolina Archives, Raleigh.

31. Chaffin, Journal, May 17, July 3, July 5, 1865; January 1, March 6, 1866.

32. Evans, *To Die Game*, p. 63.

33. RG105, National Archives (Reports of 2nd Lt. George W. Tipton, Assistant Superintendent, Bureau of Refugees, Freedmen and Abandoned Lands, Lumberton, N.C., June 30, August 7, July 15, July 26, October 22, 1866).

34. Chaffin, Journal, May 7, 1866; RG105, National Archives, Reports of William Birnie, BRFAL Agent, Lumberton, N.C. August 23, November 23, 1867.

35. W. McKee Evans, *Ballots and Fence Rails: Reconstruction of the Lower Cape Fear* (Chapel Hill, N.C., 1967), pp. 96, 102.

36. Townsend, *Swamp Outlaws*, pp. 33, 34; Evans, *To Die Game*, p. 160. Robert Chaffin's modest turpentine business is indicated in 1870 Census, Schedule 4. Industry, Robeson County, Town of Lumberton.

A mass meeting in Lumberton, March 24, 1868 was addressed by Abram Galloway, one of the state's black political leaders, and by Albion W. Tourgee, the active Northern-born radical Republican. "The radicals," Chaffin wrote, "bore the U.S. flag through the streets of Lumberton in token of negro supremacy." Chaffin, Journal, March 24 and 25, 1868.

37. Chaffin, Journal, February 21, April 5, May 20, June 19 ("[I] was at Saddletree—not a mulatto nor negro was present."), June 24, July 17, October 10, 1868.

38. Minutes of the Fifty-ninth Session of the Cape Fear Baptist Association, October 23-26, 1863 (Fayetteville, 1864), pp. 14-15; . . . Sixty-first . . . October 20-23, 1863 (Wilmington, 1866), pp. 30-32; . . . Sixty-third . . . October 25-28, 1867 (Raleigh, 1867), pp. 22-23; . . . Sixty-fifth . . . October 22-25, 1869 (Wilmington, 1870), p. 19; Minutes of the Baptist State Convention of North Carolina held in Fayetteville, N.C., Nov. 6, 7, 8 and 9, 1872 (Raleigh, 1873), p. 56; John L. Bell, Jr., "Baptists and the Negro in North Carolina During Reconstruction," *North Carolina Historical Review*, 42 (May 1965), 402; Minutes of the First Annual Session of the Burnt Swamp Baptist Association held with the church at Burnt Swamp, Robeson Co., N.C., January 21, 22, 23, 1881 (Raleigh, 1881); Norment, *Lowrie History*, p. 26; Barton, *The Most Ironical Story*, p. 95.

39. Bell, "Baptists and the Negro in North Carolina During Reconstruction," pp. 407-08.

40. Norment, *Lowrie History*, pp. 141-42; Townsend, *Swamp Outlaws*, p. 15; Gorman Papers, p. 10; Evans, *To Die Game*, p. 210; C. P. Heaton, "The 5-String Banjo in North Carolina," *Southern Folklore Quarterly*, 35 (March 1971), 62-63; Marian Hannah Winter, "Juba and American Minstrlsy," *Dance Index*, 6 (Feb. 1947), 28-29.

41. Evans, *To Die Game*, pp. 244-51; Hobsbawm, *Primitive Rebels*, p. 25.

42. A strikingly comparable reflection of modernization involved late eighteenth-century and early nineteenth-century English village laborers. See E. P. Thompson, "The Moral Economy of the English Crowd in the Eighteenth Century," *Past & Present*, February 1971, pp. 128-29.

McKenzie advertised in the Wilmington (N.C.) *Daily Dispatch*, January 17, 1866: "I want to hire for twelve months fifty freedmen, who are able and willing to work, in the turpentine and timber business in Robeson County. I will give two hundred dollars and rations for the year, and will furnish such as have families with comfortable cabins and grounds for gardens."

43. "A revitalization movement is defined as a deliberate, organized, conscious effort by members of a society to construct a more satisfying culture." Anthony F. C. Wallace, "Revitalization Movements," *American Anthropologist*, 58 (1956), p. 265; see also "Surviving Indian Groups of the Eastern United States," *Smithsonian Report for 1948* (Washington, 1949), pp. 407-38; Charles M. Hudson, *The Catawba Nation* (Athens, Ga., 1970), pp. 70-71; see also Leonard B. Glick's comments on Weston LaBarre, "Materials for a History of Studies of Crisis Cults: A Bibliographic Essay," *Current Anthropology*, 12, no. 1 (February 1971), p. 29.

Vernon Burton

Race and Reconstruction: Edgefield County, South Carolina

Historians have long acknowledged the importance of race in American history, but only recently have they begun systematically to analyze problems of racial adjustment. The most comprehensive and influential work thus far is that of C. Vann Woodward, which draws on sociologist Pierre L. Van den Berghe's bipartite race relations typology—paternalistic and competitive—to explain the rise of segregation at the end of the 19th century. In Woodward's view, slavery was a paternalistic system, characterized by intimate but unequal contact between race, that masked white racial prejudices with professions of love for subordinate blacks. This paternalistic system continued through Reconstruction until the last quarter of the 19th century. Then, with urbanization, growth and diversification of industry, and development of the New South ideology, race relations changed from paternalistic to competitive. In the competitive system of race relations, role and occupation were no longer sharply defined by race: blacks began to narrow disparities between themselves and whites in education, income, and lifestyle. Whites responded with laws regulating contact between races, and blacks and whites became more physically segregated. Recent support for Woodward's theory has come from Eugene D. Genovese, who argues that slavery's paternalism habituated Afro-Americans to an accommodationist attitude detrimental to the freedman's quest for equality during Reconstruction.[1]

To test the Woodward and Genovese theories about the nature of slavery and race relations, this paper examines the changing patterns of race relations in Edgefield County, South Carolina during Reconstruction, the formative period of southern postbellum social developments. Events in Edgefield

Source: Journal of Social History 12, no. 1 (Fall 1978): 31–56. Reprinted by permission.

during Reconstruction bring into question the positions of both Woodward and Genovese about black acquiescence in a white dominated paternalistic system in the decade following emancipation. Instead, events in that county indicate that the period from 1867 to 1877 in particular was one of fierce competition between blacks and whites for political and economic power. Edgefield County may have been typical of rural southern communities in the Reconstruction period; it certainly provided a model followed by other South Carolina counties. Edgefield County was part of the cotton-producing belt of the state; and county seat, Edgefield Village, was the commercial hub of a predominantly rural area. Because the county produced leaders who dominated South Carolina politics and loomed large in Southern history, Edgefield's impact on state and regional history, and thus on the American past, has been considerable. Even more importantly, the county led South Carolina as patterns of race relations crystallized during and after Reconstruction.[2]

In Edgefield, the period from 1865 to the 1890s, a time of transition from paternalism to competitive segregation in race relations, was characterized by uncertainty, unrest, and confusion as blacks and whites attempted to define their new social roles.[3] Under slavery, there had been no ambivalence about the relationship of blacks to whites, no crucial questions about role, and no need for whites to employ indirect methods of control over blacks. When the Civil War destroyed both the economic system of slavery and the framework of social control and discipline implicit in slavery, blacks and whites had to define new economic and social relationships in a setting that neither group completely controlled. During Reconstruction, Republicans sought to create a democratic society in which blacks were active participants along with whites. The planter class reacted by attempting to substitute for slavery new forms of social and economic dominance as similar as possible to slavery.[4] At first, this white elite was restrained by the Republican state and national governments, and blacks were able to elect political leaders and to protect themselves. In 1877, after years of inconclusive struggle, external political and military controls were removed, and southern elites drove their former slaves from positions of political authority and into renewed social, political, and economic subservience.

In Reconstruction, Edgefield County blacks outnumbered whites 25,417 to 17,040. The races continued to live in close juxtaposition to each other as they had during slavery; but during Reconstruction, when rules of intercourse had broken down, geographical intermingling only exacerbated tensions. Of the adult males in 1870, 80% of the white and 95% of the black were engaged in agriculture. There was a marked shift of both ex-slaves and whites into tenantry and cotton production throughout the period. In 1870, only 3% of Edgefield County's black compared to 65% of white household heads owned land. The whites of Edgefield were led by the antebellum upper class. Although its wealth was greatly diminished by the Civil War, the old elite still ranked in the top decile of wealth for white households, five years after Appomatox. Moreover, these elites were experienced leaders—three white Reconstruction leaders had been Confederate generals and two had served as the state's governor during the Civil War.[5]

The planter elite maintained its intellectual dominance through its superior communication system. In the postwar struggle between an oral Afro-American culture and a literate white culture, whites had a tremendous advantage in organization. As late as 1880, only 10% of Edgefield County's black household heads were literate, compared to over 90% of white household heads. Communications with the Afro-American community were conveyed through personal contact in political, educational, religious, and military institutions. For news of events beyond Edgefield, blacks relied upon their leaders.

On the other hand, blacks overcame many of the disadvantages of illiteracy by drawing upon their unexpected but considerable organizational skills. Black religious, military, and political leadership positions were occupied by the same individuals who comprised an interlocking elite within the Afro-American community. For example, Methodist minister David Harris, Sr. was at the same time preacher, state representative, and major in the militia where he served as chaplain. In addition, each Afro-American organization furthered the interests of the others. For example, Robert Brown Elliott used his post as state assistant adjutant general to organize the National Guard Service South Carolina (N.G.S.C.). While the 1870 federal census was being taken, Elliott had partisan census enumerators act as enlisted officers for the militia. Edgefield County's militia unit was one of those used by Governor Robert K. Scott for political purposes through the appointment of the county's local leaders as officers.

The role of black schools in organizing the community is less clear than that of churches or militia. Although whites detested the black militia and initially opposed efforts by Afro-American church members to form separate congregations, they viewed establishment of black schools after the Civil War with less disfavor. But churches and black education were closely related. Some black churches provided buildings and money to help support public education for Afro-Americans. In addition to public schools, by 1871 Edgefield freedmen had seventeen Sunday schools, all but one managed by blacks. Young black men throughout the South taught school in rural areas like Edgefield County to earn money to attend college and seminary, while the children of some Edgefield black preachers became school teachers. School teachers were even better represented than preachers among local black political leadership, suggesting that the school system was used as another means of politically organizing Edgefield's Afro-American community.[6]

Whites also used churches, schools, and voluntary associations for political mobilization. More important, widespread subscription to the local newspaper, the Edgefield *Advertiser*, facilitated white communication and organization in the Democratic Party. The ability to organize, persuade, propagandize, and mobilize their membership through printed media was particularly important in a farming society such as Edgefield where families lived some distance apart. Oral culture is limited in space to aural-oral relationships and thus is inefficient in communicating information rapidly over great distances. In addition, the printed word lends itself inherently to precise expression of an idea. Newspapers like the Edgefield *Advertiser* were essential media to convey the world view of planter hegemony to people in their localities. In rural areas, editors like James T. Bacon and articulate members of the white elite writing to the paper were the southern backwoods intellectuals who formulated convincing arguments for planter dominance by making them relevant to the concerns of their neighbors.[7]

To save their hegemony, white leaders exploited every advantage. Immediately after the War, however, the Freedmen's Bureau, backed by Federal troops, provided some protection for blacks and tried to mediate between ex-slaves and plantation owners. Whites from all social stations, lowest to highest, were arrested for crimes ranging from disturbing the peace and conspiracy to murder; they learned that they could no longer simply go out and shoot people. For the first time, black people received guaranteed rights of assembly and freedom of speech. Planters learned the limits of their power, but only at the expense of reducing Edgefield, from the white perspective, to an occupied territory. On July 12, 1865, James T. Bacon, editor of the Edgefield *Advertiser*, warned the abolitionist, Dr. Mansfield French, that when making speeches he had better "keep a general at his side and soldiers at his back, for on Friday last, nothing on earth but the fear of being bayonetted or thrown into prison, kept us from hurling a stone at his head. Perhaps on some future occasion, the indignation of some outraged Southern man will cause him to forget both bayonet and prison." The editorial earned Bacon two weeks in a Charleston jail.[8]

The racial conflict resolved into two spheres, political and economic. Because of black enfranchisement in 1867, the political was the more urgent. By October, 1867, 4,367 blacks and 2,507 whites were registered to vote in Edgefield. Next month, newly registered voters cast their ballots in favor of a state constitutional convention that met in January, 1868 to forge a new document that was ratified in April. The new constitution guaranteed that "distinctions on account of race or color . . . be prohibited, and all classes of citizens shall enjoy equally all common public, legal, and political privileges." Under its provisions, county elections were set for June 2 and 3, 1868.[9]

As the elections approached, newspaper editors and influential white leaders urged the formation of local Democratic clubs and agricultural societies to prevent blacks and whites from voting Republican and to formulate remedies for the landowner's plight. In Edgefield, a local landowner pleaded for creation of white men's clubs that would pledge themselves not to vote for or employ any Republican or members of the Union League. "When our present contracts with them expire," he continued, "let us cease to give them employment, cease to give them work; let them look to members of their League for support; patronize only your friends." The Edgefield *Advertiser* encouraged landowners to use "all our wealth, influence, and popularity, with the blacks, as well as the whites, to win," and reminded readers: "meat and bread are involved in these elections. White men are not going to feed their enemies." In the spring of 1868, both Democratic clubs and aricultural societies appeared in the South Carolina upcountry; significantly and as in Edgefield, the officers and members of both organizations were often the same.[10]

These societies used social and economic intimidation through threats of discharge from employment to harass black and white voters. Violence, while not freely discussed in public, emerged as a means of coercing freedmen, both as voters and as workers, and of keeping in line any whites who might threaten the social fabric. But in 1868, the landowners failed in their quest for undisputed control on the farms and in the county court house.

The organization of the elites into Democratic clubs and agricultural societies during elections might be interpreted simply as proof that landowners were determined to use their economic power against the Republican onslaught. When one examines the planters' immediate and overt actions after they failed to regain political dominance, however, their desire to regulate the social order is obvious and explicit. They tried to preserve as much of slavery as they could and prevent the advancement of blacks. Two Edgefield white leaders clearly understood the impact political developments have on economic and social developments. One week after the county elections, the "Bald Eagle of the Confederacy," General Martin Witherspoon Gary, cogently stated the argument: "It is not a question of property or mental qualifications," but if any blacks are allowed to vote, "you have consented to make this a mongrel government—to make the children of your former slaves the successful competitors of your children for the honors of the state. . . . There existed an irrepressible conflict between free labor and slave labor. . . .It still continues, in a conflict between the Caucasian and African races." Democratic leader George Tillman, pursuing the same theme, accurately prophesied the course that Edgefield's reconstruction would take: "Once break down the barrier between the races, as to political rights, on any qualifications whatever, and every succeeding election would continue to demolish more and more of the barrier until after a while there would be no barrier at all." In the sparsely settled upcountry areas like Edgefield "where land is plentiful, where labor is scarce, and wages high," he argued that blacks as voting citizens would continue to increase in number and become more and more powerful politically. They would then put their friends in offices of authority and benefit from educational opportunities that elected officials would be forced to give them. They would finally vote only for those that treated the "nigger and the nigger race as social and political equals." Tillman concluded, "Once grant a negro political privileges . . . you instantly advance his social status."[11]

Next month the Edgefield *Advertiser* printed Tillman's advocacy of denying black people their political rights. Political rights, he contended, would lead to black ownership of land. "There is nothing which makes a man so free, so independent, and so lordly in his aspirations, as ownership of land." For this reason, all white men are engaged in a mighty crusade "against the colored man." "By common consent the *land*, *labor*, and *lives* of the colored races are articles of free trade among Caucasians everywhere." This crusade against colored races made every white man a democrat to "every other white man, but an aristocrat to every colored man. It is making every white man a conqueror, a landowner and a governor, or exterminator of the colored man."[12]

In accordance with the Gary-Tillman doctrines, Edgefield Democrats used violence and fraud to prevent the November, 1868 federal election from being held rather than permit Afro-Americans to vote. Even then blacks did not yield easily to white intimidation. Among the courageous freedmen was James Martin who after declaring his intention to walk to the polls, lost his job and was warned by a white neighbor, "We intend to kill everyone who starts there, for no d——d nigger shall vote in this county." About a week before the election a crowd came to his house at night and fired repeatedly in the yard and once through his door. Despite this, Martin set out for the polls some fifteen miles away. He met two friends who had been to vote and who had been shot. "I saw their wounds," Martin testified, "They were my neighbors, and I talked with them. . . ." Undaunted, he arrived at the polls, only to find that no voting was taking place.[13]

To the Democrats' chagrin, federal and state investigations and subsequent action showed that such blatant local acts would not be tolerated. The Republican Presidential electors were returned and a congressman seated. Consequently, in 1870, planters appeared in sheep's clothing as the South Carolina Reform party with Edgefield's General Mathew Culbreath Butler as candidate for lieutenant governor. But they were again defeated at the polls in their statewide maneuver to oust the Republican party. Despite paternalistic appeals, economic intimidation, and violence, in every election throughout Reconstruction, ex-slaves continued to vote Republican against their former masters' interests and in their own. Until 1877, control of the coercive powers of both state and local government by Afro-Americans made possible real gains in their economic position and social status. In Edgefield, Reconstruction seemed to be succeeding, threatening planter hegemony and providing freedmen economic, social, and political opportunities.

Since politics and economics worked in tandem in the rural South, related to the political struggle was the struggle over land and labor control. Southern wealth was based on agriculture, and control over land and labor were central problems that southerners, black and white, had to confront immediately after the Civil War. Both black and white community leaders understood the interrelationship of politics and economics. After the abolition of slavery, a variety of choices arose in settling land tenure problems. The possibilities ranged from tenantry to wage labor or part-time employment, to a division of plantations among emancipated blacks. William Henry Trescott, South Carolina's special lobbyist in Washington during Presidential Reconstruction, wrote to Governor James L. Orr in December of 1865, "You will find that this question of the control of labor underlies every other question of state interest." Both whites and blacks in Edgefield were eager to know Federal plans for land distribution to freedmen. During a mid-December, 1865 visit to Edgefield, the chief officer of the Freedman's Bureau in northern South Carolina declared that whites would continue to own their land—blacks "owned the labor"—and recommended that blacks be paid one-third of the crop.[14]

As long as the plantocracy maintained control of the land and could find laborers, the Edgefield white elite believed it could preserve the essence of this antebellum order even without slaves. In 1865, for example, several members of the elite established an "Immigration Society" to recruit an "intelligent and thrifty white population" and to "make *ourselves independent* of the negro." Although the venture failed, it demonstrates the early determination of the upper class to preserve a plantation class society by maintaining control of both land and labor.[15] In other ways, the white elite decided soon after the war to make effective use of the power that derived from a landowning monopoly. In 1865, the Edgefield *Advertiser*, voice of the white establishment, observed that if Congress disallowed the proposed state Black Codes compelling blacks to labor, the "alternative is to keep the negro from becoming a landholder." The newspaper pointed to Trinidad as the only place where free black labor had proved successful. The reason was that all the "land . . . is owned by the white man and the negro is unable to get possession of a foot of it—he must work or perish." A law was needed to "impose a tax of one or five thousand dollars upon every white man who sells, or rents, gives, loans, or any way conveys, to a negro, any tract, parcel or messuage of land." The newspaper urged landowners to contract in writing to "pay to said negro a specified sum." Such laws would force blacks to hire themselves to white men—"they must then labor or starve." Thus, to the traditional elite, free black labor meant *landless* laborers dependent on former slaveowners for employment.[16]

After the defeat of the South Carolina Reform Party at the polls in 1870, the white elite turned to systematic economic coercion. Calls came immediately for a reorganization of the Reform political clubs (in most instances identical to the old Democratic clubs) into agricultural societies. Captain Lewis P. Jones, executive chairman of the Edgefield Reform party, was elected president of the Edgefield County "Agricultural and Police Club."

In late 1870, planters feared that whites might not hold together against Afro-Americans in conditions of Republican political power and a depressed economy. The Agricultural and Police Club rules required every white man eighteen and older to be a member of the agricultural society in his township. Moreover, the rules declared that if any white man refused to join the club or "to abide by the By-Laws, he and his family shall be socially proscribed by all the other members of the Club and their families." A white police force, reminiscent of the slave patrol, was created to ensure that all blacks and whites observed these rules. George Tillman stressed the importance of accepting the proposals. He recommended "the sternest and most unrelenting social proscription of every white man who might refuse either to join a Club, or to abide by its regulations." The threat was to cut off dissenting whites from something that really mattered, part of the existing welfare-social security system in rural communities. As Tillman put it, if any white man did not join the Club or did not submit to its regulation of the black community, then the white community was to treat the recalcitrant "as a whole nigger should be treated, pass him and his whole family with silent contempt; let him or any of his household get sick, or even die with none to cheer the lonely hours, or to bury the tainted remains but his nigger associates." If the proposals of the Agricultural and Police Club were not adopted and adhered to in Edgefield, Tillman warned, "we have but one other resource left—the Ku Kluxer's power—the assassin's privilege." The proposals were unanimously accepted.

Local clubs appeared in every township and adopted the same rules as the county club. Whites would sell *no* land to blacks or Republicans. A list of "bad characters . . . unworthy examples who ought not to be hired, or be permitted to be hired, or allowed to reside on the premises of any landowner" would be published regularly in the Edgefield *Advertiser*. No landowner would entice a laborer to break his contract with another landowner. The number of tenants a landowner could hire would be determined strictly by acres owned, and one white man would be hired for each of a specified number of blacks employed. All laborers would have to pay a portion of the landowner's land taxes.

Renting land to blacks, whether for money or for part of the crop, was forbidden; laborers were to be *hired* either for wages or for a share of the crop. White landowners wanted to use tenantry to manipulate landless laborers, both blacks and whites, and to maintain race control over freedmen. The crucial issue was who would control the labor, that is, who would decide and schedule the worker's daily chores and activities, the tenant or the landowner? A renting tenant had more control over his time and activities than someone working for wages, whether those wages were in cash or in a share of the crop. The sharecropper, unlike the renter, had little control over what crops were planted or how they were sold.[17]

Republican leaders understood the importance of land and labor control too. At the Constitutional Convention of 1868, black leaders immediately moved to petition Congress for money to buy lands for ex-slaves, but Senator Henry W. Wilson, Radical Republican from Massachusetts, replied that Congress would not accept such a proposal. Still, South Carolina's Reconstruction government gave freedmen increasingly effective controls over land and labor, which, if continued, should have provided ultimately a way for blacks to get land. In these years, Republicans in federal, state, and especially local government took a number of steps to break up the antebellum plantation system.[18]

The most important government agency for actual land distribution was the South Carolina Land Commission, established March 27, 1869 by the Republican legislature. The Commission's charge was to buy land and sell it in farm-size plots at reasonable rates to landless people. The Land Commission purchased six tracts of good quality land in Edgefield County, and divided the tracts into farms. Sixty families settled onto the tracts, their holdings ranging from 20 to a 115 acre unit held by a father and son team. Although the Commission was able to obtain land for only a small number of freedmen, it offered hope for many others and was symbolic of a changing social order. Edgefield's General Butler characterized this Commission as "the blackest spot" on Republicanism, because it was supposedly riddled by graft. But planters had other reasons to detest the Land Commission. They agreed with an upcountry newspaper editor who complained the Land Commission "will render your Negro hirelings . . . less efficient and more sullen and discontented." Moreover, since many of the fathers and sons of the Edgefield families who purchased farms were members of the black militia, it was claimed that military colonies were being set up on the land commission sites.[19]

A major Republican program shifted state and county tax bases to break up large estates. The tax burden alone, claimed a future Republican state treasurer, would "force sufficient lands upon the market at all times to meet the wants of all the landless." Edgefield plantation owners were not accustomed to even reasonable land taxes; now they faced purposefully high state, county, municipal, and educational taxes, each assessed by local Republicans. Beginning in 1870, the Edgefield *Advertiser* attacked "All the various proposed Republican measures, which let them be called by whatever technical names they may, are in the end, nothing but measures to steal money from the white people of South Carolina and increase their burden of taxation." In 1871, after the announcement of a tax increase, the editor complained, "We might as well cease all further attempt at living or breathing." By 1872, the newspaper regularly ran two to three columns of lands to be sold for delinquent taxes. Protesting Republican tax policies, Edgefield white leaders helped organize two state "taxpayers' conventions." In 1876, General M. C. Butler wrote to the governor asking for an extension on payment of taxes since many planters were "wholly unable at present" to pay. Edgefield planters had lost their slaves; now taxes were threatening their monopoly of land.[20]

The Land Commission and the state and local tax measures were complementary programs to make land available for the landless to purchase. An even more important and effective, though less dramatic, change was taking place through legal measures that gave landless blacks greatly increased control over their own labor and over the crops they raised on someone else's land. A state law strengthened the laborers' claim to the crop and thus their bargaining power with the landowners. The workers were given the first lien on the crop, and landowners were prohibited from prosecuting laborers for any unperformed work not required by a written contract.

Moreover, laborers could prosecute landowners without cost by a simple appeal to county officials who were either chosen by popular vote under home rule established by Republicans or appointed by a Republican governor on the recommendation of the elected county legislative delegation. The county commissioners were given jurisdiction over the collection and distribution of public funds. Especially important to blacks were the trial justices, who were given jurisdiction in cases that involved penalties or judgments of $100 or less. Blacks served in all county positions. More and more Afro-Americans filled these and other local offices, so that by 1872, the Edgefield *Advertiser* was claiming that no white landowner could get a fair hearing. The tenant was becoming more nearly autonomous in law and steadily gaining control of land and labor.[21]

These Republican programs damaged Edgefield County's landowning elite. In 1868, one of the wealthiest planters, ex-Governor Francis W. Pickens, had difficulty obtaining a small loan. In 1874, ex-Governor Milledge Bonham wrote that "with a large family . . . poor crops, demoralized labor, taxes, my life has been absorbed in trying to keep my head above water. The effect has been crushing. . . ." In his farm journal, one white increasingly worried about the freedmen's refusals to work under the direction of white landowners and particularly the black laborer's leaving one landowner for another who offered a higher wage. He wrote in September, 1874, that because of low cotton prices coupled with inability to control free black labor, "It goes hard with farmers especially those who work many free negroes." General M. C. Butler had returned from the Civil War impoverished except for his extensive landholdings. He was a founder of the Edgefield Agricultural and Police Club, which had pledged all members not to sell land to blacks. Yet, in 1870, he attempted to sell his 650 acre Edgefield plantation to the South Carolina Land Commission. Butler's application was rejected. In 1875, an investigator sent to Edgefield County reported to the governor that "many of the land owners are in debt being obliged to produce from their land or be sold out."[22]

The realities of increasing black power were forcing whites to deal with blacks in some important areas. One of these was white cooperation with the black-dominated county Republican legislative delegation in an effort to obtain a railroad for Edgefield County. Another was the formation of a fusion ticket of moderate Democratic and Republican candidates, which won the 1872 Edgefield municipal election. Perhaps even more disturbing to white notions of racial propriety was the marriage of a white Republican to an Edgefield ex-slave on the courthouse steps.[23]

But this promising direction of interracial relationship hardly had a chance to get started before an alternative way of dealing with black progress began to show results. To maintain their hegemony, the planters launched a systematic campaign of physical violence. Governor Chamberlain sent a special agent to Edgefield in 1875 to investigate the causes of the intense violence. The investigator attributed the disturbances in Edgefield County to a "few lawless and imprudent men of both races." A group of black militants made "incendiary remarks or suggested threats in retaliation for acts or language perpetrated or used by white people against them or some one of their race." Counterpoint to these was a small group of whites who violently opposed "any assertions of equality as a citizen when coming from a colored man, such action on his part being considered offensive and presumptuous." These few whites, wrote the investigator, held "human life at little value being as reckless in risking their own, as they are heartless in taking the lives of others." Unfortunately, the majority of whites who were a "law abiding class of citizens, who desire peace, and who are satisfied with seeking redress for their grievances only in a lawful manner" "dare not oppose or condemn" the extremist minority. To win, the extremists, who consisted largely of landowning elites, had to break the Republican party's control of the local and state government. It was somewhat similar on the black side and during the crisis of Reconstruction white and black moderates were polarized by the extremists' use of physical violence.[24]

Their failure to recapture political power in the national election of 1872 drove the white extremists into organizing irregular military companies. The white irregular militia had overlapping membership and interlocking leadership with other white voluntary organizations. Once the whites organized into military companies, they met the resistance of determined black militia. The existence of black militiamen became the symbol that the extremists used to frighten white moderates into joining their camp.[25]

Seeing blacks in positions of authority seriously upset white notions of social order. This was particularly true of black law enforcement officials, especially black militiamen who represented hope to blacks, danger to whites. The Edgefield *Advertiser* saw the influence of black troops as "intense demoralization. . . . Wherever they are that place is deeply and damnably accursed. The contagion of their influence extends not only to persons of their own color, but also to many white people who are white only as regards their skin." Ex-governor Milledge L. Bonham wrote to Governor Scott in 1868 imploring him to "arrest this tendency to anarchy and bloodshed," and warned of a race war since Confederate soldiers "will not quietly submit to unauthorized and armed negro domination." An 1874 4th of July parade by the N.G.S.C. 9th Regiment commanded by Colonel Lawrence Cain and Lieutenant Colonel Paris Simkins, represented an "insult to the white people of Edgefield as no white people upon earth had ever to put up with before," wrote *Advertiser* editor Bacon. The black regiment numbered more than a thousand armed men, and "over and above this, every negro man and *woman* in Edgefield followed it, and thirsted to be enrolled." Long to be remembered in Edgefield, it was "a splendid and embodied threat to the white people of the land, the owners of the soil. On that day, no white man dared walk the highway; no white woman dared approach her window. In fact, no orgie of the Paris Commune surpassed this in the subversion of God's law and order." A native white historian who remembered the black militiamen in Edgefield wrote that they represented "the great disintegration of the old order of things that was taking place all around... [Black militia were used to] humiliate and mortify the old masters and rulers."[26]

The most notorious black militia commander was Captain Edward Tennant who commanded one of two black militia units formed in 1870 in Edgefield County's large and remote Merriweather township. A dashing county officer, Ned Tennant, dressed in military array, rode a fine horse, and bore himself with great dignity. He was both a symbolic and substantive threat to southern white planter hegemony. Two separate incidents involving Tennant have merged through local lore into the Ned Tennant riot, which the Edgefield *Advertiser* viewed as a logical consequence of the "strife, lawlessness, and bloodshed" caused by the black militia. In July, 1874, one of the white irregular military companies, the Sweetwater Sabre Club, assembled near the place where Tennant's N.G.S.C. militia drilled. Whites were enraged by the black militia's use of large bass drums and that night shot up Tennant's house. Responding immediately to the drum's "long roll," black militiamen from Merriweather township assembled to protect Tennant. Hearing the long roll echo, whites became convinced that "negroes meant to kill all whites" and burn everything in the county. Using a prearranged system of couriers, white irregular militia with more than 200 armed men, faced 100 black militia at Tennant's home the next morning. Despite an explosive atmosphere, no bloodshed occurred as both white leaders and Tennant parleyed and agreed to dismiss their troops.

Following the first Ned Tennant riot, Edgefield planters requested newly elected Governor Daniel H. Chamberlain to disband and disarm the black militia. Whites reported that with a militia company in Edgefield, blacks "grew more impudent and unbearable every day." One white leader who helped persuade Chamberlain was General M. C. Butler. His home, four miles from Tennant's, burned soon after the meeting with Chamberlain, and it was rumored that Captain Edward Tennant had hired an arsonist to set the fire. In January, 1875, members of the Sweetwater Sabre Club rode to arrest Tennant. When black militiamen protecting Tennant fired over the posse's head, the Sweetwater Sabre Club spread the alarm of a race war. For three days, General M. C. Butler commanded over a thousand armed whites, many riding from adjoining counties, who scoured the countryside searching for Tennant and his men. Little bloodshed actually occurred because the armed and mounted white troops greatly outnumbered Tennant's black militia company, and Tennant, "a skillful tactician" was able to march "twenty-five miles through a country swarming with whites looking for him" and emerge with his full company at Edgefield Court House. There the militia company surrendered their arms to the state senator and regimental commander, Lawrence Cain, rather than risk Butler's men seizing their rifles.[27]

With whatever means at hand, elected black officials also opposed the violence and massive resistance of the planters. Early in his senate career, Lawrence Cain introduced a bill to tax the five square miles surrounding any neighborhood "in which a man shall be murdered on account of politics, race, or color to support the widows and orphans of such martyrs." But it was difficult to fight against the white planters' massive resistance. Colonel Lawrence Cain confirmed to Governor Chamberlain that "It is true that many of our men are refused employment and thrown of house, but the men are not confined to the Militia Companies. Any man who took a prominent part in the last [political] contest is proscribed." The executive report of the 1875 investigation in Edgefield County noted "that most of the white men whose buildings have been burned were those who refused to unite with others in the recent proscription against the colored people." Benjamin R. Tillman, younger brother of Democratic leader George Tillman, bragged that 200 black militia were unemployed and homeless in the southwestern section of the county where he lived, because landowners obligated themselves "not to rent land to any member of the negro militia or give them employment. . . . Those who did not sign rendered themselves very obnoxious and were almost ostracised by their fellows." Ben Tillman particularly regretted the fate of Joshua McKie, "a refined and high-toned gentleman" who, "against the wishes of his neighbors," after the first Tennant riot in 1874, gave Ned Tennant "a home." McKie, "after he had rented the land and signed the lease, . . . found himself shunned and ostracised by his friends, and even by kinsmen." Soon afterwards, he committed suicide.

State representative Paris Simkins, former Edgefield slave, demanded the state protect all black laborers who, "because of having exercised their political rights and privileges," had been discharged by white landowners in Edgefield County. He proposed a tax of two mills on all property in Edgefield County, the receipts to be given to persons discharged because of political persecution. The measure failed because the Republican state government, under the patrician reform carpetbagger Daniel H. Chamberlain, was attempting to attract the support of more white landowners. In February, 1875, Chamberlain also vetoed a bill similar to Simkins's, which had passed the General Assembly.[28]

Governor Chamberlain also disbanded all military organizations after the second Ned Tennant riot in January, 1875. Although this proclamation included whites as well as blacks, in Edgefield the white "rifle and sabre clubs" went on a rampage, attacking the jail and stealing the black militia's arms. The incident that settled the Democrats on a policy of all-out violence was the affair at Hamburg of July, 1876, in which at least four unarmed black militiamen were killed after surrendering to General M. C. Butler and his men, most of whom were members of the Sweetwater Sabre Club, the same Edgefield irregular white militia unit involved in the Ned Tennant riots.[29]

According to the early revisionist historians of South Carolina Reconstruction, Francis Butler Simkins and Robert Hilliard Woody, the events at Hamburg and Edgefield, "definitely pointed the way" for the Redemption of the state from the Republicans. In August, 1876, the Edgefield *Advertiser* favorably compared the 1876 election campaign to that of 1874. Instead of 1,000 black militia marching triumphantly through the streets of Edgefield on August 12, 1876 for a Republican election rally, 30 Edgefield County local Democratic Clubs had been summoned by the Edgefield County Executive Committee. Confederate Generals M. C. Butler and Mart Gary commanded over 700 mounted and armed Democrats, all dressed defiantly in red shirts. The presence of armed Democrats was intimidating; they pressed even harder, climbing onto the platform that held the Republican dignitaries and howling down the speakers, including Governor Chamberlain. The Democrats demanded equal time to speak at the Republican meeting and Gary and Butler delivered violent, personally abusive tirades. The *Advertiser* found the abrupt ending of the meeting symbolic—the platform constructed for the Republican rally collapsed. Again, in September, when General Butler and some 40 members of the Edgefield Sweetwater Sabre Club were to be tried for the Hamburg murders, the irregular white militia company dressed defiantly in red. Armed and on horseback, these men executed military formations and galloped through the streets of Aiken where the trial was to be held. These Edgefield whites carried a large cross that had a larger than life size effigy of an Afro-American crucified and bullet-ridden. Throughout Reconstruction, federal and state authorities had not tolerated planter-directed atrocities and political violence, but when these defiant whites were not convicted, the Edgefield former dominant planter class knew that the time had come for what Gary had earlier termed a "war of the races" to regain control of the state.[30]

Gary and George D. Tillman corresponded with leaders in Mississippi who had "redeemed" that state the previous year from Republican rule. As developed in South Carolina, the "Mississippi Plan" was accurately described as the "Shotgun Plan" and commonly referred to throughout the state as the "Edgefield Plan." Gary was the acknowledged director of the Edgefield Plan and he outlined how the state was to be "redeemed" through murder, intimidation, and bribery. It follows in part:

12. Every Democrat must feel honor bound to control the vote of at least one negro, by intimidation, purchase, keeping him away or as each individual may determine, how he may best accomplish it.
16. Never threaten a man individually if he deserves to be threatened, the necessities of the times require that he should die. A dead Radical is very harmless—a threatened

Radical or one driven off by threats from the scene of his operations is often very troublesome, sometimes dangerous, always vindictive.

Ben Tillman, a trusted Lieutenant, wrote of the 1876 campaign strategy that: "Butler, Gary, and George Tillman had to my personal knowledge agreed on the policy of terrorizing the negroes at the first opportunity, by letting them provoke trouble and then having the whites demonstrate their superiority by killing as many of them as was justifiable." Edgefield blacks were deliberately murdered in the 1876 election campaign.[31]

Reconstruction violence can best be explained if one perceives this era as did the displaced planter class. For the old elite, Republican-inspired land reform and the freedmen's support for such measures as taxes and labor laws that might promote this reform, was fundamentally a class question. Land redistribution, even more than abolition of slavery, would prevent the planter class from retaining its hegemony. Woodward argues that race divided more than class united, but Black Reconstruction's "Negro rule" confounded the traditional class and racial hierarchy. General Gary's "Edgefield Plan" illustrates the white elite's awareness of the interrelationship of race and class: "the leaders of the Radical Party" would be held responsible: "beginning *first* with the white men, second the mulatto men and third with the black leaders." This was order number 15 and the preceding order had ended with the imperative: "Treat them so as to show them, you are the superior race, and that their natural position is that of subordination to the white man."

As long as Republicans controlled national, state, and local governments, various Edgefield whites from all ranks of society became Republicans; perhaps some from ideological beliefs, obviously some for reasons of political patronage, and others in order to be elected to public office. Local government jobs that provided a regular salary were particulary prized in an agricultural community where crops were subject to vicissitudes of weather. In 1875, the governor's special investigator remained confident of Republican ascendency and reported that in Edgefield he believed the economic proscription of Republicans and black militia was dying out because of the desperate economic plight of the Edgefield landowners. And when in 1876, some remnants of the South Carolina antebellum establishment seriously discussed endorsing the moderate reform Republican Governor Chamberlain, the Edgefield white elite acted defiantly and decisively to provide a new basis for planter political hegemony. Whites were either Democrats or traitors! Because of the Republican party's guaranteed strength through the continued support of blacks and the persistent threat of white collaborators, the more "idealistic" of the planter elite felt it necessary to "redeem" the state with the "Edgefield Plan."[32]

Thirty-five Edgefield County Democratic and Rifle Clubs were active in the County on election day of 1876. The presence of two companies of federal troops did not deter the zeal or purpose of white irregular militia companies. In Edgefield Village, General Gary commanded several hundred selected armed and provisioned men and captured the Masonic Hall and Court House, the two voting establishments, thereby forcing blacks to vote in a small school inadequate to accommodate the number of freedmen voting. Edgefield blacks marched to the Court House to vote anyway, but Gary directed his men to block entrances. Freedmen protested to General T. H. Ruger, commander of the federal troops in Edgefield. Although backed by federal troops, Ruger could not budge Gary and gain entrance to the Court House for freedmen. The Confederate "Bald Eagle" defiantly answered: "By God, sir, I'll not do it." Thus, there were 2,252 more votes cast in Edgefield County than there were eligible voters. As Ben Tillman explained: "Gary's doctrine of voting early and often changed the republican majority of 2,300 in Edgefield to a democratic majority of 3,900 thus giving [Wade] Hampton a claim to the office of governor. It was Edgefield's majority alone which gave to Hampton a chance to claim to have been elected. . . "[33]

The turning point came when the federal government condoned the Edgefield Plan by withdrawing its troops from South Carolina in 1877. This enabled the planter elite to regain political power in the state and local government; that power, coupled with their economic dominance, put them in total control. In April, 1877, a black lawyer wrote from Edgefield of the great disillusionment of the freedmen who had "hazarded their lives" to elect Rutherford B. Hayes. Another black said, "to think that Hayes could go back on us now, when we had to wade through blood to help place him where he now is."[34]

Historians have long been aware of the practical disfranchisement of black South Carolinians through the eight-box law and the gerrymandering techniques after Redemption. Less well known are the changes instituted by the restored dominant planter class to ensure its hegemony. The resumption of political control by Democrats in 1877 cut short Republican efforts and effectively removed avenues of political, economic, and social advancement which had been opened for Afro-Americans during Reconstruction. Interracial marriage was prohibited in 1879. State statutes of 1878, 1880, and 1889 became the legal base for economic serfdom. The lien laws were changed to benefit the landowners: whereas, under Republican rule, the man who grew the crop (the tenant) had the first lien on the crop, the Democrats immediately reversed this and gave priority to the landowner. They also increased the percentage that the landowner could take as a lien, which had been deliberately limited by the Republicans. Moreover, the Democrats attempted to prevent tenants from obtaining liens from merchants; they wanted to prevent even this bit of independence from the landlord. Such legislation reduced the tenant to the legal position of wage earner. Moreover, since white Democratic officials at the local level were unsympathetic to a black man's grievances or his desire for landownership, arguments over rent were futile. As the Reconstruction Land Commission had been a symbol of a changing social order, the loss of the good family farms purchased by Edgefield blacks through the Commission is again symbolic. After 1878, these farms were forfeited and grabbed as large units by Edgefield white plantation owners or their sons.[35]

For many years after Reconstruction, it was impossible for black leaders in Edgefield to agitate for equality or to encourage militancy against whites. Printed in red ink for a commemorative "red-shirt" edition, the *Advertiser* pledged that Edgefield as " 'Color Bearer' of the Democratic party [would] achieve for her . . . State a victory in '78 no less glorious than the proud one of '76." And during the 1878 campaign, the *Advertiser* charged the white community: "Hang together like grim death. Let no side issues array you, one against the others." This was the context in which Edgefield blacks were forced to operate by the late 1870s. Re-establishment of planter hegemony through competitive and neopaternalistic modes of race relations elicited a changing style of black leadership. Competition gave way to accommodation. In the years after Radical Reconstruction, neopaternalism on the part of whites and accommodation on the part of blacks became reciprocal and mutually supportive styles of community leadership.[36]

Accommodationist leadership had existed throughout Reconstruction, but it had been only marginally effective, since more radical blacks had produced tangible benefits for the Afro-American community. During Reconstruction, when the planter class tried to restore their hegemony they began to understand the usefulness of black accommodationist leadership. In Edgefield, the most prominent accommodationist leader was Reverend Alexander Bettis, pastor of Mt. Canaan Baptist Church and organizer of a Baptist association.[37]

Compared to resistant Reconstruction leaders such as Lawrence Cain, Ned Tennant, and Paris Simkins, Alexander Bettis played an unglamorous role. He did, however, provide space within a restricting and suspicious white society for black institutions to grow. As a people primarily dependent upon wages from Edgefield whites for survival and welfare, Edgefield blacks utilized their cultural resources to create institutions that gave them collective security and protection, and mediated their relations with white society. Since there was no longer a black militia after 1876, the freedmen organized primarily through the churches and schools. This had the advantage of including women and children as direct participants, and of promoting the values of education and literacy. Largely through their churches and the closely related schools, Edgefield blacks transformed themselves from an oral culture to a literate one. There was never a total dichotomy between competitive and accommodationist leadership in Edgefield, but rather a continuum of leadership styles ranging from extremely militant to extremely accommodationist. Many black leaders whose actions during Reconstruction classified them as militant were also at times accommodationist in the sense that they concentrated on securing limited gains for blacks without challenging white domination. At the same time, the actions of avowed accommodationists laid the ground work that would survive past Reconstruction to challenge the basic power structure.

Alexander Bettis was able to obtain certain benefits from Edgefield white leaders after Reconstruction because he and they understood how to use each other. Because he encouraged blacks to accept a hierarchically segmented society, Bettis profited throughout his career from white support that enabled him to gain benefits through the Bettis Academy, the main institution of learning for blacks in the county. The academy was a social and economic center for the black community after Reconstruction. Its autumn fair was one of the major events of the year. Perhaps most importantly, starting in the late 1880's, the academy sponsored the purchase of land by black farmers through a self-help association, which bought large tracts of land for division into smaller farms.

In addition to the efforts of the academy, Bettis was often able to use his influence with whites to resolve disputes between blacks and whites and to clear blacks of criminal charges in the white elite dominated courts. Support for Bettis's tactics could have been a matter of life or death for Edgefield blacks.

At other times, Bettis's accommodationist role allowed his followers to have some psychological and emotional freedom. For example, drum beating, common to oral cultures and which Afro-Americans had used to summon assemblies, had been forbidden by "common law" imposed by the whites after the Ned Tennant Riot. However, exceptions were made for Bettis. "Beating of the drum" occurred "at all the gatherings" of the academy.[38]

U.S. Senator and native Edgefielden Ben Tillman reflected that Bettis "wielded great influence over his race, and . . . that influence was always exerted for good. I have never heard anyone speak ill of him in my life." Although Tillman or other whites may never have heard ill words spoken of Alexander Bettis, other Edgefield blacks did not always agree with his methods. Soon after Redemption, Edgefield's recently deposed black probate judge wrote to Bishop Henry M. Turner distressed that some Edgefield "ministers, who have fine congregations supporting them, are standing against immigration to Liberia."[39] An impressive tombstone stands at the head of Bettis's grave. It is covered by inscriptions of gratitude, love, and admiration, but one line is a reminder of the dissatisfaction some Edgefield blacks felt: "Like his Master, was by some disliked."

Because he was free from white interference, Bettis was the community's most important black leader from the end of Reconstruction until his death in 1895. His life reveals the changing nature of black leadership in Edgefield from Reconstruction to the late 19th century. Competitive race relations gave way to a new paternalistic oppression that structurally resembled the slavery system but was qualitatively different. As in slavery, most blacks were confined to one part of a southern segmented society: the special caste of the traditional agricultural laborer. But a major difference was in the amount of planter and laborer personal contact. Because of the tenant system that developed, poorer blacks and whites lived spatially dispersed in the countryside. At the same time, more of the landowning whites began to move into villages, towns, and cities in rural areas like Edgefield County. After Reconstruction, Edgefield whites came into contact with fewer and fewer individual blacks. Moreover, the legacy of Reconstruction violence prevented reestablishment of many "positive" dimensions of paternalism even after planters had regained hegemony. Therefore, from 1877 until the 1890s, when Pitchfork Ben Tillman, matured on the Edgefield Plan, took control of the state government and locked into place a more stable system of race relations to replace the style so abruptly ended by the Civil War, there continued conflicting and contending approaches to race relations. In the transition to the new system after Redemption, when Afro-Americans had no political power and no influence in forming the laws that governed them, black leaders most effective at the local level were "go-betweens," accommodationists like Bettis. In such circumstances, some competitive Reconstruction leaders left Edgefield and in one organized effort they led a large part of the community to Arkansas.[40]

Some competitive leaders also continued to live in Edgefield after Reconstruction ended. However, Lawrence Cain and Paris Simkins, who survived into the 20th century, never held political office again and, although both held law degrees, never practiced in the Edgefield court. Simkins, who died in 1930, remained a leader in one of the Baptist churches that had withdrawn from Bettis's association. In 1884, he drew up the Constitution and By-Laws of the Mutual Aid and Burial Society and became the first president. He was also the founder and leader of the secret order of Knights of Pythias in Edgefield. Urged in his old age by children and grandchildren to come to Columbia or to the North to live with them, he continued to live in his fine home, which still stands in the town today, and "loyal to the place of his birth . . . preferred to live, die, and be buried in Edgefield." Generally, the old black Reconstruction leaders' activities and influence, which would have been confined to the black community, were seldom recorded. From scattered references it is evident that other blacks continued to address the former black militia officers by their military rank. Probably these old leaders neither resisted nor accommodated. Perhaps it was enough that they were living representatives of Reconstruction's aspirations for equality in a period when whites tried desperately to suppress for blacks even the memory of those hopes.[41]

Reconstruction in rural Edgefield fits more closely with the pattern of *competitive* race relations as described by C. Vann Woodward's typology. Black leaders gained political power and used their influence to advance the status of Afro-Americans at the expense of their former white owners, thus contradicting Eugene D. Genovese's assertion that the paternalistic slavery system had ingrained an accommodationist spirit that prevented freedmen from fighting for civil rights. Antebellum paternalism did not preclude, as Genovese suggests, a viable group force in a political sense during Reconstruction, for Edgefield freedmen did develop a black political movement that succeeded in maintaining itself as long as democracy was viable. During Reconstruction, Edgefield freedmen fought their way upward in the social and political order. After Reconstruction, assertive black leadership gave way to an era of accommodation to white supremacy that structurally resembled the earlier paternalism of slavery.

In Edgefield's rural society, Woodward's models were reversed. The success of Black Reconstruction in a competitive racial system moved the whites to restore a paternalistic and oppressive segmented model as soon as federal, state, and local political and military controls were removed. This study of rural Edgefield suggests at least a modification of Woodward's typology. Reconstruction appears to have been an advanced version of 20th century race relations prematurely introduced. Competitive race relations during Reconstruction and the resumption of white control between 1877 and roughly 1910 produced a period in which competitive and paternalistic elements competed in a confused and shifting context.

The two black leadership styles that existed in Edgefield during Reconstruction and afterwards laid the foundation for the Second Reconstruction's theme of political activism united with Christian pacifism. Though the strain of militancy had been dormant for over eighty years, it had persisted through each generation of blacks since 1876, until Martin Luther King, Jr.'s message called it out into the arena of 20th-century politics. Moreover, for the literate black community, which had developed in the churches and schools during the years of accommodation, the unequal battle of the First Reconstruction was rejoined in the 20th century with the same means of communication and organization available to the white community.[42]

Notes

1. C. Vann Woodward, *The Strange Career of Jim Crow* (New York, 1955, 1957, 1966, 1974), *American Counterpoint: Slavery and Racism in the North-South Dialogue* (Boston, 1971), 234-260; Eugene D. Genovese, *In Red and Black: Marxian Explorations in Southern and Afro-American History* (New York, 1974), 102-157, *Roll, Jordan, Roll: The World the Slaves Made* (New York, 1974), especially 133-158, 661.

2. Richard Maxwell Brown, *Strain of Violence: Historical Studies of American Violence and Vigilantism* (New York, 1975), 67-90, Chapter 3 focuses on Edgefield and its crucial impact on South Carolina politics from before the Revolution to Strom Thurmond. Brown argues that Edgefield had a great impact on South Carolina history, and ultimately (through South Carolina's role) on American history. See also James G. Banks, "Strom Thurmond and the Revolt Against Modernity" (unpublished Ph.D. dissertation, Kent State University, 1970). Midway between the Smoky Mountains (143 miles) and the Atlantic (169 miles), Edgefield County is separated from Georgia by the Savannah River. Counties in South Carolina were known as districts until 1868. In 1870, Edgefield Village had only 846 residents of the 42,486 people in the county. Less than 25 miles away from Edgefield Village, a single long day's journey even on foot, Augusta, Georgia prospered as a hinterland city. For a brief period, antebellum Hamburg in Edgefield District had ri-

valed Augusta. Only two other towns in the county, Johnston and Trenton, were of notable size. Both developed during Reconstruction on railroad lines that by-passed Edgefield Court House. For more specific discussions of Edgefield County's development see John A. Chapman, *History of Edgefield County From the Earliest Settlements to 1897* (Newberry, S.C., 1897), 20, 28, 103-6, 108, 241, 316-17, 365-67; Francis Butler Simkins, *Pitchfork Ben Tillman: South Carolinian* (Baton Rouge, La., 1944), 23-56.

3. Throughout this paper I refer to the black and white community in general terms. There were nevertheless important divisions among both blacks and whites in Edgefield County. A typology of race relations depends not only on the overt relations between the powerful and powerless, but also on the relations among the powerful and among the powerless. The paternalistic-competitive typology treats only the phenomenon of inter-group relations and ignores the basic linking blocks of intra-group relations. The reader should therefore remember that political divisions emerged among Edgefield County blacks and among white Republicans and also among black and white Republicans. Economic, social, ideological, and political cleavages existed among whites in Edgefield. As elsewhere in the South, the position of yeomen and poorer whites is clearly related to violence and disfranchisement throughout the postbellum period and needs much more investigation. Some of these differences are mentioned in this essay. However, our concerns here are not to trace all the local detail, but to suggest the overall patterns of racial interaction. J. Morgan Kousser, *The Shaping of Southern Politics: Suffrage Restriction and the Establishment of the One-Party South 1880-1910* (New Haven, Conn., 1974), a superb account in almost every other respect, does not really deal with this question. Two forthcoming studies promise to shed more light on the question of yeomen and poor whites in the South's stratified society: Stephen Hahn, "The Roots of Southern Populism: White Yeoman Farmers, Tenants, and Sharecroppers in Upper Piedmont Georgia, 1850-1890" (Ph.D. dissertation, Yale University, expected 1979); William Harris, "A Social History of the Lower Georgia Piedmont, 1850-1890" (Ph.D. dissertation, The John Hopkins University, expected 1979). Even less is known about divisions in the black community. Particularly intriguing are those few Afro-Americans who aligned with Democrats.

4. Willemina Kloosterboer, *Involuntary Labor Since the Abolition of Slavery: A Survey of Compulsory Labor Throughout the World* (Leiden, Neth., 1960) documents this phenomenon in a comparative study of post-emancipation labor control in various societies around the world.

5. Information collected on Edgefield County is stored on a Statistical Package for the Social Sciences (SPSS) data file. The above computations refer to the data collected from the 1870 federal manuscript census returns and the county tax records. Applying Yule's Q to whites in 1870 to measure the strength of the relationship of color and ownership of land, on a scale of —1 to +1 the statistic shows an extraordinary high value of +0.935. Orville Vernon Burton, "Ungrateful Servants? Edgefield's Black Reconstruction: Part 1 of the Total History of Edgefield County, South Carolina" (unpublished Ph.D. dissertation, Princeton University, 1975), for wealth distributions see particularly 187, 198, 199, 201-204, 285-286; Susan Westbury, "Research Exercise in Quantitative Methods: What was the Effect of the Civil War on the Economic Status of the Wealthiest Group in Edgefield County, South Carolina," (unpublished paper in author's possession, Spring, 1975); Carlee T. McClendon, *Edgefield Marriage Records: Edgefield, South Carolina* (Columbia, S.C., 1970); William Watts Ball, *The State That Forgot: South Carolina's Surrender to Democracy* (Indianapolis, Ind., 1932), especially 22; Randolph Dennis Werner, "Hegemony and Conflict: The Political Economy of a Southern Region, Augusta, Georgia, 1865-1895" (unpublished Ph.D. dissertation, University of Virginia, 1977); Diane Neal, "Benjamin Ryan Tillman: The South Carolina Years, 1847-1894" (unpublished Ph.D. dissertation, Kent State University, 1976); Julian Landrum Mims, "Radical Reconstruction in Edgefield County, 1868-1877" (unpublished M.A. thesis, University of South Carolina, 1969); Eleanor Elizabeth Mims, "The Editors of the Edgefield *Advertiser*, Oldest Newspaper in South Carolina, 1863-1930" (unpublished M.A. Thesis, University of South Carolina, 1930); William J. Cooper, Jr., *The Conservative Regime: South Carolina, 1877-1890* (Baltimore, 1969). In addition, good discussions of the state's and Edgefield's white elite and its command of politics are found in Ralph A. Wooster, *The People in Power:*

Courthouse and Statehouse in the Lower South, 1850-1860 (Knoxville, Tenn., 1969); James M. Banner, Jr., "The Problem of South Carolina," in *The Hofstadter Aegis: A Memorial*, eds. Stanley Elkins and Eric McKitrick (New York, 1974), 60-93; William W. Freehling, *Prelude to Civil War: The Nullification Controversy in South Carolina, 1816-1836* (New York, 1965); Steven A. Channing, *Crisis of Fear: Secession in South Carolina* (New York, 1970); Diane Cooke Norton, "A Methodological Study of the South Carolina Political Elite of the 1830's" (unpublished Ph.D. dissertation, University of Pennsylvania, 1972); Robert Nicholas Olsberg, "A Government of Class and Race: William Henry Trescot and the South Carolina Chivalry, 1860-1865" (unpublished Ph.D. dissertation, The University of South Carolina, 1972); Chalmers Gaston Davidson, *The Last Foray: The South Carolina Planters of 1860: A Sociological Study* (Columbia, S.C., 1971); Simkins, *Pitchfork Ben* and his earlier *The Tillman Movement in South Carolina* (Durham, N.C., 1926); Francis Butler Simkins and Robert Hilliard Woody, *South Carolina During Reconstruction* (Chapel Hill, N.C., 1932); Joel Williamson, *After Slavery: The Negro in South Carolina During Reconstruction, 1861-1877* (Chapel Hill, N.C. 1965); Kousser, *Southern Politics*; Brown, *Strain of Violence*, 67-90; Banks, "Strom Thurmond"; Frederic Cople Jaher, *The Urban Establishment: The Upper Orders in Boston, New York, Charleston, Chicago, and Los Angeles* (University of Illinois Press, forthcoming). The antebellum politics of John C. Calhoun's state are too complicated for this paper. South Carolina did not send delegates to the national Democratic convention until 1856.

6. Percentages refer to household heads listed in the 1870 and 1880 federal population census manuscripts. "Minutes of the Edgefield Baptist Church," Edgefield, S.C.; Mrs. J. L. Mims, "History of the Edgefield Baptist Church" and Mrs. Agatha Abney Woodson, "Scrapbook of Edgefield Baptist Church," both in possession of Miss Hortense Woodson, Edgefield, S.C.; Hortense Woodson and Church Historians, *History of Edgefield Baptist Association, 1807-1957* (Edgefield, S.C. n.d.), 55-60; H. W. Purvis to F. J. Moses, Jr., July 12, 1873, in the papers of Franklin J. Moses, South Carolina Department of Archives, Columbia, S.C. (cited hereinafter as S.C.A.); H. W. Purvis to D. H. Chamberlain, Jan. 30, 1875, in the Papers of Daniel H. Chamberlain, S.C.A.; *Records of the Military Department Office of the Adjutant and Inspector General*, List of Commissions Issued, 1870-1899, Vol. 1, 58, 82-85, 114, in S.C.A.; *Records of the Military Department, Office of the Adjutant and Inspector General*, Militia Enrollments, 1869, vol. 12, in S.C.A.; Peggy Lamson, *The Glorious Failure: Black Congressman Robert Borwn Elliott and the Reconstruction in South Carolina* (New York, 1973), 86-87, 96; Simkins and Woody, *Reconstruction*, 512; William Stone to Major Horace Neide, Oct. 1, 1868, Freedmen's Bureau File, Letters and Endorsements Sent, Entry 3052, 257, in the Record of the Bureau of Refugees, Freedmen, and Abandoned Lands, National Archives, Washington, D.C. (cited hereinafter as Freedmen's Bureau File); Teachers Reports, Edgefield, 1868-1870, five folders Superintendent of Education Papers, in S.C.A.; A. W. Pegues, *Our Baptist Ministers and Schools* (Springfield, Mass. 1892), 81, 145-147, 373, 457-459; Burton, "Ungrateful Servants," 76-90, 254.

7. Mims, "Editors of Advertiser"; Werner, "Hegemony and Conflict,".19-20, 47; Walter J. Ong, *The Presence of the Word: some Prolegomena for Cultural and Religious History* (New Haven, Conn., 1967); James W. Carey, "A Cultural Approach to Communication," *Communication*, 2, no. 2 (1975), 1-22 and "Harold Adams Innis and Marshall McLuhan," *The Antioch Review*, 27 (Spring, 1967), 5-39; Jack Goody and Ian Watt, "The Consequences of Literacy," *Comparative Studies in Society and History*, 5 (1962-63), 305-45. I am most indebted to Harry S. Stout and Clifford Christians for their help in explaining to me communication networks and social organization.

8. William Stone to Major H. W. Smith, 28 Feb., 1866 Freedman's Bureau File, Entry 3051, 10-11, Lt. Charles Snyder for Brvt. Maj. Gen. R.K. Scott to Brvt. Lt. Col. H.W. Smith, 16 July, 1866, in the papers of Gov. James L. Orr, S.C.A.: *New York Times*, April 9, 1866; Williamson, *After Slavery*, 97; Simkins and Woody, *S.C. Reconstruction*, 57; Edgefield *Advertiser*, July 12, 1865, Dec. 19, 1866, June 5, 1867; Mims, "Editors Edgefield Advertiser," 72-75; Martin Abbott, *The Freedmen's Bureau in South Carolina, 1865-1872* (Chapel Hill, N.C., 1967). On September 1,

1865, James Beale Rainsford wrote from his Edgefield plantation to his brother in England, Edwin Rainsford, that "we are yet under military rule absolutely, so that none are free in the ordinary sense," in Emily A. Buckland, *The Rainsford Family with Sidelights on Shakespeare, Southhampton Hall and Hart* (Worcester, 1932), 275.

9. John Sheppard Reynolds, *Reconstruction in South Carolina, 1865-1877* (Columbia, S.C., 1905), 72-74, 76-84, 86-89, 93; South Carolina State Government, *The Constitution of South Carolina, adopted April 16, 1868* (Columbia, S.C., 1868).

10. Edgefield *Advertiser*, April 22 and 29, May 27, 1868. Apparently, Edgefield was typical in this respect. A club in Anderson County met in the morning as the "Farmers Association"; in the afternoon its members regrouped themselves as the "Democratic Club." D. Wyatt Aiken, editor of the *Rural Carolinian*, South Carolina's most influential agricultural magazine, and organizer of South Carolina's chapter of the Grange, charged landowners to "Combine agriculture and politics—and make the Democratic clubs the basis of a new organization." *Anderson Intelligencer*, July 22, 1868, Abbeville Press and *Banner*, cited in the Charleston *Daily Courier*, Aug. 10, 1868. See also J. C. A. Stagg, "The Problem of Klan Violence: The South Carolina Up-Country, 1868-1871," *Journal of American Studies*, 8, No. 3, (1974), 303-318, Stagg argues persuasively that violence was motivated by economic interest. At all times, the political, economic and social issues were interrelated, but in 1868 the violence in Edgefield had specific political targets. I greatly benefitted from discussions with my friend Stagg. For other mechanisms of social control, see Allen Trelease, *White Terror: Ku Klux Klan Conspiracy in Southern Reconstruction* (New York, 1971), xv-xlviii, 65-80, 113-126, 349-418.

11. Edgefield *Advertiser*, June 10 and 24, 1868.

12. Ibid. July 1, 1868. Gary and George Tillman were among the first white leaders to reject appeals to paternalism. They wanted Edgefield planters to create a caste system comprised of two compartmentalized groups organized in a single society with dominant and subordinate positions and each impermeable by individuals from the other group. A caste system is implicit in a competitive style of race relations.

13. *Evidence Taken by the Committee of Investigation of the 3rd Congressional District* (Columbia, S.C., 1870), 714 (hereinafter cited as *S.C. Investigation Committee*). In view of the fact that there is a very convincing argument that oral culture promotes veracity, this report is particularly relevant evidence.

14. W. H. Trescott to J. L. Orr, 13 Dec. 1865, in the papers of James L. Orr, S.C.A.: Alfred Huger. "Labor," *The Rural Carolinian*, 2 (Oct., 1870), 43: E. B. Heyward to Allen C. Izard, 16 July 1866, in the Heyward Family Papers, South Caroliniania Library, Columbia, S.C. (cited hereinafter as S.C.L.); Henry M. Christman, ed., *The South, as It Is: 1865-1866* by John Richard Dennett (New York, 1965), 246-252.

15. Edgefield *Advertiser*, June 17, 1868; Werner, "Hegemony and Conflicts," 48.

16. Edgefield *Advertiser*, Nov. 8, 1865.

17. Edgefield *Advertiser*, Nov. 3 and 10, 1870. Each club adopted the rules presented at a mass meeting on Sales Day, December 8, 1870, at the Court House. The officers and leaders of the Agricultural clubs were identical in almost every instance to those of the Democratic clubs and the Reform clubs. For a more detailed discussion of agricultural arrangements and social structure see Orville Vernon Burton, "The Development of Tenantry and the Post-Bellum Afro-American Social Structure in Edgefield County, South Carolina." in E. Le Roy Ladurie et J. Goy, eds., *Prestations Paysannes, Dimes, Rente foncière et Mouvement de la Production Agricole à l'époque Préindustrielle* (Paris, forthcoming) and Burton, "Ungrateful Servants," 194-293. Distinctions between renting and sharecropping as a tenant were not confined to Edgefield. Robert Preston Brooks, *The Agrarian Revolution in Georgia, 1865-1912* (Madison, Wisconsin, 1914), 26-27, 30, 32-68 found these differences in Georgia. Robert C. McMath, Jr. has worked through Brooks's notebooks and McMath reports that Brooks makes these distinctions even clearer in his own notes. Edmund L. Drago also found the same distinctions for renting and sharecropping for Dougherty County, Georgia. See his article in Vernon Burton and Robert C. McMath, Jr., eds.,

Nineteenth Century Southern Communities (Westport, Conn., forthcoming). See also George P. Rawick, ed., *The American Slave A Composite Autobiography* (19 vol; Westport, Conn., 1972-), *Arkansas Narrative*, 10 (6), 67, 103, 185; Thomas J. Edwards, "The Tennant System and Some Changes Since Emancipation," *The Negro's Progress in Fifty Years*, Annals of the American Academy of Political and Social Science, 49 (Sept. 1913), 38-46; Stagg, "Klan Violence," 309 argues persuasively that Klan violence was associated with renting patterns.

18. Simkins and Woody, *South Carolina Reconstruction*, 91. According to one school of thought, the failure of the Federal Government to provide lands for freedmen was the major flaw of Reconstruction strategy. I am very much in sympathy with this argument. However, these scholars have looked at the post-Reconstruction period and argued backwards. LaWanda Cox, "The Promise of Land for the Freedmen," *Mississippi Valley Historical Review*, 45 (Dec. 1958), 413-440; LaWanda Cox and John H. Cox, *Politics, Principle, and Prejudice 1865-1866: Dilemma of Reconstruction America* (New York, 1963); Staughton Lynd, *Class Conflict, Slavery, and the United States Constitution* (New York, 1967); James M. McPherson, *The Struggle for Equality: Abolitionists and the Negro in the Civil War and Reconstruction* (Princeton, N.J., 1964); William S. McFeely, *Yankee Stepfather: General O. O. Howard and the Freedmen* (New Haven, Conn., 1968). On the land question, see Herman Belz, "The New Orthodoxy in Reconstruction Historiography," *Reviews in American History*, 1 (March, 1973), 106-113.

19. South Carolina Secretary of State, Deeds for Land Sold to the State Land Commissioners (1869-1870), 71, 72, 330, 331; South Carolina Secretary of State, Purchase Book, Land Commission Office, Dec. 13, 1869; The State of South Carolina, Department of Land Commission, Settlement Book, Payment Register, Vol. 3, 1870-1887, 26, 27; The State of South Carolina, Office Secretary of State, Records of Sales of Land to the Land Commission in Acount with Settlers, not paginated, Jones Tract, Burns Tract, Walker Tract, Jennings Tract, Burton Tract, Randall Tract; The State of South Carolina, Office of Secretary of State, Department of Land Commission, Account of Sales, 1870-1875, 50-55; H. E. Hayne, Land Commissioner, (n.d.), 9-11 in Letters and Papers of the Land Commission; all of the above are in the Sinking Fund Commission, S.C.A. *Report on the Condition of Affairs in the Late Insurrectionary States* (the Ku Klux Conspiracy, Washington, D.C., 1872), 4, 1192-1194, 1214-1215; *Fairfield Herald*, Sept. 8, 1869; Stagg, "Klan Violence," 313; Reynolds, *Reconstruction*, 380; clipping from the *Carolinian Spartan*, Jan. 12, 1878, in the Papers of Martin Witherspoon Gary, S.C.L.; Carol K. Rothrock Bleser, *The Promised Land: The History of the South Carolina Land Commission, 1869-1890* (Columbia, S.C., 1969) and Williamson, *After Slavery*, 144-48, 173, 213, 258 are superb accounts of the Commission.

20. David Donald, "Reconstruction," in *Interpreting American History: Conversations with Historians*, 1, ed. John A. Garraty (New York, 1970), 357-358 notes that the subject of Reconstruction taxation "awaits further study." Donald suggests that progressive land taxes, if continued, might have had revolutionary results in a "reorganization of the economic basis of Southern society." It must be remembered that in addition to the South Carolina property tax, there was a *county* property tax administered by the local Republicans. Col. Theodore W. Parmele to Gov. Daniel H. Chamberlain, Feb. 23, 1875, Chamberlain papers; M. C. Butler to Gov. D. H. Chamberlain, March 1, 1876, Chamberlain papers; W. H. Timmerman to Gov. D. H. Chamberlain, Jan. 4, 1875, Chamberlain papers; L. E. Libendes to Johnathan C. Sheppard, Feb. 22, 1874, in the John C. Sheppard Papers, S.C.L.; James B. Campbell to M. L. Bonham, Dec. 5, 1873, in the papers of Milledge L. Bonham, S.C.L.; Milledge Lipscomb Bonham, "A Boy's Memories of War Time and the Other Times," (n.p., n.d.), 39 in S.C.L.; Milledge Louis Bonham, "The Life and Times of Milledge Luke Bonham" (unpublished ms., S.C.L.), 896, 901-902; Martin Witherspoon Gary "Speech Before the Taxpayers' Convention of S.C.," at Columbia, on February 19, 1874 (n.p., n.d.) Gary Papers; Edgefield *Advertiser*, Feb. 3 and Dec. 15, 1870, March 9 and April 6, 1871, June 6 and 13, 1872; Simkins and Woody, *S.C. Reconstruction*, 178, 180; Niles G. Parker who made the statement on taxes served as Freedman's Bureau Agent for Edgefield, before he became Republican state treasurer. In *After Slavery*, 148-159, 384, 397, Joel Williamson described

the complicated taxation system as "the core of the Republican program in Reconstruction South Carolina."

21. Edgefield *Advertiser*, Jan. 13, 1870 and June 13, 1872; R. B. Carpenter to Gov. F. J. Moses, Jr., May 22, 1973, Moses papers; Hampton M. Jarrell, *Wade Hampton and the Negro: The Road Not Taken* (Columbia, S.C., 1949), 48-49; Henry T. Thompson, *Ousting the Carpetbagger from South Carolina* (New York, 1888), 67-69, 307-311; Reynolds, *Reconstruction*, 303-305, 368-372; "Edgefield County (Edgefield)," No. 19 of the *Inventory of the Court Archives of South Carolina*, prepared by The South Carolina Historical Records Survey Project Division of Professional and Service Projects, Works Projects Administration (Columbia, South Carolina, 1940), S.C.A.; Simkins and Woody, *S.C. Reconstruction*, 101-102; *Revised Statutes of the State of South Carolina* (Columbia, S.C., 1873); Williamson, *After Slavery*, 113, 114, 172, 329-330; George Brown Tindall, *South Carolina Negroes, 1877-1900* (Columbia, S.C. 1952), 108-111; Stagg, "Klan Violence," 313; Cooper, *Conservative Regime*, 33-34.

22. H. H. Steiner to Francis W. Pickens, 1 July, 1868, in the Papers of Francis W. Pickens, S.C.L.; M. L. Bonham to Gen. J. E. Johnston, and James R. Campbell to M. L. Bonham, 5 Dec., 1873, Bonham papers; 14 Jan., 1874, James Talbert Ouzts, "Farm Journal, 1856-1898" (S.C.L.), 18 Nov., 1873, 20 Jan., 28 May, 7, 16, 27 June, 23 Sept., 1874; M. C. Butler to wife, 4 July, 1866 in the Papers of Mathew Culbreath Butler, S.C.L.; Myrta Lockett Avary, *Dixie After the War: An Exposition of Social Conditions Existing in the South, During the Twelve Years Succeeding the Fall of Richmond* (New York, 1906), 161. "Petition of Sundry Citizens of Edgefield," May, 1870, in Letters and Papers of the Land Commission, 1869-1873; M.C. Butler to C.P. Leslie, Jan., 1870, Loose Papers, Land Transfer File, 1866-1877, Questionnaire, (S.C.A.), last reference cited in Bleser, *Promised Land*, 35-36; Col. Theodore W. Parmele to Gov. Daniel H. Chamberlain, 23 Feb., 1875, Chamberlain papers; Bonham, "M. L. Bonham," 896, 901-902, 949, 951, 1005.

23. Edgefield *Advertiser* 28 March and 2 Oct., 1872, 19 June and 7 Aug., 1873; *Reports and Resolutions of the General Assembly of the State of South Carolina, 1874* (Columbia, S.C., 1874), 630-633; Mims, "Radical Reconstruction," 77-78; Werner, "Hegemony and Conflict," 82-84.

24. Col. Theodore W. Parmele to Gov. D. H. Chamberlain, 23 Feb., 1875, Chamberlain papers.

25. Ibid., Orlando Sheppard to Gov. R. K. Scott, 3 Sept., 1872, in the papers of Robert K. Scott, S.C.A.; James Boatwright to Gov. F. J. Moses, Jr., 6 Aug., 1874, Moses papers: Benjamin R. Tillman, *The Struggles of 1876: How South Carolina Was Delivered From Carpet-Bag and Negro Rule* (Speech at the Red-Shirt Reunion at Anderson, South Carolina, 1909), 40-50 and "Childhood Days," (n.p., n.d.), 1-11, both in S.C.L.; Simkins and Woody, *S.C. Reconstruction*, 499-500; Mims, "Radical Reconstruction," 60-63; Williamson, *After Slavery* 266-273 (on rifle clubs), 260-263 carefully explains the organizing and arming of the black militia; Louis F. Post, "A 'Carpetbagger' in South Carolina," *Journal of Negro History*, 10 (Jan., 1925), 49; Otis A. Singletary, *Negro Militia and Reconstruction* (Austin, Texas, 1957); Stagg, "Klan Violence," 316-17. As stated above, the black militia leaders in Edgefield were also the political leaders and the white leaders of the agricultural society, Democrat club, Reform party, Agricultural and Police Club, and irregular militia companies were the same.

26. Edgefield *Advertiser*, Jan. 3, 1866, Aug. 18 and Dec. 8, 1870, Aug. 17, 1876; M. L. Bonham to Gov. R. K. Scott, 19 Aug., 1868, Scott papers and Bonham papers; Chapman, *History of Edgefield*, 258.

27. Paris Simkins to F J. Moses, 21 Sept., 1874, and Lawrence Cain to F. J. Moses, 21 Sept., 1874, Moses papers; Col. Lawrence Cain to D. H. Chamberlain, 9 Jan., 1875, Col. Theodore W. Parmele to Gov. D. H. Chamberlain, 23 Feb., 1875, Chamberlain papers; Tillman, *Struggles of 1876*, 40-50 and "Childhood Days," 1-11; Williamson, *After Slavery*, 266-267; Allen, *Chamberlain's Administration*, 67-69, Reynolds, *Reconstruction*, 302-305, *S.C. Investigation Committee*, 708-709; Mims, "Radical Reconstruction," 62-63.

28. Edgefield *Advertiser* 19 Jan. 1871 and 27 June, 1872; Col. Lawrence Cain to D. H. Chamberlain, 9 Jan., 1875; and Col. Theodore W. Parmele to Gov. D. H. Chamberlain, 23 Feb., 1875,

Chamberlain papers; Tillman, *Struggles of 1876*, 45-46 and "Childhood Days," 7; Reynolds, *Reconstruction*, 304-305; Allen, *Chamberlain's Administration*, 74-76, Chamberlain himself denied that his attempt to win over the whites was racist. Rather, he said it was the opposite. Daniel Henry Chamberlain, "Reconstruction and the Negro," *North American Review*, 128 (Feb., 1879), 161-73.

29. R. B. Elliott to D. H. Chamberlain, 26 Feb., 1876, Hon. R. B. Carpenter to D. H. Chamberlain, 5 June, 1877, J. A. Robards and J. H. Palmer to D. H. Chamberlain, 26 June, 1876, H. Jordan to D. H. Chamberlain, 9 July, 1876, U. S. Grant to D. H. Chamberlain, 26 July, 1876, Louis Schiller to D. H. Chamberlain, 29 July, 1876, Chamberlain papers; *South Carolina in 1876: Testimony as to the Denial of the Elective Franchise in South Carolina at the Elections of 1875 and 1876*, 3 vols. (Senate Miscellaneous Documents, 44th Congress, 2d Session, No. 48); Reynolds, *Reconstruction*, 302-305; Allen, *Chamberlain's Administration*, 68-69; 307-303; Simkins and Woody, *South Carolina Reconstruction*, 485-487; Mims, "Radical Reconstruction," 65-69. Williamson, *After Slavery*, 267-271 has a concise account of the Hamburg affair. Also the notebooks of Gen. Martin W. Gary have interesting detail, in the Gary Papers; so do Tillman's *Struggles of 1876*, 14-26 and "Childhood Days," 12-24.

30. Edgefield *Advertiser*, June 10, 1868 and Aug. 17, 1876; Tillman, *Struggles of 1876*, 33-39; Simkins and Woody, *S.C. Reconstruction*, 492-493, 496, 499; Allen, *Chamberlain's Administration*, 374-377.

31. S. W. Ferguson to Maj. T. G. Baxter, Jan. 7, 1876 in Gary Papers. There are several versions of the "Edgefield Plan" in the Gary Papers. Tillman, *Struggles of 1876*, 28, 63; "Concurrent Resolution of the South Carolina General Assembly," Feb. 16, 1876, in the Chamberlain Papers; Jno. Gardner to D. H. Chamberlain, 25 Aug., 1876, Frank Arnim to D. H. Chamberlain, 18 Sept., 1876, Lawrence Cain to D. H. Chamberlain, 25 Sept., 1876, A. C. Haskell to D. H. Chamberlain, 28 Sept., 1876, James Mason to D. H. Chamberlain, 30 Sept., 1876, Chamberlain Papers; *Recent Election in South Carolina: Testimony Taken by the Select Committee on the Recent Election in South Carolina* (House Miscellaneous Documents, 44th Congress, 2d Session, No. 31); *South Carolina in 1876*; Simkins and Woody, *S.C. Reconstruction*, 564-569.

32. Col. Theodore W. Parmele to Gov. D. H. Chamberlain, 23 Feb., 1875, Chamberlain Papers; "Edgefield Plan," Gary Papers. Steven Hahn has aided me in formulating ideas on violence and class. He found similar results in a study of Mississippi. See also Manuel Gottlieb, "The Land Question in Georgia During Reconstruction," *Science & Society: A Marxian Quarterly*, 3 (1939), 356-388; Governors Papers, 1866-1876 in Orr, Scott, Moses, Chamberlain papers, passim; Mims, "Radical Reconstruction," 42-47; Simkins and Woody, *S.C. Reconstruction*, 479, 482-483, 485, 515, 556.

33. Tillman, *Struggles of 1876*, 28, 29; Simkins and Woody, *South Carolina Reconstruction*, 501, 509, 515; Francis B. Simkins, "The Election of 1876 in South Carolina," 21 (July, Oct., 1922), 225-240, 335-351; Williamson, *After Slavery*, 345.

34. John Mardenborough to William Coppinger, April 30, 1877, American Colonization Society Papers, Letters Received, Vol. 227. 86 in the Library of Congress, Washington, D.C.; W. F. Rodenbach to D. H. Chamberlain, 8 April, 1877, Chamberlain papers.

35. *S.C. Revised Statutes* (1878-1882); Tindall, *S.C. Negroes*, 108-14, 12-21; *Appleton's Annual Cyclopedia and Register of Important Events of the Year* [1876-1895] (New York); Hampton M. Jarrell, *Wade Hampton and the Negro: the Road Not Taken* (Columbia, S.C., 1949), 141, 158-159; State of S.C., Secretary of State. Settlement Book, Vol. 3, 53-62, and Daybook-Edgefield, Memoranda Concerning Land, 250, 307 both in Sinking Fund Commission; Kousser, *Southern Politics*; Robert Smalls, "Election Methods in the South," *North American Review*, 151 (1890), 593-600; Francis B. Simkins, "Race Legislation in South Carolina Since 1865," *South Atlantic Quarterly*, 20 (Jan., April, 1921), 161-171, 165-177; Burton, "Development of Tenantry," and "Ungrateful Servants," 236-283; I. A. Newby, *Black Carolinians: A History of Blacks in South Carolina from 1895 to 1968* (Columbia, S.C., 1973), 37-38.

36. Edgefield *Advertiser*, 18 July and 14 Oct., 1878; Mims, "Editors of Advertiser," 92-94; Cooper, *Conservative Regime*, 21; Tindall, *S.C. Negroes*; Newly, *Black Carolinians*; Alrutheus

Ambush Taylor, *The Negro in South Carolina During Reconstruction* (New York, 1924) 91, 290-307; Jarrell, *Wade Hampton*, 124-125; August Meier, *Negro Thought in America, 1880-1915: Racial Ideologies in the Age of Booker T. Washington* (Ann Arbor, Mich., 1963); Alfred W. Nicholson, *Brief Sketch of the Life and Labors of Rev. Alexander Bettis: Also an Account of the Founding and Development of the Bettis Academy* (Trenton, S.C., 1913). Lewis G. Jordan, *Negro Baptist History* (Nashville, Tenn., 1930), 377.

37. Edgefield *Advertiser*, 15 Nov., 1865; Woodson and Historians, *Edgefield Baptists*, 60; Tindall, *S.C. Negroes*, 187-89, 207, 225. Except where otherwise designated, the following pages drew upon my interviews with Edgefield blacks and whites, two articles by Col. E. H. Aull in the Newberry *Herald and News* (n.d., in scrapbook in possession of Miss Hortense Woodson), and especially upon Nicholson, *Bettis*, 26-27, 37, 44-49, 58, 62-66, 70-80, 88-90. The biography must be evaluated as the work of an admirer and later president of the Bettis Academy. Pages 56-68 contains testimonials from blacks and whites about Bettis. These letters are particularly useful and, like the biography, full of inadvertent revelations.

38. In antebellum South Carolina, drum beating had been forbidden by law since the Stono Rebellion in 1739. Walter J. Ong, "Trial Drum as Quintessence of Oral Culture," a talk presented at the University of Illinois in 1976, argues that drum beating is an important way of preserving oral culture.

39. Harrison N. Bouey to Rev. H. M. Turner, May 23, 1877, American Colonization Society Papers, Vol. 227, 142. Col. E. H. Aull in one Newberry *Herald and News* clipping said of Bettis's successor and biographer, Nicholson, "misunderstood by his own people, at times suspected by the white. . . ."

40. Edgefield *Advertiser*, 19 June, 1873; Werner, "Hegemony and Conflict," 48; Vernon Burton, "Town and Country in Reconstruction Edgefield County, South Carolina," paper presented at the Southern Historical Association, 41st Annual Meeting, 1975; for a detailed description of organized efforts to leave Edgefield for both Liberia and Arkansas, see Burton, "Ungrateful Servants," 157-178 and Tindall, *South Carolina Negroes*, 153-168, 170-173, Harry Hoetnik, *Caribbean Race Relations: A Study of Two Variants* (London, 1967) and Pierre L. Van den Berghe, *Race and Racism: A Comparative Perspective* (New York, 1967) develop models for segmented (Van den Berghe's term is "pluralistic") societies.

41. Joan Reynolds Faunt and Emily B. Reynolds, *Biographical Directory of the Senate of the State of South Carolina* (Columbia, S.C., 1964), 191; Lawrence C. Bryant, ed., *Negro Lawmakers in the South Carolina Legislature* (Orangeburg, S.C., 1968), 22; Mims, "Radical Reconstruction," 25-26; Edgefield *Chronicle*, Jan. 25, 1882; Edwin Booth Simkins and other children, "A Brief Narrative of the Life of Paris Simmkins, Esq., of Edgefield, S.C. who Died Sept. 26th 1930" (family typescript, 1930); Edgefield *Advertiser*, 30 Sept., 1930; C. Bruce Bailey, Sr. to author, 7 Jan., 1978; graveyard tombstones and interviews.

42. William Robert Miller, *Martin Luther King, Jr.* (New York, 1968). In many Edgefield homes today pictures of Martin Luther King, Jr., are on the walls and many people sometimes display copies of King's writings such as *Letters From a Birmingham Jail* near a *Bible*.

Frank J. Huffman, Jr.

Town and Country in the South, 1850–1880: A Comparison of Urban and Rural Social Structures

Daniel R. Hundley in *Social Relations in Our Southern States* describes an encounter in 1857 with an old gentleman from New York. The New Yorker was making his first trip South, and as they traveled down the Mississippi River, he grew increasingly restless and troubled. At last, unable to contain himself any longer, he asked Hundley, "Where's your towns?"[1] The question was both an analysis of regional distinctiveness and an accusation of regional inferiority. The shortage of towns epitomized for the northerner a certain anomalous, un-American quality of the South in the mid-nineteenth century. In other parts of the nation, towns and cities seemed to be at the heart of things. They mirrored the turbulent spirit of the times and captured the imaginations of observers. Contemporary descriptions and historical literature on the South, by contrast, concentrate on the lives of the planter, the farmer, and the rural slave. The towns and cities of the South were and are often treated as passive appendages to the system of commercial agriculture or as exotics clinging to the margins of southern life. This is especially true of scholarly writings on the antebellum period.[2] Historians of the post–Civil War years have devoted considerably more attention to urban areas, presenting them as a distinctive feature of an emerging New South, as carriers of an alien culture hostile to the native genius of the region.[3] Too often urban communities in the mid-nineteenth-century South have either been ignored or have been treated as fundamentally nonsouthern.

Certainly one of the most important things to understand about the Old South is that most of its people lived on the land, and certainly it is fruitful to

Source: South Atlantic Quarterly 76 (Summer 1977): 366–81.

consider the role of towns and cities as breeding grounds for social and economic change after 1865. But the prevalence of these two patterns of analysis has been accompanied by a relative neglect of other aspects of urban development. Happily in recent years several historians have begun to study the towns and cities of the South from a broader perspective. These scholars are beginning to fill the gaps in our literature and are subjecting southern urban communities to more varied and thorough scrutiny.

A survey of the "Urban" and "South" categories in the "Recent Articles" section of the *Journal of American History* reveals a growing interest in the urban areas of the South. Glamor cities such as New Orleans, Charleston, Memphis, and Atlanta have attracted considerable attention. This is understandable, for they dominated access to the region and were the focal points of commerce, political activity, and colorful blossomings of high and low society. Much less attention has been given the smaller towns of a few thousand inhabitants which dotted the map of Dixie. In 1850 there were 55 towns in the slave states and the District of Columbia with populations of two thousand or more. By 1860 there were 93. The same territory contained 135 such towns in 1870 and 216 in 1880. By counting only communities with two thousand or more inhabitants, many smaller places are excluded, towns which provided important economic and social services for rural southerners. If places with as many as a thousand residents are included, the number of towns at least doubles for every state and triples for some.[4] The picture which emerges from these results obviously will not overthrow the traditional image of a predominantly rural South. The point to be understood is that there were towns in the South and that they were increasing rapidly in number even before the Civil War.

These communities require attention for two reasons. The first is that even if we omit places with populations greater than 25,000 or less than 2,000, the remaining towns were home for several hundred thousand people. Such a large group merits consideration on the strength of numbers alone. Additionally, however, towns should be important to historians because they were important to that majority of southerners living in the countryside. A rural Southerner might visit a large city such as Louisville or New Orleans once or twice in his life, perhaps never. But he would make several trips, possibly several a year, to one of the small or medium-sized communities closer to his home. He would do business in that town, read its newspaper, send a promising son to school there, hire a lawyer there to handle legal matters, and base his attitudes about town life and town people upon what he observed.

Southern towns exerted an influence out of proportion to the size of their populations on the lives of rural southerners. It is therefore essential for historians to understand what these towns were like and how they differed from the countryside. This paper will focus on one southern town: Athens, Georgia, in the years from 1850 to 1880. Certain aspects of its social and economic structure will be examined and comparisons will be made between the town and a nearby rural area. The impact of the Civil War and Reconstruction on the lives of residents of town and country will be given special attention in order to judge which of the two social units weathered the disruptions of the sectional crisis with the least trouble.

Both Athens and the rural district under consideration were located in Clarke County, in the upper piedmont cottonbelt of northeastern Georgia. The population of Athens grew from 3,400 in 1850 to 6,099 in 1880. Roughly half of its residents were white and half black. (Population figures for blacks in 1850 are approximate because of the failure of enumerators to distinguish between slaves actually living in a census tract and those whose owner lived in the tract but kept his slaves elsewhere.) Athens during the 1850's was the center of an extensive upcountry wagon trade. Farmers and village storekeepers from as far away as North and South Carolina patronized its merchants. A spur of the Georgia Railroad provided a direct connection with Augusta and the coast. Commercial activity lagged during the Civil War, but with the coming of peace merchants eagerly resumed business. After the war the town succeeded in pushing its rail connection through to the Airline Railroad, which ran west of Clarke County. The Airline had cut Athens off from part of its wagon trade, but the completion of the new link in 1876 provided local merchants with a shorter route to Atlanta and made possible the expansion of their wholesale business with country merchants. Athens during these years was also the home of two banks, an insurance company, cotton mills, a woolens mill, a foundry, shoe and boot factories, flour mills, and a paper factory.

Wartime shortages stimulated demand for the products of these manufacturing establishments, and wartime profits helped the people of the town to overcome the business and financial difficulties which came with defeat. Congressman Howell Cobb and less famous politicos made Athens a center of Democratic, Whig, Republican, and Independent political activity for the Ninth District of Georgia. The University of Georgia, two boarding schools for girls, a school for freedmen, and several small academies made Athens an educational center and enriched its cultural life. Traveling circuses and lecturers included Athens on their itineraries. Churches ranging the gamut from fervor to formality competed with saloons and gambling dens to set the moral and social tone of the town. Athens was no metropolis, but it offered a variety of urban services and had a self-consciously urban ethos, a strong sense of its urban character, which separated it from the surrounding countryside.[5]

The rural district which will be discussed consists of the southwestern two-thirds of Clarke County, which was separated from Athens and the rest of the county by the Oconee River. The county seat of Clarke, the village of Watkinsville, lay in this region. Watkinsville reached a peak population of 873 in 1860. It was connected with the outside world only by poorly maintained dirt roads. Political rivalries and resentment among the city slickers of Athens at having to travel half a day into the boondocks to transact legal business led to a division of Clarke into two counties in 1875. The new county was called Oconee. Oconee County corresponds with the rural area being studied here. The population of Oconee was approximately evenly divided between the two races and grew from 4,600 in 1850 to 6,351 in 1880. The soil of the Oconee region was red clay and gray sand of good enough quality to attract a stream of planters and their slaves into the region during the 1820's and 1830's. Cotton was the primary crop, but corn, wheat, and a modest livestock industry provided some additional income for a mixed regime of planters and smaller farmers. By 1850 soil exhaustion and erosion had begun to take their toll in the Oconee district as they were doing on most of the older lands of Georgia, and cotton production had begun a slow decline. The disruption of the cotton market during the Civil War and of the labor system in 1865 aggravated the problems of local farmers. Not until the 1870's did sharecropping and the crop lien system combined with the heavy use of guano and other commercial fertilizers revive the cotton culture. By 1880 production was 65 percent greater than it had been in 1850. "Before the war," one resident complained in 1876, "the farmers bought negroes to make cotton to buy more negroes. After the war, they buy fertilizers to make cotton to buy more fertilizers."[6]

Athens and Oconee are not offered as statistically accurate microcosms of town and country in the South. No single town nor any rural area of manageable size could be. But if the areas under study here are not perfect samples of a region inhabited by eleven million people, neither are they bizarre or manifestly abnormal communities. The social and economic experiences of the people of Athens and Oconee overlapped and duplicated to greater or lesser degrees the experiences of many other southerners. If community studies are an acceptable approach to social history, then Athens and Oconee should be acceptable subjects.

One critical difference between Athens and Oconee emerges from a look at the size of their populations. The number of white males age twenty or older in Athens rose from 425 in 1850, to 458 in 1860, to 669 in 1870, and to 796 in 1880. The black population of Athens grew rapidly after emancipation from 384 adult males in 1870 to 616 in 1880. These figures indicate that the town held its own in the fifties and was an increasingly attractive place to live in the sixties and seventies. The Oconee region dropped in white adult male population from 511 in 1850 to 473 in 1860, fell to 355 in 1870 and then spurted to 757 in 1880. Its black population grew from 546 in 1870 to 810 in 1880. These changes in the population of Oconee are attributable to the slow agricultural decline of the fifties, the wrenching disruptions of the sixties, and the revival of the cotton culture during the seventies. In contrast to the abrupt reversal of population trends in Oconee, Athens experienced growth in every decade.

The drop in population reported for Oconee in 1870 may arouse suspicion among those familiar with the poor reputation of the 1870 census, but there are several reasons for believing that that census for Oconee is reliable. One is that the census marshal for that year was an old resident familiar with the region. An argument can also be made based on the census reports. If the 1870 census was badly flawed, we might expect to find the apparent rate of persistence between 1860 and 1870 to be abnormally low, but as we shall see below, this was not the case. (Persistence is here defined as the percentage of a population present in one year which is still present at some subsequent year.) We might also expect to find the percentage of young men reported in the population to be abnormally low in 1870, on the grounds that younger, less established residents would be especially likely to be overlooked in a hastily and carelessly done tally. Again this is not the case. The 1870 census reported 36.06 percent of the adult white males of Oconee as being in their twenties, a slight increase over the results for 1860, when 34.88 percent were in their twenties. The population of the rural district was low in 1870 not because established settlers abandoned the area at an abnormally high rate or because of a faulty census, but rather because few new people moved into the area during the sixties to replace the ones who moved out. In 1860, 54.11 percent of the white male residents of Oconee between the ages of thirty and fifty-nine had moved into Clarke County within the last ten years, taking the places of many of the people who had departed. In 1870, only 29.6 percent were new arrivals. By 1880, 70.92 percent were new men, drawn by the increasing ability of the fertilizer-enriched soil to provide support.

Athens experienced no such dramatic fluctuations. The percentage of newcomers there was 62.40 in 1860, 67.29 in 1870, and 57.30 in 1880. The town was apparently most attractive to outsiders during the sixties, the decade when the rural district was least attractive. It was the town, not the country, which maintained the more stable pattern of inward migration.[7]

Also related to the question of population size is the matter of persistence. Rates of persistence in both Athens and Oconee fluctuated less severely in the three decades under study than might have been anticipated.[8] Even during the decade of the Civil War, persistence remained at rates which should be considered normal relative to the fifties and the seventies. A comparison of rates of persistence among whites for Athens and for Oconee reveals that country people were consistently more stable than their town neighbors, though never by an extreme margin. This difference is a result of the above average persistence of landed farmers. Among blacks in the seventies, the result is reversed. Persistence is somewhat higher in Athens than in Oconee.

The two age groups least likely to persist, of course, were men in their twenties, who were prone to wander, and men sixty and over, whose mortality rate was high. If we eliminate these two groups and consider only the core of men thirty to fifty-nine, a slightly different picture emerges. The gap between urban and rural rates of persistence among whites nearly disappears for the fifties, remains insignificant for the sixties, and becomes greater in the seventies (49.33 percent in Athens versus 59.78 percent in Oconee). This variation is again due to the behavior of landed farmers. County-wide the rate of persistence for middle-aged landed farmers was about 58 percent in the fifties and 50 percent during the sixties, but it jumped to nearly 75 percent for the seventies.[9] No such irregularities are to be found in the persistence rates of those occupational groups which were concentrated in Athens. As a result it can be argued that while rates of persistence were somewhat higher among whites in the countryside than in town, the pattern of life was more regular and resistant to change in Athens than in Oconee.

The occupational patterns of the white male residents of Athens and Oconee stand in sharp contrast to one another. The town had a complex and highly differentiated occupational structure. The structure supported a full range of urban economic activity. Somewhat more than a quarter of the white males in all four census years studied, pursued upper white-collar callings such as merchant, lawyer, banker, insurance executive, manufacturer, wholesaler of drygoods and groceries, university professor, or physician. While much of the business activity of Athens was directly involved in providing goods and marketing services to the farmers of the region, Athens was more than just a depot where cotton was exchanged for store goods. Members of the upper white-collar group provided business, professional, manufacturing, and educational services for fellow Athenians and for farmers and nonfarmers throughout northern Georgia. A man who achieved upper white-collar status was likely to remain there. In each of the decades studied at least three-quarters of the persisting members of this group remained upper white-collar.

A second group vital to the operation of the urban economy was the large class of skilled blue-collar workers, whose occupations ranged from blacksmith to railroad brakeman to watchmaker. Fifty-nine different skilled occupations are listed in the four census years used here. Skilled workers maintained a strong position in 1850 and 1860, constituting about 30 percent of the white work force. After the Civil War they lost strength relative to the other occupational groups, declining to 15.10 percent of the work force. The increasing availability of northern manufactured goods may account for part of this drop. For example, there were nine tailors in Athens in 1860 and only four in 1870. A more important factor, however, is the decline in demand which resulted from hard times. The market for luxury items in particular had diminished. Only two men worked as carriage makers in 1870, down from nine in 1860. The logical move for a town craftsman as the demand for his service declined was to seek work as an unskilled urban blue-collar worker. Over a third of the skilled workers who persisted from 1860 to 1870 experienced such downward mobility. As a group white craftsmen had made a partial comeback by 1880, growing in number from 101 to 176 (22.11 percent of the white male work force). In addition there were nearly as many blacks as whites in skilled trades by 1880, suggesting that the craftsmen had reestablished for themselves the same major role in the urban economy which they held during the antebellum period.

Another group which provided important services for the economy of the town were the lower white-collar workers. These clerks, bookkeepers, and minor public officials supported the commercial activity of Athens, and men were recruited from their ranks to fill upper white-collar positions. They grew in number from 44 in 1850 (10.35 percent of the white adult male work force) to 67 in 1860 (14.63 percent), 76 in 1870 (11.36 percent), and 139 in 1880 (17.46 percent). The growing wholesale business of the town caused this group to double in size between 1870 and 1880.

The history of the lower blue-collar workers of Athens illustrates the impact of hard times, emancipation, and economic growth on occupational patterns. In 1850 about 9 percent of the whites (38 men) worked as teamsters, factory operatives, day laborers, or in some other unskilled or semi-skilled work in Athens. By 1870 over 16 percent of the white adult males (110 men) held such jobs. Unskilled and semi-skilled blue-collar workers remained proportionately as numerous in 1880, but with a significant difference. In 1870 about half of the members of this occupational category identified themselves simply as day laborers, specifying no particular job title, a probable indication of growing specialization and occupational security. Another clue to the growth of a sense of vocational identity among lower blue-collar workers is the organization in 1874 of a "Mechanics' and Laboring Men's Union."[10] The size and self-awareness of the white urban proletariat seemed to be increasing in post-bellum Athens. But both before and after the Civil War, a considerable range of occupational options existed for white residents of the town.

While most of the white residents of Athens were employed in urban occupations, there were always some farm owners and landless agricultural workers living there. The city limits were generous enough to include a few farms in the town, and some people lived in Athens who owned or rented farms outside of its boundaries. Among whites, however, it was only in 1870 that the agricultural population of Athens exceeded 13 percent of the total. In that year 187 men, 27.95 percent of the white adult males, reported an agricultural occupation. Ninety-seven were nonrenting farm workers. It seems likely than many of these nonrenting farm hands were occasional laborers unattached to a particular farm or employer. By 1880 the number of such floating workers had declined, suggesting the emergence of a more stable structure of employment in the countryside.[11]

The variety of occupational opportunities for blacks in Athens was not nearly so broad. Only five freedmen held white-collar positions in 1870. Twenty-four had such occupations in 1880. Freedmen were concentrated in blue-collar jobs, but they were not necessarily consigned to the margins of the urban economy. Even before emancipation slaves worked as carpenters, shoemakers, blacksmiths, and general laborers. About half of the factory operatives in antebellum Athens were slaves. So numerous were urban slave workers that white mechanics attempted, with no apparent success, to have them withdrawn from skilled jobs.[12] After emancipation blacks continued to play an important role in the economy of the town. There were 376 Negro blue-collar workers in Athens in 1870 and 611 in 1880. Agricultural occupations were reported for 157 of the adult male freedmen of Athens in 1870 and for 128 in 1880. An important shift took place in the occupational distribution of blacks during the seventies. Only 5.85 percent of the Negro blue-collar workers were upper blue-collar craftsmen in 1870. By 1880, 27.33 percent, 167 men, worked as craftsmen. Even among unskilled and semi-skilled workers, the likelihood that a specific job title would be given, increased from 6.62 percent in 1870 to 26.12 percent in 1880. None of the town's freedmen owned a farm in 1870, and only one rented land. By 1880 there were twenty-four owners and sixty-six renters. The blacks of Athens were moving toward an occupational class structure similar to that which existed among whites.[13]

The occupational profiles of both the white and black residents of Oconee are less variegated than those of their city cousins. Agriculture provided employment either as farm owners, overseers, renters, or hired hands for about 80 percent of the white adult males in all four census years. Among these agrarians, however, important changes were taking place. The percentage of these men who owned the land they were working dropped each decade. Taking all adult white males in farm-related occupations as a group, we find that 49.62 percent owned land in 1850, 47.47 percent in 1860, 37.41 percent in 1870, and 31.41 percent in 1880. The total number of farm owners rose between 1870 and 1880 from 107 to 191, but the number of nonowners rose even more from 179 to 417.

The most significant development among nonowners was the emergence of widespread tenantry during the seventies.[14] Renting was a familiar institution in antebellum Oconee, just as it was in other planting regions of Georgia.[15] Despite their familiarity with the practice of renting, however, landowners did not turn to it immediately after emancipation. They first attempted to replace slavery by hiring workers for wages. There were fewer white renters in 1870 (11) than there had been in 1860 (53), and none of the black farm workers in Oconee in 1870 can be identified as renters. Farmers were still trying to work blacks in wage gangs similar to the field gangs of slavery days and were openly hostile to the idea of renting land to the freedmen. By 1880, however, two-thirds of the white farm workers and three-fifths of the blacks were renting either for a fixed payment or on shares. The rest were nonrenting hired hands. The close supervision required under the wage system caused irritation for both employer and employee, and a chronic cash shortage made the payment of wages difficult. Tenantry offered a way out of these difficulties.[16] Farm ownership was on the rise during the seventies, but tenantry was spreading even faster.

The triumph of tenantry over ownership was even more pronounced among blacks than among whites. Only two black farm owners were identified in Oconee in 1870. By 1880, fifteen years after emancipation, the overwhelming majority of blacks continued to work the land, but there were still only thirteen farm owners among them. This record seems even more bleak when compared with the occupational progress of blacks who lived in town. There were more black farm owners living in Athens than in Oconee.

Outside of agriculture Oconee offered few choices for employment. Some whites were able to support themselves as lawyers, merchants, professional men, store clerks, or teachers, particularly in or near the village of Watkinsville. A small group of craftsmen also served local farmers, and a few men found employment as sawmill hands or in some other lower blue-collar job. Nonfarm employment opportunities were even more limited for blacks. The census reported agricultural occupations for 92.45 percent of the adult black males in 1870 and 86.69 percent in 1880. The most common alternative was domestic work. But a great majority of the people, black and white, relied directly on farming for their support, and if the land could not support them they had few alternatives within Oconee.[17] The number of men who succeeded in supporting themselves through farming expanded during the seventies, though for a growing percentage farming did not mean ownership.

The question of farm ownership is only a part of the larger issue of the distribution of all types of property. A study of amounts of property held by the citizens of Athens and Oconee reveals one of the most significant differences between town and country. The total value of all real estate held by adult white males increased in both areas during the fifties. It continued to rise in Athens through the sixties, growing by 12 percent over the decade in spite of war and reconstruction, but it declined by 44 percent in Oconee. Equally striking are the shifts in personal property. While the amount of personal property reported by Athenians fell by three-fifths between 1860 and 1870, residents of Oconee suffered a 90 percent loss.[18] The drastic drop in property values for Oconee demonstrates the special vulnerability of the two most common forms of investment in the rural area, farm land and slaves. Population growth in Athens helped to support real estate values there. In the country wartime and postwar disruptions of agriculture not only reduced the market value of cropland but also caused many farmers to take part of their land out of production, further reducing farm values. A townsman might have only a part of his personal estate tied up in slaves, but a farmer would invest all he could in slaves because that was the most obvious way to increase his income. As a result the people of Oconee were much poorer in comparison to the Athenians after the war than before.

The impact of these property losses upon the citizens of Clarke County is made more explicit in Table 1, which presents the distribution of whites among categories of total property. About a third of the residents of Athens reported no property or only insignificant amounts of personal property in 1860, and a fourth showed $10,000 or more. By 1870 only one in ten remained in this wealthiest category, but the percentage who were propertyless showed no sig-

Table 1. Distribution of White Adult Male Residents of Athens and Oconee Among Categories of Total Property, 1860–1870, and Direction of Change in Amounts of Property Reported by Persisters

		Athens					*Oconee*				
				MOVEMENT 1860–70					MOVEMENT 1860–70		
Total Wealth		**1860**	**1870**	**Up**	**Same**	**Down**	**1860**	**1870**	**Up**	**Same**	**Down**
Less than $100	N	164	229	32[a]	13[b]		143	156	20[a]	16[b]	
	%	35.81	34.23	71.1	28.9		30.23	43.94	55.6	44.4	
100–999	N	64	180	19		9	116	79	28		21
	%	13.97	26.91	67.9		32.1	24.52	22.25	57.1		42.9
1000–4999	N	68	136	11	2	19	102	95	13		29
	%	14.86	20.33	34.4	6.3	60.4	21.56	26.76	31.0		69.0
5000–9999	N	47	56	7		16	46	15	2		24
	%	10.26	8.37	30.4		69.6	9.73	4.23	7.7		92.3
10,000–	N	115	68	4		51	66	10	0		38
	%	25.11	10.16	7.3		92.7	13.95	2.82			100.0
	N	458	669	73	15	95	473	335	63	16	112
	%			39.9	8.2	51.9			33.0	8.4	58.6

[a]Includes only persons whose wealth rose above $100. In 1870, amounts less than $100 were not reported.

[b]Amounts less than $100 in 1860 are considered to be equal to $0 in 1870.

nificant change. A greater proportion of townspeople reported modest or mid-range holdings after the war. In the rural area a different picture emerges. Those who lacked property were slightly less common in antebellum Oconee (30.23 percent) than in Athens, and only one in seven fell into the $10,000 category. Small and middling holdings were more common in Oconee than in Athens. An example of rural economic democracy? Perhaps. But by 1870 the percentage of propertyless had climbed to 43.94. Only one in thirty-five owned $10,000 or more, and the percentage in the $5,000 to $9,999 group was reduced by half, indicating again the greater disruption of the rural social fabric. This is not democracy; this is poverty. Table 1 also reports direction of change in the amounts of property reported by men who were present in both 1860 and 1870. While the general trend in both Athens and Oconee was downward, town people in every category of wealth were more likely than country folk to gain and less likely to lose, another indication of the more secure economic condition of the town. Freedmen too were clearly better off in town than in Oconee. Over 28 percent of the black adult males living in Athens reported some property in 1870. This is no cause for jubilation, but it is better than the results for Oconee, where only 6.8 percent of the blacks reported ownership of property. Eight blacks in Athens had accumulated $1,000 or more, but only one black man in Oconee had that much.

This hurried survey of a few characteristics of one southern town and one rural district can not really settle any questions about urban and rural life in other parts of Dixie during the middle period. Many questions can not even be raised in so limited a space. But it is possible to begin to form impressions, which can at least guide our expectations and provide clues for subsequent research. The results reported here suggest that Athens was a mature and stable urban society even before the Civil War and that its social patterns proved remarkably resistant to the vicissitudes of economic change, war, and reconstruction. The Oconee district was by comparison a more fragile society, the vulnerability of which is reflected in shifts in patterns of persistence, occupation, and wealth. The town offered many options, both in forms of investment and in ways of earning a living. When the cotton trade declined or the demand for the services of craftsmen diminished, other forms of enterprise took up some of the slack and cushioned the blow. Savings could be invested in several ways. The result was a kind of flexibility which softened the impact of social and economic change. Blacks as well as whites found more economic opportunity in town than on the farm. The variety which gave strength and resiliency to urban society was not to be found in the countryside. Rural people had all of their eggs in a few baskets, baskets labeled slavery, cotton prices, and soil fertility. If any one of these baskets were toppled, the consequences were serious. If two or three were toppled at once, as happened during the sixties, the consequences were shattering. Because of this, historians seeking to identify links of continuity between the Old South and the New should follow the example of mid-nineteenth-century southerners and go to town occasionally.

Notes

1. Daniel R. Hundiey, *Social Relations in Our Southern States* (New York, 1860), p. 26.

2. Leonard P. Curry in a recent article on urban development in the South reported that among the authors of general histories of the antebellum South only Clement Eaton places significant emphasis on town life. See Curry, "Urbanization and Urbanism in the Old South: A Comparative View," *Journal of Southern History*, 40 (Feb. 1974), 43; and Eaton, "Town Life," in *A History of the Old South* (3d ed.; New York, 1975), pp. 247-70.

3. See for example, John S. Ezell, *The South Since 1865*, (2d ed.: New York, 1975), p. 234; W. J. Cash, *The Mind of the South* (New York, 1941), p. 184; and C. Vann Woodward, *Origins of the New South, 1887-1913* (Baton Rouge, La., 1951), p. 150.

4. If only the eleven states which joined the confederacy are considered, the results are 39 for 1850, 65 for 1860, 86 for 1870, and 140 for 1880. These figures were compiled from the printed returns of the U.S. Census, including *The Seventh Census of the United States: 1850* (Washington, D.C.: 1853); *The Population of the United States in 1860* (Washington, D.C.: 1864); *Ninth Census of the United States, 1870*, Vol. I, *Statistics of the Population of the United States* (Washington, D.C.: 1872); and *Tenth Census of the United States, 1880*, Vol. I, *Statistics of the Population of the United States* (Washington, D.C.: 1883).

5. For an important discussion of the concept of an "urban ethos" see Marvin Harris, *Town and Country in Brazil* (New York, 1971), pp. 276-89.

6. *Athens Georgian*, 1 Feb. 1876. For a more detailed discussion of Clarke County and a detailed bibliography see Frank J. Huffman, Jr., "Old South, New South: Continuity and Change in a Georgia County, 1850-1880" (Ph.D. diss., Yale University, 1974), pp. 7-25. Published works on this area include Kenneth Coleman, *Confederate Athens* (Athens, Ga., 1967); and E. Merton Coulter, *The Toombs Oak, the Tree That Owned Itself, and Other Chapters of Georgia* (Athens, Ga., 1966). Athens and the Oconee district present two different examples of life in the South. There are many points at which town and country might be compared. Those discussed here are population movement, occupational structure, and patterns of property holding. These investigations are based upon manuscript census returns.

7. See Robert Gilmour, "The Other Emancipation: Studies in the Society and Economy of Alabama Whites during Reconstruction" (Ph.D. diss., Johns Hopkins University, 1972), pp. 73, 80, 103.

8. Rates of persistence for the free adult males of Athens are as follows: 1850-60, 38.12%; 1860-70, 40.17%; 1870-80 (white), 44.23%; 1870-80 (black), 35.90%. For Oconee the results are: 1850-60, 44.03%; 1860-70, 41.44%; 1870-80 (white), 49.30%; 1870-80 (black), 31.77%.

9. The only other occupational group showing a comparable shift in persistence were the overseers, who were uprooted by emancipation. Among the overseers of Clark County whose ages ranged from 30 to 59, the rate of persistence dropped from 51.7% in the fifties to 27.6% in the sixties.

10. The importance of such specific job designations is treated in Michael B. Katz, "Social Structure in Hamilton, Ontario," in *Nineteenth-Century Cities: Essays in the New Urban History*, ed. Stephan Thernstrom and Richard Sennet (New Haven, Conn., 1969), p. 225. I have been able to discover little about the specific functions of the Mechanics' and Laboring Men's Union. It seems to have been a social organization and may have been a mutual aid society as well. See *Northeast Georgian*, 16 Dec. 1874.

11. Landed farmers accounted for 8.71% of the white male work force of Athens in 1850; 8.52% in 1860; 11.96% in 1870; and 6.28% in 1880. In order by census year, farm renters accounted for 0.24%, 0.87%, 1.49% and 4.52%. Farm laborers accounted for 2.12%, 3.28%, 14.50% and 1.13%. The rest were retired, reported no occupation, or showed an unclassifiable occupation such as "drinking and fishing."

12. J. G. Johnson, "Notes on Manufacturing in Ante-Bellum Georgia," *Georgia Historical Quarterly*, 16 (Sept. 1932), 227; James S. Buckingham, *The Slave States of America* (London, 1842), vol. 2, pp. 112-13; George P. Rawick, ed., *The American Slave: A Composite Autobiography* (Westport, Conn., 1972), vol. 12, pt. 1, p. 218, and vol. 13, pt. 3, p. 156; *Southern Watchman*, 31 Dec. 1857 and 10 March 1859: receipt for $11.00 for eleven days' work of "Billy the Carpenter," paid by M. A. Harden to Henry Hull, 22 Dec. 1856, Harden-Jackson-Carithers Collection, University of Georgia; receipt for $425.00 for carpentry work done by "the boy John," paid by William A. Carr to A. K. Patton, 28 Sept. 1858, Carr Collection, University of Georgia. Copy of Eulogy delivered to the Masonic Lodge of Athens, 27 Dec. 1871, by Howell Cobb, Jr., Cobb-Erwin-Lamar Collection, University of Georgia.

13. C. Vann Woodward discusses the tendency of blacks to create a duplicate of white society in *Origins of the New South*, p. 218.

14. Prior to 1880, renters must be identified by comparing the names of farm operators listed in the agriculture census with names in the population census to determine if the operator owned real estate. This method can not be used to distinguish between cash renters and share renters. The agriculture census for 1880 classified farm operators according to tenure and differentiates between cash and share renters. In that year about 55% of white renters and 65% of black renters were on shares.

15. Willard Range, *A Century of Georgia Agriculture, 1850-1950* (Athens, Ga., 1954), p. 7; and James C. Bonner, "Profile of a Late Ante Bellum Community," *American Historical Review*, 49 (July, 1944), 668-69.

16. *Northeast Georgian*, 14 Feb. 1873; *Southern Watchman*, 3 June 1874; Rawick, ed., *American Slave*, vol. 12, pt. 3, p. 242, and vol. 13, pt. 3, p. 272; Latimer Plantation Record Book, University of Georgia; Letter, Fannie Atkisson to L. Marion Blackshear, 25 Feb. 1866, Baber-Blackshear Collection, University of Georgia; "Monthly Report of Contracts, Wages and General Conduct and Treatment of the Freedmen, March, 1867-November, 1868, Athens Sub-district," Georgia Box #6, *Records of the Bureau of Refugees, Freedmen and Abandoned Lands*, Record Group 105, National Archives; Letter, Bvt. Major John J. Knox to Capt. Eugene Picket, 1 July 1867, *BRFAL*, 165, p. 82. For examples of disputes between freedmen and their employers see "Complaint Book, April, 1867-August, 1868, Howell C. Flournoy, Agent," *BRFAL*, 175, pp. 1-4, 9-12, 17, 18-23, 25-30, and passim.

17. Among white adult males in Oconee, 7.83% reported a white-collar occupation in 1850, 10.78% in 1860, 8.45% in 1870, and 6.08% in 1880. Blue-collar occupations were reported by 10.18% in 1850, 12.90% in 1860, 7.04% in 1870, and 6.34% in 1880. Among adult male freedmen 0.52% were white-collar and 4.43% were blue-collar in 1870. In 1880, 0.65% were white-collar and 8.93% were blue-collar.

18. The value of real property reported in the census by white male residents of Athens went from $1,173,849 in 1850 to $1,534,046 in 1860 and $1,721,300 in 1870. Personal property went from $3,754,116 in 1860 to $1,518,875 in 1870. For Oconee the amount of real property went from $540,746 in 1850 to $585,425 in 1860 and to $326,000 in 1870. Personal property went from $1,777,460 in 1860 to $178,050 in 1870 The census did not solicit information on personal property in 1850 nor on any property in 1880. Tax records do not provide comparable information.

W. E. B. Du Bois

Of the Quest of the Golden Fleece

But the Brute said in his breast, "Till the mills I grind have ceased,
The riches shall be dust of dust, dry ashes be the feast!

"On the strong and cunning few
Cynic favors I will strew;
I will stuff their maw with overplus until their spirit dies;
From the patient and the low
I will take the joys they know;
They shall hunger after vanities and still an-hungered go.
Madness shall be on the people, ghastly jealousies arise;
Brother's blood shall cry on brother up the dead and empty skies."

William Vaughn Moody

Have you ever seen a cotton-field white with the harvest,—its golden fleece hovering above the black earth like a silvery cloud edged with dark green, its bold white signals waving like the foam of billows from Carolina to Texas across that Black and human Sea? I have sometimes half suspected that here the winged ram Chrysomallus left that Fleece after which Jason and his Argonauts went vaguely wandering into the shadowy East three thousand years ago; and certainly one might frame a pretty and not far-fetched analogy of witchery and dragon's teeth, and blood and armed men, between the ancient and the modern Quest of the Golden Fleece in the Black Sea.

And now the golden fleece is found; not only found, but, in its birthplace, woven. For the hum of the cotton-mills is the newest and most significant thing in the New South to-day. All through the Carolinas and Georgia, away down to Mexico, rise these gaunt red buildings, bare and homely, and yet so busy and noisy withal that they scarce seem to belong to the slow and sleepy land. Perhaps they sprang from dragons' teeth. So the Cotton Kingdom still lives; the world still bows beneath her sceptre. Even the markets that once defied the *parvenu* have crept one by one across the seas, and then slowly and reluctantly, but surely, have started toward the Black Belt.

To be sure, there are those who wag their heads knowingly and tell us that the capital of the Cotton Kingdom has moved from the Black to the White Belt—that the Negro of to-day raises not more than half of the cotton crop. Such men forget that the cotton crop has doubled and more than doubled, since the era of slavery, and that, even granting their contention, the Negro is still supreme in a Cotton Kingdom larger than that on which the Confederacy builded its hopes. So the Negro forms to-day one of the chief figures in a great world-industry; and this, for its own sake, and in the light of historic interest, makes the field-hands of the cotton country worth studying.

We seldom study the condition of the Negro today honestly and carefully. It is so much easier to assume that we know it all. Or perhaps, having already reached conclusions in our own minds, we are loth to have them disturbed by facts. And yet how little we really know of these millions,—of their daily lives and longings, of their homely joys and sorrows, of their real shortcomings and the meaning of their crimes! All this we can only learn by intimate contact with the masses, and not by wholesale arguments covering millions separate in time and space, and differing widely in training and culture. To-day, then, my reader, let us turn our faces to the Black Belt of Georgia and seek simply to know the condition of the black farm-laborers of one county there.

Here in 1890 lived ten thousand Negroes and two thousand whites. The country is rich, yet the people are poor. The keynote of the Black Belt is debt; not commercial credit, but debt in the sense of continued inability on the part of the mass of the population to make income cover expense. This is the direct heritage of the South from the wasteful economies of the slave *régime*; but it was emphasized and brought to a crisis by the Emancipation of the slaves. In 1860, Dougherty County had six thousand slaves, worth at least two and a half millions of dollars; its farms were estimated at three millions,—making five and a half millions of property, the value of which depended largely on the slave system, and on the speculative demand for land once marvellously rich but already partially devitalized by careless and exhaustive culture. The war then meant a financial crash; in place of the five and a half millions of 1860, there remained in 1870 only farms valued at less than two millions. With this came increased competition in cotton culture from the rich lands of Texas; a steady fall in the normal price of cotton followed, from about fourteen cents a pound in 1860 until it reached four cents in 1898. Such a financial revolution was it that involved the owners of the cotton-belt in debt. And if things went ill with the master, how fared it with the man?

The plantations of Dougherty County in slavery days were not as imposing and aristocratic as those of Virginia. The Big House was smaller and usually one-storied, and sat very near the slave cabins. Sometimes these cabins stretched off on either side like wings; sometimes only on one side, forming a double row, or edging the road that turned into the plantation from the main thoroughfare. The form and disposition of the laborers' cabins throughout the Black Belt is to-day the same as in slavery days. Some live in the self-same cabins, others in cabins rebuilt on the sites of the old. All are sprinkled in little groups over the face of the land, centering about some dilapidated Big House where the head-tenant or agent lives. The general character and arrangement of these dwellings remains on the whole unaltered. There were in the county, outside the corporate town of Albany, about fifteen hundred Negro families in 1898. Out of all these, only a single family occupied a house with seven rooms; only fourteen have five rooms or more. The mass live in one- and two-room homes.

The size and arrangements of a people's homes are no unfair index of their condition. If, then, we inquire more carefully into these Negro homes, we find much that is unsatisfactory. All over the face of the land is the one-room cabin, —now standing in the shadow of the Big House, now staring at the dusty road, now rising dark and sombre amid the green of the cotton-fields. It is nearly always old and bare, built of rough boards, and neither plastered nor ceiled. Light and ventilation are supplied by the single door and by the square hole in the wall with its wooden shutter. There is no glass, porch, or ornamentation without. Within is a fireplace, black and smoky, and usually unsteady with age. A bed or two, a table, a wooden chest, and a few chairs compose the furniture; while a stray show-bill or a newspaper makes up the decorations for the walls. Now and then one may find such a cabin kept scrupulously neat, with merry steaming fireplace and hospitable door; but the majority are dirty and dilapidated, smelling of eating and sleeping, poorly ventilated, and anything but homes.

Above all, the cabins are crowded. We have come to associate crowding with homes in cities almost exclusively. This is primarily because we have so little accurate knowledge of country life. Here in Dougherty County one may find families of eight and ten occupying one or two rooms, and for every ten rooms of house accommodation for the Negroes there are twenty-five persons. The worst tenement abominations of New York do not have above twenty-two persons for every ten rooms. Of course, one small close room in a city, without a yard, is in many respects worse than the larger single country room. In other respects it is better; it has glass windows, a decent chimney, and a trustworthy floor. The single great advantage of the Negro peasant is that he may spend most of his life outside his hovel, in the open fields.

There are four chief causes of these wretched homes: First, long custom born of slavery has assigned such homes to Negroes; white laborers would be offered better accommodations, and might, for that and similar reasons, give better work. Secondly, the Negroes, used to such accommodations, do not as a rule demand better; they do not know what better houses mean. Thirdly, the landlords as a class have not yet come to realize that it is a good business investment to raise the standard of living among labor by slow and judicious methods; that a Negro laborer who demands three rooms and fifty cents a day would give more efficient work and leave a larger profit than a discouraged toiler herding his family in one room and working for thirty cents. Lastly, among such conditions of life there are few incentives to make the laborer become a better farmer. If he is ambitious, he moves to town or tries other labor; as a tenant-farmer his outlook is almost hopeless, and following it as a makeshift, he takes the house that is given him without protest.

In such homes, then, these Negro peasants live. The families are both small and large; there are many single tenants,—widows and bachelors, and remnants of broken groups. The system of labor and the size of the houses both tend to the breaking up of family groups: the grown children go away as contract hands or migrate to town, the sister goes into service; and so one finds many families with hosts of babies, and many newly married couples. but comparatively few families with half-grown and grown sons and daughters. The average size of Negro families has undoubtedly decreased since the war, primarily from economic stress. In Russia over a third of the bridegrooms and over half the brides are under twenty; the same was true of the ante-bellum Negroes. To-day, however, very few of the boys and less than a fifth of the Negro girls under twenty are married. The young men marry between the ages of twenty-five and thirty-five; the young women between twenty and thirty. Such postponement is due to the difficulty of earning sufficient to rear and support a family; and it undoubtedly leads, in the country districts, to sexual immorality. The form of this immorality, however, is very seldom that of prostitution, and less frequently that of illegitimacy than one would imagine. Rather, it takes the form of separation and desertion after a family group has been formed. The number of separated persons is thirty-five to the thousand,—a very large number. It would of course be unfair to compare this number with divorce statistics, for many of these separated women are in reality widowed, were the truth known, and in other cases the separation is not permanent. Nevertheless, here lies the seat of greatest moral danger. There is little or no prostitution among these Negroes, and over three-fourths of the families, as found by house-to-house investigation, deserve to be classed as decent people with considerable regard for female chastity. To be sure, the ideas of the mass would not suit New England, and there are many loose habits and notions. Yet the rate of illegitimacy is undoubtedly lower than in Austria or Italy, and the women as a class are modest. The plague-spot in sexual relations is easy marriage and easy separation. This is no sudden development, nor the fruit of Emancipation. It is the plain heritage from slavery. In those days Sam, with his master's consent, "took up" with Mary. No ceremony was necessary, and in the busy life of the great plantations of the Black Belt it was usually dispensed with. If now the master needed Sam's work in another plantation or in another part of the same plantation, or if he took a notion to sell the slave, Sam's married life with Mary was usually unceremoniously broken, and then it was clearly to the master's interest to have both of them take new mates. This widespread custom of two centuries has not been eradicated in thirty years. To-day Sam's grandson "takes up" with a woman without license or ceremony; they live together decently and honestly, and are, to all intents and purposes, man and wife. Sometimes these unions are never broken until death; but in too many cases family quarrels, a roving spirit, a rival suitor, or perhaps more frequently the hopeless battle to support a family, lead to separation, and a broken household is the result. The Negro church has done much to stop this practice, and now most marriage ceremonies are performed by the pastors. Nevertheless, the evil is still deep seated, and only a general raising of the standard of living will finally cure it.

Looking now at the county black population as a whole, it is fair to characterize it as poor and ignorant. Perhaps ten per cent compose the well-to-do and the best of the laborers, while at least nine per cent are thoroughly lewd and vicious. The rest, over eighty per cent, are poor and ignorant, fairly honest and well meaning, plodding, and to a degree shiftless, with some but not great sexual looseness. Such class lines are by no means fixed; they vary, one might almost say, with the price of cotton. The degree of ignorance cannot easily be expressed. We may say, for instance, that nearly two-thirds of them cannot read or write. This but partially expresses the fact. They are ignorant of the world about them, of modern economic organization, of the function of government, of individual worth and possibilities,—of nearly all those things which slavery in self-defence had to keep them from learning. Much that the white boy imbibes from his earliest social atmosphere forms the puzzling problems of the black boy's mature years. America is not another word for Opportunity to *all* her sons.

It is easy for us to lose ourselves in details in endeavoring to grasp and comprehend the real condition of a mass of human beings. We often forget that each unit in the mass is a throbbing human soul. Ignorant it may be, and poverty stricken, black and curious in limb and ways and thought; and yet it loves and hates, it toils and tires, it laughs and weeps its bitter tears, and looks in vague and awful longing at the grim horizon of its life,—all this, even as you and I. These black thousands are not in reality lazy; they are improvident and careless; they insist on breaking the monotony of toil with a glimpse at the great town-world on Saturday; they have their loafers and their rascals; but the great mass of them work continuously and faithfully for a return, and under circumstances that would call forth equal voluntary effort from few if any other modern laboring class. Over eight-eight per cent of them—men, women, and children—are farmers. Indeed, this is almost the only industry. Most of the children get their schooling after the "crops are laid by," and very few there are that stay in school after the spring work has begun. Child-labor is to be found here in some of its worst phases, as fostering ignorance and stunting physical development. With the grown men of the county there is little variety in work: thirteen hundred are farmers, and two hundred are laborers, teamsters, etc., including twenty-four artisans, ten merchants, twenty-one preachers, and four teachers. This narrowness of life reaches its maximum among the women: thirteen hundred and fifty of these are farm laborers, one hundred are servants and washerwomen, leaving sixty-five housewives, eight teachers, and six seamstresses.

Among this people there is no leisure class. We often forget that in the United States over half the youth and adults are not in the world earning incomes, but are making homes, learning of the world, or resting after the heat of the strife. But here ninety-six per cent are toiling; no one with leisure to turn the bare and cheerless cabin into a home, no old folks to sit beside the fire and hand down traditions of the past; little of careless happy childhood and dreaming youth. The dull monotony of daily toil is broken only by the gayety of the thoughtless and the Saturday trip to town. The toil, like all farm toil, is monotonous, and here there are little machinery and few tools to relieve its burdensome drudgery. But with all this, it is work in the pure open air, and this is something in a day when fresh air is scarce.

The land on the whole is still fertile, despite long abuse. For nine or ten months in succession the crops will come if asked: garden vegetables in April, grain in May, melons in June and July, hay in August, sweet potatoes in September, and cotton from then to Christmas. And yet on two-thirds of the land there is but one crop, and that leaves the toilers in debt. Why is this?

Away down the Baysan road, where the broad flat fields are flanked by great oak forests, is a plantation; many thousands of acres it used to run, here and there, and beyond the great wood. Thirteen hundred human beings here obeyed the call of one,—were his in body, and largely in soul. One of them lives there yet,—a short, stocky man, his dull-brown face seamed and drawn, and his tightly curled hair gray-white. The crops? Just tolerable, he said; just tolerable. Getting on? No—he wasn't getting on at all. Smith of Albany "furnishes" him, and his rent is eight hundred pounds of cotton. Can't make anything at that. Why didn't he buy land? *Humph!* Takes money to buy land. And he turns away. Free! The most piteous thing amid all the black ruin of war-time, amid the broken fortunes of the masters, the blighted hopes of mothers and maidens, and the fall of an empire,—the most piteous thing amid all this was the black freedman who threw down his hoe because the world called him free. What did such a mockery of freedom mean? Not a cent of money, not an inch of land, not a mouthful of victuals,—not even ownership of the rags on his back. Free! On Saturday, once or twice a month, the old master, before the war, used to dole out bacon and meal to his Negroes. And after the first flush of freedom wore off, and his true helplessness dawned on the freedman, he came back and picked up his hoe, and old master still doled out his bacon and meal. The legal form of service was theoretically far different; in practice, task-work or "cropping" was substituted for daily toil in gangs; and the slave gradually became a metayer, or tenant on shares, in name, but a laborer with indeterminate wages in fact.

Still the price of cotton fell, and gradually the landlords deserted their plantations, and the reign of the merchant began. The merchant of the Black Belt is a curious institution,—part banker, part landlord, part contractor, and part despot. His store, which used most frequently to stand at the cross-roads and become the centre of a weekly village, has now moved to town; and thither the Negro tenant follows him. The merchant keeps everything,—clothes and shoes, coffee and sugar, pork and meal, canned and dried goods, wagons and ploughs, seed and fertilizer,—and what he has not in stock he can give you an order for at the store across the way. Here, then, comes the tenant, Sam Scott, after he has contracted with some absent landlord's agent for hiring forty acres of land; he fingers his hat nervously until the merchant finishes his morning chat with Colonel Sanders, and calls out, "Well, Sam, what do you want?" Sam wants him to "furnish" him,—*i.e.*, to advance him food and clothing for the year, and perhaps seed and tools, until his crop is raised and sold. If Sam seems a favorable subject, he and the merchant go to a lawyer, and Sam executes a chattel mortgage on his mule and wagon in return for seed and a week's rations. As soon as the green cotton-leaves appear above the ground, another mortgage is given on the "crop." Every Saturday, or at longer intervals, Sam calls upon the merchant for his "rations"; a family of five usually gets about thirty pounds of fat side-pork and a couple of bushels of corn-meal a month. Besides this, clothing and shoes must be furnished; if Sam or his family is sick, there are orders on the druggist and doctor; if the mule wants shoeing, an order on the blacksmith, etc. If Sam is a hard worker and crops promise well, he is often encouraged to buy more,—sugar, extra clothes, perhaps a buggy. But he is seldom encouraged to save. When cotton rose to ten cents last fall, the shrewd merchants of Dougherty County sold a thousand buggies in one season, mostly to black men.

The security offered for such transactions—a crop and chattel mortgage—may at first seem slight. And, indeed, the merchants tell many a true tale of shiftlessness and cheating; of cotton picked at night, mules disappearing, and tenants absconding. But on the whole the merchant of the Black Belt is the most prosperous man in the section. So skilfully and so closely has he drawn the bonds of the law about the tenant, that the black man has often simply to choose between pauperism and crime; he "waives" all homestead exemptions in his contract; he cannot touch his own mortgaged crop, which the laws put almost in the full control of the land-owner and of the merchant. When the crop is growing the merchant watches it like a hawk; as soon as it is ready for market he takes possession of it, sells it, pays the land-owner his rent, subtracts his bill for supplies, and if, as sometimes happens, there is anything left, he hands it over to the black serf for his Christmas celebration.

The direct result of this system is an all-cotton scheme of agriculture and the continued bankruptcy of the tenant. The currency of the Black Belt is cotton. It is a crop always salable for ready money, not usually subject to great yearly fluctuations in price, and one which the Negroes know how to raise. The landlord therefore demands his rent in cotton, and the merchant will accept mortgages on no other crop. There is no use asking the black tenant, then, to diversify his crops,—he cannot under this system. Moreover, the system is bound to bankrupt the tenant. I remember once meeting a little one-mule wagon on the River road. A young black fellow sat in it driving listlessly, his elbows on his knees. His dark-faced wife sat beside him, stolid, silent.

"Hello!" cried my driver,—he has a most impudent way of addressing these people, though they seem used to it,—"what have you got there?"

"Meat and meal," answered the man, stopping. The meat lay uncovered in the bottom of the wagon,—a great thin side of fat pork covered with salt; the meal was in a white bushel bag.

"What did you pay for that meat?"

"Ten cents a pound." It could have been bought for six or seven cents cash.

"And the meal?"

"Two dollars." One dollar and ten cents is the cash price in town. Here was a man paying five dollars for goods which he could have bought for three dollars cash, and raised for one dollar or one dollar and a half.

Yet it is not wholly his fault. The Negro farmer started behind,—started in debt. This was not his choosing, but the crime of this happy-go-lucky nation which goes blundering along with its Reconstruction tragedies, its Spanish war interludes and Philippine matinees, just as though God really were dead. Once in debt, it is no easy matter for a whole race to emerge.

In the year of low-priced cotton, 1898, out of three hundred tenant families one hundred and seventy-five ended their year's work in debt to the extent of fourteen thousand dollars; fifty cleared nothing, and the remaining seventy-five made a total profit of sixteen hundred dollars. The net indebtedness of the black tenant families of the whole county must have been at least sixty thousand dollars. In a more prosperous year the situation is far better; but on the average the majority of tenants end the year even, or in debt, which means that they work for board and clothes. Such an economic organization is radically wrong. Whose is the blame?

The underlying causes of this situation are complicated but discernible. And one of the chief, outside the carelessness of the nation in letting the slave start with nothing, is the widespread opinion among the merchants and employers of the Black Belt that only by the slavery of debt can the Negro be kept at work. Without doubt, some pressure was necessary at the beginning of the free-labor system to keep the listless and lazy at work; and even to-day the mass of the Negro laborers need stricter guardianship than most Northern laborers. Behind this honest and widespread opinion dishonesty and cheating of the ignorant laborers have a good chance to take refuge. And to all this must be added the obvious fact that a slave ancestry and a system of unrequited toil has not improved the efficiency or temper of the mass of black laborers. Nor is this peculiar to Sambo; it has in history been just as true of John and Hans, of Jacques and Pat, of all ground-down peasantries. Such is the situation of the mass of the Negroes in the Black Belt to-day; and they are thinking about it. Crime, and a cheap and dangerous socialism, are the inevitable results of this pondering. I see now that ragged black man sitting on a log, aimlessly whittling a stick. He muttered to me with the murmur of many ages, when he said: "White man sit down whole year; Nigger work day and night and make crop; Nigger hardly gits bread and meat; white man sittin' down gits all. *It's wrong.*" And what do the better classes of Negroes do to improve their situation? One of two things: if any way possible, they buy land; if not, they migrate to town. Just as centuries ago it was no easy thing for the serf to escape into the freedom of town-life, even so to-day there are hindrances laid in the way of county laborers. In considerable parts of all the Gulf States, and especially in Mississippi, Louisiana, and Arkansas, the Negroes on the plantations in the back-country districts are still held at forced labor practically without wages. Especially is this true in districts where the farmers are composed of the more ignorant class of poor whites, and the Negroes are beyond the reach of schools and intercourse with their advancing fellows. If such a peon should run away, the sheriff, elected by white suffrage, can usually be depended on to catch the fugitive, return him, and ask no questions. If he escape to another county, a charge of petty thieving, easily true, can be depended upon to secure his return. Even if some unduly officious person insist upon a trial, neighborly comity will probably make his conviction sure, and then the labor due the county can easily be bought by the master. Such a system is impossible in the more civilized part of the South, or near the large towns and cities; but in those vast stretches of land beyond the telegraph and the newspaper the spirit of the Thirteenth Amendment is sadly broken. This represents the lowest economic depths of the black American peasant; and in a study of the rise and condition of the Negro freeholder we must trace his economic progress from this modern serfdom.

Even in the better-ordered country districts of the South the free movement of agricultural laborers is hindered by the migration-agent laws. The "Associated Press" recently informed the world of the arrest of a young white man in Southern Georgia who represented the "Atlantic Naval Supplies Company," and who "was caught in the act of enticing hands from the turpentine farm of Mr. John Greer." The crime for which this young man was arrested is taxed five hundred dollars for each county in which the employment agent proposes to gather laborers for work outside the State. Thus the Negroes' ignorance of the labor-market outside his own vicinity is increased rather than diminished by the laws of nearly every Southern State.

Similar to such measures is the unwritten law of the back districts and small towns of the South, that the character of all Negroes unknown to the mass of the community must be vouched for by some white man. This is really a revival of the old Roman idea of the patron under whose protection the new-made freedman was put. In many instances this system has been of great good to the Negro, and very often under the protection and guidance of the former master's family, or other white friends, the freedman progressed in wealth and morality. But the same system has in other cases resulted in the refusal of whole communities to recognize the right of a Negro to change his habitation and to be master of his own fortunes. A black stranger in Baker County, Georgia, for instance, is liable to be stopped anywhere on the public highway and made to state his business to the satisfaction of any white interrogator. If he fails to give a suitable answer, or seems too independent or "sassy," he may be arrested or summarily driven away.

Thus it is that in the country districts of the South, by written or unwritten law, peonage, hindrances to the migration of labor, and a system of white patronage exists over large areas. Besides this, the chance for lawless oppression and illegal exactions is vastly greater in the country than in the city, and nearly all the more serious race disturbances of the last decade have arisen from disputes in the county between master and man,—as, for instance, the Sam Hose affair. As a result of such a situation, there arose, first, the Black Belt; and, second, the Migration to Town. The Black Belt was not, as many assumed, a movement toward fields of labor under more genial climatic conditions; it was primarily a huddling for self-protection,—a massing of the black population for mutual defence in order to secure the peace and tranquillity necessary to economic advance. This movement took place between Emancipation and 1880, and only partially accomplished the desired results. The rush to town since 1880 is the countermovement of men disappointed in the economic opportunities of the Black Belt.

In Dougherty County, Georgia, one can see easily the results of this experiment in huddling for protection. Only ten per cent of the adult population was born in the county, and yet the blacks outnumber the whites four or five to one. There is undoubtedly a security to the blacks in their very numbers,—a personal freedom from arbitrary treatment, which makes hundreds of laborers cling to Dougherty in spite of low wages and economic distress. But a change is coming, and slowly but surely even here the agricultural laborers are drifting to town and leaving the broad acres behind. Why is this? Why do not the Negroes become land-owners, and build up the black landed peasantry, which has for a generation and more been the dream of philanthropist and statesman?

To the car-window sociologist, to the man who seeks to understand and know the South by devoting the few leisure hours of a holiday trip to unravelling the snarl of centuries,—to such men very often the whole trouble with the black field-hand may be summed up by Aunt Ophelia's word, "Shiftless!" They have noted repeatedly scenes like one I saw last summer. We were riding along the highroad to town at the close of a long hot day. A couple of young black fellows passed us in a mule-team, with several bushels of loose corn in the car. One was driving, listlessly bent forward, his elbows on his knees,—a happy-go-lucky, careless picture of irresponsibility. The other was fast asleep in the bottom of the wagon. As we passed we noticed an ear of corn fall from the wagon. They never saw it,—not they. A rod farther on we noted another ear on the ground; and between that creeping mule and town we counted twenty-six ears of corn. Shiftless? Yes, the personification of shiftlessness. And yet follow those boys: they are not lazy; to-morrow morning they'll be up with the sun; they work hard when they do work, and they work willingly. They have no sordid, selfish, money-getting ways, but rather a fine disdain for mere cash. They'll loaf before your face and work behind your back with good-natured honesty. They'll steal a watermelon, and hand you back your lost purse intact. Their great defect as laborers lies in their lack of incentive to work beyond the mere pleasure of physical exertion. They are careless because they have not found that it pays to be careful; they are improvident because the improvident ones of their acquaintance get on about as well as the provident. Above all, they cannot see why they should take unusual pains to make the white man's land better, or to fatten his mule, or save his corn. On the other hand, the white land-owner argues that any attempt to improve these laborers by increased responsibility, or higher wages, or better homes, or land of their own, would be sure to result in failure. He shows his Northern visitor the scarred and wretched land; the ruined mansions, the worn-out soil and mortgaged acres, and says, This is Negro freedom!

Now it happens that both master and man have just enough argument on their respective sides to make it difficult for them to understand each other. The Negro dimly personifies in the white man all his ills and misfortunes; if he is poor, it is because the white man seizes the fruit of his toil; if he is ignorant, it is because the white man gives him neither time nor facilities to learn; and, indeed, if any misfortune happens to him, it is because of some hidden machinations of "white folks." On the other hand, the masters and the masters' sons have never been able to see why the Negro, instead of settling down to be day-laborers for bread and clothes, are infected with a silly desire to rise in the world, and why they are sulky, dissatisfied, and careless, where their fathers were happy and dumb and faithful. "Why, you niggers have an easier time than I do," said a puzzled Albany merchant to his black customer. "Yes," he replied, "and so does yo' hogs."

Taking, then, the dissatisfied and shiftless field-hand as a starting-point, let us inquire how the black thousands of Dougherty have struggled from him up toward their ideal, and what that ideal is. All social struggle is evidenced by the rise, first of economic, then of social classes, among a homogeneous population. To-day the following economic classes are plainly differentiated among these Negroes.

A "submerged tenth" of croppers, with a few paupers; forty per cent who are metayers and thirty-nine per cent of semi-metayers and wage-laborers. There are left five per cent of money-renters and six per cent of freeholders,—the "Upper Ten" of the land. The croppers are entirely without capital, even in the limited sense of food or money to keep them from seed-time to harvest. All they furnish is their labor; the land-owner furnishes land, stock, tools, seed, and house; and at the end of the year the laborer gets from a third to a half of the crop. Out of his share, however, comes pay and interest for food and clothing advanced him during the year. Thus we have a laborer without capital and without wages, and an employer whose capital is largely his employees' wages. It is an unsatisfactory arrangement, both for hirer and hired, and is usually in vogue on poor land with hard-pressed owners.

Above the croppers come the great mass of the black population who work the land on their own responsibility, paying rent in cotton and supported by the crop-mortgage system. After the war this system was attractive to the freedmen on account of its larger freedom and its possibilities for making a surplus. But with the carrying out of the crop-lien system, the deterioration of the land, and the slavery of debt, the position of the metayers has sunk to a dead level of practically unrewarded toil. Formerly all tenants had some capital, and often considerable; but absentee landlordism, rising rack-rent, and falling cotton have stripped them well-nigh of all, and probably not over half of them to-day own their mules. The change from cropper to tenant was accomplished by fixing the rent. If, now, the rent fixed was reasonable, this was an incentive to the tenant to strive. On the other hand, if the rent was too high, or if the land deteriorated, the result was to discourage and check the efforts of the black peasantry. There is no doubt that the latter case is true; that in Dougherty County every economic advantage of the price of cotton in market and of the strivings of the tenant has been taken advantage of by the landlords and merchants, and swallowed up in rent and interest. If cotton rose in price, the rent rose even higher; if cotton fell, the rent remained or followed reluctantly. If a tenant worked hard and raised a large crop, his rent was raised the next year; if that year the crop failed, his corn was confiscated and his mule sold for debt. There were, of course, exceptions to this,—cases of personal kindness and forbearance; but in the vast majority of cases the rule was to extract the uttermost farthing from the mass of the black farm laborers.

The average metayer pays from twenty to thirty per cent of his crop in rent. The result of such rack-rent can only be evil,—abuse and neglect of the soil, deterioration in the character of the laborers, and a widespread sense of injustice. "Wherever the country is poor," cried Arthur Young, "it is in the hands of metayers," and "their condition is more wretched than that of day-laborers." He was talking of Italy a century ago; but he might have been talking of Dougherty County to-day. And especially is that true to-day which he declares was true in France before the Revolution: "The metayers are considered as little better than menial servants, removable at pleasure, and obliged to conform in all things to the will of the landlords." On this low plane half the black population of Dougherty County—perhaps more than half the black millions of this land—are to-day struggling.

A degree above these we may place those laborers who receive money wages for their work. Some receive a house with perhaps a garden-spot; then supplies of food and clothing are advanced, and certain fixed wages are given at the end of the year, varying from thirty to sixty dollars, out of which the supplies must be paid for, with interest. About eighteen per cent of the population belong to this class of semi-metayers, while twenty-two per cent are laborers paid by the month or year, and are either "furnished" by their own savings or perhaps more usually by some merchant who takes his chances of payment. Such laborers receive from thirty-five to fifty cents a day during the working season. They are usually young unmarried persons, some being women; and when they marry they sink to the class of metayers, or more seldom, become renters.

The renters for fixed money rentals are the first of the emerging classes, and form five per cent of the families. The sole advantage of this small class is their freedom to choose their crops, and the increased responsibility which comes through having money transactions. While some of the renters differ little in condition from the metayers, yet on the whole they are more intelligent and responsible persons, and are the ones who eventually become land-owners. Their better character and greater shrewdness enable them to gain, perhaps to demand, better terms in rents; rented farms, varying from forty to a hundred acres, bear an average rental of about fifty-four dollars a year. The men who conduct such farms do not long remain renters; either they sink to metayers, or with a successful series of harvests rise to be land-owners.

In 1870 the tax-books of Dougherty report no Negroes as landholders. If there were any such at that time,—and there may have been a few,—their land was probably held in the name of some white patron,—a method not uncommon during slavery. In 1875 ownership of land had begun with seven hundred and fifty acres; ten years later this had increased to over sixty-five hundred acres, to nine thousand acres in 1890 and ten thousand in 1900. The total assessed property has in this same period risen from eighty thousand dollars in 1875 to two hundred and forty thousand dollars in 1900.

Two circumstances complicate this development and make it in some respects difficult to be sure of the real tendencies; they are the panic of 1893, and the low price of cotton in 1898. Besides this, the system of assessing property in the country districts of Georgia is somewhat antiquated and of uncertain statistical value; there are no assessors, and each man makes a sworn return to a tax-receiver. Thus public opinion plays a large part, and the returns vary strangely from year to year. Certainly these figures show the small amount of accumulated capital among the Negroes, and the consequent large dependence of their property on temporary prosperity. They have little to tide over a few years of economic depression, and are at the mercy of the cotton-market far more than the whites. And thus the land-owners, despite their marvellous efforts, are really a transient class, continually being depleted by those who fall back into the class of renters or metayers, and augmented by newcomers from the masses. Of the one hundred land-owners in 1898, half had bought their land since 1893, a fourth between 1890 and 1893, a fifth between 1884 and 1890, and the rest between 1870 and 1884. In all, one hundred and eighty-five Negroes have owned land in this county since 1875.

If all the black land-owners who had ever held land here had kept it or left it in the hands of black men, the Negroes would have owned nearer thirty thousand acres than the fifteen thousand they now hold. And yet these fifteen thousand acres are a creditable showing,—a proof of no little weight of the worth and ability of the Negro people. If they had been given an economic start at Emancipation, if they had been in an enlightened and rich community which really desired their best good, then we might perhaps call such a result small or even insignificant. But for a few thousand poor ignorant field-hands, in the face of poverty, a falling market, and social stress, to save and capitalize two hundred thousand dollars in a generation has meant a tremendous effort. The rise of a nation, the pressing forward of a social class, means a bitter struggle, a hard and soul-sickening battle with the world such as few of the more favored classes know or appreciate.

Out of the hard economic conditions of this portion of the Black Belt, only six per cent of the population have succeeded in emerging into peasant proprietorship; and these are not all firmly fixed, but grow and shrink in number with the wavering of the cotton-market. Fully ninety-four per cent have struggled for land and failed, and half of them sit in hopeless serfdom. For these there is one other avenue of escape toward which they have turned in increasing numbers, namely, migration to town. A glance at the distribution of land among the black owners curiously reveals this fact. In 1898 the holdings were as follows: Under forty acres, forty-nine families; forty to two hundred and fifty acres, seventeen families; two hundred and fifty to one thousand acres, thirteen families; one thousand or more acres, two families. Now in 1890 there were forty-four holdings, but only nine of these were under forty acres. The great increase of holdings, then, has come in the buying of small homesteads near town, where their owners really share in the town life; this is a part of the rush to town. And for every land-owner who has thus hurried away from the narrow and hard conditions of country life, how many field-hands, how many tenants, how many ruined renters, have joined that long procession? Is it not strange compensation? The sin of the country districts is visited on the town, and the social sores of city life to-day may, here in Dougherty County, and perhaps in many places near and far, look for their final healing without the city walls.

Julie Roy Jeffrey

Women in the Southern Farmers' Alliance: A Reconsideration of the Role and Status of Women in the Late Nineteenth-Century South

In the spring of 1891, Mrs. Brown, secretary of the Menola Sub-Alliance in North Carolina, welcomed an audience of delegates to the quarterly meeting of the Hertford County Farmers' Alliance. After introductory remarks to both the women and men in the audience, Brown addressed her female listeners directly.

> Words would fail me to express to you, my Alliance sisters, my appreciation of woman's opportunity of being co-workers with the brethren in the movement which is stirring this great nation. Oh, what womanly women we ought to be, for we find on every hand, fields of usefulness opening before us. Our brothers . . . are giving us grand opportunities to show them, as Frances E. Willard says, that "Drudgery, fashion and gossip are no longer the bounds of woman's Sphere."

So enthusiastically was Brown's speech received, that the County Alliance unanimously requested its publication in the official paper of the Farmers' Alliance, the *Progressive Farmer*.[1] In a similar fashion, the Failing Creek Alliance asked the *Progressive Farmer* later that year to reprint a speech Katie Moore had delivered to them. Moore had also spoken before an audience of women and men, and she too had had some special words for the women. " 'Tis not enough that we should be what our mothers were," she told them. "We should be more, since our advantages are superior. . . . This is the only order that allows us equal privileges to the men; we certainly should appreciate

Source: This article is reprinted from *Feminist Studies* 3, nos. 1/2 (Fall 1975): 75–91, by permission of the publisher, Feminist Studies, Inc., c/o Women's Studies Program, University of Maryland, College Park, MD 20742.

the privilege and prove to the world that we are worthy to be considered on an equal footing with them."[2]

That the two audiences had approved of these speeches to the point of urging their wider circulation was not surprising. For the slogan of the Southern Farmers' Alliance itself was, "Equal rights to all, special privileges to none." As one Alliance publication explained, "The Alliance has come to redeem women from her enslaved condition, and place her in her proper sphere. She is admitted into the organization as the equal of her brother . . . the prejudice against woman's progress is being removed."[3]

Such statements about the condition of Alliance women were important, for they came from an organization which had millions of members and which was a significant force on the regional and national level in the 1880s and 1890s. In part, the Alliance was a rural protest against the inferior social, economic, and political position its members felt farmers occupied in the emerging urban-industrial society. But, like civil service reformers and other protest groups in the Gilded Age, the Farmers' Alliance argued that the finely balanced two-party system responded only to the demands of special interest groups and political machines rather than to the needs of the people. Alliance members first tried to change this situation by pressing at the state level for control of monopolies and other unfriendly interests and for favorable legislation. Better public schools for rural children, state agricultural colleges, colleges for women, laws controlling the railroads, better prices for farm products were some of the goals the Alliance sought to enable rural classes to survive within a new world. As this strategy proved frustrating, about half of the Alliance membership moved into the Populist party which ran its first presidential candidate in 1892. Although the Populist party ultimately failed, it offered the most serious challenge to the two-party system in the late nineteenth century and contributed to the reshaping of the American political system.[4]

These exhortations and demands emphasizing female equality and opportunity were important, then, because the Alliance was important, but they have an unfamiliar ring in the context of what has generally been known about sex roles and relationships in the post-Civil War South. The accepted interpretation of late nineteenth-century southern society has argued that the model of the southern lady, submissive and virtuous, "the most fascinating being in creation . . . the delight and charm of every circle she moves in," still marked the parameters of appropriate behavior for middle-class women, though the model had been predictably weakened by the traumatic experience of civil war. As for lower-class women, this interpretation suggests, they were "not much affected by role expectations," although "farmers' wives and daughters and illiterate black women . . . in some inarticulate way doubtless helped to shape [society]" and its standards.[5]

Yet an investigation of the Farmers' Alliance in North Carolina, where the Alliance had great success, indicates this explanation does not hold true for that state. If the North Carolina experience is at all typical of other southern Alliance states, and there is little reason to think it is *not*, the reality of southern attitudes toward women was more complex than recent analyses have allowed. The Civil War had been the initial catalyst for women entering new areas of activities: after the war, poverty and loss of fathers, brothers, husbands, and other male relatives forced many women to run farms, boarding houses, to become seamstresses, postmistresses, and teachers.[7] As the traditional view of woman's sphere crumbled under the impact of the post-war conditions, at least one alternative to the older view emerged in the South—one exemplified by the case of North Carolina. Responsive to social changes stemming from war and defeat, the Alliance in the 1880s and 1890s urged women to adopt a new self-image, one that included education, economic self-sufficiency, one that made a mockery of all false ideas of gentility. The activities and behavior that the Alliance sanctioned were not only considered appropriate for middle-class women but for women on all social levels.[8] Although evidence on the social class composition of the Alliance is limited, recent work suggests that approximately 55 percent of the North Carolina membership owned their land, about 31 percent were tenants, and 14 percent rural professionals. Since many wives and daughters joined the Alliance, it seems reasonable to assume that female membership, like male membership, crossed class lines.[9] Certainly, the new female role was applicable to all of them. Finally, although it was not actually created by Alliance women, the new cultural model was consciously elaborated by some of them, thus offering one way of understanding how middle-class farming women, later deemed "inarticulate" because they left so few written records, perceived and shaped their social role.

Furthermore, a case study of the North Carolina Farmers' Alliance shows that the Alliance also offered numerous rural women the rare privilege of discussing important economic and political issues with men and of functioning as their organizational equals. Few southern institutions offered women similar opportunities. The political party barred them altogether. The Methodist and Baptist churches, which with the Presbyterian claimed a majority of church members, still supported the traditional view that women ought to remain at home although they had allowed women a new area of activity in establishing female missionary societies. This expansion of their sphere was considered to be "no compromise . . . [to] female modesty and refinement," although, in reality, women could and did acquire political experience and skills in them.[10] After 1883, North Carolina women also gained valuable organizational knowledge through their involvement in the Women's Christian Temperance Union. But the W.C.T.U., the church missionary societies and women's clubs of the 1880s were all-female organizations and thus did not offer women the chance to establish a pragmatic working relationship with men as the Alliance would do.[11]

One other rural organization in the South, the Grange, which reached its height of popularity in North Carolina between 1873 and 1875, admitted both sexes before the Alliance did so. Unlike the Alliance, however, the Grange made clear distinctions between most of the offices and ranks women and men could hold. Nevertheless, the Grange clearly provided women with some practical organizational experience with men and, presumably, offered some kind of rough equality. Still, partly because of its Northern origins, the impact of the Grange was limited in the South. In North Carolina, the Grange's total membership never surpassed the 15,000 mark, and by the 1880s, numbers had dwindled.[12] Moreover, since the Grange was primarily an educational body, it failed to provide the same kind of experience for southern women as the Alliance would in the 1880s and 1890s. Ostensibly apolitical, the Alliance was actually devoted to a discussion of the "science of economical government" and was deeply involved in political questions.[13] Within the North Carolina Alliance, the spheres of women and men drew closer as both sexes voted, held office, and discussed together the stirring issues of the day as they had rarely done before.

Within the framework of the Alliance, then, southern women had the opportunity to discuss pressing economic, political, and social questions, to try out ways of behaving in mixed groups and to gain confidence in newly acquired skills. One might expect that a group of women, and perhaps men, eventually emerge whose Alliance experiences would lead them ultimately to demand or sympathize with the greater expansion of woman's role that the organization officially supported. Yet this never happened. At the same time that the Alliance offered new roles and organizational possibilities for women, the meaning of equality for women was constricted by the organization's major goal of reviving southern agriculture. Political rights within the Alliance were not seen as the first step toward political rights outside of the Alliance. The career of the North Carolina Alliance and its inclusion of women in its membership thus offers another kind of study of the slow progress of the women's rights movement in North Carolina and perhaps gives additional clues for its uncertain course in the South as a whole.[14]

The evidence for this study comes from many sources. Most useful is the State Alliance paper, the *Progressive Farmer*,[15] whose policy it was to publish the views of the Alliance membership. Few of these rural correspondents provided the leading articles for the paper, but rather they contributed letters to the correspondence page. Since these long forgotten farm women and men left virtually no other personal records, their letters, some literary, most artless, provide a crucial insight into the grassroots level of the Alliance and an important view of their responses to the opportunities the Alliance held out to them.

Initial interest in a farmers' organization in North Carolina resulted from the depressed state of southern agriculture in the 1880s. By 1886, Colonel Leonidas Polk, editor of the new agricultural weekly, the *Progressive Farmer*, was vigorously urging the paper's readers to organize local farmers' clubs as the basis for a future state wide organization. From the beginning he visualized at least some women in the clubs, for he advised they could be "elected as honorary members." Yet farmers' clubs were not to have a long life in North Carolina. By May 1887 Alliance organizers from Texas, where the agricultural order had originated, had begun to establish local Alliances in North Carolina, while a Carolinian, J. B. Barry, also began recruiting. Polk, aware of the growth potential of the Alliance, joined one of Barry's Alliances in July 1887, and was soon meeting with Texas Alliance leaders to discuss a merger between the Alliance and his farmers' clubs. After the merger was made the North Carolina Alliance grew by leaps and bounds. In the summer of 1888 the membership stood at 42,000. By 1891 the Alliance claimed 100,000 members in over 2,000 local chapters.[16]

Requirements for membership in the Alliance, formalized in the state constitution adopted in October 1887, were far more positive to female members than Polk's farmers' clubs had been. Membership was open to rural white women and men over sixteen years of age who had a "good moral character," believed in "the existence of a Supreme Being," and showed "industrious habits." While men were to pay fifty cents as an initiation fee in addition to quarterly dues of twenty-five cents, women had no required fee or dues, no doubt a recognition of their marginal economic status and their desirability as members.[17] Membership of both sexes was essential to Alliance goals as state Alliance president, Captain Sydenham B. Alexander, indicated. The purpose of the Alliance, Alexander wrote in 1887, was "to encourage education among the agricultural and laboring classes, and *elevate to higher manhood and womanhood* those who bear the burdens of productive industry."[18]

Alliance leaders did not leave the issue of female participation in the organization to chance but stressed it forcefully. Harry Tracy, a National Lecturer of the order, urged "*the ladies to come out and hear him*," and warned Alliance members: "The ladies eligible must join the order before we can succeed." Despite emphatic support from the top, however, letters from local Alliances to the *Progressive Farmer*, now the official organ of the North Carolina Alliance, indicate some male resistance to the idea of female members. As the Secretary of the Davidson College Alliance explained: "I think that the ladies are best suited to home affairs." Verbal opposition to female members led one woman to comment, "They don't want us to join, and think it no place for us." Other, more subtle techniques of discouraging female membership seem to have existed. Holding meetings in places where women would be uncomfortable or feel out of place kept the number of female members down. As the correspondent from Lenoir Alliance noted, his Alliance had fifty men and one woman because meetings were held in the court house. As one frequent contributor to the *Progressive Farmer* who favored female members pointed out: "Each Sub-Alliance needs a hall. . . . We cannot urge the ladies to attend until we can seat them comfortably."[19]

Numerous questions addressed to Polk, now secretary of the state Alliance as well as editor of the *Progressive Farmer* indicated that even if not opposed to female membership, men were often hesitant and confused about the membership of women. A variety of questions focused on what women were eligible for membership and, if elected, what their rights should be. Were women, in fact, to have the same "rights and privileges of the male members"?[20] Over and over again Polk replied that women were to have equal rights and privileges; they were to vote on new members, participate in all Alliance business and to know "all the secret words and signs" of the order.[21]

If some men were unenthusiastic about female members, so too were some of the women. As one Allianceman explained: "Our female friends seem to repose great confidence in our ability to conduct the affairs of the Alliance without their direct union and assistance. Indeed, our wives, mothers and sisters have as much as they can do to attend their own business." Other letters from men more enthusiastic about female members agreed that women refused to join because they were "too modest, or think it out of their line."[22] There was even some outright female opposition to Alliance membership as one "bright and energetic young lady," the first woman to join the Alliance in Vance County, discovered when her friends ridiculed "the idea of young ladies joining."[23] The traditional view of woman's sphere, then, constituted a barrier to active female participation in the Alliance, and it was one which female members consciously tried to undermine. When Alliancewomen wrote to the *Progressive Farmer* they frequently urged the other women to overcome feelings of timidity. "Dear Sisters, go to work; don't stay home and die, then say I have something else to do; that will never do," wrote Addie Pigford. "Sisters, what are you doing?" asked Mrs. Carver. "There is work for us to do, and we shall not be found wanting. We can help in many ways, and we must do it."[24]

Opposition and hesitation on the subject of female members obviously existed as the reports of local and county Alliances and male and female correspondents to the *Progressive Farmer* show. But evidence suggests that the message that women were to be encouraged as vigorous participants of the Alliance eventually came through clearly to most local groups. By 1889, for example, the State Line Alliance reported it was planning to discuss the desirability of female members. Rather ruefully, the writer commented: "That indicates how far we are behind, but we do not intend to remain there."[25] Questions about membership requirements and privileges, membership breakdowns sent into the *Progressive Farmer*, and local minute books, indicate that women were presenting themselves for membership. Not only did the wives and daughters of male members join but so too did unattached women. As the Alliance grew so did the number of women in the organization. In some cases, women comprised one-third to one-half of local groups.[26] "We can work just as well as the brethren," pointed out one Alliance woman. "If we want to derive good from the Alliance, we must work in love and harmony with our fellowman."[27]

As thousands of women responded to the Alliance's invitation to join "the great army of reform," there were hints that women felt increasingly at ease in their new organizational role. Although it is difficult to recover the perceptions of these rural women, their letters to the *Progressive Farmer* from 1887 through 1891 can serve as an imperfect measure for their thoughts and feelings about their participation in the Alliance.[28]

One of the most striking aspects of the women's correspondence is the initial hesitation about writing to a newspaper at all. Only one woman communicated to the editor in 1887. Gradually, however, women began to send letters, many of them conscious of departing from past patterns of behavior. "Being a farmer's wife, I am not in the habit of writing for the public prints," wrote the first female correspondent of 1888, a certain Mrs. Hogan who was concerned about stray dogs. Replied the second, "Mr. Editor:—I have never written anything for the public to read, but I feel just now, after reading Mrs. Hogan's trouble . . . that I want to tell her I truly sympathize with her."[29] Other correspondents in 1888 and 1889 often began their letters with the polite request for a "small space" for a few words from a farm woman or with the phrase, "I am but a female." "I suppose your many subscribers will not expect much from a female correspondent," wrote one corresponding secretary, "and if so, they will not be disappointed when they read this article, but if I can be of any service to the Alliance by putting in my little mite, I am willing to do what I can."[30] By 1890 such protestations and expressions of humility had disappeared. A series of letters from Evangeline Usher exemplifies the growing confidence on the part of women that their letters and reports on Alliance activities were appropriate and acceptable. In an early letter, Usher urged other women to write to the paper, with the typical hope that Polk would "give us a little space somewhere." Describing herself as fearful that her letter would go into the wastebasket, she further explained that her feelings of delicacy would prevent her from contributing her Alliance's news regularly. "I already imagine I see Brother 'R' smiling ludicrously at the idea." Within a few months, however, Usher wrote again, confessing "a kind of literary pride in seeing my name in print." By 1889, she could begin her letter, "I feel like I must intrude again, and as I am quite independent of all disfavor, I do not care whether you like the intrusion or not."[31] Though Usher was unusually outspoken, her growing boldness correlates with the straightforward and secure tone women gradually adopted in writing to the paper and suggests their greater feelings of confidence within the organization.[32]

Local reports, letters, and records also give information on another crucial consideration concerning women's involvement in the Alliance. If women only sat on the back benches during Alliance meetings, listening silently while men discussed the great economic and political issues of the day, their membership would have been insignificant. If, on the other hand, women actually helped to run the organization and helped contribute to its success, even if they were not equal in every respect to men, then the Alliance was an important departure from the typical southern organization.

Although there is no indication that women were ever elected to the office of president of local Alliances, they were occasionally, at least, voted into important positions. The Jamestown Alliance Minute Book, for example, records that a year after the subject of female members was first discussed, a woman was elected as assistant secretary; she declined, but two months later was elected a treasurer.[33] Other women held the office of secretary, with the responsibility not only for making "a fair record of all things necessary to be written," but also for "receiving all moneys due" and for communicating with Secretary Polk.[34] Still others became lecturers or assistant lecturers, both crucial positions since they were to give addresses, lead discussions, and furnish "the material of thought for the future consideration of the members."[35] Women as well as men read papers "on subjects of importance for the benefit of the order." In one Alliance, records show that women conducted the business on an Alliance meeting day.[36] At the county level where meetings were held quarterly, women were included in the membership count on which representation was based, were delegates, and at least one was elected vice-president. Others gave key addresses to large audiences.[37] Women could also be found at the annual meetings of the state Alliance. As the *Progressive Farmer* warmly replied to two women who had written to ask if they could go to the meeting, "You are not only *allowed*, but you will be most cordially welcomed to a seat."[38] Though such evidence is fragmentary, it does imply that many women took an active part in running Alliance affairs.

Women participated in the Alliance in a variety of other areas too. Several letters to the *Progressive Farmer* noted that women subscribed to the State Business Agency Fund, an important Alliance effort aimed at eliminating middlemen in purchasing fertilizers, groceries, and agricultural goods. Alliance leaders urged local groups to donate at least fifty cents a member to the fund. A few reports show women carrying their financial share. Women also sent in news to the paper, wrote articles, and worked to increased the subscription list, a job which Polk and other leaders saw as vital to Alliance success since they argued that earlier efforts to arouse farmers had foundered on ignorance and lack of proper information.[39]

If not all women were active members of the Alliance, enough were to be reported and praised in the *Progressive Farmer*. Clearly, many women welcomed the chance to work in the organization. Moreover, as their letters indicate, they shared men's interest in the compelling subjects of the day: agricultural cooperation, the role of combines and trusts in creating the farming crisis, the need to diversify southern agriculture, all standard themes for discussion and instruction in Alliance meetings and reading material.[40] But as much as women were involved with such topics, as much as they enjoyed the social conviviality of the Alliance, many must have agreed with the woman who reminded her Alliance, "This is the only order that allows us equal privileges to the man; we certainly should appreciate the privilege."[41]

North Carolina Alliance's support of "equal rights" for women within the organization and of the new role described for them outside it may seem startling, yet it corresponded to the reality of life for southern women in the late 1880s and early 1890s. It would have been surprising if the changes in southern society following the Civil War had failed to result in some ideological reconsideration of women's status. Yet the Alliance's stance was not merely a response to social change in the South. The National Alliance upheld the concept of equal rights. State leaders recognized that the farmer and his wife worked as an agricultural unit. It made sense to involve both in the Alliance for as one farmer pointed out, "We know we can scarcely dispense with the labor of our wives and children on the farm."[42] Furthermore, leaders reasoned that the Alliance could not count on continued enthusiasm and good attendance unless women as well as men came to meetings. "Meetings must be interesting" to spur membership and attendance, one pamphlet pointed out, "and the first step in this direction is to get more women and young people into the Order." At least one member agreed. The presence of women, he wrote, "cheers us on." Clearly, if the Alliance and its work were to prosper, both sexes would have to be involved.[43]

The social composition of the leadership suggests another important reason for the Alliance support for women. Although men like Colonel Polk and Sydenham Alexander, president of the state Alliance, had been or were farmers genuinely concerned with agricultural problems, they were also members of the rural upper-class. Polk had had a long career as planter, army officer, legislator, commissioner of agriculture, and editor. Alexander had headed the state Grange in the 1870s. Other leaders were teachers, doctors, and clergymen.[44] As members of North Carolina's elite, these men partitially accepted the traditional view of woman as the beacon of social morality. "If our organization means anything," one prominent supporter of female members wrote, "it means a moral reformation, morality must be our guide. The ladies are and always have been the great moral element in society; therefore *it is impossible to succeed without calling to our aid the greatest moral element in the country.*"[45]

This was how Alliance leaders conceived of the role and importance of women within their organization. But women themselves had their own ideas about their role, as an examination of their letters to the *Progressive Farmer* reveal. The writers stressed their pride in farm life, the need to throw off female passivity, the vital importance of women to the Alliance effort. "While it has been remarked that women are necessary evil," wrote Fannie Pentecost, "let us by our untiring energy, and zeal show them that it is a mistake. . . . We should devise plans and means by which we can assist those who have to bear the burdens of life." In the Alliance, another woman pointed out, women had the unique opportunity of helping men "in the thickest of the fight" by encouragement, prayers, self-denial, and endurance. Some correspondents clearly saw their role as one of moral support, but others visualized a more active role, using words like helpmate or companion to describe how they saw themselves.[46] One woman shaped the female role curiously: "Let us all put our shoulders to this great wheel, the Alliance. We, as sisters of this Alliance may feel we are silent factors in this work; we know we constantly need something to lean upon. . . . Let us so entwine ourselves around our brothers that *should we be taken away* they will feel they are *tottering*." Here, encouragement and support had beome the vital acitivity for women. So, too, one woman from Fair Grove commented that women must be "ready to hold the hands of the strong, should they become weak."[47]

That women perceived themselves occasionally as the major support for men corresponds with the way in which Alliance leaders visualized them. But there was a sharp edge to the role of moral guide as some correspondence revealed. Again, Evangeline Usher provides an insight into this kind of thinking. In a letter of September 1890, Usher wrote that someone had recently sent her a compliment, "saying they were just as strong an Alliance boy as I was an Alliance girl." Evangeline's rather surprising comment was "Brother . . . . I only hope you are, for I am one that believes in working and not talking." Other letters and articles convey a similar scepticism of men. "Why," asked assistant lecturer Lizzie Marshburn, "is it that the farmer and laboring class generally, have got no self-will or resolution of their own? . . . as a general rule they have been ever ready to link their destinies with any political aspirant who can get up and deliver a flowerly address of misrepresentation." Allie Marsh told her audience at a Randolph County meeting, "We come to these meetings with an unwritten agreement to take things as they are." Women, she said, were "perfectly content" that men exercise political rights "as long as you are vigilant in making [the ballot box] as efficient as possible." Yet the remainder of her speech suggested that she had found the men "wanting." A letter from still another woman acidly observed, "Some men can't see beyond their nose."[48]

Although most women and men probably agreed upon the function of women's participation within the Alliance, it appears that some Alliance women saw the matter differently and that they suspected that the commonly accepted view of women as the quiet impetus behind male reformers was inadequate. Their letters convey misgivings about the ability of men to persist in their support of reform and implicitly suggest that these women perceived themselves as steadier leaders than the men. As one Alliance woman explained: "My sisters, this is something we should know, that our names are on this list [of reformers] and [we should] regret we could not be allowed this opportunity years ago, for no doubt our country would be in a much better condition to-day had we taken this step." Added another, apparently filled with misgivings about men: "I would earnestly *beg the brethren* when they put their hands to the plow *not to look back . . . if they do*, they will not reap the harvest we all desire. *We must work* and *wait*, and not grow discouraged."[49] Yet, despite these indications that women suspected that they rather than men were possibly the most steadfast and reliable leaders of reform, they were hardly ready to challenge openly the Alliance's basic assumptions because of the positive support the Alliance was already providing for southern women of many areas of life.

Indeed, women's rights within the organization was only part of the Alliance's reformulation of women's status. A woman's role in the Alliance was understood to parallel the more significant role the Alliance suggested women could enjoy in society at large. The *Progressive Farmer's* policy of reporting on the achievements of women who were doctors, surgeons, journalists, lawyers, government workers, even pastors, indicated the wide range of possibilities beyond the conventional one of marriage and motherhood.[50] These career options, of course, depended on educating women, a goal that the Alliance and its official newspaper consistently supported as part of the general attempt to improve all educational facilities for "farmers and laborers."[51]

"The ability of girls," the *Progressive Farmer* stated flatly, "has been found equal to that of boys." As the resolutions of the 1890 State Alliance meeting show, the Alliance went on record that year not only in favor of public schools for boys and girls but also in support of "ample [state] appropriations [for] the training and higher education of females." The paper explained, "The lopsided system of education in North Carolina . . . provides for the education of men and neglects that of women. Gentlemanly instinct, to say nothing of justice and mercy, requires that women should be given as good a chance for education as men possess. . . . Give the noble girls of the State—those who are not able to go to our expensive colleges a chance to get an education," the paper urged. Responding to pressure from the Alliance and other interested groups, the legislature of 1891 appropriated $10,000 a year to establish a normal and industrial training school for girls.[52]

The reason for the Alliance's concern with women's education becomes obvious in the *Progressive Farmer's* discussions of private girls' schools. Traditionally, these schools had stressed teaching female accomplishments to the would-be southern lady of means. But now the *Progressive Farmer* enthusiastically reported, Salem Female Academy had expanded its offering by establishing a business course featuring music, telegraphy, phonography (shorthand), typing and bookkeeping. Such a course, the *Progressive Farmer* pointed out, was most desirable with its "studies of a practical character, fitting the learners for active avocations when required to depend upon their own efforts in the battle of life." Other schools, the paper urged, ought to follow Salem Academy's example. The fundamental point, the paper emphasized, was that *all* young women of *all* social classes should be prepared for jobs. It was true, of course, that education would help poor girls by enabling them "to make an honest living," but all women ought to learn to be self-sufficient and self-supporting.[53]

Women themselves stressed the importance of economic self-sufficiency. They did not want to "be entirely dependent upon the bounties of others" if they lost their protectors. And, as an additional point in favor of education, one Alliance woman brought up the important question of marriage. Self-sufficiency would allow women to marry because they wanted to, not because they needed financial support. Thus education of a certain kind would help women avoid the "fatal blunder," incompatibility in marriage.[54]

Alliance support for practical education for women was based on a rejection of the concept of gentility which had been such a fundamental component of the idea of the southern lady.[55] The search for a "pale and delicate" complexion, the interest in elaborate clothing and accomplishments were all denounced in the pages of the *Progressive Farmer*. These traditional female concerns were misguided since they undermined the importance of hard work and, thus, the opportunities for female independence. The idea that labor was degrading, the *Progressive Farmer* reminded its readers, was just another unfortunate remnant of slavery, and, in fact, contributed in an important way to poverty itself. True Alliance men and women wanted young people "to see that it is no disgrace, but a high honor, to know how to work and to be able to do it." The feminine ideal was the woman who was independent and practical, educated either to support herself or to marry wisely.[56]

Better education for both sexes was an issue with which many Alliance members sympathized, hoping their children's future would be more promising than their own. Yet the Alliance could not concern itself exclusively with the new options for young women who still had their lives ahead of them. With so many adult female members, the Alliance also considered how to reshape life styles for those women who would never leave the farm for school or a job. "Is the life of the Farmer's wife under present systems, calculated to give her virtue and intelligence full play," asked the Southern Alliance paper, the *National Economist*. Is she not a slave and a drudge in many cases?" The *Progressive Farmer* gave the answer: there were "thousands and tens of thousands" of farmers' wives "worked to their graves."[57] Improving this dreary situation necessitated a multipronged approach. First, the paper's scientific articles on housekeeping and cooking could show the farm wife how to lighten her work load. Then, too, her husband was to be prodded into helping her out. As one correspondent to the *Progressive Farmer* explained, men needed tough words. "Our Lecturer, in trying to discuss the social feature [of the alliance], handles husbands quite roughly, but it is received in the proper spirit. If country life is ever made more attractive, there must be more congeniality in spirit and aggressiveness between the one that follows the plow handles and the one of all beings earthly that acts as a helpmeet to man." What were "the conveniences for the good and faithful wife?" asked Colonel Polk. How far did she have to walk to the woodpile or the spring? Had the bloom on her cheeks faded prematurely? These were the subjects, he urged, that ought to be discussed in Alliance circles so that "new life, new energy, new action . . . and new views of life and living" might emerge for both sexes.[58]

The Alliance's concern with helping hard working farmwomen fused with the order's major objective, the overall improvement of agricultural life. To this end, the Alliance sought to discover "a remedy for every evil known to exist and afflict farmers and other producers."[59] The remedy of improved farming methods was especially important as the number of articles in the *Progressive Farmer* attest. The paper argued that the one-crop system was the obvious and basic cause of the state's agricultural depression. Over and over again, the paper and Alliance meetings focused on the need to farm properly and to stay out of debt. Consider the two kinds of farmers, the *Progressive Farmer* urged. One raised cotton on his land, bought milk, bread, hay and fertilizers on credit. The other chose the Alliance route and would prosper. And "his wife, dear devoted woman, instead of wearing out her life in cooking for a lot of negroes to work cotton, has time to look after the adornment and the beautifying of her home, to attend to her milk and butter, eggs, garden, bees, chickens and other poultry, and with all this they have a little time to spare socially with their neighbors and to go to church."[60]

The *Progressive Farmer* might describe the tasks of the wise farmer's wife enthusiastically, but the list of her activities highlights a crucial problem in the Alliance's approach to women. Although the Alliance supported expanding women's rights and privileges, its over-all objective was to put farmers on an economic, social, and political parity with other occupations. To do so, or to try to do so, had definite implications for women's lives and shaped the Alliance's conception of equality. If the home was to be made attractive enough to discourage children from abandoning farm life, if it was to be "a place of rest, of comfort, of social refinement and domestic pleasure," then women would have to make it so.[61] If the farm was to stay out of debt, if the farmer was to remain free of the supply merchant by raising as many of his necessities as he could, his wife must help. Woman's "judgement and skill in management may be essential to the success of her husband," one article reminded Alliance readers. "And this responsibility . . . continues to the close of her life."[62]

The Alliance proposed a position for women that embodied an equality of sorts, the economic equality of a diligent coworker. In its recognition of the importance and difficulty of woman's work, the role model differed from that of the southern lady. Nor did the model merely update the characters of the yeoman farmer's family. The Alliance's concern with diversifying southern agriculture, with eliminating the disastrous dependency on the one-crop system, was not an attempt to recreate the small farm and agricultural myth of an idealized past but to create a new kind of farm and a new cast of characters.

Agricultural reform, in fact, was seen as part of a modernizing process, and it was favored not only by the Alliance but also by leaders of the New South movement. Spokesmen for each group agreed that the South had to end its colonial status both through substantial industrial growth and through agricultural diversification.[63]

But what were the implications of such a view for women? "The housewife, who, by her industry, transforms the milk from her dairy into butter . . . is as truly a manufacturer as the most purse-proud mill-owner of Britain," explained the *National Economist*. Labeled manufacturers or helpmates, women were to carry a heavy burden in creating the new order.[64] The truth was that even though the Alliance talked of a variety of opportunities available for women, most women in North Carolina would continue to live on the farm, and Alliance leaders thought this right in terms of the world they wished to create. Farm women were important for they would share in the task of restoring agriculture to its rightful position in the economy. Even the Alliance's interest in women's education was partially tied to this goal. If women were to become efficient, modern coworkers in the task of agricultural reconstruction, they needed an education. As Polk explained: "The great and imperative need of our people and our time, is the practical education of the masses. . . . It will be a glorious day for the South when her young ladies, educated in all the higher and refined arts of life, shall boast and without blushing of equal proficiency in the management of the household and the flower-garden."[65]

Moreover, women needed to be educated so that, in turn, they could teach Alliance children, first at home and then at school. Rural children, many Alliance members were convinced, needed a special kind of education, one that embraced "the moral, physical and industrial, as well as the mental training of our children." By providing such an education, women could offer an "invaluable service." For "this system will strengthen the attachment of these classes [to agricultural life] instead of alienating [them] from it . . . it will better qualify them for success and happiness in life . . . increase the opportunity and inclination to adorn the home and practice the social virtues."[66]

Other pragmatic considerations led to the support of women's education. Education could provide poor girls with the opportunity "to make an honest living." Most, but not all, women would marry. To prepare for the possibility of spinsterhood, every careful mother must see not only that daughters were trained in their domestic and spiritual responsibilities, but would also "have them taught a trade or profession and thus equip them fully to 'face the world' if this need shall come to them."[67] No one, not even a woman, ought to be an economic drain on others. Teaching provided one means of support. So too would factory work, which the Alliance leaders, like spokesmen of the New South movement, hoped would be a growing field of employment. North Carolina's piedmont region, the *Progressive Farmer* enthusiastically suggested, should be covered with factories. "Then we could have money because our boys and girls and women who are now consumers would find constant, honorable and remunerative employment and would thus become self-supporting." Women not only had the option but, indeed, the duty of being self-supporting and of adding "to the general wealth of the place." The more educated and useful women became, "the better for them and for our State."[68]

The part that the Alliance encouraged women to play in southern life was more expansive than the traditional role of the southern lady at the same time that it had definite limitations. Women need no longer cultivate the appearance of genteel passivity; they required education as the preparation for a useful life. But the Alliance defined utility in terms of the organization's over-all objectives, the profitability of agriculture, the prosperity of the state. Thus, it was vital that women learn to be skilled managers or teachers. Whether spinsters or widows, women must never be parasites on their families or on their state. Beneath the rhetoric, the lifestyle the Alliance supported for women was one of constant hard work and low wages, if women were to be paid for their labor at all. These limitations, harsh though they seem, were realistic both in terms of the Alliance's major goals and in terms of available options in the South. As one northern observer testified, "There is yet no rapid development of opportunity for profitable labor for young white women in the South."[69]

There may be yet another reason for the contradictory meaning of equality that the Alliance proposed for women. Despite the support the Alliance gave to an expanded life style for women, Alliance leaders were affected by the circumstances of time, place, and class. Like other well-born Southerners, they had not rejected the traditional view of women as the source of morality and goodness. Because of their moral qualities, women had to participate in the Alliance, but it is doubtful whether North Carolina Alliance leaders would have supported enlarging women's sphere in any way that might threaten their own social or political position.[70]

As the *Progressive Farmer* firmly acknowledged, it had no sympathy with "that spirit which could encourage class feeling or class prejudice. . . . It is . . . subversive of the social order."[71] Leaders wanted changes, but not at the expense of social stability. Thus women might share in a kind of social and economic equality with men but they would hardly be offered political rights.

There are few indications that this strategy was unacceptable to the majority of Alliance women. Most letters from women indicate that the new parameters for female behavior were thankfully welcomed. Only occasionally can one discern an undercurrent of unrest, when women remarked on men's failure to be vigorous Alliance fighters or when they pointed out how much better a place the world would be had women, long ago, taken a more active part in shaping it.[72] Then, too, a few women dared to write on political matters, giving their own opinions and urging men to take notice.[73] At least one woman realized how far she had stepped out of her place. After mocking Alliance men who were "willing to wave Alliance principles and swallow the whole Democratic party," she observed, "I could say a good deal more on this line, but will stop, for fear some fool will ask: 'Are you a woman?' "[74]

The *Progressive Farmer* not surprisingly steered away from the explosive issue of women's participation in politics.[75] In two unusual references to the question of women's political rights, however, it is clear that the issue had come up in local meetings. At one county rally, the lecturer told the women, "He did not invite them to suffrage, though it was gaining rapidly in public favor and if they had the ballot they would drive out the liquor traffic of this country and other evils." In Alamance County, the Alliance lecturer warned his female listeners, "Do not spend your time in longing for opportunities that will never come, but be contented in the sphere the Lord hath placed you in. If the Lord had intended you for a preacher or lawyer He would have given you a pair of pantaloons."[76]

But the desire to maintain the *status quo* did not automatically succeed. Though Alliance leaders delineated definite boundaries to the theoretical and actual position women might occupy in the world, the fact that suffrage was mentioned at all may indicate a turbid undercurrent of half conscious challenge to the leadership. The way the two Alliance speakers spoke of the suffrage issue suggests that some Alliance circles had discussed it. A few letters to the *Progressive Farmer* and other fragmentary evidence point to the same conclusion. On a visit to North Carolina in 1893, for example, a Mrs. Virginia Durant who had established a suffrage organization in South Carolina, reported she found "suffrage sentiment" of an unfocused kind in the state. Perhaps she sensed incipient interest among those women exposed to the Alliance.[77]

Yet there is not enough evidence to resolve the issue. If there were some support for the further expansion of women's activities through the Alliance, however, it never had the time to grow strong and vocal. For although the Alliance lingered on into the twentieth century, by the mid-1890s it had ceased to be an institution of importance. The failure of Alliance cooperative economic ventures, continued hard times, and a split within the organization over the support of the Populist party all contributed to a decline in membership. A changing political climate brought new issues, new questions to the fore; many of them would have conservative implications.[78] By the end of the decade, the shape of southern life would be set. After the Populist challenge, franchise for both poor whites and blacks would be limited and the question of political participation closed. Voting was a privilege, not a right. "Equal rights for all, special privileges for none" was a slogan best forgotten.[79]

Though the Alliance did not survive long enough to dislodge the traditional ideas of woman's sphere, its spirited attempt to work out a new place for her both in theory and practice shows greater complexity in late nineteenth-century attitudes and behavior with respect to sex roles than previously recognized, and suggests that there may have been other attempts to create new roles for women in the South. The Alliance alternative, it is true, fell short of offering women equality in all spheres of life. Primary Alliance goals and the nature of the leadership limited the meaning of equal rights for women. Yet to expect the Alliance to propose full equality for women would be to ignore the influence of both time and place and to expect consistency of thought and action when such consistency rarely exists.

Notes

1. *Progressive Farmer,* June 23, April 21, 1891.
2. *Progressive Farmer,* December 22, 1891.
3. Nelson A. Dunning, ed., *The Farmer's Alliance History and Agricultural Digest* (Washington: The Alliance Publishing Co., 1891), pp. 309-310. See also *National Economist,* June 6, 1891.
4. For general information on the Alliance see John D. Hicks, *The Populist Revolt: A History of the Farmers' Alliance and the People's Party* (Minneapolis: University of Minnesota Press, 1931), pp. 105, 146; Theodore Saloutos, *Farmer Movements in the South: 1865-1933* (Berkeley: University of California Press, 1960), pp. 85, 123, 282-83; Hugh Talmadge Lefler and Albert Ray Newsome, *The History of a Southern State: North Carolina* (Chapel Hill: University of North Carolina Press, 1963), p. 513; John M. Dobson, *Politics in the Gilded Age: A New Perspective on Reform* (New York: Praeger, 1972), pp. 172-75, 183-86.
5. Quoted in Anne Firor Scott, *The Southern Lady: From Pedestal to Politics, 1830-1930* (Chicago: University of Chicago Press, 1970), pp. 4-5, x-xi, and Anne Firor Scott, "Women's Perspective on the Patriarchy in the 1850s," *Journal of American History* 61 (June 1974): 54, note 4.
6. Other areas in the South were more radical in their views about women than North Carolina. See *National Economist,* May 4, May 25, September 1, 1889; March 1, June 14, July 12, July 26, October 25, 1890; June 6, July 25, November 12, 1892. See also Annie L. Diggs, "The Women in the Alliance Movement," *The Arena* 6 (June 1892): 163; Dunning, *Farmer's Alliance,* pp. 308-309; A. D. Mayo, "Southern Women in the Recent Educational Movement in the South," *Bureau of Education Circular of Information,* no. 1 (Washington, D.C.: G.P.O., 1892), pp. 54, 124; Josephine K. Henry, "The New Woman of the New South," *The Arena* 11 (February 1895): 353-62; Saloutos, *Farmer Movements,* chapters 5-7.
7. Scott, *Southern Lady,* chapters 4 and 5.
8. Robert Carroll McMath, Jr., "The Farmers' Alliance in the South: The Career of an Agrarian Institution" (Ph.D. diss., University of North Carolina at Chapel Hill, 1972), pp. 88-89; Robert Carroll McMath, Jr., "Agrarian Protest at the Forks of the Creek: Three Subordinate Farmers' Alliances in North Carolina," *The North Carolina Historical Review* 51 (January 1974): 47; Philip Roy Muller, "New South Populism: North Carolina, 1884-1900," (Ph.D. diss., University of North Carolina at Chapel Hill, 1971), pp. 33-37, 148-54.
9. McMath, "Farmers' Alliance," pp. 88-89.
10. Quoted in Hunter Dickinson Farish, *The Çircuit Rider Dismounts: A Social History of Southern Methodism, 1865-1900* (Richmond, Va.: Dietz Press, 1938), pp. 327, 325-26; Scott, *Southern Lady,* pp. 137-41; Anne Firor Scott, "Women, Religion and Social Change in the South, 1830-1930, in *Religion and the Solid South,* ed., Samuel S. Hill, Jr. (Nashville, Tenn.: Abingdon Press, 1972), pp. 93-115; Marjorie Stratford Mendenhall, "Southern Women of a 'Lost Generation,'" *South Atlantic Quarterly* 33 (October 1937): 339-41; Emory Stevens Bucke, ed., *The History of American Methodism* (Nashville, Tenn.: Abingdon Press, 1964), vol. 2, pp. 291-92.
11. Daniel J. Whitener, *Prohibition in North Carolina, 1715-1935* (Chapel Hill, N.C.: Univer-

sity of North Carolina Press, 1945), pp. 104-105; Scott, *Southern Lady*, pp. 139-52. Men were admitted as honorary members to the W.C.T.U. Another organization that included both women and men was the International Order of The King's Daughters and Sons, established in 1886. As in the W.C.T.U., men played little part in the organizational activities of the charitable group. Easdale Shaw, *The History of the North Carolina Branch of the International Order of The King's Daughters and Sons* (Raleigh, N.C.: Capital Printing Co., 1929), pp. 3-4.

12. Solon Justus Buck, *The Granger Movement: A Study of Agricultural Organization and Its Political, Economic and Social Manifestations: 1870-1880* (Cambridge: Harvard University Press, 1913), pp. 41-43, 381; Saloutos, *Farmer Movements*, pp. 30-33, 42; Stuart Noblin, *The Grange in North Carolina 1929-1954: A Story of Agricultural Progress* (Greensboro: The North Carolina State Grange, 1954), pp. 2, 3.

13. Saloutos, *Farmer Movements*, pp. 32, 42; Roy V. Scott, *The Reluctant Farmer: The Rise of Agricultural Extension to 1914* (Urbana: University of Illinois Press, 1970), pp. 42-46; *National Economist*, March 14, 1889, June 7, 1890; *Progressive Farmer*, December 1, 1887, January 28, 1890. In 1889, the North Carolina State Alliance decided all political demands were to be sent to local Alliances for their approval. See "Official Circular No. 6," May 27, 1892, John R. Osborne Papers, Duke University, where Alliance secretaries are ordered to present the State Alliance resolution in favor of a secret ballot to their Sub-Alliances "for discussion and ratification."

14. In other parts of the country, the Alliance did radicalize some women and men. O. Gene Clanton, *Kansas Populists: Ideas and Men* (Lawrence: University of Kansas Press, 1969), *passim*. But for the story of the slow-moving suffrage campaign in North Carolina, see A. Elizabeth Taylor, "The Woman Suffrage Movement in North Carolina," *The North Carolina Historical Review* 38 (January and April 1961): 45-62, 173-89; Virginius Dabney, *Liberalism in the South* (Chapel Hill, N.C.: University of North Carolina Press, 1932), chapter 19.

15. Although major Alliance manuscript collections and records were utilized for this study, the most useful source for it was the official newspaper of the North Carolina Alliance, the *Progressive Farmer*. The weekly paper served as one of the major means of communication between the state Alliance and local and county groups, publishing reports, orders, and instructions for Alliance members and, in turn, including letters and reports from the membership. Its paid circulation, the largest of any North Carolina newspaper of the time, had reached 18,240 by 1891. Actually, the paper reached more readers than this figure indicates since it was passed on and often read aloud at Alliance meetings. See McMath, "The Farmers' Alliance," pp. 200-204; Stuart Noblin, *Leonidas LaFayette Polk: Agrarian Crusader* (Chapel Hill, N.C.: University of North Carolina Press, 1949), p. 210. Letters and articles for 1886, the year before the Alliance officially adopted the paper are also used since they do not differ in content or tone from what was published later. The *Progressive Farmer* is the best source for this study of Alliance thought and practice not only because of its central role in disseminating and reflecting Alliance views, but because local Alliance records are skimpy, leaders were often concerned with the "major" issues, and few of the women and men left any lasting remains at all aside from their letters to the paper. The *National Economist*, official journal of the Southern Alliance between 1889 and 1893, also proved helpful as a supplement and contrast to the *Progressive Farmer*, as did other Alliance books and pamphlets.

16. *Progressive Farmer*, March 31, 1886; McMath, "Farmers' Alliance," pp. 82-83; John D. Hicks, "The Farmers' Alliance in North Carolina," *The North Carolina Historical Review* 2 (April 1925): 169. It is difficult precisely to estimate membership in the Southern Alliance or its North Carolina branch. The organization claimed a total membership of 362,970 in July 1888, just a year after recruiting began. Of these, 42,496 or 12 percent were women. By 1890, the Alliance reported it had 3,000,000 members, a figure that some believe as inflated (Saloutos, *Farmer Movements*, p. 77). In North Carolina, the Farmers' Alliance *Daybook*, North Carolina State Archives, Raleigh, notes that the number of local Alliances had reached 2,000 in February 1890. See also *Minutes* of the Farmers' State Alliance, 1887-1893, August 14, 1888, North Carolina State Archives, Raleigh; McMath, "Farmers' Alliance," p. 139.

17. *Minutes*, Farmers' State Alliance, October 4, 1887, August 16, 1888.

18. Reprinted in *Progressive Farmer*, December 8, 1887; my italics.

19. *Progressive Farmer*, July 9, 1889, February 25, 1890, June 23, 1891. *The Sub Alliance and What It Can Accomplish: Report of the Program Committee of the North Carolina Farmers State Alliance* (no date, North Carolina State Archives, Raleigh) emphatically makes the point that female membership is a necessity. (See also *Progressive Farmer*, June 11, 1889; July 10, May 22, 1888; July 30, 1889; February 25, 1890; April 8, 1890; July 25, 1889.)

20. *Progressive Farmer*, December 18, June 12, December 4, June 12, July 24, 1888, May 14, 1889.

21. Ibid.; also *Progressive Farmer*, March 13, 1888, March 5, 1889.

22. *Progressive Farmer*, May 22, 1888; October 7, 1890. See also July 30, August 6, 1889, September 23, October 7, 1890.

23. *Progressive Farmer*, February 18, 1890, April 17, 1888.

24. *Progressive Farmer*, December 16, March 25, 1890. See also July 24, 1888, June 11, August 6, October 1, 1889; February 11, September 23, 1890; September 22, December 22, 1890, *National Economist*, June 6, 1891. Of course, men were also encouraged to be more vigorous in their support of the Alliance.

25. *Progressive Farmer*, June 11, November 19, 1889.

26. For membership ratios, see the Bethany Alliance Minute Book, John R. Osborne Papers, Duke University, Jamestown Alliance Minute Book, Duke University, and the Mt. Sylvan Alliance Minute Book, North Carolina State Archives, Raleigh. See also the Account Book of Wake City Alliance, Roll Book of L. L. Polk, Sub Alliance No. 2254, Wake County, Polk Papers, in the Southern Historical Collection, University of North Carolina Library, Chapel Hill, and the *Progressive Farmer, passim*. The Wake County Alliance Account Book, which gives membership figures for about 45 local Alliances in that County, indicates that 36 percent of the County's membership in September 1890 were women. A year later this percentage of women had risen to 38 percent.

27. *Progressive Farmer*, February 11, 1890; August 7, May 15, December 11, 1888; August 13, 1889.

28. *Progressive Farmer*, March 10, 1891. There is, of course, the possibility that any woman writing to the newspaper was atypical.

29. *Progressive Farmer*, January 19, 1887; February 16, March 13, 1888.

30. *Progressive Farmer*, April 16, April 30, 1889; October 1, 1889.

31. *Progressive Farmer*, July 24, December 11, 1888; September 23, 1889; see also her letter of March 19, 1889, and February 25, 1890. Interestingly enough, Polk saved a letter from Usher that can be found in his papers. Evangeline Usher to L. L. Polk, December 25, 1889, Polk Papers, in the Southern Historical Collection, University of North Carolina Library, Chapel Hill.

32. A letter from a Kansas woman, Mrs. S. V. P. Johnson to L. L. Polk, April 1, 1892, Polk Papers, in the Southern Historical Collection, University of North Carolina Library, Chapel Hill, discusses in detail the difficulties of throwing off female hesitancy, the opportunities she felt the Alliance offered her, and her lack of confidence.

33. Jamestown Alliance Minute Book. She subsequently left this office. "Organizers Report," November 13, 1889, Polk Papers, in the Southern Historical Collection, University of North Carolina Library, Chapel Hill, notes Miss J. M. E. Midget as treasurer. Unfortunately, inadequate records make it impossible to discover how many women held office. There are enough casual references to women in office, however, to suggest that female office holders were not unusual.

34. *National Farmers' Alliance and Industrial Union Ritual* (Washington, D.C.: National Economist Publishing Co., 1891). *Progressive Farmer*, May 28, October 1, 1889; September 23, October 7, 1890.

35. *Ritual*; *Progressive Farmer*, August 6, September 24, 1889. President Alexander stressed the crucial importance of the lecturer's position in characterizing it as "more important than any of the others" (*Minutes*, Farmers' State Alliance, August 13, 1889).

36. *Progressive Farmer*, September 11, 1888; March 31, December 22, 1891.

37. *Progressive Farmer*, June 23, 1891; July 17, October 23, 1888; April 21, 1891. There was

clearly some confusion about counting women for representation. W. M. Koonts, secretary of the Davidson County Alliance, wrote to the Bethany Alliance secretary, "You are only entitled to delegates for the *male* members clear on the books." But the previous year Polk, in answer to a question on this very point, had announced that both sexes were to be counted (S. M. Koonts, to John R. Osborne, December 27, 1889, John R. Osborne papers, Duke University, *Progressive Farmer*, July 17, 1888.

38. *Progressive Farmer*, July 9, 1889.

39. "Circular No. 3, North Carolina Farmers' Alliance Business Agency Fund," November 22, 1890, Richard Street Papers, North Carolina State Archives, Raleigh; *Progressive Farmer*, August 13, 1889; July 24, 1888, September 8, 1887; S. B. Alexander to L. L. Polk, November 14, 1885, Polk Papers, Southern Historical Collection, University of North Carolina Library, Chapel Hill; *Progressive Farmer*, May 28, October 1, 1889; Circular, "Important to Sub-Alliances: Please Read at Next Meeting," L. Polk Denmark Collection, North Carolina State Archives, Raleigh.

40. Women reported on crop information and expressed interest in a wide variety of subjects. See *Progressive Farmer*, August 14, November 6, 1888; February 26, April 30, July 9, 1889 for examples.

41. *Progressive Farmer*, December 22, 1891.

42. *Progressive Farmer*, September 11, 1888.

43. *Progressive Farmer*, June 25, 1889. For a similar view, but from Texas, see *National Economist*, September 1, 1889. *The Sub-Alliance and What It Can Accomplish*, pp. 3, 4; *National Economist*, June 7, 1890; *Progressive Farmer*, June 11, 1889.

44. See Noblin, *Polk, passim*; Noblin, *The Grange*, p. 3; McMath, "Farmers' Alliance," pp. 84-88: Muller, "New South Populism," pp. 33-37, 148-54.

45. *Progressive Farmer*, July 9, 1889; March 31, 1891; June 25, 1889; November 13, 1888. The Pleasant Garden Alliance Minute Book, William D. Hardin Papers, Duke University, shows the importance members attributed to moral and orderly conduct at meetings. *Progressive Farmer*, March 24, 1891.

46. *Progressive Farmer*, June 11, 1889; June 23, 1891; for similar views from other southern women, see *National Economist*, July 12, July 26, 1889; October 25, 1890; July 25, 1891.

47. *Progressive Farmer*, July 24, 1888, my italics; *Progressive Farmer*, June 4, 1889.

48. *Progressive Farmer*, September 23, 1890; September 24, 1889; January 22, 1889; February 25, 1890.

49. *Progressive Farmer*, September 22, 1891; December 10, 1889, my italics.

50. These items are generally given without any editorial comments, as were the other items of general interest. For examples, see *Progressive Farmer*, May 18, July 21, October 29, November 17, 1886; February 2, May 8, June 12, July 3, November 6, 1888; August 20, 1889.

51. *Progressive Farmer*, November 10, 1887.

52. *Progressive Farmer*, February 10, 1891; *Minutes*, Farmers' State Alliance, August 14, 1890; *Progressive Farmer*, January 20, 1891 and August 19, 1890; February 18, 1889; Virginia Terrell Lathrop, *Educate a Woman: Fifty Years of Life at the Woman's College of the University of North Carolina* (Chapel Hill, N.C.: University of North Carolina Press, 1942), pp. xi-xiii.

53. *Progressive Farmer*, June 19, 1888, June 23, 1887, January 12, 1888; February 19, 1889. The objectives of the Normal and Industrial School for girls were "(1) to give young women such education as shall fit them to teach; (2) to give instruction in drawing, telegraphy, typewriting, stenography, and such other arts as may be suitable to their sex and conducive to their usefulness." (quoted in Lathrop, *Educate a Woman*, p. xii).

54. *Progressive Farmer*, June 25, 1889; December 16, 1890.

55. Scott, *Southern Lady*, pp. 4-8.

56. *Progressive Farmer*, March 10, June 30, 1886; April 21, 1887; February 26, June 11, 1889; July 7, February 10, 1886; February 2, 1887; November 20, 1888; September 4, 1888; March 24, 1886.

57. *National Economist*, May 4, 1889. See also W. Scott Morgan, *History of the Wheel and Alli-*

ance and the Impending Revolution (Fort Scott: J. H. Rice & Sons, 1889), pp. 197-99; *Progressive Farmer*, June 2, 1886; September 4, 1888.

58. *Progressive Farmer*, January 19, 1887; June 30, 1886; June 5, 1888; February 28, 1888; December 8, 1886. For another southern view, see *National Economist*, June 14, 1890.

59. Dunning, *The Farmers' Alliance*, p. 257; Saloutos, *Farmer Movements*, p. 85.

60. *Progressive Farmer*, March 26, 1889.

61. *Progressive Farmer*, March 10, April 21, 1886. See *National Economist*, May 25, 1889, in which one of the Alabama Alliance's goals is to "adorn and beautify our homes, and render farm life more attractive."

62. *Progressive Farmer*, January 19, 1887; June 2, 1886; May 28, 1889; May 5, 1887. See also *The Sub-Alliance and What It Can Accomplish*, p. 6.

63. Richard H. Abbott, "The Agricultural Press Views the Yeoman: 1819-1859," *Agricultural History* 42 (January 1968): 35-48, suggests that historians have overestimated the importance of the myth of the yeoman farmer. See also, Muller, "New South Populism," p. 23; Paul. M. Gaston, *The New South Creed: A Study in Southern Mythmaking* (New York: Alfred A. Knopf, 1970), pp. 64-68, 107-108.

64. *National Economist*, April 5, 1889.

65. *Progressive Farmer*, January 12, 1888; May 12, July 7, October 13, 1886; September 15, 1887; November 20, 1888.

66. *Progressive Farmer*, November 10, 1887; *Minutes*, Farmers' State Alliance, August 11, 1892; *Progressive Farmer*, February 19, 1889.

67. *Progressive Farmer*, July 2, and April 21, 1887.

68. *Progressive Farmer*, March 2, 1887; December 8, 1886; July 28, 1887; December 3, 1889.

69. Mayo, "Southern Women," p. 170.

70. As Muller, "New South Populism," notes, p. 149, only men qualified as members of the elite.

71. *Progressive Farmer*, February 2, 1888. See Muller, "New South Populism," pp. 56-57, 177-85, for discussions of the social conservatism of Alliance leaders, pp. 104-105.

72. *Progressive Farmer*, September 22, 1891.

73. *Progressive Farmer*, June 3, September 16, December 23, 1890; July 7, December 15, 1891.

74. *Progressive Farmer*, November 4, 1890.

75. For suffrage discussions, see *National Economist*, March 1, July 12, October 18, October 25, 1890; March 5, November 12, December 24, 1892; January 21, February 18, March 11, 1893.

76. *Progressive Farmer*, September 15, 1891; December 3, 1889. There were occasionally other references to suffrage; see January 22, 1889, for example.

77. Quoted in Taylor, "Woman Suffrage," p. 46.

78. Saloutos, *Farmer Movements*, pp. 122-26; McMath, "Agrarian Protest," pp. 56-63.

79. Gerald Henderson Gaither, "Blacks and the Populist Revolt: Ballots and Bigotry in the New South (Ph.D. diss., University of Tennessee, 1972), pp. 151, 201-209; Gaston, *The New South*, pp. 38-39; J. Morgan Kousser, "The Shaping of Southern Politics: Suffrage Restriction and the Establishment of the One Party South, 1880-1910," (Ph.D. dissertation, Yale University, 1971), pp. 139-43; Guion Griffis Johnson, "The Ideology of White Supremacy, 1876-1910," in Fletcher Melvin Green, ed., *Essays in Southern History* (Chapel Hill, N.C.: University of North Carolina Press, 1949), p. 133.

Leon Fink

"Irrespective of Party, Color or Social Standing": The Knights of Labor and Opposition Politics in Richmond, Virginia

Labor reform political slates sprang up in hundreds of cities and towns across the United States in 1886–87, including at least 21 cities in eight southern states.[1] In Richmond, Virginia, following impressive economic victories by the Knights of Labor, a workingmen's ticket swept control of the municipal government in May, 1886 and went on confidently to challenge the Bourbon incumbents for Congress the coming fall. Success rested on the cooperation of disaffected white Democrats with black Republicans. Some observers felt that they were witnessing the beginning of a major political and social upheaval. Yet, on November's election day, no labor candidate appeared on the ballot and no more labor politics, to speak of, existed in Richmond.

Little is yet known about southern lower-class movements, black or white, in the Gilded Age. Recent political and social history, however, concentrated in local studies, suggests that the South was less "solid" than it once appeared. The new scholarship has challenged the view (to use Carl Degler's words) "that after the failure of Reconstruction meaningful experiments in the social order were finished . . . and that the aspirations of blacks were decisively thwarted." Nevertheless, the race question in Richmond and elsewhere proved a formidable obstacle to every political movement from below.[2]

* * *

Source: *Labor History* 19, no. 3 (Summer 1978): 325–49. Reprinted by permission of *Labor History*, original publisher and holder of copyright. Fink has restored a conclusion to the article which appears here for the first time. The author gratefully acknowledges the assistance and criticisms of Herbert Gutman, Susan Levine, Lawrence Goodwyn, David Montgomery, Eugene Genovese, Christopher Lasch, and Scott Ware in the preparation of this paper.

Richmond's post-war recovery, delayed by the panic of 1873, hit stride in the 1880s. A population climb from 63,600 to 81,388 over the decade, moderate by northern standards, accompanied a booming manufacturing product. The city's iron industry tripled in value and helped boost the state from sixteenth to seventh largest producer in the nation. Older industries including marble and stone quarries, flour mills, and boots and shoes also showed signs of growth. Most of all, however, Richmond prospered by the good fortune of King Tobacco. By 1885 its product more than tripled that of any other local trade in sales and value. The 1870s inaugurated a new branch of the tobacco industry: cigarettes. Of the latter Richmond produced three million in 1875 and 65 million six years later. By 1886 in the largest factory of its kind in the world, a thousand Richmond women and children turned out more than a million cigarettes a day. Peaking at 7300 employees around mid-decade, the tobacco work-force represented a quarter to a third of all those involved in local manufacturing.[3]

Socially, Richmond was two cities—one white, one black. Almost every area of social life indicated that white Richmond wished to distinguish itself from the more than 40 per cent of the population who were black. Following the briefest of Reconstruction periods, white officials had sought to confine black residency, social organization, and political power to the huge Jackson Ward, created in 1871 around the old free-Negro settlement area. By the late eighties official segregation in Richmond had reached the point that white and black children were walking to and from school on separate sides of the street. Howard Rabinowitz has demonstrated that even segregated access to municipal institutions was often an improvement over policies of total exclusion. But it took years, for example, before the city provided a park, adequate asylum, or almshouse for Jackson Ward.[4]

Nowhere were caste lines drawn more clearly than in the world of work. Only five per cent of the black male population in 1880 were self-employed, mainly hucksters and small food dealers; the rest were wage-earners. Indeed, the working-class population of the city was more black than white. Even within the manual working class, the racial distribution was striking. Four-fifths of the skilled workers were white; four-fifths of the unskilled work-force were black. If anything, the aggregate figures—masking the bunching of blacks in particular industries—underestimate the separateness of employment by race, the exclusion of blacks from whole categories of work, and the barriers to black occupational mobility.

The white norm of social "separatism" was most strictly enforced among women workers. White women represented less than a third of the female labor force. Even this minority, however, did not enter a general "female" labor market. More than half of all women's jobs were in domestic service, but 96 per cent of these were filled by blacks. The tobacco factories which employed large numbers of women of both races took special precautions. A visitor in 1879 did "not see any mixture of black and white women; that does not seem to be allowed."[5]

Black workers in the 1880s sought to preserve positions of employment and skill that they had occupied at Emancipation. Concentrated in the semiskilled, mass-production industries, they continued as a near labor monopoly in the tobacco trade. The only exceptions were the white skilled cigarmakers. The iron industry depended on blacks less exclusively. Since Joseph Anderson's successful experiments at the Tredegar works, blacks had provided the menial labor at the foundries, while whites generally took the more skilled, better-paid assignments as rollers and puddlers.[6]

Except for trades where free Negroes had established footholds before 1860, blacks were virtually excluded from the artisan crafts through 1890. The pattern of nearly total exclusion held for stonecutters, printers, machinists, cabinetmakers, and custom men's tailors. These crafts generally had organized early on the basis of tight control of entry. For example, not a single free-Negro machinist was found in 1860 (out of 161); only 13 (out of 462) black machinists were reported in 1890. In other skilled work including the building trades, blacksmithing, harness and saddle making, and coopering, blacks held on in varying degrees of strength to positions carved out years before through the urban employment of free Negroes and, to a lesser extent, of slaves. Black plasterers, for instance, dominated the trade in 1890 just as had free blacks in 1860. For skilled black craftsmen in general, however, the trend was indicated in the estimate of apprentices in 1890—212 whites, 24 blacks.[7]

The relative prosperity of Richmond's basic industries was especially good news to building workers and others for whose talents the city's general expansion and accumulated wealth brought increased demand. As in other sections of the country, organized, skilled Richmond workers wasted little time in taking advantage of the upswing following the trough of recession in 1885. More strikes occurred in Richmond in 1886 than in the previous five years. Of ten work stoppages in 1886–87, nine were offensive actions by craft workers for increased pay or reduced hours. Seven succeeded.[8]

The improved standing of the skilled tradesmen, particularly the building and iron workers, furnished a head of steam to the Knights of Labor, which they had recently joined. On one level the Knights represented a popular protest against the consequences of America's particular road to industrialism. Resting on the republican ideology of earlier reform movements, the Knights envisioned self-governing communities of self-respecting citizens, dedicated to productive work, sturdy families, and rational self-improvement. Much in the emerging Gilded Age landscape interfered with that vision. In the Knights eyes, the increasing concentration of capital depressed artisans into a wage-earning class and corrupted the "independence" of America's political institutions. Legislators and judges had surrendered the powers of their offices to the private purposes of money and privilege, and lawyers had effectively obfuscated political procedures from the common people, producers of the nation's wealth. To regain their democratic birthright, the producing classes—an elastic concept that excluded only bankers, lawyers, and saloonkeepers—required education (an argument for fewer hours, public schools, and support of the Knights of Labor), self-discipline (and therefore temperance), and collective independence from wage slavery (and thus cooperatives).

The Order showed greatest practical effect at the local level where labor activists added dimensions which often made their national leaders uneasy. Seeking to extend their power both within and outside the workplace, the Knights in practice sometimes resembled a city central labor union engaged in disciplined strikes and boycotts. By the same token, the realities of power sometimes dictated partisan political action, even in violation of the Order's "principled" opposition to such activity.

Jubilant Richmond participants watched "hundreds flocking in" to join the "revival of the Knights of Labor" as early as June, 1885. That summer the Order opened to black recruits; twelve "colored assemblies" formed in one two-week period alone. By the end of 1886, more than 35 local assemblies had been chartered in Richmond and Manchester (South Richmond). Contemporary estimates placed membership, arranged in two racially distinct district assemblies, around 7,000 with an overall distribution of four blacks to three whites. That a printer-editor and a tobacco engineer served as officers of the white district while a tobacco roller, a porter, and a dairyman provided leadership to the blacks, suggested the distinct social as well as racial bases brought together in one organization.[9]

By mid-1886 the Knights were a powerful local force. A general boycott of convict-made barrels in January removed them from the local market; within weeks the very threat of a boycott speedily brought wholesalers of all other prison-made products into line. Only one cigar firm remained non-union by mid-March. By May several large tobacco factories became "purely Knights of Labor." At least one granted the eight-hour day, and women cigarette makers added Progress Assembly to a list of six or seven other "lady locals." Indicative of the Order's spreading influence were the September efforts of a committee of businessmen to mediate a three-month boycott of the city's single non-union printing firm. The businessmen sought compromise on all matters of grievance, even accepting the legitimacy of the direct boycott if only the Knights would suspend their secondary "rat list." The Richmond Knights graced their work with a lecture series and performances of their own dramatics company. They also opened a cooperative soap factory and laid plans for a building association and underwear firm.[10]

Flushed with new-found strength the Knights turned to politics. Bourbon Democracy had held an easy sway in Richmond since Reconstruction. Even the Readjuster rebellion of 1879–1883 against the Bourbon commitment to full repayment of the war debt made little headway in the state's capitol city. Local power brokers, "the ring," regularly handpicked candidates for the

Democratic primary, and marched over any and all opposition. Normally, only black Jackson Ward escaped the ring's political hegemony. Perhaps it was the margin of its victories which lulled the ring into temporary somnolence. In any case it had made few overtures to the increasingly organized labor movement. Democratic candidates remained nearly all self-employed businessmen or professionals. The Bourbon Congressman, attorney George D. Wise, breathed condescension toward the workingmen whose votes he took for granted. In addition, the construction of a new city hall, eagerly awaited by building craftsmen and day laborers alike, had languished for four years in Democratic wranglings over alternate proposals and contracts.[11]

In April, 1886 white Knights of Labor moved against the "edicts of ring rule" by separating themselves from the local machinery of the Democratic Party. A convention of delegates from white District 84 authorized abstention from the April primary and fielded its own Reform slate of candidates for the May municipal election.[12]

The Reformers generally attacked the incumbent Common Council for addressing only the interests of the "wealthy class," "looking on those who earn their living by labor as secondary." Specifically, they demanded that the new city hall be built by Richmond mechanics on day labor with Virginia granite (the Knights had secured a foothold in the neighboring quarries), elimination of the contract system for city projects, and weekly cash payments to municipal employees. Condemning politically-appointed supervisory personnel, the Reformers scored "those who are required to do comparatively nothing and whose time seems to be their own . . . while those who work hard and receive nothing are watched by paid overseers and docked for 10 minutes time lost." Only a "cleaning out of the legislative departments of our city government" could correct these "class and partisan" evils. Finally the opposition platform appealed for "a general understanding and cooperation of the toiling masses, irrespective of party, color, or social standing." The weekly *Labor Herald*, edited by district master workman William Mullen, spearheaded the Reform campaign.[13]

The workingmen's political movement, like its parent organization the Knights of Labor, drew support from a broad social spectrum. Generally speaking, only the financial-industrial elite and the professional stratum were absent from Reform ranks. Workingmen's candidates for city council and board of aldermen were overwhelmingly skilled workers and small shopkeepers. Still, the Knights apparently weighed the sympathy and influence of their candidates as well as social position. Two iron manufacturers and a tobacco company manager, for example, were rewarded as "honorable" (compliant) employers with Reform endorsements. All but two of the Reform candidates had been long-time Democrats.[14]

If the white Reform movement drew a cross-section of support, its working-class core was itself heterogeneous. The prominence of names like Kaufman, Kaufeldt, Kelly, Lange, Molloy, Murphy, Parrish, and Pearce among the labor candidates suggest an ethnic as well as a class component to the disaffection from Bourbonism. To be sure, it is difficult to disentangle the immigrant from the working people of Richmond. Although only five per cent of the city's 1880 population was foreign-born, first and second-generation immigrants composed one-fourth of skilled white artisans and nearly one-third of white unskilled laborers. During the eighties the city supported daily German-language newspapers as well as two branches of the Irish National League.[15]

Blacks in Richmond held the greatest significance for the white Reformers. No accidental flourish of egalitarian rhetoric accounted for the Reformers' address to men of a different "party, color, or social standing." Rather, it was a matter of political necessity. Despite obstacles thrown in their path, black voters mobilized through the Republican party remained a formidable electoral bloc in Richmond. The arch-Bourbon *Dispatch* complained, "the typical black recognized the white Democrats as his friends during 364 days of the year. On the remaining day he is a Republican." In September, 1886 all potential voters were required to re-register within a period of only six days. To the dismay of the political establishment, blacks still managed to register a considerably greater proportion of their eligible numbers than whites, enrolling a potential 40 per cent of the electorate. Before the spring elections Richmond's white insurgents had come to terms with the black Republicans. Reformers deferred to the Republican slate in Jackson Ward and in return secured a Republican endorsement of their ticket in the rest of the city.[16]

The local Republican Party was directed by white political managers in conjunction with a group of Negro officeholders. "Boss" John S. Wise, a lawyer with important northern business connections and son of one of the state's most popular antebellum governors, had established his credentials alongside the Readjuster leader and railroad king, General William Mahone. Mahone's tenure as governor, particularly his abolition of the poll tax and educational spending for both races, had drawn him into increasingly bitter confrontation with conservative party chieftains, until finally he had bolted into the Republican Party in 1883, taking John Wise and other Readjusters with him. As a Republican John Wise proved a formidable political renegade losing a close race for governor in 1885. Besides boss Wise and a few other Republican men of standing, the party depended on Irish and German "grocers" whose grogshops served as centers of social and political influence in Jackson Ward. James H. Bahen, who had fought for the Union before settling in Richmond, was the single most powerful of these early ward heelers. For their part black Republicans dominated the party's municipal slates. This office-seeking group generally derived from the upper ranks of the Negro social ladder—the professional sector whose numbers could be counted on one hand, "businessmen" (grocers, barbers, and contractors), and skilled artisans. Tightly knit into the institutional fabric of the community, the black political leadership received strong support from ministers of the city's eighteen black churches.[17]

Probably the most important Republican organ in Richmond from the mid-eighties through the turn of the century was the weekly *Planet*, edited by John Mitchell, Jr. Born a slave in 1863, the young Mitchell turned to publishing after being dismissed along with three other black school principals in 1884. Mitchell's *Planet* emerged from the short-lived Readjuster ascendancy as a beacon of proud, defiant black Republicanism. It offered character sketches of leading citizens, boosted black candidates and business enterprises, and urged armed self-defense against southern lynchings.[18]

A querulous yet enduring unity prevailed between the black and white sections of the Republican Party. As early as 1870 the Jackson Ward organization had protested an all-white local ticket, and in 1880 it demanded that patronage be expanded beyond a narrow "Custom's House clique." Notwithstanding the internal tug-of-war for influence, black political leaders and constituents remained solidly Republican. A Bahen-Mitchell axis with ties to John S. Wise effectively beat back all opposition for control of the party in the 1880s.[19]

Within Richmond the black Republican presence immediately threatened the ruling party should white ranks ever split. Just such a coincidence of events had powered the Readjusters' success on a statewide scale. For the first time in Richmond a similar possibility had suddenly emerged in 1886, and the protagonist of the earlier contest did not hesitate to apply his winning strategy again. State Republican Chairman William Mahone seized the occasion of a local prohibition referendum in April to work some mischief in the "citadel of Bourbonism." A personal letter from Mahone, displayed "where it would do the most good," helped to spark an overwhelming defense of local licensing, with an estimated 95 per cent of the black vote contributing to the majority. This victory of the "wet" constituency represented the first electoral setback for the local Bourbons since the War. The vulnerability of the party patriarchs was not lost on their enemies; the referendum provided a direct stimulus to the Knights of Labor effort a month later. Ironically, the Knights and the Republicans—both associated nationally with strong temperance positions—enlisted the whiskey interests in their local political brew.[20]

The spring Reform campaign was capped by resounding victory. Workers trooped to the polls and carried all but one ward for the labor-Republican ticket. Reformers gained a clear majority of the city council, half the board of aldermen, as well as the city sergeant, the one contested executive office. On election day excitement ran high, fights broke out, the crowds paraded through the streets at midnight. Mahone received a gleeful Richmond report: "We had a slight volcanic eruption here on Thursday last . . . at which time all nature seemed convulsed. And all indications point to further upheavals during the year." The *Dispatch* referred to the city's "first disaster since Reconstruction days."[21]

But this initial success caused almost as much alarm within Reform ranks as among conservative Democrats. White workingmen had stepped outside the Democracy and extended a tentative hand to black Republicans to beat the Bourbons. How far should they carry this apostasy? Some of the Reformers began to take themselves seriously as an independent political force. Others balked at cutting themselves off from their traditional political guardians. Important differences of opinion also surfaced among Republicans. Mahone urged a delicate, cooperative stance towards the Reformers, but local party leaders, including John Wise, were more anxious to convert the Democratic loss to quick Republican gain. Black political leaders in turn took a wary *quid pro quo* attitude towards the Democrats-cum-insurgents. In a lead editorial entitled, "What Will Be Done For Our People?" the *Planet* demanded immediate returns in the form of jobs at the colored almshouse, appointment of a black physician, and representation in all other areas of city employment. By the second meeting of the Reform caucus, twelve whites had withdrawn to protest the outspoken presence of the Jackson Ward councilmen who had taken up the *Planet's* call.[22]

Black Republicans did not get their way with the caucus, but John Wise more or less did. Wise had been careful not to show his hand too early: "I saw that they [the Reformers] were without leadership, and wanted them to become thoroughly confused, knowing that when that occurred they would be grateful to any one who could pilot them, whereas, an earlier interference might breed resistance or a feeling of resentment." The appropriate moment of chaos finally arrived among "Reformers" and "darkies." Wise then stepped between the feuding parties and quickly secured agreements from William Mullen and Henry L. Carter, coopers' leader, to a package of compromises on municipal appointments quite favorable to Republican interests.[23]

Unfortunately for the Reform strategists, by the time they settled down to business, they had lost their council majority. With astute diplomacy "straight-out" Democrats had met repentant insurgents in a "spirit of conciliation." In addition, the Regulars had not opposed the nomination of a Reformer for city council president, effectively encouraging him to act as a non-partisan legislative steward. Finally, several Democratic officeholders had declined reappointment to allow "loyal" Knights of Labor to take their places. A Knights of Labor tinner thereby became fire department chief, and an Irishman nominated initially by the Reformers was unanimously supported for police court bailiff. But Reform choices generally were thwarted by successive 29 to 18 decisions of a joint meeting of the local legislative bodies. Four black members of the Reform coalition, which numbered 22 at full strength, withheld their votes from the caucus nominees in a gesture of pique. While Reformers still voted together more often than not, the record for the remainder of the year indicated that the initial frustrations had permanently wrecked caucus discipline.[24]

The post-election setbacks, however, only strengthened the independent political tendencies within the main body of the Knights. By August they were preparing to choose their own candidate for Congress. Not only had the Order been pushed further toward creation of an independent political party, but the momentum of events had strengthened ties between the politically-minded white locals and the black district assembly. Unlike the white-organized April movement, all locals were now invited to join the Labor Reform Committee. Names submitted to the nominating convention included Mullen, John Wise, Henry Carter, and John Bethel, city council president. With seven-tenths of his votes coming from blacks, Mullen easily captured the nomination.[25]

Contemporaries disagreed about the character of William Mullen. A confident, thirty-six-year-old Virginian, he seemed equally dedicated to his ideals and his ambition. An admirer of Henry George, Mullen nevertheless had always toed a firm Democratic line in politics. He had derided a political alliance of Richmond workingmen with liquor dealers in 1877 but had overseen the creation of just such an alliance in 1886. On the race issue as well, Mullen's principles appeared sturdiest when coupled with self-fulfillment. In 1884 Mullen had sought a local patronage appointment from the Cleveland Administration; rumor had it that he had boasted at the time of turning "the d——d Republicans and d——d Negroes out." But as a Knights' organizer, Mullen pressed vigorously for black enrollment. Mullen did not appear uncomfortable with the Republican-abolitionist heritage of the national labor reform organization. Before the 1885 general assembly, he had presented Powderly with a gravel made of three symbolic pieces of wood. The first came from the hall of Patrick Henry's "Give me liberty" address; the second was cut from a tree at Yorktown, the scene of Cornwallis' surrender to Washington; the third derived from Old Libby prison where "patriotic sons of our common country," as Mullen explained, "were confined . . . for being engaged in a struggle to liberate a race of people from the galling yoke of slavery." The Civil War, according to Mullen, had been America's "second Revolution"; he passed the gavel to "the chief of that grand army that is to work the third revolution," the liberation of "slaves of monopoly and oppression." The Order seemed to lift Mullen to his most generous sentiments and vision; for several years it practically consumed his attention. Powderly's choice of Richmond for the site of the Knights Tenth General Assembly, scheduled for October 1886, represented, in part, a tribute to his southern field marshal.[26]

Mullen's nomination for Congress precipitated a major realignment within the city's opposition forces. The Jefferson Ward Tammany Reform Club, spearheaded the Mullen campaign, arranging speakers, marches, and music. But seven anti-Mullen local assemblies, including the tinners' union, proclaimed themselves the "Democratic Knights of Labor." Two of the prominent figures in the Democratic Knights, both leaders of the typographers, had been indicted with Mullen and others in the case of the city-wide boycott of the non-union printer. Charges in the case were ultimately dismissed. It is possible that legal harassment or influence-peddling played some role in defections from the independent ticket.[27]

A more important deserter from the labor candidacy was John S. Wise.

Having been rejected as labor nominee, Wise had decided that Republicans should not go "whoring around after a lot of tramps who have no following and no principles." While publicly avowing neutrality, he privately urged Republicans to place their own candidate in the field. Republican Judge Edmund Waddill Jr., making common cause with Wise, passed along word to Mahone that "but three white men in our party [were] in favor of endorsing Mullen." The General, who had opposed a divisive partisan gathering and who was still offering encouragement to Mullen's emissary, finally withdrew his veto of the scheduled Republican convention.[28]

Approaching their October 2 conclave, Republicans split bitterly around the labor candidacy. Pro-Mullen Colored Independence Campaign Clubs opposed Regular Henrico County Republicans at each ward caucus. Anti-Mullen sentiment came from white Republicans looking to John Wise for leadership, black postal and customs house workers of federal patronage, and rural blacks untouched by the labor movement. Mullen's only reported white supporters within the party were Alderman Rowland Hill, a carpenter, and shipjoiner Dan Alley—most likely both Knights of Labor. Mullen's twenty-odd black delegates included a carpenter, a blacksmith, a plasterer, a wood and coal merchant, a saloonkeeper, and two grocers. The rest were identified in the city directories as "laborers."[29]

Even if less dramatically than among the feuding white Democrats, class differences marked the black Republican fissure. Perhaps with one or two exceptions, the blacks now pushing for power within the Republican party were not people who had figured prominently in earlier political affairs. They did not come from the tiny professional group whose dependence on governmental favor encouraged their remaining stalwart party men. On the whole they did not meet James T. Moore's categorization of Negro politicians as the "emerging middle class" of the black community. Instead, it appears that the labor movement helped to prepare or embolden a new leadership group among some Richmond blacks. Such a group overlapped in social roots with the traditional leadership, but it also represented a shift in influence toward the laboring poor.[30]

Pro-Mullen Republicans did not prevail over the party brass. Adverse rulings from the credentials committee and a hostile chair depleted the insurgents' strength, and after a spirited floor fight, Judge Waddill emerged as the Republican standard-bearer for November. Sheriff Southward, presenting himself as a Knight of Labor who had "boycotted every one Mullen blacklisted even though he lived in the county," issued the official proscription of the labor candidate; the sheriff assailed the master workman for his temperance proclivities ("a milk and cider man"), for refusing to campaign openly for Republican favor, and for lack of commitment to "national issues," meaning that Mullen had not endorsed the high tariff.[31]

Despite the division in opposition ranks, no one counted Mullen out. The

Dispatch accorded him good odds for election. Mahoneite Republicans, still trying to arrange a last-minute compromise with the labor men, were even more emphatic. They believed John Wise and Edmund Waddill had committed "political suicide." A Petersburg paper warned, "The labor element will dominate *both* parties henceforth, and gentlemen who rashly incur the animosity of those elements may as well get out of politics as soon as possible."[32]

Tensions mounted in Richmond with the approach of the federal election. Even the Democratic majority on the Common Council had accommodated to demands of the new political forces, and multiple signs of labor influence drew harsh reaction from the city's old guard. In early September "A Taxpayer" complained, "Will a man who is not a Knight of Labor be allowed to work on the City Hall?" A howl of disapproval followed news that public works employees had received a wage boost allegedly "50% above the market place."[33]

The shift in tone in the city's politics was most clearly illustrated by the deflated influence of the Chamber of Commerce. Holding a public meeting to aid the Charlestown, S.C., victims of the earthquake which struck the Southeast on August 31, the businessmen (apparently acting according to custom) decided on an appropriate amount for relief, determined that it must be taken from the public treasury ("the fairest and most equitable method"), then approached the city government for ratification. The city council, approving its own contribution, refused even to consider the Chamber's resolution. "As a representative of the people," Democrat Andrew Pizzini explained, "[he] did not require the Chamber of Commerce to tell him his duty."[34]

To its critics the reform movement had grown ominously larger than life. It no longer expressed particular grievances but seemed bent on a redistribution of political power. Conservatives worried that the Reformers "have become more partisan in the support of class doctrines and the demand for class legislation than they ever were as members of the Democratic and Republican parties." More disquieting still was the possibility that the Richmond movement was only a link in a chain of political and industrial insurrection slowly encircling the nation. With one eye on Henry George in New York and the other on Mullen at home, the *Whig* uncovered "socialistic and agrarian elements" threatening the "genius of our free institutions." In late September, a local merchant despaired of "this terrible social earthquake." Evoking "the scenes enacted at Pittsburg[h] in 1875 (or thereabouts)," he pointed to "what has actually been done in our own city during the past twelve months. Think of the boldness, the insolence, and some of the leaders of this fearful movement." By the time the Tenth General Assembly of the Knights opened in Richmond even Democratic Governor Fitzhugh Lee was trying to steer the emerging southern labor movement into calmer waters. Addressing the first session of the Knights convention on October 3, the governor expressed general agreement with the "original" aims of the Order. But, in pointed reference to events in the host city, he underscored General Master Workman Powderly's "assertion that the

Knights of Labor would never be a political party . . ." and asserted "There has always been and always will be two great political parties. Room has never been found for a third. . . . Let us follow your chief's advice and keep politics out [of the Order]."[35]

The general assembly and its attendant racial "events" caught the political process in Richmond at both a revealing and decisive moment. To be brief, the events included a direct attack on the color line by District Assembly 49 of New York and its black delegate Frank Ferrell. This pointed, crusading show of principle spread with the initial support of Powderly to encompass many other northerners among the 800 delegates. Virginians were shocked by the sight of Ferrell following Governor Lee to the podium to reaffirm the Order's commitment to the "abolition of distinctions maintained by creed and color," by inter-racial delegations inhabiting their hotels, and especially by the mixed company in public of men and women of the opposite race. The Bourbon press excoriated the Knights for their display of "social equality in its richest phase."[36]

A showdown came midway through the convention. Invited by the visiting Shakespearian actor Daniel Bandmann to a performance of *Hamlet*, Ferrell and sixty other members of DA 49 took orchestra seats at the Mozart Academy. This breach of the traditional gallery-only restriction on Negroes, coming as it did at the city's most fashionable concert hall, nearly led to violence. The next day, the local Law and Order League, formed to protect businesses from labor boycotts and containing "the best families in the city," had its members "armed and ready for bloodshed" in the event of further depredations of the city's cultural monuments. Shouts of "Coons and Forty Niners" were heard in the streets. Heeding the warnings of police chief Thomas Poe, Powderly quickly moved to avert calamity. The general master workman promised *de facto* compliance with the local social code and exacted a similar pledge from DA 49. An uneasy truce prevailed for the duration of the convention.[37]

The "social equality" issue pointed to the dilemma of the Knights of Labor in the South. Crusading egalitarianism mixed uneasily with practical considerations of the Order's survival and growth. Massachusetts' delegate and labor editor Frank Foster reflected the ambivalence within the general assembly over how far to push an issue like racial equality. Foster believed that "perhaps a little too much of this color line question" had been agitated for the Order's own good: "Still, our southern brethren must learn. . . ."[38]

Southern white Knights of Labor greeted the practical application of "equality" doctrines by the general assembly with varying degrees of resentment. In Augusta the Richmond "events" set off "near panic" among striking Georgia textile workers already aroused by rumors of the importation of black strikebreakers. In addition an Oxford, North Carolina, master workman reported that "disregard of the 'color line' " by the general assembly alongside local political gains by Republicans had set off a wave of recriminations against the order: "They pointed at us with scorn and kept crying 'Nigger! Nigger!' until the two words 'nigger' and Knight became almost synonymous terms." That happened even though the Oxford mayor and ex-mayor were Knights; as a consequence the Order suffered a serious loss of support there. Augusta and Oxford constituted extreme reactions, but the likely fallout from the race issue was not lost on the southern convention delegates. White southerners successfully steered a resolution through the assembly specifying that the Order had no intention "to disrupt the social relations . . . in various parts of the country." At the last moment the Knights' executive board cancelled a fancy-dress ball in deference to southern opposition to mixed social gatherings. Local white Knights of Labor shared in the opposition to any attempt "to build a new social fabric during a two-week visit." While no mass exodus was recorded, a New York *Times* correspondent noted "a storm of indignation and a new hesitancy by whites in their relation to the order." One reporter heard that "a few" local Knights intended to quit the Order to join the Law and Order League."[39]

A different response was accorded the gestures of the general assembly by Richmond blacks. The white supremacy press turned up only a solitary black voice, an unnamed out-of-town delegate, to protest the "stirring up of the race issue at the convention." More typical reactions were readily apparent. Local black families threw open their homes to mixed delegations of Knights refused lodging at white-only hotels. Enthusiasm was undisguised. A wealthy white woman complained nervously that since the convention had opened, "her colored cook and servant have been trifling and inclined to be impudent." A labor parade and day of festivities heralded the mid-point of the convention. White Richmond citizens symbolically avoided the activities, but blacks turned out in force. One correspondent believed the "the entire colored population of Richmond" was present along the parade route, "including a few colored women in carriages." Two blacks and a white served as the parade marshalls. The *Whig* found in the procession more than a good-humored throng of three thousand marchers: "It was a small army of workingmen, white and black, animated by a common purpose, and marching under a common flag. It was the outward manifestation of a great movement, yet in its incipiency perhaps, the ultimate results of which only the revolving years can reveal."[40]

Richmond blacks reserved their boldest gestures for those most responsible for the provocative racial events. As the general assembly neared its end, a banquet was held in honor of DA 49 in the Negro hall above Harris's funeral parlor. The occasion seemed to signal a semi-official and non-partisan expression of gratitude to the New Yorkers and their friends by leaders of the local black community. Carefully tempering with words an act that doubtlessly infuriated the city's patriarchs, "each one of the colored orators" dismissed the social equality question "in good set terms." Said Republican District

Attorney Walter Scott, a Yale Law School graduate: "The only social equality that had ever existed had been thrust upon them by whites." As if to underscore the refutation of any interest in racial amalgamation black women did not attend the banquet. While the blacks painstakingly tailored their public words, the response to New York socialist Victor Drury's address was uncensored. Reported one newspaper: "He said that what Forty-Eight was to the oppressed millions of Europe, it was hoped Forty-Nine might be to the struggling masses of Americans in this day, and this play upon words and reference to a red-letter period of the revolutionary spirit nearly forty years ago abroad were received with cheers."[41]

Cleavage between whites and blacks on the equality issue at the general assembly created an immediate impact upon local politics. A Virginia organizer protested to Powderly, that the racial events had done "great injury . . . to our labor candidate for Congress." The southern version of the bloody shirt, with its appeal to the deepest of race loyalties, wreaked havoc on the independent campaign. In attempting to sidestep the race issue—appealing to both whites and blacks solely on class terms—Mullen himself permitted both of his opponents to cast him in the worst possible light. Ten days before the November 2 election, Democrats revealed positive evidence of Mullen's sympathy "with what '49' had done." In the company of one black and one white campaign associate near the Goochland County courthouse, Mullen had sat down at the refreshment stand of Martha Cousins, "an old colored woman." When, according to custom, she refused to serve the mixed party at the same table, Mullen reportedly had risen and indignantly turned away with his friends, vowing to take his supper elsewhere. The "Goochland courthouse" incident soon was picked up by Republicans as well—only with a different twist. At a Waddill rally John Wise claimed that the story had not ended with Mullen's declaration of principle. Rather, "half an hour afterwards Mullen shook his colored friend and sneaked back to the stand and bought a pie." Wise warned his audience, "you see how he went back on the negro there, don't you? and if you vote for him he will fool you."[42]

The campaign's direction pushed Mullen permanently onto the defensive. Democratic orators reviled Mullen as a secret Republican agent intent on the ruin of the South, while Democratic councilmen passed election-eve wage increases to selected city workers and Congressman Wise offered a smile of friendship to the Knights of Labor. The Republican campaign apparatus was also in high gear and operated smoothly above and below ground. Expecting whites to split their votes, Waddill promised a glorious victory if blacks remained solid. Meanwhile, organized disruptions made it increasingly difficult for Mullen to venture into Jackson Ward. The highlight of the labor campaign was a march and rally of fifteen hundred supporters, mostly blacks. But it was nearly broken up by black hecklers organized by John S. Wise. By the end of October, both the *Dispatch* and the *Whig* were marvelling at the Republicans' effectiveness: "Two or three weeks ago all the Negroes were said to be for Mullen. Today they are said to be for Waddill."[43]

The heated congressional campaign came to a quick and unexpected end. At the decision of his campaign committee, Mullen dropped out of the race and threw his support to the Democrat George Wise "to kill Waddill, [J. S.] Wise, and Co., the deadliest enemies of the Reform party." In a bitter message to his followers, the ex-candidate explained that the Republican county leaders had first induced him to run then had "switched their minds and effectively sabotaged his campaign." In Mullen's mind both the party's chiefs and its rank and file bore the onus for his dashed hopes: "While this is slander on those of our colored brethren who have stood firm, a sufficient number have gone over to make our success doubtful. They have permitted themselves to be whipped into line by the party lash and are alone responsible for the defeat of the labor candidate." The mere likelihood of defeat, by transforming the "independent" third political alternative into a broker for one of the old parties, had created an impossible situation for the biracial ticket. "As workingmen," argued Mullen, "we cannot afford to assume . . . responsibility for taking a Democratic district and putting it in the hands of the Republican party."[44]

With only slightly less vituperation, Mahone Republicans concurred in the verdict of the labor leader. "Our friends ran the labor people back into the Democratic camp," C. C. Clark wrote to Mahone. "I voted for Judge Waddill of course—through party fealty as well as personal friendship—but it was like casting the ballot in [the] James River—his defeat was a foregone conclusion after Mullen withdrew—and Mullen's withdrawal was also a foregone conclusion after they brought out a candidate against him and then abused him like a pickpocket." The black grocer, Colin Payne, who had resigned from the Republican city committee after Waddill's nomination, revealed that black Republicans were "very much divided" by the election. "The laboring men thinks it was done to defeat them and something have to be done to homonize [sic] our party."[45]

Republican strategy in the fall campaign was bitterly disputed for years afterwards. John Wise would cling to the view that the party would have enjoyed a pure, uncompromised triumph had Mullen not hung on until he received an unspecified "deal" from the Democrats. Defeat in the Third Congressional District stimulated an escalating disaffection between Wise and Mahone, leading to an open break in 1888. As late as 1890 Mullen's black aide, J. T. Wilson, was still fulminating against John Wise as "a man who had come as a Moses and betrayed us." By the time Wilson spoke, Wise had already left town. Counsel for the first electric street railroad in Richmond, he moved to New York City to represent numerous urban transit companies.[46]

A period of demoralization, distrust, and recrimination followed immediately upon the Mullen fiasco in labor circles. The campaign that had begun with such bright prospects "had not been advantageous to the order here," according to one Richmond Knight. Politically, the labor bubble had burst. On the Common Council, swing voters, recalculating where the political future lay, snuggled back among Conservative Democrats. In its first meeting since the election, the council excluded black mechanics from work on the city hall. Only a black councilman opposed the move. At the same time labor's bid to restrict the construction project to local workers and apprentices was rejected. In April, 1887 the council elected with labor votes heard a protest from Mullen and boilermaker J. P. Devine that workers who had shown "reform" sympathies on election day in 1886 later had been frozen out of city jobs. Collapse of labor's political power was evident in Devine's pleadings: "We didn't come here as a big railroad corporation, in royal array, we are but poor workingmen. I have just laid down my hammer. We represent the sons and daughters of men who are strewn over your battlefields." Within months of his aborted candidacy, Mullen was finding it difficult to get work. Within a year he had suspended publication of the *Labor Herald*, and in 1889 Powderly learned that Mullen had been dropped as master workman in an internal reorganization of the Richmond district. By the time of the biennial municipal elections of May, 1888, the Reform movement in Richmond politics had vanished.[47]

Local circumstances combined with influences affecting the Order elsewhere to drive the Richmond Knights of Labor into steady decline. A white iron-molder reported succinctly in March 1888, "the order here is not holding its own." As aggressive, class-based organizations of workingmen fell away, a few, more conservative adaptations to the industrial order rose to take their place. In mid-1888, for example, the YMCA established an educational program aimed specifically at Tredegar iron workers. The same period marked the reappearance of the Colored Mercantile Association, a group set up to sell stock in land for homes and businesses "instead of allowing the best land . . . to pass into the hands of white foreigners." The *Dispatch* noted that the Association had been founded "two or three years ago . . . but just at that time the Knights of Labor excitement started. The originators decided to let this movement rest until the labor agitation quieted somewhat."[48]

For Richmond's blacks the late 1880s onward were increasingly desperate years. With a new vehemence, Bourbons preached total exclusion of blacks from public office. Facing additional impediments, nearly two thousand fewer blacks in Richmond voted in Mahone's 1889 losing bid for Governor than in the legislative election two years previously. In 1890, despite local black protest, the Republican Party did not field a congressional candidate in the Third District. At the Colored Men's Convention of that year, after the final defeat in Washington of the Force Bill, J. T. Wilson raged, "We saved the National Government from dissolution to be treated as orphan children, apprenticed to the rice, cotton, and tobacco growers of the South." In 1896 the first all-white Common Council since the War took office in Richmond, and the year 1902 witnessed the official disfranchisement of Virginia blacks.[49]

Nevertheless, even in this period of decline, there remained glimmerings of the common aspirations which had surfaced in 1886. George Duncan, then master workman of white D.A. 84, filed a complaint against harassment of Jackson Ward voters by Democratic poll-watchers in the fall of 1888. His petition led ultimately to the seating of the persistent Republican candidate, Edmund Waddill, by the U.S. Congress. A Knights of Labor newspaper backed Mahone in 1889. Three years later only fraud prevented a Populist victory in the Fourth Congressional District. In 1888 this same district had elected the black Republican John Mercer Langston to Congress. As late as 1895, Terence Powderly received a letter from organizer W. T. Booze, asking him to allow ninety black men and women from Richmond to form a local. The evidence suggests that the core of the Knights which survived into the 1890s had finally moved into a close working relationship with the state Republican Party. Only now, the Order no longer represented a movement vying for power, but a lonely legion of dissenters.[50]

The Knights of Labor loomed in the mid-1880s as a beacon of racial enlightenment in a dark sea. Never, however, were the Knights so foolish as to think that the past had been overcome. The white master workman of Natchez, Mississippi, was hopeful of organizing women cotton operatives. He warned Powderly, however, that "the Colored race for the present at least had better be formed into separate assemblies." A black master workman from Montgomery, Alabama, delicately explained to the national leader, "As a general thing the colored people of the South cannot understand the whites and the white organizer cannot do just what is necessary for the up-building of the order." From Florence, S.C., the message was more blunt, "Our white Brothers down South is not eager to organize the Negro Race, thats why we appeal to you for a colored organizer."[51]

Black embrace of the Knights of Labor was neither uncritical nor unlimited. The Washington *Bee*, for example, warned the Order to put its resolutions "into practical form before we would advise colored people to go too far." T. Thomas Fortune, the editor of *The Freeman* and a strong pro-labor voice, chided Powderly for having pulled back on the race issue at the end of the general assembly "in craven deference to the yell of the Southern white press and the demands of Southern Knights of Labor."[52]

The record indicates that the Knights had not organized many blacks in the South; rather, blacks had adopted the Knights. No other conclusion makes sense given the lightning-like speed of formation of black assemblies in Richmond in 1885 and in other parts of the South. With black workers as with other groups in labor history, the image of movement from "the unorganized" to "the organized" may sometimes misrepresent the situation. Richmond black workers had organized as early as 1867 into benefit societies with names like the Stevedores and Waggoners Association, Baley factory hands, and Union Laboring Class. During the late 1860s and early 1870s organized strikes were conducted by Negro stevedores, coopers, railroad construction laborers, and waiters. Workingmen expressed themselves through various instruments. Thirty black laborers petitioned the federal government in 1885 for back pay due them in "services rendered" in 1865. Their agent of persuasion then was Mahone and the resources of the state Republican Party. When black Richmond D.A. 92 was formed, we must suppose the reality to have been in part a shading of existing community organization into the new structure.[53]

To be sure, there was "organizing" to be carried out among black workers, in the classic sense of education, persuasion, and agitation. Yet, the equal-rights doctrines of the labor organization did not by themselves induce whites to expand their area of contact and cooperation with black workers. The calculation of Paul Chotier, Morgan City, Louisiana, master workman "that the Colored Laborers should be organized in this place as it will work detrimental to us if not taken in," suggests that necessity was often the handmaiden of progress. C. Vann Woodward has offered an analytic framework for Chotier's opinion:

> Two possible but contradictory policies could be used by the labor movement towards the Black worker: eliminate the Negro as a competitor by excluding him from the skilled trades either as an apprentice or as a worker, or take him in as an organized worker committed to the defense of a common standard of wages. Southern labor wavered between these antithetical policies from the seventies into the nineties, sometimes adopting one, sometimes the other.[54]

Accepting that Woodward's alternate poles of economic logic mark the long-term dilemma of the labor movement, one might question whether they describe the real options usually encountered in the late nineteenth century. The tentative, precarious relations of southern white and black workers assumed numerous intermediary positions, each with distinct degrees and limits of cooperation. If blacks and whites were not actively competing for the same jobs, choices might present themselves as other than full economic partnership *versus* total exclusion. In Richmond white Knights need not have greeted blacks directly as competitors *or* as brothers. The unskilled black laborer or factory operative posed little threat to the skilled white worker, especially during a period of local economic expansion. No self-interested white worker would have called for exclusion of blacks from the tobacco trade, the city's productive dynamo.

The relative absence of direct economic friction left the course of race relations all the more to the influence of non-economic factors. For whites a political, cultural, and ideological tug-of-war between traditional allegiances and fragile, new opportunities could be played out on more neutral ground. For blacks the stakes were much higher. Were they really prepared to leave the Republican Party? The party in the South had become a caste-confined institution, yet it remained the major protection of that caste. Should blacks desert the John Wises, Edmund Waddills, and James Bahens to join a fledgling reform movement of former Democrats? In the process, they would bear the double burden of race and class insurgency and risk what one skeptic called the jump "from the frying pan into the fire." In the end, black citizens, including many Knights, surrendered to the logic as well as the muscle of their local party leaders.[55]

In the circumstances the efforts of the Ben Scotts and J. T. Wilsons are more remarkable than their failures. Instead of retreating in the mid-eighties to "weather a storm," they imagined a dramatically different scenario. Their perspective judged in the light of ultimate "realities" must appear illusory or at best utopian. But only in acknowledging their vision can one explain certain behavior, including the true ending—unacceptable to both Democratic and Republican chroniclers—of the Goochland courthouse story. According to the sworn affidavit of Martha Cousins, "the colored man [not Mullen] remarked that if all of them could not sit together, no one of the three would eat at her table." A similar spirit was registered in Montgomery, Alabama, in April 1886. On the same day that Jefferson Davis was laying a cornerstone for a Confederate monument, a black man named W. J. Campbell arrived in town to begin organizing for the Knights of Labor. Elsewhere, the white master workman of an interracial Jackson, Mississippi, assembly declared his faith that "the clouds of superstition will gradually roll away and the destiny of man will be viewed in a new light. The relics of barbarism will tumble down and we can extend our hands clean across this broad land and know that we are Brothers in a common cause."[56]

Suggesting a radical shift in the social distribution of power, political reform efforts like the one in Richmond were seeds which did not germinate. The plowing under of such possibilities affected later southern and American political history. Defeats of attempted coalitions between skilled and unskilled workers in the late 1880s and early nineties left a labor movement generally bereft of social initiative. Exclusionist trade unions, disfranchisement, a virulent Tom Watson, a conservative T. Thomas Fortune, and the self-help ideology of a Booker T. Washington were mutually reinforcing, dominant strains by the turn of the century. In this sense, the "Progressive" Age inaugurated a social and political retreat for many Americans.

Notes

1. Labor tickets appeared in Raleigh, Durham, Fayetteville, Burlington, and Statesville, N.C.; Key West and Jacksonville, Fl.; Selma, Mobile, and Anniston, Al.; Ft. Worth and Houston, Texas; Macon, Ga.; Hot Springs, Ark.; Chattanooga, Tenn.; Vicksburg, Miss.; and Lynchburg, Alexandria, West Point, Kanawha Falls, and Richmond, Va. No doubt these listings are incomplete.

2. See for example Carl N. Degler, *The Other South, Southern Dissenters in the Nineteenth Century* (New York, 1974); John Strawn, "Black History and Black Culture," *Journal of Ethnic Studies*, I (1974), 99-108; Lawrence C. Goodwyn, "Populist Dreams and Negro Rights: East Texas as a Case Study," *American Historical Review*, 76 (December 1971), p. 1451.

3. U.S. Tenth Census, 1880, *Report on the Social Statistics of Cities* (Washington, 1887), 85; U.S. Eleventh Census, 1890, *Report on the Population*, Pt. II (Washington, 1895), 128; U.S. Eleventh Census, 1890, *Report on Manufacturing Industries in the U.S.*, Pt. III, 385-88; B. W. Arnold, Jr., *History of the Tobacco Industry in Virginia from 1860 to 1894*, John Hopkins University Studies . . . , Series 15, Nos. 1-2 (1897), 64-66; Trade Committee of the Chamber of Commerce, "Advantages of Richmond, Virginia as a Manufacturing and Trading Centre" (Richmond, 1882), 37-42; James P. Wood, "The Industries of Richmond . . ." (Richmond, 1886), 11-13.

4. Howard Rabinowitz, "The Search For Social Control; Race Relations in the Urban South 1865-1890" (unpublished Ph.D. diss., Univ. of Chicago, 1973), 56, 82, 808-10.

5. U.S. Eleventh Census, 1890, *Population*, Pt. II, 716-18; testimony of Sir George Campbell reported in A.A. Taylor, *The Negro in the Reconstruction of Virginia* (Washington, 1926), 117.

6. Taylor, 118; Charles B. Dew, *Ironmaker to the Confederacy: Joseph R. Anderson and the Tredegar Iron Works* (New Haven, 1966), 27, 28, 262.

7. U.S. Eleventh Census, 1890, *op. cit.*, 716-18. Figures for 1860 courtesy of Herbert Gutman; the 1860 census did not list occupations of slaves, but Gutman has argued persuasively with other data that what little skilled work blacks performed was done by free Negroes, not slaves. *Slavery and the Numbers Game* (Urbana, 1975), 48-61.

8. *John Swinton's Paper* (hereafter *JSP*). March 21, 1886. See also Rendigs Fels, *American Business Cycles 1865-1897* (Chapel Hill, 1959), 138; U.S. Labor Bureau, *Annual Report of the Commissioner*, III (Washington, 1887), 588-95.

9. *JSP*, June 21, 1885; Jonathan Garlock and N. C. Builder, *Knights of Labor Data Bank: Users Manual and Index to Local Assemblies* (unpublished ms., Rochester, 1973); Richmond *Dispatch* September 30, October 9, 1886; *Knights of Labor, Proceedings of the General Assembly*, Richmond, 1886.

10. *JSP*, January 24, February 4, March 7, 1886; Haverhill *Laborer*, March 15, 1886; *JSP*, May 23, 1886. Richmond organizers appealed in vain against General Master Workman Powderly's 40-day freeze on new assemblies. Henry Trimble to Powderly, March 5, 1886, Terence V. Powderly Papers, Catholic University, Washington, D.C.; Richmond *Dispatch*, October 9, 1886; *JSP*, November 22, December 13, 1885; *Journal of United Labor* (hereafter *JUL*), August 25, 1886; Raymond Pinchbeck, *The Virginia Artisan and Tradesman* (Richmond, 1926), 74.

11. Rabinowitz, 25; Richmond *Whig*, September 1, 25, 1886; Richmond *Dispatch*, May 3, 1884.

12. Richmond *Dispatch*, May 2, 1886.

13. Ibid.

14. Richmond *Dispatch*, May 30, 1886; Richmond city directories, 1886-1887, 1889.

15. Access to 1880 manuscript census occupational breakdowns courtesy of Herbert Gutman; Richmond city directory, 1889. The Irish presence within the southern Knights was apparent in a rumor circulated in Natchez, Miss., that the order admitted only Catholics. The Irish miner Nicholas Byrne Stack headed the organization in Alabama. John S. Power to Powderly, April 12, 1886, Powderly Papers; *JUL*, June 16, 1888.

16. Richmond *Dispatch* as quoted in Rabinowitz, 758. See also ibid., 66-68; Richmond *Whig*, September 26, 28, 30, 1886. Statistics from the 1890 census (the first to break cities down into nativity groups) indicate that 8308 Richmond black males, 20 and older, were outnumbered by 22,471 whites in the same age range. In this light a registered electorate 40 per cent black is all the more striking. Black voting strength at mid-decade was symbolized by the 1886 election in neighboring Manchester of that town's first black councilman and justice of the peace. U.S. Eleventh Census, 1890, 128; Richmond *Dispatch*, May 28, 1886; Charles Wynes, *Race Relations in Virginia, 1870-1902* (Charlottesville, 1961), 34.

17. Ann F. Alexander, "Black Protest in the New South: John Mitchell, Jr. (1863-1929) and the Richmond *Planet*" (unpublished Ph.D. diss., Duke Univ., 1972), 219-20, 223-24; Luther Porter Jackson, *Negro Office-Holders in Virginia 1865-1895* (Norfolk, 1945), 57-58; Rabinowitz, 168-69, 495-500, 724, 742; Alexander, 72.

18. Richmond *Planet*, February 21, 1885; June 12, 1886; July 12, 1890. Only scattered issues of the black newspaper remain.

19. Rabinowitz, 697-700; James T. Moore, "Black Militancy in Readjuster Virginia 1879-1883," *Journal of Southern History*, 41 (1975), 172-75; Alexander, 224.

20. R. F. Walker to William Mahone, May 2, 1886, William Mahone Papers (Duke University, Durham, N.C.).

21. R. T. Hubard to Mahone, June 1, 1886, ibid.; Richmond *Dispatch*, May 28, 1886. The *Dispatch* reacted with characteristic alarm to threats from below. During a war-time Richmond printers' strike the paper had called for the hanging of the miscreants. Susan Stone, "Workers in Richmond, 1861-1865" (unpublished MA essay, Columbia Univ., 1972), 58-59.

22. C. C. Clarke to Mahone, May 29, 1886; B. Taylor McCue to Mahone, July 17, 1886; R. F. Walker to Mahone, May 26, 1886; John S. Wise to Mahone, July 2, 1886, Mahone Papers; Richmond *Planet*, June 12, 1886; Richmond *Dispatch*, June 23, 24, 30, July 1, 1886; whites like John S. Bethel and A. L. Owen who remained in the Reform caucus admitted their political debts to the blacks but still rejected black patronage demands on grounds that the present moment was "impolitic" for such advances, "as the movement is young and must be surrounded by every safeguard." Richmond *Dispatch*, June 30, 1886.

23. John S. Wise to Mahone, June 25, 1886, Mahone Papers.

24. Richmond *Dispatch*, July 2, 1886; Richmond, Va. Common Council *Journal* (minutes), July 6, August 2, 1886.

25. Richmond *Dispatch*, September 11, 1886.

26. William Mullen to Henry George, June 8, 1885. Henry George Papers, New York Public Library, New York City; Richmond *State*, October 17, 1877, courtesy of Peter Rachleff, University of Pittsburgh, who is completing an exhaustive study of 19th century labor organization in Richmond. Mullen, who had come to Richmond as a young apprentice printer, had been active in the labor movement since the mid-1870s and had joined the Knights in 1884; Richmond *Whig*, September 25, 1886; R. J. Steele to Powderly, February 17, 1886; R. W. Cruse to Powderly, April 28, 1886, Powderly Papers; *JUL*, October 25, 1885 (quotation) courtesy Peter Rachleff.

27. Richmond *Whig*, October 6, 23, 1886; Richmond *Dispatch*, May 10, 1887.

28. John S. Wise to Mahone, September 27, 1886. In June, Wise's "understanding" with the Reform leaders had entailed mutual acceptance of a "labor man" for Congress "who will agree to sustain the tariff policy, vote with the Republicans in organizing the House and not go into the Democratic caucus." At that time, however, Wise had personally believed, "they will have no man" and would have to turn to him to fulfill the bargain. John S. Wise to Mahone, June 25, 1886; Edmund Waddill Jr. to Mahone, September 27, 1886, Mahone Papers.

29. Richmond *Dispatch*, October 2, 9, 1886; Rabinowitz, 845-46, 707-08, 736. The tug of competing loyalties was suggested by the presence of W. W. Fields, an officer in black D. A. 92 of the Knights among the anti-Mullen delegates.

30. L. P. Jackson, 57-59; Moore, "Black Militancy . . . ," 172.

31. Richmond *Whig*, October 3, 1886; Richmond *Dispatch*, October 3, 1886.

32. *Valley Virginian*, September 25, 1886; quotation from Petersburg *Index-Appeal* as cited in Richmond *Whig*, October 10, 1886.

33. Quotations from Richmond *Whig*, September 12 and September 8, 1886, respectively.

34. Richmond *Whig*, September 8, 1886.

35. Quotations from Richmond *Whig*, September 18, 25, 1886, respectively; Governor Lee's comments were reported in both the Richmond *Whig* and *Dispatch*, October 5, 1886.

36. Quotations from Richmond *Dispatch*, October 5, 12, 1886, respectively. Among incidents that the Bourbon press found repugnant were these. A black delegate from Baltimore was spotted

one morning in a Richmond hotel asking white delegates to join him for breakfast. Two white delegates from Boston reportedly stopped at the house of one of the most distinguished white residents in the city and asked to speak with "Miss . . . ." The lady of the house told them that there was "no one here by that name except our colored servant girl." "Lucy" then received the men in the servants' room where she was given letters from a mutual acquaintance, "a colored gemmon" from Boston whom she had met several weeks before. Two white women delegates, strolling through the rotunda of the state capitol, stopped to chat with the black janitor and urged him to join the Knights. Richmond *Dispatch*, October 7; Richmond *Whig*, October 10; Richmond *Dispatch*, October 8, 1886.

37. New York *Sun*, October 7, 1886; Richmond *Dispatch*, October 6, 7, 8 (quotation re. law-and-order league), 1886; Burlington, Vt. *Free Press*, October 8, 1886. Bandmann had met Ferrell and company on the boat from New York to Richmond. Afterwards, the actor continued to defend his action. "As an artist and a free-thinking American citizen I shall be only too proud to play before so many colored people as the houses will hold." Starke and Hamm, p. 77; Trenton, N.J. *Daily Gazette* as quoted in New York *Freeman*, October 30, 1886.

"Aristocratic" Richmonders had similarly picked up their guns to intimidate Mahoneite blacks on election day in 1883 (Moore, 185). Following the law-and-order outburst, Knights of Labor leaders limited themselves to quieter demonstrations of their beliefs. Powderly and Thomas McGuire, master workman of D.A. 49, for example, attended mass at the city's black Catholic church. (New York *Herald*, October 11, 1886; Richmond *Dispatch*, October 19, 1886).

38. Haverhill, MA *Laborer*, October 16, 1886.

39. Melton McLaurin, *Paternalism and Protest, Southern Cotton Mill Workers and Organized Labor 1875-1905* (Westport, CT, 1971), 107, 116 (quotation); *JUL*, June 11, 1887; Richmond *Whig*, October 17, 1886; Chicago *Tribune*, October 12, 1886; Richmond *Dispatch*, October 8, 1886 (statement of local Knight); New York *Times*, October 7, 1886; Bay City, MI *Evening Press*, October 6, 1886.

40. Richmond *Dispatch*, October 9, 1886; New York *Tribune*, October 9, 1886; Richmond *Whig* comment on parade, October 12, 1886. Frank Foster reported the turnout on parade day as "90 to 1" black (Haverhill *Laborer*, October 23, 1886).

41. Pittsburgh *Dispatch* report as cited in Richmond *Dispatch*, October 17, 1886.

42. Ibid., October 19, 1886; R. J. Steele to Powderly, October 21, 1886, Powderly Papers; Richmond *Dispatch*, October 24, 1886; ibid., October 23 (Democratic story), 29 (Republican story), 1886.

43. Richmond *Whig*, November 2, 1886; Common Council *Journal*, November 6, 1886; Richmond *Dispatch*, October 31, 1886; Richmond *Whig*, October 27, 30 (quotation), 1886.

44. Ibid., November 2, 1886; Richmond *Dispatch*, October 31, 1886.

45. C. C. Clarke to Mahone, December 6, 1886; C. Payne to Mahone, October 24, November 3, 1886.

46. Richmond *Dispatch*, April 7, 26, 1888; Alexander, 218-20; Richmond *Dispatch*, April 16, 1890; April 24, 1888.

47. *JSP*, November 14, December 12, 1886; Richmond *Dispatch*, December 11, 24, 1886; April 19, 1887 (quotation); Mullen to Powderly, February 28, 1887, Powderly Papers; Richmond *Dispatch*, April 19, May 22, 25, 1888.

48. C. E. Hills to Powderly, March 23, 1888, Powderly Papers; Richmond *Dispatch*, May 18, 1888. For the YMCA's role in socializing an industrial work force, see Gerd Korman, *Industrialization, Immigrants, and Americanizers. The View from Milwaukee 1866-1921* (Madison, 1967), 73-74, 89, 141-47.

49. Rabinowitz, 791; Richmond *Dispatch*, April 16, 1890; Alexander, 192.

50. Richmond *Dispatch*, November 25, 1888; August 26, 1890; Degler, 333; William Dubose Sheldon, *Populism in the Old Dominion, Virginia Farm Politics, 1885-1900* (Princeton, 1935), 55, 92, 61, 102-03; Booze to Powderly, August 12, 1895, Powderly Papers.

51. John L. Power to Powderly, January 20, 1886; A. J. Loveless to Powderly, April 1, 1887; S. T. S. Sweet to Powderly, March 4, 1887; A Gadsden, Alabama, master workman confessed that "some of our brothers have misgivings about the Negro getting the same signs and Password as are in possession of white assemblies. Could the password given to them not be changed a little . . . ?" E. P. S. Dum to Powderly, November 15, 1883, Powderly Papers.

52. Washington *Bee*, October 23, 1886; New York *Freeman*, October 30, 1886; Pierre L. Van der Berghe, *Race and Racism, A Comparative Perspective* (New York, 1967), p. 15.

53. Records of the Freedmen's Savings Bank, Richmond, Va., microfilm copy courtesy of John O'Brien, Dalhousie University; Rabinowitz, pp. 193-94; letter May 18, 1885 to Mahone, Mahone Papers.

54. Chotier to Powderly, March 6, 1886, *ibid.*: C. Vann Woodward, *Origins of the New South 1887-1913* (Baton Rouge, 1971), p. 229.

55. Staunton, Va., *Critic*, October 16, 1886.

56. Richmond *Whig*, October 29, 1886; *JSP*, May 9, 1886; Phil Hammond to Powderly, January 4, 1886; Powderly Papers.

Lawrence C. Goodwyn

Populist Dreams and Negro Rights: East Texas as a Case Study

Nearly a century later the Populist decade lingers in historical memory as an increasingly dim abstraction. The very word "Populism" no longer carries specific political meaning. It is now invoked to explain George Wallace, as it was used to explain Lyndon Johnson in the sixties, Joe McCarthy in the fifties, and Claude Pepper in the forties. Though afflicting principally the popular mind, this confusion is at least partly traceable to those historians who have insisted on concentrating on Populism as exhortation, so that Ignatius Donnelly's utopian novels or Mary Lease's pronouncements on the respective uses of corn and hell became the explanatory keys to agrarian radicalism. For scholars who mine political movements with a view to extracting cultural nuggets, the focus has been chiefly upon the word, not the deed; in the process the agrarian crusade has become increasingly obscure.[1]

Much of the difficulty centers on the subject of race. There is essential agreement that, on economic issues, Populists were men of the Left, primitive to some, prophetic to others, but leftists to all. But did their banner indicate a highly selective nativist radicalism for whites only, or did they grapple with the inherited legacies of the caste system as part of an effort to create what they considered a more rational social and economic order? The analysis of Populist rhetoric has left us with contradictory answers.

While party platforms can be useful tools in determining professed attitudes, the gap between asserted ideals and performance is sufficiently large to defeat any analysis resting on the implicit assumption that political manifestos have an intrinsic value apart from the milieu in which they existed. In America the

Source: American Historical Review 76 (December 1971): 1435–56. Reprinted by permission of the author.

distance between assertion and performance is especially evident in matters of race; as a result, on this issue above all, the context of public assertions is central to the task of their political evaluation.[2] An inquiry into the murkiest corner of Populism, interracial politics, should begin not merely with what Populists said but what they did in the course of bidding for power at the local level. What was the stuff of daily life under Populist rule in the rural enclaves where the third party came to exercise all the authority of public office, including police authority? What can we learn not only about Populist insurgency but also about the orthodoxy the third party opposed?

Grimes County, Texas, was one of many counties scattered across the South and West where the People's party achieved a continuing political presence in the latter part of the nineteenth century. Located some sixty miles north of Houston in the heart of what the natives call the Old South part of Texas, Grimes County displayed the cotton-centered economy typical of rural East Texas in 1880. Its largest town, Navasota, contained 1,800 persons in 1890 and its second largest town, Anderson, the county seat, only 574 persons as late as 1900. Farms in Grimes County ranged from plantation size in the rich bottomland country of the Brazos River on the county's western border to small, single-family agricultural units on the poorer land of the northern part of the county.[3] The 1890 census revealed a county population of 21,312, of which 11,664 were black.[4]

Populism in Grimes County is the story of a black-white coalition that had its genesis in Reconstruction and endured for more than a generation. In time this coalition came to be symbolized by its most enduring elected public official, Garrett Scott. The Scotts had roots in Grimes County dating back before the Civil War. Their sons fought for the Confederacy and returned to face a postwar reality by no means unique in the South; possessing moderately large holdings of land but lacking necessary capital to make it productive, the Scotts did not achieve great affluence. During the hard times that continued to afflict undercapitalized Southern agriculture through the 1870s Garrett Scott became a soft-money agrarian radical.[5] His stance was significant in the political climate of Grimes County in the early 1880s. During Reconstruction Negroes in the county had achieved a remarkably stable local Republican organization, headed by a number of resourceful black leaders. When Reconstruction ended and white Democrats regained control of the state governmental machinery in Texas, Grimes County blacks retained local power and sent a succession of black legislators to Austin for the next decade.[6] The local effort to end this Republican rule took the usual postwar Southern form of a political movement of white solidarity under the label of the Democratic party. In supporting the Greenback party Garrett Scott not only was disassociating himself from the politics of white racial solidarity, he was undermining it.

In 1882 a mass meeting of various non-Democratic elements in Grimes

County nominated a variegated slate for county offices. Among the candidates were black Republicans, "lily-white" Republicans, and Independent Greenbackers. Garrett Scott was on the ticket as the Independent Greenback candidate for sheriff.[7] Not much is known about the racial climate in Grimes County in 1882, but it must not have been wholly serene, because the "lily-white" nominee for county judge, Lock MacDaniel, withdrew from the ticket rather than publicly associate with black candidates.[8] Garrett Scott did not withdraw, and in November he was elected. Also elected, as district clerk, was a black man who became a lifelong political ally of Scott, Jim Kennard.[9] Thus began an interracial coalition that endured through the years of propagandizing in Texas by the increasingly radical Farmers Alliance and through the ensuing period of the People's party. The success of the coalition varied with the degree of white participation. After the collapse of the Greenback party in the mid-eighties visible white opposition to the Democratic party declined for several years before Grimes County farmers, organized by the Alliance, broke with the Democracy to form the nucleus of the local People's party in 1892. Scott and Kennard were the most visible symbols of the revitalized coalition, but there were others as well. Among them were Morris Carrington, a Negro school principal, and Jack Haynes, both staunch advocates of Populism in the black community, as well as J. W. H. Davis and J. H. Teague, white Populist leaders. These men led the People's party to victory in the county elections of 1896 and again in 1898.[10]

A subtle duality creeps into the narrative of events at this point. To the world outside Grimes County in the 1890s, to both Populists and Democrats, Garrett Scott was simply another Populist officeholder, distinguished for his anti-monopoly views and his generally radical approach to monetary policy. To his white supporters within Grimes County he was doubtless respected for the same reasons. But to the Democrats of Grimes County the sheriff symbolized all that was un-Southern and unpatriotic about the third party. Under Populist rule, it was charged, Negro school teachers were paid too much money; furthermore, in Scott's hands the sheriff's office hired Negro deputies. The two Democratic newspapers in Navasota were fond of equating Populist rule with Negro rule and of attributing both evils to Scott. The Navasota *Daily Examiner* asserted that "the Negro has been looking too much to political agitation and legislative enactment. . . . So long as he looks to political agitation for relief, so long will he be simply the means of other men's ambition."[11] To the Navasota *Tablet* Scott was simply "the originator of all the political trouble in Grimes County for years."[12] Both these explanations oversimplify Grimes County politics. The political presence and goals of blacks were definite elements of local Populism, as was, presumably, the personal ambition of Garrett Scott. But the Populists' proposed economic remedies had gained a significant following among the county's white farmers, and this was of crucial importance in inducing white Populists to break with Democrats and ally themselves with blacks. Garrett Scott was a living embodiment of white radicalism; he did not cause it.[13] Beyond this the political cohesion of blacks was a local phenomenon that had preceded Scott's entry into Grimes County politics and had remained relatively stable since the end of the war. The ease with which Democratic partisans saw the fine hand of Garrett Scott in Negro voting was more a reflection of their own racial presumptions than an accurate description of the political dynamics at work in the county.

Through the election of 1898 Democrats in Grimes County had labored in vain to cope with the disease of Populism among the county's white farmers. Finally, in the spring of 1899, the Democrats moved in a new direction. The defeated Democratic candidate for county judge, J. G. McDonald, organized a clandestine meeting with other prominent local citizens and defeated Democratic office seekers. At this meeting a new and—for the time being—covert political institution was created: the White Man's Union. A charter was drawn providing machinery through which the Union could nominate candidates for county offices in elections in which only White Man's Union members could vote. No person could be nominated who was not a member; no person could be a member who did not subscribe to these exclusionary bylaws; in effect, to participate in the organization's activities, so adequately expressed in its formal title, one had to support, as a policy matter, black disfranchisement.[14] Throughout the summer and fall of 1899 the White Man's Union quietly organized.

Writing years later McDonald explained that care was taken not to launch the organization publicly "until the public attitude could be sounded."[15] By January 1900 the covert organizing had been deemed sufficiently successful to permit the public unveiling of the White Man's Union through a long story in the *Examiner*. During the spring the *Examiner*'s political reporting began to reflect a significant change of tone. In April, for example, the *Examiner*'s report of a "quiet election" in nearby Bryan noted that friends of the two mayoral candidates "made a display of force and permitted no Negroes to vote. All white citizens went to the polls, quietly deposited their ballots for whom they pleased and went on about their business."[16] The *Examiner* had progressed from vague suggestions for disfranchisement to approval of its forcible imposition without cover of law.

The first public meetings of the White Man's Union, duly announced in the local press,[17] occupied the spring months of 1900 and were soon augmented by some not-quite-so-public night riding. The chronology of these events may be traced through the denials in the local Democratic press of their occurrence. In July the *Examiner* angrily defended the county's honor against charges by the Negro Baptist State Sunday School Conference that the county had become unsafe for Negroes. The Austin *Herald* reported from the state's capital that the Sunday School Board, "after mature thought and philosophical deliberation," had decided to cancel its annual meeting scheduled for Navasota.[18] The *Examiner* cited as "irresponsible slush" the charge that Negroes were being threatened and told to leave the county, but within weeks reports of just such events began cropping up in the *Examiner* itself.[19] One example of terrorism left no one in doubt, for it occurred in broad daylight on the main street of the county seat: in July Jim Kennard was shot and killed within one hundred yards of the courthouse. His assailant was alleged to be J. G. McDonald.[20]

Intimidation and murder constituted an even more decisive assault on the People's party than had the ominous bylaws of the White Man's Union. The Populist leadership recognized this clearly enough, and Scott went so far as to attempt to persuade Southern white farmers to shoulder arms in defense of the right of Negroes to vote.[21] Beyond this we know little of the measures attempted by the local Populist constabulary to contain the spreading terrorism. A well-informed member of the Scott family wrote a detailed account of these turbulent months, but the manuscript was subsequently destroyed. In the early autumn of 1900 members of the White Man's Union felt sufficiently strong to initiate visits to white farmers with a known allegiance to the People's party. Under such duress some of these farmers joined the White Man's Union.[22]

In August the Union, aided by a not inconsiderable amount of free publicity in the local press, announced "the Grandest Barbecue of the Year," at which the "workings of the White Man's Union" would be explained to all. The leadership of the People's party objected to announced plans to include the local state guard unit, the Shaw Rifles, in the program. After some discussion the Texas adjutant general, Thomas Scurry, placed at the discretion of the local commander the question of the attendance of the Shaw Rifles in a body. The commander, Captain Hammond Norwood, a leading Navasota Democrat and a member of the White Man's Union, exercised his option, and the Shaw Rifles appeared en masse at the function. Populist objections were brushed aside.[23]

Shortly after this well-attended barbecue had revealed the growing prestige of the White Man's Union as well as the inability of the People's party to cope with the changing power relationships within the county, a black exodus began. People left by train, by horse and cart, by day and by night. The *Examiner*, with obvious respect for the new political climate its own columns had helped engender, suggested elliptically that the exodus could produce complications. Some citizens, said the *Examiner*, "are beginning to feel a little nervous as the thing progresses, and lean to the idea that the action will bring on detrimental complications in the labor market."[24]

The next day, however, the paper printed a public address that it said had been "ordered published by the executive committee of the White Man's Union in order to combat the many reports that are calculated to injure the Union." After reaffirming the Union's intent to end "Negro rule" in the county, the report concluded with a message "to the Negroes":

> Being the weaker race, it is our desire to protect you from the schemes of those men who are now seeking to place you before them. . . . Therefore, the White Man's Union kindly and earnestly requests you to keep hands off in the coming struggle. Do not let impu-

dent men influence you in that pathway which certainly leads to trouble. . . . In the future, permit us to show you, and convince you by our action, that we are truly your best friends.[25]

Fourteen days later a black Populist leader, Jack Haynes, was riddled with a shotgun blast by unknown assailants. He died instantly in the fields of his cotton farm.[26]

The White Man's Union held a rally in Navasota two nights later that featured a reading of original poetry by one of the Union's candidates, L. M. Bragg. The verse concluded:

> Twas nature's laws that drew the lines
> Between the Anglo-Saxon and African races,
> And we, the Anglo-Saxons of Grand Old Grimes,
> Must force the African to keep his place.[27]

Another White Man's Union rally held in Plantersville the same week displayed other Union candidates whose conduct won the *Examiner*'s editorial approval: "They are a solid looking body of men and mean business straight from the shoulder."[28] Apparently this characterization of the Plantersville speakers was not restricted to approving Democrats; Populists, too, responded to events initiated by the men who "meant business." In October the Plantersville school superintendent reported that only five white families remained in his school district and that all the Negroes were gone. The superintendent stated that twelve white families had left that week, and "the end is not in sight."[29]

Amid this wave of mounting terror the People's party attempted to go about its business, announcing its nominating conventions in the local press and moving forward with the business of naming election judges and poll watchers. But there were already signs of a fatal crack in Populist morale. The People's party nominee for county commissioner suddenly withdrew from the race. His withdrawal was announced in the *Examiner*, and no explanation was offered.[30]

Throughout the late summer and autumn of 1900 the demonstrated power of the White Man's Union had protected McDonald from prosecution in the Kennard slaying. Nothing short of a war between the Populist police authority and the White Man's Union could break that extralegal shield. An exasperated and perhaps desperate Garrett Scott angrily challenged a White Man's Union official in October to "go and get your Union force, every damn one of them, put them behind rock fences and trees and I'll fight the whole damn set of cowards."[31] That Scott had to use the first person singular to describe the visible opposition to the Union underscores the extent to which terror had triumphed over the institutions of law in Grimes County. By election eve it was clear that the Populist ticket faced certain defeat. The third party had failed to protect its constituency. White Populists as well as black were intimidated. Many would not vote; indeed, many were no longer in the county.[32]

Over 4,500 votes had been cast in Grimes in 1898. On November 6, 1900, only 1,800 persons ventured to the polls. The People's party received exactly 366 votes. The Populist vote in Plantersville fell from 256 in 1898 to 5 in 1900. In the racially mixed, lower-income precinct of south Navasota the Populist vote declined from 636 to 23. The sole exception to this pattern came in a geographically isolated, lower-income precinct in the extreme northern part of the county that contained few Negroes and thus, presumably, fewer acts of terrorism. The Populist vote in this precinct actually increased from 108 to 122 and accounted for one-third of the countrywide vote of 366. In north Navasota, almost all white but not geographically isolated from the terror, the Populist vote declined from 120 to 3.[33] An additional element, nonstatistical in nature, stamped the election as unusual. The underlying philosophy of the South's dominant political institution, the Democratic party, has perhaps never been expressed more nakedly than it was in Grimes County in 1900 when "the party of white supremacy," as C. Vann Woodward has called the Southern Democracy, appeared on the official ballot as the White Man's Union.[34]

On the way to its landslide victory the Union had grown more self-confident in its willingness to carry out acts of intimidation and terrorism in defiance of the local Populist police authority. Now that that authority had been deposed and a sheriff friendly to the White Man's Union had been elected, would terrorism become even more public?

On November 7, 1900, the morning after the election, a strange tableau unfolded on the streets of Anderson, the tiny county seat.[35] Horsemen began arriving in town from every section of the county, tied their horses all along the main street, and occupied the second floor of the courthouse. In a nearby house Garrett Scott's sister, Cornelia, and her husband, John Kelly, watched the buildup of Union supporters on the courthouse square, not fifty yards from the sheriff's official residence on the second floor of the county jail. They decided the situation was too dangerous to permit an adult Populist to venture forth, so the Kellys sent their nine-year-old son with a note to warn Scott not to appear on the street.

At about the same time that this mission was carried out Garrett Scott's younger brother, Emmett Scott, came into town from the family farm, rode past the growing clusters of armed men, and reined up in front of the store belonging to John Bradley, his closest friend in town. Bradley was a Populist but, as befitting a man of trade, a quiet one. His store was adjacent to the courthouse.

Cornelia Kelly's son found the sheriff at Abercrombie's store across the street from the jail and delivered the warning note. As Scott read it an outbreak of gunfire sounded from the direction of Bradley's store. Scott stepped to the street and peered in the direction of the fusillade. Rifle fire from the second floor of the courthouse immediately cut him down. Upon hearing the gunfire Cornelia Kelly ran out of her house and down the long street toward the courthouse. The gunsights of scores of men tracked her progress. Seeing her brother's body in the street she turned and confronted his attackers. "Why don't you shoot me, too," she yelled, "I'm a Scott." She ran to her brother and, with the assistance of her son, dragged him across the street to the county jail. He was, she found, not dead, though he did have an ugly wound in his hip. Inside Bradley's store, however, three men were dead—Emmett Scott, Bradley, and Will McDonald, the son of a Presbyterian minister and a prominent member of the White Man's Union. McDonald had shot Scott shortly after the latter had entered the store; the two men grappled for the gun, and the fatally wounded Scott fired one shot, killing McDonald. Bradley was killed either by a shot fired from outside the store where Union forces had gathered near the courthouse or by a stray bullet during the struggle inside.[36]

The siege of Anderson continued for five days, with the wounded sheriff and his deputies—black and white—in the jail and the White Man's Union forces in the courthouse. Shots crossed the fifty yards between the two buildings intermittently over the next several days. On the evening of the fatal shooting another member of the Scott clan, Mrs. W. T. Neblett, had left Navasota for Austin to plead with the governor, Joseph D. Sayers, for troops. On Friday she returned, accompanied by the adjutant general of the State of Texas, Thomas Scurry—the same official who had earlier acquiesced in the participation of the state guard in the White Man's Union barbecue. After conferring with the contending forces Scurry pondered various methods to get the wounded Scott out of town and into a hospital; gangrene had set in. For protection, Scurry suggested that he be authorized to select a group of twenty prominent citizens of Navasota to escort the sheriff from the jail to the railroad station. Since most of the "prominent citizens" of Navasota were members of the White Man's Union, it is perhaps understandable that Scott declined this offer. The adjutant general then suggested that the Shaw Rifles be employed as an escort. This idea was respectfully declined for the same reason. Asked what he would consider a trustworthy escort, the wounded sheriff suggested a state guard unit from outside the county.[37]

On Saturday, four days after the shooting, a company of Houston light infantry of the Texas Volunteer State Guard detrained at Navasota and marched the eleven miles to Anderson. On Sunday morning Garrett Scott was placed on a mattress, the mattress put in a wagon, and the procession began. In the wagon train were most of the members of the large Scott clan—Emmett Scott's widow and children, the Kelly family, and the Nebletts, all with their household belongings piled in wagons. A file of infantrymen marched on either side as the procession formed in front of the jail, moved past hundreds of armed men at the courthouse and onto the highway to Navasota, and then boarded a special train bound for Houston.[38]

The scene of the postelection gun battle between Populists and supporters of the White Man's Union. The photograph was taken in about 1915 and is an accurate picture of Anderson at the time of the battle. The courthouse is at the end of Main Street. Photograph courtesy of Barker History Center, University of Texas.

Thus did Populism leave Grimes County. From that day in 1900 until well after mid-century Negroes were not a factor in Grimes County politics. J. G. McDonald regained his judgeship and served for many years. The White Man's Union continued into the 1950s as the dominant political institution in the county. None of its nominees, selected in advance of the Democratic primary, was ever defeated.[39] The census of 1910 revealed the extent of the Negro exodus. It showed that Grimes County's Negro population had declined by almost thirty per cent from the 1900 total.[40] School census figures for 1901 suggest an even greater exodus.[41]

To this day the White Man's Union, as a memory if no longer as an institution, enjoys an uncontested reputation among Grimes County whites as a civic enterprise for governmental reform. In this white oral tradition the general events of 1900 are vividly recounted. Specific events are, however, remembered selectively. The exodus of Negroes from the county is not part of this oral tradition, nor is the night riding of the White Man's Union or the assassination of the Negro Populist leaders.

As for Garrett Scott, he endured a long convalescence in a San Antonio hospital, regained his health, married his nurse, and moved to a farm near Houston. He retired from politics and died in his bed. He is remembered in the oral tradition of the black community as the "best sheriff the county ever had." Kennard and Haynes were killed because they "vouched" for Scott among Negroes.[42] In this black oral tradition the Negro exodus plays a central role. It is perhaps an accurate measure of the distance between the races in Grimes County today that two such contradictory versions of famous events could exist side by side without cross-influence.

To these two oral traditions a third must be added—the Scott tradition. The Scotts were, and are, a proud family. One by one, as they died, they were brought home to be buried in the family plot in the Anderson cemetery, little more than a mile from the site of the bloody events of 1900. Tombstones of female members of the clan bear the Scott middle name, defiantly emblazoned in marble. Edith Hamilton of Richards, Grimes County, was ten years old in November 1900 and remembers vividly the day her nine-year-old brother carried her mother's message to Garrett Scott. She remembers the defiance of her mother, the political commitment of her father, the acts of intimidation by the White Man's Union, the Negro exodus, and what she calls the "intelligence of Uncle Garrett." "They said that Uncle Garrett was a nigger-lover," recalls Mrs. Hamilton. "He wasn't a nigger-lover, or a white-lover, he just believed in being fair to all, in justice."[43]

The Scott oral tradition—similar to the black oral tradition and at odds with the white tradition—is virtually the only legacy of the long years of interracial cooperation in Grimes County. Beyond this the substance of political life that came to an end in Grimes County in 1900 cannot be measured precisely from the available evidence. Very little survives to provide insight into the nature of the personal relationship that existed between Garrett Scott and Jim Kennard, between any of the other Populist leaders of both races, or between their respective constituencies. Scott and his third-party colleagues may have been motivated solely by personal ambition, as the White Man's Union charged; on the other hand, the impulses that made them Populists in the first place may have led them toward public coalition with blacks. It is clear that such stridently white supremacist voices as the Navasota *Tablet* were unable to project any reason other than personal ambition to explain the phenomenon of white men willingly associating themselves politically with black men. To what extent this attitude reflected Populist presumptions is another question. White Populists and black Republicans shared an animosity toward the Southern Democracy that grew in intensity during the bitter election campaigns of the 1890s. Democratic persistence in raising the cry of "Negro domination" to lure Populist-leaning voters back to the "party of the fathers" was effective enough to keep white Populists on the defensive about the race issue throughout the agrarian revolt in the South. The circumstance of a common political foe nevertheless provided Populists and Republicans with a basis for political coalition that was consummated in a bewildering variety of ways—and sometimes not consummated at all. The stability of local black organizations and their demonstrated capacity to withstand Democratic blandishments or acts of intimidation were only two of the factors governing the complex equation of post-Reconstruction interracial politics. A stable, local black political institution existed in Grimes County, and its enduring qualities obviously simplified the organizational task confronting Garrett Scott. What might be regarded as "normal" Bourbon efforts to split blacks from the Populist coalition—mild intimidation, petty bribery, campaign assertions that the Democrats were the Negroes' "best friends," or a combination of all three—failed to achieve the desired results in Grimes County in the 1890s. The precise reasons are not easily specified. The Navasota *Tablet*, seeing the world through lenses tinted with its own racial presumptions, ascribed the credit for Negro political cohesion solely to the white sheriff. In the face of all Democratic stratagems, the third party's continuing appeal to Negroes was, in the *Tablet's* view, a thing of "magic." A white supremacist view does not automatically exclude its holder from rendering correct political analyses on occasion, and it is possible that the *Tablet's* assessment of the cause of Negro political solidarity was correct; however, such an analysis does not explain how the Negro Republican organization was able to send a succession of black legislators to Austin in the 1870s and 1880s, before Garrett Scott became politically active. It seems relevant that when Grimes County Democrats decided upon an overt campaign of terrorism, the men they went after first were the leading black spokesmen of Populism in the county rather than the third party's white leadership. To this extent the actions of Democratic leaders contradicted their public analysis of the causal relationships inherent in the continuing Populist majorities.

Before they indulged in terrorism the Democrats already possessed another method of splitting the Populist coalition: regaining the loyalty of white Populists. Against the historic Democratic campaign cry of white supremacy, the People's party had as its most effective defense the economic appeal of its own platform. The persuasiveness of Populism to white farmers in Grimes County was confirmed by newspaper accounts of the public reaction to the Populist-Democratic debates that occurred during the years of the agrarian uprising. While the reports in the *Examiner* were uniformly partisan and invariably concluded that Democratic spokesmen "won" such debates hands down, the papers conceded that Populist speakers also drew enthusiastic responses from white residents. The absence of reliable racial data by precincts renders a statistical analysis of the Populist vote in Grimes County impossible; however, the fragmentary available evidence suggests that the People's party was generally able to hold a minimum of approximately thirty per cent of the county's white voters in the four elections from 1892 to 1898 while at the same time polling approximately eighty to ninety per cent of the Negro electorate. The inability of the Democratic party to "bloc vote" the county's white citizenry, coupled with the party's failure to win black voters by various means or, alternatively, to diminish the size of the Negro electorate, combined to ensure Democratic defeat at the polls. The fact merits emphasis: both the cohesion of black support for the People's party and the maintenance of substantial white support were essential to the local ascendancy of Populism.

This largely deductive analysis, however, reveals little about the internal environment within the third-party coalition during the bitter struggle for power that characterized the decade of Populist-Democratic rivalry. However scrutinized, the bare bones of voting totals do not flesh out the human relationships through which black and white men came together politically in this rural Southern county. In the absence of such crucial evidence, it seems prudent to measure the meaning of 1900 in the most conservative possible terms. Even by this standard, however, a simple recitation of those elements of Grimes County politics that are beyond dispute isolates significant and lasting ramifications.

An indigenous black political structure persisted in Grimes County for thirty-five years following the Civil War. Out of his own needs as a political insurgent against the dominant Southern Democratic party, Garrett Scott decided in 1882 to identify his Greenback cause with the existing local Republican constituency. Once in office as sheriff he found, among other possible motives, that it was in his own self-interest to preserve the coalition that elected him. It is clear that the style of law enforcement in Grimes County under Scott became a persuasive ingredient in the preservation of black support for the People's party. The presence of black deputy sheriffs and Scott's reputation within the black community seem adequate confirmation of both the existence of this style and its practical effect. The salaries paid Negro school teachers constituted another element of third-party appeal. Comparisons with white salaries are not available, but whatever black teachers received, partisans of the White Man's Union publicly denounced it as "too much." It is evident that Grimes County Negroes supported the People's party for reasons that were grounded in legitimate self-interest—an incontestable basis for political conduct. The point is not so much that the county's Negroes had certain needs, but that they possessed the political means to address at least a part of those needs.

From this perspective the decisive political event of 1900 in Grimes County was not the overwhelming defeat of the local People's party but the political elimination of that part of its constituency that was black. Scott was valuable to Negroes in short-run terms because he helped to translate a minority black vote into a majority coalition that possessed the administrative authority to improve the way black people lived in Grimes County. In the long run, however, it was the presence of this black constituency—not the conduct of a single white sheriff nor even the professed principles of his political party—that provided the Negroes of the county with what protection they had from a resurgent caste system. As long as Negroes retained the right to cast ballots in proportion to their numbers they possessed bargaining power that became particularly meaningful on all occasions when whites divided their votes over economic issues. Disfranchisement destroyed the bargaining power essential to this elementary level of protection. Arrayed against these overriding imperatives for Negroes such questions as the sincerity of Garrett Scott's motives fade in importance. Whatever the sheriff's motives, both the political realities that undergirded the majority coalition and Scott's ability to respond to those realities shaped a course of government conduct under the People's party that was demonstrably of more benefit to Negroes than was the conduct of other administrations before or since. The permanent alteration of those realities through black disfranchisement ensured that no other white administration, whether radical, moderate, or opportunistic, would be able to achieve the patterns in education and law enforcement that had come to exist in the county under Populism. Stated as starkly as possible, after 1900 it was no longer in the interest of white politicians to provide minimal guarantees for people who could not help elect them.

Beyond this crucial significance for the county's black people, disfranchisement also institutionalized a fundamental change in the political environment of whites. More than a third party passed from Grimes County in 1900; in real political terms an idea died. Though a new political idea invariably materializes in democratic societies as an expression of the self-interest of a portion of the electorate, the party that adopts the idea in the course of appealing for the votes of that sector of the electorate inevitably is placed in the position of having to rationalize, defend, explain, and eventually promote the idea. If the concept has substance, this process eventually results in the insinuation of the idea into the culture itself. In this sense it is not necessary to know the precise depth of the commitment to Negro rights of the Grimes County People's party to know that the *idea* of Negro rights had a potential constituency among white people in the county as long as black people were able to project its presence through their votes. Given the endurance of this real and potential constituency, one could reasonably intuit that twentieth-century politics in Grimes County would have contained one, or a dozen, or a thousand Garrett Scotts—each more, or less, "sincere" or "ambitious" than the Populist sheriff. Disfranchisement destroyed the political base of this probability. A political party can survive electoral defeat, even continuing defeat, and remain a conveyor of ideas from one generation to the next. But it cannot survive the destruction of its constituency, for the party itself then dies, taking with it the possibility of transmitting its political concepts to those as yet unborn. It is therefore no longer possible to speak of two white political traditions in Grimes County, for the White Man's Union succeeded in establishing a most effective philosophical suzerainty. Seventy years after disfranchisement Mrs. Hamilton can recall the racial unorthodoxy of Uncle Garrett; she cannot participate in such activity herself. "The Negro people here don't want this school integration any more than the whites do," she now says. "They're not ready for it. They don't feel comfortable in the school with white children. I've talked to my maid. I know."[44]

While Garrett Scott's memory has been preserved, the local presence of the creed of his political party died with the destruction of that party. There has been literally no political place to go for subsequent generations of Scotts and Teagues, or Kennards and Carringtons. This absence of an alternative political institution to the Democratic party, the party of white supremacy, has been a continuing and unique factor in Southern politics.[45] The circumstance is based on the race issue, but in its long-term political and social implications it actually transcends that issue.

The Populist era raises a number of questions about the interaction of the two races in the South, both within the third party and in the larger society. It is widely believed, by no means merely by laymen, that after the failure of Reconstruction meaningful experiments with the social order were finished in the South and that the aspirations of blacks were decisively thwarted. The example of Grimes County suggests, however, the existence of a period of time—a decade perhaps, or a generation—when nascent forms of indigenous interracial activity struggled for life in at least parts of the old Confederacy. Was some opportunity missed and, if so, how? How widespread through the South, and the nation, was this opportunity?

The White Man's Union was organized and led by men who considered themselves the "best people" of the South. If this attitude was typical, major adjustments must be made in our understanding of precisely how, and for what reasons, the antebellum caste system, in altered form, was reinstitutionalized in Southern society a generation after the formal ending of slavery. Was the "red-neck" the source of atrocity, or was he swept along by other stronger currents? And what of the Populist role? To what extent was agrarian racial liberalism in Texas traceable to an overall philosophy within the third-party leadership? Through what intuition of self-interest did the radical organizers of the Farmers Alliance, the parent institution of the People's party, accept the political risks of public coalition with blacks? What were their hopes and fears, and where did they falter? And, finally, what does the substance of their effort tell us about the Democrats in the South and the Republicans in the North who opposed them?

Answers to these questions rest, in part, on detailed knowledge of such events as those in Grimes County, but they require more than compilations of local histories, just as they assuredly require more than cultural assessments based on novels, speeches, and party manifestoes considered apart from their organic milieu. These answers will not provide much of a synthesis—Populism was too diverse, too congregational, and too ideologically thin—but they should tell us more about the larger society that, along with the Populists, failed to erect the foundations for a multiracial society in the nineteenth century. As the inquiry proceeds, it should be remembered that Populism perished before developing a mature philosophy—on race, on money, or on socialism. One must generalize, therefore, not only from contradictory evidence but, more important, from incomplete evidence. An analogy, doubtless unfair, could be made with the plight that would face modern historians of Marxism had that movement been abruptly truncated at the time, say, of the Brussels Conference in 1903. Who could have predicted on the evidence available to that date the Stalinist reign of terror that evolved from the mature, victorious revolutionary party of 1917? By the same token sweeping generalizations about what Populist radicalism could have become are not only romantic but historically unsound.

It should be sufficient to observe that in the long post-Reconstruction period—a period not yet ended— during which the social order has been organized hierarchically along racial lines, Populism intruded as a brief, flickering light in parts of the South. For a time some white Southerners threw off the romanticism that has historically been a cover for the region's pessimism and ventured a larger, more hopeful view about the possibilities of man in a free society. Under duress and intimidation this public hope failed of persuasion at the ballot box; under terrorism it vanished completely.

The Grimes County story dramatically illustrates this failure, but in the insight it provides into the underlying politics of black disfranchisement and the achievement of a monolithic one-party political environment in the American South it is not unique. Other Populists in East Texas and across the South—white as well as black—died during the terrorism that preceded formal disfranchisement. In Texas the extraparliamentary institutions formed by white

Democrats to help create the political climate for disfranchisement bore a variety of local names: The Citizens White Primary of Marion County; the Tax-Payers Union of Brazoria County; the Jaybird Democratic Association of Fort Bend County; and the White Man's Union of Wharton, Washington, Austin, Matagorda, Grimes, and other counties.[46] The available historical material concerning each of these organizations comes largely from the founders themselves, or their descendants, reflecting an incipient or a mature oral tradition—one oral tradition.[47] The secondary literature based on these accounts, including scholarly works used in graduate schools as well as primary and secondary textbooks, is correspondingly inadequate.[48]

A surprising amount of uninterpreted material from violently partisan white supremacist sources has found its way into scholarly literature. One example from the Grimes experience pertains directly to the scholarly characterization of Negro political meetings during the Populist era. It is worth attention as an illustration of the impact of white supremacist modes of thought on modern scholarship. The sunup-to-sundown work routine of Southern farm labor obviously precluded daytime political meetings. Accordingly, Kennard, Haynes, and Carrington campaigned among their black constituents by holding political meetings in each of the towns and hamlets of the county at night. Democratic partisans termed these rallies "Owl Meetings" and characterized black Populist leaders as " 'fluence men." Drawing upon their own party's time-honored campaign technique with Negroes, Democrats further asserted that owl meetings were more concerned with sumptuous banquets and whisky than with politics. If partisans of white supremacy had difficulty finding reasons for white acceptance of political coalition with blacks, they were culturally incapable of ascribing reasons for Negro support of the third party to causes other than short-run benefits in terms of money and alcohol. The point is not that Democrats were always insincere in their descriptions (as white supremacists they were quite sincere), but that scholars have subsequently accepted such violently partisan accounts at face value. The darkly sinister picture of " 'fluence men" corrupting innocent blacks with whisky at surreptitious owl meetings served to justify, at least to outsiders, the use of terrorism as the ultimate campaign technique of Democratic interracial politics. This sequential recording of events has found its way into scholarly monographs that otherwise demonstrate no inherent hostility to the Populistic inclinations of Southern farmers, black or white. In *The People's Party in Texas* Roscoe Martin precedes his brief allusion to the White Man's Union with a resumé of owl meetings and " 'fluence men" that reflects in detail the bias of white supremacist sources.[49] Other scholars writing broadly about Gilded Age politics have routinely drawn upon such monographs as Martin's, and by this process " 'fluence men" have materialized as an explanation of Negro political insurgency in the nineties.[50] In the heat of local political combat, however, Democratic leaders often were able to face a wholly different set of facts in the course of persuading their followers, and the citizenry as a whole, to adjust to the necessity of terrorism. As the time approached for actual precinct campaigning in Grimes County in the autumn of 1900, the executive board of the White Man's Union published a notice of the Union's intentions, climaxed by a "fair distinct warning" to the county's Negro leadership. The statement is revealing—not only of the transformation visited upon normal campaign practices when they were viewed through the cultural presumptions of white supremacy but also of the dangers of uncritical acceptance of such perspectives by scholars relying upon monoracial sources. The notice read in part:

> The Union is largely composed of the best citizens of the county. . . . They are the tax payers, representing the worth, the patriotism, the intelligence, and the virtues of the county. . . . We are not fighting any political party or individuals, but only those who band together under any name, who seek to perpetuate negro rule in Grimes County. [Good citizens] are astounded at the manner in which the children's money has been expended. Colored teachers with fat salaries and totally incompetent have been appointed for political "fluence." Our white teachers, male and female, enjoy no such fat salaries as these colored politicians or these sweet colored girls. . . . One of the most corrupting practices in the past has been the system of Owl Meetings which has been in vogue for years. . . . This is the school and hot bed where the negro politician received his inspiration, and riding from one end of the county to the other as an apostle of his race, corrupting his own people who may be in the honest pathway of duty. We give fair warning that any effort to continue these Owl Meetings—by the appointment of special deputies sheriffs to organize and carry them on—will be prevented. No threat of shotguns will deter us from the discharge of this duty.[51]

Even without recourse to other perspectives this view of the existing political situation in Grimes County contains serious internal contradictions. Black Populist leaders were "incompetent" but as "apostles of their race" they had been so effective that their efforts needed to be stopped. Black teachers were paid "fat salaries" solely for political reasons, but among those receiving such gross patronage were "sweet colored girls," who obviously were not conducting owl meetings. The assertion that black teachers were actually paid more than white teachers must be rejected out of hand. In addition to the compelling fact that such an arrangement would have constituted poor political behavior on the part of a third party strenuously endeavoring to hold a substantial portion of the white vote and the further reality that such expenditures were unnecessary since parity for blacks in itself would have represented a notable accomplishment in the eyes of Negro leaders, Democrats had access to the records of all county expenditures and no such charge was ever leveled, much less documented, at any other time during the Populist decade. Whites complained that Negro teachers received "too much," not that they received more than white teachers. In any case, it seems necessary only to observe that American political parties have routinely utilized night gatherings without having their opponents characterize them as owl meetings and that persons who benefited from incumbency were not presumed to be acting in sinister ways when they campaigned for their party's re-election. The only thing "special" about Garrett Scott's deputies was that some of them were black. Viewed as some sort of black abstraction Jim Kennard might appear convincing as a shadowy " 'fluence man," but as an intelligent and determined voice of the aspirations of Negro people he merits scholarly attention from perspectives not bounded by the horizons of those who murdered him. To an extent that is perhaps not fully appreciated, decades of monoracial scholarship in the South have left a number of Jim Kennards buried under stereotypes of one kind or another. They sometimes intrude anonymously as " 'fluence men," but they simply do not appear as people in books on Southern politics.

This circumstance suggests that not only the broad topic of interracial life and tension but the entire Southern experience culminated by disfranchisement needs to be tested by a methodology that brings both black and white sources to bear on the admittedly intricate problem of interpreting a free society that was not free. At all events, evidence continues to mount that monoracial scholarship, Northern and Southern, has exhausted whatever merit it possessed as an instrument of investigating the variegated past of the American people. The obvious rejoinder—that written black sources do not exist in meaningful quantity—cannot, of course, be explained away; at the same time, this condition suggests the utility of fresh attempts to devise investigatory techniques that offer the possibility of extracting usable historical material from oral sources. The example of the erroneous report in the Navasota *Examiner* of Morris Carrington's death[52] illustrates, perhaps as well as any single piece of evidence, not only the dangers inherent in relying on such "primary sources" for details of interracial tension in the post-Reconstruction South but also the value of received oral traditions in correcting contemporary accounts. Nevertheless, the problem of evaluating such source material remains; white and black versions of the details of racial conflicts are wildly contradictory. When they are measured against other contemporary evidence, however, the interpretive problem becomes considerably less formidable; indeed, the task of penetrating the substance behind partisan contemporary accounts may be lessened through recourse to available oral sources, as I have attempted to demonstrate.

Since much of the *Realpolitik* of the South, from Reconstruction through the modern civil rights movement, rests on legal institutions that, in turn, rest on extralegal methods of intimidation, the sources of political reality may be found less in public debate than in the various forms of intimidation that matured in the region. However determined a historian may be to penetrate the legal forms to reach this extralegal underside of the political culture of the South he is, in our contemporary climate, blocked off from part of his sources by his skin color. For black scholars there are limits to the availability both of courthouse records in the rural South and of responsive white oral sources. There are corresponding limits to the information white scholars can gain from interviews in black communities. Here, then, is fertile ground for scholarly cooperation. Methods of achieving this cooperation need to be explored. In its fullest utilization the subject is not black history or Southern history but American history.

Notes

1. Such careful inquiries as C. Vann Woodward, *Origins of the New South* (Baton Rouge, 1951); Woodward, *Thomas Watson, Agrarian Rebel* (New York, 1938); and Walter T. K. Nugent, *The Tolerant Populists* (Chicago, 1963), demonstrate how regional and state studies can reconstruct the milieu within which men performed their public political labors. Both historians are careful to set the words of Populists, Democrats, and Republicans against their respective acts. In contrast Richard Hofstadter and Norman Pollack, though in healthy disagreement in their assessment of the quality of Populist agitation, both rest their analysis on elusive cultural and ideological categories that often seem far removed from the inner workings of the agrarian crusade. In *The Populist Response to Industrial America* (Cambridge, 1962), Pollack strains to find an authentic socialist basis for Populist criticisms of American capitalism. The attempt has the effect of diminishing the provincial generosity and innocence of Populism as well as socialist claims to ideological consistency; it also carries Pollack's inquiry toward the upper reaches of the party hierarchy in a manner frequently unrelated to the substance of third-party survival at the local level. The scholarly assault on Hofstadter's *The Age of Reform* (New York, 1958) has been both telling and recurring—the recurrence a testament to the vitality of this creative and persuasively written book. The criticism that Hofstadter selected a small number of Populist writings as a basis for sweeping generalizations about the nature of the agrarian crusade remains as true as ever.

2. For example, a central aspect of race relations in the South concerns the question of which classes in Southern society took the lead in the successive processes—black disfranchisement being one of the more essential ones—by which the antebellum caste system, in altered form, was reinstitutionalized after Reconstruction. Analysis of rhetoric that is not intimately related to these processes as they occur cannot be expected to produce evidence that bears on the crucial causal relationships involved. In this connection a recent study by William I. Hair touches directly on one of these processes—the violent suppression of black trade unionism. Hair asserts that the gentry "embraced the kind of Negrophobia elsewhere usually attributed to ignorant poor whites." When Louisiana planters crushed a Knights of Labor strike in the lower delta parishes in 1887 casualties among cane field workers "ran into the hundreds." *Bourbonism and Agrarian Protest: Louisiana Politics, 1877-1900* (Baton Rouge, La., 1969), 184.

3. The author wishes to acknowledge the assistance of Marcus Mallard of Navasota, chairman of the Grimes County Historical Society. Mr. Mallard provided social, economic, and genealogical information on the county and many of its prominent families.

4. Bureau of the Census, *Thirteenth Census of the United States, Abstract with Supplement for Texas* (Washington, D.C., 1913), 620; *Texas Almanac, 1910* (Dallas, Tex., 1910), 133.

5. Galveston *News*, Sept. 10, 1882; Navasota *Tablet*, Nov. 11, 1900.

6. Harrell Budd, "The Negro in Politics in Texas, 1877-1898" (master's thesis, University of Texas, 1925), 83; J. Mason Brewer, *Negro Legislators of Texas* (Dallas, Tex., 1935), 64, 74-75, 81.

7. Galveston *News*, Sept. 10, 1882.

8. Ibid., Sept. 21, 1882.

9. Ibid., Nov. 11, 1882.

10. Carrington and Haynes as well as Kennard had been active in the county Republican organization prior to the emergence of the third party. The information from contemporary sources on the political lives of Negro leaders in Grimes County that was used in this paper was augmented by oral interviews with their descendants. The author wishes to express his gratitude to Maurice Lyons and B. T. Bonner, both former students at the University of Texas, for their assistance in the conduct of oral interviews in the black communities of Navasota, Anderson, Plantersville, and Richards in Grimes County. Largely through the efforts of Mr. Lyons and Mr. Bonner, the author was able to locate the descendants of every known black leader of the People's party in Grimes County. With respect to the third party's white leadership, the political histories of Teague, Davis, and Scott, traced through both oral interviews and contemporary sources, stand as examples of the diverse sources of Southern Populism. Teague, like Scott, spent his entire political life in opposition to the Democratic party—but as a Republican rather than as an agrarian radical. Quietly progressive on the race issue, Teague possessed considerable administrative talents and eventually became chairman of the third party for the first congressional district of Texas. He was elected county judge in 1896 and was reelected in the local third-party sweep of 1898. Davis, a Democrat, became quite radical on economic issues, broke with his party, and became a third-party editor. He displayed an ambivalent stance on the race issue and was not prominent in the events described in this paper.

11. Navasota *Daily Examiner*, Oct. 13, 1898.

12. *Tablet*, Nov. 11, 1890.

13. The characterization of third-party rule as "Negro rule" was common in the Democratic press in counties where Populism was strong. Such accounts must be weighed against other stories, appearing in the same newspapers, that acknowledged the strong appeal of the People's party among white farmers. In this connection, see the *Examiner*, Nov. 4, 1898.

14. The bylaws of the White Man's Union were published in the *Examiner*, Jan. 6, 1900.

15. J. G. McDonald to E. L. Blair, July 10, 1928, in E. L. Blair, *Early History of Grimes County* (Austin, 1930), 197.

16. *Examiner*, Apr. 4, 1900.

17. Ibid., Apr. 2, 3, June 4, 6, 11, July 17, 18, 19, 20, 30, 1900.

18. Austin *Herald*, reprinted in *Examiner*, July 17, 1900.

19. *Examiner*, Sept. 4, 13, Oct. 19, Nov. 5, 1900.

20. Carrie Meacham, private interview near Plantersville, Texas, Aug. 12, 1970. Mrs. Meacham is the daughter of the slain Populist leader. W. F. McGowan, private interview in Navasota, Apr. 14, 1970. Mr. McGowan, now ninety-four years old, was a personal friend of Jim Kennard. A. P. Wickey, private interview in Anderson, May 14, 1970. Mr. Wickey is the source of the statement attributing Kennard's death to Judge McDonald, Mr. Wickey's stepfather was a prominent member of the White Man's Union; the younger Wickey, now in his eighties, was present in Anderson the day of the slaying. His account is supported by Mrs. Meacham: "Judge McDonald shot my father off his horse on the main street of Anderson."

21. The Navasota *Tablet* accused Scott of attempting to rally Populists in defense of Negro voting rights, describing his public appeals as "raving speeches." *Tablet*, Nov. 11, 1900.

22. Edith Hamilton, private interview in Richards, Texas, May 24, 1970. Though specific information about the night-riding activities of the White Man's Union can occasionally be found in the local Democratic press, that source cannot be characterized as zealous in its reporting of extra-parliamentary aspects of the campaign of 1900. Accounts of intimidation of Negro Populists have been preserved in the oral tradition of Grimes County Negroes; accounts of intimidation of white Populists have been preserved in the oral tradition of the Scott family. Mrs. Hamilton, now eighty years of age, is the niece of Garrett Scott. Richards, Texas, is located in Grimes County, a few miles from the county seat of Anderson. The lost "Populist history" of Grimes County was written by Mrs. Hamilton's father. It was destroyed after his death by his wife, Cornelia Kelly, because, says Mrs. Hamilton, "my mother felt we had all suffered enough and no purpose would be served by keeping my father's manuscript."

23. *Examiner,* July 30, Aug. 8, 17, 18, 24, 1900. The affair of the Shaw Rifles was described in the *Examiner,* Aug. 21, 1900. The *Examiner* had by this stage become quite committed to the cause of extraparliamentary disfranchisement. On August 24 the paper described the White Man's Union picnic in terms of triumph, asserting that five thousand people had feasted at "1500 feet of tables . . . laden with well-turned and thoroughly seasoned barbecue, pork and mutton." Replying a week later to out-of-town dispatches that Grimes County politics had become complicated by the presence of four political tickets (Democratic, Republican, Populist, and White Man's Union), the paper replied: "Grimes County is in better shape politically than most counties in Texas. There is only one ticket and one piece of a ticket in the field. Anyone who viewed the Anderson picnic parade last week would have left little room for doubt as to which side would win." *Examiner,* Aug. 31, 1900.

24. Ibid., Sept. 13, 1900.

25. Ibid., Sept. 14, 1900. The promptness of the reply by the White Man's Union to the *Examiner's* gentle admonition may be taken as an indication of the confidence and aggressiveness of the organization's leadership.

26. Jack Haynes, Jr., private interview, Navasota, Texas, Apr. 14, 1970. Mr. Haynes is the son of the slain Populist leader. W. F. McGowan, interview, Apr. 14, 1970. The *Examiner,* Sept. 27, 1900, carried a one-paragraph story on Haynes's murder without, however, attributing to it any political implications. Haynes was not identified as a Populist leader. The murder of another black Populist leader, Morris Carrington, was also reported in the same issue, again without specifying Carrington's role in the People's party. This report had no foundation in fact and was printed either through error or by design to frighten the county's black population. Mr. Carrington died in 1923. The value of received oral traditions in correcting primary—and partisan—sources is briefly discussed at the conclusion of this paper.

27. *Examiner,* Sept. 29, 1900.

28. Ibid.

29. Ibid., Oct. 24, 1900.

30. Ibid., Oct. 30, 1900.

31. *Tablet,* Nov. 11, 1900.

32. The *Examiner*'s pre-election issue foresaw a "quiet election" despite "some unmistakable bitterness in some quarters." The paper reported that "everything points to the success of the White Man's Union ticket." *Examiner,* Nov. 5, 1900.

33. *Examiner,* Nov. 10, 1898, Nov. 9, 1900. Official Texas election returns are available in the state archives only on a countywide basis.

34. The twenty-five per cent decline in the Democratic vote showed that not everyone was wholly content with the climate of violence that had developed. The *Examiner* somewhat opaquely expressed this anxiety. After noting that the Negro exodus was not confined to Grimes County, the White Man's Union and its tactics having spread to other counties, the newspaper felt constrained to add: "Yet there is a positive indication that something deep is at the bottom of the removal—some source for the frightful, unchristian and willful fabrications circulated." *Examiner,* Nov. 5, 1900. The *Examiner* can perhaps be pardoned for its failure to comment on its own role as a "source" if not of fabrications then of the advantages of the exclusionary administration of the ballot.

35. The ensuing account of the events of November 7-11 is derived from a variety of sources. Both Navasota newspapers published versions of the Anderson affair, the *Tablet,* in a lengthy story on November 11 and the *Examiner* on November 8-10. The Galveston *News* carried increasingly detailed accounts on November 8-12. In addition to those persons cited elsewhere herein, a number of Grimes County residents supplied information on a basis not for attribution. In the black community the effect of the terrorism of 1900 has not yet run its course. The adjutant general's account, which is available in the Texas State Archives, Austin, is quite brief. *Report of the Adjutant General, 1899-1900* (Austin, 1900).

36. The *Tablet* leaves open the question of how Bradley's death occurred. White oral tradition

holds that Scott killed Bradley. This is disputed by the Scott family oral tradition, supplied by Mrs. Hamilton, that Bradley was Scott's "best friend." The Galveston *News* supports Mrs. Hamilton's version: "As a result of some words, McDonald emptied his revolver into Emmett Scott, killing him, hitting him every time. He grabbed Scott's pistol, and the two began scuffling when a shot rang out and Bradley fell." *News*, Nov. 8, 1900. A subsequent bulletin, also printed in that issue, revises the story: "It was first thought Bradley received an accidental shot from Scott's pistol but later reports say he was shot by someone else. It is claimed Bradley had nothing to do with the fight between Scott and McDonald." The *News* described all three victims as men "prominent in the county."

37. *Report of the Adjutant General*, 12. Both the *Tablet*, November 11, 1900, and Mrs. Hamilton agree in principle on this summation of the conversation between Garrett Scott and the adjutant general.

38. Galveston *News*, Nov. 12, 1900; *Tablet*, Nov. 11, 1900; *Report of the Adjutant General* says that eight men and six women had taken refuge in the jail (p. 12).

39. On this point all oral traditions in Grimes County correspond.

40. *Thirteenth Census*, 822. The Negro population declined from 14,327 in 1900 to 9,858 in 1910. In 1890, the black population of Grimes had been 11,664.

41. *Scholastic Population and Apportionment of Available School Fund for 1901* (Austin, 1901), 7. While school census figures are available for 1901, I have been unable to locate comparable data for 1900. Nearest available figures prior to 1901 are for 1889. The 1901 school census, though taken a year after the exodus and presumably reflecting the return of some Negroes in addition to in-migration encouraged by the labor shortage, reveals a decline in the number of Negro pupils of fifteen per cent from the 1889 total, despite the fact that census returns show an increase of almost twenty per cent in Negro population between 1890 and 1900. This comparison suggests that the thirty per cent decline in Negro population evident from the census returns for 1900 and 1910 probably substantially minimizes the actual exodus that occurred in the late summer and fall of 1900. An exodus in the range of from forty to fifty per cent probably would be a reasonable estimate.

42. W. F. McGowan, interview, Apr. 14, 1970.

43. Edith Hamilton, interview, May 13, 1970.

44. Ibid., May 24, 1970.

45. V. O. Key, *Southern Politics* (New York, 1949), is an authoritative study of the forms of Democratic orthodoxy in the various states of the old Confederacy, including the dominating orthodoxy of white supremacy; Vincent P. DeSantis, *Republicans Face the Southern Question* (Baltimore, 1959), summarizes the Republican failure to cope with the same imperatives.

46. J. A. R. Moseley, "The Citizens White Primary of Marion County," *Southwestern Historical Quarterly*, 49 (1946): 524-31; Pauline Yelderman, "The Jaybird Democratic Association of Fort Bend County" (master's thesis, University of Texas, 1938); Millie L. Kochan, "The Jaybird-Woodpecker Feud: A Study in Social Conflict" (master's thesis, University of Texas, 1929); Ira Brandon, "The Tax Payers Union in Brazoria County," *Texas History Teachers Bulletin*, 14 (1926): 86-92. Roscoe Martin reflects a knowledge of these extraparliamentary institutions, though the closest the author comes to exploring the topic is the following footnote: "One who is willing to undergo the hardships involved may learn many interesting things concerning the White Man's Party from those who have a first hand knowledge of the organization. Practically nothing, however, has been written on the subject." *The People's Party in Texas* (2d ed.; Austin, 1970), 236n. Other than accounts reflecting the perspective of the founders of these institutions, the statement is as true in 1971 as when Martin wrote in 1933.

47. J. A. R. Moseley is the son of the founder of the Marion County Citizens White Primary. Both the Yelderman and Kochan manuscripts on the Jaybird Democratic Association rest on versions supplied by founders, as does the Brandon article on Brazoria County. The following extract from Brandon may be taken as indicative of the style of this genre: "On the night before the returns were canvassed, a comparatively small band of determined, conservative, honest, white,

Christian, representative men of the county assembled . . . and the result of their deliberations was the creation of the present Tax Payers' Union of Brazoria County. . . . According to the rules, only white men can be members of this union and . . . vote in the 'Tax Payers' Primary.'" "Tax Payers Union," 87. Douglas G. Perry makes no inquiry into the structure of the party at the local level, in Grimes or any other Texas county, nor does he investigate the politics of black disfranchisement as it affected the People's party. "Black Populism: The Negro in the People's Party" (master's thesis, Prairie View Agricultural and Mechanical College, 1945).

48. Dewey Grantham, *The Democratic South* (Athens, Ga., 1963), is but one of the more recent manifestations of a long scholarly tradition in the South reflecting an unconscious assumption that reform politics is a function of white Southerners and that the observable victims of "Negrophobia" are Southern white progressives who are forced to employ race-baiting demagoguery in order to prevail at the polls. In this context see also Grantham's *Hoke Smith and the Politics of the New South* (Baton Rouge, 1958), 178: "The publicity given [Smith's] anti-Negro measures during the years 1905-1909 stamped him in the eyes of the nation as a Southern demagogue. It was unfortunate for his reputation as a Progressive leader that his work should have been marred in this respect." The failure of this kind of monaracial Southern scholarship rests less in its detail than in its underlying perspective on the qualifications for being "Southern" and the criteria upon which progressive "reputations" are based. Negroes lived desperately "political" lives during the period covered by Professor Grantham's books, though the substance of this politics, after disfranchisement, rarely took the form of decisions made at a ballot box.

49. Martin, *People's Party* 179-83, 236.

50. See, for example, H. Wayne Morgan, *From Hayes to McKinley* (New York, 1969), 382.

51. *Examiner*, Sept. 13, 1900. Jack Haynes was murdered two weeks after publication of this statement.

52. See note 26 above.

David Montgomery

On Goodwyn's Populists*

"THEY'RE HERE! THE GREAT INDUSTRIAL ARMY!" announced the *Cincinnati Enquirer* in welcoming 1,400 delegates of Farmers Alliances, cooperative exchanges, the Knights of Labor, the reform press, and third-party movements to the city where they would create a provisional national committee for the People's Party. Lawrence Goodwyn's *Democratic Promise* has conveyed the spirit of that occasion and of the movement it represented more clearly and vividly than any other book since C. Vann Woodward's *Tom Watson*.[1] Like Woodward, Goodwyn is not in the least embarrassed at the spectacle of sun-burned and toil-worn men and women engaging in serious political discussion and deciding together to destroy both the banking and commercial webs that enmeshed them and the two political parties that had commanded their loyalties since the Civil War. In fact, this historic "moment" of popular initiative represented for him the last hope of democracy about to be crushed beneath the weight of the "economic, political, and moral authority that 'concentrated capital' was able to mobilize in 1896" and that was to gather "in intensity until it created new guidelines for the entire society in twentieth-century America" (p. 515).

The central theme of Goodwyn's interpretation of Populism is simple: Squeezed between staggering interest rates charged for store "furnishings" and chronically falling prices, farmers on the western agricultural frontier of Texas organized cooperative buying and selling schemes, which spread

Source: This article originally appeared in *Marxist Perspectives*, No. 1 (Vol. I, No. 1), New York 1978. Reprinted by permission.

*Lawrence Goodwyn, *Democratic Promise: The Populist Government in America*, Oxford University Press, 1976.

rapidly throughout their state during the second half of the 1880s and fanned out northward across the wheatlands. To break the relentless grip of crop liens and mercantile debts they not only had to replace the cash-and-carry tradition of the older Grange cooperatives with "joint note" devices for pooling their debts, but also had to organize such huge cooperative exchanges as the marketing and purchasing warehouse of the Texas Alliance Exchange in Dallas.

The vast organizational network created by these farmers in scarcely five years provoked intense hostility from local merchants and bankers and was dramatically rescued from bankruptcy in June 1888 only by contributions from the meager funds of farmers at 175 simultaneous Texas county courthouse rallies. The Farmers Alliance generated a "movement culture" through regular meetings of thousands of suballiances, stimulated by a small army of lecturers and cooperative functionaries, and supporting a reform press which boasted more than 150 papers at its peak. This political milieu warmly received the Greenbacker analysis of capitalist society, which focused on the exploitative character of the banks' control of the money supply. Out of it grew the famous "subtreasury" plan, which simultaneously promised a governmental source of the money that cooperative exchanges so desperately needed for advances against crops—vehemently refused by the banks—and an agency through which flat currency could be efficiently distributed into the economy as needed. Through this plan the Alliance sought to bring about the abolition of national banks for which Greenbackers had so long aspired.

Realization of the "subtreasury" dream, not to mention such other objectives as public ownership of railroads and telegraphs, required political action. "If Texas led the farmers to the Alliance," says Goodwyn, "Kansas led the Alliance to the people's Party" (p. 195). In fact, the cotton farmers, who provided the movement's center of gravity, faced special difficulties in entering the politics, for to do so meant to break with the white-supremacist Democratic "party of the fathers." Goodwyn recounts that rupture's pitiless battles at length.

The movement collapsed as abruptly as it had risen. By 1890 the cooperative exchanges of the South were crumbling in financial ruin. Parallel to the vibrant political initiatives nurtured by the Alliance movement in Texas, Alabama, Georgia, and Kansas, a "shadow movement" imitative of Populism but without organic roots in the Alliance network and its political culture emerged in Nebraska, Iowa, and Minnesota. And racist demagogues of the "Pitchfork Ben" Tillman variety challenged the Populists in the cotton belt itself. The officials and elected office holders of the People's Party jettisoned their own program in pursuit of electoral victory through fusion with the Democrats. "After the defeat of the cooperatives, the pressure was too great for the People's Party, alone, to bear. The movement lost its animating reality and, in the end, became like its shadow and succumbed to hierarchical politics" (p. 547). Like Woodward, but unlike Richard Hofstadter, Norman Pollack, and most recent interpreters of the movement, Goodwyn rightly sees the nomination of Bryan as the coup de grace to Populism.[2]

Since those who learned about Populism from the scholarship of an earlier vintage than the Eisenhower Era will find much of the argument familiar, do we need a massive new study? Part of the answer lies in the intellectual hegemony established by Richard Hofstadter's *Age of Reform*, which blended so perfectly with the dominant prejudices of its time that overnight it became established historical wisdom. As Goodwyn rightly says, Hofstadter "managed to frame his interpretation of the intellectual content of Populism without recourse to a single reference to the planks of the Omaha Platform . . . or to any of the economic, political, or cultural experiences that led to the creation of those goals" (p. 602). If nothing else, historians do need to look again at what Populists actually did and thought. The loose way in which the word "Populist" is used in current political discussion makes that need urgent.

Goodwyn's analysis of the institutional base of Populism has no precedent among the histories of the movement and provides the book's most solid contribution to our understanding of late nineteenth-century popular politics. Hundreds of thousands of farmers created a network of suballiances, cooperative exchanges, informal "bulking" of cotton sales, joint notes, lectures, reform press, wagon parades, mass rallies, and picnics. The collective political wisdom they distilled generated not only a massive rejection of the political economy of laissez-faire, but also a distinct language through which they identified themselves as "labor" and their movement as one of the "industrial classes"—in marked contrast to the protectionist movements of Prussian Junkers and French peasants during the same crisis. That language came from the urban and workingclass sources of Greenback doctrine, to which Goodwyn pays all too little attention, but most significantly, millions of farmers adopted it to describe their plight and aspirations. Not so Bryan, who described farmers and workers in his Cross of Gold speech as "all businessmen."

An important antidote emerges here to the conception now in vogue of a late nineteenth-century "search for order."[3] The creative struggles of cotton and wheat farmers contributed a major component to the broad popular effort to impose order on laissez-faire capitalism—order from below. The organizational and educational work of the Knights of Labor, the scores of workers' cooperatives that appeared in the 1880s, and the standard wage rates, regional agreements, and elaborate work rules of the trade unions were all collective efforts of working people to bring order into the exploitative chaos of capitalism. These efforts of the workingclass, together with the sophisticated devices used by the Alliances to telegraph the latest market prices to remote rural areas, to circumvent local cotton buyers and grain elevators by "bulking," and to buy machinery directly from distant manufacturers, mock the current historical fad of contrasting the "cosmopolitanism" of business and professional leaders to the "localism" of the lower classes. But the bourgeoisie's "search for order" could succeed only at the expense of the comparable quests of workers and farmers. Popular initiatives had to be suppressed, and workers and farmers reduced to individuals competing with each other if corporate-style "order" was to prevail.

Yet, some functional features of Goodwyn's analysis of plebeian initiative are not convincing. Goodwyn is not simply a historian who understands Greenback doctrine—the quintessence of Populism. He *is* a Greenbacker. "How money was created," he argues, "and on what basis it circulated, defined in critical ways the relationships of farmers, urban workers, and commercial participants in the emerging industrial state" (p. 10).

Genuine pleasure awaits readers who, wearied by the ideological homogeneity of contemporary American historiography, seek distinctive intellectual presuppositions. But Goodwyn's interpretation obscures relationships other than those defined by money. Consider those missing from his catalogue of social groups: bosses. Goodwyn is at a loss to understand the relationship of industrial workers to Populism, for his theoretical categories take no account of the wage-labor relationship and comprehend no exploitation except that which arises in the realms of credit and commodity exchange. Labor reformers, among whom Greenback theories enjoyed their first wide diffusion, had criticized them as early as the 1860s, for they recognized that the problems of interest rates and money supply bore directly only on the relations between owners of the means of production (their employers) and the bankers. Even labor papers as friendly to the Greenback cause as the *National Labor Tribune* insisted that the money issue "does not go to the bottom" of the labor question.[4]

Goodwyn can imagine only three possible causes for the lack of enthusiasm for the Greenback cause among workers: "because the entire matter seemed too difficult to grasp, or because they never heard of it, or because they developed other priorities" (p. 17). The explanation like so many of his references to workers seems gratuitous and condescending; the second is preposterous to anyone familiar with the late nineteenth-century labor movement; and the third remains uninvestigated. The large numbers of workers who, unlike the Populist farmers, could not qualify under residency or citizenship requirements to vote at all, or who, like the majority of the nation's farmers outside of the cotton and wheat belts, continued to vote Republican or Democrat, receive no analysis at all.[5] Consequently, the Republican electoral triumphs of 1894–1896, which began thirty-six almost unbroken years of national hegemony, remain incomprehensible in the terms offered by this study.

More directly relevant to the "Populist moment" itself, Goodwyn gives short shrift to the tens of thousands of workers who directly participated in it—that is, little more than observations about a few leaders. Accepting the customary view that the Knights of Labor collapsed abruptly after 1886, he ignores evidence of resurgence after 1890, especially among southern and western workers.[6] Through exchange of memberships, the Order practically fused with the American Railway Union, in 1894, creating a combined membership larger than that of the American Federation of Labor, committed to the People's Party. Although Goodwyn recounts Chester M. Destler's analysis of labor Populism in Illinois, he pays no attention to the large Populist votes cast by immigrants in Milwaukee, coal miners in Ohio, and shoe workers in Massachusetts.[7] If the "agrarian revolt was over" in 1896 (p. 492), the march of these workingclass voters through Populism into the Social Democracy of America and later the Socialist Party had only begun. While they shared with wheat and cotton farmers the experience of self-education through their own institutional networks, their vision went beyond the abolition of the banker to the abolition of the boss, and thus of wage-labor itself.

Even more serious, Goodwyn offers no class analysis of rural America. For him, a farmer was a farmer, whether he was a cropper, chopped cotton for daily wages, rented land for cash, owned a large plantation, or coupled agricultural pursuits with owning stores and lending money. Hence, although a state like Alabama exhibited complex class relations—black tenants, rich planters, upcountry yeomen, workers in large steel and textile enterprises, Birmingham businessmen, northern investors—Goodwyn explains the defeat of the Populists, despite the mass desertion of the Democratic Party by poor white farmers, simply by pointing to voting frauds in the Black Belt and adding that "the Alabama Alliance never produced a consummate organizational spokesman" like L. L. Polk or Tom Watson, and thus was left in the hands of Reuben Kolb, "a hesitant politician" (p. 402). Fraud and demagogues abounded throughout the South. The question therefore remains: What social relationships in Texas, piedmont Georgia, and northern Alabama fostered the emergence of Alliances with greater vitality than those of South Carolina, Mississippi, and the Black Belt generally?

Closely related to this problem is the thin quality of Goodwyn's treatment of the Colored Farmers' National Alliance and Cooperative Union and of the Knights of Labor among rural blacks. The author pleads lack of sources related to this largely secret and opaque movement (p. 276n), and that remains a serious problem despite the success of Nell Irvin Painter and William Ivy Hair in recreating rural black life and consciousness during this epoch.[8] One recently discovered source has, however, indicated the essential importance of class analysis and the inadequacy of a Greenback interpretation of blacks and the Alliance movement. Evidence of a black rural assembly of the Knights was found in the papers of John B. Grimes, a leader in the Farmers Alliance of Pitt County, North Carolina. The blacks were croppers and laborers on one of Grimes' several plantations. His records reveal that blacks kept their activities secret even from white Alliancemen; for Grimes was trying to discover the participants and break up the organization.[9] Like the hundreds of members of the Colored Farmers Alliance who provoked the wrath of the (white) National Farmers Alliance by going on strike for higher wages in 1891, the Black Knights were the Alliance members' employees.

Goodwyn ends his book with condemnations of both the social order of corporate capitalism, which strode to unchallenged dominance in American life over the corpse of the popular search for order, and its modern socialist alternative, which has meant only "victory through a red army directed by a central political committee" (p. 538). It is unfortunate, indeed, that instead of depicting a world's end in 1896, he did not stay with his farmers through the days when many of them played a prominent role in the American socialist movement, and especially through those of the Non-Partisan League which, during 1916–1920, created the closest thing this country has yet seen to a democratic government in operation. He might better have understood the attitude of those farmers who concluded that more was needed to secure farmers' control in agriculture than just the abolition of banks. They envisaged public ownership of the whole industrial sector as the necessary precondition of their own freedom from exploitation.

Nevertheless, there is considerable merit in Goodwyn's argument that "The entire subject of large-scale agriculture in the modern state, both under capitalist and communist systems of organization, needs thorough reevaluation" (p. 569). Twentieth-century federal farm programs have encouraged the domination of American farming by large-scale capitalist enterprises and the corresponding expulsion of millions of small farmers to the urban slums. The failure of Soviet agriculture has been the Achilles Heel of European socialism and the direct cause of the emergence of that authoritarian state which has mocked socialist dreams.[10] Perhaps one basic lesson to be learned from the "Populist Moment" is that no successful socialist design for agriculture can be drawn up except by the people who work the land themselves. The cooperatives of the Farmers Alliance and the ingenious subtreasury plan showed how creative the collective imagination of the rural working population could be. Comparable popular initiatives will be needed once again to create the agricultural component of a socialist America.

Notes

1. *Tom Watson: Agrarian Rebel* (New York, 1938).

2. Richard Hofstadter, *The Age of Reform, From Bryan to F.D.R.* (N.Y., 1955); Norman Pollack, *The Populist Response to Industrial America: Midwestern Populist Thought* (Cambridge, Mass., 1962).

3. Robert H. Wiebe, *The Search for Order, 1877-1920* (N.Y., 1967); Gabriel Kolko, *Main Currents in Modern America* (New York, 1976); Samuel P. Hays, "Political Parties and the Community-Society Continuum, 1865-1929," in William N. Chambers and Walter Dean Burnham, eds., *The American Party System* (New York, 1967), pp. 152-181.

4. *National Labor Tribune*, Aug. 26, 1876.

5. Even those of us who remain unconvinced of the adequacy of "ethno-cultural determinants" to explain political behavior cannot simply ignore what historians who march under that banner have to say about the late nineteenth century. See Paul Kleppner, *The Cross of Culture: A Social Analysis of Midwestern Politics, 1850-1900* (New York, 1970); Richard J. Jensen, *Winning of the Midwest: Social and Political Conflict, 1886-1896* (Chicago, 1971).

6. See Jonathan E. Garlock, "A Structural Analysis of the Knights of Labor: A Prolegomenon to the History of the Producing Classes" (Unpublished Ph.D. diss., University of Rochester, 1974).

7. Chester M. Destler, *American Radicalism, 1865-1901* (New London, 1946). On working-class votes for Populism, see Kleppner, pp. 190, 199-201, 248-249, 288; Alan Dawley, *Class and Community: The Industrial Revolution in Lynn* (Cambridge, Mass., 1976), pp. 212-213; Henry F. Bedford, *Socialism and the Workers in Massachusetts, 1886-1912* (Amherst, Mass., 1966), pp. 11-135.

8. Painter, *Exodusters: Black Migration to Kansas after Reconstruction* (New York, 1977); William Hair, *Carnival of Fury: Robert Charles and the New Orleans Race Riot of 1900* (Baton Rouge, La., 1976).

9. Robert C. McMath, Jr., "Southern White Farmers and the Organization of Black Farm Workers: A North Carolina Document," *Labor History*, 18 (1977), pp. 115-119.

10. See Moshe Lewin, *Russian Peasants and Soviet Power: A Study of Collectivization* (Evanston, Ill., 1968); Stephen F. Cohen, *Bukharian and the Bolshevik Revolution: A Political Biography, 1888-1938* (N.Y., 1973).

Dale Newman

Textile Workers in a Tobacco County: A Comparison Between Yarn and Weave Mill Villagers*

The cotton textile industry was concentrated in the northeastern part of the United States until the late nineteenth century. Around 1880, the industry began a gradual and continuous shift to the South.[1] The Southeast's share of spindles in cotton-goods manufacture increased from 22 percent to 73 percent of the nation's total between 1899 and 1939.[2] By the mid-twentieth century, more than 80 percent of the active spindles were in the cotton states.[3]

Such shifts in location of major industries are rare,[4] and a thorough explanation of the phenomenon lies beyond the scope of this essay.[5] However, the initial specialization of the southern mills upon the production of coarse yarns was integrally related to technological improvements in ring spinning and widespread poverty in the South. Ring spindles were invented in 1828, but the technical difficulties of high-speed spinning were not overcome until 1871.[6] Unlike mule spinning, which relied upon skilled male labor, ring spinning could be performed by unskilled women and children.[7] The lesson taught by the Fall River, Massachusetts, strike of 1879 was not lost on would-be textile manufacturers below the Mason-Dixon line: Mills that used mules shut down; those which used rings continued to operate.[8] As their efforts to ameliorate the destitution of landless whites impoverished by slavery, civil war, and declining cotton prices culminated in the crusade for cotton mills,[9] the new industrialists

Source: This essay is based upon a presentation at the Second Southern Labor History Conference, Atlanta, May 4, 1978, titled, "Comparison of the Living and Working Conditions in a Cotton Yarn Mill to Those in a Weave Mill Village in a Rural-Industrial County of Piedmont North Carolina." I am indebted to Jonathan Levine and David Montgomery for their criticisms of the original version.

*Pseudonyms have been used for proper names. See the Appendix to this essay for an abbreviated methodological statement.

installed almost exclusively ring spindles.[10] As the rhetoric of the cotton mill campaign echoed throughout the southeast, "Bring the cotton mills to the cotton fields,"[11] the South welcomed the manufacturing jobs that would provide its industrial base for the next one hundred years.

The shift of the American cotton textile industry from the North to the South was a shift not only in the geographic and economic center of the industry.[12] More importantly, it was a shift from the exposed textile communities of the northern cities to the concealed mill villages of the rural South.[13] Students of life and labor in the villages have devoted most of their attention to mills located in urban settings or in "mill chains."[14] Scant regard has been paid to the isolated rural mill,[15] and even less to those located in non-cotton agricultural counties. Villages located in tobacco agriculture counties have been almost totally neglected by students of southern textile labor.[16] While half (551) of the South's 1,104 counties specialized in cotton culture on the eve of the Great Depression, a significant minority produced tobacco as their single money crop. There were approximately 125 such counties in 1930.[17] Since World War I, cotton culture has declined in importance and tobacco agriculture has increased in the South.[18]

"Carol County" is located in the Old Bright Tobacco Belt of Piedmont North Carolina. During the nineteenth century, the area was a remarkably barren section in a state noted for general poverty.[19] Since 1900, tobacco agriculture and textile manufacturing have shaped the socioeconomic characteristics of the majority of the county's nearly 100 percent native-born population.

Study of a rural-industrial[20] county in Piedmont North Carolina from 1900 to 1950 reveals that the daily lives of cotton mill workers under the paternalism[21] of local ownership and management varied considerably from the daily lives of operatives in a nearby weave mill village owned and operated by a northern firm. There were four main differences between the two: (1) cotton mill village workers had less control over their non-work activities than did weave mill workers; (2) cotton mill workers received lower wages and fewer fringe benefits than those employed by the weaving company; (3) cotton mill employees occupied a social status inferior to those in the weave mill; and (4) weave mill operatives worked consistently harder and *demonstrated* more discontent with their working conditions than their cotton mill counterparts.

The relative superiority of living and working conditions in the weave mill village was the direct result of differences between the two major occupations of the industries (spinning and weaving), the differences between the socioeconomic climates in which each village evolved, and differences in the composition of the two work forces. The cotton mill began operations early in the twentieth century when tobacco agriculture in the one-crop county necessitated skill and maturity; coarse yarn, however, could be easily produced on ring spindles operated by unskilled and youthful hands. Consequently, the first generation of cotton mill operatives was comprised primarily of large tenant-farm families ill-suited to growing tobacco. The weave mill was constructed more than twenty years later when changes in tobacco culture were reducing the skill and age levels of agricultural laborers; weaving fine quality fabrics on complex looms, on the other hand, required skillful and mature operators. Thus the first generation of weave mill employees consisted primarily of adult males. Intersecting with the changes in local agriculture and the more complicated technology of the weave mill was an increasing social awareness of industrial working conditions. When the cotton mill was built, child labor was prevalent and labor legislation was minimal; when the weave mill was constructed, more effective labor legislation had reduced child labor in the factories.

To understand the differences between the two villages and their significance for those who experienced them, it is necessary to examine the origins and subsequent development of the two firms. The Roseville Cotton Mills[22] were incorporated in 1899 in Carol County, North Carolina. The corporation was organized by Lee Edward Clay,[23] a local merchant, banker, and farm owner who was instrumental in bringing the railroad through the county during his tenure in the state legislature. Construction of the first Roseville Cotton Mill, a 3,000-spindle plant located one-half mile from the town after which it was named, but across the railroad tracks, was completed early in the new century. It provided employment for fifty people, whose efficiency is evidenced by the doubling of the mill's capacity in 1904 and the construction of a second mill—the subject of today's analysis—in 1907. When the founder of the mills died in 1915, he left an entire business block in town, seven to eight thousand acres in real estate holdings, two cotton mill villages with a total employment of 500 persons, the title of Town Father, a reputation for being a modern capitalist, and the county's only millionaire.[24] He also left a son, Lee Edward Clay, Jr., to carry on the family's interests.

The population of Carol County throughout the twentieth century has been nearly 100 percent native-born, of which approximately two-thirds were white, and the remainder black.[25] The white world consisted of a rigid class structure, and the Clays occupied the pinnacle of the social pyramid; their industrial employees were at the bottom. When the spinning mill was built, tobacco was harvested by the cutting method. Determining the optimum time for harvesting the ripening plant and slicing downward through the four-feet high stalk with a sharp curved knife without damaging the leaves or cutting through the base of the plant required judgment, skill, strength, and height. Cutting was a difficult task and usually performed by males sixteen years old or over.[26] The process of curing tobacco—hanging twenty-five pound tobacco-laden sticks on tiers in the barn—and maintaining carefully regulated temperatures in the wood-fueled flues required similar expertise.[27] Without adequate manpower—either as a result of age,[28] sex,[29] health,[30] or size of the individual family members—to farm profitably, sharecroppers suffered extreme deprivation.[31] A former spooler in the mill recalled memories of farm life and partially reveals the poverty which was the common characteristic of the first generation of cotton mill families:

> Why wouldn't we want to come! . . . six rooms—plastered, painted, a bathroom in the house. . . . In the country, I had to go down hill to a spring for water. . . . My job was carrying water to the field and tending to the baby. Mother worked in the fields some but usually had to carry at least two babies. I took care of them at home and in the field on a pallet. . . . Mother was trying to have a living. With a family of girls, girls can't do but so much.[32]

The cracks in the kitchen floor of their three-room farmhouse showed the chickens underneath by daylight; those in the ceiling revealed the stars at night. Eight members of the family slept in their one "good" room, and three slept upstairs.[33] The initial cotton mill labor force was composed primarily of such large tenant families which were ill suited to growing the golden weed. In choosing the immediate material benefits of life in the mill village[34]—a better house, more frequent and higher income, "work for all of us"—these families sacrificed the respect not only of their agricultural neighbors, friends, and relatives, but they were also subjected to the disapproval of the townspeople.[35] These families went to work in the mill with the knowledge that they had taken a step downward on the social ladder. One woman was told by her relatives that she might as well be taking her eight children (six girls, two boys) to a "whore house" as to the mill.[36]

Town attitudes toward the cotton mill workers are reflected in a novel written by one of the county's farm-owning families: "The inhabitants of Milltown had come from the farms, landless and homeless whites, living from day to day, a lazy, shiftless, unimaginative lot. Poor whites who had never known a surplus of anything except misery. . . ."[37] Referred to as "cotton mill tackies" living on "mill hill" or "cotton hill," the industrial villagers were ostracized by the "town" people. Life in the mill village nurtured attitudes of low self-esteem and perpetuated the rigidities of the closed society. Considered and treated as inferior by society, cotton mill workers came to feel inferior. Their feelings were reinforced by the physical and social isolation of the industrial community as it developed.[38]

In 1923, Lee Edward Clay, Jr., persuaded a Philadelphia weave mill to open a plant one-half mile north of his LeClay village in order to provide a local market for his yarns. Profits from World War I had been ploughed into expanding both of his mill facilities: Spindlage increased from 21,000 to 38,000; the number of company houses was doubled, and a mercantile store, school, church, theatre, and bank were built in LeClay. After the prosperity related to the war abated, an improvement in marketing arrangements was needed to utilize the company's increased capacity.[39] Induced to construct a small mill as an experiment, the northern firm installed only thirty looms initially; the venture was so successful that they doubled the number within a year. In 1927, the weave firm merged with K & O Fabrics, another Philadelphia company, which launched an expansion that has continued till the present decade.[40]

K & O Fabric Corporation was typical of many northern firms which began operations in the South during the twenties as the depression in textiles accelerated following the reconversion to production for civilian markets after World War I.[41] There were many benefits to be derived from the North Carolina plant: Four years of operation had established the existence and efficiency of the labor force, as well as the reliability of the cotton mill in providing yarn. In addition, the local wage structure was even lower than that of the southern textile industry generally. The purchase and initial expansion of K & O coincided with declining tobacco prices and changing crop culture in Carol County. As prices of bright leaf plummeted from $24.62 per 100 pounds in 1926 to $7.73 in 1931,[42] farmers supplemented their meager returns with textile work at K & O.[43] They also began to switch from cutting to priming individual leaves of the ripening plant. The change in harvesting decreased the demand for adult labor in the fields and barns as children as young as ten were capable of priming—snapping off single leaves—and anyone over six could hand leaves without difficulty.[44]

These agricultural changes contributed to a quite different labor force working in the weave mill. Whereas, that in the cotton mill was family labor, that in the weave plant was primarily adult males whose average age was twenty-seven years;[45] in contrast, nearly half of fifty workers whose age is known, who began work in the spinning mill before 1920, were fifteen or younger.[46] Men outnumbered women two to one at K & O, which employed no one under sixteen and few under eighteen.[47] Weave mill employees were not only older; they were better educated; more than half had graduated high school, and the average grade level was eighth.[48] Cotton mill employees had much less formal education: 1915 birth records reveal more than 40 percent of fifty employees becoming parents that year were without any schooling; an equal percent were able simply to read and write, and a mere 12 percent had common or public school education. Only two of the fifty cotton mill parents had high school experience.[49] Unlike spinning mill operatives who lived in the company-owned village,[50] approximately one-half of the weave mill's 1,000 employees lived on farms or in town, and K & O operated a bus for their convenience.[51]

The differences between the two groups of employees derive not only from tobacco culture which affected the labor *supply*, but also from the differences in technology between the two industries, as well as the social climate in which each firm was established, which affect the labor *demands* of the employer. Spinning, spooling, and doffing cotton yarn were easily performed by young, unskilled children;[52] learning these jobs was usually a matter of days. In contrast, weaving, winding, beaming, dyeing, and twisting, to mention a few of the K & O operations, required much more skill, strength, and consequently, maturity; learning was usually a matter of weeks, with proficiency coming long after.[53]

Exercising greater skill in producing a higher-grade product and possessing more formal education, weave mill operatives occupied a social status superior to that of workers in the spinning mill. The employment of farm *owners*, and during the depression even some leading businessmen,[54] contributed to the higher ranking of the K & O employees. As a landowner and former mechanic at the weave mill explained: "I don't think [K & O] was ever considered in that class. It was not a cotton mill. It was a manufacturing establishment . . . viewed in a different light."[55] According to a former weaver, the people at the weave mill felt superior to those at LeClay, and the townspeople felt superior to both groups. He said working in K & O was "definitely" better than working in the cotton mill, where the people "were looked down on by everybody."[56]

Although child labor laws had existed in North Carolina since 1903, cotton mill officials violated them often until the federal minimum wage and age provisions made it uneconomical to do so.[57] In the first generation of mill workers, mothers with many children who could earn wages did not work in the factory.[58] After the short-lived Federal Child Labor Law of 1917,[59] violations were less flagrant and less frequent. When the North Carolina minimum age was raised to fourteen, more mothers began to work in the mill. The first "Little Mother's League" was organized in Carol County in 1922 for girls between the ages of ten and fourteen who were "occasionally or regularly assuming charge of their baby brothers and sisters. . . ."[60] With the introduction of minimum wage and age laws and the addition of second and third shifts in the mill, this trend intensified; subsequent generations of wives and mothers worked in the spinning mill and their adolescent children continued to drop out of school—but to care for younger siblings, rather than to work in the mill.[61]

Any failure on the part of the K & O Company to observe the North Carolina child labor laws would have been much more visible to the community at large because of the complement of rural and town operatives. But the main reason K & O did not employ laborers under sixteen years of age is that work was too difficult to be mastered easily, thus rendering training expensive.

The Roseville Cotton Mills maintained strict supervision over LeClay village. The company was able to effect its control in several ways: (1) by close proximity and high visibility of supervisory personnel who imposed and enforced a rigid moral code; (2) by domination of community institutions which functioned to serve the best interests of the company; (3) by constant threats of unemployment and eviction of its captive work force, which lacked the education, experience, esteem, and opportunity for alternative employment; (4) by persistent *underemployment* of its laborers, whose substandard wages necessitated that all able-bodied members of the family work for daily subsistence; (5) through the vulnerability of the whole family to reprisals against individual members; (6) and, finally, through the vulnerability of individuals aspiring to personal advancement, who could only succeed by ingratiating themselves with bosses, by conforming to company rules and informing on friends, neighbors, and sometimes relatives.

The superintendent of the mill and his overseers lived in the five houses leading into the main part of the cotton mill village where they could observe who came and went.[62] The superintendent held a dominant position in LeClay for nearly sixty years, during which time he molded would-be fixers and foremen into the image of God-fearing, church-attending, alcohol-abstaining, loyal, punctual, and hard-working employees. The company also paid an employee to serve as a police officer and patrol LeClay.[64] With few exceptions, the cotton mill operatives lived in the company's 100 houses until the introduction of second and third shifts; New Deal legislation resulted in the hiring of workers who commuted from the farms.[65] Only those houses built after World War I had inside plumbing (no bathtub); nearly half of them were without water until 1950,[66] and families on the "old hill" used outside pumps and privies for basic needs. It was the responsibility of children to carry the water for household use, a duty which contributed to high absenteeism from school on Monday mornings as that was wash day.[67] Pouring kerosene oil down the outdoor toilet as a sanitary measure was also a chore assigned to youngsters, with on one occasion disastrous consequences: Unable to locate any kerosene, the young son poured gasoline down the seat. When his father was using the facility a short while later and tossed a cigarette butt down the hole, he was exploded right out the door and into the yard.[68]

Cotton mill village residents risked eviction if they disturbed their neighbors[69]—many of whose houses were only twenty-five feet distant.[70] As family size decreased with the second and third generations of mill workers who grew in the village,[71] it becamc increasingly difficult not to disturb neighbors, since the three-, four-, and five-room houses had to accommodate two separate families instead of the one large one as had been the case with their parents and grandparents.[72] After the mid-twenties, LeClay workers found their leisure curtailed. Dancing, card playing, partying, and drinking alcoholic beverages in the houses were prohibited; previously popular pound parties—to which everyone would bring a pound of something—coffee, cabbage, potatoes, peaches—continued as a form of economic aid for those who were especially indigent.[73] For minor infractions of rules such as riding a mule into a store, a person was forced to "rest" for two weeks;[74] for more serious ones, such as persistent alcohol consumption, the offender would be fired;[75] if a woman became pregnant out of wedlock—and the town doctors would inform the mill office—, she would have to leave the village and visit her family only at night when she would not be seen by others.[76] The company concerned itself not only with what employees did, but what they wore—women could not wear shorts to the company store[77]—and what they said: Swearing or cursing were not allowed.[78] As one woman expressed it, "They knew your thoughts almost."[79]

The Baptist church was an important instrument of social control in LeClay village because of its domination by the company. The superintendent of the mill was also superintendent of the Sunday school, chairman of the board of deacons, chairman of the pulpit committee, and church treasurer. In the mid-thirties, he advised the Baptist minister that his task "was to save souls and not to deal in problems that were none of his business." When the minister sermonized, "The Lord calls a true pastor to speak to the sheep and not to run about here and there dressing their sores," the mill officials were pleased.[80] The espousal of the doctrine that one's position in life is ordained by God led to long-suffering resignation in anticipation of heavenly rewards; worshipers were encouraged in the belief that only God can eliminate wordly evils, which are a part of His grand, if mysterious, design. One of the 1951 "Come to Church" advertisements which the company sponsored regularly in the biweekly newspaper captures this attitude: Grandmother Knows . . . that spiritual things are far more important than material things. She knows that God rules in the kingdom of men, that the Church is His messenger, and faith is man's hope of salvation.[81] Such views were deterrents to the concepts of self-help and collective action which had been an important aspect of daily life on the farms.[82]

By operating a mercantile store, for which deductions were made by the mill office before workers received their pay, the company contributed to the dependency of employees, whose earnings were expended primarily on food.[83] Poor learning environment and experience in the mill school reduced the children's potential for independence. Hopefully atypical but revealing of the educational atmosphere was the experience of a third-generation mill worker who repeated the fifth and sixth grades during the mid-forties:

> Teacher in the fifth grade played music all the time. She [told me] get up and sing a solo, and I got up and asked the kids if they knew the Billy Goat's Song. They said, "No," and I said, "Baaaaaaaa!" and [the teacher] slapped the *fool* out of me three times [first one side of the face, then the other, and back around again].[84]

Roseville Cotton Mills further controlled LeClay residents by paying low wages, which were inferior to those paid by K & O. Department of Labor statistics averaged by the National Association of Cotton Manufacturers in 1926 determined northern operatives received 44.8 cents per hour, and southern ones 28.8 cents.[85] LeClay spinning mill workers, however, were paid at the rate of approximately 15 cents per hour;[86] K & O paid at the rate of 20 cents per hour.[87] The discrepancy between cotton operatives' wages locally and those of other southerners generally had existed since the construction of the mills and persisted until the Fair Labor Standards Act of 1938.[88] Perhaps apocryphal, but accurate in substance, is a statement attributed to the grandson of the original founder of the mills when his father's (Lee Edward Clay, Jr.'s) business acumen was being praised: "I don't know. Is that genius or damned rascality—

He was paying one-third of what they were in New England."[89] Unlike the cotton mill, which paid learners nothing, the weave mill paid them $1.50 a day.[90]

The weave mill not only paid higher wages, but it also gave frequent bonuses, and paid incentives to operatives who exceeded the production standard. In 1936, for example, workers at K & O received a 10 percent wage increase and two separate bonuses of $20 and $25 each.[91] Few cotton mill employees were paid piece rates before the National Industrial Recovery Act;[92] most were paid by the day and enjoyed a work schedule that allowed more leisure than was true for the weave mill. Doffers at LeClay could leave the mill to play outside or stand around the store; spinners and spoolers played mumblety-peg in the aisles.[93] Horseplay was prevalent and persisted throughout generations: sending "green hands" for skyhooks, frame stretchers, and left-handed monkey wrenches, or asking them to move the frames which were bolted to the floor.[94] Since most of the spinning mill employees began work so young, many of them met their future spouses in the plant, and courting was widespread.[95]

Clowning and courting occurred in the weave mill also. While asleep on third shift one night, a weaver was doused with a foul bucket of stagnant water which had hung in the mill for months in case of fire. But as he and others noted, they never joked around with anyone who was trying to do his job.[96] Weave mill employees earned their higher wages, incentives, and bonuses by working at a much more intense pace than did the spinning mill operatives. Frequent bonuses granted by K & O appear to have been designed for increasing production and decreasing workers. When the company paid its bonus in December 1936, 1,100 employees were the recipients; in April 1937 there were only 950.[97] As the number of looms operated and the amount of production expected increased, so did the pressures from the bosses. As a former weaver who became a fixer and "little boss" before he finally quit said:

> I hated every minute that I worked at [K & O]; supervisors drove you; it was slavery. Only poor white trash can be drove—They kept everybody scared to death all the time; they just talked to you like you was dogs all the time. [ ] was the big superintendent on day, [ ] was night superintendent; those fellows never stayed long. They were drove by the Company; they drove the foremen; the foremen drove section bosses; and we in turn drove the weavers.[98]

Wages received by operatives at both mills were irregular. Each company was subject to seasonal slumps, as well as recession and depression.[99] Temporary interruptions of work because of over- or underruns in different departments were also frequent.[100] Although subject to more layoffs, weave mill workers had the opportunity to receive unemployment checks.[101] Rarely was the cotton mill laborer eligible for such compensation, as the cotton mills' practice of hiring "spare hands" (more workers than there were jobs) resulted in greater underemployment for operatives; "resting" for one or two days per week was customary in order to spread the work, and spinning mill employees never got overtime.[102] LeClay laborers also had to "rest" for infractions of village rules against swearing, drinking, creating a "fuss" or "talking back" to bosses on the job.[103]

Workers at both mills were penalized for poor work, but the weave mill employee was more likely to have his wages docked for defects. Asked if he were ever docked, one weaver replied:

> Oh Lord, Yes!! Everybody [was]! [There was] no way to make that cloth perfect. . . . [I] have known some to be docked $10.00 in one week . . . when you not making [but] $20 . . . I've seen poor weavers bawling and crying they was docked so bad . . .[104]

Nepotism and favoritism existed at both mills, but were most prevalent in the cotton mill, where a few families maintained supervisory control—hiring, firing, assigning, or promoting for three generations; fathers trained their sons; daughters of the favored became winders.[105] These familial relationships reduced the frequency of docking at the cotton mill. But workers at both plants were subject to "compulsory rest" periods of one to two weeks for excessive amounts of poor work.[106]

Employees at both plants labored five and a half days, sixty hours a week until the thirties, but the weave mill operated a night shift soon after opening.[107] Supervision varied between the two companies, as well as between individuals and shifts worked, and labor supply.[108] The long range trend at each mill was toward an increased work load: more machines to operate, at faster speeds, on larger packages with greater output per man-hour.

Despite low and irregular wages for both groups of workers, the economic status of weave mill employees was superior to that of the LeClay operatives. In addition to providing relatively higher wages and more opportunity to work, K & O Fabrics maintained a clinic for workers and their families with a nurse on duty twenty-four hours a day, and a physician available one hour each morning and afternoon for treatment at no cost. The company was quite candid about its motives, acknowledging its recognition of the principle that "good health is a necessary adjunct to work at peak capacity."[109] K & O had instituted hospital insurance and part-time insurance for unemployment, as well as $25 for mothers at childbirth by the late thirties.[110]

Roseville Cotton Mills, on the other hand, refused to provide group insurance for its employees. Although the company would lend money to operatives for hospital bills, it would not do so for physicians' fees. Consequently, many cotton mill laborers postponed medical care. One father of thirteen had been told three times by his doctor that he should receive surgical treatment before he finally succumbed to the humiliating procedure of having the superintendent of the mill sign a statement authorizing a loan which the worker had to carry to the president of the company in his town office. Employees were sometimes repaying their medical loans for more than three years.[111]

Two questions occur immediately: (1) Why did the weave mill provide more benefits and higher pay? (2) Why didn't all the cotton mill employees quit their jobs for the better ones at the weave mill? The answer to the first question is complex: (1) the nature of the work in the weave mill required a more skilled work force which was necessarily older, with the corollary that the *potential* labor supply was smaller than for the cotton mill. (2) The fabric company produced upholstery fabrics primarily for the expanding transportation industry. The large size of its local plant, which employed over a thousand by 1934,[112] and the ownership of eight mills by then, may be presumed to have provided K & O with economies of scale not possible for Roseville Cotton Mills. The latter operated in a contracting market as rayon and synthetics competed with cotton, and as the cotton textile industry continued its migratory habits to underdeveloped areas.[113] (3) As a northern firm of long standing, there can be no doubt that K & O was aware of and anxious to avoid the adverse publicity surrounding the low wages, long hours, and child labor in southern textiles.[114] (4) Though ostensibly welcomed to Carol County by the elites, K & O was sensitive to their anti-industrial bias and the undercurrent of criticism occasioned by their profits going elsewhere.[115] (5) The company prided itself as a pace setter in adopting personnel benefits.[116]

Cotton mill workers did not quit for work in the weave mill because the two companies had an agreement not to hire each other's help.[117] The owner of the mill village in which one was born had the first option on one's labor. One woman quit her job at LeClay and moved to another state for several months in order to establish a non-local residence and employment; her objective was to obtain a job at K & O because: "[They] paid better. . . . When they gave you a job, you worked. [They] didn't tell you to go home and rest today. . . . [You] didn't have a *piece* of a job like at [LeClay]."[118] If a woman married a K & O employee, however, she was automatically allowed to transfer. Many Roseville Cotton Mill employees would have preferred working for K & O weave mill. But no one employed by the latter has ever indicated a preference for labor in the spinning plant.

K & O village residents enjoyed not only higher incomes but also more freedom over their non-work activities, which the weave company did not restrict. It was not the habit of the northern executives to visit or patronize stores in the village.[119] Nor did they interfere in the personal relationships of their villagers. Quarreling, fighting, and getting drunk were common occurrences, as were extramarital affairs. In 1929, an enraged husband in Koville shot a man who had been visiting his wife "frequently."[120] This could never have happened in LeClay as the company would have known and prevented "frequent" visits by a man with someone else's wife. A former weaver and resident in the village made home brew regularly, and on one occasion climbed the mill tower while under its influence; he was ordered down by the mill guard, and slept off the effects in a pig pen (a clean one) without encountering the wrath of his supervisors. As he stated, the company "didn't care what you done as long as you was on your job when your time come, [but] they didn't want you to destroy their property."[121]

Squabbles within families and between neighbors were commonplace in the weave mill village.[122] Crowded living conditions contributed to the dissension; there were nearly nine (8.7) persons per household in Koville compared with seven (6.5) in LeClay;[123] though houses in the weave mill village were no closer together than those at the spinning community, they occupied a much smaller total land space. Although families in both sections took in boarders to supplement low wages, occupants in the Koville households were less likely to be related.[124] One woman who lived in a four-room house at K & O during the depression, with both her parents and six brothers and sisters, noted that her mother always had two or three boarders who slept in the beds while the children were in school.[125] Workers' constant fear of being docked, continuous pressure of working under top speed while on the job, and the strain of keeping children quiet so that the night shift could sleep also added to tensions among Koville residents.

The weave mill did not impose rigid controls for several reasons: First, the impermanence of its top officials whose values, culture, policies, and procedures reflected their northern background was not conducive to a consistent and continuous set of *mores*. K & O had three resident managers between 1929 and 1951, and was operating five years before constructing its executive housing. Approximately 25 percent of the personnel at the weave mill came from outside Carol County. These top officials did not attend the churches organized by operatives in the weave mill village; some attended the churches in town, and others helped to establish a Catholic church. The cultural differences between K & O and Roseville Cotton Mill officials were clearly demonstrated when the weave company served beer at its first employee social.[126]

Second, and more importantly, the weave company lacked the institutional bases of power possessed by the cotton mill. The necessity for providing housing, as well as all goods and services for destitute tenant families which Roseville Cotton Mills confronted in the first two decades of its operation, did not exist for the weave mill when it was constructed. The proximity of Koville to LeClay village with its boardinghouses, churches, school, and store[127] obviated any urgency for building extra-work institutional structures in the weave mill village. More widespread ownership of automobiles and the company's bus operation reduced housing and transportation problems for potential employees. K & O did build 126 houses for employees, some with each phase of its expansion before 1940 as an attraction to more highly skilled and transient operatives. The three-, four-, and six-room bungalows for workers were well constructed, with interior plumbing and electricity, and were located on paved streets which were swept weekly.[128] In 1931, the company built a modern grammar school, but it did not establish a church; operatives formed their own—Methodist—in 1933. Baptists organized a year later. Although it leased land for grocery stores, a barber shop, and a drugstore, the northern firm did not operate any commercial establishment and did not deduct store accounts from employee wages, as did the cotton mill.[129] By employing predominantly young adult males—many of whom belonged in the landowning class and thus did not live in the village, but a significant minority of whom were highly skilled, difficult to replace, and potentially mobile—the weave mill was unable to exercise restraints on the *family as an institution.*

Third, the physical layout of Koville made surveillance of employees by management difficult. The company's ten executive houses—two-story colonial structures—were located on an exclusive crescent-shaped driveway immediately off the main highway and sufficiently north of the mill to protect their occupants from the clackety-clack of the looms. Employees, on the other hand, occupied houses south and directly behind the plant where the roar of machinery accompanied the coal soot which settled over the backyard clotheslines.[130]

The fourth reason why K & O was unable to maintain strict discipline over its village residents stems from internal class lines and ethnic differences between top officials and lower-level bosses and foremen. There were sharp social divisions within both industrial villages which were not visible to the larger community. In the cotton mill village, the top-ranking group consisted of the superintendent, his overseers, and foremen, who along with their families comprised the bulk of the Baptist church membership; the second highest group consisted of operatives and their families who made up the Methodist church roll; and the lowest ranking was held by families newly arrived from the farms and occasionally from other mills.[131] The subdivisions at the weave mill were more complex: At the top were the officials from the North occupying Executive Crescent; second were the overseers, heads of departments, who often lived uptown; third were the loom fixers, electricians, carpenters, knifemen, mechanics, and to some extent the weavers; this third group lived with and among the operatives but was excluded from the social life of the top two. As a result, these "little bosses" did not always identify with white-collar executives who held "a position." A fourth group included less skilled employees—operatives whose status quite often depended upon the socioeconomic backgrounds of their families: Those of the landowning class or the highly skilled employees were above the "poor folks." The fifth and lowest rank was held by persons with whom no one associated—publicly—such as women who bore children outside of wedlock with different fathers.[132]

The final reason the northern company abstained from interfering in the personal lives of employees in their village may be attributed to an astute awareness of the firm's vulnerability to collective action by operatives.[133] Weave mill workers demonstrated their dissatisfaction with the intensity of the work pace and attitude of supervisors on more than one occasion. In 1932, workers at K & O walked out for three days in protest against the work pace; their picket line was crossed by a fellow weaver who helped the mill start up.[134] In 1937 and 1942, K & O employees attempted unsuccessfully to form a union. The company responded by instituting an employees' council and instituting its first "Family Day" stew, abandoning the separate-sex socials it had customarily sponsored, in an apparent response to the young male leaders of the organizing effort. By not curbing workers' rights to swear, drink, fight, dance, play cards, and run around with someone else's spouse, K & O provided a safety valve for employees' emotions in their potentially explosive work environment.[135]

K & O's non-interference in the private lives of village residents did not reflect disinterest in their activities. The company tried to stay informed about them. A deputy sheriff was hired to protect the company's property, and supervisors encouraged employees to inform on fellow workers. Internal industrial class lines facilitated the company's communication system and undermined employees' integrity. According to a former weaver and loom fixer:

> Bosses didn't associate with those in the village at all. . . . They was poor white trash—*We was*! [There were] three or four different classes. People in my social standing didn't associate with those below. [We] were encouraged to be that way; they'd call a person in and try to get you to tell something on somebody. They knew what you had in your house, wasn't anything they didn't know.[136]

In conclusion, the comparison of living and working conditions in LeClay cotton mill village with those in K & O weave mill village from 1900 to 1950 reveals that life was not easy for either the weavers or the spinners. But the weave mill village residents enjoyed greater freedom and exercised more control over their non-work activities, received higher wages and more fringe benefits, and occupied a higher rung on the social ladder than those in the locally owned community. In exchange for their relative advantages, weave mill operatives worked consistently harder than those at the spinning mill. The failure of workers at both plants to form a viable union reflects the superior social, political, and economic power of their industrial employers, not an "individualism rooted in agrarian origins."[137] Nor does it denote, as Robert Blauner has suggested, that objective tendencies in the southern textile industry are overcome by the integration of work and non-work concerns, such as family, religion, and community.[138] On the contrary, the company-controlled mill village was an insidious violation of individual rights.

Notes

1. Broadus Mitchell, *The Rise of Cotton Mills in the South* (Baltimore, 1921), pp. 77-159; Marvin N. Fischbaum, "An Economic Analysis of the Southern Capture of the Cotton Textile Industry Progressing to 1910" (unpublished Ph.D. diss., Columbia University, 1965), pp. 1-22;

John Garett Van Osdell, Jr., "Cotton Mills, Labor, and the Southern Mind: 1880-1930" (unpublished Ph.D. diss., Tulane University, 1966), pp. 1-36.

2. *Labor in the South*, Bureau of Labor Statistics Bulletin No. 898 (Washington, D.C., 1947), p. 8.

3. James A. Morris, "Cotton and Wool Textiles—Case Studies in Industrial Migration," *The Journal of Industrial Economics* 2 (November 1953): 66.

4. Ibid. See also Fischbaum, "An Economic Analysis of the Southern Capture of the Cotton Textile Industry," p. 2.

5. For general accounts, see Fischbaum, Mitchell, and Morris *op. cit.*; Ben Lemert, *The Cotton Textile Industry of the Southern Piedmont* (Chapel Hill, N.C., 1933); Richard Woods Edmonds, *Cotton Mill Labor Conditions in the South and New England* (Baltimore, 1925); Victor R. Fuchs, *Changes in the Location of Manufacturing in the United States Since 1929* (New Haven, Conn., 1962).

6. Herbert Jay Lahne, *The Cotton Mill Worker* (New York, 1944), pp. 13, 153; Sister Mary J. Oates, *The Role of the Cotton Textile Industry in the Economic Development of the American Southeast* (unpublished Ph.D. diss., Yale University, 1969), pp. 6-7.

7. Lars Sandburg, "American Rings and English Mules: The Role of Economic Rationality," *The Quarterly Journal of Economics* 83 (February 1969): 25-43. Sandburg claims the replacement of mules by ring spinning was the most important technological improvement in the spinning industry during the past 100 years (p. 25).

8. Lahne, *The Cotton Mill Worker*. Though appearing to discount the impact of the mule spinners on the shift to rings, Sandburg concludes: "Although the quantitative data are not strong enough to prove the point, I suspect there may have been some substance to the many comments by contemporary observers that employer dislike of unions caused them to avoid mule spinning" (p. 43). Not only were the mule spinners the most effectively organized union in cotton textiles, but they also took an aggressive role in encouraging organization among other operatives (p. 33).

9. It was the poverty of the region that provided an abundant and cheap labor supply which was the primary attraction to industrialists. See Lemert, Van Osdell, Jr., Fischbaum, "An Economic Analysis . . ."; C. Vann Woodward, *Origins of the New South, 1877-1913* (Baton Rouge, La., 1951); Rupert Vance, *Human Geography of the South: A Study in Regional Resources and Human Adequacy* (Chapel Hill, N.C., 1932); Mildred R. Mell, "A Definitive Study of the Poor Whites of the South" (unpublished Ph.D. diss., University of North Carolina, 1938).

10. This conclusion is based upon the repeated references to child and female spinners. Scattered evidence suggests that mules may have been used in some of the earlier and larger mills, particularly in South Carolina mills which employed male spinners and produced fine goods. Examples can be found in "Working Conditions of the Textile Industry in North Carolina, South Carolina, and Tennessee," *Hearings Before the Committee on Manufactures United States Senate*, 71st Cong., 1st sess., on Senate Res. 49 (May 8, 9, and 20, 1929), hereafter referred to as Senate Res. 49. It is also true that during "hard times," mills regularly employing females on ring spindles would re-assign men to work while the females were laid off. There has been no study of the extent and impact of mules in the South.

11. Mitchell, *Labor in the South*.

12. The situation is analogous to that of the British coal industry as revealed in Christopher Storm-Clark's "The Miners, 1870-1970: A Test Case for Oral History," *Victorian Studies* 15 (September 1971): 49-74.

13. "Decentralization" is the term used to describe the rural setting of many southern mills and has been suggested as a partial explanation for the absence of unionization among the workers. Villages existed in a wide variety of settings, and their "characters" were the product, not only of the proximity of an urban network or a dozen other mills, but also of the demographic characteristics of the workers and the technology of the plant, as well as the socioeconomic and cultural milieu of the area.

14. For examples of the former, see Melton McLaurin, *Paternalism and Protest: Southern Cotton Mill Workers and Organized Labor, 1875-1905* (Westport, Conn., 1971), and Merl E.

Reed, "The Augusta Textile Mills and the Strike of 1886," *Labor History* 14 (Spring 1973): 228-46; for studies of mills located in the "chains," see Jennings J. Rhyne, *Some Southern Cotton Mill Workers and Their Villages* (Chapel Hill, N.C., 1930); Bernard M. Cannon, "Social Deterrents to the Unionization of Southern Cotton Mill Workers" (unpublished Ph.D. diss., Harvard University, 1952).

15. This neglect is partly explained by the unwillingness of textile employers to permit researchers to enter and question their employees in the rural villages. Two employers refused to cooperate with Rhyne in his study of Gaston County, which contained 100 mills in 1930; Cannon encountered considerable difficulty before he discovered a cooperative management for his investigation in a South Carolina county having 43 plants and more than 24 corporations. One vice-president told Cannon, "You ought to know I can't let you come in here and talk to my workers. That is unthinkable. Indeed, you might start them thinking and they could go union overnight.... We don't want any outsider disturbing the village" (p. 16). (Cannon was a middle-class native of the region.) It is also true that mill workers have been suspicious of researchers and afraid and unwilling to cooperate on some occasions. See Donald Roy, "The Role of the Researcher in the Study of Social Conflict: A Theory of Protective Response," *Human Organization* 24 (1965): 262-66. Even though he received full cooperation from officials and operatives, Kenneth Morland noted that he never completely overcame the suspicions of the mill workers in Kent. See *Millways of Kent* (New Haven, Conn., 1964), p. 3.

16. The origins of operatives in Reed's, McLaurin's, Morland's, Cannon's, and Mitchell's studies derive from cotton agriculture. Fischbaum ignores the impact of tobacco tenancy, 67-88; and Rhyne, although undoubtedly aware of tobacco agriculture as the source of Gaston's labor, makes no distinction between tenants from cotton or tobacco. Even Robert Sidney Smith's *Mill on the Dan* (Durham, N.C., 1960) fails to analyze the origins of workers in Danville who were clearly drawn from the region of the Old Tobacco Belt.

17. Charles S. Johnson, *Statistical Atlas of Southern Counties: Listing and Analysis of Socio-Economic Indices of 1104 Southern Counties* (Chapel Hill, N.C., 1941), pp. 1-39. According to Johnson, there were 167 crop-specialty counties other than cotton in 1930, and three-fourths of them specialized in tobacco. As he notes, the principal type of farming in a one-crop county can tell us much about the characteristics of the county; the system of tobacco culture involves a quite different cultivation, harvesting, and marketing than cotton; the two are not so dissimilar in financing.

18. On the decline in cotton, see T. J. Woofter, Jr., "The Status of Racial and Ethnic Groups," *Recent Social Trends in the United States, I* (New York, 1933), pp. 568-69, and James H. Street, *The Revolution in the Cotton Economy: Mechanization and Its Consequences* (Chapel Hill, N.C., 1957); for the expansion of tobacco culture, see Nannie May Tilley, *The Bright Tobacco Industry 1860-1929* (Chapel Hill, N.C., 1948), and W. W. Gardner et al., "History and Status of Tobacco Culture," United States Department of Agriculture *Yearbook*, 1922, pp. 395-468.

19. Tilley, *The Bright Tobacco Industry*, pp. 15-17.

20. The usage of "rural-industrial" denotes the small and scattered plants imbedded in the large agricultural sector as described by Sister Mary J. Oates, "The Role of the Cotton Textile Industry in the Economic Development of the American Southeast: 1900-1940" (unpublished Ph.D. diss., Yale University, 1969), p. 73; it does *not* derive from Johnson's *Statistical Atlas*, under which classification "Carol County" was small town, industrial in 1930.

21. "Paternalism" is used to denote the company's ownership of the land, structures (including mill, houses, stores, and churches) in the unincorporated villages and the provision of goods and services (coal, credit, electric, etc.). For a detailed discussion of southern textile mill village paternalism, see Harriet L. Herring, *Welfare Work in Mill Villages: The Story of Extra-Mill Activities in North Carolina* (Chapel Hill, N.C., 1929).

22. Pseudonyms are used for all proper names and places pertaining to the county; numbers and statistics have been rounded off to protect the identity of the community and its residents. Using an official North Carolina highway map distributed by the local Chamber of Commerce to

assure that no such places actually existed, I created the names of "Roseville" and "Carol County" in 1971. While driving across the state in 1976, I discovered a community by the name of Roseville, which was apparently too small for the 1970 map; I know nothing about this community, and any similarity between it and the mill town under study is coincidental. The names of the companies are fictitious, but the names of the real villages derive as indicated: The cotton mill community was named after the founder; the weave mill village became known as "Koville" based on the *first* Philadelphia company to build in Carol County; this community also acquired a second name based on its second owner, which has not been used in this presentation.

23. *The Roseville Messenger* (pseudonym—cited hereafter as RM) (August 8, 1935), Section 1, p. 6.

24. *RM* (January 31, 1917), p. 2, (August 8, 1935), see 1, p. 7, and [Withheld], *Historical Sketch of [Carol County]* (Danville, 1974), quoting *RM* of September 13, 1899, p. 170.

25. U.S. Census Statistics of population indicate a declining black population from 1900 to 1960. The historical experience of blacks has not been dealt with in this presentation because operatives in both firms were white until the sixties. For a comparison of black experiences under the caste system to white experiences under paternalism and the effects of integration, see my "Work and Community Life in a Southern Textile Town," *Labor History* 19, no. 2 (Spring 1978): 204-25.

26. Interviews with agricultural laborers, tenants, and landlords—male and female, black and white—who farmed during the cutting era. See Tilley, *The Bright Tobacco Industry*, pp. 57-58, 71-81 for comparisons between cutting and priming. The more economically advantaged the farm family was, the less likely that a female or younger adolescent would cut; children of poor sharecropping families were often assigned farm tasks before they were physically equipped to handle them; boys seven to ten, for example, often had to lead a double-horse plow.

27. Women and children helped to hang the tobacco by standing on a platform laid across the tiers. Sleeping at the barn in order to tend the fire during curing was an occasion for pleasure; families would sing, and roast potatoes and corn at the end of the flue. But adult supervision was essential to keep the fire from getting too low or too hot.

28. Interview with a white female (hereafter designated WF, WM, BM, or BF to indicate race and sex) first-generation spinner, WF spooler, and WF whose grandmother came to work in the mill with her five daughters after she was widowed.

29. *Ibid.*

30. Interview with WM, former bandmaker, and WF, former spinner.

31. While conducting interviews with white and black cotton mill workers, the writer noted the diminutive stature of many whites in contrast to the blacks. In 1933, a Public Health service report observed the striking tendency for the workers to be under the average weight of other industrial employees by about ten pounds. See Rollo Britten, J. J. Bloomfield, et al., "The Health of Workers in a Textile Plant," U.S. Treasury Department, Public Health Service, *Public Health Bulletin* No. 207 (Washington, D.C., 1933). The physical difficulty of meeting the heavy labor requirements of tobacco harvesting resulted in a self-selection process that reproduced itself in the mill village.

Sharecroppers who farmed on "halves"—receiving land, house, and equipment in exchange for their labor and half the crop—were usually "furnished" by their landlords throughout the year. Frequently, the tenant was unable to pay off his "due bill" and half the fertilizer costs; consequently, his indebtedness would run over into the next year. For vivid portraits of tenant hardships, see J. A. Dickey and E. C. Branson, "How Farm Tenants Live," University of North Carolina Extension Bulletin (Chapel Hill, 1922). (The conditions of Chatham County, which had two money crops—tobacco and cotton—probably were superior to those of Carol County.) Also Margaret J. Hagood, *Mothers of the South* (New York, 1972) is an excellent portrayal of white tenant farm women.

32. Interview with WF, former spooler, who came to the village when she was ten years old in 1918.

33. Ibid. The woman's mother bore thirteen children in all, but there were never more than

eight living at any one time. Infant and maternal mortality were high among the first generation of mill families.

Carol County textile mills contrast sharply with the French linen mills studied by Reddy, who found the spinning factories made up primarily of secondary breadwinners and without family solidarity, and the weave mills made up of greater family concentration. K & O weave mill probably had as much relatedness among weavers as did French weavers—50 percent. No one has been interviewed who worked at K & O who did not have some relative working there *eventually*, and most had a relative employed at the same time, but the point remains, it was not the *whole* family during a life cycle covering childhood, adolescence, and adulthood. The degree to which employees at the LeClay spinning mill were related approximates 95 percent or more. In fact, only one individual has been discovered who arrived at the mill from outside the community without relatives; he was the superintendent, and married a fellow worker soon after arriving, thus acquiring relatives in short order. See William Reddy, "Family and Factory: French Linen Weavers in the Belle Epoque," *Journal of Social History* 8, no. 1 (Winter 1975): 102-12.

34. Interviews with WM, former foreman; WF, former spinner; WF spinner; WM, former opening room operative; WM, former bandmaker.

35. Low social status was characteristic of cotton mill workers throughout the South. See Senate Document No. 645, *Women and Child Wage Earners in the United States, Volume I: Cotton Textile Industry* (Washington, D.C., 1910) 585-87; also Van Osdell, Jr., "Cotton Mills, Labor, and the Southern Mind," p. 37; Morland, *Millways of Kent* (Chapel Hill, N.C., 1958), pp. ix, 174-77.

36. WF, former spooler.

37. Name of author and title withheld, p. 39.

38. See Rhyne, *Some Southern Cotton Mill Workers and Their Villages*, p. 197; Lahne, *The Cotton Mill Worker*, pp. 65-66.

39. Overcapacity was a pervasive problem after the war; see "Cotton Textile Industry: Message from the President of the United States" transmitting *A Report on the Conditions and Problems of the Cotton Textile Industry, Made by the Cabinet Appointed by Him*, Senate Document No. 126, 74th Cong., 1st sess. (G.P.O. 1935), hereafter cited as Senate Doc. 126.

40. Based on "History of [K & O] Corporation" published in a company brochure entitled *Family Day* 1960, as well as numerous newspaper articles.

41. See Van Osdell, Jr., "Cotton Mills, Labor, and the Southern Mind," pp. 31-34. Whereas the earlier shift of the industry was related to technological improvements in ring spinning, the second phase in the transfer of cotton textiles to the South was related to advances in weaving and increased use of automatic looms. See Irwin Feller's "The Diffusion and Location of Technological Change in the American Cotton-Textile Industry, 1890-1970," in *Technology and Culture* (October 1974): 569-93. K & O did not use automatic looms in its Roseville plant initially, however.

42. *President's Annual Report: 1959* (Danville Tobacco Association, Incorporated, Danville, Virginia), pp. 9-10. The prices given for the Danville Market are indicative of the declining tobacco profits throughout the bright leaf area.

43. Interviews with farm owners and operators who began work in the mill after 1925. The phenomenon of working in the factory and operating a small farm at the same time was not peculiar to Carol County; see the government's study of part-time farmers in the Southeast: R. H. Allen L. S. Cottrell, et al., *Part-Time Farming in the Southeast*, Works Progress Administration, Research Monograph IX (Washington, D.C., 1937). This study, as do the historical experiences of agricultural and industrial workers in Carol County, contradicts the commonly held myth that southern textile workers' agricultural origins account for their failure to unionize.

44. Interviews with black and white, male and female farm owners and operators who had used both methods. For a detailed description of children's contributions to tobacco agriculture under both systems of harvesting, consult Harriet A. Byrne, *Child Labor in Representative Tobacco-Growing Areas*, USDL Childrens Bureau Publication No. 155 (Washington, D.C., 1926); the data pertaining to Halifax, Virginia, are analogous to Carol County procedures before 1930;

the data relating to Florence, South Carolina, would correspond to the priming era.

45. RM (December 1937), nd, p. 1.

46. Based on interviews, birth and death records.

47. At the Fourth Annual outing for K & O male employees in early August 1938, there were 600 present; four weeks later, the company entertained 300 ladies at its first stew for females. See RM (August 2, 1938), p. 1; and (August 28, 1938), p. 1.

48. RM (December 1937), nd, p. 1; interview data reveal no discrepancies with newspaper figures.

49. Interview data with fifteen persons beginning work before 1920 reveal an even higher rate of illiteracy; approximately half had no formal schooling; the highest achieved was eighth grade; seven had elementary education. Although there has been no evidence of high mobility into or out of the LeClay community before World War II, these interviews suggest the exodus of whites from the cotton mill in the sixties was comprised of the better educated, a suggestion reinforced by interviews with the personnel managers of the largest industrial firms in the county in 1974.

50. Interview data.

51. Interview data; also RM (April 26, 1934).

52. In 1905, nearly one-half of the frame spinners in the South were children; nearly two-thirds of the rest were women. See *Manufactures*, 1905, Part III, "Special Reports on Selected Industries," Department of Commerce and Labor, Bureau of the Census (Washington, D.C., 1908) 30.

53. Interviews with former weavers, male and female; and two loom fixers; former mender, former winder (all white).

54. [Withheld] Historical Sketch of [Carol County] (Danville, 1974) 184.

55. Interview with WM.

56. Interview with WM now living in Lenoir County, North Carolina.

57. See Senate Doc. 645; U.S.D.L. Children's Bureau Publication No. 78, "Administration of the First Federal Child-Labor Law" (Washington, D.C., G.P.O., 1921), and M. H. Ross, "The Operation of the Wage and Hour Law in North Carolina and the South," *North Carolina Law Review* 30 (1952): 248-74 for the prevalence of child law, especially in North Carolina. Violations did not cease with legislation, but were clearly reduced. During the 1917 legislation, one of the overseers at LeClay changed birth dates in the family Bible of one family. In July 1942, a number of minors were discovered by a representative of the Department of Labor to be at work illegally in Carol County, but the newspaper failed to specify the employers. See RM (July 23, 1942), p. 1. Among the former employees at LeClay who began work while under legal age are a WF spinner who began as a "helper" in 1916; a WM who began in 1917 "to run slubbers right along side my Daddy" when he was nine; and a WF spooler who began helping her mother when she was in the third grade. During her first year in school, the child's teacher wanted her to skip a grade because she was so "smart." In October 1924, her name appeared in the newspaper for making the honor roll in the *fifth* grade. Born in 1911, she was then thirteen years old, which suggests the retardative effects of her mill labor! She wanted an education for herself desparately, but was unable to acquire it because she was the youngest child and her labor was required to enable her mother to keep the mill house after older siblings had married and left the home. Vowing never to live in a mill house when she became an adult, she left home in 1937 to establish a residence and employment in another state in order to acquire work at K & O without their knowing she had been working at LeClay and *quit*. She became a weaver in 1938 and worked until 1976 when she retired; although she liked her job, she did not want her seven children (all of whom she supported through college, except one who did not care for school) to work there, and she said she "would switch handles all her life to keep them out of the mill." The extent of child labor law violations is suggested by the oft-occurring statement: "Everybody began when they were *big* enough," and "A lot of them, they put their age up." Others when asked how old they were when they began work would answer, "You'd have to put *fourteen* 'cause it was the law."

58. Interviews with WF, former spinner; WM, former slubber; WM, former maintenance

overhauler; WF, former spooler; WF, former winder; WM, former cardroom supervisor. This same pattern of family labor for the first quarter of the century—that is, mothers staying at home, fathers and children nine and up working in the mill—is revealed by the Senate's investigation of women and child wage earners; see Senate Document No. 645, *Woman and Child Wage Earners in the United States, Volume XVI: Family Budgets of Typical Cotton-Mill Workers* (Washington, D.C., 1911); families nos. 17-21 are most analagous to LeClay.

59. Persons who began work before 1917 usually gave no indication of being aware of child labor laws, even though laws were in existence from 1903 on; evasiveness about revealing age was most apparent for those who began working in the mill from 1917 to 1938; frequently, such persons would admit to knowing how to do the job when they began because they used to "drift in and out" of the mill before they actually were put on the payroll.

60. RM (June 28, 1922), p. 5.

61. Interviews with WF spare hand, WM electrician, WF winder, WF spinner, WM supervisor in spinning.

62. Interview with WM, former card grinder; WF former spooler, and map (1925) of LeClay.

63. Interviews with WF, former spooler; WF, non-employed mother whose five children worked in the mill; WM, former "little boss" who blackmailed the superintendent into this position after observing that the superintendent had been arrested in another town for drunk driving; the official fought the charge all the way to the North Carolina Superior Court and was found not guilty, but operatives in LeClay assert he forced an overseer who was with him to take over the wheel. Interview with WF, whose father stoked the superintendent's furnace every morning and night, says her father received a "drink" in the evening as part of his payment.

64. Interview with WM, former overseer in spinning; wife of former deputy.

65. Examination of birth records from 1914 to 1930 reveals few births for townships other than that where the mills were located for persons employed in textiles. Interview data are consistent with birth records.

66. RM (January 11, 1951), p. 1.

67. Interview with WF, former mill teacher.

68. Interview with WM, former slubber and son of the man who dropped the cigarette. The K & O fire company was called to hose down the yards in the vicinity.

68. Interviews with WM, former overhauler and traveler changer; WF, former spooler; WM, former construction foreman; WM, former chief maintenance overhauler.

70. From a 1925 map of LeClay and observation of the community.

71. Of eight families coming to the mill before 1919, for whom the details are known, the average size of the nuclear unit was 12. In 1938, of 109 families who supplied the minister with the information, the average was 5.78. As the first generation of children grew up and married, they lived with one set of parents until they began to have children. By the time the second generation of children brought up in the village was ready for work, their grandparents had to be taken in as boarders because they were too old for the mill (according to the company) and had nowhere else to go.

A former Methodist minister in LeClay during the depression made a covert study of the mill for a master's thesis. Even though he used pseudonyms, I recognized many of the particulars, and was able to confirm his presence, but I have not informed respondents of his study. His study will be cited hereafter as Minister's thesis (pp. 72-74).

72. Interviews with three generations of residents and families.

73. Interviews with WM, former card grinder; WF, wife of former maintenance overhauler; WF, wife of former store manager; WF, former spooler.

74. Interview with WM, former carpenter.

75. Interview with WM, former card room employee; WM overseer.

76. Interviews with WF, spinner; WM, former spare hand whose paternal grandfather was evicted because of his unwed daughter's pregnancy; WF, wife of overhauler whose father was in charge of the "unpleasant" duty of telling people they had to move.

77. Interview with WF, former spinner.

78. Interview with WM, former overhauler, traveler changer.

79. Interview with WF, mother of five children who worked in the mill and had to give up her company house in World War II when they (the children) left the community.

80. Minister's thesis.

81. RM (December 6, 1951), p. 12.

82. Interviews with black and white, male and female, farm owners and operators. Swapping labor was common; social events often were held in conjunction with work: corn huskings, pea shellings; cutting (wood) frolics. See also Tilley, chap. 10, and the government's study of part-time farmers, which found more labor union membership among textile workers living on farms than in mill villages, as well as more propensity toward organizational membership in general.

83. See "Industrial and Labor Conditions: Company Stores and the Scrip System," *Monthly Labor Review* (July 1935): 53. Also Senate Doc. 645, Vol. 16, and interview data.

84. Interview with WM, former spare hand. He dropped out of school when he was sixteen, primarily because he was ashamed of his clothes and could not tolerate the class distinctions at the high school. Few respondents are critical of the teachers at the mill school, but the inadequacy of facilities is indicated in *Survey of School Plants and Facilities Carol* [pseudonym] *County Schools* (Chapel Hill, N.C., 1960), which ranked LeClay mill 296 out of a possible 1,000 points.

85. Senate Res. 49, p. 38.

86. Interview with WF spinner; WF former spooler.

87. Interviews with two WMs, former weavers.

88. According to Senate Doc. 645, Vol. 1, female spinners in North Carolina under sixteen years of age earned an average of $3.69 in late 1907, early 1908; males under sixteen earned an average of $4.48. Children at LeClay that year learned for "nothing" and then received 25-35 cents a day; their older siblings and fathers earned 50 to 70 cents per day. Even if they had worked full time, the highest earnings would have been only $4.20, which is less than the average of southern workers. But they did not work full time, and only the oldest and most skilled member of the family received the highest wage of 70 cents. At least a dozen respondents volunteered the effect of the minimum wage on their salary, and praised Roosevelt for the law. People could not believe their wages would go from $1.50 or in one case from $1.30 to $2.10 for only eight hours when they had been working ten hours and fifty-five minutes per day. Quite a few employees received no increase because they worked outside. See Moss, and Charles H. Livengood, Jr., *The Federal Wage and Hour Law Including the Fair Labor Standards Amendments of 1949* (American Bar Association, Philadelphia, 1951), for exemptions.

89. Interview with WM, former weaver, now professional employee of the state.

90. Ibid.

91. RM (November 12, 1936), p. 1; (December 17, 1936), p. 1.

92. Interview data. Even some employees who theoretically were paid for production rarely received more than the prevailing day wage in the mill.

93. Interviews with WF, former spinner; WF, former spooler.

94. Interviews with WM, former doffer; WM, former spare hand; WF, former spooler; WM, supervisor.

95. WF spinner; WM supervisor; Minister's thesis.

96. WM, former weaver; WM former loom fixer, smash hand.

97. RM (December 17, 1936), p. 1; (April 16, 1937), p. 1.

98. Interview with WM, former weaver, section boss.

99. See Senate Doc. 126; also interview with WM supervisor; WM, former section boss at K & O.

100. Interviews with WF spinner, WM supervisor; WM, former weaver.

101. Interviews with WF, former weaver; WF, former spinner. RM (February 15, 1938) for example, reported more than 100 of the 700 laid off the first of the year went back to work—all in finishing, none in weaving. On March 1, the newspaper announced 1,200 benefit checks received for the employees who had received no income since the first of year. Checks also arrived on March

15 and 26.

102. Interviews with WM, former card grinder; WF, former spooler; WF, mother of five who worked in the mill, and was deserted by her husband.

103. Ibid.

104. Intgerview with WM, former weaver, section boss; WF, former weaver; WF, former mender, inspector, weaver.

105. Interview data.

106. Interviews with WF, former weaver; WM, former section boss.

107. Interview data.

108. Ibid.

109. Special edition of RM following the December 2, 1937, issue.

110. Minister's thesis.

111. Ibid.

112. *RM* (April 26, 1934), K & O edition.

113. See Senate Doc. 126.

114. Publicity surrounding the wave of strikes in the Southern Piedmont in 1929 (Elizabethton, Marion, Gastonia, Danville, and South Carolina), the "rolling strikes" in 1932, and the national textile strike in 1934 undoubtedly gave the northern firm much to ponder; countering criticism incurred by other "absentee" employers may account for the frequent announcements in the local press of benefits for K & O employees. (Local coverage of external labor conflicts was not sympathetic, however.)

115. RM (March 6, 1952), editorial, p. 4.

116. *Family Day.* Their pride as a leader after 1936 in setting trends is justified.

117. This agreement was observed until the integration of the mills occurred with the industrial diversification of the county in the mid-sixties. Interviews with WM, roving frame tender; WF, former winder; WM, former overhauler.

118. WF, former weaver.

119. *Decisions of National Labor Relations Board.* "In the Matter of [Name Withheld] and Textile Workers Union of America, C.I.O." Case No. (withheld).

120. Interview data.

121. Interview with WM, former weaver.

122. Interviews with WM, former weaver; WF, former winder; WF, wife of supervisor in dye house; newspaper articles of disturbances.

123. Minister's thesis.

124. Based on interview data. There was very low turnover in LeClay; according to interviews, people who came to either village (but mostly K & O) from other villages "never stayed long."

125. WF, former winder. Interview with WM, former section boss who said his family had two double beds in every room but the kitchen, and possibly three beds in one room.

126. RM (August 2, 1938), p. 1.

127. Interview data. Birth records indicate boarding of Koville workers in LeClay also.

128. Special edition of RM following December 2, 1937, issue, p. 1.

129. Interview data.

130. Map constructed by observation and with the aid of WM, former construction foreman who helped to build most of the additions to K & O before he retired.

131. Interview data, and Minister's thesis.

132. Interview with WM, former weaver and section boss.

133. This conclusion is based upon examination of NLRB Trial Examiner Reports of cases involving southern mills and TWUA during the late 1930s and early 1940s. K & O was a large plant, with skilled employees producing primarily for the transportation industry; this combination of factors coupled with their being an "absentee landlord" made them a prime candidate for organizational efforts. What is relevant here is producing for the customer and shipping directly. Textile firms shipping to middlemen (or dealing with commission houses) as did Roseville Cotton Mills

were more difficult for the employees to organize. By knowing the peak demand seasons, K & O employees could more easily predict the "best" times to organize. Community attitudes are also important in assessing probable success of employees in their efforts to unionize. In the K & O community, the prestige and power of the Roseville Cotton Mills was a deterrent to unionism by both plants; in other communities, where the absentee employer was the only mill employer, workers' chance for successful organization were greater.

134. Interview with WM, former section boss.

135. *RM* (October 23, 1944), p. 1. Also interview with WM smash hand; data regarding speed up and stretch out, and the Gastonia, Marion, experiences are based on interviews.

136. Interview.

137. See G. T. Schwenning, "Prospects of Southern Textile Unionism," *Journal of Political Economy* 39 (December 1931): 802-3; and "Labor in the South," USDL Bulletin No. 898 (Washington, D.C., 1947), p. 174.

138. "The Textile Worker: Integration Without Freedom in a Traditional Community," in *Alienation and Freedom: The Factory Worker and His Industry* (Chicago, 1964), p. 88.

Appendix

The bulk of the data examined during the course of this investigation is documentary in nature and includes U.S. Census Data on Commerce, Agriculture, Vital Statistics, Social and Economic Characteristics of the County; City and County Data Books; State and County Educational, Agricultural, Economic and Health Reports; local newspapers, histories, National Labor Relations Board Trial Examiner's Reports, and available company records.

The lack of continuous and consistently classified data for analysis poses serious problems for the historian of Carol County. The local newspaper is available for 1900 to 1917, which precedes the construction of K & O. Fire destroyed the newspaper office in the twenties, and there is a total gap in press coverage for the years 1918 to 1921. There are unbound papers available for the years 1922 to 1939; these vary in condition of legibility and completeness, but tend to improve with the later dates. From 1940, coverage is available.

In general, newspaper treatment of the two mills has differed in quantity and quality. Coverage of the cotton mills has been primarily of the owners and sympathetic to their interests. Treatment of K & O operatives has been much more descriptive and detailed. News stories about the weave company suggest the public was being consciously reminded of the northern firm's economic contributions to the county.

The published censuses excluded much data about rural-industrial counties for fear of disclosing individual firms. These documents also combine much data about the two textile firms, which prevents extracting particulars for each. In addition to these problems, the classifications of census data change. The category of "rural-nonfarm" is not used before 1930; prior to that time, the mill village populations were lost in the township figures. In 1930, all three villages are combined in the rural-nonfarm figures; it is not until 1950 that the rural-nonfarm classification is further subdivided into the three separate mill communities.

Birth records for the years 1914 to 1930 were examined in order to obtain data about the earlier generation of mill workers. These documents are also flawed. Interview data reveals information on the birth records was frequently inaccurate. The unavailability of the birth records before 1914 prevents analysis of the first generation of cotton mill workers. The frequent designation of occupation as "mill work" after 1923 prevents distinguishing from between the two firms. The birth records provide the educational attainments for the mill-working parents of newborns for 1914 and 1915, and not for subsequent years.

Because of the inadequacy and incompleteness of written evidence, oral data have provided a major resource for learning about people's experiences, perceptions, purposes, motives, and goals. Childhood, adolescent, and continuing adult experiences in the community under study have enabled the writer to return to the county for research purposes. While acting as a participant observer and interviewer on twenty visits between Fall 1971 and Winter 1977, I have conducted over two hundred interviews with residents of Carol County. Pseudonyms have been used for all proper names of people and places; and numbers and statistics have been rounded off to protect the identity of respondents, most of whom were workers and former workers for Roseville Cotton Mills. The better newspaper coverage of K & O operatives and the higher turnover of that work force made oral history less useful for the study of the weave mill village.

Part II:

Suggested Readings

The notes following each of the selections in Part II contain a rich literature to which readers may turn for further study of the issues they document. The following articles and books should prove useful as well.

On southern social structure in the late nineteenth century see Roger W. Shugg, *Origins of Class Struggle in Louisiana* (1939, rev. 1968), C. Vann Woodward, *Origins of the New South, 1877–1913* (1951), Allison Davis et al., *Deep South: A Social Anthropological Study of Caste and Class* (1941). A backward glance to the Confederacy's home front problems may also offer suggestions of sharp social differences: Ella Lonn, *Desertion During the Civil War* (1928); Paul W. Gates, *Agriculture and the Civil War* (1965); Bell I. Wiley, *The Plain People of the Confederacy* (1943); Charles W. Ramsdell, *Behind the Lines in the Southern Confederacy* (1944). Literary impressions of lower-class whites are analyzed in Shields McIlwaine, *The Southern Poor White from Lubberland to Tobacco Road* (1939). See also a useful local history: William Warren Rogers, *Thomas County Georgia During the Civil War* (1964).

Study of black roles in Reconstruction should begin with W. E. B. Du Bois, *Black Reconstruction in America* (1935; reissue 1956) and should be supplemented with Vernon L. Wharton, *The Negro in Mississippi: 1865–1890* (1947); Joel Williamson, *After Slavery: The Negro in South Carolina During Reconstruction, 1861–1877* (1965); Alrutheus Ambush Taylor, *The Negro in the Reconstruction of Virginia* (1926), *The Negro in South Carolina During Reconstruction* (1924), and *The Negro in Tennessee, 1865–1880* (1938); Joe M. Richardson, *The Negro in the Reconstruction of Florida, 1865–1877* (1966); Peter Kolchin, *First Freedom: The Responses of Alabama Blacks to Emancipation and Reconstruction* (1972); Edward

Magdol, *A Right to the Land: Essays on the Freedmen's Community* (1977); LaWanda Cox and John H. Cox, eds., *Reconstruction, the Negro and the New South* (1973); Thomas Holt, *Black Over White: Negro Political Leadership in South Carolina During Reconstruction* (1977); Carol K. Bleser, *The Promised Land: The History of the South Carolina Land Commission, 1869–90* (1969). Useful in this connection is one of the best of the 1865–66 travelers' accounts, John Dennett, *The South as It Is: 1865–1866* (1967).

Post-Reconstruction social and economic relations in the agriculture sector may be studied in F. A. Shannon, *The Farmer's Last Frontier: Agriculture, 1860–1897* (1945); Theodore Saloutos, *Farmer Movements in the South* (1960); Robert C. McMath, Jr., *Populist Vanguard: A History of the Southern Farmers' Alliance* (1975); Michael Schwartz, *Radical Protest and Social Structure, The Southern Farmers' Alliance and Cotton Tenancy, 1880–1890* (1976); William F. Holmes, "The Arkansas Cotton Pickers' Strike of 1891 and the Demise of the Colored Farmers' Alliance," *Arkansas Historical Quarterly* 32 (Summer 1973); William Warren Rogers, "The Negro Alliance in Alabama," *Journal of Negro History* 45 (January 1960); Robert C. McMath, Jr., "Agrarian Protest at the Forks of the Creek: Three Subordinate Farmers' Alliances in North Carolina," *North Carolina Historical Review* 51 (Winter 1974); Roger L. Ransom and Richard Sutch, *One Kind of Freedom: The Economic Consequences of Emancipation* (1977); Gavin Wright, *The Political Economy of the Cotton South, Households, Markets, and Wealth in the Nineteenth Century* (1978); LaWanda Cox, "The American Agricultural Wage Earner," *Agricultural History* 22 (April 1948); Jay R. Mandle, "The Plantation Economy: An Essay in Definition," *Science and Society* 36 (Spring 1972); "The Reestablishment of the Plantation Economy in the South, 1865–1910," *Review of Black Political Economy* 3 (1973); Jonathan M. Wiener, "Planter-Merchant Conflict in Reconstruction Alabama," *Past & Present* 68 (August 1975); "Planter Persistence and Social Change: Alabama, 1850–1870," *Journal of Interdisciplinary History* 7 (Autumn 1976); "Class Structure and Economic Development in the American South, 1865–1955," and "Comments" by Robert Higgs, Harold Woodman, and "Reply" by Wiener, all in *American Historical Review*, 84 (October 1979).

On farmer political action and economic organization see Lawrence C. Goodwyn, *Democratic Promise, The Populist Movement in America* (1976); William Ivy Hair, *Bourbonism and Agrarian Protest: Louisiana Politics, 1877–1900* (1969); William Warren Rogers, *The One-Gallused Rebellion: Agrarianism in Alabama, 1865–1896* (1970); C. Vann Woodward, *Tom Watson: Agrarian Rebel* (1938, reissue 1973); Woodward, *Origins of the New South* (1951); Shugg, *Origins of Class Struggle in Louisiana* (1968 reissue); Albert D. Kirwan, *Revolt of the Rednecks: Mississippi Politics, 1876–1925* (1951); J. Morgan Kousser, *The Shaping of Southern Politics, Suffrage Restriction and the Establishment of the One-Party South, 1880–1910* (1974); Joseph H. Cartwright, *The Triumph of Jim Crow: Tennessee*

Race Relations in the 1880s (1976); Charles Crowe, "Tom Watson, Populists, and Blacks Reconsidered," *Journal of Negro History* 55 (1970); Jack Abramowitz, "The Negro in the Populist Movement," *Journal of Negro History* 38 (1953); Herbert Shapiro, "The Populists and the Negro: A Reconsideration," in August Meier and Elliot Rudwick, eds., *The Making of Black America*, vol. II (1969); William F. Holmes, "Whitecapping in Mississippi: Agrarian Violence in the Populist Era," *Mid-America* 55 (April 1973); "Whitecapping: Agrarian Violence in Mississippi, 1902–1906," *Journal of Southern History* 35 (1969); E. C. Branson, "Farm Tenancy in the Cotton Belt: How Farm Tenants Live," *Journal of Social Forces* 1 (1923); James O. Nall, *The Tobacco Night Riders of Kentucky and Tennessee, 1905–1909* (1939); John G. Miller, *The Black Patch War in Kentucky and Tennessee Tobacco Fields* (1936).

For industrial and agricultural labor organization see Shugg, *Origins of Class Struggle*; Woodward, *Origins of the New South*; Gary M. Fink and Merl E. Reed, eds., *Essays in Southern Labor History: Selected Papers, Southern Labor History Conference, 1976* (1977); Sterling D. Spero and Abram L. Harris, *The Black Worker, The Negro and the Labor Movement* (1930, reissue 1969); Melton A. McLaurin, *Paternalism and Protest: Southern Cotton Mill Workers and Organized Labor, 1875–1905* (1971); "The Knights of Labor in North Carolina Politics," *North Carolina Historical Review* 49 (July 1972); Frederic L. Myers, "The Knights of Labor in the South," *Southern Economic Journal* (April 1940); Sidney H. Kessler, "The Organization of Negroes in the Knights of Labor," *Journal of Negro History* (July 1952); Katherine A. Harvey, "The Knights of Labor in the Maryland Coal Fields, 1878–1882," *Labor History* 10 (Fall 1969); F. Ray Marshall, "Some Reflections on Labor History," *Southwest Historical Quarterly* 75 (1971); Herbert G. Gutman, "Black Coal Miners and the Greenback Labor Party in Redeemer, Alabama, 1878–1879," *Labor History* 10 (Summer 1969); James Green, "The Brotherhood of Timber Workers, 1910–1913," *Past & Present* 60 (August 1973); Paul B. Worthman, "Black Workers and Labor Unions in Birmingham, Alabama, 1897–1904," *Labor History* 10 (Summer 1969); James V. Reese, "The Early History of Labor Organizations in Texas, 1838–1876," *Southwestern Historical Quarterly* 72 (1968); Ruth A. Allen, *Chapters in the History of Organized Labor in Texas* (1941); J. Carlyle Sitterson, *Sugar Country: The Cane and Sugar Industry in the South, 1753–1950* (see Ch. 15, "Planters, Tenants, and Laborers, 1880–1910") (1953); United States Commissioner of Labor, *Second Annual Report, 1886* (1887); United States Department of Labor, Bureau of Labor Statistics, *Labor in the South* (Bulletin 898) (1947).

On women and women's movements in the South see A. Elizabeth Taylor, *The Woman Suffrage Movement in Tennessee* (1957), and "The Origin of the Woman Suffrage Movement in Georgia," *Georgia Historical Quarterly* 28 (June 1944); Anne Firor Scott, "The 'New Woman' in the New South,"

South Atlantic Quarterly (Autumn 1962); Aileen S. Kraditor, "Tactical Problems of the Woman Suffrage Movement in the South," *Louisiana Studies* 4 (Winter 1966).

On immigration and white ethnic groups, a topic omitted from this volume, see Rowland Berthoff, "Southern Attitudes Toward Immigration, 1865–1914," *Journal of Southern History* 40 (February 1974); Jean A. Scarpaci, "A Tale of Selective Accommodation: Sicilians and Native Whites," *Journal of Ethnic Studies* 5 (Fall 1977), and "Immigrants in the New South: Italians in Louisiana's Sugar Parishes, 1880–1910," *Labor History* (Spring 1975); Durward Long, "An Immigrant Co-operative Medicine Program in the South, 1887–1963," *Journal of Southern History* 31 (November 1965); Louis A. Perez, Jr., "Reminiscences of a *Lector*," *Florida Historical Quarterly* (April 1975); George E. Pozzetta, "Foreigners in Florida: A Study of Immigration Promotion, 1865–1910," *Florida Historical Quarterly* 53 (1974), and "Foreign Colonies in South Florida, 1865–1910," *Tequesta* 34 (1974); Jacek Przygoda, "New Light on the Poles in Texas," *Polish American Studies* 27 (1970); Joseph P. O'Grady, "Immigrants and the Politics of Reconstruction in Richmond, Virginia," *Records of the American Catholic Historical Society of Philadelphia* 83 (June 1972).

On socialist activity see James R. Green, *Grass-Roots Socialism: Radical Movements in the Southwest 1895–1943* (1979); Grady McWhiney, "Louisianna Socialists in the Early Twentieth Century: A Study of Rustic Radicalism," *Journal of Southern History* 20 (1954); Emilio Zamora, Jr., "Chicano Socialist Labor Activity in Texas, 1900–1920," *Aztlan* 6 (1976); Malcolm Sylvers, "Sicilian Socialists in Houston, Texas, 1896–98," *Labor History* 11 (1970).

On religion see John Bell, Jr., "Baptists and the Negro in North Carolina During Reconstruction," *North Carolina Historical Review* (May 1965); Frederick A. Bode, "Religion and Class Hegemony: A Populist Critique in North Carolina," *Journal of Southern History* 37 (August 1971); John B. Holt, "Holiness Religions: Cultural Shock and Social Disorganization," *American Sociological Review* 5 (1940); David E. Harrell, Jr., "The Agrarian Myth and the Disciples of Christ in the Nineteenth Century," *Agricultural History* 41 (April 1967); J. L. Eighmy, *Churches in Cultural Captivity: A History of the Social Attitudes of Southern Baptists* (1972); H. D. Farish, *The Circuit Rider Dismounts: A Social History of Southern Methodism, 1865–1900* (1938); Leonard Dinnerstein and M. D. Palsson, eds., *Jews in the South* (1973); R. B. Spain, *At Ease in Zion: A Social History of Southern Baptists, 1865–1900*; Liston Pope, *Millhands and Preachers: A Study of Gastonia* (1942, reissue 1970); Wayne Flynt, "Alabama White Protestantism and Labor, 1900–1914," *The Alabama Review* 25 (July 1972), and "Dissent in Zion: Alabama Baptists and Social Issues, 1900–1914," *Journal of Southern History* 35 (November 1969).

Afterword

The common folk—the mass of independent, property-holding whites with their aspirations of upward mobility and their ideology of equal opportunity—once loomed large in the study of southern society. Historians observed that they composed the majority of the southern people, that they owned considerable property in a society that celebrated capitalism, and that they voted regularly in a nation that applauded republicanism. From these observations, scholars concluded that the white majority dominated southern life and set the tone of agrarian republicanism from Tom Jefferson to Tom Watson and beyond.

During the past two decades, the common folk have been pushed from the center stage of southern historiography. Students of southern life, led by Eugene D. Genovese, have argued that even in a democratic republic numbers were not everything. Although small farmers, crossroad storekeepers, rural artisans, and urban merchants were numerous, propertied, and politically active, they did not dominate antebellum southern society. Instead, a small group of planters who controlled the best land, owned most of the slaves, and grew the staple-export crops ruled the South. As the South's ruling class, slaveholding planters set the tone of southern society, dominated southern politics, and shaped southern culture. In this view, upward-striving southerners aspired to be planters, not yeomen farmers. The gentleman aristocrat with his military title, easy hospitality, courtly manners, and quick-fire temper and not the horny-handed son of the soil became the southern ideal. And the planter's paternalism, not the yeoman's equalitarianism, informed social relations in the South, not only between master and slave but also between planters and common folk and presumably among the common folk themselves.

The dispute over the nature of southern society has been most clearly defined in the historiography of the antebellum years. But the debate has spilled over into the postwar period as well. To be sure most scholars admit that the demands of newly freed and enfranchised blacks forced a reorganization of the plantation. Planters appeared in a variety of new guises as landlords, furnishing merchants, and factors. They also made important concessions to the new realities of northern dominance, and these concessions were not just cosmetic but led ultimately to a re-working of the planter's world view and the rise of a new entrepreneurial one. However, the reorganized plantation remained the central institution within southern society well into the twentieth century.

The plantation-centered historiography has not gone unchallenged. Some scholars have continued to argue that the equalitarianism of the common folk, not the paternalism of the planter class, shaped southern life. George Fredrickson has called the South a *herrenvolk* or white man's democracy in the South African mode, where race not class was the chief determinant of status and belief. In this view, planters may have gained the lion's share of the economic benefits of southern life, but the common folk, by using their political power, set the direction of southern society. Other scholars have questioned the unique character of the plantation itself. Economist Gavin Wright has suggested that the plantation might better be thought of as a bloated farm and planters, by implication, as nothing more than successful yeomen.

Such profound differences in scholarly views of the fundamental character of southern society raise important questions about the nature of the common folk, their relationship to other classes and races, and their behavior and belief. Few have been explored. In some measure, these questions have been overshadowed by the present generation's preoccupation with the role of race in the making of southern life. Propelled by the events of the sixties, scholars have subjected all aspects of black life and race relations to close investigation. The investment of scholarly energies has yielded enormous dividends. But the new interpretations of the pervasive influence of race in the formation of southern society and the reciprocal interaction of whites and blacks in the making of southern culture has only revealed more fully the poverty of the present understanding of the white majority. The study of the common folk remains the largest question now facing students of southern life.

In bringing together some of the most recent work on the common folk, Jon Wakelyn and Edward Magdol have performed an extraordinarily valuable service. First, they have begun the difficult but essential task of defining the composition of the common folk. No history of the southern common people can be written until this sprawling and seemingly formless group has been dissected into its constituent parts. Second, they have begun to outline the chronology and geography of the common folk. Failure to respect the force of time and space has dogged studies of the plantation South during the past generation. It is well that any history of the common folk begin by placing these variables at the center. Third, by their selections, Wakelyn and Magdol have demonstrated how recent scholarly interest in social structure, institutional development, and ideology can inform the history of the common folk. Finally, by doing so much, they suggest how much there is to do. One can hardly ask for more in an anthology.

Ira Berlin

College Park, Maryland

Index

Contributors to Part I

Ira Berlin, Associate Professor of History at the University of Maryland, is the author of *Slaves Without Masters* (1974). He has published in a number of scholarly journals, including the *Journal of Social History*, and is editor of the Freedman's Bureau Papers.

Walter J. Fraser, Jr., is Associate Professor of History at The Citadel, Charlestown. He directs the Citadel Conference on the South and is the author of *Patriots, Pistols, and Petticoats: Charles Town in the American Revolution* (1976).

Richard H. Haunton, Professor of History at Appalachian State University, has published in journals such as the *Tennessee Historical Quarterly* and the *Georgia Historical Quarterly*. He is writing a history of antebellum Savannah.

Guion Griffis Johnson is emeritus Professor of History at North Carolina State University. She is the author of *A Social History of the Sea Islands* (1930); *Ante-bellum North Carolina: A Social History* (1937); and *Volunteers in Community Service* (1967).

Forrest McDonald is Professor of History at the University of Alabama. Among his many publications on the constitutional period are *We the People: The Economic Origins of the Constitution* (1958), *E pluribus unum: The Formation of the American Republic* (1965), *Confederation and Constitution, 1781–1789* (1968), *The Presidency of George Washington* (1974), and *The Presidency of Thomas Jefferson* (1976).

Grady McWhiney is Professor of History and chairman of the Department at the University of Alabama. Among his many books on the South are *Grant, Lee, Lincoln and the Radicals* (1964), *Braxton Bragg and Confederate Defeat* (1969), and *Southerners and Other Americans* (1973).

Randall M. Miller, Associate Professor of History at Saint Joseph's College, Philadelphia, has published in many scholarly journals. Among his books are *The Cotton Mill Movement in Antebellum Alabama* (1978), *"Dear Master": Letters of a Slave Family* (1978), and *Ethnic Images in American Film and Television* (1978).

Frank L. Owsley (1890–1956) was Professor of History at Vanderbilt University and the University of Tennessee. He wrote *State Rights in the Confederacy* (1925), *King Cotton Diplomacy* (1931), *Plain Folk of the Old South* (1949), and contributed to the Vanderbilt agrarian study, *I'll Take My Stand* (1930).

Alden B. Pearson, Jr., Assistant Professor of History at the University of Alabama, Huntsville, has published in the *Tennessee Historical Quarterly* and *World Affairs.*

Robert Royal Russel is emeritus Professor of History at Western Michigan University. He is the author of *Economic Aspects of Southern Sectionalism, 1840–1861* (1924), *Antebellum Studies in Slavery, Politics and the Railroads* (1960), *A History of the American Economic System* (1964), and *Critical Studies in Antebellum Sectionalism* (1972).

Contributors to Part II

Vernon Burton, Assistant Professor of History at the University of Illinois, Urbana, is a co-editor (with Robert C. McMath) of a volume of studies of southern communities in the nineteenth century, to be published by Greenwood Press.

W. E. B. Du Bois (1868–1963) was the author of more than a dozen books and hundreds of articles, reviews, editorials, and addresses. He received his Ph.D. degree from Harvard University in 1895. Dr. Du Bois was a pioneering and dominant force in American scholarship, and a leader of the equal rights movement.

Leon Fink, Assistant Professor of History at the University of North Carolina, Chapel Hill, is also the author of "Class Conflict in the Gilded Age: The Figure and the Phantom," *Radical History Review* (1975).

Lawrence C. Goodwyn, Professor of History at Duke University and Co-director of the Oral History Project of the Center for Southern Studies, is the author of *Democratic Promise: The Populist Movement in America* (1976).

Frank J. Huffman, Jr., received his Ph.D. from Yale University and taught history at the University of Houston. He is currently assistant to the Executive Vice-President of E. H. Crump Companies, Inc., in Memphis, Tennessee. His essay is a revision of a paper presented at the November 1975 meeting of the Southern Historical Association at Washington, D.C.

Julie Roy Jeffrey, Associate Professor at Goucher College, Towson, Maryland, is a member of the editorial board of the *Journal of Social History*, and the author of *Frontier Women, The Trans-Mississippi West, 1840–1880* (1979).

Edward Magdol, Associate Professor of History at the State University College at Potsdam, New York, is also the author of *A Right to the Land: Essays on the Freedmen's Community* (1977) and *Owen Lovejoy, Abolitionist in Congress* (1967).

David Montgomery, Professor of History at Yale University, is a prominent historian of the American working class. Among his influential published works are *Workers' Control in America: Studies in the History of Work, Technology, and Labor Struggles* (1979) and *Beyond Equality, Labor and the Radical Republicans, 1862–1872* (1967).

Dale Newman, Teaching Fellow and doctoral candidate in History at the University of Pittsburgh, is also the author of "Work and Community Life in a Southern Textile Town," *Labor History* (Spring 1978), and guest editor, *Pennsylvania Oral History Newsletter* (June 1977) devoted to "Labor and Oral History: Substance and Method."